The Medical-Legal Aspects of Acute Care Medicine

James E. Szalados
Editor

The Medical-Legal Aspects of Acute Care Medicine

A Resource for Clinicians, Administrators, and Risk Managers

Springer

Editor
James E. Szalados
Director, Surgical and Neurocritical Care Units
Rochester Regional Health System at Rochester General Hospital
Rochester, NY
USA

The Szalados Law Firm
Hilton, NY
USA

ISBN 978-3-030-68569-0 ISBN 978-3-030-68570-6 (eBook)
https://doi.org/10.1007/978-3-030-68570-6

This Springer imprint is published by the registered company Springer Nature Switzerland AG
The registered company address is: Gewerbestrasse 11, 6330 Cham, Switzerland

This project could not have been possible without the constant support of my family.

To my mom, who gave me positive energy, who raised me to work hard and never, ever, give up.

To my dad, who taught me to stand for what I believe but also to understand, respect, and care for others.

For my sister Liz, whose gentle spirit taught me about the magic in believing.

Finally, but not lastly, for my wife and love of my life, my constant life companion, my anchor, my best friend, and soulmate, Doris, who shares in all that we have accomplished because she has been there with me and for me, on every step on this journey.

James E. Szalados

Preface

This book could not have been possible without the hard work and support of so many. I would like to thank all my contributors for their hard work and insight. Taking the time to help write a book, especially given the events of the past year, is an extraordinary commitment and achievement. I would also like to thank my support staff, especially Abha Krishnan and her editorial team at Springer, for their patience, hard work, and dedication in helping bring this project to completion.

I have the privilege of practicing multiple professions. On any given day, I have the opportunity of helping, patients, clients, or others as I work on their behalf as a physician, attorney, or consultant. I take great satisfaction in being able to help others in need; it is my life's work. This book crosses the boundaries between the professions from a single multidisciplinary lens. My hope is that it is both engaging and practical.

The healthcare team is comprised of many professionals of diverse training and backgrounds who work in what is possibly the most regulated of any area of public service or commerce in the USA. To a large extent, deep ethical and moral convictions, internal fortitude, work ethic, and dedication provide the momentum for healthcare professionals and their support teams to perform the work of patient care. Healthcare entails enormous personal commitment and sacrifice, from the beginning of one's training to the daily rigors of practice. Moreover, healthcare is not devoid of risk, as the recent COVID-19 pandemic has underscored. Throughout the moment-to-moment and day-to-day controlled chaos, it is often the shared goals and the team spirit that helps us all make a difference. It is not inconsequential that when the world ground to a halt in the COVID epidemic, the frontline healthcare teams were there, every day, every night, making a difference, doing what we were born to do.

However, take one step back and healthcare workers immediately realize the regulatory and legal complexity of the system in which we work each day. We seem to prefer the term "administrative complexity" to address the regulatory framework in which our healthcare system is embedded. We prefer the term "population health" to address the deep importance of the social and economic support system upon which our public health infrastructure is precariously balancing. The law is something healthcare practitioners and administrators hope to avoid; however, it is always there. Nonetheless, there are healthcare attorneys, who also want to help; healthcare attorneys understand the regulations, laws, and the processes that are so essential to effective patient care. The task of the healthcare attorney is to help busy healthcare practitioners focus on patients, their families, and the community. The goal of healthcare attorneys is to provide guidance and counsel, when needed, to navigate the regulatory world. In a sense, healthcare attorneys are also a part of the healthcare team, perhaps not at the front lines, but on the sidelines helping to make it all work.

Morality and ethics will always be at the foundation of healthcare, as much as patients and families will always be our focus. Advances in medical technology should never overtake the relationships we have with our patients, although technology helps us provide better care for them. New technology will pose ethical, legal, and regulatory problems, and technology, as it progresses, will inevitably "force" new laws and regulations. Laws rarely force technology, although they may enable innovation; technology, on the other hand, will inevitably and always force new laws and regulations into existence. It is inevitable that healthcare providers maintain their situational awareness and participate fully in their organizations, public policy development, and regulatory agencies to help develop and drive technology and laws and to help enable a better tomorrow.

Rochester, NY, USA James E. Szalados

Author's Note and Disclaimers

This book is intended for students, teachers, clinicians, administrators, and other attorneys.

The material presented herein is intended to provide readers with a rich and practical overview of the enormous complexity of the ethical and legal framework in which healthcare professionals practice. This work is intended to serve both as a practical reference and also as a basis for further inquiry.

The information presented herein focusses on the laws and regulations related to the practice of healthcare in the USA and is not intended to address international laws or procedures.

The material presented herein is not intended to and must not be construed in any way to represent legal advice. This book in no way implies the existence of an attorney–client relationship. No legal actions should be taken solely in reliance on this material. The editors and authors disclaim any legal responsibility for actions taken or not taken in reliance of the material herein to the fullest extent.

The laws of the USA are constantly in flux, with new regulations, statutes, and case law. In addition, the laws regarding or impacting healthcare vary between states.

Please consult with a qualified attorney for legal advice on any specific legal issue.

The opinions of the editor or the authors represent the opinions of each individual contributor and may not reflect the opinions or policies of any institutions, firms, or other entities with which the contributors are, or have previously been, affiliated.

Contents

Contributors

Zohair Ahmed Al Aseri, MD Departments of Emergency Medicine and Critical Care, College of Medicine, King Saud University, Riyadh, Saudi Arabia

Christian Becker, MD, PhD eHealth Center, Westchester Medical Center Health Network, Taylor Pavilion, Valhalla, NY, USA

Department of Medicine, Division of Pulmonary, Critical Care and Sleep Medicine, Westchester Medical Center and New York Medical College, Valhalla, NY, USA

Marianne Chiafery, DNP, MS, Clin. Eth., PNP, HEC-C Division of Medical Humanities and Bioethics, University of Rochester School of Medicine and Dentistry, Rochester, NY, USA

Joette Derricks, MPA, FACMPE, AAPC, CHC, CPC Derricks Consulting, LLC, Hunt Valley, MD, USA

Mario V. Fusaro, MD eHealth Center, Westchester Medical Center Health Network, Taylor Pavilion, Valhalla, NY, USA

Department of Medicine, Division of Pulmonary, Critical Care and Sleep Medicine, Westchester Medical Center and New York Medical College, Valhalla, NY, USA

Taylor Hughes, RN, CCRN Surgical Intensive Care Unit, Rochester General Hospital, Rochester Regional Health System , St. John Fisher College AGACNP Candidate, Rochester, NY, USA

Tiffany M. Ingham, MD Envision Physician Services, Houston, TX, USA

Marcin Karcz, MD, PhD, MSc Columbia University Vagelos College of Physicians and Surgeons, New York, NY, USA

David C. Kaufman, MD, FCCM, HEC-C Division of Medical Humanities and Bioethics, University of Rochester School of Medicine and Dentistry, Rochester, NY, USA

Nicole Keenan, DNP, CRNA, RN University of Rochester Medical Center, Rochester, NY, USA

Brenton LaRiccia, PA-C, MS, MBA University of Rochester Medical Center, Rochester, NY, USA

Cheryl Lustik, RN, MSN, APN-C University of Rochester Medical Center, Rochester, NY, USA

Daniel Miller, MD eHealth Center, Westchester Medical Center Health Network, Taylor Pavilion, Valhalla, NY, USA

Department of Medicine, Division of Pulmonary, Critical Care and Sleep Medicine, Westchester Medical Center and New York Medical College, Valhalla, NY, USA

Peter J. Papadakos, MD, FCCM, FAARC Critical Care Medicine, Anesthesiology, Surgery, Neurology, and Neurosurgery, University of Rochester, University of Rochester School of Medicine and Dentistry, Rochester, NY, USA

Corey Scurlock, MD, MBA eHealth Center, Westchester Medical Center Health Network, Taylor Pavilion, Valhalla, NY, USA

Department of Medicine, Division of Pulmonary, Critical Care and Sleep Medicine, Westchester Medical Center and New York Medical College, Valhalla, NY, USA

Department of Anesthesiology, Westchester Medical Center and New York Medical College, Valhalla, NY, USA

Margie Hodges Shaw, JD, PhD, HEC-C Division of Medical Humanities and Bioethics, University of Rochester School of Medicine and Dentistry, Rochester, NY, USA

James E. Szalados, MD, MBA, MHA, JD Director, Surgical and Neurocritical Care Units, Rochester Regional Health System at Rochester General Hospital, Rochester, NY, USA

The Szalados Law Firm, Hilton, NY, USA

Samuel A. Tisherman, MD, FACS, FCCM Department of Surgery, Program in Trauma, University of Maryland School of Medicine, RA Cowley Shock Trauma Center, Baltimore, MD, USA

Wendy L. Wright, MD, JM, FCCM, FNCS Emory University Hospital Midtown, Emory University School of Medicine, Atlanta, GA, USA

Chapter 1
Morality, Ethics, the Foundations of the American Legal System, and Ethical Challenges in the Digital Age

James E. Szalados

Cultural Norms, Morality, Ethics, and the Law

The norms of behavior within a society are culturally defined. Such cultural definitions of behavioral norms are largely rooted within religion, custom, and tradition. The course of human history is defined by diverse groups and cultures which developed and unified around specific and often unique sets of purpose, value, and principles. Thus, norms of behavior can vary significantly between cultures (e.g., eastern and western values) and even between common root cultures with divergent traditions (e.g., English, Australian, Canadian, and American values) and even among the various states within a country. Codes of conduct, regulations, and laws evolve from shared ethical and moral values when individuals with a shared culture form a society and then a system of government. Thus, each society in some fashion will define its values and authorize its government to enforce shared values through legislation, regulation, and laws.

Societies cannot function or preserve their existence without oversight and enforcement mechanisms for upholding shared values. Regulations and laws are the mechanism by which societies enforce compliance with shared norms and preserve the deeply held, widely shared, and relatively stable values of that society. Without defined standards of tolerance and standards for behavioral conformity, social order is compromised. The distinctions between moral and immoral, ethical and unethical, and legal or illegal are thus defined in the context of shared cultural values [1].

J. E. Szalados (✉)
Director, Surgical and Neurocritical Care Units, Rochester Regional Health System at Rochester General Hospital, Rochester, NY, USA

The Szalados Law Firm, Hilton, NY, USA
e-mail: james.szalados@rochesterregional.org; jszalados@aol.com

J. E. Szalados (ed.), *The Medical-Legal Aspects of Acute Care Medicine*,
https://doi.org/10.1007/978-3-030-68570-6_1

Thus, morality refers to a shared system of behavior within a society whereby standards are defined, and shared, regarding the "rightness" or "wrongness" of certain behaviors. Durkheim observed that "man is a moral being, only because he lives in society. Let all social life disappear and morality will disappear with it" [2]. Morality is an increasingly complex notion in an increasingly complex world: "the word carries the concepts of: (1) moral standards, with regard to behavior; (2) moral responsibility, referring to our conscience; and (3) a moral identity, or one who is capable of right or wrong action. Common synonyms include ethics, principles, virtue, and goodness. Morality has become a complicated issue in the multi-cultural world we live in today" [3].

Whereas morality may restrict behaviors, it can also promote rights and freedoms by opening the scope of intellectual inquiry, argument, innovation, and experimentation. Therefore, if the moral code of a society says that a certain action is right, then that action is right, at least within that society.

Freedoms will both liberate and protect. In a perfect world, liberties are endless limited only where one's liberty interests encroach on those of others. Thus, the *freedom to* is the freedom to pursue one's own individuality and personal goals and interests; *freedom from* is the freedom from encroachment upon one's rights by others. In order to be just, laws must be crafted so as to maintain the delicate balance of personal freedoms against societal interests. In a free society, laws must reconcile "principles of conformity and individual initiative, group living and private freedom of choice, social regulation and personal autonomy" [4]. Thus, "to individuality should belong the part of life in which it is chiefly the individual that is interested; to society, the part which chiefly interests society… everyone who receives the protection of society owes a return for that benefit, and the fact of living in society renders it indispensable that each should to observe a certain conduct towards the rest" [5]. Within Mill's utilitarian framework, the function of laws and regulations within a society is to provide for the "the greatest good for the greatest number."

Thus, the concept of "justice" is defined as a socially mandated conformity with existing law and regulations. Justice also presupposes that laws are enforced uniformly and that people can expect equal and impartial treatment in the eyes of the law. In the words of Aristotle, "The only stable state is the one in which all men are equal before the law" [6]. The Declaration of the Rights of Man and of the Citizen was drafted by the Abbé Sieyès and the Marquis de Lafayette, in consultation with Thomas Jefferson and was adopted in 1789 by the National Constituent Assembly of France, during the period of the French Revolution, as a human civil rights document, and presumably, the first step toward writing a constitution for France. The French *Declaration* espoused the principles of secular natural rights and law and accordingly defined universal individual and collective rights applicable to all men. The Declaration contains 17 articles, and a preamble which describes the document to represent a "solemn declaration [of] the natural, inalienable, and sacred rights of man." For example and in part, Article I states that "Men are born and remain free and equal in rights;" Article IV states that "Liberty consists of doing anything which does not harm others;" and Article VI states that "The law is the expression of the general will. All the citizens have the right of contributing personally or through their representatives to its formation. It must be the same for all, either that it protects, or that it punishes" [7]. With respect to the just enforcement of laws, the French Declaration, (in contrast to prevailing notions ...surrendered to government), instead advocated that the power to enforce rights, rather than the rights themselves, be delegated to government. Furthermore, the Declaration, stated that such "executive power" was voluntarily delegated and revocable. The "executive power" of the government could thus be rightly reclaimed by the citizens in the event that the government become despotic or tyrannical.

The U.S. Declaration of Independence may be considered to be a product of the Enlightenment. Philosophers such as John Locke, David Hume, and others espoused humanistic principles to emphasize human liberty, human rights, and social justice as the foundation for a social contract between government and its governed. Subsequently in 1776, in the United States, The Declaration of Independence was adopted by the Second Continental Congress meeting at the Pennsylvania State House in Philadelphia and stated, in part:

> When in the Course of human events it becomes necessary for one people to dissolve the political bands which have connected them with another and to assume among the powers of the earth, the separate and equal station to which the Laws of Nature and of Nature's God entitle them, a decent respect to the opinions of mankind requires that they should declare the causes which impel them to the separation.
>
> We hold these truths to be self-evident, that all men are created equal, that they are endowed by their Creator with certain unalienable Rights that among these are Life, Liberty and the pursuit of Happiness. — That to secure these rights, Governments are instituted among Men, deriving their just powers from the consent of the governed, — That whenever any Form of Government becomes destructive of these ends, it is the Right of the People to alter or to abolish it, and to institute new Government, laying its foundation on such principles and organizing its powers in such form, as to them shall seem most likely to effect their Safety and Happiness [8]....

The United States Constitution was enacted September 17, 1787, at the Pennsylvania State House in Philadelphia and represents the foundational legal principles from which all laws in the United States are derived. The Preamble to the Constitution articulates its guiding principles to be unity, domestic tranquility, and general welfare. The US Constitution is remarkable in that it assumed that both individual rights and natural rights were secured and articulated that the Constitution did not grant rights, but secured those natural personal rights and instead imposed limits upon the power of government. The link between morality and the law is underscored by the words of John Adams: "Our Constitution was made only for a moral and religious People. It is wholly inadequate to the government of any other" [9]. Thus, the US Constitution was built upon a long history of philosophical inquiry into the nature of man; the Framers' views on moral philosophy were influenced by the intellectual traditions which guided their views on morality and politics such as natural law theory and Scottish Enlightenment thinking on issues of morality, humanism, social justice, and ethics.

Ethics and the Law

A nation's laws are usually founded on moral and ethical principles which demand just enforcement to promote societal harmony. Ethics have been generally considered to be abstract, internalized, and non-binding; they are, in a sense, opinions regarding appropriate behavior and construct. Similar to morality, ethics provide guidelines regarding norms of behavior within certain situations, although ethics are individual norms whereas moral are collective, or social norms. Whereas morality is a social construct, ethics are more personal. Nonetheless, ethical principles are linked to culture: Western ethics are derived from Judaic-Christian principles and the subsequent teachings of Aristotle (virtue ethics), Kant (duty-based ethics), and Bentham and Mill (utilitarian and consequentialist ethics). Eastern ethical principles are derived from diverse sources including Buddhist, Taoist, Confucian, Hindu, and the Islamic Hadith. Therefore, and arguably, western ethics may be more concerned with the exploration of universal truths, whereas eastern ethical principles may be more concerned with protocol and respect; however, it is evident that within all social constructs there are in fact recognizable and non-distinct universally shared ethical principles [10].

Typically, it was believed that what is lawful may not be ethical, and what is ethical may not be lawful. Nonetheless, ethical principles have increasingly formed the basis for legal analysis. The Greek philosopher Plato is credited with the statement that "ethics belongs to the body polis" referring to that what a society determines to be either ethical or unethical is ultimately determined through the courts and through the political bodies which establish laws through legislation. Ethical duties more often than not are increasingly associated with regulatory and legal ramifications. The judicial system has increasingly relied on generally accepted ethical doctrine to delineate and codify concrete duties into regulations and law which are generally accepted as necessary to maintain equality, social order, and to provide a predictable and uniformly applied framework for preventing and resolving disputes. For example, ethical principle of respect for autonomy has formed the basis for regulations and laws regarding assault and battery, informed consent, informed refusal, and right to die; whereas ethical principles of justice form the basis for laws regarding triage, resource allocation in emergency response, and biomedical research.

Professionalism and Professional Ethics in Medicine

Professional societies represent diverse professionals who are united by a common educational background, professional training, and the same or similar interests. The four hallmarks of a profession are as follows: (1) an extensive specialized education in a specialized field of abstract, specialized knowledge with further extended practical training which lead to defined reasoning and skills; (2) the rendering a basic and essential societal service; (3) practitioners usually have a high degree of autonomy in in decision-making and in practice; and, (4) practitioners must undergo a process of legislatively mandated certification or licensing for eligibility to practice. Certification and licensure accords professionals with an exclusive legal right to provide the specific services associated with a profession.

A meaningful and enforceable code of ethics can be considered a hallmark of professionalism. Professionals subscribe to a set of values specific to a given profession, and such values are typically codified as oaths and/or codes. Individual diversity with respect to moral viewpoints among individual practitioners within a profession mandates that the professional society, academy, or association establish its own standards, beyond what law, market, morality, and public opinion would otherwise require, in order to uphold the integrity and public image of the profession. A professional code of ethics thus represents a set of guiding principles intended to inspire and guide professionals in the conduct of their business. Codes can serve as the formal basis for investigating claims of conduct that may be potentially unethical within a profession. Professional codes may hold members to an even higher standard than imposed by regulations or the law, and, in some professional societies, codes of conduct are enforceable through sanctions. Violations of a code of ethics code may represent grounds for revocation of the right practice a profession, which is the case with the American Bar Association's Model Rules of Professional Conduct which may be used in in disbarment procedures [11]; or, the American Academy of Neurosurgeons standards for expert opinion services which, if violated can result in formal discipline [12].

Professions are grounded in a fiduciary relationship between the professional and the client. A fiduciary relationship is defined as "a relationship in which one party places special trust, confidence, and reliance in and is influenced by another who has a fiduciary duty to act for the benefit of the party" [13]. In general, the fiduciary is a professional, who must knowingly accept his or her role in the fiduciary relationship, accept the attendant relationship of trust and confidence, and exercise his or her discretion or expertise in acting on behalf of his or her client. Thus, the oaths or codes of a profession reinforce a duty to uphold the ethical duties inherent in a higher calling.

"Medicine is a moral enterprise; the diligent efforts and work of medical providers converge ultimately on decisions and actions presumed to be directed toward furthering the good of another person, the patient, in need of help and healing" [14]. Thomas Percival published a Code of Medical Ethics in 1803 which outlined professional duties and ideal behaviors for providers and hospitals [15]. Percival's Code is widely recognized to have been the foundation for the American Medical Association's Code of Ethics, first passed at the initial meeting of the AMA in Philadelphia in 1847. The American Medical Association Principles of Medical Ethics and the Opinions of the AMA Council on Ethical & Judicial Affairs comprise the AMA Code of Medical Ethics [16]. The AMA's Council on Ethical and Judicial Affairs (CEJA) publishes an annual report chronicling each year's judicial activities adjudicating the complaints presented before it [17].

Morals are validated by social attitudes, more so than by individual attitudes. What is "right" and what is "good" may vary between societies. Morality refers to a set of deeply held, widely shared, and relatively stable values within a community. In our complex society, every medical encounter raises a potential conflict between the intersecting moral values of physician, or provider, and patient. Thus, where a diverse society-at-large may be composed of a variety of moral values, professional codes of ethics have the important role of unifying and codifying the values of a profession.

Whereas codes are written documents, oaths represent promises, aspirational statements, of idealized ethics typically ritualized through spoken vows witnessed by peers. Oaths outline the ethical elements within a professional relationship but have meaning when the Oath is taken in a free and heartfelt fashion. Adherence to the elements of an oath are typically not enforceable. Oaths may be characterized by a "greater moral weight compared with promises because of their public character, their validation by transcendent appeal, the involvement of the personhood of the swearer, the prescription of consequences for failure to uphold their contents, the generality of the scope of their contents, the prolonged time frame of the commitment, the fact that their moral force remains binding in spite of failures on the part of those to whom the swearer makes the commitment, and the fact that interpersonal fidelity is the moral hallmark of the commitment of the swearer" [18].

The most well-known is the Hippocratic Oath, in either its classical version [19] or its modern version [20, 21], written in 1964 by Louis Lasagna then Academic Dean of the School of Medicine at Tufts University. The modern version of the Hippocratic Oath [22] states:

- I swear to fulfill, to the best of my ability and judgment, this covenant:
- I will respect the hard-won scientific gains of those physicians in whose steps I walk, and gladly share such knowledge as is mine with those who are to follow.
- I will apply, for the benefit of the sick, all measures [that] are required, avoiding those twin traps of overtreatment and therapeutic nihilism.
- I will remember that there is art to medicine as well as science, and that warmth, sympathy, and understanding may outweigh the surgeon's knife or the chemist's drug.
- I will not be ashamed to say "I know not," nor will I fail to call in my colleagues when the skills of another are needed for a patient's recovery.
- I will respect the privacy of my patients, for their problems are not disclosed to me that the world may know. Most especially must I tread with care in matters of life and death. If it is given me to save a life, all thanks. But it may also be within my power to take a life; this awesome responsibility must be faced with great humbleness and awareness of my own frailty. Above all, I must not play at God.
- I will remember that I do not treat a fever chart, a cancerous growth, but a sick human being, whose illness may affect the person's family and economic stability. My responsibility includes these related problems, if I am to care adequately for the sick.
- I will prevent disease whenever I can, for prevention is preferable to cure.
- I will remember that I remain a member of society, with special obligations to all my fellow human beings, those sound of mind and body as well as the infirm.

- If I do not violate this oath, may I enjoy life and art, respected while I live and remembered with affection thereafter. May I always act so as to preserve the finest traditions of my calling and may I long experience the joy of healing those who seek my help.

Some examples of other less widely known professional oaths specifically written for medical professionals include the Oath of Maimonides and The Physicians' Oath codified by the World Medical Association. The Physician's Oath was authored in response to atrocities committed in Nazi Germany during World War II and reads:

- I solemnly pledge myself to consecrate my life to the service of humanity;
- I will give my teachers the respect and gratitude which is their due;
- I will practice my profession with conscience and dignity;
- The health of my patient will be my first consideration;
- I will respect the secrets which are confided in me, even after the patient has died;
- I will maintain by all the means in my power, the honor and the noble traditions of the medical profession;
- My colleagues will be my brothers;
- I will not permit considerations of religion, nationality, race, party politics or social standing to intervene between my duty and my patient;
- I will maintain the utmost respect for human life from its beginning even under threat and I will not use my medical knowledge contrary to the laws of humanity;
- I make these promises solemnly, freely and upon my honor [22].

The Nightingale Pledge, authored in 1893, is a statement of the ethics and principles of the nursing profession in the United States, it is, for intents and purposes, a professional oath and stems from the Hippocratic Oath. The Oath was revised in 1935 to read:

- I solemnly pledge myself before God and in the presence of this assembly to pass my life in purity and to practise my profession faithfully.
- I will abstain from whatever is deleterious and mischievous, and will not take or knowingly administer any harmful drug.
- I will do all in my power to maintain and elevate the standard of my profession and will hold in confidence all personal matters committed to my keeping and all family affairs coming to my knowledge in the practice of my calling.
- With loyalty will I aid the physician in his work, and as a missioner of health, I will dedicate myself to devoted service for human welfare [23].

Humanism in the Health Sciences

Humanism can be defined as "any system or mode of thought or action in which human interests, values and dignity predominate" [24]. Specifically, in medicine, humanism describes the attitudes and behaviors which demonstrate interest in and respect for patients' psychological, social, and spiritual concerns and values [25].

Nonetheless, medicine has always been firmly grounded within the principles of humanism from the Hippocratic Oath through the teachings of the medieval physicians Avicenna and Maimonides. The Renaissance ideal of the physician was of a person who was learned both in the humanities and the medical sciences.

The latter decades of the twentieth century witnessed a renewed attempt to reestablish humanism within the medical profession. Arguably, the contemporary "humanism in medicine" movement represented a response to perceived external forces such as the "corporatization of the practice of medicine, the increasing role of business and finance in medicine, the fragmentation of patient experiences, the reduced time for clinical encounters, the increasing reliance on technology as a substitute for human interaction, and a de-emphasis on the humanities in the education of physicians" [26]. Increasingly, within the context of provider "burnout," the adoption of humanism within the practice of medicine has been identified as a core tenet of not only patient care but of provider wellness.

The specific traits of a humanistic provider are not clearly defined; however, they include (a) humility, respect, and the ability to listen; (b) relationship building and the ability to build a connection with the patient as a person; (c) compassion, empathy, sincere caring, mindfulness, and self-reflection including the ability to treat the patient as the provider would himself or herself want to be treated; and, (d) curiosity as a lifelong learner and communication with patients through support and teaching. Although in the past, professionalism and humanism were traditionally learned informally during a provider's training through role-modeling, it is now being formally integrated into the curricula of physicians and other providers as a core body of knowledge.

The Principles of Biomedical Ethics

Morality, ethics, and the law merge within the principle of biomedical ethics. Beauchamp and Childress originally developed four principles, which represent the foundation for modern bioethical decision-making: (1) respect for individual autonomy; (2) the principle of beneficence; (3) the principle of nonmaleficence; and (4) the principle of justice [27]. These principles are widely considered and well accepted to represent a standard theoretical framework from which to analyze ethical situations in medicine, and these four principles will generally encompass most of the moral dilemmas that arise in healthcare.

The Principle of Respect for Autonomy: Consent, Refusal, and Right to Die

The principle of respect for autonomy presumes that rational persons have the right to make uncoerced, informed, and voluntary decisions regarding their personhood. The antithesis of autonomy is paternalism, whereby individual choice is subjugated to the dictates of a superior father-like figure who "knows" what a person needs, rather than considering what that person actually wants.

The respect for autonomy is exemplified by the principles of informed consent and informed refusal. Consent constitutes a permission and represents the legal defense to potential allegations of both civil and criminal assault, and battery, which are predicated in a showing of unpermitted bodily contact. In order to be valid in the medical treatment setting, consent or refusal must be "informed." Informed consent and refusal presuppose that an uncoerced voluntary decision is made after a competent patient has received an unbiased, truthful, and full disclosure of the indications for, and the risks, benefits, and alternatives to a proposed medical therapy. Thus, the notion of "informed" requires a "meeting of minds" and requires that a critical process of communication has transpired including, but not limited to, due diligence by the provider including consideration of one's capabilities, evidence-based practice and standards of care, and patient circumstances, followed by a true opportunity of the patient to ask questions and to finally decide for his or herself [28].

Capacity is at the basis of informed consent. True medical decision-making capacity can apply only if one can demonstrate one's understanding of the situation and the issues, the consequences of a decision, reasonable reasoning or thought process, and effectively communicate. Thus exercise of one's autonomy presupposes capacity which in turn requires understanding, reasonable consideration, and communication. Reasonable decision-making is weighed by others in a moral sense; every carefully considered decision may not be morally acceptable, even if it falls squarely under the principle of autonomy; additive behaviors and suicide are some examples of potentially unacceptable exercises of autonomy subject to challenges on moral grounds. Moreover, in order to meet legal criteria for capacity, both situational capacity, such as intoxication, and, competency which relates to more permanent impairments such as mental illness, dementia, or acute or chronic neurological injuries must be considered. The potential lack of capacity underlies the legal remedies of healthcare proxies or legal guardians whereby surrogate decision-makers are appointed and empowered to make substituted judgments on behalf of the incapacitated, based on some understanding of the patient's needs or preferences, as the patient would choose if he or she had the capacity to do so, thereby imputing some element of autonomy in decision-making.

The traditional antithesis of autonomy is paternalism. Medical paternalism occurs when a provider decides what is best for the patient, either in the absence of shared decision-making, or without consulting the patient regarding their preferences or wishes. In the past, when there was little or no understanding of science or medicine by the lay public, paternalism was seen as necessary to guide patients in their decision-making. More recently, as public education has increasingly provided lay persons with a foundation for their medical decision-making, paternalism has increasingly been replaced by shared decision-making and a respect for the patient's autonomy.

The Principle of Beneficence and the Fiduciary Duty

Beneficence is generally defined as an obligation to help others further their personal goals and interests. Beneficence is strongly rooted within the notion of fiduciary duty and the duty of care that is a tenet upon which all professional relationships are based. A fiduciary relationship arises in every professional relationship because professionals work for the good of their clients; professionalism traditionally places a greater priority on the duty to serve than it does on productivity of profit. Encounters between clients or patients, and their professional, are characterized by an imbalance of education, training, and experience that results in a position of dependence by, and substantial confidence extended to the fiduciary. Patients do not understand the intricacies of physiology, disease, and treatment; therefore, patients largely depend on the beneficence of providers to "take care of them." In medicine, the concept of beneficence is rooted within the values expressed in the Hippocratic Oath. However, as evidenced in the Hippocratic Oath, beneficence can be at odds with the principle of autonomy because it removes the element of risk balancing from the patient and places that obligation within the responsibility of the provider, thus promoting paternalism.

The Principle of Nonmaleficence and "Primum non Nocere"

The principle of nonmaleficence mandates that professional actor takes care so as to avoid causing harm; the principle of *primum non nocere*—or—"above all (or alternatively "first") do no harm." The principles of beneficence and nonmaleficence are closely interrelated because they both require the balancing of respect for individual autonomy, explorations of professional and personal values, and utilitarianism. The Hippocratic Oath enjoins the principles of beneficence and nonmaleficence where it states that "I will use treatment to help the sick according to my ability and judgment, but I will never use it to injure or wrong them." Therefore, in cases of conflict between beneficence and nonmalfeasance, nonmalfeasance will normally override beneficence.

The principle of nonmaleficence and it translation, "first do no harm," because of the implication that healthcare professionals will cause harm if left unchecked, has recently launched a quality movement intended to monitor medical errors and protect the patient from harm through regulatory and administrative oversight [29]. It has been well publicized that patient during the delivery of healthcare is a leading cause of morbidity and mortality [30]. The 1999 Institute of Medicine (IOM) report entitled "To Err is Human: Building a Safer Health System" underscored the impact of medical errors to the US healthcare system and posited that the prevention of death and injury from medical errors would require dramatic, systemwide changes in the US healthcare delivery model [31]. On the other hand, preventable, or foreseeable, medical errors, may legitimately constitute medical negligence, and therefore be actionable under the law of medical malpractice. Negligence is defined as a foreseeable imposition of unreasonable risk of harm upon another, and the occurrence of that harm causing quantifiable damages. Moreover, the importance of avoiding harm affirms the need for competence among all medical providers and support staff [28].

The Principle of Justice and the Equitable Distribution of Resources

The notion of justice is fundamental to Western morality, ethics, and law. Justice, however, is a complex and poorly defined term. Although everyone believes that justice is a fundamental liberty right, not everyone agrees on how it is applied. Justice implies equitable distribution of benefits and burdens to individuals in society, and the rights of individuals to resources. Justice is implicated in discussions of fairness, entitlement, and equality.

There are many forms of justice: (1) distributive justice which represents the equitable allocation of scare resources in society; (2) retributive justice which imposes punishment upon wrongdoers in a presumably objective and proportionate manner through a fair and impartial judicial system; (3) restorative justice which seeks to compensate those wronged—to "make whole" those injured under the tort law system; and finally, (4) procedural justice refers to predictable, structured, and transparent processes.

Distributive justice is especially important to public policy, public health, and emergency response preparedness. The principle of distributive justice addresses the equitable distribution of benefits and burdens to individuals in society:

- To each person an equal share
- To each person according to need
- To each person according to effort
- To each person according to contribution
- To each person according to merit
- To each person according to free-market exchanges [32].

Nonetheless, the concept of justice represents something greater than equality since persons can be treated unjustly even if they are treated equally. Where individuals lose capacity, freedom, or autonomy, they are at risk of losing their access to justice.

Clinical Ethical Challenges and Ethics Committees

Although informal hospital-based ethics committees have been in existence since at least the 1960s [33], it was the New Jersey Supreme Court in its opinion *In re Quinlan* which suggested that ethics committees might play an advisory role in such cases as an alternative to resorting to litigation within the court system [34]. Thereafter, in 1983, the President's Commission which addressed life-sustaining treatment provided further impetus regarding hospital ethics committees to assist with decisions regarding the use and the foregoing of life-sustaining interventions [35].

Hospital ethics committees (or, institutional ethics committees (IECs)), are, in general, quasi-formal advisory groups who assemble ad hoc to discuss the management of cases which raise ethical or moral dilemmas. IECs review, on request, ethical or moral questions that may arise during inpatient care. IECs are usually composed of interested members such as providers, nurses, and social workers. In more complex, and arguably more credible variations, ethics committees may also include, for example, bioethicists, lay persons, and/or attorneys. IECs also vary not only by structure but also by mode of operation; for example, individual consultants may investigate and then report to committee, a small team of IEC members may address a specific case, or, the entire committee may function as a unit.

The role and importance of IECs will vary by institution. In general, IECs provide the following: (1) consultation in complex clinical cases; (2) guidance or education for the healthcare team; and/or (3) development and review of institutional policies regarding the management of ethical issues arising during the delivery of patient care. The American Society for Bioethics and Humanities (ASBH) has identified two main objectives for clinical ethics case consultation: (1) identify and analyze the nature of the value uncertainty and (2) facilitate the building of a "principled ethical resolution" [36]. Hurst and colleagues identified the main reasons for ethics consultations:

- To obtain needed help in deciding what to do
- To identify a practical way of doing what had already been decided should be done
- To implement a practical solution
- To obtain reassurance that the correct decision was being made
- To better to face people who might otherwise think that the decision was inappropriate
- To seek consensus [37].

Ethical dilemmas frequently arise when there are conflicts or uncertainty about the goals of care, the value of a specific intervention as it relates to those goals, and the moral implications of medical choices and when communication about these conflicts breaks down. IECs may also support clinical staff who may suffer moral distress stemming from internal or external conflicts in complex clinical situations [38].

The American Academy of Pediatrics (AAP) has articulated its standards regarding ethics consultation:

1. Any patient, parent or guardian, or family member should be able to initiate an ethics consultation.
2. The patient and parent or guardian should be able to refuse to participate in an ethics consultation without concern for negative repercussions.
3. The refusal of a patient or parent or guardian to participate in an ethics consultation should not obstruct the ability of an ethics committee to provide consultation services to physicians, nurses, and other concerned staff.
4. Any physician, nurse, or other healthcare provider who is involved in the care of the patient should be able to request an ethics consultation without fear of reprisal.
5. The process of consultation should be open to all persons involved in the patient's care yet conducted in a manner that respects patient and family confidentiality and privacy.
6. Anonymous requests for consultation are not recommended. In situations in which fear of reprisal limits open discussion of the issues, the identity of the person(s) requesting consultation may be kept confidential.
7. The primary care pediatrician should be invited to participate in the consultation to support existing physician-family relationships [38].

Perhaps the greatest significance of the AP guidelines is its focus not only on patient and caregiver autonomy but also its respect for the healthcare team. In general, IECs which function in a vacuum, without stressing communication and consensus, are likely to fail not only in individual case circumstances but also in their mission.

Moral Distress in Clinical Care

The term "moral injury" was popularized by Johnathan Shay after the Vietnam War [39]. The clinical healthcare environment is characterized by one or more subcultures, which individuals must navigate, as they perform their patient care duties within the system in which they work. Where morality forms the basis of laws because morality generally represents shared societal values which demand enforcement to promote societal harmony, ethics more properly address each person's internal and more personal moral compass [28]. Although arguably, in an anthropological sense, culture creates shared ethical systems, healthcare workers do not create but rather join the healthcare system and are generally expected to conform to rather than create the culture. The term "moral distress" refers to a phenomenon originally described by Andrew Jameton in 1984 [40]. According to Jameton, moral distress occurs "when a clinician makes a moral judgment about a case in which he or she is involved and an external constraint makes it difficult or impossible to act on that judgment, resulting in painful feelings and/or psychological disequilibrium" [41].

Moral distress represents a cognitive dissonance similar to that described in military veterans. Cognitive dissonance was first described by Leon Festinger in 1957 from his work on the behavior of cult members [42]. Festinger proposed that individuals have an innate need to maintain harmony between their attitudes and behaviors; in other words, to avoid disharmony (or dissonace) - this forms the basis for the "principle of cognitive consistency." On the other hand, when inconsistency arises between attitudes or behaviors, dissonance arises, individuals try to take steps to either reduce the extent of, or eliminate, that dissonance. Forced compliance occurs in situations where one must act, either because of rules or social pressure, in ways that are inconsistent with his or her beliefs [43].

Until recently, the literature has been silent on the moral distress of healthcare trainees, staff, and providers. Moreover, moral distress has now been identified in multiple professions [44] including medicine, nursing [45], pharmacy [46], and respiratory therapy [47].

The importance of strong and cohesive teamwork, communication, and shared decision-making as ways of mitigating moral distress cannot be underestimated. Transparency, especially with respect to critical decision-making in complex ethical dilemmas, fosters such communication and can help minimize misperceptions and confusion. Of course, reasonable persons might always reasonably disagree with respect to the applicable ethical principles, the application of ethical principles, and with respect to individual value judgments. However, where individuals and the group together participate in honest and open discourse, there is opportunity to reconcile differing beliefs and points of view. In the end, transparent and well-considered reasons for implementaing one course of action over another (through evidence based decision making, application of ethical principles, and recognition of uncertainities) may actually stregnthen emotional bonds between patients and caregivers, and within the team itself. Thus, the powers of honesty and respect, with patients and caregivers, and among the care team, cannot be over-emphasized.

The Challenges of Biomedical Ethics in the Technological and Digital Age

Where morality and ethics represent the shared values of a society, technological changes through innovation can shift social norms and that in turn can result in changing social values. Technological innovation is inextricably linked to moral, ethical, and legal innovation. In the past, physicians were limited by the availability of technology; now technology can provide interventional opportunities which may or may not be ethically sound; for example, continued life support in the setting of futility. In some cases, morality and law may stifle technological innovations; however, increasingly technological innovation is forcing re-evaluation of traditional ethical beliefs and therefore "forcing" the development of laws to manage the evolving technology.

Health information technology (HIT) is continually evolving via technology such as Electronic Medical Records (EMRs), Clinical Decision Support Systems (CDS), Health Information Exchanges (HIEs), Computerized Physician Order Entry (CPOE), mHealth, telemedicine, and remote monitoring. Although such technological innovation improves the efficiency and arguably the safety of care delivery, these advances have also led to large-scale privacy breaches. Thus the HIT, together with the internet and social media, has redefined the public notion of privacy; therefore arguably, regulations and laws governing the privacy of health information may become outdated.

Within the field of neurosciences, advances in functional neuroimaging, neurogenetics, neurobiomarkers, neuro-psychopharmacology, brain stimulation, neural stem cells, neural tissue transplants have created the newly recognized disciplines of neuroethics [48] and neurolaw [49]. Future responsible advances in the neurosciences will necessitate interdisciplinary collaboration between neuroscientists and scholars from ethics, philosophy, law, and others who focus on the implications and applications of science and the associated ethical, legal, social, and policy implications [50]. For example, in the field of criminal law, functional magnetic resonance imaging (fMRI), neurogenetics, biomarkers, and neuropharmacology are challenging traditional notions of responsibility, moral responsibility, free will, and autonomy [51]. Innovation in imaging technology may delineate the neurobiological correlates of human behaviors. The promise of fMRI may lie in its ability to allow communication with individuals previously believed to be comatose, and, alternatively, as a more reliable lie detector.

The Ethics of Practical Wisdom

Practical wisdom has been recognized as a key concept in the field of virtue ethics [52]. Practical wisdom (Aristotle's concept of *phronesis*) refers to the pragmatic process of perceiving the relevant issues within the situation, recognizing the feelings provided by one's internal moral compass, deliberating upon and considering the options, and ultimately acting thereupon. Aristotle argued that each of us need to develop character traits such as self-control, love, generosity, gentleness, truthfulness, friendliness, and courage. Aristotle termed these traits virtues (*arete*) and argued that these virtues provided a conduit for the practical application of wisdom [53].

The role that *phronesis* plays in ethical medical decisions is arguably central to the skill of clinical judgment. There is an increased recognition of the importance of moral virtues such as care, honesty, and courage to medical practice and also argued that ethical physicians and providers embody a practical moral know-how (*phronesis*), now increasingly seen to be a term synonymous with "professionalism," "professional judgment," or "clinical judgment" which is necessary if good moral motivations (dispositions or virtues) are to translated into ethical and effective patient care. Phronesis is the link between a physician's medical knowledge, clinical reasoning, and the physician's internal moral compass providing the foundations by which to navigate the competing scientific and humanistic demands of ethical medical practice [54].

Technological complexity will increasingly challenge the moral code of medical practice. Practical wisdom has been proposed as part of the solution to navigate complexity, aiming at the provision of morally good care. The focus of medicine must remain the delivery of the best possible morally sound care to each individual patient.

Conclusion

Morality, ethics, and the law are the basis for and the products of the societies in which they are defined. Morality and ethics are in themselves insufficient unless they become guiding principles in everyday transactions; alternatively, they are codified into regulations and law which then become enforceable. The moral and ethical foundations upon which our societies are founded will become increasingly important to navigate effectively through a rapidly evolving technological revolution which remains in the end, the humanistic care of the sick by providers.

References

1. Szalados JE. Morality, ethics, and the law: an overview of the foundations of contemporary clinical ethical analysis in ethics and law for neurosciences clinicians: foundations and evolving challenges. New Brunswick: Rutgers University Press; 2019.
2. Durkheim E. In: Bellah RN, editor. Emile Durkheim on morality and society. Chicago: University of Chicago Press. Heritage of Sociology Series; 1973.
3. All about philosophy. https://www.allaboutphilosophy.org/morality.htm. Cite verified May 12, 2019.
4. Lee D. Freedom and culture. Saddle River: Prentice Hall; 1959.
5. Mill JS. On liberty. Mineola: Dover Press; 2002.
6. Aristotle. Aristotle's politics. Oxford: Clarendon Press; 1905.
7. France: declaration of the right of man and the citizen. National Legislative Bodies/ National Authorities. 26 August 1789. Available online at: https://www.refworld.org/docid/3ae6b52410.html.
8. The U.S. Declaration of Independence; John Hancock, et al.; 1776.
9. From John Adams to Massachusetts Militia, 11 October 1798. Available online at: https://founders.archives.gov/documents/Adams/99-02-02-3102.
10. Widdows H. Western and eastern principles and globalised bioethics. Asian Bioethics Rev. 2011;3(1):14–22.
11. American Bar Association. Model Code of Judicial Conduct. 2011 Edition. Available online at: https://www.americanbar.org/groups/professional_responsibility/publications/model_code_of_judicial_conduct/.
12. AANS Code of Ethics. Available online at: https://www.aans.org/-/media/Images/AANS/Header/Govenance/AANS_Code_of_Ethics_11-22-2014.ashx?la=en&hash=124B159D6B41ACF78DFB0110EB55B10E68D5D3DD.

13. "Fiduciary relationship." The Merriam-Webster.com legal dictionary, Merriam-Webster Inc., https://www.merriam-webster.com/legal/fiduciary%20relationship. Accessed 30 Nov 2019.
14. Pellegrino ED. Ethics and the moral Center of the Medical Enterprise. Bull NY Acad Med. 1978;54(7):625–40.
15. Pellegrino ED. Thomas Percival's ethics: the ethics beneath the etiquette. 1985:1–52. In: Thomas Percival, medical ethics. Birmingham: Classics of Medicine Library.
16. AMA Code of Medical Ethics. Available online at: https://www.ama-assn.org/delivering-care/ama-code-medical-ethics. Verified November 11, 2017.
17. Council on Ethical and Judicial Affairs, American Medical Association. Chicago, IL: CEJA Rep. 5-A-13; 2013.
18. Sulmasy DP. What is an oath and why should a physician swear one? Theor Med Bioeth. 1999;20(4):329–46.
19. Hippocratic oath. Translation from the Greek by Ludwig Edelstein. From the hippocratic oath: text, translation, and interpretation, by Ludwig Edelstein. Baltimore: Johns Hopkins Press; 1943.
20. Orr RD, Pang N, Pellegrino ED, Siegler M. Use of the hippocratic oath: a review of twentieth century practice and a content analysis of oaths administered in medical schools in the U.S and Canada in 1993. J Clin Ethics. 1997;8(4):377–88.
21. Kao AC, Parsi KP. Content analyses of oaths administered at U.S. medical schools in 2000. Acad Med. 2004;79(9):882–7.
22. Available online at: http://www.aapsonline.org/ethics/oaths.htm. Verified November 11, 2017.
23. Florence Nightingale Pledge. Nightingalesnursing. Online at: http://nightingalesnursing.net/florence-nightingale-pledge/.
24. Webster's New Universal Unabridged Dictionary. New York, NY: Barnes & Noble Publishing, Inc.; 2003.
25. Branch WT, Kern D, Haidet P, et al. The patient-physician relationship. Teaching the human dimensions of care in clinical settings. JAMA. 2001;286(9):1067–74.
26. Thibault GE. Humanism in medicine: what does it mean and why is it more important than ever? Acad Med. 2019;94(8):1074–7.
27. Beauchamp TL, Childress JF. Principles of biomedical ethics. 3rd ed. Oxford, UK: Oxford University Press; 1989.
28. Id. Szalados JE. Morality, ethics, and the law; 2019.
29. The Joint Commission. Leading the way to zero. https://www.jointcommission.org/performance-improvement/joint-commission/leading-the-way-to-zero/. See also.
30. de Vries EN, Ramrattan MA, Smorenburg SM, Gouma DJ, Boermeester MA. The incidence and nature of in-hospital adverse events: a systematic review. Qual Saf Health Care. 2008;17(3):216–23.
31. Kohn LT, Corrigan JM, Donaldson MS, editors. To err is human: building a safer health system. Washington, DC: National Academy Press, Institute of Medicine; 1999.
32. Id. Beauchamp & Childress; 1994. p. 330.
33. Youngner SJ, et al. A National Survey of Hospital Ethics Committees. Crit Care Med. 1983;11(11):902–5.
34. In re Quinlan 70 NJ 10, 355 A2d 647 (NJ 1976).
35. President's Commission for the Study of Ethical Problems in Medicine and Biomedical and Behavioral Research. Deciding to forego life-sustaining treatment: a report on the ethical, medical, and legal issues in treatment decisions. Washington, DC: US Government Printing Office; 1983.
36. American Society for Bioethics and Humanities. Core competencies for health care ethics consultation. Glenview: American Society for Bioethics and Humanities; 2010.
37. Hurst SA, et al. How physicians face ethical difficulties: a qualitative analysis. J Med Ethics. 2005;31(1):317–4.
38. Moon M, AAP Committee on Bioethics. Institutional Ethics Committees. Pediatrics. 2019;143(5):e20190659.

39. Shay J. Achilles in Vietnam: combat trauma and the undoing of character. New York: Atheneum; 1994.
40. Jameton A. Nursing practice: the ethical issues. Englewood Cliffs: Prentice-Hall; 1984.
41. Perni S. Moral distress: a call to action. AMA J Ethics. 2017;19(6):533–6.
42. Festinger L. A theory of cognitive dissonance. Stanford: Stanford University Press; 1957.
43. Festinger L, Carlsmith JM. Cognitive consequences of forced compliance. J Abnorm Soc Psychol. 1959;58(2):203.
44. Allen R, Judkins-Cohn T, deVelasco R, et al. Moral distress among healthcare professionals at a health system. JONAS Healthc Law Ethics Regul. 2013;15(3):111–8.
45. Burston AS, Tuckett AG. Moral distress in nursing: contributing factors, outcomes and interventions. Nurs Ethics. 2013;20(3):312–24.
46. Sporrong SK, Höglund AT, Arnetz B. Measuring moral distress in pharmacy and clinical practice. Nurs Ethics. 2006;13(4):416–27.
47. Swenzer KD, Wang L. Assessing moral distress in respiratory care practitioners. Crit Care Med. 2006;34(12):2967–297.
48. Roskies A. Neuroethics for the new millenium. Neuron. 2002;35(1):21–3.
49. Szalados JE. Neurlolaw and the integration of neuroscience, ethics, and the law. In: Ethics and law for neurosciences clinicians: foundations and evolving challenges. New Brunswick: Rutgers University Press; 2019.
50. Illes J. Empowering brain science with neuroethics. Lancet. 2010;376(9749):1294–5.
51. Vincent NA. Neuroscience and legal responsibility. Oxford, UK: Oxford University Press; 2013.
52. Russell D. Practical intelligence and the virtues. Oxford: Oxford University Press; 2009.
53. Schwartz B, Sharpe K. Practical wisdom: the right way to do the right thing. New York: Riverhead Books; 2010.
54. Pellegrino E, Thomasma D. The virtues in clinical practice. Oxford: Oxford University Press; 1993.

Chapter 2
Traditional and Applied Clinical Ethics: Contemporary and Evolving Challenges

Margie Hodges Shaw, Marianne Chiafery, and David C. Kaufman

Taking care of patients is a moral endeavor. In 1847, the newly established American Medical Association adopted its first Code of Medical Ethics, largely embracing the code developed in 1803 by the English physician and philosopher Thomas Percival [1]. Philosophers, theologians, and clinicians contributed to early medical ethics scholarship. German theologian Fritz Jahr published articles, starting in 1927, arguing for a broader conception of medical ethics and the establishment of an academic discipline, "Bio-Ethik" [2]. The scope of medical ethics expanded with advances in sciences and technology and in reaction to perceived failures in ethical decision-making, in both human research and patient care. It also expanded as the care of patients became interprofessional and team-based. The American Nurses Association adopted the first Code of Ethics for Nurses in 1950 [3].

In America, the term "bioethics" gained traction in the late 1960s and early 1970s as scholars embraced the language and created institutions dedicated to the examination and analysis of ethical issues facing science, medicine, and technology. Philosopher Daniel Callahan and psychoanalyst Willard Gaylin founded the Hastings Center in 1969 [4]. In 1971, Georgetown University established a Bioethics Research Library and founded the Kennedy Institute of Bioethics within the Kennedy Institute for Ethics [5]. However, the specific scope of the term "bioethics" varied; it often included the study of ethics in human research, human health, environment, sciences, technology, and animal research and rights. Today, "bioethics" is understood to be a relatively young multi- and interdisciplinary field applying ethical reasoning and methods to the health sciences, life sciences, and computer sciences when they interface with patient care. "Bioethics" includes

M. H. Shaw · M. Chiafery · D. C. Kaufman (✉)
Division of Medical Humanities and Bioethics, University of Rochester School of Medicine and Dentistry, Rochester, NY, USA
e-mail: Margie_Shaw@urmc.rochester.edu; Marianne_Chiafery@urmc.rochester.edu; David_Kaufman@urmc.rochester.edu

J. E. Szalados (ed.), *The Medical-Legal Aspects of Acute Care Medicine*,
https://doi.org/10.1007/978-3-030-68570-6_2

decision-making in the care of patients. As such, it is important to consider which values are fundamental to the care of patients, and whose values.

In 1979, Tom Beauchamp and James Childress published the Principles of Biomedical Ethics, introducing the four principles of bioethics as an approach to resolving dilemmas in clinical ethics [6]. "Principlism" offered an alternative to deontology and utilitarianism, the traditional moral theories applied to medical ethics and to other approaches including virtue ethics, casuistry, and feminist ethics [7]. Beauchamp and Childress argue that the four principles of bioethics – *beneficence (do good), nonmaleficence (do no harm), justice (be fair),* and *autonomy (respect the right of self-determination)* – in combination with rules and virtues provide a sufficient method for resolving clinical ethics conflicts. Most health professional schools teach principlism while acknowledging the limitation of applying any particular ethical theory to ethical dilemmas in clinical care. Gert and Clouser identify two limitations of the principles approach: (1) it merely offers clinicians an unsound checklist and (2) it does not provide a mechanism for conflict resolution between the principles [8]. These criticisms notwithstanding, principlism identifies values important in the care of patients. One can trace two of these principles, *beneficence* and *nonmaleficence*, to the first care of patients and the Hippocratic tradition. Abuses of the principles of *justice* and *autonomy* in research and in clinical care led to the inclusion of these as additional prima facie principles. These abuses came to light through the efforts of activists, journalists, clinicians, and patients who pursued remedies through the legal system. As a result, there are laws relating to the field of bioethics.

Ethical Versus Legal Decision-Making

It is important to understand when law regulates actions in the clinical setting and to also understand the limitations of the law. As the President's Commission for the Study of Ethical Problems in Medicine (Presidential Commission) observed, one cannot create and nurture a positive patient-provider relationship "primarily though reliance on the law" [9]. An act may be ethical and legal, ethical and illegal, unethical and legal, or unethical and illegal. Caring for patients is a team-based human practice that requires relationships complicated by values-based decisions. The law is rights based and does not provide guidance on all the ethical questions clinicians face. In the ICU, the issues that most commonly raise ethical dilemmas and challenge the provider-patient relationship include informed consent, surrogate decision-making, parental authority and pediatric patient advocacy, attempted suicide, death, organ donation, the rationing of treatment, and, increasingly, moral distress.

Informed Consent

The idea that physicians know best what is in their patients' best interest has a long history. In the Silent World of Doctor and Patient, Jay Katz describes doctors as historically deeply caring individuals wholly committed to their patients' best interest who were also inattentive "to the patient's rights and needs to make their own decisions" [10]. Most trace the origin of the American legal doctrine of informed consent to *Schloendorrf v. The Society of New York Hospital* (1914) and Judge Cardozo's declaration: "Every human being of adult years and sound mind has the right to determine what shall be done with his own body…." [11] Despite ruling against Schloendorrf, this decision upheld the general legal rule, and standard clinical practice, that the patient must consent to surgery; however, it did not address the concept of *informed* consent. Subsequent legal decisions, including *Salgo v. Leland Stanford Hospital* (1957) and *Natason v. Kline* (1960), built to the conclusion in *Canterbury v. Spence* (1972) that "true consent to what happens to oneself is the informed exercise of a choice, and that entails an opportunity to evaluate knowledgably the options available and the risks attendant upon each" [12]. Acknowledging the history of the doctor-patient relationship, also described by Katz, the court further concluded that "respect for the patient's right of self-determination on particular therapy demands a standard set by law for physicians rather than one which physicians may or may not impose upon themselves" [13]. Patients, who have capacity, have the legal right to consent or refuse to consent to any and all treatment options, including life-sustaining treatment. Patient's decisions may conflict with the values and beliefs of health care providers.

Respect for autonomy, therefore, is both a bioethical and a legal concept. While few clinicians today dispute the right of a patient with capacity to exercise autonomy, the concept of *informed* consent can remain challenging in the ICU. Clinicians often still think they know what is in the patient's best interest, leading some to question patients' capacity when the patient makes a different decision than the one recommended. Under these circumstances, it may help to focus on encouraging the patient to articulate his or her values and preferences with the goal of maximizing the patient's participation. In 1982, the Presidential Commission recommended a flexible, collaborative, and shared decision-making model to support informed medical decisions. In 2001, the Institute of Medicine (now the National Academy of Medicine) released a report reiterating the need for patient values and preferences to "guide all clinical decisions" [14]. While helping a patient make decisions in concordance with the patient's values is ideal, many patients in the ICU lack the capacity to begin that conversation.

Surrogate Decision-Making

In 1976, the Supreme Court of New Jersey decided *In the Matter of Karen Quinlan*, a case involving an adult patient diagnosed to be in a permanent vegetative state [15]. The patient's parents requested health care providers withdraw ventilator support, with the expectation that Quinlan would die. The medical team refused, asserting both ethical and legal concerns. The court concluded that when patients lose capacity, they do not lose the right of self-determination and granted the father authority to make treatment decisions according the patient's values, including removal of the ventilator. This ruling identified the Health Care Agent (HCA) as the appropriate person to express the moral views of the patient and protected the health care team from legal liability. After the court decision, physicians still refused to remove ventilator support, maintaining that removing the patient from the ventilator, knowing that she would die, was unethical. Ultimately, the medical team weaned Quinlan from the ventilator. She lived in a permanent vegetative state for over 9 years, dying from complications from pneumonia. Her parents never requested discontinuation of artificial nutrition and hydration and refused cardiopulmonary resuscitation at the time of her death.

In 1990, the Supreme Court of the United States, in *Cruzan v. Director, Missouri Department of Public Health*, determined the rights of an HCA to refuse or remove artificial nutrition and hydration, while upholding the right of states to set the evidentiary standard required for such a decision [16]. As a result, some states have a higher standard for decisions about artificial nutrition and hydration. For example, Missouri and New York require an HCA to demonstrate "clear and convincing" evidence of the patient's wishes. While these cases illustrate the moral complexity of treatment decisions at the end of life when there is a disagreement between heath care providers and family, the life and death of Terri Schiavo illustrates the complexity when there is disagreement between family members [17].

Each state has a process for designating an HCA and, ideally, the patient would have designated an HCA before losing the capacity to do so. Each state also has a process for determining an appropriate surrogate decision maker in the event the patient did not designate one; often it is a sequential list of family members, but sometimes it must be a court-appointed guardian. This legal status has an ethical justification: family members are in a better position to know the patient's values and preferences than health care providers. Family members, however, may have different views on what the patient would want. In 1990, Terri Schiavo collapsed at home and was subsequently diagnosed to be in a permanent vegetative state. After unsuccessful rehabilitation efforts, in 1998, her husband, who was also her legal guardian, made the decision to withdraw life-sustaining treatments. Schiavo's parents disagreed with the decision. The local court, following the law established by *Quinlan* and *Cruzan* and consistent with Florida legislation, affirmed the guardian's authority to withdraw life-sustaining treatment. Schiavo's parents continued to fight: filing multiple motions, petitions, over a dozen appeals to the State court decisions; five lawsuits in federal district court; four petitions to the US Supreme Court;

and advocating for legislative and executive interventions on both the state and federal levels. The cases finally concluded in 2005: Terri Schiavo was permanently removed from life-sustaining treatment and allowed to die. The story both reinforces the settled law on the rights of HCAs and demonstrates the limitations of the law as a mechanism for cultivating positive working relationships in the face of conflicting values.

When patients do not have family, friends, or a guardian, states may, as a last resort, permit health care providers to make certain decisions for patients under limited circumstances, including appointing an HCA. For example, the state of Oregon permits the hospital to "appoint a health care provider who has received training in health care ethics, including identification and management of conflicts of interest and acting in the best interest of the patient, to give informed consent to medically necessary health care services on behalf of a patient admitted to the hospital…." [18]

The responsibility of an HCA, regardless of whether they are designated by the patient or appointed in compliance with law, is to make decisions about medical treatment that the patient would have made. Ideally, the HCA would know, from previous conversations or advance directives, exactly what decision the patient would make. In those circumstances, the HCA merely makes the patient's prior decision known. If the HCA does not know what the patient would decide in the specific circumstances, they should use their knowledge of the patient's values, beliefs, and preferences to apply the substituted judgment standard. This means they make the decision the patient would make based on the patient's values, not the one they wish the patient would make or the one they might make for themselves. If the HCA does not know the patient's values under the circumstances, then the HCA is to decide what is in the patient's best interest. This standard is intended to be an objective standard, one that balances the burdens and benefits of treatments and makes the decision that most people would make under the circumstances. This standard is challenging since it requires an HCA to consider the quality of life of the patient and to make judgments about that quality of life without input from the patient experiencing the life. It is preferable to base decisions on the known values of the patient

In the 1990s, patients and surrogates began to assert the right to demand treatment. Clinical judgment is not value free and health care providers have an obligation to uphold the ethical standards of their profession. Therefore, an important question in critical care is how to balance the right of patients to exercise self-determination and the obligation of health care providers to act in the best interest of their patients, especially when the values of the patient conflict with the values of the professions. This is an ethical dilemma that courts occasionally consider. For example, in 1989, the daughter of Catherine Gilgunn filed a negligence lawsuit against the Massachusetts General Hospital and two physicians for refusing to continue life-sustaining treatment for her mother, a 71-year-old woman with diabetes, heart disease, chronic urinary tract infections, breast cancer, Parkinson's disease, and a history of a stroke [19]. Gilgunn entered the hospital on the last occasion for a broken hip following a fall. Before her surgery, she had two grand mal seizures.

She continued to have seizures and neurologic damage. Several weeks after Gilgunn became unresponsive, physicians entered a Do Not Resuscitate Order over the surrogates' objection. The surrogate insisted her mother always said she wanted all medical treatment possible. Ultimately, a physician, determining medical interventions inappropriate, began to wean Gilgunn from the ventilator. Around this time, her daughter claimed to have a rehabilitation facility willing to accept her mother. Gilgunn died in the hospital, without resuscitation attempts, on the third day of the weaning process. The testimony before the trial court uncovered a flawed ethical decision-making process, and while the jury failed to find the physicians negligent, the ruling does not resolve the ethical issues, nor does it create legal precedent [20].

In another case, Helga Wanglie, an active and healthy 85-year-old woman, fell and broke her hip. Her medical course included multiple cardiopulmonary arrests and ultimately resulted in a diagnosis of persistent vegetative state [21]. When her husband of 53 years refused to consent to the withdrawal of life-sustaining treatment, the hospital ethics consultant filed a petition to replace the husband with a guardian. The judge ruled that Wanglie's husband was "the most suitable and best qualified" surrogate and he had the authority to make decisions about her medical treatments. Absent strong evidence to the contrary, courts consider family members to be in the best position to know and advocate for treatment decisions that align with the patient's values. These cases illustrate the importance of health care providers having conversations with patients and family members, when patients still have capacity, about values and beliefs important to medical decision-making.

Parental Authority and Pediatric Patient Advocacy

Historically, health care providers deferred to parents' representations of family values and preferences for decisions of pediatric patients. Parents were given the authority to make almost all medical decisions for their children, but these decisions were influenced by societal morals, those of the medical profession, and the emerging field of bioethics. For example, in the 1940s, it was not uncommon for physicians to recommend immediate commitment to an institution when an infant was born with a disability such as trisomy 21 [22]. However, there is evidence of provider moral distress around complete parental authority that coincides with the birth of bioethics. For example, in 1971, the Johns Hopkins Hospital created a dramatization, financed by the Joseph P. Kennedy Jr. Foundation, of the death of a baby with trisomy 21 whose parents refused surgical intervention for a duodenal atresia [23]. This production, "Who Should Survive? One of the Choices on Our Conscience," questioned whether the parents made the decision that was in the best interest of the infant, and began a public conversation about parental authority to make decisions for pediatric patients with disabilities. In 1982, a family accepted the obstetrician's recommendation to not treat the tracheoesophageal fistula in an infant born with trisomy 21. Disagreeing with the decision, other health care providers sought judicial intervention, filing the first of the Baby Doe cases. The local court, following contemporary precedent to allow parents to make decisions supported by physicians, declined to intervene. The baby died before the US Supreme Court heard the appeal.

In response to this case, the US Surgeon General, C. Everett Koop, campaigned the Reagan administration to interpret §504 of the Rehabilitation Act of 1973 to apply to the withholding of medical treatment on the basis of a disability [24]. The court ultimately ruled this interpretation unconstitutional and the US Congress passed the Child Abuse Amendments of 1984 (P.L. 98–457) [25]. This amendment to the Child Abuse Prevention and Treatment Act (CAPTA) of 1974 prohibited the "withholding of medically indicated treatment" except "(A) if the infant is chronically and irreversibly comatose; (B) the provision of such treatment would (i) merely prolong dying; (ii) not be effective in ameliorating or correcting all the infant's life threatening conditions; or (iii) otherwise be futile in terms of survival of the infant; or (C) the provision of such treatment would be virtually futile in terms of the survival of the infant and the treatment itself under such circumstances would be inhumane" (§5106 g) [25].

In 1984, the American Academy of Pediatrics (AAP) created a task force, which recommended the creation of Infant Bioethics Committees, and developed guidelines on how to approach decisions to forgo or withdraw life-sustaining treatment [26]. The Infant Bioethics Committees were the precursors to bioethics committees. The guideline endorsed the position of the President's Commission, recommended use of the best interest standard when making decisions for pediatric patients, and emphasized the legal obligations to report suspected instances of child abuse or neglect. CAPTA severely limits the cases in which parents and clinicians can determine whether it is in the best interest of the pediatric patient to forgo life-sustaining treatment.

Even when ethical reasoning and CAPTA permitted the withdrawal of treatment for pediatric patients, fear of legal liability could lead hospitals and health care providers to make unethical and illegal decisions [27]. In 1988, a six-month old, Sammy Linares, choked at a birthday party and lost consciousness [28]. A team of providers were able to reestablish a heartbeat approximately 20 minutes later, but Linares never regained consciousness and remained ventilator dependent. Despite CAPTA and precedent in bioethics, the hospital's legal counsel advised the medical team that removing Linares from the ventilator would create criminal and civil liability. Upon receipt of this controversial legal advice, the hospital refused the father's repeated requests to discontinue ventilator support and allow his son to die. "Once while visiting his son in the middle of the night, he disconnected the ventilator himself, but security guards wrestled him to the ground and the medical staff reconnected the machine" [27]. Nine months after the initial injury, the father displayed a gun, unplugged the ventilator, and waited for his son to die before turning himself in to police. A grand jury refused to indict the father for the death of his son.

Other cases can be even more legally and morally complex. In 1990, a pregnant woman presented to Woman's Hospital of Texas in premature labor and an infection [29]. Her fetus was 23 weeks old and the consulting neonatologist told the parents that he had never seen a baby born alive at that gestational age. The parents, believing this was a "tragic miscarriage," made the difficult decision to refuse "heroic" measures in the delivery room. They did not want their baby to suffer. The hospital, concerned about compliance with the Baby Doe cases, decided that the parents did not have the authority to make this decision: an attending neonatologist would make decisions about resuscitation at delivery. The hospital gave the parents the option to have an abortion, but the family refused believing abortion to be a morally different decision [30]. The neonatologist at the delivery was able to resuscitate the infant, who survived with the expected comorbidities of extreme prematurity. The parents took their infant home. The family filed a lawsuit when Sidney, at age seven, exhausted the lifetime cap on her medical insurance benefits. On appeal, the court found for the hospital, holding that under "emergent" circumstances, the physician could provide life-saving treatment without parental consent.

It is difficult to resolve the legal and bioethical issues in Sidney Miller's treatment. One could argue, as the hospital legal team did, that the birth presented an emergent situation and the infant's condition did not meet the criteria set forth in CAPTA, a law intended to protect pediatric patients with disabilities; therefore, the decision was legal. One could also argue, as the family's lawyer did, that the birth was not emergent, and CAPTA was not intended to control decisions in cases like this one: Sidney Miller's case is very different from the Baby Doe cases; therefore, the decision should not have been legal. How one thinks about parental authority, disabilities, and the role of the health care providers in protecting the rights of pediatric patients will influence whether one thinks this resuscitation was ethically necessary, ethically defensible, or an ethical travesty.

In addition to experiencing moral distress when parents decided to forgo medical treatment, health care professionals also experienced moral distress in some cases when parents request medical treatments. In 1992, Baby K was diagnosed in utero with anencephaly [31]. Health care providers told the mother that babies born with this condition would be unable to see, hear, or feel and that the standard medical practice was to withhold medical treatment. The mother continued the pregnancy and insisted the medical team place her baby on mechanical ventilation at birth. The team complied to give the mother time to accept the diagnosis and prognosis. Despite the team's recommendations, the mother, believing that her daughter's life was precious, insisted on continued treatment and refused to sign a Do Not Resuscitate order. The hospital attempted unsuccessfully to transfer the baby to another hospital and continued treatment until able to transfer the baby to a nursing home. The nursing home sent the baby to the hospital when she experienced respiratory distress. The health care team believed treating the infant was both "medically and ethically inappropriate" and, after the second admission, requested a court to declare that the hospital was not required to provide medical treatment. The Fourth Circuit Court of Appeals held that the Emergency Medical Treatment and Active Labor Act (EMTALA) required the hospital to treat Baby K's respiratory distress [32]. She lived 2 years and 6 months, dying in the Emergency Department during her sixth admission for respiratory distress.

Ethical Issues Regarding the Patient Who Has Attempted Suicide

The law distinguishes between various decisions and acts that lead to death – refusing or withdrawing life-sustaining treatment, suicide, physician aid in death, and active euthanasia. These laws reflect a balancing of the principles of bioethics, including the right of autonomy, the state's interest in protecting and promoting life, and the state's interest in upholding the standards of the health professions. Moral attitudes about these decisions and acts vary.

Suicide is defined as the purposeful taking of ones' own life. Decades ago it was illegal in the USA to attempt suicide, but this is no longer the case in most states. While suicide is not illegal, there is no general law creating a "right" to commit suicide. It is illegal for a person to assist a suicide except in those states where physician aid-in-dying (PAD) or medical-aid-in-dying (MAID), also pejoratively termed physician-assisted-suicide, is legal. It is important to note that there are specific guidelines, procedures, and safety measures mandated for PAD so that it is not an impulsive act.

Beliefs about suicide are as controversial as abortion because of the conflicting views on the rightness or wrongness of the act. Personal spiritual beliefs and contextual factors contribute to how a suicide attempt is regarded and can confuse clinicians as to how to proceed. To elucidate, many religions condemn suicide as a mortal sin and in violation of the sanctity of human life, but doctrine may embody different response to suicide. Some religions note that God will forgive the person who attempts to end their life, while others believe the soul will be damned forever. Some believe suicide is the ultimate expression of autonomy, thus rendering the decision to end one's own life as a personal choice that should be honored.

Some cultures view suicide as honorable in the right context, such as WWII Japanese Kamikaze pilots who flew suicide missions or "suicide bombers." Others believe that fasting for a cause and dying a martyr is a worthwhile endeavor. Given the various beliefs surrounding suicide, it is easy to see why the care of a patient who has attempted suicide is fraught with moral overtones. Individual health care team members may have differing views on the attempt and resuscitation based on contextual factors as well as personal beliefs on suicide.

The most common reason for a suicide attempt is an underlying mental health problem, ranging from schizophrenia to depression that causes the person to think irrationally. Usually the suicide attempt is due to a situation that is reversible or impermanent, such as a relationship problem (42%), acute crisis (29%), substance abuse (28%), physical health problem (22%), job or financial loss (16%), or legal trouble (9%) [33].

Given the presumed lack of capacity and reversibility of the problem, it is ethically obligatory for health care providers to intervene and aggressively treat a patient who has attempted suicide. The ethical justification is that health providers have an obligation to treat a reversible situation that is a result of a decision made when the patient lacked capacity to make a reasoned and well-thought out decision.

Often the attempt is a cry for help, and the person is testing to see if anyone cares [34]. Indeed, most patients who have attempted suicide are grateful that they were saved, and the vast majority do not attempt suicide again [35].

Some situations are more nuanced and require more thoughtful deliberation, such as the person who has a failed suicide attempt and presents with an MOLST (Medical Orders for Life Sustaining Treatment) forms are intended to document patient's wishes regarding cardiopulmonary resuscitation (CPR) and other life sustaining treatments. Depending on the state, these documents may have different names, e.g. Physician Orders for Scope of Treatment (POST) or Pennsylvania Orders for Life Sustaining Treatment (POLST). This form allows patients to document preferences for life sustaining treatments or limitations of life sustaining treatments, such as Do Not Resuscitate (DNR) orders. This is based on the premise that treatment that is started can be stopped, but once the patient is dead, there is no second opportunity to do the right thing. On the other hand, some argue that suicide can be a reasoned or rational decision informed by the patient's lived experience and the treatment of such a patient over objection is a violation of the patient's right to self-determination [36]. It is important to carefully explore, over a period of time, with the patient and family the reason for the attempt, including whether this was impulsive or carefully thought out; the patient's burden of suffering and whether that suffering has been and can be adequately treated; and the family's perceptions of the patient's wishes and intent.

Some persons who are successfully resuscitated suffer severe, often permanent, damage and persistent complications as a result of the suicide attempt. The decision to stop life support for the person who has attempted suicide is a difficult one. Brown et al. [37] suggest that careful deliberation be undertaken when reliable surrogates request withdrawal of life support. The process should be thoughtful and not rushed and include a reasonable period of time (several days) with no action to withdraw treatment. This time allows for careful assessment and discussion to clarify prognosis, ascertain patient wishes, and assess surrogate appropriateness. These authors suggest that the patient be treated as if they were "psychiatrically healthy" based on the premise that many psychiatric illnesses can be treated and become less burdensome with time; therefore, psychiatric morbidity ought to be removed from the deliberation. Further, a long history of severe refractory mental illness should be carefully considered and not ignored. They pose the question, "If this were not an attempted suicide, would a request to withdraw treatment be reasonable?" [29]

Some may believe the decision to refuse life-sustaining treatment, such as renal dialysis or enteral feedings, is an act of suicide. The law does not equate these actions. The court ruled in the case of Elizabeth Bouvia that patients with capacity have the right to refuse unwanted treatments and have a right to privacy about such decisions [38]. The ethical justification lies in the autonomous right of a person to decide what they are willing to tolerate, what constitutes a good enough quality of life, and to decide when extraordinary treatment no longer meets the patient's goals and should be stopped. The law explicitly promotes the decision to try life-sustaining treatment by not requiring continuation of such treatment if the benefit is less or the burden is greater than anticipated.

Physician aid in dying (PAD), also termed medical aid in dying (MAID), death with dignity (DWD), or physician-assisted suicide (PAS) is a controversial topic among health care providers and the general public. First legalized in Oregon in 1997, the Oregon statute has become the model for other states. The Oregon Death with Dignity Act (DWDA) allows those who are "terminally-ill to end their lives by voluntary self-administration of lethal medications expressly prescribed by a physician for that purpose" [39]. To proceed, patients must meet specific requirements: two physicians must verify that the patient has a terminal illness, has capacity, and is making an informed choice free of coercion. Other safeguards in the law include a waiting period between the time of patient's request and provision of the lethal medication prescription, witness specifications, protection of minor children and vulnerable populations, as well as oversight via a state-wide monitoring and reporting system [39].

The trend to legalization of PAD has continued across the USA. As of 2019, California, Colorado, the District of Columbia, Hawaii, Oregon, Vermont, and Washington have passed legislative statutes legalizing PAD, while Montana supported the right via court decision [40]. PAD laws in other states are similar but have nuances that physicians must understand. PAD is not a right supported by the US Constitution, as determined by the US Supreme Court in the case of *Gluckerberg v Washington* [41]. The Court has left the decision for legalization up to each state to decide [38].

A recent survey indicates that physicians are split on whether PAD is a morally acceptable practice, with just over half in support [42]. After holding steady for many years, the opinion of the general public has shown increasing support, with nearly seven in ten Americans in favor of PAD [43]. The arguments and counterarguments from both sides of the controversy are supported by ethical principles and views on the role of the physician.

Arguments in support of PAD are framed in the concepts of autonomy and right to privacy, justice, and the role of the physician to prevent suffering and act with the intent to do good (beneficence). Supporters believe that patients should have the autonomous right to control the circumstances of their death when suffering becomes too great [44] and that such action should be decided in private conversation with their physician and loved ones. Another argument notes that all patients on life support systems such as dialysis and mechanical ventilation have the right to terminate that machinery when their suffering is too great, and patients who do not have this path should be allowed PAD as a just and fair path to end their suffering. Finally, physicians who support PAD base it on an obligation to relieve suffering and not abandon their patient at the time of greatest need [44].

Counterarguments to PAD are framed in the concepts of nonmaleficence, the sanctity of life, concerns of active versus passive killing, and violation of the physician role as a healer, thus rendering the act as harmful to the patient and the integrity of the profession [45]. Those opposed to PAD view the act of hastening death as directly opposed to the centuries-old medical call to "do no harm."

The term euthanasia is often equated with PAD; however, euthanasia is clinically different from PAD: euthanasia is the act of a third party directly administering lethal medication to another with the intent to end the life [45]. Some do not see a distinction between euthanasia and PAD and view PAD as a passive form of euthanasia.

As more states move to legalize PAD, physicians and other care providers will need to consider their stance and, if opposed, refer patients to physicians who can provide the help they seek. If willing to support PAD, then careful review of and adherence to state law is required.

Distress among those caring for patients who seek to end their life is not uncommon. The juxtaposition of differing beliefs among key stakeholders as well as confusion regarding the patient's mental status, intent, and reason for the decision can result in significant moral distress. Paramount is the question: what action is in the best interest of this patient and promotes personal caregiver integrity?

Death

We live in a society that cannot agree on when life begins, so it is no great surprise that, with the advent of life-support technology, there is controversy surrounding the determination of death. The two accepted methods of determining death are the cardiorespiratory criteria and the neurological criteria [46]. Most people are pronounced dead utilizing the cardiorespiratory criteria: heart function ceases and this phenomenon leads to the cessation of breathing or, alternatively, they stop breathing and lack of oxygen results in cessation of heart function. People who are pronounced dead utilizing the neurologic criteria are said to have irreversible cessation of the entire brain, including the brainstem.

The development of neurological criteria is the result of the invention of mechanical ventilation, which forces oxygenated gas into the lungs utilizing positive pressure and, with subsequent lung recoil as with normal ventilation, exhaled gas to leave the lungs. This maintenance of respiration allows for oxygenation of the myocardial tissue and continued heart function in the absence of brain function. Both modalities for death pronouncement have recently become controversial. The cardiorespiratory criteria, which have seemed noncontroversial, have become complicated with the routine use of extracorporeal membrane oxygenation (ECMO) which maintains cardiac output and has been compared to continuous cardiopulmonary resuscitation (CPR). The criteria for brain death have also fallen under scrutiny 50 years after its inception as it becomes apparent that it is more of a social rather than a scientific construct.

Until 1968, persons were pronounced dead when they had no heart function. That year, a committee of physicians and non-physicians from Harvard decided that the time had come to state that people who were permanently unconscious could be pronounced dead [47]. Supporters of the committee's report claim that the authors were driven to make this determination because of (1) a belief that these patients were a burden to their families and (2) their organs could be used by people awaiting transplantation. Critics of the committee's report claim the authors were driven first by a desire to grow the field of solid-organ transplantation.

These criteria for brain death lent itself to a checklist that allowed doctors to reproducibly determine that persons who met the criteria were dead. Although there were some "fits and starts" in the early years, there was general acceptance of death determination using this approach in the USA. In 1981, the National Conference of Commissioners on Uniform State Law approved the Uniform Determination of Death Act (UDDA). Under UDDA, death can be determined if there is either (1) irreversible cessation of circulatory and respiratory function or (2) irreversible cessation of all functions of the entire brain, including the brainstem [47]. Lately, however, more cases have surfaced suggesting that the determination of death is more a matter of values or beliefs rather than a matter of science. The most famous patient who seemed to meet clinical criteria for brain death, Jahi McMath, became well known because her family refused to accept the criteria [48] and successfully moved her to the State of New Jersey. New Jersey law does not allow persons to be pronounced dead if it would "violate the personal religious beliefs of the individual" [49].

Before the history of Jahi McMath is described, it is necessary to explore the concept of the Dead Donor Rule (DDR). The DDR states that a person must be declared dead prior to organ donation. If death can be pronounced due to the irreversible loss of circulatory and respiratory function or the irreversible loss of the function of the entire brain, then there are two potential avenues open to obtaining organs for donation. In 1968, when the Harvard Brain Death Committee issued their report, it was not routine to remove people from life support since the act leads to death and, therefore, it could be argued, constitutes homicide. Seven years later, in 1975, the case of Karen Ann Quinlan changed how clinicians approach this situation. As discussed above, Karen Ann Quinlan was in a Permanent Vegetative State (PVS) in which the person has preserved brainstem function but no higher brain function. Her parents petitioned the New Jersey court system to support their contention that the withdrawal of mechanical ventilation was not homicide and won. Although brain death is a very different entity from PVS, the fact that it was no longer considered homicide to remove a person from life support means that it may have been possible to donate organs after life-support withdrawal without the requirement of the DDR if history were reversed and the case of Karen Ann Quinlan had predated the work of the Harvard Brain Death Committee. Jettisoning the DDR would dramatically increase the organ donor pool since now, if you are not brain dead, your organs can only be donated if you first die by cardiorespiratory criteria after life support is withdrawn. Organs are injured between the withdrawal of life support and the pronouncement of death, the so-called "warm ischemia" time and, if transplantable, increase the morbidity of the recipient. In an ironic but predictable twist of fate, Karen Ann Quinlan lived for 9 years after she was disconnected from mechanical ventilation because, as is usually the case in persons in PVS, she was able to breathe on her own.

Jahi McMath was a 13-year-old California girl with sleep apnea who underwent uvulopalatopharyngoplasty and suffered a postoperative hemorrhage into her airway that resulted in respiratory arrest and, ultimately, cardiac arrest. Despite attempts at resuscitation, she suffered anoxic brain injury and met the clinical criteria for brain death on two separate examinations using two different confirmatory tests. Her family did not accept the clinical determination that she was dead, so crowdfunded her transfer to New Jersey where state law does not recognize brain death if the family objects. Before she was pronounced dead by cardiorespiratory criteria there was evidence that she no longer met the California criteria for brain death [49]. This case raises serious questions: What would it mean to be dead and subsequently alive? Could the doctors in California be sued to financially support her for her remaining life if she no longer met the standard for brain death? Should death be a personal decision that requires an advanced directive or substituted judgment? These questions do not have a binary answer. They are complex and require an individual dialogue.

New Jersey is the only state in the USA that requires surrogate-decision makers agree that a person can be declared dead by neurological criteria before proceeding with brain death testing. This approach may be the most rational; it allows a personal decision about a topic, that if we accept that brain death is not a scientific diagnosis like myocardial infarction, prostate cancer, or a pulmonary embolism, but rather is a cultural concept that is accepted by some people but not all. It would allow people to circumvent the DDR and donate organs without waiting for the heart to stop. Potentially transplantable organs are damaged while waiting for the heart to stop beating in order to pronounce a person dead by cardiorespiratory criteria. As cardiac output decreases, the body shunts blood to the brain by increasing the arteriolar resistance to the other organs. This shunting results in poor perfusion and injury to the organs prior to removal. It also increases warm ischemia time, when organs receive inadequate oxygen and glucose while they are warm with a higher metabolism than when they are cooled. If potential donors are considered brain dead or the DDR requirement is relinquished, then there is the potential for healthier organs for transplant. Some people worry that jettisoning the DDR will lead to public mistrust and a slippery slope where vital organs will be removed without consent. It may be that doctors and nurses are presuming there is a public concern where none exists and, frankly, the slippery slope is considered by logicians to be fallacious. Safeguards could be put into place, making it unlikely that perverse actions would occur.

How does the concept of brain death fit into the science of medicine? Is it a theory? A fact? A disease? A syndrome? It cannot be any of these. If a person met the criteria originated by the Harvard Brain Death Committee or any of the subsequent variations codified by future committees, but then regained consciousness, it would certainly disprove that the criteria set forth were evidence that they were permanently unconscious. The fact would be evidence that the criteria for permanent unconsciousness have been falsified. It would not, however, prove that a person who is permanently unconscious *is* dead. That supposition is not falsifiable and therefore not subject to the scientific method. That supposition that someone who is permanently unconscious is dead is a matter of belief and, more or less in most jurisdictions, a matter of law. Laws are not scientific theories that need to be falsified but constructs that are created by people for one purpose or another. Whether that purpose was to sidestep the DDR and allow organs for transplantation at a time when there was no other way to obtain viable organs because of beliefs surrounding the withdrawal of life support that have changed since that time or a sincere rationale is moot. Science changes because new truths are uncovered but the law changes to better serve a society. When we conflate science and the law, we run the risk of developing rules that are not able to change or evolve as society changes. Equating permanent unconsciousness with death is done by consensus but good science is always falsifiable and unrelated to consensus.

As mentioned earlier, the Harvard Brain Death Committee's report was published over half a century ago. Most of today's physicians were taught about brain death in medical school. They did not have to grapple with the concept after reading a report in the medical literature. In addition to technology allowing for the assumption that some who are permanently unconscious are dead, a newer technology has worked in reverse. Extracorporeal membrane oxygenation (ECMO) allows perfusion to continue despite a nonfunctioning heart. In these situations, a person is only dead if we accept and pronounce death by neurological criteria or discontinue ECMO. In these situations, the problem of what it means to be pronounced dead is equally complicated. When Morris B. Abram, the chairman of the 1981 presidential commission on Defining Death, said in a letter to the Speaker of the House that "we are grateful for the opportunity to assist in resolving this issue of public concern and importance" [46], it is likely that he was hoping that brain death would be resolved and not concerned that the concept of cardiorespiratory death would become confusing.

In summary, dying and the determination of death have been complicated by technology. In the not-so-distant past, if the heart or lungs stopped functioning, the brain would follow, and if the brain stopped functioning, the lungs and heart would follow. This interdependence kept the concept of death straightforward, despite the fact that it was possible to be wrong, given the limitations in the technology. Over the years, both the diagnostic and supportive technologies have improved. In the past, it was not necessary to define death by evaluating the organs separately since they could not be supported separately. Since technology has outpaced our definitions regarding death and there is a lack of consensus, it seems that the only honest way forward is to treat these confounding situations as we treat all patient/family-physician interactions and explain the complexities to patients and families and give people a choice. It is a mere supposition that organ donation would not be accepted without the DDR. In his 1996 editorial entitled "Odds and Ends: Trust and the Debate over Medical Futility" [50], Arthur Caplan expresses the opinion that if patients and families do not *trust* their doctors, then they are more likely to desire, what we would call in 2019, ineffective care. Trust requires the truth, however complex, and might actually increase the organ-donor pool. It is important to realize that the DDR is a historically relevant approach rather than a scientifically grounded concept. If the perceived resistance to the DDR could be overcome, perhaps organs could then be removed before the heart stops and, therefore, all organs would be healthier at the time of transplantation.

Rationing Care in the ICU

The most apropos definition in the Merriam-Webster dictionary for the verb "rationing" is "to distribute equitably." When used clinically in the health care setting, the term rationing invokes a sense of unfairness. There are numerous ways to approach an ethical problem but, as noted earlier in this chapter, one of the most popular frameworks used by physicians is principlism [46]. The basic premise is that the four ethical principles apply in all clinical encounters: autonomy, nonmaleficence, beneficence, and justice. Autonomy is the principle that makes self-rule the primary focus. Nonmaleficence is the moral principle that is the rightful heir of the ancient wisdom "primum non nocere," which translates to "first, to do no harm." Beneficence is the alter ego of nonmaleficence, where caregivers are charged to "do good" rather than "do no harm." The fourth principle is justice which takes us out of the realm of the single patient and asks what is *fair* for a group in a society [6].

The relationship among the four principles is best underscored by a case that is reminiscent of the Japanese play Rashomon, where four witnesses tell a different version of a murdered samurai. Imagine there is an 85-year-old woman who underwent elective colectomy for cancer with a primary anastomosis complicated by an anastomotic leak. She is now critically ill with a high risk of mortality due to septic shock, acute kidney injury (AKI), and the acute respiratory distress syndrome (ARDS). The patient's husband believes that his wife would want life support withdrawn and be allowed to die peacefully. Since he believes this choice is her wish, he is invoking the principle of autonomy, albeit through the lens of substituted judgment, to arrive at this perspective. The patient's primary care physician believes the medical team is causing harm by continuing life support when there is so little likelihood that the outcome of any of the patient's suffering will result in a good quality of life. This physician is invoking the principle of nonmaleficence. Her surgeon feels it would be in her best interest to continue life support for another week and see if her critical illness is reversible, so is invoking the principle of beneficence. The patient's nurse wonders whether it is fair to use an ICU bed for this patient when there are ICU patients in the Emergency Department and Post-Anesthesia Care Unit (PACU) who would benefit from transfer to the ICU. The nurse is invoking the principle of justice. Justice and fairness in health care and patient care can be viewed from multiple levels. At the most global level, justice relates to the distribution of services and access to health care for populations. Governments determine what is deemed to be most fair for the majority of its constituents at this level. As levels are descended, choices are made for smaller and smaller groups. Eventually the hospital and the ICU level are reached, and choices are made that affect individual patients. Hospital and ICU policies set boundaries and guidelines, but individual providers make choices that are based on fairness. These choices are not independent. If one patient is in respiratory distress and requires intubation, that patient will be given priority over other less ill patients. A choice is made and care is rationed. Another patient on the same unit, when evaluated an hour later may be determined to be septic. Even if antibiotics are started as soon as possible, it would have been better if this patient had been evaluated earlier and started on antibiotics sooner. The second patient's care has been *rationed,* even though it was unavoidable. Doctors are often perfectionists and like to believe they can give equal care to all patients and, although this is aspirational, it is not realistic.

It would be better if doctors accepted rationing as a reality and did not try to pretend that it does not exist. Perhaps it is a desire to convince patients and their families that they are receiving the best care or perhaps it is an outcome of the perfectionist personality prevalent among doctors that lead doctors into denial regarding rationing care. Whatever the etiology, the belief leads to both dissatisfaction from patients and their families and moral distress among caregivers. What might happen if rationing is acknowledged? It can become part of the decision-making equation, a new and honest variable that can be applied, more or less, depending on the circumstances. The potential emphasis or de-emphasis on rationing requires an appreciation of the two dichotomous theories of justice: consequentialism and deontology. Consequentialism is a philosophy where outcomes matter most. Deontology is a philosophy where the fairness of the process is most important and the outcome is secondary. As an example, in the classic philosophical trolley problem, a trolley is heading toward five people on a track and you are standing next to a switch that would redirect the trolley down a different track toward one person with the pull of a lever. A consequentialist may pull the lever and the deontologist would not. Rounding in the ICU when there are plenty of empty beds would allow the intensivist to play the role of deontologist but, during a pandemic, the intensivist would have to play the role of consequentialist but during a pandemic, unless the hospital invoked a protocol to direct decision-making, the intensivists.

Physicians are usually on the deontological end of the deontological-consequentialist spectrum, and make just decisions considering only what is best for their individual patient based on the primacy of the patient-physician relationship and duty owed, while consequentialist forces only influence but do not determine decisions. When medicine turns to human-subjects research, it becomes a pure deontological system because the researcher must primarily care about the subject and only secondarily care about the results of the research. Human subject researchers who forget or ignore this prime directive put their subjects in harm's way. The Tuskegee experiment is one such situation where the researchers ignored their obligation. In the mid-twentieth century at Tuskegee University in Alabama, US Public Health Service physicians experimented on African-American men, without informing them of the purpose of the study and, most egregiously, denying them treatment with penicillin when it became available in 1947 [51]. The proposed research goal was to follow the course of syphilis. This incident, where the rights of the individual were viewed as less important than the research goal, contributed to the development of the Belmont Report and Institutional Review Boards (IRBs). IRBs are necessary entities to protect the individual and deontological principles and prevent consequentialism.

Occasionally situations arise, when physicians are forced to choose among different people to receive a limited resource. Transplantation of limited organs and pandemics when life-support measures like ventilators are in short supply are two such examples. In these circumstances, the consequentialist outcome desired must be determined at the outset: Who should be saved? Should it be the youngest people? Or those who will most likely live the longest, or parents of young children? People who support and care for others? These examples reveal that the actual consequences in consequentialism require a value to be applied to the outcomes, so an appropriate algorithm can be mapped out.

Ultimately, the question of rationing, if we are to be honest, is really a question of demarcation and degree. If it is only rationing when one life is saved and another one is lost, then it is true that the concept of rationing only comes into play in situations such as organ transplants where there are more people who need organs than potential donors, or pandemics where a limited resource like a ventilator has to be given to one person instead of another. On the other hand, if we define rationing more broadly, then we are rationing when we round on one person before another, assign one person and not another to our most skilled ICU nurse, board patient "X" in another unit to make a bed for patient "Y", or put the 20-year-old but not the 90-year-old on VA-ECMO (veno-arterial extracorporeal membrane oxygenation) for heart failure. Rationing in the intensive care unit, like beauty, may actually be in the eye of the beholder.

Moral Distress

Ethical dilemmas are not uncommon in the acute care setting. High technology often blurs the boundaries between life and death, making treatment decisions challenging. Moreover, the patient, patient's family, and individual health team members may have differing values, beliefs, and obligations that may result in conflicting opinions of the best course of action. Moral distress is the "psychological response to morally challenging situations such as those of moral constraint, moral conflict, or both" [52]. It is a complex phenomenon which includes the impact of personal and relational factors [53] as well as contextual factors [54]. The causes of greatest moral distress for direct care personnel are reported as following surrogate's wishes to continue life support when not seen as being in the patient's best interest, actions that prolong death [55–57], and actions that are viewed as futile [58, 59]. Ineffective communication and collaboration among team members, particularly around prognosis and end-of-life care, is often cited as a significant cause of moral distress among nurses [58, 60]. Lack of continuity of care due to frequently changing health care providers is also cited as contributing to poor patient care and moral distress [61].

Moral distress is felt by all health care professionals but is highest in those with direct patient contact such as nurses and physicians [61]. Work-related moral distress may take a toll on the staff that can manifest in physical, emotional, and psychological responses such as exhaustion, anger, sleeplessness, guilt, absenteeism, fleeing the work setting or the profession, and suicide [57, 62, 63]. In addition, over time, unaddressed distress may cause some providers to become immune to unethical care, creating a dulling effect on morality [63]. The results of such malaise may be poor patient care and outcomes [54, 59], exacerbating a negative environment and culture.

There is growing awareness that moral distress is not necessarily bad, but rather an indication that staff have moral sensitivity and moral agency, qualities that should be fostered. Expressions of moral distress may be viewed as a sign that conversation needs to occur to address a problem. Leaders who are morally sensitive and courageous, who trust and listen to the insights of team members and treat them as moral equals, can set the ground work for a stronger ethical unit and organizational climate. There are multiple ways to address moral distress.

Hospital-wide moral distress consultation teams may decrease distress by providing an opportunity for interprofessional discussion about ethically challenging cases, enabling teams to find common ground, share, and accept differing values; identifying recurring issues; and providing validation to staff members that their insights are valued [59, 64, 65]. Moral distress may also be decreased by unit-based discussions led by a clinical nurse ethicist [66]. Continued ethics education and case discussion in an interprofessional setting may promote team collaboration, team trust, and understanding of the ethical obligations/beliefs held by individual team members [59].

The overarching ethical climate of an organization is perhaps the most important factor to mitigate and prevent moral distress. Perhaps the most important factor to mitigate and prevent moral distress is the ethical climate of an organization is shared understanding of criteria that guides moral decision-making, has leaders that strive to include all interprofessional team members in case discussion and solicit all points of view. Staff care for each other, recognize personal and professional boundaries, and use a shared decision-making model to make decisions that demonstrate primary concern for the patient and family [67–69]. Leaders must work to minimize barriers to open communication and flatten the power imbalances among staff, with the goal to promote intra-team trust [70]. De Boer and colleagues [71] implemented and analyzed a five-step process to promote ethical decision-making among a team of interprofessional caregivers in a neonatal intensive care unit. Steps in the process include (i) group exploration of medical facts and contextual factors such as psychosocial, cultural, and religious influences, (ii) description of the ethical dilemma and possible solutions, (iii) discussion and analysis among all group members of the pros and cons and likely effects of each option, (iv) a decision made by consensus with recognition that the physician is responsible for the decision, and (v) development of an action plan to implement the decision. Participants reported better understanding about the ethical dilemma and perceived that all points of view were considered.

In summary, the phenomenon of moral distress among ICU providers is not uncommon and should be taken seriously. Moral distress on an individual level may contribute to personal and professional dissatisfaction and staff turnover and, at the organizational level, may be viewed as a barometer of a system's ethical climate. Careful monitoring of moral distress and situations that trigger such feelings may provide information about problems that should be addressed proactively. Recurring problems may indicate the need to develop policies or guidelines to help with similar scenarios in the future. Careful appointment of clinical leaders who are good communicators and willing to include key stakeholders in the ethical decision-making process can help ameliorate moral distress and promote an ethical environment.

References

1. Percival T. Medical ethics: or a code of institutes and precepts, adapted to the professional conduct of physicians and surgeons. London: Johnson & Bickerstaff; 1803.
2. Jahr F. Bio-Ethik. Eine Umschau über die ethischen Beziehungen des Menschen zu Tier und Pflanze. Kosmos Handweiser für Naturfreunde. 1927;24(1):2–4.
3. Fowler M. Evolution of the code. In: White GB, editor. Ethical dilemmas in contemporary nursing practice. ANA: Washington, DC; 1992.
4. Callahan D. Bioethics as a discipline. Stud Hastings Cent. 1973;1(1):66–73.
5. March 13, 2000. Interview with LeRoy Walters, PhD, Director, Kennedy Institute of Ethics, and Joseph P. Kennedy, Sr. Professor of Christian Ethics, Kennedy Institute of Ethics, Washington, DC. The interview was conducted by Dr. Judith P. Swazey at the Kennedy Institute of Ethics, Georgetown University. Available at: https://repository.library.georgetown.edu/bitstream/handle/10822/557055/WaltersL.pdf?sequence=6&isAllowed=y.
6. Beauchamp TL, Childress JF. Principles of biomedical ethics. Oxford: Oxford University Press; 2013. p. 2013.
7. Jonsen AR, Toulmin S. The abuse of casuistry: a history of moral reasoning. Berkeley: University of California Press; 1988. Kopelman LM. Case method and casuistry: the problem of bias. Theor Med. 1994;15(1):21–37; Noddings N. Caring: a feminine approach to ethics and moral education. Berkeley: University of California Press; 1984. Pellegrino E. Toward a virtue-based normative ethics for the health professions. Kennedy Inst Ethics J. 1995;5(3):253–77; Rawlinson MC. The concept of a feminist bioethics. J Med Philos. 2001;26(4):405–16; Shelp E. Virtue and medicine. Explorations in the character of medicine. Dordrecht: D. Reidel; 1985; Sherwin S. No longer patient: feminist ethics and health care. Philadelphia: Temple University Press; 1992; and Tomlinson T. Casuistry in medical ethics: rehabilitated, or repeat offender. Theor Med. 1994;15(1):5–20.
8. Gert B, Clouser KD. A critique of principlism. J Med Philos. 1990;15(2):219–36.
9. President's Commission for the Study of Ethical Problems in Medicine and Biomedical Research: making health care decisions, vol. 1. Washington, DC, Government Printing Office. 1982. Available at: https://repository.library.georgetown.edu/handle/10822/559354. Last accessed on 31 Mar 2019.
10. Katz J. The silent world of doctors and patients. Baltimore: The Johns Hopkins University Press; 1984. p. 28.
11. Schloendorff v. Society of New York Hospital, 211 N.Y. 125 (1914).
12. Salgo v. Leland Stanford Jr. Univ. Bd. Trustees. 154 Cal. App. 2d 560, 317 P.2d 170 (1957); Natanson v. Kline, 186 Kan. 393, 411, 350 P. 2d 1093 (1960); and Canterbury v. Spence, 464 F.2d 772 (DC Cir. 1972).
13. Canterbury v. Spence, 464 F.2d 772 (DC Cir. 1972).
14. National Research Council. Crossing the quality chasm: a new health system for the 21st century. Washington, DC: National Academies Press; 2001.
15. In the Matter of Karen Quinlan. 70 N.J. 10; 355 A.2d 647 (1976).
16. Cruzan v. Director, Missouri Department of Health, 497 U.S. 262; 110 S. Ct. 2841 (1990).
17. Schiavo v. Schiavo, 916 So. 2d. 814; 2005 Fla. App. (2005).
18. Oregon 2017 ORS, (Vol.3):127 §127.269 Consent to health care services by person appointed by hospital. Available at: https://www.oregonlaws.org/ors/127.760.

19. Gilgunn v. Massachusetts General Hospital, Super. Ct. Civ. Action No. 92–4820, Suffolk Co., Mass., verdict, 21 April 1995.
20. Capron AM. Abandoning a waning life. The Hastings Center Report; Hastings-on-Hudson. Jul 1995;25(4):24–6.
21. In re Helga Wanglie, Fourth Judicial District (Dist. Ct., Probate Ct. Div.) PX-910283. Minnesota, Hennepin County.
22. Aldrich CA. Preventive medicine and mongolism. Am J Ment Defic. 1947;52:127–9.
23. Produced and directed by Werner Schumann. for the Guggenheim Productions, Inc. Washington DC; 1971. Funded by The Joseph P. Kennedy, Jr. Foundation, Who should survive. Available at: http://mn.gov/mnddc/ada-legacy/who-should-survive.html. Last accessed on 31 Mar 2019.
24. National Library of Medicine. The C. Everett Koop papers: congenital birth defects and the medical rights of children: the "Baby Doe" controversy. http://profiles.nlm.nih.gov/ps/retrieve/Narrative/QQ/p-nid/86. Last accessed on 31 Mar 2019.
25. The Child Abuse Prevention and Treatment Act (CAPTA) 42 U.S.C. chapter 67, sections 5101-5116i. Available at: https://www.govinfo.gov/content/pkg/USCODE-2017-title42/html/USCODE-2017-title42-chap67.htm. Last accessed on 31 Mar 2019.
26. American Academy of Pediatrics Infant Bioethics Task Force and Consultants. Guidelines for infant bioethics committees. Pediatrics. 1984;74(2):306–10.
27. Schneiderman LJ, Jecker NS. Wrong medicine. Baltimore: The Johns Hopkins University Press; 1995. p. 90.
28. New York Times. "Father is Cleared In ill Baby's Death." May 19, 1989. Available at: https://www.nytimes.com/1989/05/19/us/father-is-cleared-in-ill-baby-s-death.html. Last accessed on 1 Apr 2019.
29. Miller ex rel. Miller v. HCA, Inc., 118 SW 3d 758 (2003).
30. Bender M. The Palm Beach post. Preemie birth case ignites GOP race for Governor. July 3, 2010. Available at: https://www.palmbeachpost.com/article/20100703/NEWS/812027539. Last Accessed on 1 Apr 2019.
31. In The Matter Of Baby "K", 16 F.3d 590; 1994 U.S. App. Lexis 2215; 3 Am. Disabilities Cas. (BNA) 128.
32. The Emergency Medical Treatment and Active Labor Act, 42 U.S.C. §1395dd (1994).
33. Centers for Disease Control. National Violent Deaths reporting system. 2015. Retrieved from: https://www.cdc.gov/vitalsigns/suicide/.
34. Verhey A. 'No' can be a gracious word. Health Progress, January–February. 2014. Retrieved May 5, 2019 from https://www.chausa.org/publications/health-progress/article/january-february-2014/%27no%27-can-be-a-gracious-word.
35. Owens D, Horrocks J, House A. Fatal and non-fatal repetition of self-harm: systematic review. Br J Psychiatry. 2002;181:193–9.
36. Koenig K, Salvucci A. Should we honor pre-hospital DNR orders in patients who attempt suicide? J Emerg Med. 1998;16(5):761–2.
37. Brown S, Elliott C, Paine R. Withdrawal of non-futile life support after attempted suicide. Am J Bioeth. 2013;13:3–12.
38. Bouvia v Superior Court, California Court of Appeals, 225 Cal . Rptr (Cal.Ct. App.1986).
39. Oregon Health Authority. Oregon Death with Dignity Act. 2019. Retrieved May 2, 2019 from: https://www.oregon.gov/oha/PH/ProviderPartnerResources/Evaluationresearch/deathwithdignityact/Pages/index.aspx.
40. ProCon. n.d. Retrieved May 2, 2019 from https://euthanasia.procon.org/view.resource.php?resourceID=000132.
41. Washington v Gluckersberg 521 U.S. 702 (1997) Retrieved from: https://www.oyez.org/cases/1996/96-110.
42. Ault A. Doctor support for assisted death rises, but debate continues. 2017. Retrieved May 2, 2019 from https://www.medscape.com/viewarticle/882334.
43. Galllup. In U.S., Support up for doctor-assisted suicide. 2017. Retrieved May 3, 2019 from: https://news.gallup.com/poll/183425/support-doctor-assisted-suicide.aspx.

44. Quill T, Sussman B. Physician-assisted dying. Hastings center bioethics briefings. 2018. Retrieved May 5, 2019 from https://www.thehastingscenter.org/briefingbook/physician-assisted-death/.
45. Starks H, Dudzinksi D, White N. Physician aid-in-dying. Ethics in medicine. University of Washington. 2013. Retrieved from https://depts.washington.edu/bioethx/topics/pad.html.
46. Defining death: a report on the medical, legal and ethical issues in the determination of death. President's Commission for the Study of Ethical Problems in Medicine and Biomedical and Behavioral Research; 1981.
47. A definition of irreversible coma: report of the ad Hoc Committee of the Harvard Medical School to examine the definition of brain death. JAMA;205(6):337–40.
48. Aviv, Rachel. "What does it mean to die", The New Yorker, February 5, 2018.
49. New Jersey Declaration of Death Act, N.J. Sess. Law Serv. Ch. 90, 26:6A–5(1991).
50. Caplan AL. Odds and ends: trust and the debate over medical futility. Ann Intern Med. 1996;125(8):688–9.
51. U.S. Public Health Service Syphilis Study at Tuskegee (2015 December 22). Retrieved from https://www.cdc.gov > Tuskegee > timeline.
52. Foure C. Moral distress and moral conflict in clinical ethics. Bioethics. 2015;29(2):91–7.
53. Lutzen K, Kvist B. Moral distress: a comparative analysis of theoretical understandings and inter-related concepts. HEC Forum. 2012;24:13–25. https://doi.org/10.1007/s10730-012-9178-9.
54. Corley M. Nurse moral distress: a proposed theory and research agenda. Nurs Ethics. 2002;9(6):636–6560.
55. Nathaniel A. Moral reckoning in nursing. West J Nurs Res. 2006;28(4):419–38.
56. Varcoe C, Pauly B, Storch J, Newton L, Makaroff K. Nurses' perceptions of and responses to morally distressing situations. Nurs Ethics. 2012;19(4):488–500.
57. Austin C, Saylor R, Finlay P. Moral distress in physicians and nurses: impact on professional quality of life and turnover. Psychol Trauma Theory Res Pract Policy. 2017;9(4):399–406.
58. Piers R, Azoulay E, Ricou B, Ganz F, Decruyenaere J, Max A, Benoit D. Perceptions of appropriateness of care among European and Israeli intensive care unit nurses and physicians. JAMA. 2011;306(24):2694–703. https://doi.org/10.1001/jama.2011.1888.
59. Hamric A, Blackhall L. Nurse-physician perspectives on the care of dying patients in intensive care units: collaboration, moral distress and ethical climate. Crit Care Med. 2007;35(2):422–9.
60. Epstein E, Delgado S. Understanding and addressing moral distress. Online J Issues Nurs. 2010;15(3):manuscript 1.
61. Whitehead P, Herbertson R, Hamric A, Epstein E, Fisher J. Moral distress among healthcare professionals: report of an institution-wide survey. J Nurs Scholarsh. 2015;47(2):117–25.
62. Privatera M, Rosenstein A, Plessow F, Lo Castro T. Physician burn-out and occupational stress: an inconvenient truth with unintended consequences. J Hosp Admin. 2015;4:27–35.
63. Metzer L, Huckabay L. Critical care nurses' perceptions of futile care and its effect on burnout. Am J Crit Care. 2004;13(3):202–8.
64. Vig E. Weekly rounding with the MICU team: description of a clinical ethics project. Am J Hosp Palliat Med. 2019;36(4):290–3.
65. Wocial L, Ackerman V, Leland B, Benneyworth B, Patel V, Tong Y, Nitu M. Pediatric ethics and communication excellence (PEACE) rounds: decreasing moral distress and patient length of stay in the PICU. HEC Forum. 2017;29:75–91. https://doi.org/10.1007/s10730-016-9313-0.
66. Chiafery M, Hopkins P, Norton S, Shaw M. Nursing ethics huddles to decrease moral distress among nurses in the intensive care unit. J Clin Ethics. 2018;29(3):214–23.
67. Victor B, Cullen J. The organizational bases of ethical work climates. Adm Sci Q. 1988;33:101–25.
68. Edmondson A. Psychological safety, trust and learning in organizations: a group level lens. In: Kramer R, Cook K, editors. Trust and distrust in organizations: dilemmas and approaches. Russell Sage: New York; 2004. p. 239–73.

69. Rathert C, Fleming D. Hospital ethical climate and teamwork in acute care: the moderating role of leaders. Health Care Manage Rev. 2008;33:323–31.
70. Nembhard I, Edmondson A. Making it safe: the effects of leader inclusiveness and professional status on psychological safety and improvement efforts in health care teams. J Organ Behav. 2006;27:941–66.
71. DeBoer J, van Blijderveen G, Dijk G, Duvenvoorden H, Williams M. Implementing structured, multi-professional medical ethics decision-making in a neonatal intensive care unit. J Med Ethics. 2012;38:596–601. https://doi.org/10.1136/medethics-2011-100250.

Chapter 3
The Ethics and Laws Governing Informed Decision-Making in Healthcare: Informed Consent, Refusal, and Discussions Regarding Resuscitation and Life-Sustaining Treatment

James E. Szalados

Autonomy and Free Will: The Ethical and Moral Basis of Informed Decision-Making

Respect for autonomy is rooted in cultural, social, and political values which respect individual "personhood" and is exemplified as individual choice: the choice to consent or refuse. Within the medical-legal context, consent addresses an individual's right to make uncoerced, informed, and voluntary decisions regarding their personhood and their bodies in a fashion that is respectful of one's individual philosophy and values [1].

The word "patient" derives from the Latin *pati* meaning "to suffer." The word "agent" is rooted in the Latin *agere* meaning "to act." Thus, the healthcare provider can be seen as the agent of the patient, working on the patient's behalf to cure or alleviate suffering. In addition, the patient is not seen the actor in his or her disease; rather, the actor is the provider. Morally, a provider who takes actions on the person of another must do so with permission, if he or she acts with respect upon the personhood of the patient.

Historically, the motivation for physicians to share information with patients was to facilitate patient understanding of the treatment plan and to motivate compliance with physician directives. In *Epidemics I*, Hippocrates wrote that the patient must cooperate with the physician in combating the disease [2]. Nonetheless, in the Hippocratic Oath, Hippocrates did not mention consent to treat; rather, the Oath advocates a paternalistic view of the provider-patient relationship. In fact,

J. E. Szalados (✉)
Director, Surgical and Neurocritical Care Units, Rochester Regional Health System at Rochester General Hospital, Rochester, NY, USA

The Szalados Law Firm, Hilton, NY, USA
e-mail: james.szalados@rochesterregional.org; jszalados@aol.com

J. E. Szalados (ed.), *The Medical-Legal Aspects of Acute Care Medicine*,
https://doi.org/10.1007/978-3-030-68570-6_3

Hippocratic philosophy cautioned against untimely and excessive sharing of information.

Plato connected the notion of consent with the quality of personal freedom [3]. Aristotle described *autarkeia*, or self-sufficiency, as an essential ingredient of happiness. However, as important as individual autonomy was to everyday life, it was held to be an attribute relinquished in the face of authority.

In *Medical Ethics*, Thomas Percival espoused the notion that a patient's right to the truth was subject to the physician's obligation to act in the benefit of the patient, thus advocating benevolent deception:

> [T]o a patient … who makes inquiries which, if faithfully answered, might prove fatal to him, it would be a gross and unfeeling wrong to reveal the truth. His right to it is suspended, and even annihilated; because its beneficial nature being reversed, it would be deeply injurious to himself, to his family, and to the public. And he has the strongest claim, from the trust reposed in his physician, as well as from the common principles of humanity, to be guarded against whatever would be detrimental to him …. The only point at issue is, whether the practitioner shall sacrifice that delicate sense of veracity, which is so ornamental to, and indeed forms a characteristic excellence of the virtuous man, to this claim of professional justice and social duty [4].

Percival's *Medical Ethics* represented the dominant influence in Anglo-American medical ethics and was the paradigmatic source for the *Code of Medical Ethics of the American Medical Association* (AMA) [5]; nonetheless, it represented a philosophy of paternalism couched in an overarching objective of benevolence. The 1847 AMA *Code of Medical Ethics* adopted Percival's writings in an almost verbatim fashion, highlighting the nineteenth-century conflict between paternalism and autonomy within the medical profession. In a more theoretical than pragmatic fashion, philosopher Kant developed the idea of moral autonomy as the power of authority over one's own actions [6]. Later, the connection between autonomy and the ideal of developing one's own individual self was incorporated into the views of humanistic psychology espoused by Maslow and Rogers, who viewed the goals of human development as "self-actualization" and "becoming a person," respectively.

The ideal of uniting the freedom of choice and the freedom of action is exemplified within the Declaration of Independence which affirms autonomy and personal self-determination stating that "[w]e hold these truths to be self-evident, that all men are created equal, that they are endowed by their Creator with certain unalienable Rights, that among these are Life, Liberty and the pursuit of Happiness." The United Nations Universal Declaration of Human Rights (UDHR) holds that all human beings are born free and equal in dignity and rights [7]. The UNESCO International Bioethics Committee (IBC) states that the power to decide for one's self entails acceptance of the consequences of one's actions, which can have far-reaching consequences especially in matters of health [8].

The freedom to choose and the freedom to act are not synonymous. Autonomy relates to free will, and thus an "autonomous agent" is a person with free will, whereas liberty relates to freedom to act without the interference of others. "Freedom from" and "freedom to" are not necessarily equivalent freedoms; however, freedom from deception is a necessary prerequisite to a freedom to act autonomously. Thus, autonomy presupposes the ability to gather information, reason, and consider choices. The most basic of all human freedoms is the freedom of choice. The ability to choose is an expression of one's personal identity and autonomy. However, freedom of choice is meaningless unless it is accompanied by a capacity to understand the present and future implications of that choice. Fundamental to the notion of autonomy is the exercise of reason; and fundamental to the notion of rational reasoning is a prerequisite of knowledge and understanding. Thus, the conveyance of information to the patient is, in itself, insufficient to uphold the value of autonomy; the reasonable belief must be that the patient can understand the information and act reasonably upon that information to reach a decision. Simple communication in disregard of the capacity to understand protects the liberty to make decisions but not the patient's autonomy. Beauchamp equated autonomy with "privacy, voluntariness, self-mastery, choosing freely, choosing one's own moral position and accepting responsibility for one's choices." True respect for the value of autonomy requires empowerment of both freedom of reason and freedom of action. Mutual trust is fundamental to an effective therapeutic relationship. The healthcare provider has a fiduciary obligation toward the patient (Fig. 3.1).

Thus, although healthcare providers are considered to have a moral obligation to consider a patient's autonomy and self-determination, even autonomy is not absolute and may be subject to moral constraints, as in the case of self-destructive behaviors or suicide, or legal and administrative constraints, as in the case of medical care of minors. Practical wisdom involves general knowledge, particular knowledge, an ability to reason toward a choice, and an ability to act on that choice.

Lu and Adams list five basic tenants that are accepted as the foundation of informed consent:

1. The patient must have sufficient information about his or her medical condition.

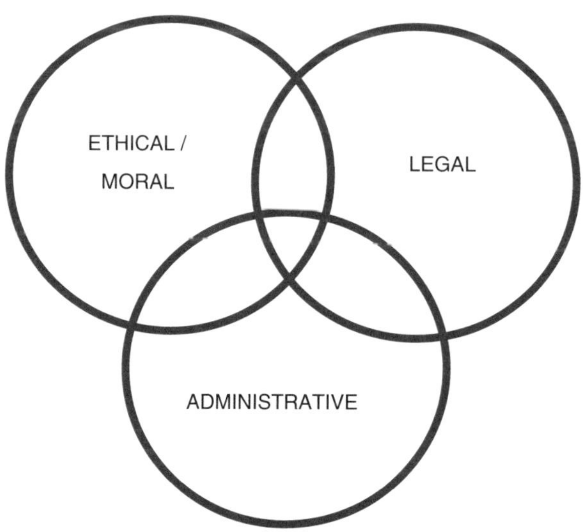

Fig. 3.1 Intersecting implications of informed decision-making in healthcare

2. The patient must understand the risks and benefits of available options, including the option not to act.
3. The patient must have the ability to use the above information to make a decision in keeping with his or her personal values.
4. The patient must be able to communicate his or her choices.
5. The patient must have the freedom of will to act without undue influence from other parties, including family and friends [9].

Informed Consent as Shared Decision-Making

Shared decision-making is a new term which embodies all elements of the informed consent process; however, shared decision-making further employs materials such as visual, graphic or printed decision aids, and a more comprehensive discussion of treament options, so as to better align the proposed treatment options and choices with the patient's values and goals. Shared decision-making is based on a model of the therapeutic alliance which arguably transcends the administrative requirement of informed consent and promotes the dialogue necessary to achieve a common understanding of therapeutic goals and their attendant implications.

Shared decision-making is believed to represent a high-value, patient-centered process for informed consent. Individuals who actively participate in their health-care decisions have been shown to have better understanding of their choices and are more likely to receive care consistent with their preferences, values, and goals [10]. The notion of shared decision-making is also very much related to evolving concepts such as patient-centered care, patient empowerment, and evidence-based patient choice [11].

Nonetheless, from a strictly legal point of view, shared decision-making in fact represents the classical doctrine of informed consent, with its attendant requirements not only for disclosure but for discourse, ultimately memorialized in a written consent form. Classically, it has always been held that informed consent is not the consent document per se but the process underlying the decision-making. Where the legal standard for informed consent is based within the reasonable person standard, it is both ethically and legally incumbent that practitioners adhere to the shared decision-making process.

Autonomy as a Legal Construct: The History of the Informed Consent Doctrine in the USA

The modern history of informed consent based on an obligation of disclosure respectful of a patient's autonomy and self-determination evolved gradually and is largely the result of successive legal rulings which established precedential authority which was subsequently incorporated into statutes, regulations, medical education, codes of conduct, and standards of care. Thus, the rights (and the duties) inherent in the doctrines of informed consent and refusal of medical care can be traced to seminal judicial opinions which arose in the context of battery cases. Consent is a legal defense to a legal charge of battery. These early cases established that patients have the right to protect their bodily integrity through the right to make their own decisions about proposed medical treatments and that a doctor's interference with this right may be considered a battery. The legal definition of battery is generally any physical contact with another person, to which that person has not consented. A person is liable to another for battery if (1) he or she acts intending to cause a harmful or offensive contact with the person of the other or a third person or an imminent apprehension of such a contact (2) and an offensive contact with the person of the other directly or indirectly results from that action.

In *Pratt* [12], the Illinois Appellate Court opined that "Under a free government, at least, the free citizen's first and greatest right, which underlies all others—the right to the inviolability of his person; in other words, the right to himself…". In the case of *Mohr*, Mrs. Mohr sued a surgeon after an operation further impaired her hearing claiming that the operation, "not having been consented to by her, was wrongful and unlawful, constituting an assault and battery." The Supreme Court of Minnesota, citing *Pratt*, ruled that the surgeon should have consulted with the patient and obtained her consent before performing surgery. In the case of *Pratt*, Mrs. Pratt sued a physician for battery after he performed a hysterectomy.

In *Union Pacific Railway Co.* [13], the court opined that "No right is held more sacred, or is more carefully guarded by the common law, than the right of every individual to the possession and control of his own person, free from all restraint or interference of others, unless by clear and unquestionable authority of law." Subsequently, in *Schoendorff* [14], a patient consented to an examination of a fibroid tumor under ether anesthesia but specified that she did not want an operation, and, once she was unconscious, the tumor was removed, and the patient then developed gangrene in her left arm, which later required amputation of several fingers. The court in *Schoendorff* opined that "Every human being of adult years and sound mind has a right to determine what shall be done with his own body; and a surgeon who performs an operation without his patient's consent, commits an assault, for which he is liable in damages."

The 1957 court case of *Salgo* [15] first introduced the term "informed consent." In *Salgo*, Mr. Salgo brought a malpractice suit against his physicians alleging negligence after he was left permanently paralyzed after a translumbar aortography. Salgo claimed that the doctor failed to disclose the various possible complications of the procedure; and specifically, to warn him about the risk of paralysis. The California Court of Appeals ruled that that the physician was liable for not disclosing all the relevant information during the consent process. The court in Salgo opined that "a physician violates his duty to his patient and subjects himself to liability if he withholds any facts which are necessary to form the basis of an intelligent consent by the patient to the proposed treatment," such a heightened disclosure requirement would exceed the basic elements simple consent necessary to defeat a potential claim of battery. Importantly, the Salgo court also introduced the concept of "therapeutic exception" to informed consent, whereby a doctor felt that he or she could potentially cause harm to a patient by creating sufficient fright so the patient refuses a necessary treatment and instead use his or her discretion in the disclosure process.

Whereas *Salgo* first introduced the legal duty of informed consent, the 1960 court case of *Natanson* [16] represents the first case in which a physician was premised in a theory of negligence rather than battery. In *Natanson*, a patient with breast cancer underwent a mastectomy followed by cobalt radiation during which she was injured by the cobalt radiation. Mrs. Natanson then sued her radiologist for negligence both in the performance of the procedure and for failing to warn her about the nature and hazards of the treatment. The Kansas Supreme Court on appeal, in *Natanson*, held that the radiologist was liable in medical negligence for failing to meet the duty of disclosure. The *Natanson* court thus firmly established that the theory of medical negligence was applicable to informed consent cases.

Traditionally the legal standard for the extent of disclosure during the informed consent process was that of the "reasonable practitioner" or that information which a majority of physicians within a particular community would customarily discuss. *Natanson* defined the standard of disclosure for informed consent as the "reasonable doctor" standard which was then widely adopted by most states in the USA. The "reasonable physician" standard was limited by difficulties arising from its definition and in legally and practically defining the reasonable practitioner standard.

In 1972, the case of *Canterbury v. Spence* [17] caused a shift in the disclosure standard from the "reasonable practitioner" to that of the "reasonable person." In *Canterbury*, a patient underwent a laminectomy and alleged that he had not been informed of a risk of paralysis. Although the operation was successful, Mr. Canterbury fell from his hospital bed the day after surgery and developed paralysis involving the lower half of his body; a second operation failed to correct the paralysis. Canterbury brought suit alleging that the physician negligently failed to disclose the risk of paralysis before the first operation. The *Canterbury* court held that the doctor was liable for failure to disclose the risk of paralysis. Although the *Canterbury* court affirmed the disclosure requirement for informed consent, it departed from prior cases through its adoption of a new "reasonable person standard" to replace the existing "professional practice standard" determining that the extent of disclosure required to make consent "informed" needed to be measured according to what would be important to the average patient rather than what a reasonable physician revealed in the course of his or her usual practice and thereby affirmed concerns for patients' rights.

In the California case of *Truman v. Thomas* [18], the court extended the duty of disclosure to encompass potential risks associated with not consenting to treatment. In Truman, the court held that a physician had a duty to disclose a woman who had refused a Pap smear the possibility that precancerous cells might develop into cervical cancer if she declined to undergo the procedure.

General Exceptions to the Disclosure Mandate During Informed Consent

Many courts have recognized two exceptions to the requirement where providers disclose all relevant risks, benefits, and alternatives during the informed consent process: (1) where a competent patient refuses to hear the information and (2) where the benefit of treating the patient outweighs any potential harm of the treatment [19, 20].

State statutes regarding informed consent vary; however, for example, the New York-informed consent statute states, in part:

> 4. It shall be a defense to any action for medical, dental or podiatric malpractice based upon an alleged failure to obtain such an informed consent that:
> (a) the risk not disclosed is too commonly known to warrant disclosure; or
> (b) the patient assured the medical, dental or podiatric practitioner he would undergo the treatment, procedure or diagnosis regardless of the risk involved, or the patient assured the medical, dental or podiatric practitioner that he did not want to be informed of the matters to which he would be entitled to be informed; or
> (c) consent by or on behalf of the patient was not reasonably possible; or
> (d) the medical, dental or podiatric practitioner, after considering all of the attendant facts and circumstances, used reasonable discretion as to the manner and extent to which such alternatives or risks were disclosed to the patient because he reasonably believed that the manner and extent of such disclosure could reasonably be expected to adversely and substantially affect the patient's condition [21].

It is however axiomatic that whenever consent is discussed, or the exceptions are invoked, a suitable documentation of the process by which the decision-making occurred should be memorialized.

The Provider as Fiduciary

The doctrine of informed consent is based on both (a) respect for patient autonomy and (b) the fiduciary duty of the physician/provider toward the patient. The process of informed consent provides a reasonable assurance that a patient has not been deceived or coerced. The reasonable assurance inherent in the informed consent process represents a legally enforceable evidentiary threshold demonstration that the process was followed, memorialized, and witnessed.

Within the traditional Hippocratic physician-patient relationship, the patient is portrayed as silent and dutifully obedient to a beneficent and trusted physician. Patients voluntarily seek out the aid of the physician; however, once the physician agrees to treat and the patient agrees to be treated, there is an implied trust that the physician will act in their interest, or at least will do no harm.

Fiduciary relationships are characterized by an imbalance of knowledge, training, and skill between the fiduciary and the principal, and therefore, fiduciary duties oblige all professionals to act as fiduciaries for their clients. The physician-patient relationship is a member of a special class of legal relationships called fiduciary relationships. In a fiduciary relationship, the "fiduciary" is the party the duty is imposed on (the provider), whereas the "principal" is the party that is owed the duty (the patient). The main elements of fiduciary duty in healthcare are (a) duty of care, (b) duty of competence, (c) duty of good faith and fair dealing, (d) duty of loyalty, and (e) duty to avoid conflicts of interest.

Thus, in healthcare, fiduciary relationships describe interactions between providers and patients, wherein patients depend and rely upon those more knowledgeable, skillful, and powerful than themselves to act in their best interest [22]. In *Canterbury*, Judge Robinson reasoned that "The average patient has little or no understanding of the medical arts, and ordinarily has only his physician to whom he can look for enlightenment with which to reach an intelligent decision … The patient's reliance upon the physician is a trust of the kind which traditionally has exacted obligations beyond those associated with arms-length transactions."

The essence of the fiduciary relationship is that the patient's interests must be paramount. The AMA Code of Medical Ethics clearly states that the "relationship between a patient and a physician is based on trust, which gives rise to physicians' ethical responsibility to place patients' welfare above the physician's own self-interest or obligations to others, to use sound medical judgment on patients' behalf, and to advocate for their patients' welfare" [23].

> [T]he physician-patient relationship has: ... its foundation on the theory that the former [physician] is learned, skilled and experienced in those subjects about which the latter [the patient] ordinarily knows little or nothing, but which are of the most vital importance and interest to him, since upon them may depend the health, or even life, of himself or family. [T]herefore, the patient must necessarily place great reliance, faith and confidence in the professional word, advice and acts of the physician [24].

Nonetheless, it is important to distinguish the fiduciary obligation recognized in law from the duty imposed on providers to act non-negligently and in accordance with the standard of care.

Legal Cause of Action for Failure to Obtain Informed Consent

Treatment with no consent at all, actual or implied [25], treatment substantially different from that to which the patient consented [26, 27], or unauthorized substitution of one treater for another [28] come within the definition of battery, especially when involving invasive procedures. That an unpermitted medical treatment may be lifesaving or curative, except in situations where consent would be implied, does not excuse battery [29]. On the other hand, consent is a defense to the tort of battery. Early decisions by courts at times characterized a lack of consent claim under the intentional tort of battery; however, the modern trend is to base such claims on professional negligence.

Nonetheless, the Arizona case of *Duncan* is relevant since it is a case where the court upheld a claim of battery based on an allegation of consent obtained by a healthcare provider's fraud or misrepresentation. In this case, Duncan, scheduled to receive a magnetic resonance imaging (MRI) study, consented to preimaging injection with sedation but explicitly informed the imaging staff that she did not want to receive the narcotic fentanyl, a request she repeated three times. The nurse assured Duncan that only Demerol or morphine would be administered. During the procedures, after receiving fentanyl, Duncan experienced severe complications including severe headache, projectile vomiting, breathing difficulties, post-traumatic stress disorder, and vocal cord dysfunction. Following the procedure, Duncan learned that, contrary to the prior express understanding, she had indeed been administered fentanyl for the procedure and brought suit predicated in (1) lack of informed consent and (2) battery. On appeal, the Supreme Court of Arizona relied on the Second Restatement of Torts [30] which defined "battery" as an intentional act wherein the actor engages in harmful or offensive contact with the person of another and case law [31] which had upheld causes of action for battery within the healthcare context. In this case, although Arizona Statute precluded such a claim for battery, the Supreme Court held the Statute unconstitutional and remanded the case to trial under a cause of action for battery. Malpractice liability policies do not universally indemnify against charges of battery.

Legal theories predicated in a lack of informed consent are more commonly generally based on either (1) medical malpractice or (2) lack of informed consent. Medical malpractice, or medical negligence, is variably defined as a deviation by a medical professional to follow the accepted standards of practice of his or her profession, resulting in harm to a patient. On the other hand, lack of informed consent is an independent cause of action, wherein a provider fails to obtain informed consent for non-emergency treatment, with specific exceptions. Lack of informed consent can reinforce a claim of medical malpractice or serve as an alternative point of attack when the case is otherwise weak.

The laws regarding informed consent vary among the individual states; however, in a very general sense, a civil lawsuit predicted upon a provider's failure to obtain informed consent requires that specific elements be proven by a preponderance of the evidence. For example, in the State of Illinois:

1. The physician had a duty to disclose medical information.
2. The physician failed to inform or inadequately informed the patient of medically material information which a reasonably well-qualified physician would have disclosed under the same or similar circumstances.
3. If the physician had disclosed the material information, a reasonable person in the plaintiff's position would have chosen a course of treatment different from that actually undertaken (or have chosen no treatment instead of what was done).
4. The patient was injured by the proposed treatment or failure to treat [32].

- The New York Statute requires proof that the physician or other medical provider failed to fully disclose alternative courses of treatment and reasonably foreseeable risks associated with the treatment rendered, as well as risks associated with all alternative courses of treatment, that a reasonable physician or other medical provider would have disclosed under the same circumstances; and. that "[f]or a cause of action therefor it must also be established that a reasonably prudent person in the patient's position would not have undergone the treatment or diagnosis if he had been fully informed and that the lack of informed consent is a proximate cause of the injury or condition for which recovery is sought." [33]

Recent Case Law Impacting Informed Consent

In 2017, the Pennsylvania Supreme Court decided *Shinal v. Toms, M.D.* [34], wherein the issue was based on Section 504 of the MCARE Act which imposed a legal duty for a physician "to obtain the informed consent of the patient" prior to surgery, the insertion of a surgical device, radiation or chemotherapy, and blood transfusions. In 2007, Megan L. Shinal and Dr. Toms met for a 20-minute initial consultation to discuss removing a recurrent non-malignant tumor from the pituitary region of Shinal's brain. Following initial discussions with Dr. Toms regarding surgical options, Shinal, the plaintiff, had a telephone conversation with Dr. Toms' physician assistant whom she asked about scarring, whether radiation would be necessary, and about the date of the surgery; the record of this telephone call indicated that Dr. Toms' physician assistant also answered questions about the craniotomy incision. In 2008, Shinal met with the physician assistant at the Geisinger Medical Center's Neurosurgery Clinic where the physician assistant obtained Shinal's medical history, conducted a physical, and provided Mrs. Shinal with information relating to the surgery and had Shinal sign an informed consent form. Subsequently and shortly thereafter, Shinal underwent an open craniotomy for total resection of the brain tumor at Geisinger Medical Center during which Toms punctured Shinal's carotid artery and the procedure was complicated by hemorrhage, stroke, brain injury, and partial blindness. The plaintiff argued that her consent for the surgery was not sufficiently informed because the information provided to her should have been provided by Dr. Toms. The Pennsylvania Supreme Court, in its 4-3 decision, held that physicians in Pennsylvania must directly "disclose the information required to obtain informed consent." The Court, in its decision, relied on the case of *Valles* [35] which had previously held that the duty to obtain informed consent is the sole responsibility of the physician and that it is non-delegable. In its decision, the Shinal court reasoned that "[w]ithout direct dialogue and a two-way exchange between the physician and patient, the physician cannot be confident that the patient comprehends the risks, benefits, likelihood of success, and alternatives" [36].

Although the *Shinal* decision is not binding to states other than Pennsylvania, such cases may be used as persuasive authorities in other jurisdictions. Of note, controversy ensued following the rulibng in Shinal; the American .... disagreed; dissenters argued that physicians and providers should have the right to delegate elements of the informed consent process to other members of the patient care team. Nonetheless, in most states, liability for failure to obtain informed consent rests solely with the physician.

Informed Decision-Making as a Regulatory Mandate

The Patient Self-Determination Act (PDSA) was introduced in 1990 as H.R.4449 of the 101st Congress as an amendment to titles XVIII (Medicare) and XIX (Medicaid) of the Social Security Act, requiring hospitals, skilled nursing facilities, home health agencies, hospice programs, and health maintenance organizations to "(1) inform patients of their rights under State law to make decisions concerning their medical care; (2) periodically inquire as to whether a patient executed an advanced directive and document the patient's wishes regarding their medical care; (3) not discriminate against persons who have executed an advance directive; (4) ensure that legally valid advance directives and documented medical care wishes are implemented to the extent permitted by State law; and (5) provide educational programs for staff, patients, and the community on ethical issues concerning patient self-determination and advance directives" [38]. The Patient Self-Determination Act became effective as federal law in 1991, and therefore compliance is mandatory.

Compliance with the Centers for Medicare and Medicaid Services (CMS) Conditions of Participation (CoP) is required to meet Medicare and Medicaid hospital regulations. Those hospitals which participate in Medicare and Medicaid undergo onsite surveys by State Survey Agencies and private Accrediting Organizations to ensure compliance with Federal Regulations. CMS CoP has outlined mandatory requirements for informed consent or refusal of treatment:

1. The patient has the right to participate in the development and implementation of his or her plan of care.
2. The patient or his or her representative (as allowed under State law) has the right to make informed decisions regarding his or her care. The patient's rights include being informed of his or her health status, being involved in care planning and treatment, and being able to request or refuse treatment [39].

CMS Interpretive Guidelines elaborate by noting that "[t]he right to make informed decisions means that the patient or patient's representative is given the information needed in order to make 'informed' decisions regarding his/her care" and that "[t]he right to make informed decisions regarding care presumes that the patient has been provided information about his/her health status, diagnosis and prognosis" [40]. Moreover, CMS notes that "[h]ospitals must utilize an informed consent process that assures patients or their representatives are given the information and disclosures needed to make an informed decision about whether to consent to a procedure, intervention, or type of care that requires consent" [40].

The Joint Commission (TJC) has published its requirements surrounding the informed consent process and safe care. Specifically, The Joint Commission defines "informed consent" to be:

> Agreement or permission accompanied by full notice about the care, treatment, or service that is the subject of the consent. A patient must be apprised of the nature, risks, and alternatives of a medical procedure or treatment before the physician or other health care professional begins any such course. After receiving this information, the patient then either consents to or refuses such a procedure or treatment [41].

and TJC further states:

> To establish a mutual understanding between the patient and the licensed independent practitioner or other licenses practitioners with privileges about the care, treatment and services that the patient will receive. Informed consent is not merely a signed document. It is a process that considers patient needs and preferences, compliance with the law and regulations and patient education. Using the informed consent process helps the patient to participate fully in decisions about his or her care, treatment and services [42].

TJC requires that the informed consent process complies with hospital policy and requires that the hospital's medical staff bylaws address the process of informed consent.

Although non-binding, the American Medical Association (AMA) Code of Medical Ethics Opinion 2.1.1(b)–(c) states, in part, that relevant information should be presented to the patient "accurately and sensitively, in keeping with the patient's preferences for receiving medical information". The physician should include information about (1) the diagnosis (when known), (2) the nature and purpose of recommended interventions, and (3) the burdens, risks, and expected benefits of all options, including forgoing treatment. (c) Document the informed consent conversation and the patient's (or surrogate's) decision in the medical record in some manner. When the patient/surrogate has provided specific written consent, the consent form should be included in the record [43].

Informed Consent and Human Subject Research

The issue of clinical research was addressed early in the US legal system in the 1871 legal case of *Carpenter v. Blake* [44] where Carpenter sued her physician for negligence and malpractice alleging that the physician did not properly set the dislocated arm and did not attempt to reset the bones after the patient developed swelling in the elbow joint. The physician, Blake, defended his actions claiming that his chosen method of treatment was not negligent but rather represented a new treatment approach. Although Blake did not specifically claim to be engaging in research, there was no true systematic clinical research at the time. The court in Carpenter held that a physician who departs from usual, established methods of treatment is liable for resulting injury and viewed experimentation as a departure from standard care until the validity of experimental treatments could be established stating "the rule protects the community against reckless experiments, while it admits the adoption of new remedies and modes of treatment only when their benefits have been demonstrated." In 1935 however, in the case of *Brown v. Hughes*, the Supreme Court of Colorado opined that a degree of clinical experimentation was essential to scientific advancement stating that "there must be a clearer case of total abandon than here attaches before liability occurs, otherwise the learned judgment of our skilled profession would be lost to the human race. Without such, we could not enjoy the advancement of science" [45]. Furthermore, in the case of *Fortner v. Koch*, the court again expressed the opinion that "we recognize the fact that, if the general practice of medicine and surgery is to progress, there must be a certain amount of experimentation carried on; but such experiments must be done with the knowledge and consent of the patient or those responsible for him, and must not vary too radically from the accepted method of procedure" [46].

At the end of World War II, in 1946, Nazi physicians were brought to trial in Nuremberg, Germany, and prosecuted for war crimes conducted under the pretense of "medical experimentation" on concentration camp prisoners. In *United States v. Karl Brandt*, also known as "the 'Doctor's Trial,'" the first of 12 sequential trials, the court set out 10 "certain basic principles [that] must be observed in order to satisfy moral, ethical, and legal concepts" as prerequisite to research on human subjects:

1. The voluntary consent of the human subject is absolutely essential. This means that the person involved should have legal capacity to give consent; should be so situated as to be able to exercise free power of choice, without the intervention of any element of force, fraud, deceit, duress, over-reaching, or other ulterior form of constraint or coercion; and should have sufficient knowledge and comprehension of the elements of the subject matter involved as to enable him to make an understanding and enlightened decision. This latter element requires that before the acceptance of an affirmative decision by the experimental subject, the nature, duration, and purpose of the experiment, the method and means by which it is to be conducted, all inconveniences and hazards reasonable to be expected, and the effects upon his health or person which may possibly come from his participation in the experiment should be made known to him. The duty and responsibility for ascertaining the quality of the consent rests upon each individual who initiates, directs, or engages in the experiment. It is a personal duty and responsibility which may not be delegated to another with impunity.
2. The experiment should be such as to yield fruitful results for the good of society, unprocurable by other methods or means of study, and not random and unnecessary in nature.
3. The experiment should be so designed and based on the results of animal experimentation and knowledge of the natural history of the disease or other problem under study that the anticipated results will justify the performance of the experiment.

4. The experiment should be so conducted as to avoid all unnecessary physical and mental suffering and injury.
5. No experiment should be conducted where there is an a priori reason to believe that death or disabling injury will occur, except, perhaps, in those experiments where the experimental physicians also serve as subjects.
6. The degree of risk to be taken should never exceed that determined by the humanitarian importance of the problem to be solved by the experiment.
7. Proper preparations should be made and adequate facilities provided to protect the experimental subject against even remote possibilities of injury, disability, or death.
8. The experiment should be conducted only by scientifically qualified persons. The highest degree of skill and care should be required through all stages of the experiment of those who conduct or engage in the experiment.
9. During the course of the experiment, the human subject should be at liberty to bring the experiment to an end if he has reached the physical or mental state where continuation of the experiment seems to him to be impossible.
10. During the course of the experiment, the scientist in charge must be prepared to terminate the experiment at any stage if he has probable cause to believe, in the exercise of the good faith, superior skill, and careful judgment required of him, that a continuation of the experiment is likely to result in injury, disability, or death to the experimental subject.

These ten principles became known as the Nuremberg Code, codified by the Nuremberg Military Tribunal in 1947. Informed consent was articulated as the core principle of the Nuremberg Code. Thus, the Nuremberg Code requires that physician-researchers act in the best interests of their subjects but also states that the subjects may actively protect themselves as well. The key contribution of the Nuremberg Code was to merge Hippocratic ethics and the protection of human rights. Nonetheless, the Nuremberg Code has not been specifically adopted as law by any nation or as ethics by any major medical association; however, the lasting influence on global human rights law and medical ethics has been profound [47].

The Declaration of Geneva was promulgated by the World Medical Association (WMA), which represented the previous Association Professionnelle Internationale des Médecins, and was published in 1949. The Declaration of Geneva was criticized for its vague language and was the subject of ongoing debate until the WMA reconvened in Geneva where it drafted the subsequent Declaration of Helsinki, which was adopted in 1964 by the 18th World Medical Assembly [48]. The Declaration of Helsinki was heavily influenced by the Nuremberg Code. The original document notably relaxed requirements regarding consent for participation in research, modifying the Nuremberg requirement that consent is "absolutely essential" to instead urge consent "if at all possible" and to allow for proxy consent, such as from a legal guardian. In addition, and perhaps indirectly, by order of priority, the Declaration of Helsinki accorded scientific expertise and the goals of medical advancements ahead of the informed consent requirement. The Declaration distinguished therapeutic from non-therapeutic research. The 2013 version of the Declaration of Helsinki follows seven revisions but has evolved to encompass frontiers and also improves clarity regarding specific issues such as underrepresented groups, compensation and treatment for individuals who are harmed as a result of their participation in research, post-trial access to interventions and care for participants from limited-resource countries, registration of trials in publicly accessible databases, and publication of negative, inconclusive, and positive results and continued to elaborate on the role of research ethics committees [49].

The National Research Act [50] was signed into law in 1974 resulting in the creation of the National Commission for the Protection of Human Subjects of Biomedical and Behavioral Research. The Commission was charged with identification of the basic ethical principles which should guide the conduct of biomedical and behavioral research that involved human subjects and then develop guidelines to assure that research is conducted in accordance with such principles. The Commission was directed to consider:

(i) The boundaries between biomedical and behavioral research and the accepted and routine practice of medicine
(ii) The role of assessment of risk-benefit criteria in the determination of the appropriateness of research involving human subjects
(iii) Appropriate guidelines for the selection of human subjects for participation in such research
(iv) The nature and definition of informed consent in various research settings [51]

In 1978, the International Committee of Medical Journal Editors, originally known as the Vancouver Group, convened to discuss requirements for the publication of medical research. Importantly, the group set standards regarding authorship, editorial obligations, peer review, conflicts of interest, privacy and confidentiality, and human/animal protections.

The Belmont Report was authored by the National Commission for the Protection of Human Subjects of Biomedical and Behavioral Research and published in 1979 a statement of basic ethical principles and guidelines that should assist in resolving the ethical problems that surround the conduct of research with human subjects. The Belmont Report, formally entitled "Ethical Principles and Guidelines for the Protection of Human Subjects of Research," was created specifically for the Department of Health and Human Services (formerly the US Department of Health, Education, and Welfare) and was named for the Smithsonian Institution's Belmont Conference Center where the Commission held its hearings [52]. In brief, the Commission concluded that the primary principles underlying ethical research with human beings were respect for persons, beneficence, and justice and that adherence to these principles was based in the principles of informed consent, risk-benefit analysis, and appropriate patient selection. Informed consent emphasized the sharing of information including "the research procedure, their purposes, risks and anticipated benefits, alternative procedures (where therapy is involved), and a statement offering the subject the opportunity to ask questions and to withdraw at any time from the research." The Belmont Report states that an autonomous agent is "an individual capable of deliberation about personal goals and of acting under the direction of such deliberation." Special issues addressed in the report included classes of potential research subjects with potentially limited comprehension, vulnerable populations, and voluntariness of the decision to participate. The Belmont Report also introduced the concept of the Institutional Review Board (IRB) and required IRB oversight of intuitional research as a condition of research funding.

In 1991, the Belmont Report, together with its evolving regulatory reach, morphed into the Common Rule [53], which was endorsed by 16 federal agencies including the Departments of Health and Human Services, Agriculture, Energy, Commerce, Housing and Urban Development, Justice, Defense, Education, Veterans Affairs, and Transportation and the National Aeronautics and Space Administration, the Consumer Product Safety Commission, the Agency for International Development, the Environmental Protection Agency, the National Science Foundation, and the Central Intelligence Agency. Importantly, the US Food and Drug Administration, although it concurred with the Common Rule, did not adopt it in its entirety. The FDA made selected changes to its IRB and informed consent regulations of the Common Rule, and, where a protocol is subject to review under more than one department or agency's regulations, the requirements of each set of regulations must be met. FDA regulations [54] apply to all clinical investigations as well as clinical investigations that support applications for research or marketing permits for products regulated by the FDA.

HHS regulations which codify the Common Rule are published in US statute at Title 45: Public Welfare, Part 46 [55]. The components of informed consent under the Common Rule also include an identification of the project as research, its purpose, and its duration; a description of the procedure, risks/benefits, and possible alternatives to participation; information on who to contact with questions or, if injury were to occur, limits of compensation provided by the researchers; and assurance that participation is voluntary. HHS regulations require that an investigator obtain the legally effective informed consent of the subject or the subject's legally authorized representative, unless (1) the research is exempt under 45 CFR 46.101(b), (2) the IRB finds and documents that informed consent can be waived (45 CFR 46.116(c) or (d)), or (3) the IRB finds and documents that the research meets the requirements of HHS Secretarial waiver under 45 CFR 46.101(i), an exception which permits a waiver of the general requirements for obtaining informed consent in a limited class of research in emergency settings. When informed consent is required, it must be sought prospectively and documented to the required extent.

In order to facilitate oversight of clinical research, the National Institutes of Health (NIH) developed the Office for Protection from Research Risks (OPRR) which was the precursor to the Office for Human Research Protections (OHRP). OHRP is administered under the Office of the Assistant Secretary for Health in the Office of the Secretary of the US Department of Health and Human Services (HHS) and provides leadership in the protection of the rights, welfare, and well-being of human subjects involved in research conducted or supported by HHS. OHRP reviews allegations of noncompliance involving human subject research projects. The issue of compliance with informed consent mandates is an especially important function of the OHRP:

> The informed consent process should be an active process of sharing information between the investigator and the prospective subject. The exchange of information between the investigator and prospective subjects can occur via one or more of the following modes of communication, among others: face-to-face contact; mail; telephone; video; or fax. Prospective subjects should be provided with ample opportunity to ask questions and seek clarification from the investigator. The prospective subjects should be in a position to freely decide whether to initially enroll in the research, or later, to withdraw or continue participating in the research. The informed consent process should ensure that all critical information about a study is completely disclosed, and that prospective subjects or their legally authorized representatives adequately understand the research so that they can make informed choices [56].

Implied Consent

Consent may be either express or implied. Express consent is consent which is clearly communicated; the acceptable manners of communication are contextual. Informed consent is the same as express consent. The most common form of expressed consent is communicated through the signing of a pre-printed consent form; however, express consent may be obtained through a nod of assent or a verbal assent. Thus, a person who is unable to use his or her hands may still be able to consent, or refuse to consent, through alternate modes of communication. In some situations, such as plastic surgery, informed consent may even be documented by way of a videotaped discussion. In general, the more intimate, invasive, or riskier a procedure may be, the more likely that informed consent will be necessary. Nonetheless, since informed consent cannot be realistically obtained under emergency circumstances, the doctrine of implied consent serves to protect both patients and providers.

Implied consent on the other hand is consent in the absence of a formal discussion, disclosure, or documented agreement. The issue of implied consent was first addressed in the 1905 case of *Mohr* where the court, in addressing the requirement for informed consent to treatment, acknowledged situations in which implied consent could arise in emergencies such as where a patient was unconscious, if the injuries were so serious as to require immediate attention, or if during the course of an operation, previously-unknown conditions arose that without redress would endanger the patient's life. Whether implied consent is legally valid depends on the circumstances and the applicable law. In general, the implied consent is based on the prior behaviors of the patient and is generally invoked in emergent and life-threatening situations where a patient is unable to consent and no surrogate is available. There is a long-standing assumption that an unconscious person would consent to emergency care if that person were conscious and able to provide consent since, under a "reasonable person" standard, such a person would want medical care if indicated. Thus, the doctrine of implied consent is based on the assumption that the patient is a "reasonable person" and that consent would have otherwise been reasonable under the circumstances.

Informed Consent of Minors

Minors are presumed to lack capacity to consent, or refuse to consent, to emergency care. In life-threatening emergencies, the consent to treat is generally presumed under implied consent. However, a minor's lack of capacity is rebuttable, and minors may, under certain circumstances, have legal capacity. In most states, 18 years of age defines the age of majority; therefore in the case of patient under the age of 18, except in cases of emergency, informed consent must be obtained from the adolescent minor's parent or legal guardian. The parent(s) or legal guardian(s) of a minor generally provide informed consent for most medical decisions on behalf of the minor. Where a parent or guardian refuses to provide consent for recommended medical treatment, a third party may petition, through the probate court, to order the treatment against the parent's or guardian's wishes. In general, consent from one parent within an intact marriage is usually sufficient; however, if treatment poses a significant risk to the minor or violates the personal or religious beliefs of one or both parents, it may be advisable for the provider to obtain the consent of both parents. If there is an unresolved disagreement among the parents regarding consent, it may be necessary for a juvenile court to intervene. In order for a parent to give informed consent on behalf of their child, they themselves must meet legal requirements for decisional capacity.

There are, however, three broadly recognized situational categories under which adolescent minors may direct their own medical decision-making: (a) exceptions based on specific diagnostic categories, (b) the "mature minor" exception, and (c) legal emancipation. The precise legal definitions for these categories can vary substantially by state, and providers are reminded to consult their specific state laws [57] (Table 3.1).

In most states, minors may legally consent to treatment for issues such as substance abuse, sexual abuse, sexually transmitted diseases, mental health care, and birth control; in the states of Vermont and California, this right may be accorded to minors as young as 12 years of age. In such cases, the reasoning and justification upon which the provider's decision to treat the minor is based should be clearly documented in the medical record, and there should be an accompanying signed consent obtained from the minor. Some states require that providers specifically document that (a) the minor would reject treatment if consent from a parent was required, (b) the treatment is clinically indicated, (c) the failure to provide treatment

Table 3.1 Exceptions to the informed consent rule for minors

In general, a minor patient may consent/refuse treatment if he/she is:
Emancipated by legal decree
Pregnant at the time treatment is rendered
12 years of age or older, requesting treatment for sexual assault/abuse, a sexually transmitted disease, alcohol or drug abuse, or limited outpatient mental health counseling
A member of the US Armed Forces
16 years of age or older presenting with a psychiatric emergency

would be detrimental to the minor's well-being, (d) the minor has knowingly and voluntarily sought the treatment, and (e), in the opinion of the provider, the minor demonstrates sufficient maturity to participate in treatment.

The mature minor doctrine provides that adolescents who are not otherwise legally emancipated may participate in decisions regarding their own medical care, generally when the care is not of a serious nature. The mature minor doctrine is a relatively new legal concept, and few states have enacted the doctrine into statute, although some states have adopted the doctrine as law. The mature minor is usually 14–16 years of age and can demonstrate that he or she fully understands the treatment and the consequences.

Emancipation accords minors the legal right to make independent decisions. An emancipated minor is considered a competent adult with the legal authority to accept or refuse medical treatment. Not all states have emancipation statutes. There are two basic types of emancipation: (a) court-ordered emancipation is granted by the decree of a court. In order to petition a court for emancipation, a minor must be within a state-specific age category, live independent of his or her parents or guardians, be capable of managing his or her financial affairs, and have the ability to provide for his or her general well-being. A copy of an emancipation decree should accompany each emancipated patient's medical record; and (b) situational emancipation confers decision-making capacity upon minors who are married, are parents of living children, do not live with their parents, or serve in the military.

Where possible, even if the child or adolescent cannot legal consent or decline consent, it may be reasonable to include the minor patient, especially an older child or adolescent, in the decision-making process. The American Academy of Pediatrics (AAP) has published statements regarding informed consent for treatment of children, first in 1976 [58] and subsequently revised in 1995 [59] and in 2016 [60]. The AAP document states that "[p]ediatricians should be adept at using developmentally appropriate language during discussions with minors, and information must be provided in a manner that respects the cognitive abilities of the child or adolescent," and therefore "patients should participate in decision-making commensurate with their development; they should provide assent to care whenever reasonable." The AAP recommends assent from children as young as 7 years of age since it may foster moral growth and development of autonomy at a concrete operations stage of development. Later, adolescent decision-making is dependent on factors such as cognitive ability, maturity of judgment, and moral authority, understanding that adolescent decision making may rely more on mature limbic, or socioemotional, cognition rather than on impulse-controlling, less-developed prefrontal cognitive system.

Against Medical Advice and Refusal to Consent: Legal Pitfalls

When a patient refuses to consent to treatment, the result is a potential legal landmine for the provider. In most cases of "refusal to consent," the medical record is either silent as to the consent process or the documentation of the discussion is superficial. Patients leave the hospital "against medical advice," and the documentation reflects only that "the patient left AMA." In most cases where litigation arises from either "informed refusal" or "against medical advice," the common denominator is not whether a plan of care was recommended and subsequently refused; the litigation hinges on whether the material risks were disclosed, discussed, and understood.

Informed consent and informed refusal each balances the ethical principles of respect for the patient's autonomy and minimization of paternalism, balanced as against the provider's fiduciary and legal duty to care for the patient in a manner consistent with accepted standards of care. The California case of *Truman v. Thomas* not only defined the requirements for informed consent but also the basis for informed refusal. In *Truman*, the court extended the duty of disclosure to encompass potential risks associated with not consenting to, or refusing, treatment. Recall that in *Truman* the court held that a physician had a duty to disclose to the patient the possibility that precancerous cells might develop into cervical cancer if she declined to undergo a Pap smear test. Where the physician did not disclose the risks of not having the test, and the patient later died from metastatic cervical cancer, the court determined that that the physician had a fiduciary duty to explain the potentially fatal consequences of a decision to forgo testing.

Furthermore, since informed decision-making is a two-part process, patients may choose to accept or waive either part of the process. Patients may refuse to be informed about their diagnosis or medical treatment plan; or alternatively they may choose to waive their right to be informed about the risks. Moreover, after choosing to hear or choosing not to discuss the diagnosis, plan, and risks, they may abdicate their choice to proceed or not with the plan. In such instances, patients may relate that they "don't want to hear about that," request that the provider "do what you think is best," or request that another make the decisions on their behalf such as "talk to my daughter about that." In all such circumstances, the overarching principle of autonomy can be respected through effective communication, discussion, and documentation.

State laws may also support patient choice about whether they want to receive information. It may be inappropriate to force patients to accept information that they are unready to accept; this may provoke a claim for intentional, or negligent, infliction of emotional distress. The right of patients to choose, the right to accept or to decline information, may be legally enforceable [61]. For example, under the laws of New York State:

> …
>
> (4) It shall be a defense to any action for medical, dental or podiatric malpractice based upon an alleged failure to obtain such an informed consent that:

> …
>
> (b) the patient assured the … practitioner he would undergo the treatment, procedure or diagnosis regardless of the risk involved, or the patient assured the … practitioner that he did not want to be informed of the matters to which he would be entitled to be informed;… [62]

However, in any such process, the usual levels of inquiry form the basis for a provider's due diligence:

1. The patient must be competent to make his or her own decisions. Most patients are competent by default; however, patients for whom a legal guardian or surrogate decision-maker has been appointed, minors, wards of the state, those with cognitive impairment, or those in custody may be considered to lack competency. In such cases, providers generally have a legal duty to provide care until the guardian can direct otherwise.
2. The patient must also have the capacity to make a decision about his or her care. Although the competence and capacity are often debated, there is an arguable distinction, based on the chronicity of the condition. Capacity relates more patient's immediate abilities demonstrate an understanding of their medical condition and subsequently make an informed decision. The state of mental capacity may fluctuate and may be variable. Capacity is based upon a medical evaluation and its subsequent documentation. For example, patients deemed to be psychotic, suicidal, or homicidal probably lack capacity; patients with head injuries, acute encephalopathy, severe sepsis, or other acute cognitive impairment may lack capacity, and finally patients who are intoxicated may lack capacity. In the case of a refusal to consent, the issue of capacity to refuse emergency treatment can be seen as a rebuttable presumption; the question often becomes whether an impartial subsequent reviewer will believe that it was appropriate to accept the request for refusal of care from an acutely impaired patient.

Thus, the minimum basic legal requirement to support "informed refusal" or "against medical advice" is the same as those necessary to establish informed consent. The principles of informed refusal apply the concepts of informed consent to refusal of care. The provider must discuss with the patient, or their caregiver, in a manner so that the patient or caregiver understands (1) the proposed examination, test, and/or treatment, (2) the potential risks and benefits of acceptance and/or refusal, and (3) any potential alternative approaches or therapies.

Finally, the medical record should clearly document the elements of the discussion, the important risks accepted and the potential benefits forgone, and the fact that all questions and concerns were addressed. Where standard practice dictates a written and signed documentation of consent, "refusal to consent" and "against medical advice" should be similarly documented in a signed writing. In instances where "refusal to consent" or "against medical advice" is accompanied by a refusal to sign a consent form, that itself should be carefully documented.

Informed Refusal and the Right to Die

Although a complete discussion of refusal of life support and right to die is beyond the scope of this chapter, it is important to note that the corollary to informed consent is the right to expressly refuse medical treatment, even where such refusal represents the withdrawal of previously instituted life support.

In 1960, the *Natanson* court extended the informed consent doctrine to include a right to refuse treatment:

> Anglo-American law starts with the premise of thorough-going self-determination. It follows that each man is considered to be master of his own body, and he may, if he be of sound mind, expressly prohibit the performance of life-saving surgery, or other medical treatment. A doctor might well believe that an operation or form of treatment is desirable or necessary but the law does not permit him to substitute his own judgment for that of the patient by any form of artifice or deception.

In the 1970s, the right to refuse medical treatment was extended to justify the removal of life support in patients in persistent vegetative states. It is now well established, under American law, that a mentally competent adult has the right to refuse medical treatment, even if, in doing so, he or she will hasten his or her death [63].

In 1975, Karen Quinlan sustained a respiratory arrest and after a period of anoxia was resuscitated to a "chronic persistent vegetative state" wherein she was dependent on mechanical ventilator support. Quinlan's parents requested termination of mechanical ventilator support, a request which was contested by the treating physicians. In its analysis, the Supreme Court of New Jersey invoked the right of privacy. Recognizing that the US Constitution does not explicitly mention a right of privacy, the Court noted that prior Supreme Court decisions had recognized that a right of personal privacy exists and that certain areas of privacy are guaranteed under the Constitution. Specifically, the New Jersey Court cited *Griswold v. Connecticut* in which the US Supreme Court found the unwritten constitutional right of privacy to exist in the penumbra of specific guarantees of the Bill of Rights "formed by emanations from those guarantees that help give them life and substance" [64]. In this context, the *Quinlan* court saw the issue to be the "claimed interests of the State … essentially the preservation and sanctity of human life" and the "defense of the right of the physician to administer medical treatment plan according to his best judgment." The court weighed Quinlan's right to privacy against the state's interest in preserving human life and defending the right of a physician to administer medical treatment according to his or her best judgment. Thus the NJ court determined that as the degree of bodily invasion increased and the prognosis for the patient's recovery worsened, the patient's right to privacy increased and the state's interest weakened. In its analysis, the court deferred to the expertise of the medical profession with respect to prognosis and the initial presumption of entitlement to guardianship in the next of kin stating that "decision-making within health care if it is considered as an expression of a primary obligation of the physician, *primum non nocere*, should be controlled primarily within the patient-doctor-family relationship."

Importantly, the NJ court also ruled that if the medical consensus determined that Quinlan had no reasonable possibility of recovery, and, after consultation with the family, they acted in accordance with the family's wishes, then the physicians could not be subject to criminal or civil liability for that decision. The importance of the Quinlan case is that it laid the foundation and framework for the right of kin to speak on behalf of an incapacitated and incompetent critically ill family member on life support with no reasonable hope of recovery.

In *Matter of Farrell*, Judge Garibaldi wrote [65]:

> Death comes to everyone. However, in our society, due to great advances in medical knowledge and technology over the last few decades, death does not come suddenly or completely unexpectedly to most people. Instead, most people who die are under the treatment of health care professionals who are able to continue physical existence for human beings "even when most of our physical and mental capacities have been irrevocably lost." While medical advances have made it possible to forestall and cure certain illnesses previously considered fatal, they also have prolonged the slow deterioration and death of some patients. Sophisticated life-sustaining medical technology has made it possible to hold some people on the threshold of death for an indeterminate period of time, "obfuscat[ing] the use of traditional definition of death." Questions of fate have thereby become matters of choice raising profound "moral, social, technological, philosophical, and legal questions involving the interplay of many disciplines." (*internal citations omitted*)

Nevertheless, the right to refuse life-sustaining medical treatment is not absolute. The state has at least four potentially countervailing interests in sustaining a person's life: preserving life, preventing suicide, safeguarding the integrity of the medical profession, and protecting innocent third parties [66].

The first "right-to-die" case to reach the US Supreme Court was the case of Nancy Cruzan. Cruzan was rendered incompetent as a result of severe injuries sustained during an automobile accident. Cruzan's parents and family sought the withdrawal of artificial feeding and hydration after it became apparent that Cruzan had virtually no chance of recovering her cognitive faculties. The Supreme Court of Missouri held that, because there was no clear and convincing evidence of Nancy's desire to have life-sustaining treatment withdrawn under such circumstances, her parents lacked authority for such a request. In the US Supreme Court, the common law doctrine of informed consent is viewed as generally encompassing the right of a competent individual to refuse medical treatment. The court ruling supported the idea that patients have a fundamental right to refuse life-sustaining treatments but added that states may regulate the circumstances under which life-sustaining treatments may be withdrawn when the patient cannot speak on his or her own behalf.

The right to die a natural death, free of unwanted medical interventions, is not legally the same as the right to hasten one's death. In Conroy, the NJ court decided that the value of life is not diminished through a decision to refuse medical treatment but "by the failure to allow a competent human being the right of choice." Thus, "[i]n cases that do not involve the protection of the actual or potential life of someone other than the decision-maker, the state's indirect and abstract interest in preserving the life of the competent patient generally gives way to the patient's much stronger personal interest in directing the course of his own life."

In Conroy, the court also explained that declining life-sustaining medical treatment may not properly be viewed as an attempt to commit suicide. Refusing medical intervention merely allows the disease to take its natural course; if death were to eventually occur, it would be the result primarily of the underlying disease, and not the result of a self-inflicted injury.

The Disenfranchised: Time for Circumstantial Reevaluation of Paternalism?

The concept of a healthcare proxy presumes that every patient will have someone available to speak on their behalf in the event that they become ill or incapacitated without a living will [67]. There is a presumption that every person has someone who cares about them enough to direct their healthcare, either as informed consent or informed refusal, so as to respect their wishes and their autonomy. However, not everyone does; the American Bar Association's Commission on Law and Aging has estimated that approximately 4% of older adults constitute a group referred to as "the unbefriended elderly" – those patients who are unable to make decisions for themselves; have no advance directive, living will, or surrogate decision-maker; and also have no family or friends to speak on their behalf [68]. Variably those who have no one to speak on their behalf are also referred to as the "disenfranchised," the "elder orphans," or the "unrepresented." The more common terminology is "unrepresented" patients defined as hospitalized patients who lack decision-making capacity but have no advance directive and no one to serve as a legally authorized surrogate [69]; these patients have lost the capacity to make their own healthcare decisions and also do not have anyone who is authorized by law to make decisions so as to provide directions regarding their wishes for interventions, ongoing care, or resuscitation. Although such labels arguably stigmatize individuals, these individuals are unarguably vulnerable.

However, despite the common assumption that patients who are hospitalized and have no surrogate decision-maker are friendless and alone, many patients actually have family member available but that family member was either unable or unwilling to act as surrogate decision-maker or guardian [70]. The unbefriended population also includes those who have outlived family members, immigrants (both documented and undocumented), transients, the mentally ill, and the homeless, and therefore, this population is rapidly increasing. Nonetheless, even in the event that an otherwise unbefriended individual has written advance directives, someone must bring those documents to the attention of healthcare providers and forcefully advocate on the basis of the patient.

Although the exact prevalence of unrepresented patients remains unknown, a 2006 study found that 16% of patients in the medical ICU of a metropolitan hospital lacked decision-making capacity and had no surrogate decision-maker [71]; 5.5%

of deaths in seven geographically diverse ICUs were unrepresented patients [72], and 3–4% of those living in nursing homes are unrepresented [73].

There is no standardized process for making healthcare decisions on the behalf of unrepresented patients. Guardianship is a legal tool that allows one person or entity to make decisions for another who is referred to as "the ward." State laws vary with respect to mandatory appointment of a guardian to act on behalf of incapacitated patients. In many states, there is only one legally authorized decision-maker for unrepresented patients: a *guardian* ad litem who is appointed by a judge to make medical decisions [74]. The traditional court-appointed guardianship process is lengthy and may take weeks or months depending on the jurisdiction, and court-appointed guardians are likely unfamiliar with the patient and may have little understanding of the healthcare or treatment issues. In addition, many critical healthcare decisions are necessary while patients are awaiting guardianship. Healthcare facilities may act as petitioner or assist a petitioner for guardianship in order to facilitate a treatment plan. In the event of an emergency, a probate court may appoint a temporary guardian, or an expedited temporary medical consent guardian, to act on the patient's behalf until the court can appoint a permanent guardian.

Decisions to withdraw life support in the absence of guardianship or a legal surrogate are often made by an ICU physician (with the concurrence of another physician) or the ICU team [75], decisions to write DNR orders were made mostly by the ICU physician and the medical team or the ICU physician with the concurrence another physician, and, less commonly, the DNR orders were written in conjunction with a hospital ethics committee or following petition for a court-appointed guardian.

Once again, state laws vary; however, for example, Georgia, state law provides a mechanism for decisions regarding resuscitation of unrepresented patients:

> (a) It shall be lawful for the attending physician to issue an order not to resuscitate pursuant to the requirements of this chapter. Any written order issued by the attending physician using the term "do not resuscitate," "DNR," "order not to resuscitate," "no code," or substantially similar language in the patient's chart shall constitute a legally sufficient order and shall authorize a physician, health care professional, or emergency medical technician to withhold or withdraw cardiopulmonary resuscitation.
>
> …
>
> (e) If none of the persons specified in subsections (b), (c), and (d) of this Code section is reasonably available or competent to make a decision regarding an order not to resuscitate, an attending physician may issue an order not to resuscitate for a patient, provided that:
>
> (1) Such physician determines with the concurrence of a second physician, in writing in the patient's medical record, that such patient is a candidate for nonresuscitation;
> (2) An ethics committee or similar panel, as designated by the health care facility, concurs in the opinion of the attending physician and the concurring physician that the patient is a candidate for nonresuscitation; and
> (3) The patient is receiving inpatient or outpatient treatment from or is a resident of a health care facility other than a hospice or a home health agency [76].

Furthermore, under Georgia law, a "candidate for non-resuscitation" includes patients who based on a determination to a reasonable degree of medical certainty by an attending physician with the concurrence of another physician:

(a) Has a medical condition which can reasonably be expected to result in the imminent death of the patient
(b) Is in a noncognitive state with no reasonable possibility of regaining cognitive functions
(c) Is a person for whom CPR would be medically futile in that such resuscitate will likely be unsuccessful in restoring cardiac and respiratory function or will only restore cardiac and respiratory function for a brief period of time so the patient will likely experience repeated need for CPR over a short period of time and so such resuscitation would be otherwise medically futile [77]

The legislative complexity, as it varies from state to state, is illustrated by New York State law which has continued to evolve. New York's former DNR Law [78], which went into effect in 1988 and remained effective until 2010, stated, in relevant part, that a physician could write a DNR order for a patient who lacked capacity if he or she determined, among other circumstances, that resuscitation would be "medically futile," another physician concurred, and a surrogate decision-maker consented to the DNR order [79]; moreover, if a patient had no surrogate, the physician could write the DNR order based on medical futility without surrogate consent, with the concurrence of another physician [80]. In 2010, the passage of the Family Health Care Decisions Act (FHCDA) [81] repealed New York's former DNR Law with respect to DNR orders and made such decisions subject to FHCDA's more general standards stating, in part, that:

> treatment can be withheld (and therefore a DNR order can be issued) if the attending physician and another physician determine to a reasonable degree of medical certainty that:
>
> (i) life-sustaining treatment offers the patient no medical benefit because the patient will die imminently, even if the treatment is provided; and
> (ii) the provision of life-sustaining treatment would violate accepted medical standards [82].

In 2016, a proposed NY State Senate Bill, S4796, supported by the New York State Bar Association aimed to improve end-of-life decisions by clarifying that a physician can write a DNR order for a patient who lacks capacity, among other circumstances, when the attending physician finds that resuscitation would be "medically futile," another physician concurs, and a surrogate decision-maker consents to the DNR order; and, if the patient has no surrogate, an attending physician, with the concurrence of another physician, could write the order based on medical futility in the absence of a surrogate [83].

In 2016, Colorado passed House Bill 1101 which stated, in relevant part, that:

- An attending physician may designate another willing physician to make health care treatment decisions as a patient's proxy decision-maker if:

- After making reasonable efforts, the physician cannot locate any interested persons, or none of the interested persons are willing and able to serve as proxy decision-maker;
- The attending physician has obtained an independent assessment of the patient's lack of decisional capacity by another health care provider;
- The physician has consulted with and obtained a consensus on the proxy designation with the medical ethics committee of the health care facility where the patient is receiving care; and
- The identity of the physician designated as proxy decision-maker is documented in the medical record.
- The authority of the proxy decision-maker terminates in the event that an interested person is willing to serve as proxy decision-maker, a guardian is appointed, the patient regains decisional capacity, the proxy decision-maker decides to no longer serve as the patient's proxy decision-maker, or the patient is transferred or discharged from the facility, if any, where the patient is receiving care (unless the proxy decision-maker expresses his or her intention to continue to serve as proxy decision-maker).
- The act establishes guidelines to which an attending physician and proxy decision-maker shall adhere for proxy decision-making.
- When acting in good faith as a proxy decision-maker, a physician is not subject to civil or criminal liability or regulatory sanction [84].
- With respect to unrepresented patients who present for medical care, there is often a tacit or implied presumption of implied consent to treatment. Where there is an unequivocal lacking of reasonably conclusive evidence of unrepresented patients' preferences the healthcare provider team has no basis upon which to make decisions respecting of a person's autonomy and therefore must rely on a form of substituted judgement, or, arguably a form of paternalism. Although paternalism in its purest form represents a usurpation of a patient's decision-making power through the substitute one's judgment for theirs, expressly for the purpose of promoting their welfare [85]. In the context of the unrepresented, there is no evidence to support a countervailing expression of autonomy, and therefore the pure definition of the term paternalism cannot apply. Once again, in the context of the unrepresented, unilateral decisions by healthcare providers on the behalf of the patient to further the goal of that patient's best interests are bare human values judgments.[1] Bare human values judgments do not represent universal truths but rather imply a shared norm of morality to justify what 'should 'be done under a set of circumstances; this presupposes an absence of bias, conflict of interest, or coercion. Moral distress and a sense fairness must be optimized within the healthcare team so that where the clinical team caring for the patient become the default decision makers for the unrepresented patient do not present an ethically troubling dilemma. The importance of the healthcare team and the considered buy-in of the team members, who are most intimately famil-

[1] *See* Ozar, *supra*.

iar with the patient's clinical condition and course, cannot be over-emphasized; since those caregivers will have a perspective that is arguably superior even to that of an internal (ethics committee) or external (court-based) reviewer. Protection of the interests of the unrepresented, and other similar disenfranchised patients, will ultimately require a clinically, legally, and administratively accepted approach, which ensures "that (1) decision-making is not unduly delayed, (2) alternatives that may benefit the patient are fairly considered, and (3) patients are protected from decisions that may be harmful." [86]

Summary and Conclusions

Many would argue that there can never be a truly "informed" consent because of the enormous technological complexities of modern medicine and the significant gap in education, training, and experience between the patient and the provider. However, it is axiomatic that from a moral and ethical analysis, and certainly from a regulatory and legal perspective, informed consent for treatment is mandatory. Consent not only is a legal defense to battery but is a legal documentation of a patient's understanding of and permission for medical care.

References

1. Szalados JE. Morality, ethics, and the law. An overview of the foundations of contemporary clinical ethical analysis. Ethics and law for neurosciences clinicians: foundations and evolving challenges. New Brunswick: Rutgers University Press; 2019.
2. Jones WHS. Hippocrates, vol. vol II. London: Heinemann; 1923: 6–7; 165; 192–3.
3. Bury RG. Plato laws. London: Heinemann; 1926: 212–3; 238–9; 306–9; 454–7.
4. Percival T. Medical ethics: or a code of institutes and precepts adapted to the professional conduct of physicians and surgeons. Manchester: J Johnson; 1803.
5. Pellegrino ED. Percival's medical ethics: the moral philosophy of an 18th-century English gentleman. Arch Intern Med. 1986;146(11):2265–9.
6. Kant I. Practical philosophy. ed. and trans. Mary Gregor; 1996.
7. United Nations. Universal declaration of human rights. United Nations; 1948.
8. International Bioethics Committee (IBC) Report of the International Bioethics Committee of UNESCO on consent. Social and Human Sciences Sector, Division of Ethics of Science and Technology, Bioethics Section SHS/EST/CIB08–09/2008/1, UNESCO; 2008.
9. Lu DW, Adams JG. Ethical issues. In: Bass RR, editor. Medical oversight of EMS. Dubuque: Kendall/Hunt Publishing Company; 2009. p. 117–24.
10. Spatz ES, Krumholz HM, Moulton BW. The new era of informed consent: getting to a reasonable-patient standard through shared decision making. JAMA. 2016;315(19):2063–4.
11. Whitney SN, McGuire AL, McCullough LB. A typology of shared decision making, informed consent, and simple consent. Ann Intern Med. 2004;140:54–9.
12. Pratt v. Davis, 118 Ill., App. 161 (1st Dist. 1905).
13. Union Pacific Railway Co., v. Botsford, 141 US. 250, 251 (1891).

14. Schoendorff v. Society of New York Hosp., 105 N.E. 92, 93 (N.Y. 1914) relying on Pratt v. Davis, 224 Ill. 300, 79 N.E. 562 (1906) and Mohr v. Williams, 95 Minn. 261, 104 N.W. 12 (1905).
15. Salgo v. Leland Stanford Jr. University Board of Trustees 154 cal. App 2d 564 (1957).
16. Natanson v. Kline 186 Kan. 393; 350 P.2d 1093 (1960); Natanson v. Kline 187 Kan. 186; 354 P.2d 670 (1960).
17. Canterbury v. Spence, 464 F.2d 772, 778 (D.C. Cir. 1972).
18. Truman v Thomas, 27 Cal 3d, 611 P2d 902 (1980).
19. Dunham v Wright, 423 F2d 940 (3rd Cir 1970).
20. Stewart-Graves v Vaughn, 162 Wash 2d 115, 170 P3d 1151 (2007).
21. NY Pub Health L § 2805-D (2019). Limitation of medical, dental or podiatric malpractice action based on lack of informed consent.
22. 49 A.L.R. 3d 501 § 2(a) (1973).
23. AMA principles of medical ethics, in AMA code of medical ethics. Available online at: https://www.ama-assn.org/sites/ama-assn.org/files/corp/media-browser/principles-of-medical-ethics.pdf. Accessed 30 Sept 2019.
24. Witherell v. Weimer, 421 NE2d 869 (1981).
25. Mink v. University of Chicago. U.S. District Court, N.D. Illinois, E.D. Fed Suppl. 1978 Oct 13; 460:713–23.
26. Cobbs v Grant, 502 P2d 1 (Cal 1972).
27. Gaskin v Goldwasser, 520 NE2d 1085 (Ill App Ct 1988).
28. Tom v Lenox Hill Hosp, 627 NYS2d 874 (NY App Div 1995).
29. Raab EL. The parameters of informed consent. Trans Am Ophthalmol Soc. 2004;102:225–32.
30. Restatement (Second) of Torts §§ 13, 18 (1965).
31. Hales v. Pittman, 118 Ariz.305, 576 P.2d 493, 498 (1978).
32. See IPI.105.0.03; *see also*, Davis v. Kraft, 405 Ill.App.3d 20, 29 (1st Dist. 2010).
33. NY Pub Health L § 2805-D (2014).
34. Shinal v. Toms 162 A3d 429 (2017).
35. Valles v. Albert Einstein Medical Center, 805 A.2d 1232 (Pa. 2002).
36. Shinal at 162 A.3d 453.
37. Lynch HF, Joffe S, Feldman EA. Informed consent and the role of the treating physician. NEJM. 2018;378(25):2433–8.
38. H.R.4449 - Patient Self Determination Act of 1990. Available online at https://www.congress.gov/bill/101st-congress/house-bill/4449. Verified October 11, 2020.
39. 42 CFR § 482.13(b)(1)–(2). CMS Condition of participation: Patient's rights.
40. Department of Health & Human Services. Centers for Medicare & Medicaid Services. Director, Survey and Certification Group. Revisions to the hospital interpretive guidelines for informed consent. S&C-07-17. April 13, 2007. Available online at: https://www.cms.gov/Medicare/Provider-Enrollment-and-Certification/SurveyCertificationGenInfo/downloads/SCLetter07-17.pdf. Verified October 11, 2020.
41. The Joint Commission. 2016. Comprehensive accreditation manual glossary.
42. TJC. Standard RI0103.01 (2017).
43. American Medical Association. Code of medical ethics opinion 2.1.1. Available online at: https://www.ama-assn.org/delivering-care/ethics/informed-consent.
44. Carpenter v. Blake, 60 Barb NY 488 (1871).
45. Brown v. Hughes, 94 Colo. 295, 30 P.2d 259 (1934).
46. Fortner v. Koch, 272 Mich. 273, 261 N.W. 762 (1935).
47. Shuster E. Fifty years later: the significance of the Nuremberg code. N Engl J Med. 1997;337:1436–40.
48. The declaration of Helsinki. Available online at: https://history.nih.gov/research/downloads/helsinki.pdf.
49. Ndebele P. The declaration of Helsinki, 50 years later. JAMA. 2013;310(20):2145–6.
50. National Research Act. Pub. L. 93–348. July 12, 1974.

51. The Belmont Report. Ethical Principles and Guidelines for the Protection of Human Subjects of Research. The National Commission for the Protection of Human Subjects of Biomedical and Behavioral Research. Department of Health, Education, and Welfare. April 18, 1979. Available online at: https://www.hhs.gov/ohrp/regulations-and-policy/belmont-report/read-the-belmont-report/index.html. Verified October 11, 2020.
52. National Commission for the Protection of Human Subjects of Biomedical and Behavioral Research. Ethical Principles and Guidelines for the Protection of Human Subjects of Research (aka the Belmont Report). 1979. Available at http://ohsr.od.nih.gov/guidelines/belmont.html. Verified October 11, 2020.
53. Department of Health and Human Services, National Institutes of Health, Office for Protection from Research Risks. Title 45: public welfare, part 46: protection of human subjects (aka the common rule). 2001. Available at www.hhs.gov/ohrp/humansubjects/guidance/45cfr46.htm.
54. Code of Federal Regulations Title 21. Part 50 Protection of human subjects. 21 CFR 50. (2019).
55. Electronic Code of Federal Regulations. Title 45: public welfare. Part 46—protection of human subjects. Available online at: https://www.ecfr.gov/cgi-bin/retrieveECFR?gp=&SID=83cd09e1c0f5c6937cd9d7513160fc3f&pitd=20180719&n=pt45.1.46&r=PART&ty=HTML.
56. HHS. Office for Human Research Protections. Informed consent. Available online at: https://www.hhs.gov/ohrp/regulations-and-policy/guidance/faq/informed-consent/index.html.
57. Minor Consent to Medical Treatment Laws. National District Attorneys Association. Updated January 2013. Available online at: https://ndaa.org/wp-content/uploads/Minor-Consent-to-Medical-Treatment-2.pdf.
58. American Academy of Pediatrics. Consent. Pediatrics. 1976;57(3):414–6.
59. American Academy of Pediatrics. Committee on bioethics. Informed consent, parental permission, and assent in pediatric practice. Pediatrics. 1995;95(2):314–7.
60. American Academy of Pediatrics. Committee on bioethics. Informed consent in decision-making in pediatric practice. Pediatrics. 2016;138(2):2016–1484.
61. Beauchamp TL, Childress JF. Principles of biomedical ethics. 7th ed. New York: Oxford University Press; 2013.
62. NY Pub Health L § 2805-D(4)(2014).
63. See *In re* Brooks' Estate, 32 Ill. 2d 361, 205 N.E.2d 435 (1965); *In re* Osborne, 294 A.2d 372 (D.C. 1972); Lane v. Candura, 6 Mass. App. Ct. 377, 376 N.E.2d 1232 (1978), cited with approval in Brophy v. New England Sinai Hosp., 398 Mass. 417, 497 N.E.2d 626 (1986); *In re* Quackenbush, 156 N.J. Super. 282 (Morris County Ct. 1978; Satz v. Perlmutter, 362 So. 2d 160 (Fla. Dist. Ct. App. 1978), aff'd, 379 So. 2d 359 (Fla. 1980); Bartling v. Superior Court, 163 Cal. App. 3d 186, 209 Cal. Rptr. 220 (Cal.Ct.App. 1984); *In re* Conroy, 98 N.J. 321, 343 (1985); Bouvia v. Superior. Court, 179 Cal. App. 3d 1127, 225 Cal. Rptr. 297 (Cal.Ct.App. 1986), review denied (June 5, 1986).
64. Griswold v. Connecticut, 381 U.S. 479, 85 S. Ct. 1678, 14 L. Ed. 2d 510 (1965).
65. Matter of Farrell. 108 N.J. 335, 529 A.2d 404 (1987).
66. Conroy, supra, 98 N.J. at 348–49 (citing Satz v. Perlmutter, supra, 362 So. 2d at 162; In re Spring, 380 Mass. 629, 640, 405 N.E.2d 115, 123 (1980); Commissioner of Correction v. Myers, 379 Mass. 255, 261, 399 N.E.2d 452, 456 (1979); Saikewicz v. Superintendent of Belchertown State School, 373 Mass. 728, 738, 370 N.E.2d 417, 426 (1977); In re Torres, 357 N.W.2d 332, 339 (Minn. 1984); In re Colyer, 99 Wash. 2d 114, 121, 660 P.2d 738, 743 (1983).
67. Paula Span. When there's no family. The New York Times September 23, 2013. Available online at: https://newoldage.blogs.nytimes.com/2013/09/23/when-theres-no-family/.
68. Karp N, Wood E. Incapacitated and alone: healthcare decision-making for unbefriended older people. American Bar Association Commission on Law and Aging; 2003.
69. Ozar D. Who are "Unrepresented" patients and what count as "Important" medical decisions for them? AMA J Ethics. 2019;21(7):E611–6.
70. Bandy RJ, Helft PR, Bandy RW, Torke AM. Medical decision-making during the guardianship process for incapacitated, hospitalized adults: a descriptive cohort study. J Gen Intern Med. 2010;25(10):1003–8.

71. White DB, Curtis JR, Lo B, Luce JM. Decisions to limit life-sustaining treatment for critically ill patients who lack both decision-making capacity and surrogate decision-makers. Crit Care Med. 2006;34:2053–9.
72. White DB, Randall Curtis J, Wolf LE, Prendergast TJ, Taichman DB, Kuniyoshi G, Acerra F, Lo B, Luce JM. Life support for patients without a surrogate decision maker: who decides? Ann Intern Med. 2007;147(1):34–40.
73. Karp N, Wood E. Incapacitated and alone: healthcare decision making for unbefriended older people. Hum Rights. 2004;31(Spring):20–5.
74. Pope TM. Making medical decisions for patients without surrogates. N Engl J Med. 2013;369(21):1976–8.
75. Bandy 2010 *supra*.
76. Georgia Code. TITLE 31 – HEALTH; Chapter 39 - cardiopulmonary resuscitation. GA Code § 31–39-4 (2010).
77. 2010 Georgia Code. Title 31 – Health; Chapter 39 - cardiopulmonary resuscitation. GA Code § 31–39-2. O.C.G.A. 31–39-2 (2010) Definitions: § (F)(4) §§ a-c.
78. NY Public Health Law (PHL) Article 29-B, added by NY Laws of 1987, chapter 818, eff. April 1 1988. See also the Department of Health's nearly identical hospital regulations. 10 NYCRR § 405.43 (repealed March 11, 2014).
79. NY PHL § 2965.3(c)(1988).
80. Ibid., § 2966.1.
81. PHL Article 29-CC, added by NY Laws of 2010, chapter 8.
82. NY Public Health Law § 2994-g.5.
83. Fins JJ, Swidler RN. New York State Bar Association. A proposal to restore medical futility as a clinical basis for a DNR order under NY law. Available online at: https://www.nysba.org/CustomTemplates/SecondaryStandard.aspx?id=72612.
84. Colorado General Assembly. First Regular Session | 72nd General Assembly. HB16–1101 medical decisions for unrepresented patients. Concerning medical decisions for unrepresented patients. Bill summary. Available online at: https://leg.colorado.gov/bills/hb16-1101.
85. Buchanan DR. Autonomy, paternalism, and justice: ethical priorities in public health. Am J Public Health. 2008;98(1):15–21.
86. Kinlaw K. "Unrepresented patients" and vulnerability: patients without decision makers. THE HEALTHCARE.

Chapter 4
The Laws and Regulations Governing Hospitals and Healthcare Entities

James E. Szalados

Introduction

American healthcare systems, hospitals, clinics, and other points of healthcare delivery are subject to a myriad of laws and regulations promulgated by federal, state, agency, and local entities. In general, regulation is largely intended to best ensure that patients receive safe, high-quality care, in facilities that are operated in a clean and safe fashion, by appropriately trained and supervised employees. Healthcare entities are subject to HIPAA, HITECH, EMTALA, HCQIA, Anti-Kickback and Stark, false claims, CLIA, OCR, human resources laws, and other regulation addresses in detail elsewhere in this text [see Chaps. 12, 13, 25, and 27]. The resultant administrative burden to healthcare entities is substantial and adds not only to the cost of American healthcare at every level from the entities' operations, compliance programs, and governmental oversight and enforcement. At the present time, it is estimated that health systems, hospitals, and post-acute care providers (PACs) must comply with approximately 630 discrete federal regulatory requirements across nine domains, exclusive of intermittent compliance requirements such as antitrust and land use regulations; these include 341 hospital-related requirements and 288 PAC-related requirements. The American Hospital Association has described the array of regulations as "regulatory overload" and has estimated that the annual administrative cost of regulatory compliance to health systems, hospitals, and PACs and hospitals is approximately $39 billion [1]. The pace at which new rules and regulations are adopted and the sheer volume or verbiage of information within each rule make compliance challenging. The AHA also notes that an average

J. E. Szalados (✉)
Director, Surgical and Neurocritical Care Units, Rochester Regional Health System at Rochester General Hospital, Rochester, NY, USA

The Szalados Law Firm, Hilton, NY, USA
e-mail: james.szalados@rochesterregional.org; jszalados@aol.com

J. E. Szalados (ed.), *The Medical-Legal Aspects of Acute Care Medicine*,
https://doi.org/10.1007/978-3-030-68570-6_4

size community hospital must dedicate 59 full-time equivalents (FTEs) of person power to regulatory compliance, of which more than 25% are physicians and nurses; the regulation of PACs is more complex, requiring on average an additional 8.1 FTEs to ensure compliance. The average-sized hospital spends nearly $760,000 to meet Meaningful Use (MU) administrative requirements annually, devotes 4.6 FTEs, more than 50% of whom are clinical staff, and spends approximately $709,000 annually on the administrative aspects of quality reporting [1].

The First Hospitals

The first institutions devoted specifically to the care of the injured, sick, and infirm were military hospitals which date to ancient antiquity, generally providing more comfort and care than treatment. Perhaps the earliest known civilian, or public, hospitals date to Sri Lanka to a period between 100 BC and 150 AD, described in the Sanskrit encyclopedia of medicine, the Compendium of Caraka. The Academy of Gondishapur was established as a hospital and center for medical education at Gundeshapur in Persia in the year 271 AD [2]. Early Christian and Islamic Hospitals were devoted to the care of lepers and the blind. In ancient Greece, temples dedicated to the healer-god Asclepius were organized as centers of medical learning, care, and healing, frequently in the course of religious rituals and rites. A large number of hospitals were built in Italy during the thirteenth century, especially in Milan and Florence. Between years 1414 and in 1444, in Italy, the Padua hospital "San Francesco Grande" was founded with the specific purpose of caring for the sick and subsequently became an institution for the advancement of medical research and teaching.

Medieval "hospitals" were based in the notion of social charity. The societal obligation to care for its less-fortunate fellow citizens is a global construct found throughout history. Societies and cultures, united in such interest, raised resources necessary for the care of the disadvantaged through tithes (a proportion of one's produce or earnings collected as a tax to support a religious organization) or through voluntary charitable contributions. Charitable care, through community donations of food, orphanages, and "poorhouses" were not specifically organized for the purpose of caring for the sick, but rather to care for those who could not care for themselves, the homeless, the orphaned, the infirm, the elderly, and the sick. In England, medieval and Tudor-era laws established a legal duty to care for the disadvantaged. In general, benevolent care was provided through religious institutions, generally organized at the level of local congregations or parishes. With the advancement of medical science and training, medical rather than comfort goals became the focus of hospitals, which then also evolved into medical schools providing teaching and apprenticeships.

The evolution of hospitals in the Western world from charitable guesthouses to centers of scientific excellence has been influenced by a number of social and cultural developments which include changes in our understanding of disease, economics, geographic location, religion and ethnicity, socioeconomics, scientific and technological progress, and the perceived needs of society and the population [3]. Thus, "modern medicine is one of those extraordinary works of reason: an elaborate system of specialized knowledge, technical procedures, and rules of behavior. ... From a relatively weak, traditional profession of minor economic significance, medicine has become a sprawling system of hospitals, clinics, health plans, insurance companies, and myriad other organizations employing a vast labor force. ... The history of medicine has been written as an epic of progress, but it is also a tale of social and economic conflict over the emergence of new hierarchies of power and authority, new markets, and new conditions of belief and experience" [4].

The first hospitals in the USA were probably the Bellevue Hospital (established in 1736 as the New York City Almshouse) and the Pennsylvania Hospital (jointly established in 1751 by Dr. Thomas Bond and Benjamin Franklin with the intent of caring "for the sick-poor and insane who were wandering the streets of Philadelphia") [5].

Benjamin Franklin was instrumental in the founding of Pennsylvania Hospital in 1751 [6]. Nonetheless, throughout the eighteenth and even into the early twentieth centuries in America, physicians' offices were within their own homes, from where healthcare to the sick was delivered primarily at home; physicians visited patients at their homes where they performed surgery and deliveries at their homes and cared for the sick. Families and neighbors, as laypersons, would participate in the care of the sick and provide support to the families of the afflicted [7]. With the development of industrialization and urbanization and the accompanying shifts in social structure, in the early eighteenth century, almshouses or poorhouses were established to shelter and treat the indigent ill; and with the recognition of contagion, government-operated pesthouses segregated those who are at risk of spreading diseases such as cholera or tuberculosis. General care was provided to the sick, but there was little ability or attempt to treat or cure. Therefore the role of physicians at such institutions was merely peripheral. Thus, for most of the nineteenth century, hospitals were places where the poor and the "insane" were sent to die. Moreover, almshouses were not intended strictly to provide medical care since they also provided custodial care to the poor and destitute [8]. The vast majority of the care provided at such institutions was by nurses and not physicians. Although such institutions were supported through the philanthropy of the wealthy and by religious organizations and to a lesser extent government funding, the wealthy did not utilize such institutions for their own healthcare; since the conditions were generally deplorable, the physicians were generally unskilled, and there was little hope of healing. Rather, the wealthy continued to be either cared for at home or at hospitals owned and established by more prominent physicians [9].

Nonetheless, scientific advances in asepsis, radiology, and pharmacology provided the framework for the early hospitals. Developments in medical science and technology both led to a widespread hope that some diseases could be cured and a need for more formal education for physicians. The germ theory of disease was published by Koch in 1861; in 1879 Toussaint identified bacteria in chicken, and in

1880 Pasteur identified bacteria as the cause of spread for infections. In 1847, the American Medical Association (AMA) was established as a professional membership organization for physicians. Simultaneously, in 1847, Semmelweis proposed that handwashing was effective in reducing infections in obstetrical patients, and in 1867 Lister published his work on antiseptic techniques using disinfectants. In 1895 Roentgen took the first medical X-ray of his wife's hand, and soon afterward radiology became an accepted diagnostic technique. In the early twentieth century, through the establishment of a more standardized medical education, hospitals slowly became more accepted across socioeconomic classes, and the reputation of providers improved [10]. Through these developments, hospital infections dramatically dropped and became safer and more accepted places for medical care. Hospitals became centers for clinical teaching and by the turn of the twentieth century were recognized as places where medical care was provided for the entire community. Hospitals in the USA began to gain increasingly more credibility and respectability; by 1910, there were over 4000 acute bed hospitals in the USA.

The early education of physicians in the USA was largely by apprenticeship and later through small private medical schools with limited faculty and non-standardized curricula. Prior to the widespread implementation of educational reforms, medical training was highly variable and often considered inadequate [11]. The Carnegie Foundation for the Advancement of Teaching, commissioned in the Flexner Report, published in 1910, challenged the state of medical education at the time and provided a foundation for more standard criteria for the accreditation of medical schools, criteria for student admissions, standardization of curricula, and testing [12].

In 1929, the Great Depression caused almost all privately financed hospital construction in the USA to cease; and between the years 1928 and 1938, nearly 800 hospitals closed, compounding access to healthcare. Subsequently, during the 1930s and 1940s, the ownership of the hospitals changed from physician-owned to church-related and government-operated. Charity remained a cornerstone for early hospitals which were largely established and operated by religious organizations such as the Catholics, Jesuits, Methodists, and Baptists. However, wealthy donors were also instrumental in establishing hospitals such as the Massachusetts General Hospital and Johns Hopkins often as a means of both providing medical education and as a source of prestige.

State Regulation of Hospitals and Healthcare Facilities

The source of the states' power to regulate healthcare institutions is the "police power" derived from the Tenth Amendment of the US Constitution wherein states retain the "powers not delegated to the United States…" [13]. Thus, states are granted, by default, necessary powers to establish and enforce laws protecting the welfare, safety, and health of the public. The state also derives the authority to regulate healthcare through the enforcement of the federal-state Medicaid program; however, the states' authority under Medicaid is subject to federal authority.

In 1946, the Hospital Survey and Construction Act, better known as the Hill-Burton Act, was enacted by the US Congress and authorized federal grants, loans, and loan guarantees to assist states and communities in constructing acute care general hospitals, special hospitals, nursing homes, public health centers, and rehabilitation facilities [14]. In its original form, the Act established a 5-year program authorizing $75 million annually for hospital construction. In order to be eligible for Hill-Burton funds, a hospital could be organized as either a public or not-for-profit entity. As a condition of funding, recipient facilities contracted, for a period of 20 years, to be available to "all persons residing in the territorial area" of the facility and to make available "a reasonable volume of hospital services to persons unable to pay therefor" – two obligations termed, respectively, the "community service" and "uncompensated care" components of the Act. Thus, the Hill-Burton Act indirectly established the first American program to fund healthcare to underserved areas.

In response to rising healthcare costs, the Social Security Amendment of 1972 contained Section 1122, legislation intended as an oversight mechanism requiring states that participated in the Medicare capital reimbursement program to review and submit recommended capital expenditures to the Secretary of Health, Education, and Welfare for prior approval [15]. New York was the first state to enact a CON law in 1964. Congress enacted the National Health Planning and Resources Development Act's ("NPHRDA") Certificate of Need (CON) program in 1975 [16], in effect a precursor to the future state-based CON laws. The NHPRDA required states to create State Health Planning and Development Agencies (SHPDA) to further develop and administer state-based CON programs and is therefore considered to represent the federal legislation which effectively required states to adopt CON laws. The NHPRDA was repealed in 1986; however, states continued to administer their CON statutes. CON laws are variably in effect in 36 states.

Certificate of Need (CON) laws are state regulatory mechanisms which, in brief, require that a state oversight or health planning agency approves the construction of healthcare facilities, expansion of facilities, and plans for major capital expenditures or service line expansions. CON laws generally intend to ensure access to healthcare resources, promote healthcare quality, control statewide healthcare costs through the avoidance of needlessly duplicative services, and ensure that services are aligned with the community need. Although New York State enacted the first CON program in the USA in 1964 as the state's Metcalf-McCloskey Act, the current CON program is a product of the National Health Planning and Resources Development Act of 1974 which, inter alia, withheld federal funds from states that did not adopt CON laws. In 1986 Congress repealed the federal CON act, thereby eliminating federal incentives to states to maintain their CON programs. Subsequently, 15 states abolished their CON regulations; however, at present, 35 states and Washington DC continue to operate their CON programs.

The term "reasonable volume" was not defined until 1979, where "not less than the lesser of (i) three percent of its operating costs for the most recent fiscal year for which an audited financial statement is available or (ii) ten percent of all Federal assistance provided to or on behalf of the facility, adjusted by a percentage equal to the percentage change in the national Consumer Price Index for medical care between the year in which the facility received assistance or 1979, whichever is later, and the most recent year for which a published index is available" [17].

At the present time, there are approximately 300 Hill-Burton healthcare facilities nationwide; however, several states (such as Alaska, Indiana, Minnesota, Nebraska, Nevada, Rhode Island, Utah, and Wyoming) have no Hill-Burton healthcare facilities [18]. In the wake of the COVID-19 pandemic, 22 states with existing CON laws repealed or suspended them all or in part, for indeterminate periods of time. Individual state statutes provide additional regulatory authority over the healthcare institutions within that state.

The Joint Commission (on Accreditation of Healthcare Organizations)

The history of standardization of the quality of patient care in hospitals is widely credited to begin with a surgeon, Dr. Ernest Codman, who, in 1910, advocated that hospitals should be able to track the outcomes of every patient treated to determine if that treatment was effective and that reasoning led to the establishment of the American College of Surgeons. In 1917 following the Conference on Hospital Standardization, the American College of Surgeons formally established the Hospital Standardization Program, and in 1918, the College published a "Standard on Efficiency" in the Bulletin. The perceived need to extend the Hospital Standardization Program to include the American Hospital and medical arena soon became costly, and in 1951, the American College of Physicians, the American Hospital Association, the American Medical Association, and the Canadian Medical Association united with the American College of Surgeons to form the Joint Commission on Accreditation of Hospitals (JCAH). The Canadian Medical Association withdrew in 1959 to pursue its own standardization program, Canadian Council on Hospital Accreditation, and in 1970 published its Accreditation Manual for Hospitals. In 1965, the Medicare Act included a provision that hospitals accredited by the Joint Commission were "deemed" to be in compliance with most of the Medicare Conditions of Participation (COP) for Hospitals and therefore were considered to meet the requirements for participation in the Medicare and Medicaid programs [19]. In 1987 the JCAH was renamed as the Joint Commission on Accreditation of Healthcare Organizations (JCAHO). In 2007 the JCAHO simplified its name to The Joint Commission (THC). Effective as of 2010, the Medicare Improvements for Patients and Providers Act of 2008 (MIPPA) removed the Joint Commission's statutorily guaranteed accreditation authority for hospitals as it's related to COP [20]. Nonetheless, despite statutory deference to accreditation by THC, CMS continues to require accreditation by a CMS-approved accrediting organization or review by a state survey agency as a fundamental element of the Medicare COP [21].

THC continues to dominate the healthcare institution accreditation filed and accounts for greater than 80% of the accreditation market as the accrediting agency of choice for nearly all major hospital systems. To a large extent, THC domination is consumer-driven, based on marketing; it is also costly [22]. The effectiveness of THC accreditation as a surrogate for overall quality of care at any institution continues to be debated [23, 24]. For example, Barnett et al. found that patients admitted to hospitals during TJC survey weeks have significantly lower mortality than during non-survey weeks, particularly in major teaching hospitals [25]; and Lam et al. found no evidence to indicate that patients choosing a hospital accredited by The Joint Commission confer healthcare benefits over choosing a hospital accredited by another independent accrediting organization [26].

THC accreditation is awarded upon successful completion of an onsite survey conducted by trained surveyors who assess an institution's compliance to predetermined and published standards. THC accreditation is generally awarded for a 3-year period; however, laboratory accreditation is a 2-year award.

In addition to TJC, numerous other American organizations perform accreditation and establish standards with respect to healthcare delivery, including the National Committee for Quality Assurance (NCQA), the American Medical Accreditation Program (AMAP), the American Accreditation HealthCare Commission/Utilization Review Accreditation Commission (AAHC/URAC), the Accreditation Association for Ambulatory HealthCare (AAAHC), the Foundation for Accountability (FACCT), and the Agency for Healthcare Research and Quality (AHRQ). Furthermore, a newer accrediting organization, Det Norske Veritas and Germanischer Lloyd (DNV GL), also performs annual onsite inspections and accredits hospitals as well as specialized hospital programs such as stroke care.

As an alternative to Joint Commission accreditation, CMS-approved accreditation, an acceptable substitute accreditation is through a survey conducted by a respective state survey agency, usually through the state Department of Health. Through a state survey venue, surveyors assess a hospital's compliance with the Medicare Conditions of Participation (CoP) for all services, areas, and locations covered by the hospital's provider agreement under its CMS Certification Number (CCN) in accordance with the CMS State Operations Manual (SOM) which outlines the CMS policies. For example, in New York State, the Division of Hospitals and Diagnostic and Treatment Centers (D&TCs) is under the statutory authority of Article 28, Section 3401 of the Public Health Law (PHL), and Title 10 of the New York Codes of Rules and Regulations (NYCRR), Section 405 which, in part, issues and oversees each facility's Operating Certificate, the hospital license issued by the NYS Department of Health (DOH). In the State of New York, licensed acute care hospitals are therefore sometimes referred to as "Article 28 facilities" each identified by a unique number, the Permanent Facility Identifier (PFI), assigned to each hospital or clinic by the DOH. State health departments will also investigate complaints, issue citations, request a Plan of Correction (POC), and maintain a state database containing, for example, the demographic data of each hospital and the number of complaint investigations completed during the previous year. Thus, specific compliance of hospitals with Medicare CoPs are actually monitored on behalf of the federal government by the respective state agency that licenses hospitals.

Classification of Healthcare Institutions

The notion of healthcare facilities has evolved from the simple designation of "hospitals" into a large array of institutions which have evolved with time to respond to patient and community needs and changes in healthcare markets, payment and reimbursement models, and federal and state regulations, laws, and mandates. In turn, with the evolution of various subtypes of healthcare instructions, the economic models, payment structure, and the regulatory landscape are adapted so as to maintain structural and quality oversight. Present-day hospitals are classified in many ways using a variety of criteria, for example, acuity or length of stay, number of beds, financial organization, ownership and control, academic status, or specialization. Examples of such designations may include, for example, public versus private, general versus specialty (i.e., pediatrics, veterans, women's health, psychiatric or mental health), for-profit versus not-for-profit, short-term versus long-term acute care hospitals, and academic versus community hospitals. Public hospitals are funded and owned by local, state, or federal governments. Private hospitals are owned by investors with a goal of profit, often concentrating services to one or a few service lines such as plastic surgery, cardiology, or neurosurgery. Increasingly, individual hospitals are a part of a healthcare system. The American Hospital Association (AHA) reports that 67% of AHA member hospitals are part of health systems, the majority consisting of three to ten hospitals [27]. Nonetheless, the definition of what constitutes a healthcare system is highly variable; for example, the Dartmouth College Center of Excellence defines a health system as an organization that consists of either at least one hospital plus at least one group of physicians (must include at least three primary care physicians) or more than one group of physicians; the National Bureau of Economic Research (NBER) Center of Excellence defines a health system based on the nature of the relationships between two or more healthcare provider organizations: (1) organizations with common ownership, (2) contractually integrated organizations (e.g., accountable care organizations), and (3) informal care systems, such as common referral arrangements; and the RAND Center of Excellence defines a health system as two or more healthcare organizations that are affiliated through shared ownership or a contractual relationship for payment and service delivery [28]. When a healthcare system also provides a form of insurance services to patients, it becomes an Integrated Delivery Network (IDN), which is then a formal system of providers and sites of care that provides healthcare services and a health insurance plan to a patient population. An IDN may vary in the scope of services it offers but can include, for example, acute care services, long-term health services, specialty clinics, primary care, and home care services, together with a plan of health insurance.

At the turn of the twentieth century, hospitals were unregulated entities, which, together with physician's offices, represented the cottage industry which was healthcare at the time. The earliest attempts at developing uniform standards for the organization and operation of hospitals were developed by the American College of Surgeons (ACS), first published as the "Minimum Standard" set circa 1918. The Minimum Standard requirements both challenged and changed the landscape of hospitals, medical staff, and teaching programs. In 1946 the Hospital Survey and Construction (Hill-Burton) Act required states to establish minimum standards for hospitals that were constructed through aid provided by the Act. In 1951 the ACS partnered with the American College of Physicians, AHA, and the American Medical Association (AMA) to form the Joint Commission on Accreditation of Hospitals (JCAH). The JCAH was created in 1951 to develop minimum health and safety standards for hospitals and subsequently to provide a uniform structure and methodology for the survey, review, and accreditation of US hospitals. In 1987, JCAH became the Joint Commission on Accreditation of Healthcare Organizations (JCAHO) based on its extended oversight of long-term care facilities, ambulatory healthcare, home care, hospice care, mental healthcare, and managed care organizations; and in 2007 the name was subsequently shortened to The Joint Commission (TJC). Nonetheless, widespread state oversight, regulations, and licensing standards for hospitals did not begin until the 1950s. Medicare was signed into law in 1965, at which time there remained wide variation in the application of Joint Commission on Accreditation of Hospitals (JCAH) standards and a substantial number of US hospitals were not participating in the voluntary accreditation program administered by JCAH. Thus, the 1965 amendments to the Social Security Act which established Medicare also contained certain minimum requirements for hospitals, the Conditions of Participation (CoPs) which were first developed in 1965 by the Bureau of Health Insurance (BHI) of the Social Security Administration's Medicare Bureau.

CMS defines a "hospital" as "an institution primarily services in providing, by or under the supervision of physicians, inpatient diagnostic and therapeutic services or rehabilitation services". Facilities must meet the federal statutory definition of a hospital to participate in Medicare as a hospital, with the specific requirement that the hospital be primarily engaged in providing inpatient care. Hospitals must then meet CMS CoPs to be recognized by CMS as a hospital.

Federal rules and regulations regarding hospitals and healthcare facilities generally apply only to those which participate in federally funded payment programs, generally Medicare ("participating hospitals"), although nonparticipating hospitals may also be reimbursed through federal funds if certain conditions are met. Current federal standards for hospitals participating in Medicare are presented in the Code of Federal Regulations (CFR) as 24 separate CoPs which are presently 75 specific requirements or standards. The Bureau of Eligibility, Reimbursement and Coverage of the Health Care Financing Administration (HCFA) is charged with the responsibility for the review and revision of CoPs. A separate unit within HCFA unit, the Bureau of Health Standards and Quality (HSQB), is responsible for the administration and enforcement of CoP standards. CMS recognizes that it is possible for a hospital to have multiple inpatient campuses and outpatient locations; however, then the entire healthcare system must be certified since it is not permissible to certify only part of a participating hospital.

Under Section 1861 of the Social Security Act, hospitals that participate in Medicare must meet certain requirements as specified in the Social Security Act with the caveat that the Department of Health and Human Services (DHHS) may impose additional requirements as it deems necessary. Section 1865 of the Social Security Act provides that hospitals accredited by TJC or the American Osteopathic Association (AOA) are automatically '"deemed"' ("deemed status") to meet all the health and safety requirements for participation; although both the federal conditions and the Joint Commission standards also require hospitals to be licensed by their respective states.

Critical Access Hospitals

Congress created the Critical Access Hospital (CAH) designation through the Balanced Budget Act of 1997 [29] in an attempt to reduce the financial vulnerability of rural hospitals and improve access to healthcare in rural settings. The Act also contained the Medicare Rural Hospital Flexibility Program (Flex Program) to support CAHs. In order to be eligible for CAH status, hospitals must in general meet at least the following conditions: (a) 25 or fewer acute care inpatient beds, (b) located more than 35 miles from another hospital, (c) maintain an annual average length of stay of 96 hours or less for acute care patients, and (d) provide 24/7 emergency care services. CAHs are designated by CMS. Financial incentives to CAHs include the following: (1) CAHs are paid for most inpatient and outpatient services to patients at 101% of reasonable costs; (2) Medicare does not include CAHs in the hospital Inpatient Prospective Payment System (IPPS) or the hospital Outpatient Prospective Payment System (OPPS); and (3) Medicare pays CAH services according to Part A and Part B deductible and coinsurance amounts and does not limit most of the 20% CAH Part B outpatient services copayment charges by the Part A inpatient deductible amount [30].

CAHs are eligible for participation in the 340B Drug Pricing Program, based in the Section 340B of the Public Health Service Act which requires pharmaceutical manufacturers participating in Medicaid to provide outpatient drugs at discounted prices to healthcare organizations which serve uninsured and low-income patients [31]. In addition to CAHs, the 340B program is also available to sole community hospitals (SCHs), rural referral centers (RRCs), and public and nonprofit disproportionate share hospitals (DSH). Through participation in the 340B program, these institutions can potentially achieve an average savings of 25 to 50% in pharmaceutical costs.

Medicare Critical Access Hospitals (CAHs) are certified under separate standards [32]. CAHs are a distinct type of provider with their own Medicare CoPs and also reimbursed under a separate payment method [33]. For example, CAHs are reimbursed by CMS for most inpatient and outpatient services to patients at 101%

of reasonable costs; they are not included in the Medicare hospital Inpatient Prospective Payment System (IPPS) or the hospital Outpatient Prospective Payment System (OPPS); and Medicare pays CAH services according to Part A and Part B deductible and coinsurance amounts. Nonetheless, although CAHs are treated distinctly by the CMS for purposes of accreditation and reimbursement, they are entities that are created by state designation [34]. A Medicare-participating hospital must meet the following criteria to be designated by CMS as a CAH:

- Be located in a state that has established a State Medicare Rural Hospital Flexibility program.
- Be designated by the state as a CAH.
- Be located in a rural area or an area that is treated as rural.
- Be located either more than 35 miles from the nearest hospital or CAH or more than 15 miles in areas with mountainous terrain or only secondary roads; OR prior to January 1, 2006, were certified as a CAH based on state designation as a "necessary provider" of healthcare services to residents in the area.
- Maintain no more than 25 inpatient beds that can be used for either inpatient or swing-bed services.
- Maintain an annual average length of stay of 96 hours or less per patient for acute inpatient care (excluding swing-bed services and beds that are within distinct part units).
- Demonstrate compliance with the CAH CoPs found at 42 CFR Part 485 subpart F.
- Furnish 24-hour emergency care services 7 days a week [35].

Nonetheless, a CAH may be granted "swing-bed" approval to provide post-hospital skilled nursing facility-level care in its inpatient beds, and, in addition, a CAH may also operate a psychiatric and/or a rehabilitation distinct part unit of up to ten beds each [35].

Acute Care Hospitals

Although reasonably constant, there has been a slow but steady decline in the number of hospitals over the past decades, for a variety of reasons including insolvency as well as merger and acquisitions. At the time of this writing, based upon the most recent available data, there are approximately 6146 hospitals in the USA (7156 in 1975) with approximately 924,000 hospital beds (1.5 million in 1975), accounting for 34.3 million hospital-reported admissions for year 2018. Hospital care accounts for approximately one-third of all healthcare costs, and the healthcare sector employs more than six million people in the USA [36].

The AHA classifies most hospitals in the USA to be community hospitals; of these, two-thirds are located in large cities. Community hospitals are sub-classified as (1) teaching or (2) non-teaching hospitals. Teaching hospitals are generally affiliated with a medical school, provider training program, or university or college and are active in teaching and training of healthcare professionals, conduct clinical research, and usually provide complex and specialized care such as trauma, transplant, and a wide array of specialty and subspecialty care [37]. Acute care hospitals are divided into hospitals which provide (1) short-term acute care or (2) long-term acute care. This classification of facilities is jointly governed by the federal and state statutes and regulations.

Short-term acute care hospitals (STACHs) are also referred to as a Short Stay Hospital (SSH). For example, NYS defines "acute care" as "inpatient general routine care provided to patients who are in an acute phase of illness, but not to the degree which requires the concentrated and continuous observation and care provided in the intensive care units of an institution" [38]. An acute care hospital may be defined as "any institution, place, building, or agency providing accommodations, facilities, and services over a continuous period of twenty-four hours or more for observation, diagnosis, or care of two or more individuals not related to the operator who are suffering from illness, injury, deformity, or abnormality, or from any other condition for which obstetrical, medical, or surgical services would be appropriate for care or diagnosis" [39]. For example, Connecticut Public Health Code (PHC) defines a short-term hospital as one "that has facilities, medical staff and all necessary personnel to provide diagnosis, care and treatment of a wide range of acute conditions, including injuries."

On the other hand, a long-term acute care hospital (LTAC, LTCH, or LTACH) is a special type of hospital, certified as an acute care hospital, which is focused on the care of patients with complex acute medical issues which require intense, special treatment for a longer period of time, on average 25 days generally admitted to the LTACH from intensive care, or step-down intensive care, units in SSHs. LTACHs specialize in treating patients who may have more than one serious condition; often these are patients who have three to six concurrent active diagnoses or are patients who have suffered an acute episode on top of several chronic illnesses. Accordingly, LTACHs provide complex care such as mechanical ventilation via tracheostomies, complex respiratory therapy, dialysis, heart failure care, sepsis care with a need for long-term antibiotics, complex wound care, and subacute brain trauma care [40]. The diagnostic codes (DRGs) for such diagnoses, where the stay is prolonged, will generally result in an outlier payment to the STACH due to extensive resource consumption; however, that outlier payment will usually not be sufficient to compensate the STACH for the added costs of care, resulting in a loss to the institution both as a real loss (reimbursement lower than the cost of care) and also an opportunity cost (potential shortage of acute care beds for non-outliers). LTACHs are designed to deliver care for medically complex patients who were initially admitted to an STACH, at a lower overall cost than would be possible if the patients received their entire care in STACHs for the same duration. LTACHs may be affiliated with healthcare systems and hospitals or be managed by corporations or privately. LTACHs are different from Long-term care (LTC) facilities, which do not provide acute acre, are primarily custodial, and are discussed in detail below.

Long-Term Care Facilities

A Long-term care facility (LTC facility) can be defined as "A facility that provides rehabilitative, restorative, and/or ongoing skilled nursing care to patients or residents in need of assistance with activities of daily living" [41]. LTC facilities are a type of PAC. Long-term care facilities include skilled nursing facilities (SNF), nursing homes, rehabilitation facilities, inpatient behavioral health facilities, and long-term chronic care hospitals. LTC facilities are regulated jointly by CMS [42] and the states. LTC facilities are subject to CMS CoPs and Conditions for Coverage (CfCs).

In 1986 the Institute of Medicine (IOM) published recommendations intended to comprehensively and radically reform the regulations and thereby improve the quality of care provided in nursing homes [43]. These IOM recommendations were largely accepted by Congress, enacted through the Nursing Home Reform Act as part of the Omnibus Budget Reconciliation Act (OBRA) of 1987 and, subsequently, generally implemented by CMS. CMS has regulatory authority and responsibility for federal regulations regarding the CoPs which must be met by nursing homes in order to receive Medicare and Medicaid funding.

Most residents of LTC facilities are elderly, infirm, and likely to have one or more chronic health conditions and the average length of stay (ALOS) for a LTC resident is substantially longer than for acute care facilities. In addition, LTC resident are likely to be dependent on caregivers for activities of daily living (ADLs) such as transferring, eating, bathing, and toileting. In some cases, residents with debilitating injuries or progressive neurologic conditions will require continuous custodial care in a LTC facilty throughout their lifetime. Therefore, although patients in LTC are not acutely ill, they are nonetheless frail and pose significant challenges to caregivers. The recent rapid growth in litigation against LTFs which allege negligence in the care provided to LTC facility residents, despite intense federal and state regulations, suggests persistent quality challenges [44]. A review of nursing home litigation claims by Stevenson and Studdert found that state statutes (49%) and common law causes of action (36%) represented the primary legal bases of claims that more than half of claims nationwide involved deaths, followed in frequency by alleged harms that included pressure ulcers/bed sores, dehydration/weight loss, and emotional distress. Notably, suit was brought most frequently by children of nursing home residents, followed by residents' spouses and lastly by the residents themselves. Lastly, the authors found that 7.9% of claims reached trial with almost and that on national average 46.2% resulted in verdicts for the plaintiff. Importantly, the authors conclude that, on the basis of the rates and the outcomes of litigation in the nursing home sector, there are likely persistent issues regarding the quality of care in LTC facilities [45]. On the other hand, Studdert et al. later found an inverse relationship between nursing home performance on quality measures and litigation although the risk of litigation was only fractionally lower for the best-performing nursing homes as compared to their worst-performing counterparts [46].

Federal Oversight: CMS (Medicare and Medicaid)

The increasing availability of healthcare, the growth in the population, changes in lifestyle, and the costs of new technology created debate over access. Reinhardt and Relman framed the debate as follows:

> We have a crisis in the private sector because employers can't continue adding the rising costs of their employees' health insurance to the price of their products without becoming non-competitive in world markets. And we have a crisis in the public sector because the government, having made a commitment to provide care for the poor and the elderly, is no longer willing to pay the bills, and local taxpayers are unwilling to pick up the slack. So, I don't think you help the public understanding of our dilemma by asserting that there is no "crisis." The problem is that we want to have our cake and eat it too. We want more and better health care, but we don't have a system of paying for it that distributes the cost equitably or assures equal access for all citizens [47].

A Brief Overview of Medicare

Private health insurance in America became accepted in the 1930s and 1940s (9% of the population had some form of private health insurance in 1940) and by 1950 more than half of the population (more than 40 million people) had some form of private insurance [48]. Legislative proposals for national health insurance appeared in 1943, 1945, and 1947, initially under the Roosevelts and subsequently under Truman, although such proposals did not pass into legislation. In 1965, President Johnson signed into law the bill that led to Medicare and Medicaid. Medicare [49] was established as a federally funded program to help provide healthcare for Americans age 65 and older. The original Medicare program included Part A (hospital insurance) and Part B (medical insurance), and the budget for Medicare in 1965 was approximately $10 billion. Medicare coverage became effective in 1966; and 19 million individuals enrolled in Medicare the first year of the program. Medicare eligibility requires the participant to have paid into the system through payroll taxes. Medicare is composed of four parts, titled A, B, C, and D. Part A provides coverage for inpatient hospital, skilled nursing, hospice, and home services. Part B provides coverage for physician, laboratory, outpatient, preventive care, and other similar services. Medicare Part C or Medicare Advantage is a combination of parts A and B. Part D provides coverage for prescription medications.

In 1972, President Nixon enacted legislation to expand Medicare coverage to include individuals under the age of 65 with long-term disabilities and individuals with end-stage renal disease (ERSD) requiring dialysis or kidney transplantation. The Omnibus Reconciliation Act of 1980 expanded home health services and created Medigap, Medicare supplement insurance. In 1982, hospice services for the terminally ill were added to existing Medicare benefits. Arguably, as an indirect product of access to healthcare, American life expectancy increased from an average of 70.2 years in 1965 to 78.8 years in 2012 [50].

Congress created the Medicare Part C program through the Balanced Budget Act of 1997. The Children's Health Insurance Program (CHIP) was also created in 1997 and provided health insurance and preventive care to, at the time, 11 million, or 1 in 7, uninsured children largely from uninsured working families whose earnings disqualified them from Medicaid eligibility. Today, all of the 50 states, the District of Columbia, and the territories have enacted CHIP plans.

The Medicare Prescription Drug, Improvement, and Modernization Act of 2003 (MMA), private health plans approved by Medicare, became known as Medicare Advantage Plans sometimes termed "Part C" or "MA Plans" and also laid the foundation for a prescription drug benefit designed for seniors and people with disabilities on Medicare. Thus, the MMA subsequently expanded Medicare to include an optional prescription drug benefit, termed "Part D" which took effect in 2006.

In March of 2020, President Trump enacted a coronavirus emergency stimulus package, called the CARES (Coronavirus Aid, Relief, and Economic Security) Act, to provide expanded coverage expands for treatment and services for those affected by COVID-19. The CARES Act also broadened reimbursement for telehealth services; Medicare certification for home health services provided by physician assistants, nurse practitioners, and certified nurse specialists; and increased Medicare payments for COVID-19-related hospital stays and durable medical equipment.

A Brief Overview of Medicaid

In 1960, Congress established the Kerr-Mills program (Public Law 86-778) which enabled federal grants to the states to pay for medical services for the medically indigent elderly. In 1965, the Child Health and Medical Assistance Act was submitted for consideration to the 1965 federal legislative program. The Medical Assistance Program (Title XIX) commonly known as Medicaid was enacted as Title XIX of the Social Security Amendments of 1965 (Public Law 89-97), jointly funded by the states with federal matching funds, provides medical assistance to certain categories of the poor regardless of age and the chronically ill. Through the Medicaid program, low-income children have gained access to vaccinations and preventive and primary care; and elderly patients unable to afford Medicare premiums or long-term care have alternative options for healthcare. Medicaid eligibility for low-income families was linked to Aid to Families with Dependent Children (AFDC).

The growth in Medicaid enrollment and hospital caseload prompted states to develop alternative financing mechanisms, such as disproportionate share hospital (DSH) payments to help fund the state share of Medicaid spending at the hospital level. The Omnibus Budget Reconciliation Act of 1981 (OBRA-81) required states to provide hospitals with DSH payments to hospitals with higher Medicaid volumes.

Medicaid enrollment grew from 4 million in 1966 to exceed 33 million in 2000; throughout the same time period, per enrollee grew from $200 to more than $6000 per enrollee per year. From less than $1 billion in 1966, Medicaid expenditures exceeded $200 billion in fiscal year (FY) 2000 [51]. Together, Medicare and

Medicaid serve nearly 25% of Americans and finance about $1 in every $3 that the nation spends on healthcare [52].

The Centers for Medicare & Medicaid Services (CMS)

In 1965, at the inception of Medicare and Medicaid, the responsibility for the administration of Medicare fell under the Social Security Administration (SSA), and the administration of Medicaid fell under the aegis of the Social and Rehabilitation Service (SRS); both are organized under the Department of Health, Education, and Welfare (HEW). In 1977, the administrative responsibility for both Medicare and Medicaid programs was merged through the creation of the Health Care Financing Administration (HCFA) under the oversight of HEW. In 2001, the Centers for Medicare & Medicaid Services (CMS) was formally organized under the Department of Health and Human Services (DHHS). Although CMS is based in Maryland, it also has ten regional offices throughout the USA: in Boston, New York, Philadelphia, Atlanta, Dallas, Kansas City, Chicago, Denver, San Francisco, and Seattle.

In addition to CMS, important divisions of the HHS include the Office for Civil Rights which has administrative oversight for and enforcement authority over the Health Insurance Portability and Accountability Act (HIPAA) and the Health Information Technology for Economic and Clinical Health (HITECH) Act of 2009; the Office of Inspector General (OIG) which provides oversight and enforcement of violations of Medicare and Medicaid Integrity (false claims, Stark, self-referral) and also for the Centers for Disease Control and Prevention, the National Institutes of Health, and the Food and Drug Administration; the Office of the National Coordinator for Health Information Technology; the National Institutes of Health (NIH); and the Food and Drug Administration (FDA).

Key Federal Regulations Affecting Acute Care Facilities

In addition to local and federal rules, regulations, laws, and ordinances which govern healthcare entities, additional important federal regulations and programs include:

Constitutional Authority over Healthcare

The US Constitution does not make mention of the words "health," "healthcare," or "medical care," and the US Constitution does not explicitly address either the right to healthcare or its regulation. The scope of Congressional powers is enumerated in the Constitution. The authority of Congress legislate in the areas of health and healthcare derives from the enumerated powers set forth in Article I, Section 8 of the Constitution which states, in part, that "[t]he Congress shall have Power to lay and collect Taxes, ... to ... provide for the ... general Welfare of the United States."

The Commerce Clause of the US Constitution states that "Congress shall have the Power… to regulate Commerce… among the several States…" [53]. Constitutional constructions of the Commerce Clause have resulted in expanded federal powers to regulate public health issues. Supreme Court interpretations of the Commerce Clause empowered the US Congress to regulate labor, agriculture, manufacturing, and education. The federal government has the resources to survey the population's health status and health needs, set policies and standards, pass laws and regulations, support biomedical and health services research, help finance and deliver personal healthcare services, and provide technical assistance and resources to state and local health systems [54].

Moreover, a legal doctrine called the "dormant Commerce Clause" may not only empower Congress to act, but it can also bar state and local actions that could interfere with interstate commerce even when Congress has not acted. Thus, in effect, there is no constitutional provision to prohibit Congress from regulating inactivity when exercising its enumerated powers. Of course, legislation enacted under the Commerce Clause must be rationally related to a legitimate constitutional end, which in the case of healthcare is founded in the general welfare, conversely healthcare and health.

Since the Commerce mandate provides a reasonable foundation for Congressional regulation of healthcare, it bolstered through the Necessary and Proper Clause which provides that Congress shall have the authority "to make all Laws which shall be necessary and proper for carrying into Execution the foregoing Powers."

Administrative Procedure Law: Agency Structure and Function

Under the US Constitution, two distinct principles, separation of powers and due process, resulted in the development of the nondelegation doctrine, the theory that one branch of government may not delegate its own constitutionally authorized power to another. However, with the need for administrative efficiency in an increasingly complex world, the courts found a contrast between the delegation of authority between branches of government and the delegation of authority to a public agency. Supreme Court Chief Justice Marshall recognized in the 1825 ruling in *Wayman v. Southard*, that, although Congress may not delegate powers that "are strictly and exclusively legislative," it may delegate "powers which [it] may rightfully exercise itself" [55]. The Court recognized that the administration of the law requires exercise of discretion and that "in our increasingly complex society, replete with ever changing and more technical problems, Congress simply cannot do its job absent an ability to delegate power under broad general directives" [56].

Article I, Section I, of the US Constitution provides that all legislative power is vested in Congress; however, Congress may delegate legislative power to an administrative agency. Although the Constitution does not recognize agencies, the US Supreme Court accorded legitimacy to federal administrative agencies and empowered them to enact rules, regulations, and standards that are binding to the same extent as statutes enacted by Congress. Thus, delegation of powers, under US constitutional law, represents the transfer of a specific authority by one of the three branches of government (executive, legislative, and judicial) to another branch or to an independent agency. Justice Marshall distinguished between "important" subjects, "which must be entirely regulated by the legislature itself," and subjects "of less interest, in which a general provision may be made, and power given to those who are to act under such general provisions, to fill up the details" [55]. Through the delegation of powers doctrine, a regulatory agency is established by Congress, empowered by statute to exercise quasi-legislative authority over a specific segment of economic activity, such as healthcare, technology, communications, or transportation. The US Congress, for example, has created government agencies to which it has delegated authority to promulgate and enforce regulations pursuant to law. Agencies are thus empowered with quasi-legislative functions, executive functions, and quasi-judicial functions which allow them to regulate and oversee areas of administrative law, regulatory law, secondary legislation, and rulemaking. Regulatory agencies are empowered with broad powers to oversee activities within their designated field of jurisdiction, to enact laws and regulations, to investigate violations, and to enforce compliance [57].

The Administrative Procedure Act (APA) [58] is a federal statute which prescribes the processes by which agencies may propose and enact regulations, emphasizing transparency and public input at each stage of rule enactment. The statute which confers authority to an agency is termed an "enabling statute." Under the APA, administrative functions are categorized as either formal or informal rulemaking or adjudication, all of which have binding effects on the field which is being regulated.

The term "rulemaking" refers to the "agency process for formulating, amending, or repealing a rule" [59]. The rulemaking process first requires publication of proposed rules in the Federal Register, followed by a prescribed period of public notice and opportunity for comment, and subsequent publication of the final rule. A rule is defined to mean "the whole or a part of an agency statement of general or particular applicability and future effect designed to implement, interpret, or prescribe law or policy or describing the organization, procedure, or practice requirements of an agency" [60]. Finally, agencies must annually publish a "regulatory plan" or "work plan" in the Federal Register subsequently compiled within the Code of Federal Regulations (CFR).

The substantive standard for rulemaking by an agency is that the rules and regulations must not be arbitrary or capricious and they must fall within the scope of statutory authority granted to the agency by Congress. The APA describes the necessary procedures for agency rulemakings and adjudications, as well as standards for judicial review of final agency actions, and the DHHS, of which CMS is a part, is bound by the rulemaking process [61]. In general, the standard for judicial review of an agency's rulemaking presents a formidable barrier to a substantive legal challenge. In estate of Smith v. Heckler, the Tenth Circuit Court of Appeals held that the "judiciary is not a 'super agency' controlling the affairs of an agency which is part of another branch of government" [62]. State legislatures empower state agencies under the respective state Administrative Procedures Acts of the individual states.

Regulatory agencies have statutory authority to function with oversight, but their actions are also subject to legal review. Controversies arising from agency actions are adjudicated in Administrative Courts, by administrative law judges. Nonetheless, controversies generally favor agencies since courts accord deference agencies, with the presumption that agencies have sought and used specialized knowledge regarding the technical aspects of the issues that they regulate. Agencies frequently work with panels of experts during the rulemaking process to define problems and regulate them.

The US Supreme Court has promulgated three standards of judicial deference to agency decisions: (1) under *Chevron v. NRDC* [63], courts will defer to agency interpretations of their enabling statutes unless they are unreasonable on their face; (2) under *Auer v. Robbins* [64], courts defer to an agency's interpretations of its own regulations, even in the case of ambiguity; and (3) under *Skidmore v. Swift* [65], courts do not unconditionally defer to an agency's interpretation, but rather give varying amounts of deference in recognitions of that agency's expertise within a specific subject matter.

The classic legal test to guide the analysis of whether a court should defer to a ruling made by an agency in its interpretation of its enabling statute is derived from Chevron,[1] in which the court's opinion developed a two-part framework of review:

> First, always, is the question whether Congress has directly spoken to the precise question at issue. If the intent of Congress is clear, that is the end of the matter; for the court, as well as the agency, must give effect to the unambiguously expressed intent of Congress. If, however, the court determines Congress has not directly addressed the precise question at issue, the court does not simply impose its own construction on the statute . . . Rather, if the statute is silent or ambiguous with respect to the specific issue, the question for the court is whether the agency's answer is based on a permissible construction of the statute.

Federal (CMS) and state regulators function as administrative agencies and are therefore bound by the procedural requirements of the Administrative Procedures Act [66].

[1] See Chevron, *supra.*

Diagnosis-Related Groups and the Prospective Payment System

Fee-for-service (FFS) reimbursement for healthcare services provided by physicians represented a long-standing industry norm, especially within the private healthcare sector. With greater access under the Medicare and Medicaid programs, the rising costs of healthcare served as an impetus for cost containment strategies. Health maintenance organizations (HMOs) were incepted ion the 1960s. Under the HMO model, the HMO receives a flat per person per month amount for which it provides all necessary health. The fee cap was thought to provide an incentive to providers to provide diagnostic and treatment services as efficiently as possible. In 1985, HCFA began to encourage the development of health maintenance organizations (HMOs) to provide Medicare coverage to enrolled beneficiaries.

The Medicare risk program became operational in 1985 under the Tax Equity and Fiscal Responsibility Act (TEFRA) of 1982 (Public Law 97-248) and allocated responsibility to HMOs for the provisions of Medicare-covered services to beneficiaries in return for a capitated payment. In addition to the objective of cost control, additional goals of the HMO program included the following: (1) more efficient healthcare with improved healthcare quality and (2) to provide Medicare beneficiary access to the same range of choices of healthcare delivery systems available to the non-Medicare population. At its inception, HCFA set the capitation payment to an HMO, on behalf of an enrolled beneficiary, at 95% of HCFA's actuarial estimate of the average amount that HCFA would spend in FFS reimbursements on a typical Medicare beneficiary a particular geographically defined county [67].

The Medicare Inpatient Prospective Payment System (IPPS) was introduced in 1983. The IPPS classified each patient's hospital admission into a diagnostic category (DRG) on the basis of the documentation in the medical record which translates into an International Classification of Diseases (ICD) nomenclature; then, extraction of additional data from the record is used to define a Medicare Severity-Adjusted Diagnosis-Related Group (MS-DRG) based on data including (a) the principal diagnosis, (b) complications and comorbidities (secondary diagnoses), (c) surgical procedures required during the admission, (d) age, (e) gender, and (f) discharge destination (routine, transferred, or expired). The assignment of an MS-DRG is calculated by computer through the use of a program known as the "grouper" designed for use by hospitals and Medicare Administrative Contractors (MACs). Using the MS-DRG, CMS pays hospitals by a predetermined fee schedule, although allowances are made for patients who incur exceptionally length of stay or costs ("outliers"). Each MS-DRG is assessed annually by CMS for its relative weight, which is indexed to the relative costs for treating patients with that MS-DRG during the prior year; this ratio is published annually in the Federal Register for each MS-DRG. The average MS-DRG weight for a hospital's Medicare admission is referred to as the Case Mix Index (CMI) which indicates the severity of illness for a hospital's patient population. In 2007, CMS revised its method of calculating relative weights, so as to base relative weights on allocated costs instead of charges.

DRG reimbursement affects only facility, not professional fee reimbursement. Traditionally, Medicare reimbursement was based on a payment methodology of a provider's customary, prevailing, and reasonable charges. In 1989, the Omnibus Budget Reconciliation Act (OBRA) of 1989 implemented the Medicare fee schedule which effectively changed the basis for physician reimbursement from charges to relative values that reflected the costs of resources consumed during patient care for a specific condition. The basis for Medicare reimbursement became the relative value unit (RVU) based on three categories of resources: (a) physician work, (b) practice expense (PE), and (c) malpractice (MP) expense. The Medicare Physician Payment Schedule also incorporates, and annually updates, geographic adjustments to reflect the variations in the costs of furnishing services in a specific geographic area using three factors: (a) the resource-based relative value scale (RBRVS), (b) the geographic practice cost indexes (GPCI), and the monetary conversion factor.

Hospital Readmissions Reduction Program (HRRP)

Readmissions after inpatient hospitalizations are common, costly, and in many cases potentially preventable. In 2009, a review of Medicare beneficiaries observed that 19.6% patients were readmitted within 30 days of discharge, and Medicare was paying more than $17 billion annually on unplanned rehospitalizations [68]. The Hospital Readmissions Reduction Program (HRRP), an initiative required under Section 3025 of the Affordable Care Act (2012), is a Medicare value-based purchasing (VBP) program that requires the Secretary of the Department of Health and Human Services (HHS) to implement a reduction in payments, or impose financial penalties, upon hospitals with excess readmissions for defined conditions or procedures: (1) acute myocardial infarction (AMI), (2) chronic obstructive pulmonary disease (COPD), (3) heart failure (HF), (4) pneumonia, (5) coronary artery bypass graft (CABG) surgery, and (6) elective primary total hip arthroplasty and/or total knee arthroplasty (THA/TKA) [69]. In addition, the twenty-first Century Cures Act directs CMS to assess a hospital's performance relative to other similar hospitals. The intent of the HRRP is to improve communication and care coordination between hospitals, caregivers, and patients so as to improve discharge planning, reduce avoidable readmissions, improve the quality of hospital care, and decrease utilization costs due to readmissions. As of 2017, of the participating sites, the CBOs demonstrated lower readmission rates and Medicare Part A and Part B expenditures as compared with comparable nonparticipants [70].

A "readmission" is defined as the admission of a patient to the same hospital from which the patient was discharged or to another hospital within a time period specified by the Secretary from the date of the patient's discharge.

At present, CMS includes the following six condition–/procedure-specific 30-day risk-standardized unplanned readmission measures in the program: (1) acute myocardial infarction (AMI), (2) chronic obstructive pulmonary disease (COPD), (3) heart failure (HF), (4) pneumonia, (5) coronary artery bypass graft (CABG) surgery, and (6) elective primary total hip arthroplasty and/or total knee arthroplasty (THA/TKA) [71]. Those hospitals with relatively high readmission rates for patients with these conditions have Medicare payments adjusted by the greater of a "ratio" or a "floor adjustment factor." Hospitals are also mandated to publish their hospital readmission rates on the Hospital Compare website.

Readmissions or rehospitalizations among Medicare beneficiaries have been repeatedly demonstrated to be prevalent and associated with poor quality of care outcomes and significant financial costs [72]. Historical data has shown that nearly 20% of all Medicare discharges had a readmission within 30 days [68], 12% of readmissions are potentially avoidable, and that prevention of as few as 10% of these readmissions could save Medicare $1 billion [73]. The Community-based Care Transitions Program (CCTP), created under Section 3026 of the ACA, launched in 2012, was developed as a system to test models for improving care transitions and reducing readmissions.

The Hospital Value-Based Purchasing (VBP) Program

Intuitively, in any enterprise costs can generally be trimmed without impacting quality; however, beyond a point, costs begin to impact quality. The goal of value-based care is the advancement of healthcare quality while increasing patient access and while keeping reimbursement constant. CMS developed several models of value-based care, each with a phase-in period, first associated with incentive payments and subsequently with penalties for nonperformance. Value-based purchasing (VBP) is a program that increases the accountability of healthcare providers for both the cost and quality of care.

The Hospital VBP Program was established to reward acute care hospitals with incentive payments, as payment adjustments under the Inpatient Prospective Payment System (IPPS) as an incentive for achieving higher quality of care provided in the inpatient hospital setting. The Hospital VBP Program incentivizes the (1) elimination of or reducing the incidence of healthcare errors' adverse events, (2) adoption of evidence-based care standards and protocols in order to obtain the best outcomes for Medicare patients, (3) the incentivization of hospitals to develop processes to improve patient experience (patient satisfaction scores), (4) improved transparency of care quality, and (5)

a recognition that hospitals that provide high-quality care at a lower cost to Medicare should be rewarded for performance [74]. VBP programs depend on three main factors: the external environment, provider characteristics, and program features. The external environment of VBP includes factors such as the regulatory environment, payment policies, patient treatment preferences, and compliance with prescribed care. Provider characteristics important to VBP include structure of the healthcare system, leadership commitment, the organizational culture, available resources and capabilities (including information technology), and demographics of the population served. Program features which impact VBP include the targeted patient population, program goals, the metrics used, financial incentives, and risk structure [75].

In 2015, based on early success, DHHS announced their intent to tie 85% of all traditional Medicare payments to quality or value by 2016 and 90% of payments by 2018. With the passage of the Accountable Care Act, a voluntary program of "pay-for-reporting" evolved into the "pay-for-performance" (P4P) Physician Quality Reporting System (PQRS) program which instead imposed penalties for not reporting quality data [75]. P4P was later extended to performance-based penalties and bonuses through implementation of the Value-Based Payment Modifier (Value Modifier) [76].

The Hospital VBP Program incentivizes performance through measures of quality, efficiency, patient experience, and safety. The Medicare Access and CHIP Reauthorization Act of 2015 (MACRA) was signed into law in 2015 and created the Quality Payment Program that created the Merit-Based Incentive Payment System (MIPS); repealed the long-standing, unsuccessful Sustainable Growth Rate (SGR) formula for Medicare; and allocated bonus payments for participation in eligible alternative payment models (APMs) [77].

Hospital VBP indicators include (a) the elimination or reduction of adverse event, (b) the adoption of evidence-based care standards and protocols in order to obtain optimal patient outcomes, (c) the development of processes which improve patient experience, (d) methods to increase the transparency of care quality, and (e) recognition of those hospitals which provide high-quality care at a lower cost [78]. The quality domain measures are weighted each year; for the year 2020, (i) clinical outcomes (25%), (ii) person and community engagement (25%), (iii) safety (25%), and (iv) efficiency and cost reduction (25%).

The Medicare Access and CHIP Reauthorization Act (MACRA) of 2015

The Medicare Access and CHIP (Children's Health Insurance Program) Reauthorization Act of 2015 replaced the Sustainable Growth Rate formula as a means of updating Medicare physician compensation. MACRA revised the reimbursement formula for physicians and providers under the Quality Payment Program (QPP) which linked Medicare Part B payment to measures of quality and resources use and adoption of Certified EHR Technology (CEHRT). The Merit-Based Incentive Payment System (MIPS) was a key component of the MACRA Quality Payment Program (QPP) which was more popular for the first performance year. Under MIPS, the Meaningful Use (MU) Medicare incentive program, Physician Quality Reporting System (PQRS), and the Value-Based Modifier (VBM) program will be consolidated into one program. MACRA represents a financial incentive for hospitals to make providers adopt advanced Alternative Payment Models (APMs) allowing hospital-based providers to participate in shared savings and incentives, possibly though a Professional Services Agreement (PSA) although hospitals will also be in a position to leverage MACRA to incentivize the quality of care provided by employed providers.

Hospital-Acquired Condition (HAC) Reduction Programs

The Hospital-Acquired Condition (HAC) Reduction Program (HACRP) is a Medicare pay-for-performance program. Value-based purchasing is a form of pay-for-performance, which, in turn, is a tiered system of reimbursement based on provider or entity performance as based in established quality metrics [79]. The ACA established the HAC Reduction Program under Section 1886(p) of the Social Security Act to link Medicare payments to healthcare quality in the inpatient hospital setting beginning in 2015. CMS established a scoring methodology used to rank hospitals based upon their performance with respect to risk-adjusted HAC quality measures. The worst-performing hospitals which fall into a rank (scores greater than the 75th percentile of all Total HAC Scores that is in the lowest quartile-based on their HAC score) are subject to a 1% reduction in their total Medicare reimbursements. HACs are divided into two domains: (1) Domain 1 represents the Agency for Healthcare Research and Quality (AHRQ) composite Patient Safety Indicators (PSI) 90 scores, and (2) Domain 2 is composed of the Centers for Disease Control and Prevention's (CDC) National Healthcare Safety Network (NHSN) measures.

The CMS PSI 90 measure is represented by the following ten CMS PSI component measures [80]:

- PSI 03 – Pressure Ulcer Rate
- PSI 06 – Iatrogenic Pneumothorax Rate
- PSI 08 – Inhospital Fall with Hip Fracture Rate
- PSI 09 – Perioperative Hemorrhage or Hematoma Rate
- PSI 10 – Postoperative Acute Kidney Injury Requiring Dialysis Rate
- PSI 11 – Postoperative Respiratory Failure Rate
- PSI 12 – Perioperative Pulmonary Embolism or Deep Vein Thrombosis Rate
- PSI 13 – Postoperative Sepsis Rate
- PSI 14 – Postoperative Wound Dehiscence Rate
- PSI 15 – Unrecognized Abdominopelvic Accidental Puncture/Laceration Rate

Domain 1 constitutes 35% of the total score and is solely based on the Agency for Healthcare Research and Quality's (AHRQ) Patient Safety for Selected Indicators (PSI) 90 composite measure. The scores for the PSIs from 1–12 are allocated on a 110 basis, where a score of 1 indicates the best performance and a score of 10 indicates the worst performance.

CDC NHSN is represented by the following hospital-associated infections (HAI) measures [80]:

- Central line-associated bloodstream infection (CLABSI)
- Catheter-associated urinary tract infection (CAUTI)

- Surgical site infection (abdominal hysterectomy and colon procedures) (SSI)
- Methicillin-resistant *Staphylococcus aureus* (MRSA) bacteremia
- *Clostridium difficile* infection (CDI)
- *Total HAC Score*
- *Payment* Reduction Indicator

Domain 2 accounts for the remaining 65% of the total score and consists of an average of two intensive care unit-based nosocomial infections: central line-associated bloodstream infections (CLABSI) and catheter-associated urinary tract infections (CAUTI).

Nonetheless, there is a controversy regarding the effectiveness of the HACRP program since there is data to suggest that minority-serving hospitals are being disproportionately penalized [81] and because of the sensitivity of the HACRP penalties to small changes in performance and correlation of the HACRP score with hospital characteristics also potentially challenges the validity of the HACRP measure and method of risk adjustment [82].

Patient Safety and Quality Improvement Act (PSQIA) of 2005

The Patient Safety and Quality Improvement Act (PSQIA) protects healthcare workers who report unsafe conditions [6]. Legislators created the law to encourage the reporting of medical errors while maintaining patients' confidentially rights. To ensure patient privacy, the HHS levies fines for confidentially breaches. The law also authorizes the Agency for Healthcare Research and Quality (AHRQ) to publish a list of patient safety organizations (PSOs) that record and analyze patient safety data. The Office for Civil Rights (OCR) enforces the law among national healthcare facilities. The regulation implementing the Patient Safety and Quality Improvement Act of 2005 (PSQIA) was published on November 21, 2008, and became effective on January 19, 2009.

Compliance with Healthcare Regulations

Healthcare compliance ("compliance" or "corporate compliance") is a critical administrative function in all highly regulated industries, such as healthcare, banking, charitable not-for-profits, finance, universities, and government contractors. The many government agencies that regulate healthcare will necessarily approaches its regulatory framework based upon its own area of control; for example, the Drug Enforcement Administration (DEA), the Food and Drug Administration (FDA), the Occupational Safety and Health Administration (OSHA), the Equal Employment Opportunity Commission (EEOC), and the Department of Health and Human Services (HHS) Office of Inspector General (OIG) will each focus on an area of regulation – the corporate compliance program must ensure compliance with all regulations. The purpose of a compliance program is to align administrative practices within an institution with the relevant internal and external rules, regulations, law, and policies. Compliance is not only a good practice for legal, ethical, and strategic reasons but is also mandated by law. The Deficit Reduction Act of 2005 § 6032 required all Medicaid providers receiving $5 million a year or more to have an effective compliance program [83]. The HHS Office of Inspector General (OIG) has published guidelines on the development of model corporate compliance programs [84]. Federal Sentencing Guidelines allow for reduced penalties for those organizations which have enacted an "effective" corporate compliance program [85]. The seven components of an effective program as defined in the Guidelines are (1) standards and procedures, (2) oversight responsibilities, (3) employee training, (4) monitoring and auditing, (5) reporting systems, (6) enforcement and discipline, and (7) response and prevention [86].

The governing body (BOD) of a healthcare organization is responsible for the conduct of the organization and bears responsibility for a healthcare organization's compliance or lack of compliance. Thus, the healthcare compliance program necessarily reports directly to the BOD. The oversight and review of compliance program functions by a BOD include the (1) roles of, and relationships between, the organization's audit, compliance, and legal departments; (2) mechanism and process for issue-reporting within an organization; (3) approach to identifying regulatory risk; and (4) methods of encouraging enterprise-wide accountability for achievement of compliance goals and objectives [87].

Antitrust

Antitrust litigation involving hospitals has been common and is increasingly common in the setting of current healthcare market consolidations including practice acquisitions and merger and acquisition activities. In the perspective of antitrust laws, healthcare institutions and medical practices are business firms which are engaged in the economic activity of providing medical services. Modern antitrust law focuses on corporate behavior and not business objective. The Department of Justice (DOJ) notes that "competition in the healthcare industry benefits consumers because it helps contain costs, improve quality, expand choice, and encourage innovation. The Antitrust Division enforces the antitrust laws in healthcare to protect competition and to prevent anticompetitive conduct" [88]. The USA has enacted three major federal antitrust laws: (1) the Sherman Antitrust Act of 1890, (2) the Clayton Act of 1914, and (3) the Federal Trade Commission Act of 1914 [89].

Section 1 of the Sherman Act prohibits all contracts, combinations, and conspiracies that unreasonably restrain interstate commerce and foreign trade, including agreements among competitors to fix prices, rig bids, and allocate customers, practices which are punishable as criminal felonies. Section 2 of the Sherman Act makes it a crime to monopolize any part of interstate commerce. An unlawful monopoly exists when one firm controls the market for a product or service, and it has obtained that market power, not because its product or service is superior to others, but rather through abusive suppression of competition with anticompetitive conduct. The "rule of reason" is a judicial doctrine of antitrust law which states that a practice is in violation the Sherman Act only if the practice is an unreasonable restraint of trade, based on economic factors.

The Clayton Antitrust Act is a civil (as opposed to criminal) statute which, in Section 7, prohibits mergers or acquisitions that are likely to substantially lessen competition and are likely to increase prices for consumers. The Robinson-Patman Act [90] is a federal law which was enacted in 1936 as an amendment to the Clayton Act to prevent price discrimination in interstate commerce or the charging of different prices to equally-situated distributors, when the effect of such sales is to reduce competition and may give favored customers an advantage in the market unrelated to their actual efficiency. The Robinson-Patman Act has been invoked, generally unsuccessfully, against health maintenance organizations (HMOs) because of a broad exception to the prohibition against price discrimination when one of the sales is made to any of certain entities listed in the Nonprofit Institutions Act. The Celler-Kefauver Act further amended the Clayton Antitrust Act through prohibition of practices that would reduce market as a result of the asset acquisitions, or mergers, to prevent vertical and conglomerate mergers that would limit competition. The Federal Trade Commission Act created the Federal Trade Commission and as a civil statute reiterated the prohibition against unfair methods of competition in interstate commerce, intended to monitor and regulate any "unfair or deceptive" trade practices. The FTC and the Department of Justice are the enforcers of antitrust laws in the USA.

The Hart-Scott-Rodino Act requires certain types of mergers and consolidations, where party acquiring has total assets or annual net sales of more than $100 million and the acquired party has total assets or annual net sales of more than $10 million, to be reported to the FTC or the Department of Justice (DOJ) before the transaction occurs [91].

The Emergency Medical Treatment and Active Labor Act

In 1986, the Emergency Medical Treatment and Active Labor Act (EMTALA) [92] was enacted by Congress as part of the Consolidated Omnibus Reconciliation Act (COBRA) with the intent of both ensuring access to emergency medical care and to deter the then-prevalent practice of "patient dumping" [93] by which uninsured patients were transferred from private to public hospitals, solely for financial reasons, without consideration of their medical stability. Although EMTALA applies only to facilities which participate in Medicare, it thus applies to over 98% of all US hospitals.

EMTALA-participating hospitals with Emergency Departments (EDs) must screen and treat the emergency medical conditions of all the patents who present there for care in a nondiscriminiatory manner, regardless of their ability to pay, insurance status, national origin, race, creed, or color. EMTALA imposes three distinct legal duties on Medicare-participating hospitals: (1) the duty to perform a mandatory medical screening examination (MSE) on all patients who present for medical care in order to determine whether an emergency medical condition (EMC) exists; (2) if an EMC is determined to exist, the patient must either be stabilized medically in accordance with the hospitals' capabilities or transferred to another hospital with the requisite capabilities; and (3) hospitals with specialized capabilities or facilities (such as trauma centers or burn units) are required to accept transfers of patients in need of such specialized services if they have the capacity to treat them.

Obligations under EMTALA are considered to arise when an individual first presents to the ED, more specifically, when an individual first arrives on hospital property. However, under some circumstances, EMTALA obligations may be triggered before the patient's actual arrival; for example, in those instances where a patient is en route and the ED has been previously been notified of the patient's pending arrival [94]. EMTALA prohibits a hospital or its staff from delaying a screening examination or the initiation of stabilizing care "in order to inquire about the individual's method of payment or insurance status," although the collection of basic demographic information prior to the MSE is considered acceptable [95]. The term "individual" has been interpreted to refer to any person with a potential EMC who presents for care regardless of whether that person is a Medicare patient or even a US citizen. EMTALA further defines an EMC as "[a] medical condition manifesting itself by acute symptoms of sufficient severity such that the absence of immediate medical attention could reasonably be expected to result in—(1) [p]lacing the health of the individual . . . in serious jeopardy; (2) [s]erious impairment to bodily functions; or (3) [s]erious dysfunction of any bodily organ part" [96]. The transfer protocol of patients requires that the referring hospital (1) provides ongoing care within its capability until transfer to minimize transfer risks, (2) provides copies of medical records, (3) confirms that the receiving facility has space and qualified personnel to treat the condition and has agreed to accept the transfer, and (4) ensure that the transfer be made with qualified personnel and appropriate medical equipment. In general patients may be reasonably transferred when the treating physician, in his or her best judgment, documents that the benefits of transfer outweigh the risks and accepting facility and provider are identified and the transfer is conducted with appropriate equipment and personnel. In the event that the patient is not transferred, and the hospital instead accepts the patient as an inpatient for further treatment, the obligations under EMTALA are considered met [97].

EMTALA also governs obligations for on-call providers, including generalists and specialists. EMTALA requires healthcare facilities to maintain a list of physicians who are on call, as either treating or consulting physicians. On-call physicians may provide consultation by telephone, video conferencing, or any other reasonable means of communication, and there is no specific requirement that the on-call physician evaluates the patient in person. However, the on-call physician must evaluate a patient in person if specifically requested to do so; failure to do so is considered a violation under EMTALA [98].

In 2020, during the SARS-CoV-2 virus pandemic, which caused the 2019 Novel Coronavirus Disease ("COVID-19"), the Centers for Medicare & Medicaid Services ("CMS") issued a memorandum waiving certain EMTALA obligations deemed to apply only if the hospital's actions did not discriminate on the basis of a patient's source of payment or ability to pay. The CMS memorandum, issued March 9, 2020, entitled QSO-20-15 (Emergency Medical Treatment and Labor Act (EMTALA) Requirements and Implications Related to Coronavirus Disease 2019) [99], addressed how hospitals and Critical Access Hospitals could best fulfill EMTALA obligations while continuing to minimize the risk of exposure of ED patients from those already infected with COVID-19. Furthermore, in addition to the QSO, the Secretary of the Department of Health and Human Services ("Secretary") invoked his waiver authority and waived sanctions under EMTALA for certain medical screening exams ("MSEs") and stabilization requirements, effective March 1, 2020 [100]. Specifically, the EMTALA waiver allowed hospitals to:

1. Direct or relocate individuals who come to the emergency department ("ED") to an alternative off-campus site for the MSE, in accordance with a state emergency or pandemic preparedness plan.
2. Effect transfers normally prohibited under EMTALA of individuals with unstable emergency medical conditions ("EMCs"), so long as the transfer is necessitated by the circumstances of the declared emergency for the COVID-19 pandemic, without sanction.

Hospitals have a duty to report EMTALA violations to the CMS. Allegations of EMTALA violations are investigated by the Office of the Inspector General (OIG). Where alleged violations are found, potential penalties include termination of the hospital's and/or physician's Medicare provider agreement and also civil monetary penalties (CMPs or fines) imposed on hospitals and/or physicians. In violation of EMTALA, a hospital may be fined up to $50,000 per violation ($25,000 for a hospital with fewer than 100 beds); physicians may be fined up to $50,000 per violation, and these fines may also extend to on-call physicians. A receiving facility that has suffered a financial loss as a result of another hospital's violation of EMTALA may further bring a suit to recover any damages sustained. The statute of limitations under EMTALA is 2 years, and, under federal law, whistleblowers are protected by law. Moreover, EMTALA violations are not covered by standard malpractice insurance policies, since EMTALA violations in themselves may not represent malpractice, although derivative actions for malpractice stemming from negligent screening examinations or stabilization are possible and actions under negligence or abandonment may also ensue.

EMTALA is now considered one of the most comprehensive laws guaranteeing nondiscriminatory access to emergency medical care, became the de facto national healthcare policy for the uninsured, and now applies to virtually all aspects of patient care in the hospital setting.

Federal Taxation Status of Hospitals

Hospitals may be classified as either "for-profit" or "not-for-profit" entities, a designation separate from whether or not he healthcare entity is indeed profitable or not. Tax exemption is complicated and largely beyond the scope of this discussion however; in general tax exemption status refers to exemption from state and local taxes (such as real estate tax and state corporate tax) and federal corporate income tax. Requirements for exemption from state and local taxes can vary substantially between state localities. In order to qualify for federal tax exemption, a healthcare institution organized under one of the sections of Internal Revenue Code (IRC) § 501 is considered exempt from taxation [101]; and, the (c) designation denotes a not-for-profit or a charitable organization. Of the potential § 501(c) classifications, § 501(c)(3) status is potentially the most desirable since it confers benefits such as the ability to accept tax deductible contributions and the ability to issue tax-exempt bonds. Organizations under § 501(c)(3) must be organized and operated exclusively for one or more of (a) religious, (b) charitable, (c) scientific, (d) testing for public safety, (e) literary, (f) educational, or (g) prevention of cruelty to children or animals. In order to qualify for § 501(c)(3) status, the organization must meet both organizational and operational test requirements. Under the organizational test, the entity's articles of incorporation must specify that the organization is limited to the performance of exempt purposes, and under the operational test, the entity must be operated for the stated exempt purposes.

Hospitals have traditionally been exempt from federal taxation if they are "organized and operated exclusively for... charitable... purposes" which in its initial iteration in 1956 was that not-for-profit hospitals provide free or discounted medical services. Thus, prior to 1969, the IRS specified that to maintain tax-exempt status, hospitals were simply required to provide charity care, although there was latitude to define the amount of care required. In 1969, however, the IRS issued a ruling that created a more ambiguous standard and also eliminated the obligation to provide charity, or uncompensated, care [102]. In order to be considered a "charitable hospital," the entity must meet the general requirements for tax exemption under Internal Revenue Code (IRC) Section 501(c)(3), Revenue Ruling 69-545, and IRC Section 501(r)(1):

> Section 501(c)(3) organizations must be organized and operated exclusively for specific tax-exempt purposes to be exempt from federal income tax. In addition to being a type of organization that is specifically described within Section 501(c)(3), these organizations must also have the following characteristics [103].
>
> **Organizational Test**
>
> An organization must be organized exclusively for one or more exempt purposes. Generally, an organization is organized exclusively for one or more exempt purposes only if its organizational documents:
>
> - Limit the purposes of such organization to one or more exempt purposes.
> - Do not expressly empower the organization to engage, other than as an insubstantial part of its activities, in activities which in themselves are not in furtherance of one or more exempt purposes.
> - Do not expressly empower it to.
> - Devote more than an insubstantial amount of its activities to attempting to influence legislation.

- Participate or intervene in any political campaign on behalf of or in opposition to any candidate for public office.
- Engage in activities which characterize it as an "action" organization.
- The organizational documents must also permanently dedicate the organization's assets to charitable purposes upon dissolution.

Operational Test

The operational test for exemption under Section 501(c)(3) consists of four broad categories:

1. Requirement to operate exclusively for exempt purposes
2. Prohibition against inurement
3. Prohibition against becoming an action organization
4. Prohibition against substantial private benefit

An organization is considered to operate exclusively for one or more exempt purposes if it engages primarily in activities that accomplish one or more exempt purposes as specified in Section 501(c)(3).

Patient Protection and Affordable Care Act (ACA) §9007 further amended the IRC and added §501(r) entitled "Additional Requirements for Charitable Hospitals" [104] that required four elements to meet tax-exempt status: (1) community health needs assessment and implementation strategy; (2) financial assistance policies, including adherence to the hospital's Emergency Medical Treatment and Active Labor Act emergency care obligations (which are expressly identified in the statute); (3) policies related to hospital charges; and (4) policies related to billing and collections [105]. The IRS prescribed penalties for noncompliance including loss of tax-exempt status and a monetary penalty of $50,000 per year for failure to satisfy the community health needs assessment requirements.

Nonetheless, private causes of action by indigent patients who received bills for payment [106] or alleging the illegality of balance billing [107] have not been successful. On the other hand, states have been successful in their attempts to quantify and challenge the level of charity care required to qualify for tax-exempt status under state law. In the Illinois case of *Provena Covenant Med. Cent. v. Dep't. of Revenue*, Provena was alleged to charged uninsured patients "established rates, which were more than double the actual costs of care" while charging privately insured patients or patients enrolled in Medicare or Medicaid discounted rates for the same medical care; Provena was found to have waived $831,724 in actual costs while receiving a benefit of $1.1 million in property tax exemptions. Here the Illinois Supreme Court held that Provena failed to qualify as a tax-exempt hospital for purposes of a state property tax exemption [108].

Healthcare Entity Organization

Hospitals, as incorporated entities, have fairly uniform organizational structures which are composed of diverse employees with multiple layers of accountability. The administrative structure of an accredited hospital is defined by TJC within the Comprehensive Accreditation Manual for Hospitals chapter on "Leadership." Early guidance from TJC, prior to 1994, included standards and chapters addressing, for example, "Management," "Governance," "Medical Staff," and "Nursing Services"; however, TJC, beginning in 1994 adopted a systemic approach to organizational leadership. Healthcare systems are generally characterized by three groups of leaders: (1) the governing body; (2) the chief executive officer (CEO), chief medical officer (CMO), chief nursing officer (CNO), chief operating officer (COO), chief financial officer (CFO), and other senior managers (which may be referred to collectively as the "C-suite"); and (3) the medical staff leadership. Hospital leadership is accountable to the Board of Directors.

The Healthcare Board of Directors (Board)

The Board of Directors (BOD), or the Board of Trustees, is the legally constituted governing body of the hospital, with full responsibility for the financially viable and quality/safety practices of the hospital. The BOD is responsible for the establishment and oversight of the hospital's bylaws and policies, establishes new policies, and, on the advice of a medical advisory board, appoints senior leadership and medical staff. The BOD can be variable with respect to size and membership, often a reflection of the type and location of the hospital. BODs of for-profit organizations govern on behalf of shareholders, and the primary obligation is to increase shareholder value. On the other hand, nonprofit corporations do not have shareholders, community leaders, legislators, and regulators such as the state Attorney General has the authority to hold board members accountable for actions and inactions. Board members are the fiduciaries with three primary legal duties known as the "duty of care," "duty of loyalty," and "duty of obedience." The duty of care refers to prudent stewardship; the duty of loyalty requires that the fiduciary acts in the best interest of the corporation; and the duty of obedience requires that the member follows applicable laws, regulations, and bylaws, and adheres to the stated corporate mission [see Chap. 29 "Corporate Structure"]. Members of the BOD must maintain confidentiality and carefully manage potential conflicts of interest. In order to perform its functions efficiently and expeditiously, the BOD relies on committees and C-suite status reports. The "balanced scorecard" or "dashboard" concept includes four key dimensions of performance: financial, organizational, executive, and quality [109].

TJC defines the roles of the BOD in Standard LF.01.03.01 as "the body ultimately accountable for the safety and quality of care, treatment, and services… the governing body's ultimate responsibility for safety and quality derives from its legal responsibility and operational authority for hospital performance. In this context, the governing body provides for internal structures and resources, including staff that supports safety and quality" and lists the elements of performance [110]:

1. The governing body defines in writing its responsibilities.
2. The governing body provides for organization management and planning.
3. The governing body approves the hospital's written scope of services.

4. The governing body selects the chief executive.
5. The governing body provides for the resources needed to maintain safe, quality care, treatment, and services.
6. The governing body works with the senior managers and leaders of the organized medical staff to annually evaluate the hospital's performance in relation to its mission, vision, and goals.
7. The governing body provides a system for resolving conflicts among individuals working in the hospital.
8. The governing body provides the organized medical staff with the opportunity to participate in governance.
9. The governing body provides the organized medical staff with the opportunity to be represented at governing body meetings (through attendance and voice) by one or more of its members, as selected by the organized medical staff.
10. Organized medical staff members are eligible for full membership in the hospital's governing body, unless legally prohibited.

The effectiveness of a hospital BOD has been shown to be related to hospital financial performance. With respect to financial oversight, a BOD has six core financial responsibilities, to (1) specify financial objectives, (2) review and align the management financial plan with stated objectives, (3) enhance creditworthiness, (4) ensure capital is effectively allocated, (5) monitor financial performance, and (6) verify financial statements [111]. Important financial indicators include cash flow, efficiency, charity care, debt structure, return on investment, operating expenses, profitability, liquidity, creditworthiness, capital structure, and asset activity. Boards must be able to understand the key elements of financial performance and prescribe appropriate corrective or strategic interventions. In addition, financial and performance metrics must be compared with local, regional, and national benchmarks.

Hospital BOD also has a responsibility for hospital quality performance, even as quality performance is increasingly linked to financial performance. In 2007 the Institute for Healthcare Improvement (IHI) developed the "Boards on Board" program, with the intent of engaging BOD leadership in clinical quality. Increasingly, the notion of a "culture of quality" is used to discuss the engagement of senior leadership, specifically including the BOD, in the elements that comprise the safety and quality of care environment. Often, safety, quality, and finance are closely linked. Medical errors are costly and are an increasingly visible competitive metric.

The National Quality Forum (NQF) has also called on hospital BODs to focus on quality [112]. Provonost et al. discuss six principles for governance oversight of hospital quality of care and patient safety: (1) ensure oversight for quality everywhere within the system that care is delivered, (2) create a framework to organize and report the safety and quality-related work and metrics, (3) identify care areas where quality is ambiguous or underdeveloped and ensure reporting and accountability in such areas, (4) create a consolidated quality dashboard to track safety and quality performance, (5) ensure the integrity of the data used to measure and report quality and safety performance, and (6) transparently report performance and create an explicit accountability model [113].

Administration and Executives

The chief executive officer is the chief administrator of the hospital and is responsible to the BOD. In a large hospital, there are many separate departments, each of which is controlled by a department head. The CEO operates an executive leadership team, with second-level executives including the COO, CFO, CMO, and CNO, designations which may variably be referred to as "vice president" of operations, financer, medical affairs, and nursing, respectively. Further, in some cases the CMO/VPMA and CNO/VPN may be referred to as Medical Director and Director of Nursing, respectively.

TJC defines the roles of the chief executive of a hospital in Standard LD.01.04.01 as "a chief executive manages the hospital" and lists the elements of performance as:[2]

1. The chief executive provides for information and support systems.
2. The chief executive provides for recruitment and retention of staff.
3. The chief executive provides for physical and financial assets.
4. The chief executive identifies a nurse leader at the executive level who participates in decision-making.
5. When the chief executive is absent from the hospital, a qualified individual is designated to perform the duties of this position.

In addition to TJC, state statutes address the duties of hospital administrative staff. For example, in NYS, NYCRR Title 10 Section 405.3 lists and details, in part:

> The hospital shall be managed effectively and efficiently in accordance with hospital bylaws and policies and procedures. The daily management and operational affairs of the hospital shall be the responsibility of the chief executive officer.
>
> (a) The chief executive officer shall be responsible for the development, submission and implementation of all plans to correct operational deficiencies identifed by regulatory agencies on a timely basis and shall report to the governing body progress in developing and carrying out plans of correction.
>
> (b) Personnel. The chief executive officer develops and implements personnel policies and practices with regard to at least the following…

Additional hospital executives are responsible for managing the organization, making financial decisions, overseeing business strategy, and indirectly managing the hospital support staff infrastructure.

The Medical Staff

Physicians traditionally have been relatively independent of hospitals and have used them as "workshops" in which to carry out their professional services [4]. The medical staff of a hospital are integral to the healthcare mission; in essence, the medical

[2] See The Governance Institute, supra.

staff define the healthcare entity. The medical staff are composed of the physicians, dentists, podiatrists, psychologists, and advanced practice providers (APPs), often collectively referred to as "providers." APPs are composed of, for example, physician assistants, nurse anesthetists, anesthesiologist assistants, nurse practitioners, and nurse midwives. In a regulatory nomenclature, providers are often referred to as "licensed independent practitioners." An unlicensed person who diagnoses and/or treats a patient through activities that are covered by any of the licenses is considered to be practicing illegally and is "practicing without a license." Laws vary by state, an activity that is illegal in all states. Although the classification of the crime will vary by state and by circumstances, the practice of medicine without a license may be charged as either a misdemeanor or felony offense, punishable by fines and prison terms that range from 1–8 years, depending on the jurisdiction. In addition a person harmed through the unlicensed practice of medicine may sue in civil court for assault/battery and be entitled to restitution as monetary damages and possibly punitive damages.

Physicians and licensed independent practitioners (collectively "the medical staff") bring to the healthcare entity the technical knowledge and training necessary to provide patients with the requisite preventive, diagnostic, and therapeutic medical care that is essential to the hospital mission. In addition, the medical staff are authorized to provide clinical supervision of support staff.

TJC first defined the organized medical staff as a hospital standard in 1951. TJC defines its medical staff leadership as "an organized medical staff that is accountable to the governing body" in TJC Leadership Standard LD.01.05.01. The elements of medical staff performance according to TJC are:

1. There is a single organized medical staff unless criteria are met for an exception to the single medical staff requirement.
2. The organized medical staff is self-governing.
3. The medical staff structure conforms to medical staff guiding principles.
4. The governing body approves the structure of the organized medical staff.
5. The organized medical staff oversees the quality of care, treatment, and services provided by those individuals with clinical privileges.
6. The organized medical staff is accountable to the governing body.

EP 2 requires that the medical staff be self-governing, and EP 6 requires the medical staff to be accountable to the governing body. TJC defines self-governance to include:

- The initiation, development, and approval of medical staff bylaws and rules and regulations
- The approval or disapproval of amendments to the medical staff bylaws and rules and regulations
- The selection and removal of medical staff officers
- The determination, establishment, and enforcement of criteria and standards for membership on the medical staff

- The determination, establishment, and enforcement of criteria for the delegation of oversight responsibilities to practitioners with independent privileges
- The establishment of mechanism for maintaining patient care standards and credentialing and delineation of clinical privileges
- Performance improvement activities

The organized medical staff has a critical role in the oversight of safety and quality through setting of rules, regulations, and internal standards and review of adverse outcomes, credentialing, peer review, and punitive actions. However, smaller community hospitals may face significant challenges with respect to peer review and credentialing by virtue of their limited resources, difficulty in medical staff recruitment, and limited medical staff size [114]. For examples, hospitals that have a Department of Surgery composed of two partners may have difficulty conducting an effective peer review and may restrict competition through control of credentialing in the institution [See also Chap. 7].

The 2009 Comprehensive Accreditation Manual for Hospitals further elaborates on the responsibilities of the medical staff's including, for example:

- Oversight of care provided by physicians and other licensed independent practitioners in the hospital
- A role in graduate medical education programs, when the hospital has one (or more)
- A leading role in performance improvement activities to improve the quality of care and patient safety
- Collection, verification, and evaluation of each licensed independent practitioner's credentials
- Recommending to the governing body that an individual be appointed to the medical staff and be granted clinical privileges, based on his/her credentials
- Participating in continuing education

The relationship between the hospital and the medical staff continues to evolve as physicians and physician practices are increasingly acquired and owned by hospitals; thereby transforming an independent medical staff into medical staff who are employees of the hospital, and therefore, at least partly or potentially, subject to administrative control. The changing physician practice environment has wide-ranging potential implications from voluntary involvement in medical staff governance and duties, medical staff socialization, and even burnout.

Conclusion

Compliance with regulatory mandates is mandatory to healthcare entities. The regulatory and legal environment of healthcare is both de facto complex but is also constantly changing. Therefore, in order to remain compliant with the regulatory mandates that govern healthcare, both fluency with respect to terminology and its implications and competence with respect to an appreciation of the scope of potential regulatory impact are important. Although few will be able to recite the regulations, it is perhaps more important to appreciate the potential regulations that are applicable to any one circumstance and know where to find the law.

References

1. American Hospital Association (AHA). Regulatory overload: assessing the regulatory burden on health systems, hospitals and post-acute care providers. Available online at: https://www.aha.org/system/files/2018-02/regulatory-overload-report.pdf. Verified 11 Oct 2020.
2. Söylemez MM. The Jundishapur School: its history, structure, and functions. Am J Islam Soc Sci. 22:2. Available online at: https://www.academia.edu/14579207/The_Jundishapur_School_Its_History_Structure_and_Functions. Verified 11 Oct 2020.
3. Guenter B. Risse, mending bodies, saving souls: a history of hospitals. New York: Oxford University Press; 1999.
4. Starr P. The social transformation of american medicine. New York: Basic Books; 1982. p. 3–4.
5. Penn Medicine. History of Pennsylvania Hospital. Available online at: http://www.uphs.upenn.edu/paharc/features/creation.html#:~:text=The%20Story%20of%20the%20Creation%20of%20the%20Nation%27s,the%20fastest%20growing%20city%20in%20the%2013%20colonies. Verified 11 Oct 2020.
6. Williams WH. The early days of Anglo-America's first hospital: The Pennsylvania Hospital, 1751-1775. J Am Med Assoc. 1972;220(1):115–9.
7. Vern L, Bullough B. Medieval Nursing. Nurs Hist Rev. 1993;1:89–104.
8. James H. Cassedy, medicine in america: a short history. Baltimore: Johns Hopkins University Press; 1991.
9. Rosen G. The structure of American medical practice 1875–1941. Philadelphia: University of Pennsylvania Press; 1983.
10. Nancy G. Siraisi, medieval and early renaissance medicine: an introduction to knowledge and practice. Chicago: University of Chicago Press; 1990.
11. Beck AH. The flexner report and the standardization of American medical education. JAMA. 2004;291(17):2139–40.
12. Flexner A. Medical education in the United States and Canada: a report to the Carnegie foundation for the advancement of teaching. New York: The Carnegie Foundation for the Advancement of Teaching; 1910.
13. U.S. Const. amend. X.
14. Title VI of the Public Health Service Act, Pub. L. No. 79-725, 60 Stat. 1040 (1946) (codified, as amended, at 42 U.S.C. §§ 291-291o (1976)) [hereinafter referred to as the Act or Title VII. In 1975 Congress enacted Title XVI of the National Health Planning and Resources Development Act of 1974 to supplant the original Hill-Burton Act. Pub. L. No.93-641, 88 Stat. 2258 (codified at 42 U.S.C. §§ 300o-300t (1976)) [hereinafter referred to as the new Act or Title XVI].
15. Pub. L. No. 92–603, § 1122, 86 Stat. 1386–90 (1972).
16. National Health Planning and Resources Development Act of 1974, Pub. L. No. 93–641, 88 Stat. 2225 (repealed 1986).
17. Compliance level. 42 C.F.R. § 124.503 (1979).
18. Hill-Burton Facilities. MedicareFAQ. Available online at: https://www.medicarefaq.com/blog/hill-burton-act/. Verified 12 Jun 2020.
19. Roberts JS, Coale JG, Redman RR. A history of the joint commission on accreditation of hospitals. JAMA. 1987;258(7):936–40.

20. Medicare and Medicaid Programs; Survey, Certification and Enforcement Procedures. 42 CFR Parts 488 and 489. Federal Register / Vol. 78, No. 66 / Friday, April 5, 2013.
21. Centers for Medicare & Medicaid Services. Conditions for Coverage (CfCs) & Conditions of Participations (CoPs). https://www.cms.gov/Regulations-and-Guidance/Legislation/CFCsAndCoPs/index.html?redirect=/CFCsAndCOPs/. 2013. Verified 11 Oct 2020.
22. Joint Commission International Accreditation and Certification Policies. Accreditation and certification fee policies. 2015. http://www.jointcommissioninternational.org/assets/3/7/06-Accreditation-Fee-Policies.pdf. Verified 11 Oct 2020.
23. Armour S. House panel probes organizations that accredit most U.S. Hospitals. https://www.wsj.com/articles/house-panel-probes-organizations-that-accredit-most-u-s-hospitals-1520871334. Verified 11 Oct 2020.
24. Griffith JR, Knutzen SR, Alexander JA. Structural versus outcomes measures in hospitals: a comparison of joint commission and medicare outcomes scores in hospitals. Qual Manag Health Care. 2002;10(2):29–38.
25. Barnett ML, Olenski AR, Jena AB. Patient mortality during unannounced accreditation surveys at US Hospitals. JAMA Intern Med. 2017;177(5):693–700.
26. Lam MB, Figueroa JF, Feyman Y, Reimold KE, Orav EJ, Jha AK. Association between patient outcomes and accreditation in US hospitals: observational study. BMJ. 2018;363:k4011.
27. AHA. Health care systems. Available online at: https://www.aha.org/advocacy/health-care-systems. Verified 11 Oct 2020.
28. AHRQ. Defining Health Systems. Content last reviewed September 2017. Agency for healthcare research and quality, Rockville, MD. Available online at: https://www.ahrq.gov/chsp/chsp-reports/resources-for-understanding-health-systems/defining-health-systems.htm. Verified October 11, 2020.
29. Public Law 105–33, 111 Stat. 251 (1997).
30. Critical Access Hospitals Fact Sheet. CMS. Available online at: https://www.cms.gov/Outreach-and-Education/Medicare-Learning-Network-MLN/MLNProducts/downloads/CritAccessHospfctsht.pdf. Verified 11 Oct 2020.
31. Limitation on prices of drugs purchased by covered entities. 42 USC 256b(a)(4)(L)(i).
32. CMS. Hospitals. Online at: https://www.cms.gov/Medicare/Provider-Enrollment-and-Certification/CertificationandComplianc/Hospitals. Verified 11 Oct 2020.
33. 42 CFR 485 subpart F.
34. CMS.CriticalAccessHospitalAvailableonlineat:https://www.cms.gov/Outreach-and-Education/Medicare-Learning-Network-MLN/MLNProducts/Downloads/CritAccessHospfctsht.pdf. Verified 11 Oct 2020.
35. CMS. Critical Access Hospitals. https://www.cms.gov/Medicare/Provider-Enrollment-and-Certification/CertificationandComplianc/CAHs.
36. John Elflein. Number of all hospitals in the U.S. 1975–2018. Statista. July 2, 2020. Available online at: https://www.statista.com/statistics/185843/number-of-all-hospitals-in-the-us-since-2001/. Verified 11 Oct 2020.
37. Liu JB, Kelz RR. Types of hospitals in the United States. JAMA. 2018;320(10):1074.
38. NYCRR 10. 441.8. Acute Care.
39. Definition of Acute care hospital. Law Insider. Available online at: https://www.lawinsider.com/dictionary/acute-care-hospital. Verified 11 Oct 2020.
40. CMS. What are long-term care hospitals? Revised June 2019. Available online at: https://www.medicare.gov/Pubs/pdf/11347-Long-Term-Care-Hospitals.pdf. Verified 11 Oct 2020.
41. Schiel WC. Medical definition of long-term care facility. MedicineNet. Available online at: https://www.medicinenet.com/script/main/art.asp?articlekey=24859. Verified October 11, 2020.
42. 42 CFR Part 483. Requirements for states and long term care facilities. Available online at: https://www.law.cornell.edu/cfr/text/42/part-483. Verified 11 Oct 2020.
43. Jost TS. Regulation of the quality of nursing home care in the United States. Qual Assur Health Care. 1990;1(4):223–8.

44. Kapp MB. Malpracxtice liability in long term care: a changing environment. 24 Creighton L Rev. 1235 (1191).
45. Stevenson DG, Studdert DM. The rise of nursing home litigation: findings from a national survey of attorneys. Health Aff. 2003;22(2):219–29.
46. Studdert DM, Spittal MJ, Mello MM, et al. Relationship between quality of care and negligence litigation in nursing homes. N Engl J Med. 2011;364:1243–50.
47. Institute of Medicine (US) Committee on Implications of For-Profit Enterprise in Health Care. In: Gray BH, editor. For-profit enterprise in health care. Washington, DC: National Academies Press (US); 1986. An exchange on for-profit health care. Available from: https://www.ncbi.nlm.nih.gov/books/NBK217899/. Verified 11 Oct 2020.
48. Berkowitz E. America's welfare state: from Roosevelt to Reagan. Baltimore, MD: Johns Hopkins University Press; 1991.
49. Title XVIII, Social Security Act of 1965, Pub. L. No. 89-97, 79 Stat. 286 (codified in scattered sections of 26, 42 & 45 U.S.C. (1976)). The elderly are the chief beneficiaries of the program, although persons with certain disabilities and those with end-stage renal disease are eligible regardless of age. Need is not a factor in entitlement to benefits. "Part A" Medicare benefits, which provide hospital insurance, are funded primarily through the Social Security tax.
50. Xu J, Kochanek KD, Murphy SL, Arias E. Mortality in the United States, 2012. October 2014.
51. Health Care Financing Administration, Office of the Actuary. Data from estimates based on President's fiscal year 2001 budget. Jan, 2000.
52. DeParle NA. Celebrating 35 years of medicare and medicaid. Health Care Financ Rev. 2000;22(1):1–7.
53. U.S. Constitution, Art. 1, §8, cl. 3.
54. Galva JE, Atchison C, Levey S. Public health strategy and the police powers of the state. Public Health Rep. 2005;120 Suppl 1(Suppl 1):20–7.
55. Wayman v. Southard. 23 U.S. (10 Wheat) 1, 41, (1825).
56. Mistretta v. United States, 488 U.S. 361, 372 (1989). See also Sunshine Anthracite Coal Co. v. Adkins, 310 U.S. 381, 398 (1940) ("Delegation by Congress has long been recognized as necessary in order that the exertion of legislative power does not become a futility").
57. Szalados JE. Regulatory law and the clinical practice of the neurosciences. Chapter 5. In: Szalados JE, editor. Ethics and law for neurosciences clinicians: foundations and evolving challenges. New Jersey: Rutgers University Press; 2019. p. 81–103.
58. Administrative Procedure Act, 5 U.S.C. § 551 et seq. and 5 U.S.C. § 701 et seq. (1946).
59. Administrative Procedure Act (APA). 5 U.S.C. §551(5) (2005).
60. Administrative Procedure Act (APA). 5 U.S.C. §551(4) (2005).
61. HHS. HHS Regulations Toolkit. Available online at: https://www.hhs.gov/regulations/regulations-toolkit/index.html.
62. Estate of Smith v. Heckler. 747 F.2d 583 (10th Circ. 1984).
63. Chevron U.S.A., Inc. v. Natural Resources Defense Council, 467 U.S. 837 (1984).
64. Auer v. Robbins, 519 U.S. 452 (1997).
65. Skidmore v. Swift, 323 U.S. 134 (1944).
66. Administrative Procedure Act. 5 USC §551 et seq. (1946).
67. Brown RS, Clement DG, Hill JW, Retchin SM, Bergeron JW. Do health maintenance organizations work for Medicare? Health Care Financ Rev. 1993;15(1):7–23.
68. Jencks SF, Williams MV, Coleman EA. Rehospitalizations among patients in the medicare fee-for-service program. N Engl J Med. 2009;360(14):1418–28.
69. CMS. Hospital Readmissions Reduction Program (HRRP). Available online at: https://www.cms.gov/Medicare/Medicare-Fee-for-Service-Payment/AcuteInpatientPPS/Readmissions-Reduction-Program. Verified 11 Oct 2020.
70. Econometrica, Inc. Final Evaluation Report. Evaluation of the community-based care transitions program. November 2017. Available online at: https://www.ncbi.nlm.nih.gov/pmc/articles/PMC4439931/#R5. Verified 11 Oct. 2020.

71. Hospital Readmissions Reduction Program (HRRP). CMS. Available online at: https://www.cms.gov/Medicare/Medicare-Fee-for-Service-Payment/AcuteInpatientPPS/Readmissions-Reduction-Program.
72. Jencks SF, Williams MV, Coleman EA. Rehospitalizations among patients in the medicare fee-for-service program [published correction appears in N Engl J Med. 2011 Apr 21;364(16):1582]. N Engl J Med. 2009;360(14):1418–28.
73. Medicare Payment Advisory Commission. Report to the congress: promoting greater efficiency in medicare. Available online at: https://www.ncbi.nlm.nih.gov/pmc/articles/PMC4439931/#R5. Verified 11 Oct 2020.
74. CMS. The hospital value-based purchasing (VBP) program. Available online at: https://www.cms.gov/Medicare/Quality-Initiatives-Patient-Assessment-Instruments/Value-Based-Programs/HVBP/Hospital-Value-Based-Purchasing. Verified 11 Oct 2020.
75. Chee TT, Ryan AM, Wasfy JH, Borden WB. Current state of value-based purchasing programs. Circulation. 2016;133(22):2197–205. https://doi.org/10.1161/CIRCULATIONAHA.115.010268.
76. Szalados JE. "P4P as a performance-based compensation arrangement in health care: foundation, administrative structure, and legal pitfalls" in Managed care litigation. 2007 Supplement. Barnes J. ed. BNA Books. pp. 129–180. 2007.
77. Centers for Medicare & Medicaid Services. Accessed 15 Oct 2015. MACRA: MIPS & APMs. https://www.cms.gov/Medicare/Quality-Initiatives-Patient-Assessment-Instruments/Value-Based-Programs/MACRA-MIPS-and-APMs/MACRA-MIPS-and-APMs.html. Verified 11 Oct 2020.
78. The Hospital Value-Based Purchasing (VBP) Program. Centers for medicare and medicaid. Available online at: https://www.cms.gov/Medicare/Quality-Initiatives-Patient-Assessment-Instruments/Value-Based-Programs/HVBP/Hospital-Value-Based-Purchasing. Verified 11 Oct 2020.
79. Szalados JE. "P4P as a performance-based compensation arrangement in health care: foundation, administrative structure, and legal pitfalls" in managed care litigation. 2009 Cumulative Supplement. Barnes J. ed. BNA Books. pp. 129–180. 2007. ISBN: 978-1-57018-766-7.
80. CMS. Hospital-Acquired Condition Reduction Program Fiscal Year 2020 Fact Sheet. Available online at: https://www.cms.gov/Medicare/Medicare-Fee-for-Service-Payment/AcuteInpatientPPS/Downloads/HAC-Reduction-Program-Fact-Sheet.pdf. Verified 11 Oct 2020.
81. Zogg CK, Thumma JR, Ryan AM, Dimick JB. Medicare's hospital acquired condition reduction program disproportionately affects minority-serving hospitals: variation by race, socioeconomic status, and disproportionate share hospital payment receipt. Ann Surg. 2020;271(6):985–93.
82. Fuller RL, Goldfield NI, Averill RF, Hughes JS. Is the CMS hospital-acquired condition reduction program a valid measure of hospital performance? Am J Med Qual. 2017;32(3):254–60.
83. Deficit Reduction Act, Pub. L. No. 109-1711, Chap. 3, § 6032; *see also* Deficit Reduction Act. 42 U.S.C. 1396a(a)(68) (2005). See also OIG. Compliance Resource Portal. Available online at: https://oig.hhs.gov/compliance/compliance-resource-portal/index.asp. Verified 11 Oct 2020.
84. Publication of the OIG compliance program guidance for hospitals--OIG. Notice. Fed Regist. 1998;63(35):8987–98.
85. U.S. Sentencing Commission. Guidelines Manual (Nov. 2013) (USSG). http://www.ussc.gov/sites/default/files/pdf/guidelines-manual/2013/manual-pdf/2013_Guidelines_Manual_Full.pdf. Verified 11 Oct 2020.
86. Saum TB, Byassee J. Effective health care corporate compliance. Physician Exec. 2000;26(3):56–9.
87. Office of Inspector General, U.S. Department of Health and Human Services. Practical Guidance for Health Care Governing Boards on Compliance Oversight. April 20, 2015. Available online at: https://ahia.org/assets/Uploads/pdfUpload/WhitePapers/

PracticalGuidanceForHealthCareGoverningBoardsOnComplianceOversight.pdf. Verified 11 Oct 2020.
88. Unites States Department of Justice. Antitrust division. Healthcare. Available online at: https://www.justice.gov/atr/health-care.
89. Satiani B. Relevance of federal antitrust statutes to clinical practice. J Vasc Surg. 2003;37(6):1334–40.
90. Robinson-Patman Act, 15 U.S.C. §§ 13 et seq.
91. Hart-Scott-Rodino Act. U.S.C. 15 (1013 b).
92. Examination and treatment for emergency medical conditions and women in labor. 42 U.S. Code § 1395dd (2005).
93. Ansell DA, Schiff RL. Patient dumping. Status, implications, and policy recommendations. JAMA. 1987;257(11):1500–2.
94. Morales v. Sociedad, 524 F.3d 54 (1st. Cir. 2008).
95. Examination and treatment for emergency medical conditions and women in labor. 42 USC 1395dd (1986).
96. 42 Code of Federal Regulations § 489.24(b).
97. Medicare Program: Changes to the Hospital Inpatient Prospective payment Systems and Fiscal Year 2009 Rates; Payments for Graduate medical Education in Certain Emergency Situations; Changes to Disclosure of Physician Ownership in Hospitals and Physician Self-Referral Rules; Updates to the long-Term Care Prospective Payment System; Updates to Certain IPPS-Excluded Hospitals; and Collection of information Regarding Financial Relationships between Hospitals. 73 Fed. Reg. 48434–48659 Vol 73 no. 161 (Aug. 19, 2008).
98. 42 CFR Parts 413, 482, and 489. Medicare program: clarifying policies related to the responsibilities of medicare-participating hospitals in treating individuals with emergency medical conditions; final rule. 68 Fed. Reg. 53221-53264. Vol. 68 no. 174 (Sept. 9, 2003).
99. Emergency Medical Treatment and Labor Act (EMTALA). Requirements and implications related to coronavirus disease 2019 (COVID-19). QSO-20-15 Hospital/CAH/EMTALA. CMS. March 9, 2020. Available online at: https://www.cms.gov/files/document/qso-20-15-hospitalcahemtala.pdf.
100. 1135 Waiver- At A Glance. CMS. Available online at: https://www.cms.gov/Medicare/Provider-Enrollment-and-Certification/SurveyCertEmergPrep/Downloads/1135-Waivers-At-A-Glance.pdf. Verified 11 Oct 2020.
101. 26 CFR § 1.501(a)-1. Exemption from taxation.
102. IRS (US) Revenue ruling 69-545, 1969-2, C.B. 117. Available online at: http://www.irs.gov/pub/irs-tege/rr69-545.pdf.
103. IRS. Charitable Hospitals – General Requirements for Tax-Exemption Under Section 501(c)(3). Available online at: https://www.irs.gov/charities-non-profits/charitable-hospitals-general-requirements-for-tax-exemption-under-section-501c3.
104. Internal Revenue Code. 26 U.S.C. §501(r).
105. Rosenbaum S, Margulies R. Tax-exempt hospitals and the patient protection and affordable care act: implications for public health policy and practice. Public Health Rep. 2011;126(2):283–6.
106. Lorens v. Catholic Health Care Partners, 35.6 F. Supp. 2d 827 (N.D. Ohio 2005).
107. Vencor, Inc. v. Physicians Mut. Ins. Co., 211 F.3d 1323 (D.C. Cir. 2000).
108. Provena Covenant Med. Ctr. v. Dep't of Revenue, 925 N.E.2d 1131, 236 Ill. 2d 368, 2010 Ill. LEXIS 289, 339 Ill. Dec. 10 (Ill. Mar. 18, 2010).
109. Pointer DD, Totten MK, Orlikoff JE. Trustee workbook 2. The balanced scorecard: a tool for maximizing board performance. Trustee. 2005;58(4):17–20.
110. The Governance Institute. Leadership in healthcare organizations. A guide to joint commission leadership standards. 2009. Available online at: https://www.jointcommission.org/-/media/deprecated-unorganized/imported-assets/tjc/system-folders/topics-library/wp_leadership_standardspdf.pdf?db=web&hash=86F0223A5C016F833DA3DDB1C62F5D20. Verified 11 Oct 2020.

111. Culica D, Prezio E. Hospital board infrastructure and functions: the role of governance in financial performance. Int J Environ Res Public Health. 2009;6(3):862–73. https://doi.org/10.3390/ijerph6030862.
112. Jha A, Epstein A. Hospital governance and the quality of care. Health Aff. 2010;29(1):182–7.
113. Pronovost PJ, Armstrong CM, Demski R, Peterson RR, Rothman PB. Next level of board accountability in health care quality. J Health Organ Manag. 2018;32(1):2–8. https://doi.org/10.1108/JHOM-09-2017-0238.
114. Spaeth RG, Pickering KC, Webb SM. Quality assurance and hospital structure: how the physician-hospital relationship affects quality measures. Ann Health Law. 2003;12(2):235–47.

Chapter 5
The Timeline of a Medical Malpractice Lawsuit

James E. Szalados

Introduction

Medical malpractice is governed by the law of torts, or personal injury, through which a liability arises under civil (as opposed to criminal) law. A tort is defined as an act, or an omission, which causes injury to another; however, there are three main types of torts: [1] intentional torts such as assault/battery or deliberate infliction of emotional distress; [2] unintentional torts, such as negligence; and [3] strict liability torts such as defective product actions. Professional negligence is one type of unintentional tort whereby a professional breaches the duty of care to a client, thereby causing harm to the client. Medical malpractice, or medical negligence, is a type of professional negligence, whereby a medical provider or medical professional, though a negligent act or omission, causes an injury to a patient. The law of medical negligence is governed by civil law and therefore subject to variations between the states; however, the main variability between the states is less in the substantive laws (the statutes) and more in the procedural law (which governs the procedures to be followed during a lawsuit. The variations in procedure are most likely, but not absolutely, to apply to definitions, deadlines, court rules, and the judicial procedure. This chapter will outline the steps of a malpractice lawsuit in a generic fashion. A Glossary of Terms is provided in the Appendix, and Fig. 5.1 generally illustrates the timeline and process.

J. E. Szalados (✉)
Director, Surgical and Neurocritical Care Units, Rochester Regional Health System at Rochester General Hospital, Rochester, NY, USA

The Szalados Law Firm, Hilton, NY, USA
e-mail: james.szalados@rochesterregional.org; jszalados@aol.com

J. E. Szalados (ed.), *The Medical-Legal Aspects of Acute Care Medicine*,
https://doi.org/10.1007/978-3-030-68570-6_5

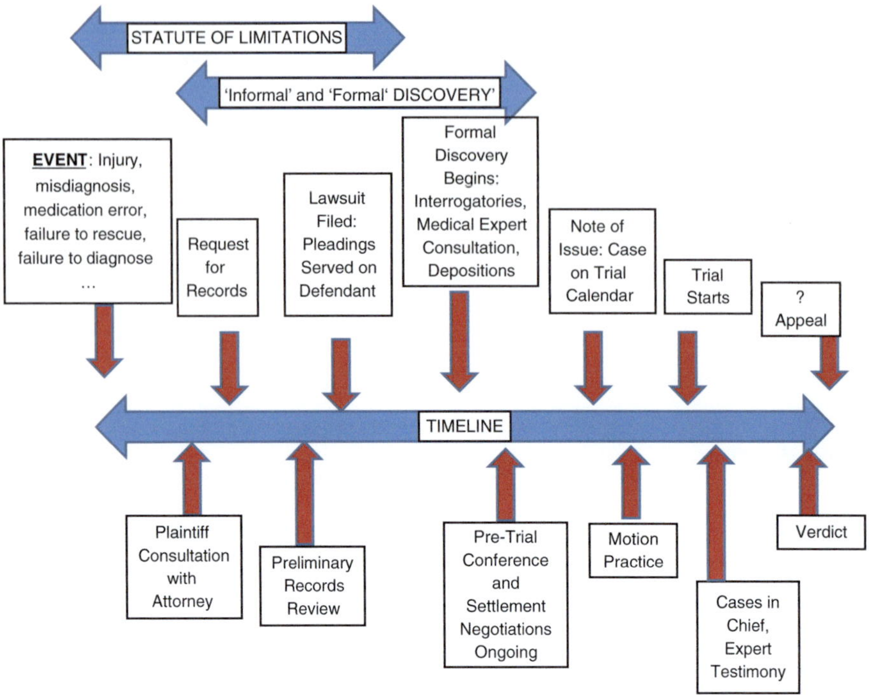

Fig. 5.1 The general timeline of a civil medical malpractice lawsuit

The Cause of Action

The cause of action is legally defined as the set of facts, and the applicable legal theory, which taken together serve as justification for a legal remedy. The cause of action accrues at the time that an allegedly negligent event occurred. In a practical sense, within the ambit of medical negligence, the cause of action is the actual act or omission, which causes harm to the patient. The cause of action may be, for example, a mistaken or delayed diagnosis, a medication error, a procedural or surgical error, or failure to treat. In general, a complication, in itself is not strictly malpractice. Medicine is not a perfect science mainly because there is a large variability between patients and their responses to treatment and because there are a large number of unknowns in all medical treatment encounters. Complications may be foreseeable or unforeseen. Most complications are foreseeable and are generally discussed in the context of informed consent and may include bleeding during surgery, side effects of medications, or postoperative infections. Foreseeable complications can rise to the level of negligence if they are not discussed as part of the informed consent process, if reasonable steps to prevent or prepare for a complication are omitted or if a complication which would be recognized and treated by a reasonably prudent practitioner is overlooked, ignored, or mistreated. For example, injury to the common bile duct can occur during gallbladder surgery; it may require intraoperative repair if recognized during surgery, or it may present later, possibly after hospital discharge. The act of causing injury to the common duct is not in itself malpractice, especially if the surgeon documents that appropriate steps were taken to avoid injury; however, a recognized injury is not immediately addressed by repair or transfer or where a patient develops jaundice and upper abdominal pain and the surgeon fails to address a post-cholecystectomy complication. There may be a cause of action for medical malpractice. Unforeseen complications are, by their nature, not addressed during informed consent; however, the provider's duty to rescue, in accordance with standard of care, is nonetheless the same as that for a foreseeable complication.

The Statute of Limitations

A statute of limitation (SOL) is by definition a state-specific statutory law, which defines a set period of time, subject to some exceptions, after which a lawsuit for a particular tort or crime can no longer be filed. After the applicable SOL expires or "has run," a plaintiff cannot file, or initiate, a legal action, even if the underlying facts would otherwise have substantive merit. For example, if the applicable SOL is 3 years, then a lawsuit that would be initiated 3 years and 1 day after the barring exceptions and after the inciting incident would be disallowed on the basis that it is "time-barred." A potential cause of action begins, or accrues, as of the date of the event that is the basis for the claim. The expiration of the SOL is in itself a defense to a potential lawsuit, since after the SOL has run, the court which would otherwise hear the suit no longer has jurisdiction over the parties for that matter. Running of the SOL is an affirmative defense, which would need to be pleased by the defendant in the answer to a complaint; a failure to raise the affirmative defense in the answer can result in the defendant unknowingly waiving the protection of the SOL. It is important to note that once a case is timely filed, the actual period of litigation can outlast the SOL; the SOL applies only until the point in time that a case is actually filed in court. Thus, the period which defines the SOL will vary by jurisdiction and the type of claim. The SOL is a procedural rule and is separate from the substantive law governing an act. There is an associated SOL that is defined in both civil and criminal causes of action, although certain federal crimes do not have SOLs. The intent of a SOL is to ensure that controversies can be reasonably diligently addressed in a timely fashion and convictions are based upon evidence (physical or eyewitness) that has not deteriorated with time. Widespread variation in state laws produces significant differences in state-to-state liability risk and insurance cost. The SOL is important to clinicians with respect to the type of medical liability insurance they carry, since the SOL is perhaps the most basis for the tail or nose coverage that is required for claims-made policies [see Chap. 10]. Table 5.1 illustrates the SOLs, by state, for medical malpractice, which may be affected by the exceptions discussed below [1].

Table 5.1 State-specific states of limitations for medical malpractice

State	SOL	Code
Alabama	2 years	Ala. Code Sec. 6-2-38
Alaska	2 years	Alaska Stat. Sec. 9.10.070
Arizona	2 years	Ariz. Rev. Stat. Sec. 12-542
Arkansas	3 years	Ark. Stat. Sec. 16-114-203
California	2 years	Cal. Code of Civ. Proc. Sec. 335.1
Colorado	2 years	Colo. Rev. Stat. Sec. 13-80-102
Connecticut	2 years	Conn. Gen. State. Sec. 52-584
Delaware	2 years	Del. Code Ann. Title 10, Sec. 8119
District of Columbia (DC)	3 years	D.C. Code Ann. Sec. 12-301
Florida	4 years	Fla. Stat. Ann. Sec. 95.11
Georgia	2 years	Ga. Code Ann. Sec. 9-3-33
Hawaii	2 years	Haw. Rev. Stat. Sec. 657.7
Idaho	2 years	Idaho Code Sec. 5-219
Illinois	2 years	Ill. Ann. State. Ch. 735, Art. 5, Sec. 13-202
Indiana	2 years	Ind. Code Ann. Sec. 34-11-2-4
Iowa	2 years	Iowa Code Ann. Sec. 614.1
Kansas	2 years	Kan. Stat. Ann. Sec. 60-513
Kentucky	1 year	Ky. Rev. Stat. Sec. 413.140
Louisiana	1 year	La. Civ. Code Ann. Art. 3492
Maine	6 years	Maine Rev. Stat. Ann. Title 14, Ch. 205, Sec. 752
Maryland	3 years	Md. Ann. Code Sec. 5-101
Massachusetts	3 years	Mass. Gen. Laws, Art. 260, Secs. 2A, 4
Michigan	3 years	Mich. Comp Laws Sec. 600.5805(9)
Minnesota	2 years	Minn. Stat. Ann. Sec. 541.05, 541.07
Mississippi	3 years	Miss. Code Ann. Sec. 15-1-49
Missouri	5 years	Missouri Ann. Stat. Title 35, Sec. 516.120
Montana	3 years	Mont. Code Ann. Sec. 27-2-204, 27-2-207
Nebraska	4 years	Neb. Rev. Stat. Sec. 25-207
Nevada	2 years	Nev. Rev. Stat. Sec 11.190
New Hampshire	3 years	N.H. Rev. State. Sec. 508.4
New Jersey	2 years	N.J. Stat. Ann. Sec. 2A:14-2
New Mexico	3 years	N.M. Stat. Ann. Sec. 37-1-8
New York	3 years	N.Y. Civ. Prac. R. Sec. 214
North Carolina	3 years	N.C. Gen. Stat. Sec. 1-52
North Dakota	6 years	N.D. Cent. Code Sec. 28-01-16, 28-01-18
Ohio	2 years	Ohio Rev. Code Sec. 2305.10
Oklahoma	2 years	Okla. Stat. Ann. Title 12, Sec. 95
Oregon	2 years	Ore. Rev. Stat. Sec. 12.110
Pennsylvania	2 years	42 Pa. Con. Stat. Sec. 5524
Rhode Island	3 years	R.I. Gen. Laws Sec. 9-1-14
South Carolina	3 years	S.C. Code Ann. Sec. 15-3-530

Table 5.1 (continued)

South Dakota	3 years	S.D. Comp. Laws Ann. Sec. 15-2-14
Tennessee	1 year	Tenn. Code Ann. Sec. 28-3-104
Texas	2 years	Tex. Civ. Prac. & Rem. Code Sec. 16.003
Utah	4 years	Utah Code Ann. Sec. 78-12-28
Vermont	3 years	Vt. Stat. Ann. Title 12, Sec. 512
Virginia	2 years	Va. Code Sec. 8.01-243
Washington	3 years	Wa. Rev. Code Ann. Sec. 4.16.080
West Virginia	2 years	W. Va. Code Sec. 55-2-12
Wisconsin	3 years	Wisc. Stat. Ann. Sec. 893.54
Wyoming	4 years	Wy. Stat. Ann. Sec. 1-3-105

NOTE: This table is intended as a general guide for reference and educational purposes only. Not legal advice. Laws are amended and change. There are also state-specific exceptions and statutes of repose which may apply. Readers are strongly advised to consult their individual state laws and with experienced counsel

The procedural rules that govern the SOL differ in substance from, and should not be confused with, the common law legal doctrine of "laches" which states that a legal right or claim may, at the discretion of the court, not be enforced or allowed if an unreasonable delay by the plaintiff in the assertion of his or her right or claim has prejudiced the other party. Latches is an equitable defense to a lawsuit, and therefore, by raising the defense of latches, one is asking the court for equitable relief, in essence a form of "estoppel." Laches is ""'a defense developed by courts of equity' to protect defendants against 'unreasonable, prejudicial delay in commencing suit'" [2]. In general, the elements of latches are therefore (1) knowledge of a potential claim by the plaintiff, (2) a neglectful delay in filing the legal action, (3) which is unreasonable, and (4) that prejudices the defendant. Examples of prejudice to the defendant might include loss or degradation or evidence, loss of witness testimony by death or recollection, or changes in position. Latches may apply even in cases where the SOL has not run; "laches may bar a legal claim even if the statutory period of limitations has not yet expired" [3].

The SOL can be suspended, by state-specific statutorily defined circumstances, to cause an extension of time during which a case may be filed. Exceptions by which a SOL may be extended include (1) the discovery rule and (2) tolling.

The "discovery" (or "discovery of harm") rule can, under some circumstances, extend the SOL to either the date in time when the person actually discovered the injury or the malpractice or to the date in time when the patient reasonably should have known that malpractice occurred. State statutes address the discovery rule differently. The discovery rule applies in situations where a harm caused is not obvious. Examples where the discovery rule may apply in medical malpractice cases include inadvertently retained foreign bodies, wrong site surgery, fraudulent concealment, erroneous or incomplete radiology reports, and incomplete surgery (incomplete tumor removal). In the case of *Kaplan v. Mamelak*, surgery was performed to relieve plaintiff's back pain with the intention to excise the herniated portion of disk T8–T9; during the operation, the surgeon in fact operated on the disc at T6–T7 and T7–T8, rather than T8–T9. Following the surgery, the plaintiff, Kaplan, continued to suffer pain, and a subsequent MRI revealed persistent disc protrusion at T8–T9 and that the operation was performed at the incorrect site. The California Appellate Court reversed the trial court's determination that the actions for battery and medical malpractice were time-barred [4]. In 2018, New York State enacted Lavern's Law [5] which applies to malpractice actions related to the alleged failure to diagnose cancer and extended the NYS SOL from 2½ years to 7 years from the date of the missed diagnosis through a special application of the discovery rule. The NYS law is based in the case of Lavern Wilkinson presented to a hospital with symptoms of chest pain in 2010 where a chest x-ray was performed which was interpreted by a radiologist to show a suspicious mass on Ms. Wilkinson's right lung, but this information was not communicated to her. In 2012 with complaints of a chronic cough, Ms. Wilkinson had a repeat chest x-ray that revealed cancer which had spread to both lungs; additional imaging revealed tumor spread to the liver, brain, and spine. Ms. Wilkinson was advised that the cancer diagnosis had not been appreciated by the hospital's treating clinicians in 2010 when it was still potentially treatable.

The "continuous treatment doctrine," in those states which apply the doctrine may toll the SOL during the time that a provider continues a course of treatment for the same condition from which a potential lawsuit would arise. The intent of the continuous treatment doctrine is to allow the completion of a course of therapy without interfering adversely with the patient-provider relationship or potentially for the correction of a deviation from standards of care, while the treatment is ongoing. There are differing versions of the continuous treatment doctrine. For example, "under the continuing treatment doctrine, a plaintiff's cause of action does not accrue until the tortious continuing treatment ends, even if the plaintiff is aware of the facts constituting negligence before that time" [6]. A different version of the doctrine is where courts do not require that the entire course of treatment be negligent, but only that some portion of the ongoing treatment be negligent; here the statute of limitations may be tolled during subsequent continuing treatment, even if non-negligent [7]. The failure to diagnose or treat a condition does not qualify as a continuous course of treatment under the doctrine.

The statute of limitations may also be suspended by "tolling," for example, in the event of acute disability, mental state, or age of minority. Those unable to bring suit may benefit from a SOL toll which extends the applicable statute of limitations until the condition resolves. For example, in NYS NYS CPLR §208 states, in part:

(a) If a person entitled to commence an action is under a disability because of infancy or insanity at the time the cause of action accrues, and the time otherwise limited for commencing the action is 3 years or more and expires no later than 3 years after the disability ceases or the person under the disability dies the time within which the action must be commenced shall be extended to 3 years after the disability ceases or the person under the disability dies, whichever event first occurs; if the time otherwise limited is less than 3 years, the time shall be extended by the period of disability. The time within which the action must be commenced shall not be extended by this provision beyond 10 years after the cause of action accrues, except in any action other than for medical, dental, or podiatric malpractice, where the person was under a disability due to infancy. This section shall not apply to an action to recover a penalty or forfeiture or against a sheriff or other officers for an escape.

Pretrial Process

Consultation and Informal Fact Acquisition

When a prospective plaintiff first consults with an attorney, future litigation becomes a possibility. In some cases, a plaintiff may consult with more than one attorney in contemplation of a lawsuit. In the case of potential clients that allege medical malpractice, a substantial number of such potential cases do not advance beyond the initial "intake" analysis. Threshold questions which may arise during the initial interview may include conflicts of interest, attorney competence or areas of expertise, the events and the timeline of the case such as the SOL, and a general overview of the acts of the case. Client screening is also used by attorneys to avoid forming a representation relationship with potential clients who are demanding, vengeful, and untruthful, have unreasonable expectations, or those who have been unable to form relationships with other attorneys with which they have consulted on the same matter.

The initial interaction will define the attorney-client relationship and discuss the issues of confidentiality and representation. Confidentiality relates to the attorney-client privilege which, under a majority rule, attaches at the time that a prospective client consults with a licensed attorney, seeking legal advice or potential representation, and where the prospective client reasonably believes that the communication will be confidential, then that consultation is privileged. The holder of the privilege of confidentiality is the prospective client, or client, who is free to break the confidentiality; the attorney is, generally, not. The attorney-client privilege attaches even if an ongoing attorney-client relationship is not formed. The attorney-client relationship begins at the time that both the client and the attorney agree to the relationship; the attorney-client relationship requires both that the client request representation and that the attorney agree to provide such advice and representation. In most cases, representation will entail a formal signed engagement letter or retainer agreement. The fee arrangement in personal injury litigation, including medical malpractice, is usually a contingency fee, for which the relationship is formed through a written contract. In a contingency fee arrangement, the attorney provides representation to the client for a predetermined percentage of the amount recovered on behalf of the client; the fee is deducted from the net award. Under a contingency agreement, the attorney is not compensated unless he or she prevails and recovers damages on behalf of the client. The contingency fee may be adjusted as based on relevant statutes or laws, agreed upon based on the expected complexity and risk, and the costs of litigation. In New York State, the contingency fees for attorneys in claims or actions for medical, dental, or podiatric malpractice are statutorily defined as:

- 30% of the first $250,000 of the sum recovered
- 25% of the next $250,000 of the sum recovered
- 20% of the next $500,000 of the sum recovered
- 15% of the next $250,000 of the sum recovered
- 10% of any amount over $1,250,000 of the sum recovered [8].

The attorney will perform a preliminary case valuation; where the expected costs of case filing, records acquisition, records reviews, and experts are likely to outweigh the likelihood of success and the potential recovery, the attorney will likely decline to represent the client. If the case proceeds, informal fact acquisition will include general information about the client, the treating provider, the institution, and the circumstances; it begins the formation of the "story" which will be important in litigation. Informal fact acquisition will also include requests for medical records – perhaps the first time that a healthcare professional may become aware of potential litigation. In some larger institutions, providers are not routinely made aware when an attorney's office makes a request for medical records. The interviews will identify potential witnesses and additional sources of information for later discovery. Finally, at this stage, additional details such as Internet or social media, billing records, or prior claims histories for the providers may be obtained and reviewed.

Legal Foundations Preparation

The laws regarding medical malpractice and other potentially applicable state civil statutes (e.g., assault/battery, informed consent, emotional distress) vary between the states; these represent the substantive law of the jurisdiction and will entail specific elements of proof necessary to maintain a cause of action. The appropriate court is identified; subject-matter jurisdiction refers to the power of a court to adjudicate a particular type of matter and provide the remedy demanded. The court with subject-matter jurisdiction in most medical malpractice cases will be the state trial court; however, in cases that involve the government, such as the Veteran's Administration, the court with subject-matter jurisdiction may be the district federal court.

Venue refers to the specific court in which an action is filed, usually a trial court within a specific county. Venue is based on personal jurisdiction, which refers to a court's power to exercise authority over a party. In contradistinction, *forum non conveniens* means "inconvenient forum" which implies a venue that is inconvenient or not as appropriate as another forum may be. Proper venue is a personal right. Choice of venue is based on the procedural rules for state civil cases and varies by state; federal venue rules apply to federal courts. In state actions, a reasonable or the most appropriate venue could be based on where the plaintiff or defendant resides or where the cause of action arose. Venues may be changed after the lawsuit is filed through objections in the answer or through motions, which are requests to the court. When a venue is changed, the substantive and other elements of procedural law will follow the venue. In some jurisdictions, before a malpractice compliant can be formally filed with a court, there must have been a general review of the facts of the case by an expert; this review and the attendant certification may be referred to as a Certificate of Merit, Affidavit of Merit, or an Offer of Proof. In general, the Certificate of Merit is a statement based on a written opinion from a suitably qualified professional certifying that he or she has reviewed the medical records and that, in the certifier's opinion, the plaintiff's claim has merits. Usually, the expert who signs the Certificate of Merit must qualify as an expert in the same medical field as the defendant health provider. Generally, the Certificate of Merit is signed by the reviewing medical professional; however, in some states, the person executing the certification may be, or included, the plaintiff's attorney who certifies the consultation. The intent of the Certificate of Merit is to decrease the number of frivolous lawsuits since; in the theory, the case has been certified as meritorious by a medical professional.

The lawsuit is commenced when pleadings are filed in the court with appropriate subject-matter and personal jurisdiction [Fig. 5.1] [see Chap. 17]. Strategically sound pleadings are a combination of (1) a theory of the case that is legally and medically sound, (2) a good litigation plan, and (3) technically precise and complete drafting. The requirements for and the structure of pleadings may vary between jurisdictions. In general, the pleadings are composed of a notice and compliant, which, depending on jurisdiction, may be accompanied by a summons. Generally, the requirements of a notice are simple and must contain only sufficient information to fairly notify the defendant(s) of the existence of and the basis of the claim(s). The complaint will detail the jurisdiction, briefly state the facts, specify the allegations, and demand relief. A summons is an order from the court where the lawsuit will be heard and contains the docket, or file, number. Together, the pleadings begin the lawsuit; under many circumstances, they represent the first time that a provider is aware that a legal process is underway. Upon receiving the pleadings, the provider should immediately notify appropriate administrative staff, risk management, insurance carriers, and seek legal counsel.

The summons and complaint or the summons with notice are served on the defendant by a person and in a manner authorized by law in the applicable jurisdiction. The requirement for due process stipulates that one must be given notice of a lawsuit and also be accorded and opportunity to be heard; Rules of Civil Procedure and Criminal Procedure determine the proper form of legal process and how it must be served. Process must be properly and individually served on all parties to an action. Service of process may occur by either (1) actual, or personal, service, (2) substituted service, or (3) service by publication. Often, substituted service may be used only after diligent efforts to effect personal service have failed. The person who delivers the process papers is referred to as a process server, who is qualified by the law of the jurisdiction and who, following delivery, must file an Affidavit of

Service with the court, giving the details of the delivery. Improper service is a defense to lawsuit, and therefore defendants should carefully note the exact details surrounding any service of process upon them.

The defendant has a statutorily specified period of time in which he or she must answer the complaint. Failure to timely answer the pleadings will result in a default judgment. The time allowed for the answer may depend on jurisdiction and also the means by which service of process was completed. The answer will usually deny allegations and also raise defenses (e.g., SOL, jurisdiction, venue, contributory/comparative negligence). In the event that the answer is not timely filed, the defendant is in default and loses the opportunity to defend the lawsuit; at that time the court will "skip" the hearings and move directly to a determination of damages.

In jurisdictions that allow for a Bill of Particulars, a request for a Bill of Particulars will be requested from the plaintiff by the defendant when the defendant responds to the complaint in his or her answer. The Bill of Particulars is a particularization and a detailed version of the complaint, the details of which are usually governed by statute.

Motions are written or oral applications made to a court or judge in to obtain a ruling or order. The rules regarding motions are governed by local laws and court rules. Motion practice is a significant part of the litigation process. There are a variety of motions which may be made by either party in a malpractice lawsuit. Typically, some first motions may include motions to dismiss the lawsuit, dismiss a party, motion to compel release of evidence, motion for summary judgment, motion to change venue, or motions for time extensions. Motions in limine are motions made in front of a judge, in closed chambers, usually immediately before or during trial, whereby an attorney will request that the court preclude certain evidence or testimony from the courtroom.

A motion for summary judgment is a request for the court to rule in the moving party's favor before a lawsuit goes to trial and based on the evidence at hand claiming that all factual and legal issues can be decided in the moving party's favor without a need for trial. In order to overcome a motion for summary judgment, the opposing party must show that "triable issues of fact" and/or of law remain which must be resolved in court.

Discovery

Discovery is the principal pretrial method whereby the facts surrounding a controversy are gathered and shared. Discovery in preparation for trial is both an art and a science, usually accounts for most of the time spent by the counsel during litigation, and will develop the foundations upon which a case is won or lost. Discovery can include interrogatories which are written questions requiring a timely answer; depositions which are structured interviews under oath conducted with representation by both parties' respective counsel; subpoenas, expert guidance and testimony; and a relatively new form of discovery electronic discovery (e-discovery) which can be sweeping in its scope.

A deposition (sometimes referred to as an "examination before trial" or "EBT") is an oral testimony and is under oath, in the presence of counsel and a court reporter who generates a transcript, and may sometimes also be recorded or videotaped. Parties are served with notice regarding their appearance at a deposition, which is most often performed at a mutually convenient time and place, usually in a law office or meeting room. Depositions are scheduled after the exchange of interrogatories, after the release of documents, and after consultation with experts, since the structure of the depositions will be based upon the prior evidence obtained. Nonparty witnesses must also be served with a subpoena which requires their appearance at a deposition. Testimony during a deposition is under oath and therefore may be introduced at trial in order to contradict or impeach future testimony or to substantiate a charge of perjury. During the deposition, the witness may be asked to identify or authenticate documents, photographs, and other evidence referred to during the deposition which are then admitted as exhibits. Preparation of a witness for a deposition, similar to a preparation of a witness for trial is essential; these preparations are based on document review, strategies, and discussion of sample questions or perhaps as mock deposition. The deposition is an important tool to obtain testamentary evidence, impeach witnesses at trial, find avenues for additional evidence, preserve evidence for trial, and assess a witness' poise and presentation abilities during questioning. Each party must review the deposition transcript for accuracy prior to the admission of the deposition transcript into evidence.

Electronic discovery refers to discovery of evidence that is stored in an electronic format (electronically stored information or ESI) using digital forensic processes. Electronic discovery applies not only to electronic medical records (EMRs) but also to email, websites, digital databases, the Internet of things, social media, and electronic presence tracing. Electronic discovery has been widely codified in the Federal Rules of Civil Procedure and in state statutes governing evidence.

Court orders, warrants, summons, and subpoenas are examples of legal documents by which a court enforces personal jurisdiction over persons or property. A subpoena is a written order from a court. The term "subpoena" means "under penalty." There are two forms of subpoenas: (1) a *subpoena ad testificandum*, a subpoena compelling a witness to testify, and a *subpoena duces tecum*, a type of subpoena that requires production of a document or documents pertinent to a proceeding. In general, any person or material can be the subject of a subpoena although the scope of the subpoena must be reasonable. A subpoena is typically requested by an attorney and issued by a court clerk, a notary public, or a justice of the peace. A subpoena can also be issued and signed by an attorney on behalf of a court in which the attorney is authorized to practice law. A subpoena can be served by a process server, sent via the mail or email, and read out loud, as per the applicable procedural rules for service of process within the jurisdiction. Subpoenas are time-sensitive with court-imposed deadlines, and a delay or failure to reply is considered contempt of court. A "motion to quash" is a request that a judge nullify or cancel a subpoena; grounds to quash may include privilege or privileged material, vagueness, short notice, or overly burdensome. Notably, a legal entity such as a corporation or partnership has no privilege against self-incrimination under the Fifth Amendment, whether or not the subject of the subpoena may incriminate the company [9]. With respect to individual natural persons, the Fifth Amendment again generally does not shield the incriminating contents of private documents from court inquiry; however under the "act of production doctrine," it may offer protection where the act of production in itself is incriminating [10]. On the other hand, a warrant is a court order that permits a law enforcement officer to perform a search and seizure of persons or property.

Pretrial negotiated settlement is a mechanism to avoid trial, with its attendant financial costs, time commitments, and emotional impact on parties and witnesses. In general, the large majority of medical malpractice cases are settled prior to trial. Options for settlement and the details of a settlement are often coordinated with the medical liability carrier who may require the plaintiff provider's consent to settle and who may impose "high-low" parameters to a potential settlement deal. Thus, the process of reaching a settlement is process of negotiation, especially with respect to any claims for noneconomic damages; successful negotiation requires skill, data, and effective communication. Settlements, like adverse verdicts, must be reported to the National Practitioner Databank and will appear on all future provider credentialing verifications; therefore providers with reasonably strong cases will often have an incentive not to settle, whereas insurers may be averse to the potentially unpredictable nature of trials and juries. Settlements will often require a court approval, either as a structured payment over time or as a lump sum payment.

In some situations, prior to or at any point during a lawsuit, the defendant party may file a counterclaim. Following the pretrial completion of discovery, the parties will file a Certificate of Readiness (may also be referred to as a "Note of Issue" or "at-issue memorandum") whereby they attest that they are ready to proceed to trial.

Trial

Medical malpractice trials are generally intense structured confrontations during which each side presents the facts of their case through party, nonparty, and expert witness testimony, exhibits, and argumentation. The trial will be a recreation of the realities surrounding the event giving rise to the cause of action. Some will argue that rather than reality, trials are more represent of a surreality since decisions and actions that occurred in a moment will be dissected and analyzed in the context of retrospection, enhanced context, and opposing points of view. Retrospection and enhanced context will introduce information that may or may not have been available or obvious at the time treatment was rendered, possible courses of action which may or may not have been logistically possible under the circumstances, and with a hindsight knowledge of the implications of clinical decisions made in real time. Consequently, the trial will develop three versions of reality, respectively, that of the plaintiff, the defendant, and the jury. The psychology of persuasion and the skill of storytelling are essential skills for litigators, since, in the end, the reality as developed by the jury will determine the outcome of the trial.

Judge, Jury Selection, and Juries

The presiding judge in a medical malpractice case may bring attitudes and implicit biases to their interpretation of the rules of evidence and may or may not have experience and knowledge specifically relevant to medical malpractice trials. The judge, court clerk, and court reporter will be present for the trial: the judge will rule on issues of evidence and procedure, the court clerk will admit witnesses and evidence, and the reporter will develop a transcript of the trial. The judge and court clerk must at all times be treated with respect. Contempt of court is defined as being any act of willful disobedience to, or disregard of, a judge or court order or any misconduct in the presence of a court. Civil contempt may be punished by fine, incarceration, or both.

In most jurisdictions, the right to a jury trial is presupposed under the Seventh Amendment of the US Constitution but may be waived. Juries are complex and diverse body of persons assembled under oath to render an impartial verdict based on the evidence presented to them at trial. Potential jurors are randomly selected from voters' list or other public databases. Jury selection is the process whereby potential legally qualified jurors are screened, dismissed, or selected for jury service at a particular trial. *Voir dire* is the process by which potential juries are interviewed in order to identify prejudices, involvement, relationship, implicit biases, beliefs or attitudes, or other conflicts of interest. Civil trials require six jurors, although there may be one or more alternatives in the event of inability, illness, or misconduct.

Juries are necessarily composed of affective and cognitive decision-makers. Affective ("right brain") decision-makers (1) are emotional and creative, more interested in people and drama than problems; (2) use deductive reasoning which is primarily emotional and impulsive; and (3) become committed to their decisions early and subsequently filter, accept, discard, or distort additional new information to maintain internal consistency with the decision they have reached. On the other hand, cognitive ("left brain") decision-makers are (1) more interested in problems than people, (2) use logic and inductive reasoning to make decisions, and (3) will not decide until they feel satisfied that all available information has been presented. Moreover, all jurors will bring implicit cognitive biases and subconscious attitudes to the courtroom. Biases subconsciously affect the manner by which individuals process information and make decisions, even when the biases themselves are contrary to expressed beliefs or attitudes [11]. The jury will be influenced by perceptions of the credibility of counsel, plaintiff and defendant, and witnesses: their ability to contrite on and understand the evidence presented, their interest in learning, and their perception of and engagement in the "story." Jurors will also differ in the way they respond to aural, as opposed to visual information.

Opening statements are critical to the outcome of a case since they provide initial impressions and also a framework for the jury into which they often incorporate all subsequent evidence. The opening statement is both a story and a theory of the case. Plaintiff attorneys will often outline a case based on commonly accepted notions of right and wrong behaviors or "rules of the road" [12]. The "rules of the road" strategy is to deflect the focus of the jury to the large volume of potentially confusing and conflicting information and to focus on commonly accepted undisputable standards of behavior. Nonetheless, opening statements should not be argumentative and "do no more than to inform the jury in a general way of the nature of the action and defense so that they may better be prepared to understand the evidence" [13]. The plaintiff, who has the burden of proof, will open first, although courts may at their discretion change the order of the opening statements. The outcome of a trial is usually a result of the strength of one's case rather than the weakness of the opponent's case.

Following the opening statements, the prosecution, and then the defense will present their cases in chief. The plaintiff has the burden of proof with respect to the facts and the essential elements of the cause of action (duty, breach, causation, and damages) by a preponderance of the evidence standard. The plaintiff will call and examine witnesses under oath and introduce illustrative or demonstrative evidence. At times, the plaintiff will call the defendant physician as an adverse witness for a direct examination.

Good trial testimony tells a story and repeatedly reinforces the theme of the story. The theme, usually a short phrase, is what the jury will use to draw meaning from the testimony and to maintain a sense of direction during the trial. The witnesses tell the story but the attorneys will guide the storytellers. How the story is received will have much to do with the demeanor of the storytellers, the credibility of the story, and the tone and cadence of the conversation between the attorney and the storyteller on stage (at trial). In a medical malpractice trial, the emotional elements can be overwhelming; the provider is accused and attacked on his or her knowledge, skill, or judgment, whereas the plaintiff may arrive visibly injured and tell a story of how his or her life has been forever altered. The use of drama can captivate and control a jury. Important elements of a story include the "who," "when," "what," "where," and "why." Good stories have a beginning, a middle, and an end, again tied together with a theme.

In general, the person testifying will be introduced to the jury through questions posed by counsel. Stipulation refers to an agreement between attorneys concerning any matter, such as facts and issue, prior to a deposition or prior to trial. Common stipulations may include agreements to allow copies rather than original documents to be admitted into evidence or qualifications of a witness. The trial court judge has discretion to accept or reject any stipulation made by counsel. Stipulations can save a great deal of time; however, especially with qualifications of expert witnesses, stipulations may result in opportunities gained and lost.

The advance preparation of witnesses for trial, like for deposition, is an expectation. There are magic words that arise during testimony such as the reliability of a treatise, standards, or probable which should be defined in advance since their legal implications may differ from common usage. Witnesses should have reviewed relevant documents, including the depositions of opposing parties and those of experts. During direct examination, the attorney will question a witness they have called upon to testify; defense may call the defendant provider on direct exam; and similarly plaintiff's counsel may call the plaintiff on direct exam. Every question asked during a direct examination should have a purpose in relation to the theory of the case or the elements of the cause of action; often the questioning will follow the jury instructions for the action. Direct examination is the opportunity for the plaintiff, defendant, and witnesses to tell their stories through a logical sequence of open-ended ("non-leading") questions. Direct examination is the chance to "humanize" the witness, establish their credibility, and develop a relationship between the witness and the jury. Questioning on direct examination is designed to elicit the background to the story and for the courtroom to collectively relive a reality from the testifying witness' perspective.

Cross-examination is the examination of a witness by opposing counsel and occurs immediately after the conclusion of a direct examination. Cross-examination is composed of only leading questions. Leading questions are phrased so as to contain the answer within the question. Examples of leading questions might include the following:

- You examined Ms. Jones, did you not?
- Ms. Jones complained of chest pain, didn't she?
- It is true that one would order EKG on a patient with chest pain, isn't it?
- You did not order an EKG on Ms. Jones at that time, did you?

During a cross-examination, counsel will not ask questions to which they do not already know the answer. In addition, the witness on cross-examination is prevented from elaboration or explanation. The presentation of anything other than a simple answer by the witness will be immediately interrupted by counsel. The questioning on cross-examination is highly structured and require simple answers, usually "yes" or "no." A good cross-examination represents a yes-no logic diagram where the answers lead the witnesses' testimony down a path to a desired end.

Following the completion of a cross-examination, counsel who called the witness may conduct

a redirect examination to allow for some clarification or explanation of the answers elicited from the witness during the cross-examination. The redirect examination is an opportunity to "rehabilitate" a witness and to rebut or clarify potentially inconsistent or misspoken testimony, rebut evidence, or address insinuations or inferences which may have been raised during cross-examination. The scope of redirect examination is limited to the scope of cross-examination and cannot be used to introduce new evidence or theories. Finally, the redirect examination occurs only at the discretion of the judge.

Impeachment of a witness occurs when an attorney notes an inconsistency in statements made at deposition or at prior testimony, with what is stated in court under oath. Counsel will not usually impeach his or her own witness.

Objections will be common at trial; sometimes for strategic reasons, an attorney may choose not object when an objection would otherwise be reasonable. Rules of evidence govern what may and may not be considered when the jury decides the outcome of a case. The reasons behind objections are many and may include relevance, hearsay, leading, asked and answered/repetitious, speculation, and argumentative, for example. Following an objection, the judge will rule as to the objection: an objection is "sustained when the judge upholds the objection and disallows the question, testimony, or evidence; an objection is 'overruled' when the judge does not uphold the objection and allows the question, testimony, or evidence to proceed. In general, following an objection, the judge will help the witness by asking him or her to proceed. Nonetheless, with objections 'a bell once rung cannot be unrung," and even if the testimony is overruled or stricken from the record, the jury will have heard it.

The admissibility of evidence requires authenticity and materiality; however, in order to be admissible, the probative value of the evidence must outweigh any potential to prejudice or bias the proceedings. The rules of evidence govern the admissibility of evidence, and evidence must be introduced after a foundation is laid by counsel for the proof it would offer. Evidence at trial may be (1) real, (2) demonstrative, (3) documentary, or (4) testimonial. Real evidence is physical evidence. Demonstrative evidence is illustrative usually in the form of charts and diagrams. Documentary evidence include chart entries, letters, or other documents in physical or electronic form. Testimonial evidence is related by testimony. Courtroom exhibits include models, machines, diagrams, charts, photographs, videos, or anything else, other than testimony which may be presented at trial. Today's courtrooms are increasingly sophisticated with respect to technology, and many have not only large video screens to allow projection to the entire courtroom but also individual screens from of the jury members, the judge, and the counsel, to allow for close-up and undistracted viewing. Exhibits need to be admitted through a foundation to ensure relevance and through a strict procedural process.

Expert witnesses are necessary to help judges and juries interpret complex fields of knowledge wherein the expert has a specialized knowledge that will assist the court in its understanding of the issues in a case. The Federal Rules of Evidence [14] state:

> A witness who is qualified as an expert by knowledge, skill, experience, training, or education may testify in the form of an opinion or otherwise if:
> (a) the expert's scientific, technical, or other specialized knowledge will help the trier of fact to understand the evidence or to determine a fact in issue;
> (b) the testimony is based on sufficient facts or data;
> (c) the testimony is the product of reliable principles and methods; and,
> (d) the expert has reliably applied the principles and methods to the facts of the case.

Federal Rules of Evidence. Rule 702. Testimony by Expert Witnesses. 2017.

US Courts will use either the Frye [15] or Daubert [16] standards to qualify an expert witness; Daubert is the federal standard, and Frye still remains in effect in many states, such as NY. Under the *Frye* standard, the only inquiry for the trial court is whether the scientific techniques used are generally accepted by other scientists as reliable. The Daubert standard considers the validity of a scientific methodology by weighing: (1) whether the theory or technique in question can be and has been tested; (2) whether it has been subjected to peer review and publication; (3) its known or potential error rate; (4) the existence and maintenance of standards controlling its operation; and (5) whether it has attracted widespread acceptance within a relevant scientific community [17]. Accordingly, experts may testify about their conclusions in a case so long as their analysis is scientifically sound. In reaching their conclusions, experts can rely on information that similar professionals normally rely upon and draw inferences and conclusions of the elements of a cause of action, regarding especially: (1) delineation of the applicable standard of care and (2) determination of whether the defendant provider deviated from the applicable standard of care and whether the deviation proximately caused the injuries to the plaintiff. Additional experts may be called to help with discovery such as computer forensic experts; and additional experts commonly called upon at trial to assess damages and determine a fair monetary award as damages include physiatrists and vocational experts to determine the level of functioning and prognosis; psychologists to assess the impact of pain and suffering; and economists to help determine lost wage and opportunities, the costs of future care, and other expenses.

The closing argument is an argument, not simply a summary. The closing argument will be a logical reiteration of key facts together with reasonable inferences. Frequently the closing argument will include key portions of the jury instructions and a discussion of the necessary burden of proof with a lay translation of the meaning of "preponderance of the evidence." The closing argument is part theory, theme, facts, expert opinion, the law, and reasonable inference.

The exact wording of jury instructions in a civil trial may vary by jurisdiction and is a statement of the law, read to the jury at the conclusion of a trial by the judge, and an iteration of the burden of proof. In some cases, the jury instructions may have been partially discussed at opening and closing arguments by counsel; however, here the judge reads the instructions aloud to the jury. Publications of Pattern Jury Instructions or PJIs are available by jurisdiction. Requests for the use of one of the potential alternate wordings of jury instruction may be requested by counsel, but not necessarily honored by the court. One of the jurors will be elected to the role of foreperson or presiding juror. The bailiff will ensure that there is no communication with the jury during deliberations. Following the jury charge, the jury will deliberate and return a verdict. If the jurors cannot agree on a verdict, a hung jury results, leading to a mistrial; in such a rare case, the case may be retried at a later date before a new jury.

Post-Trial

In general, the non-prevailing party in a lawsuit may seek to appeal the final verdict to a higher court; however there must be grounds for an appeal, beyond that of an adverse verdict. State and federal appeal courts review the decisions of lower trial courts, depending on the court of prior jurisdiction. Appellate courts will review the evidence, the application of the laws, and the findings of a lower court to determine if the determination made by the lower court was reasonable. The reviewing appellate court also will review the lower court's record for "reversible errors" such as rulings on objections, evidentiary rulings, or other procedural errors.

Conclusions

Lawsuits are intimidating to providers since the emotional impact of an accusation can be devastating to a conscientious provider who has had a poor clinical outcome; the courtroom is a foreign place, where the persons and procedures are unfamiliar. In the event of a poor outcome, early involvement of risk management and counsel can be helpful to advise and guide even if a lawsuit has not been filed. Evidence should be preserved, often in accordance with protocols, especially if the evidence may be evanescent. Providers must be careful to not discuss the case with anyone, since in some states, even peer-reviewed statutes offer only superficial protection. Providers should choose their counsel carefully, consider the engagement of a consulting attorney where it may be potentially useful, and work closely with their counsel to help prepare every aspect of their defense.

References

1. Szalados, J.E. Statutes of limitations. In Szalados JE, Smith W, Wright W. Law and ethics in neurocritical care. Neurocritical Care Society. 2019. pp 22–23.
2. SCA Hygiene Prods. Aktiebolag v. First Quality Baby Prods., LLC, 137 S. Ct. 954, 960 (2017) (quoting Petrella v. Metro-Goldwyn-Mayer, Inc., 134 S. Ct. 1962, 1967, 1973 (2014)).
3. Tenneco Inc. v. Amerisure Mut. Ins. Co., 281 Mich. App. 429, 456–57, 761 N.W.2d 846, 863–64 (2008); see also Veysey v. Nelson, 2017 UT App 77, 7, 397 P.3d 846, 848.
4. Kaplan v. Mamelak, 162 Cal. App. 4th 637 (2008).
5. NYS CPLR § 214-(a)(2018). ("An action for medical, dental or podiatric malpractice must be commenced within two years and six months of the act, omission or failure complained of or last treatment where there is continuous treatment for the same illness, injury or condition which gave rise to the said act, omission or failure; provided, however, that: (a) where the action is based upon the discovery of a foreign object in the body of the patient, the action may be commenced within one year of the date of such discovery or of the date of discovery of facts which would reasonably lead to such discovery, whichever is earlier; and (b) where the action is based upon the alleged negligent failure to diagnose cancer or a malignant tumor, whether by act or omission, the action may be commenced within two years and six months of the later of either (i) when the person knows or reasonably should have known of such alleged negligent act or omission and knows or reasonably should have known that such alleged negligent act or omission has caused injury, provided, that such action shall be commenced no later than seven years from such alleged negligent act or omission, or (ii) the date of the last treatment where there is continuous treatment for such injury, illness or condition.").
6. Wehrman v. United States, 830 F.2d 1480 (8th Cir.1987) at 1483.

7. Otto v. Nat'l Inst. of Health, 815 F.2d 985, 988 (4th Cir.1987).
8. NY Jud L § 474-A (2015).
9. Braswell v. United States, 487 U.S. 99, 107–08 (1988).
10. Fisher v. United States, 425 U.S. 391 (1976) (rejected but discussed the doctrine); see United States v. Doe (Doe I), 465 U.S. 605 (1984). *See also* Charles Doyle. Supreme Court Recognition of Fifth Amendment Protection for Acts of Production. Congressional Research Service. The Library of Congress. January 2, 2004. Available online at: https://fas.org/sgp/crs/misc/RL32184.pdf.
11. Cherry K. What is cognitive bias? Verywellmind. July 19, 2020. Available online at: https://www.verywellmind.com/what-is-a-cognitive-bias-2794963.
12. Friedman R, Malone P. Rules of the road. 2nd ed. Portland: Trial Guides, LL; 2010.
13. Best v. District of Columbia, 291 U.S. 411, 54 S. Ct. 487, 78 L. Ed. 882 (1934).
14. Federal Rules of Evidence. Rule 702. Testimony by expert witnesses. 2017. Available online at: https://www.uscourts.gov/sites/default/files/evidence-rules-procedure-dec2017_0.pdf.
15. Frye v. United States, 293 F. 1013 (D.C. Cir. 1923).
16. Daubert v. Merrell Dow Pharmaceuticals, Inc., 509 U.S. 579 (1993).
17. Daubert at 592–595.

Chapter 6
Regulation of Provider Practice: State Oversight, Licensing, Credentialing, Peer Review, and the National Practitioner Data Bank

James E. Szalados

Licensing of Healthcare Professionals

Licensure may be generally defined as the process by which a regulatory body or agency attests and certifies that a healthcare practitioner meets the standard requirements to practice a specific profession within the state issuing the license. State constitutions contain enabling acts which are the legislative basis for boards; these acts or statutes define the board missions, define the grounds for discipline, and establish sanctions. Statutes which define and regulate the licensing of healthcare providers are state-specific and are justified on the basis of states' interests to regulate the behaviors within their boundaries for the promotion and maintenance of the health, safety, morals, and general welfare of their citizens. State statutes will define the particulars of, for example, requirements for licensure, criteria for licensure renewal, scope of practice, and the mechanisms for quality oversight and the processes by which actions such as review, sanction, probation, or revocation of licensure are conducted.

State Board Oversight of Medical Practice

State medical licenses are considered to be "undifferentiated" which means that medical licensure is not specialty or practice focus-based, and, in general, a board certification in a medical specialty is not an absolute requirement for medical

J. E. Szalados (✉)
Director, Surgical and Neurocritical Care Units, Rochester Regional Health System at Rochester General Hospital, Rochester, NY, USA

The Szalados Law Firm, Hilton, NY, USA
e-mail: james.szalados@rochesterregional.org; jszalados@aol.com

J. E. Szalados (ed.), *The Medical-Legal Aspects of Acute Care Medicine*,
https://doi.org/10.1007/978-3-030-68570-6_6

licensure. State medical boards are state-level agencies, authorized by state constitution and statutes, which serve the public through the oversight of medical practice within that state [1]. Approximately 70 state and territorial medical boards regulate the practices of medicine within their borders at present. Medical licensure is also not transferrable between the states; each state sets its own rules, regulations, and process for licensure. Nonetheless, there is some level of reciprocity between some states through the Interstate Medical Licensure Compact (IMLC). The IMLC is a process by which a physician holding a valid medical license in one of the participating states can obtain a license in another participating state through a simplified procedure. Although the IMLC creates a simplified pathway for licensure through reciprocity, it does not otherwise change the requirements and standards for licensure and does not modify any of the participating states' Medical Practice Acts [2].

Professional practice, granted through state licensure, is a privilege and is not a right. Thus, a duly educated, trained, and certified individual has neither a right to licensure nor a right to practice their profession without state approval. The laws and regulations of each state specify the rights and responsibilities of practitioners and those of the board; these laws and regulations are well defined within individual state statutes, commonly referred to as the state Medical Practice Act. Boards are accorded broad state agency powers to interpret and enforce the Medical Practice Act. It is widely held that professional disciplinary boards meet two complementary public policy purposes: (1) to protect the public and (2) to protect the standing of the profession in the eyes of the public. Thus, character-based misconduct, albeit unrelated to professional capabilities, may cause public mistrust of the profession, which in turn reflects on the state Board. The standing of a profession in the eyes of the public is vital to the element of trust that is at the core of professional relationships; without trust, patients would be hesitant to seek healthcare [3]. Boards which oversee a group of professionals will almost uniformly have leadership or representation profession, either as a board chair or a chair of its operating committees; often such professional leadership is mandated by statute in the relevant practice act. Licensing statutes are a mechanism for physicians to control entry into the medical profession, enforce disciplinary actions against their colleagues, and control the delivery of healthcare to the community. Professional oversight is considered important because it is widely recognized that "the lay public is incapable of evaluating the quality of medical services" and that only the "professionals themselves have sufficient control over specialized knowledge required for such an evaluation" [4]. Therefore, the protection of the public is generally recognized as the main rationale for the state medical boards [5].

Unauthorized Practice of Medicine

One mechanism by which states regulate the quality of medical care provided is through medical licensure. A legal definition for the unauthorized practice of medicine might be "a person providing medical advice or treatment without a medical license." The unauthorized practice of medicine may include diagnosis, treatment, or the prescribing of medications, is illegal in all states, and may subject violators to criminal and civil liability. In 1889, the US Supreme Court in *Dent v. West Virginia* unanimously held that states could regulate medicine, and other professions, via professional licensing boards [6]. *Dent* resulted in the delegation of wide discretion to the states with respect to the content and enforcement of medical licensing laws, subject to state and federal constitutional law protections. Subsequently, the US Supreme Court, in *Hawker v. New York*, further clarified that states could regulate professional licensees by adding new qualifications, which could be applied to those who had previously been licensed and were in practice as well as new applicants. The ruling in *Dent* also reinforced the precepts that states had the authority to revoke professional licensure based on a conviction that supported a reasonable belief of an applicant's or licensee's poor moral character [7].

In *Board of Medical Quality Assurance v. Andrews* [8], the Religious School of Natural Hygiene (RSNH), a healing church which operated the California Health Sanctuary near Hollister, California, provided supervised fasting for those "who seek health restoration, knowledge of health maintenance and experience in healthful living." Business cards stated that the organization specifically did not use drugs, medicines, vaccinations, blood transfusions, or X-rays. Nonetheless, the organization articulated a philosophy that many physical conditions could be cured by undergoing supervised periods of fasting. RSNH was brought to the attention of the California Board of Medical Quality Assurance (Board) on appeal from a trial court which had determined that pursuant to Business and Professions Code § 125.5 1, RSNH had engaged in the unlawful practice of medicine. The board issued an injunction against RSNH and upheld the decision of the trial court. Appellants then challenged the ruling and the injunction based on an argument that the board and its position infringed the constitutional rights of RSNH to a free exercise of religion under the First Amendment. The board determined that:

> First, there is no evidence that [the] statute was meant to confer protection for religious practices beyond that already conferred by the free exercise clause of the United States Constitution. The absence of any such evidence is itself persuasive of the contrary conclusion. This is so because to confer such extraordinary protection by means of the unusual route of an exemption from a licensing scheme would be a remarkable exercise of legislative power. Statutes conferring exemptions from regulatory schemes are narrowly construed. … Here what is involved is not faith healing but the practice of medicine, and therefore the exemption does not apply. The record here is replete with examples of appellants' conduct in purporting to have special knowledge of the body's physical symptoms and needs and further undertaking to diagnose ailments and to prescribe treatment for those ills. The conduct and the treatment goes far beyond prayer and reliance on divine intervention.

In the case of *Board of Medical Quality Assurance v. Andrews*, the state board of medicine exercised its jurisdiction not only over matters specifically pertaining to the practice of medicine but also "activities that are customarily performed by licensed providers" even where similar activities might otherwise be constitutionally protected (such as freedom of speech or religion). A similar finding was reached in North Carolina in the case of *State v. Nelson*, where an unlicensed iridologist prescribed colonic irrigations to the public. This case underscores the broad reach of Medical Practice Act powers in the protection of the public [9].

More recently, in *Brooks v. Tex. Med. Board* [10], the Texas Medical Board issued a cease-and-desist order to a chiropractor, Brooks, after determining that she had engaged in the unlicensed practice of medicine through offerings of treatments on her website, which exceeded the scope of practice for chiropractic. Brooks' website identified her as a "biomedical doctor," "board certified pediatric chiropractor," "craniosacral therapist," and "one of only a few pediatric biomedical doctors in the area." Brooks' website went on to state that Brooks engaged in "mentoring and consulting other physicians and practitioners," that she "assists her patients in achieving optimum health by utilizing biomedical and functional medicine," was concerned about "dysfunction in the body" rather than "the label of the disease;" and that she focused on "diagnosing the cause of the problem rather than treating just the symptoms." Listed "Services" offered by Brooks included autism, craniosacral therapy, chiropractic, pediatric nutrition, and biomedical intervention. In response to a complaint, the board conducted an investigation and convened a disciplinary panel of board representatives which resulted in a cease-and-desist hearing. Brooks challenged that order by filing suit in a Travis County district court which then affirmed the Board's decision; and Brooks appealed. In its consideration of the evidence, the appellate court noted that chiropractors, when using their names on any written or printed professional identification, must designate the healing art that they are licensed to practice by using either "chiropractor," "doctor, D.C.," "doctor of chiropractic," or "D.C.," and here, Brooks had identified herself as a "biomedical doctor" and, moreover, "one of only a few pediatric biomedical doctors in the area." Further, the court noted that Brooks' website implied that she was a physician through references to her "mentoring and consulting *other* physicians and practitioners" [emphasis added]. Brooks also contended, in her appeal, that the district court had erred in concluding that the Board's order "was not made through unlawful procedure, was not in excess of statutory authority, and does not violate any statutory or constitutional provision." Specifically Brooks argued that her cease-and-desist order was the result of an improper hearing before the board rather than the State Office of Administrative Hearings (SOAH); the court again also ruled against Brooks citing the precise language of the state statute with respect to the procedural requirements.

In the case of *State v. Pac. Health Ctr.*, [11] a practitioner of "Qi," the Oriental medicine concept of managing energy flow in the body using electrodermal testing ("EDT"), offered his services to "diagnose" physical conditions and then provided remedies, such as dietary changes, nutritional supplements, homeopathic mixtures, and herbs, to "treat" such conditions. The appellate court in its ruling stated, in part:

> Whether a person is engaged in the practice of medicine within the meaning of [Washington law] and is, therefore, required to have a valid license under [Washington law] depends on the facts of the case and not on the name of the procedure employed, the origin of the procedure, or a legislative lack of clairvoyance.... Using EDT as an instrumentality to determine, or 'diagnose,' medical conditions in a patient and then recommending and selling specific remedies to that person to address those conditions are practices that unquestion-

> ably fall within the valid police power the legislature exercised when it regulated the practice of medicine.
>
> *State v. Pac. Health Ctr., Inc.*, at 166–167

Thus, a substantial amount of court litigation resulting from state medical board actions is based on decisions regarding "the practice of medicine" and "scope of practice." [See also Chap. 7.] It is clear that the medical boards must protect the public from non-providers claiming to offer diagnostic and therapeutic services which are traditionally or specifically under the purview of the practice of medicine. The scope of practice of advanced practice providers continues to evolve; however, where medical services are advertised or offered by naturopaths [12], homeopaths, iridologists [13], alternative medical treatments, acupuncturists [14], or even chiropractors, the state boards of medicine is authorized to, has, and will likely exercise its jurisdictional authority.

There is a split in the courts regarding the issue of whether the medical director of an insurance company or health plan is practicing medicine under his or her utilization review function in the course of coverage/coverage denial decisions. In 1999, the Ohio Attorney General determined that physicians performing utilization review for insurance companies are not practicing medicine, and therefore the decisions of medical directors in Ohio were beyond the disciplinary reach of the Ohio State Medical Board [15].

On the other hand, in *Murphy v. Board of Medical Examiners of the State of Arizona* [16], the Arizona Court of Appeals held that a medical director's conduct was in fact subject to review by the Board of Medical Examiners to the extent that he or she makes medical decisions regarding "medical necessity." Murphy is a lead case which directly addressed the question of whether a medical director in an MCO is practicing medicine when that medical director is prospectively reviewing a treatment, for medical necessity, when that treatment was recommended by the patient's provider. In *Murphy*, the medical director of Arizona's Blue Cross and Blue Shield plans refused to authorize gall bladder surgery on a patient, finding it was not "medically necessary" after reviewing the patient's medical records, thereby contradicting the advice of the patient's surgeon. After the pathology substantiated the need for surgery, the patient filed a complaint with the state Insurance Department alleging that Blue Cross failed to honor its subscriber contract; this complaint was dismissed. The surgeon then filed a complaint against Murphy with the Arizona Board of Medical Examiners, alleging that Murphy's coverage denial constituted "unprofessional conduct" and "medical incompetence" and that it interfered with the physician-patient relationship. The board investigated and issued an "advisory letter of concern" to Dr. Murphy citing "an inappropriate medical decision which could have caused harm to a patient." Murphy then appealed the decision of the board in court where the trial court held that the board had the right to determine if Murphy's decision was medically reasonable. On appeal, the appellate court affirmed the jurisdiction of the board to review Murphy's medical decisions, since he was a state-licensed physician, citing the Blue Cross subscriber contract which read, in part:

> . . . Dr. Murphy is an employee who makes medical decisions for his employer on whether surgeries or other non-experimental procedures are medically necessary. Such decisions are not insurance decisions but rather medical decisions because they require Dr. Murphy to determine whether the procedure is "appropriate for the symptoms and diagnosis of the condition," whether it is to be "provided for the diagnosis" care or treatment and whether it is "in accordance with standards of good medical practice in Arizona."
> 949 P2d at 536

Finally, in the DC case of *Morris v. Dist. of Col. Bd. of Medicine*, the District of Columbia Court of Appeals reached a different decision but on a substantially different fact pattern. Here, Morris, a physician licensed in Maryland but not in DC, was employed as medical director of Blue Cross in DC. Subsequently, some 2 years after beginning his employment, the District of Columbia Board of Medicine notified the President and CEO of Blue Cross that Morris had not obtained a license to practice in the district and that he should either complete an application or "cease and desist from the unlicensed practice of medicine." Simultaneously, the board assessed Morris with a fine of $3600 and warned of disciplinary action. Since Morris contested the decision, the board served Morris with a letter stating its intent to deny Morris' licensure application. Testimony at the hearing established that Blue Cross did not require a license to practice medicine for a person to perform Dr. Morris's functions; in addition, in this case, the medical director participated solely in post-treatment certification, participated in a committee hearing which reviewed the individual cases but was not a voting member of the committee, and reviewed the committee's decisions but only for purposes of clarity. The Board, despite its conclusion that Dr. Morris had practiced medicine during the relevant time, found that "[t]he duties and responsibilities of [his] position were exclusively administrative." Here, based on the specific facts of this case, the court found that Morris was not engaged in the practice of medicine while performing his administrative duties at Blue Cross.

> On the record of this case, however, no substantial evidence supports the finding that Dr. Morris practiced medicine during the time alleged. A contrary determination would subject a person in Dr. Morris's position not just to denial of a license and a civil fine, but also to the possibility of criminal punishment. See § 2-3310.7. And that could be so even if the person were not a trained physician such as Dr. Morris but, say, a business executive experienced in medical administration. Hence, the deference this court owes the Board's interpretation of the statute must be accompanied by concern that an overbroad reading of "practice of medicine" would be a trap for the unwary.
> *Morris v. Dist. of Col. Bd. of Medicine* at 368

Unauthorized Practice of Nursing

Nursing is a licensed profession subject to laws and regulations similar to those applicable to medicine. Nursing Practice Acts parallel the Medical Practice Acts and establish the requirements for licensure, scope of practice, grounds and procedures for discipline, and the penalties pertaining to the practice of nursing within a particular state. The practice of nursing without a license is a crime, generally a misdemeanor; however, felony charges may be possible in some states. The training of nurses may endorse different specialties and practice styles; some states may recognize additional nursing certifications beyond that of the basic registered nurse license, but some do not. In addition to the state boards of medicine, the state boards of nursing examiners have also enforced actions against the unauthorized practice of medicine by nurses. Thus, nurses are subject to potential discipline for the unauthorized practice of medicine; however, lay persons and others are potentially subject to prosecution for the unauthorized practice of nursing.

Although the traditional nurse licensing statutes portrayed nursing practice as a profession that required the supervision or direction of a physician, the contemporary recognized scope of nursing practice has become broader to establish nursing as a profession providing independent nursing diagnosis and treatment and the exercise of independent nursing judgment.

The issue of whether the practice of midwifery in fact falls within the scope of medical practice and therefore prohibited to any but licensed providers has been extensively litigated. In the case of *Leigh v. Board of Registration in Nursing* [17], the Supreme Court of Massachusetts upheld the disciplinary actions imposed by the Board of Registration in Nursing which had concluded that the alleged violations constituted "gross misconduct in the practice of nursing." Here, Leigh was a professional midwife who attends women at normal, uncomplicated, home births, the Board of Nursing regulated "nurses practicing in the expanding role," and the "Nurse Midwife" represented one such expanded role. The Board's regulations mandated certification requirements for nurses to practice as a nurse midwife. Leigh, not certified as a nurse midwife, contended that she practiced as a "lay midwife," for which no regulations were established, and was therefore not subject to the Board's regulations. The court rejected Leigh's claims.

The Process of Disciplinary Actions of State Medical (and Nursing Boards)

Discipline of licensees is a substantial function of boards. Disciplinary board actions against physicians, pharmacists, providers, and other healthcare professionals are not malpractice actions, although the two may co-exist simultaneously or in sequence. Thus, it is critical to realize that disciplinary actions may not be covered under professional liability insurance policies, although some carriers do offer optional riders for such coverage. Disciplinary board actions against professionals generally do not presume innocence at the onset; rather, in contradistinction to judicial process, the proceedings by which disciplinary boards conduct investigations and gather evidence and witnesses are vastly different from malpractice actions (Table 6.1).

Health professionals should also realize that the consequences of disciplinary actions by a state licensing or professional regulatory board are significantly more serious than professional malpractice since board actions affect licensure and therefore one's ability to practice and earn a living in one's profession. Disciplinary actions related to unprofessional or criminal misconduct are much more straightforward for a board to pursue than issues which are based on challenges to professional competence [18]. Penalties imposed by licensing boards include censure, reprimand, fines, license suspension, probation, or license revocation.

Disciplinary boards are comprised of investigators and medical coordinators, who investigate and evaluate complaints, attorneys who prosecute cases, and administrative law judges who preside over hearings and support staff. Almost uniformly, states require representation by some number of lay members on the Disciplinary Board, partly on the theory that lay people are more likely to hold professionals accountable. Disciplinary boards often include other peer and frequently the chair is a physician. Grounds for professional discipline by state boards include impairment, practicing without a license, and a general category of actions labeled "unprofessional conduct." Definitions of "professional misconduct" will vary by jurisdiction and by profession. Professional misconduct may range, for example, from professional conduct that is "fraudulent, grossly negligent, grossly incompetent" so as to arguably render a licensee "professionally incompetent" or "morally unfit" to practice under his or her license; a pattern of complaints, malpractice, or other similar quality concerns; failure to maintain adequate medical records; the ordering of excessive tests and treatments; failure to respond to board correspondence; or failure to wear one's identification badge. For example, a list of violations which constitute professional misconduct in the State of New York are listed in Table 6.2. Each state will define its own bases for misconduct; however, states also reciprocate with each other, so that where one has been found in violation of misconduct definitions in one state, other states will use that sanction to enforce their own restrictions. In the case of *Haley v. Medical Disciplinary Board*, the Supreme Court of Washington determined that a physician's sexual conduct with his patient indicates a "lack of trustworthiness," increasing a "reasonable apprehension" that he may "abuse the trust inherent in professional status" [19]. The case of *In re Kindschi* [20] addresses a situation where the Medical Board of Washington had suspended a physician's license to practice medicine after he was convicted of tax fraud; although the tax fraud was not specifically related to the physician's diagnosis, care, or treatment of any patient, the court nonetheless adopted a broad view of improper conduct and the professional practice.

Administrative agencies must follow fair procedures and provide due process. The principle of substantive due process derives from the Constitution. In *Dent*, the Supreme Court stated that when challenging a licensee's ability to practice, disciplinary actions must be clear and detailed while showing common sense rationality [21]. The 14th Amendment of the US Constitution § 1 states that:

> All persons born or naturalized in the United States, and subject to the jurisdiction thereof, are citizens of the United States and of the state wherein they reside. No state shall make or enforce any law which shall abridge the privileges or immunities of citizens of the United

Table 6.1 Comparison of legal and disciplinary processes

Process	Legal action	Board action
Event	Cause of action arising from discrete diagnostic or therapeutic encounter	
Complaint	Plaintiff Matter of public domain Defendant on notice through service of process at onset Complaint details of allegations and relief sought	Complainant (or board survey) Public domain: allegations posed on website Defendant need not be on notice Nature of allegations need not be disclosed to the accused
Discovery	Rules governing discovery outlined in Rules of Civil Procedure, Rules of Evidence, or similar documents	"Informal" discussions or conversations with investigators are admissible Anything considered relevant may be introduced
Representation	Self or attorney	Self or attorney
Adjudication	Court usually as jury trial	Administrative hearing by a Hearing Committee of the Board
Location of hearing	Courtroom	Board offices Boardroom Hotel conference room
Rules of Evidence at trial or hearing	Rules of Evidence Hearsay prohibited Plaintiff present Evidence and witnesses generally known and disclosed	Wide range of admissible evidence Any similar cases or complaints Evidence and witnesses may or may not or be disclosed Complainant need not attend Hearsay permitted Confidential testimony permitted Human resources, employment, quality assurance files, etc.
Pre-trial or pre-hearing outcomes	Settlement Discontinuation Dismissal	Discontinuation Consent Agreement or Non-Disciplinary Order of Consent (NDOC)
Potential penalties	Financial (generally as insurer indemnification) National Practitioner Data Bank (NPDB) reporting Credentialing reporting	Licensure censure, reprimand, sanction, revocation Stipulation of additional education, proctoring, or supervision Monetary fines NPDB reporting Credentialing reporting Potential exclusion from federally funded payment programs or insurer panels
Appeal	Courts of Appeal	Administrative Court

Table 6.2 National Practitioner Data Bank (NPDB) reporting requirements (after the US Department of Health and Human Services. National Practitioner Data Bank) [52]

Applicable law	Reporting entity	Data and/or information reported	Reported professional
Title IV	Medical malpractice insurers, self-insured healthcare entities	Payments made on behalf of a healthcare practitioner resulting from a written claim or judgment	Practitioners
	State medical and dental boards	Adverse licensure actions related to professional competence or conduct	Physicians and dentists
	Hospitals Healthcare organizations or entities engaged in peer review	Professional review actions related to professional competence or conduct adversely affecting clinical privileges for a period longer than 30 days Voluntary surrender or restriction of clinical privileges while under review, or in order to avoid an investigation	Physicians and dentists Other practitioners (optional)
	Professional societies engaged in formal peer review	Professional review actions related to professional competence or conduct that adversely affects society membership	Physicians and dentists
	Drug Enforcement Administration (DEA)	DEA controlled substance registration actions	Practitioners
	Department of Health and Human Services (HHS); Office of Inspector General (OIG)	Exclusions from participation in Medicare, Medicaid, and/or other federally funded health programs (i.e., CHAMPUS)	Practitioners
§ 1921	Peer review organizations	Negative actions or findings by peer review organizations	Practitioners
	Private accreditation organizations	Adverse actions or findings	Healthcare entities, providers, suppliers
	State licensing and certification authorities	State licensure and certification actions as a result of a formal disciplinary proceeding Adverse actions such as licensure revocation, suspension, reprimand, censure, probation Dismissal or closure of the formal proceedings by reason of surrendering the license or certification agreement or contract for participation in a government healthcare program or leaving the state or jurisdiction Loss of the right to apply for, or to renew, a professional license or certification agreement or contract for participation in a government healthcare program Publicly available negative action or finding	Practitioners, healthcare entities, providers, suppliers
	State law enforcement agencies State Medicaid Fraud Control Units (MFCUs) State agencies administering or supervising a state healthcare program	Exclusion from a state healthcare program Healthcare-related civil judgments in state court Healthcare-related state criminal convictions Adjudicated actions or decisions arising from payment, provision, or delivery of a healthcare	Practitioners, providers, suppliers

§ 1128E	Federal government agencies Health plans	Federal licensure and certification actions Formal or official actions including but not limited to revocation, suspension, reprimand, censure, or probation of DEA certification or licensure, for example Dismissal or closure of the proceedings by reason of surrendering the license or certification agreement or contract for participation in a government healthcare program or leaving the state or jurisdiction Loss of the right to apply for, or renew, a license or certification agreement or contract of participation in a government healthcare program Publicly available negative action or finding Healthcare-related civil judgments in federal or state court Healthcare-related criminal convictions in federal or state court Exclusions from participation in a federal healthcare program Other adjudicated actions or decisions related to the payment, provision, or delivery of a healthcare item or service	Practitioners, providers, suppliers

> States; nor shall any state deprive any person of life, liberty, or property, without due process of law; nor deny to any person within its jurisdiction the equal protection of the laws.

State courts have further recognized that professional regulation must follow due process. In the NY case of *Barsky v. Board of Regents of University of State of New York* [22], the US Supreme Court opined that:

> It is one thing thus to recognize the freedom which the Constitution wisely leaves to the States in regulating the professions. It is quite another thing, however, to sanction a State's deprivation or partial destruction of a man's professional life on grounds having no possible relation to fitness, intellectual or moral, to pursue his profession. Implicit in the grant of discretion to a State's medical board is the qualification that it must not exercise its supervisory powers on arbitrary, whimsical or irrational considerations. A license cannot be revoked because a man is red-headed or because he was divorced, except for a calling, if such there be, for which red-headedness or an unbroken marriage may have some rational bearing. If a State licensing agency lays bare its arbitrary action, or if the State law explicitly allows it to act arbitrarily, that is precisely the kind of State action which the Due Process Clause forbids.

The implications of due process increase as the potential severity of the disciplinary action increases; the greater the potential penalty, the greater the due process implication.

The Complaint Process

The states of board complaint resolution are composed of four main stages: (1) intake, (2) investigation, (3) pre-hearing preparations, and (4) and the administrative hearing. The exact process by which state boards provide oversight and discipline varies by state. Allegations or suspicions of misconduct may originate, confidentially, from almost any source, including the general public, hospital administration, or colleagues [23]. In general, complaints are generated mostly from patients, former patients, and their friends and family members who report being treated poorly. Many states have provisions in their laws and regulations that govern professionals so that other licensed health professionals are legally required to report colleagues whom they suspect may be guilty of misconduct, unprofessional conduct, or impairment. In many states, an abject failure to report suspected instances of misconduct itself is misconduct. Reports by colleagues may also be channeled through a hospital committee, a local or state medical society, or a professional practice association, who then are similarly mandated to pass such a report to the state. At least one study has suggested that disciplinary action among practicing physicians by medical boards is strongly associated with unprofessional behaviors while in medical school [24].

Once an allegation is made against a professional, it may be immediately made public, often posted on the board's website, even before any investigation, hearing, or board decision has occurred. In general, even if the preliminary investigations fail to produce evidence to proceed with further investigations and a hearing, and the case is closed, the record of the investigation will remain in board files for future reference.

The Process of Disciplinary Boards

Discovery is the process by which evidence is gathered in preparation for a trial or an administrative hearing. In a criminal or civil action, plaintiff's counsel or prosecutors must conform to rules by which evidence is gathered. For example, in a criminal trial, investigative errors such as failures to obtain warrants or administer a Miranda warning will result in that evidence being inadmissible; moreover all future evidence stemming from improperly obtained evidence will be inadmissible as stemming from "the fruit of a poisoned tree." Similarly, civil actions, such as malpractice, the rules regarding interrogatories, subpoenas, witness testimony, depositions, and the scope of discovery, are limited by the Rules of Civil Procedure and the Rules of Evidence. Board investigation, following the initial intake, may or may not require review by a medical consultant.

Complaints are referred to investigators and staff of the disciplinary board who often have a professional background in healthcare or law and who will interview the professional by telephone or in person. Although such interviews may appear informal in the eyes of the professional, they are actually often taped or transcribed without the professional being made aware, and those statements may be later introduced into evidence. Nonetheless, licensees must cooperate with board investigations, and failure to do so may constitute professional misconduct in itself. Nonetheless, licensees may invoke their right to consult with counsel before speaking with a board investigator.

During the pre-hearing process, the board will make a decision as to whether to discontinue an investigated case, to issue a letter of warning, or to render another non-prejudicial action. If the board chooses to proceed with charges against the professional, based on probable cause, the professional must be then notified of such charges under due process. The prosecutorial staff may or may not be those that conducted the investigation.

Scope of Practice

State laws and regulations define legal scopes of practice for healthcare practitioners. The term "scope of practice" refers to the breadth and extent of privileges permitted by state law for a given class of health professional based on specific criteria such as education, training, experience, and special additional qualifications. Scope of practice for physicians, like licensure, is undifferentiated. The laws of most state laws permit physicians to perform any of the duties associated with the practice of medicine, including those duties that would otherwise fall to other allied health support staff [25] such as nurses, therapists, or nutritionists. It is necessary to distinguish between "professional scope of practice" and "legal scope of practice." Professional scope of practice, sometimes referred to as "professional competence," relies on each profession to describe the functions its members are trained and competent to perform. Such "professional competence" may evolve and change with time to include new developments in science, technology, and practice norms. On the other hand, "legal scope of practice" refers to how individual state laws and regulations define the scope of services which may be provided by members of each profession [26]. Thus, a physician's scope of practice is the sum of the relevant national certification bodies, state regulations, and hospital privileging and credentialing bodies; and thus, in reality, physician scope of practice is more based on specialty training and certification rather than within the medical degree itself.

Provider Credentialing and Privileging

Certification is a voluntary demonstration, by an individual or an institution, of successful completion of a defined set of predetermined standards defined by a non-governmental body. With respect to individuals, certification usually refers to specialty board certification for physicians, nursing certifications such as CCRN or CCRC, advanced practice nursing certification, or National Commission certification for physician assistants, for example. Certification by a national certifying body underscores the existence of a national standard of care for such professionals. Professional licensure is the process by which a governmental agency grants permission to a qualified person to practice in his or her professing or occupation. Although certification is usually a prerequisite to licensure, it is not necessarily so. A licensed provider may practice within their scope of practice without necessarily being credentialed or privileged by any institution or system, especially if their practice is a private one and does not rely on third-party reimbursement. However, by and large, both certification and licensure are usually prerequisites to either provider status on a third-party payer (insurer or managed care organization) panel and medical staff membership at a healthcare institution.

Credentialing and privileging are not synonymous. Credentialing refers to a process of credential verification, whereby an institution grants a privilege of medical staff membership, whereas privileging refers to an individual's allowed scope of practice especially as it relates to permissions to admit and discharge patients, the population one may serve, and the procedures that he or she may perform at that institution. Thus, a provider credentialed at one institution may not be granted credentials at another similar nearby facility. Similarly, a provider privileged to perform a specific procedure at one institution at which he or she is credentialed may not be granted privileges at a similar nearby institution, even though he or she is otherwise duly credentialed there. Finally, peer review is a process whereby a provider's performance is evaluated by his or her peers as a requisite to continued credentialing and privileging.

In general, the importance of the credentialing and privileging to hospitals and other healthcare institutions is threefold: (1) to protect patient safety through an oversight of the care provided at the institution, (2) to mitigate and manage liability and risk, and (3) to maintain accreditation and regulatory compliance mandates.

Hospital Staff Credentialing

Credentialing is the procedure whereby a healthcare entity, or a related organization, formally determines whether a prospective licensed healthcare provider meets the minimum criteria for admission to the medical staff. Entities which perform credentialing include hospitals, clinics, ambulatory centers, medical groups, managed care (MCO) and provider (PPO) organizations, and third-party payers (insurers). The credentialing of providers for appointment to an entity's medical staff is a procedural legal minefield with potential regulatory and liability implications for (1) the credentialing entity, (2) those serving on the evaluation committee(s), and (3) the provider submitting the credentialing application [27].

Prior to 1957, a hospital was largely immunized against liability for the actions of its employees under the *Schloendorff* Rule [28]. Under *Schloendorff*, if an employee caused a patient to be injured as part of a clinical act, the hospital was immune from liability, whereas if the patient was injured as a result of an administrative action, then the hospital could be found legally liable. The reasoning upon which the Schloendorff Rule was based argued that physicians and nurses functioned as independent contractors when treating patients and their work involved the exercise of special skills that were beyond the control of the hospital. To a large extent, the Schloendorff Rule was based on the prevailing view of charitable immunity to publically funded hospitals.

The 1957 landmark NY case of *Bing v. Thunig* [29] firmly established that hospitals do, in fact, have a responsibility for the medical care received by patients. In *Bing*, a hospital-employed nurse spilled an inflammable antiseptic on the operating room sheets while an anesthetized patient was being prepared for surgery. When the surgeon engaged the cautery device, the sheets ignited and caused serious burn injuries to the patient. The prevailing view at the time of *Bing* was that hospitals were charitable trusts deserving of special treatment under liability law and, thus, that holding hospitals liable for patient harm would constitute a misuse of public funds allocated to the hospitals. The Bing court reviewed and abolished the charitable immunity status of hospitals, establishing for the first time a rule of direct hospital liability, outside the boundaries of agency theory or employment. Specifically, the holding in Bing states that hospitals perform their mission through their doctors and nurses and that patients reasonably "expect" that the hospital as a whole will undertake to care for them.

> The conception that the hospital does not undertake to treat the patient, does not undertake to act through its doctors and nurses, but undertakes instead simply to procure them to act upon their own responsibility, no longer reflects the fact. Present-day hospitals, as their manner of operation plainly demonstrates, do far more than furnish facilities for treatment. They regularly employ on a salary basis a large staff of physicians, nurses and interns, as well as administrative and manual workers, and they charge patients for medical care and treatment, collecting for such services, if necessary, by legal action. Certainly, the person who avails himself of 'hospital facilities' expects that the hospital will attempt to cure him, not that its nurses or other employees will act on their own responsibility.
>
> Bing, 143 N.E.2d at 8

Darling v. Charleston Community Memorial Hospital [30] in 1965 set the legal precedent that a hospital could be held negligent for a failure to assess or monitor the competency of the medical staff.

> At the core of the Illinois Supreme Court's decision is its holding, for the first time ever, that hospital entities themselves, acting through both their employees and independent (non-employed) medical staff members, undertake to treat patients and that in their capacity as providers of care, hospitals owe separate duties of care to their patients directly (hence, "direct liability") which, if violated, will result in liability for the hospital entity. These direct duties of care owed by hospitals are in addition to the vicarious liability exposures hospitals have under the doctrine of *respondeat superior* for their agents' breaches of other independent duties of care owed by those agents to patients (typically having to do with the standards of hands-on medical or clinical care). [31]

Hospitals therefore began a process whereby physicians would be subject to a process of credential verification as a condition to medical staff membership. However, three key legal issues associated with credentialing duties arose: (1) the confidentiality of credentialing and peer review information, (2) restraint of trade issues, and (3) scope of immunity. Physicians denied with medical staff privileges then brought litigation against hospitals relying on the Sherman Act and state antitrust laws claiming that the credentialing process constituted an anti-competitive and potentially collusive practice of restraint of trade. The likelihood that credentialing has and continues to be used as a means for physicians to limit competition at their respective institutions, especially smaller institutions with few but powerful legacy medical staff members, is a certainty. Moreover, credentialing decisions are increasingly complicated by economic and quasi-economic pressures ("economic credentialing"); these may include, for example, (1) DRG and case mix index profiles, (2) average length of stay, (3) pay for performance data, and (4) economic performance. The AMA strongly opposes privileging or credentialing decisions based on economic factors.

Thus, credentialing is not a perfect mechanism because it was controlled by physicians whose personal interests were sometimes at odds with the hospital's interests. In 1986, the Congress enacted the Health Care Quality Improvement Act (HCQIA) which provided physicians involved in credentialing, privileging, and peer review activities a layer of immunity against retaliation for a negative peer review. The HCQIA confers a qualified procedural confidentiality and a qualified limited immunity to members of a professional review body, except in cases of alleged civil rights violation, antitrust cases, and alleged violations of Americans with Disabilities Act (ADA) and/or the Age Discrimination in Employment Act (ADEA) statutes.

The courts will, in general, respect the decisions of the credentialing body in the absence of a convincing evidence of discriminatory intent. In addition, Section 1 of the Sherman Act [32] imposes two basic requirements for a prima facie claim: the plaintiff must prove (1) the existence of a "contract, combination . . ., or conspiracy" that (2) imposes an unreasonable restraint on trade [33]. Thus, unilateral conduct cannot, by itself, constitute a Section 1 violation because the statute prohibits only concerted actions [34]. However, the courts remain divided in their views as to whether a hospital may be legally capable of conspiring with the members of its medical staff on privilege matters. Nonetheless, although there is no clear rule regarding the ability of a hospital and its medical staff members to enter into a conspiracy during the credentialing process, it is legally well accepted that the members of a hospital's medical staff do in fact have the legal capacity to conspire among themselves and therefore violate Section 1 of the Sherman Antitrust Act [35]. *Weiss v. York Hospital* [36] is an antitrust case which arose from a hospital's refusal to grant hospital staff privileges to an osteopathic physician; at the time, York Hospital was controlled by and exclusively staffed by doctors who graduated from allopathic medical schools. Weiss claimed that although allopaths and osteopaths were both trained and qualified to practice medicine, his application for staff privileges at York Hospital was denied solely because he was an osteopath. The appellate court in *Weiss* found that (1) the medical staff violated Sherman Act §1 which was supported by sufficient evidence but that (2) since there was no evidence adduced at trial that York engaged in any willful conduct designed to acquire or maintain its monopoly power, the appellate court reversed the district court's finding of liability in favor of Weiss and against York and that (3) Weiss' application was properly refused on the grounds of lack of professional competence or character. On the other hand, in the case of *Patrick v. Burget* [37], the medical staff of a geographically isolated community hospital with a monopoly over the local market had a business dispute that resulted in the termination of a physician's medical staff privileges. The case arose in Astoria, then a city of approximately 10,000 people located in the northwest Oregon with a solitary hospital, Columbia Memorial Hospital (CMH), and a private group medical practice called the Astoria Clinic. Patrick, a general and vascular surgeon, became an employee of the Astoria Clinic and a member of the CMH's medical staff in 1972; the clinic invited Patrick to become a partner of the clinic, but he declined the offer and instead began an independent practice in competition with the surgical practice of the clinic. As a result of a peer review, Patrick's credentials at CMH were restricted; Patrick sued for restraint of trade. The *Patrick* case addressed the issue of former partners weaponizing the peer review process for financial advantage. The court held that the state action doctrine did not protect Oregon physicians from federal antitrust liability for their activities on hospital peer review committees. Furthermore, in total, Dr. Patrick was awarded over two million dollars.

The HCQIA defines "sham peer review" as a "corrective action proceeding commenced by a hospital medical staff against a physician to discipline the physician motivated by other concerns than the quality of patient concerns such as hospital politics, competitive advantage or retaliation" [38].

CMS requires that a healthcare entity comply with The Joint Commission (JC) and National Committee for Quality Assurance (NCQA) accreditation guidelines for privileging and credentialing as Conditions of Participation (CoP). However, these Title 42 Conditions of Participation (CoPs) only apply to hospitals as a condition to participate in Medicare and Medicaid. The Code of Federal Regulations (CFR) parts 42 CFR 482.12 and 482.22 outline the credentialing and privileging practices that hospitals must implement as CoPs for the CMS programs; these include the general requirements medical staff credentialing and privileging requirements. The CFR specifies, in relevant part, that:

42 CFR § 482.12. Condition of Participation: Governing body.

There must be an effective governing body that is legally responsible for the conduct of the hospital. If a hospital does not have an organized governing body, the persons legally responsible for the conduct of the hospital must carry out the functions specified in this part that pertain to the governing body.

(a) Standard: Medical staff. The governing body must:

(1) Determine, in accordance with State law, which categories of practitioners are eligible candidates for appointment to the medical staff;

(2) Appoint members of the medical staff after considering the recommendations of the existing members of the medical staff;

(3) Assure that the medical staff has bylaws;

(4) Approve medical staff bylaws and other medical staff rules and regulations;

(5) Ensure that the medical staff is accountable to the governing body for the quality of care provided to patients;

(6) Ensure the criteria for selection are individual character, competence, training, experience, and judgment; and

(7) Ensure that under no circumstances is the accordance of staff membership or professional privileges in the hospital dependent solely upon certification, fellowship, or membership in a specialty body or society.

…

42 CFR § 482.22. Condition of Participation: Medical staff.

The hospital must have an organized medical staff that operates under bylaws approved by the governing body, and which is responsible for the quality of medical care provided to patients by the hospital.

(a) Standard: Eligibility and process for appointment to medical staff. The medical staff must be composed of doctors of medicine or osteopathy. In accordance with State law, including scope-of-practice laws, the medical staff may also include other categories of physicians (as listed at § 482.12(c)(1)) and non-physician practitioners who are determined to be eligible for appointment by the governing body.

(1) The medical staff must periodically conduct appraisals of its members.

(2) The medical staff must examine the credentials of all eligible candidates for medical staff membership and make recommendations to the governing body on the appointment of these candidates in accordance with State law, including scope-of-practice laws, and the medical staff bylaws, rules, and regulations. A candidate who has been recommended by the medical staff and who has been appointed by the governing body is subject to all medical staff bylaws, rules, and regulations, in addition to the requirements contained in this section.

(b) Standard: Medical staff organization and accountability. The medical staff must be well organized and accountable to the governing body for the quality of the medical care provided to patients.

(1) The medical staff must be organized in a manner approved by the governing body.

(2) If the medical staff has an executive committee, a majority of the members of the committee must be doctors of medicine or osteopathy.

(3) The responsibility for organization and conduct of the medical staff must be assigned only to one of the following: …

(c) Standard: Medical staff bylaws. The medical staff must adopt and enforce bylaws to carry out its responsibilities. The bylaws must:

(1) Be approved by the governing body.

(2) Include a statement of the duties and privileges of each category of medical staff (e.g., active, courtesy, etc.)

(3) Describe the organization of the medical staff.

(4) Describe the qualifications to be met by a candidate in order for the medical staff to recommend that the candidate be appointed by the governing body....

...

(6) Include criteria for determining the privileges to be granted to individual practitioners and a procedure for applying the criteria to individuals requesting privileges. ...

The JC standards require that the medical staff be organized under a set of bylaws, rules, and regulations which define the duties and functions of the staff medical staff. A demonstrable lack of strict and effective credentialing standards and processes will result in (1) exclusion from federal and state-funded programs, (2) loss of commercial payer contracts, and (3) loss of JC accreditation.

The legal standards to which hospitals are held are that of due diligence and reasonable care; in the event that an entity fails to meet these legal standards and a substandard provider is credentialed who subsequently causes patient harm, the healthcare entity itself can be held liable to injured parties under the legal theory of "negligent credentialing." Since hospitals administer their credentialing processes through committees of the medical staff and the Board of Directors, there is an additional potential individual liability to members of the respective committees and the board for negligent credentialing.

Individual providers are also at risk for liability and sanctions during the credentialing process since provider statements or attestations are certified by the provider's signature to be true and accurate. Thus, where a provider makes an error, even an inadvertent error, misstatement, omission, or inaccuracy; such an error will colorably constitute "misrepresentation." In essence, a misrepresentation is a lie. Depending on the intentions, circumstances, and personalities involved, an error may either be addressed or corrected, or submitted for disciplinary action. An error on a credentialing or privileging application may either simply result in a procedural delay or request for correction or, under the worst-case scenario, result in a denial of credentials or privileges, or civil charges. Where the credentialing application is retrospectively found to be submitted under false pretenses, the Department of Justice may even invoke a violation of the Federal False Claims Act where federal reimbursement is involved. Finally, denial of an application for medical staff membership, denial of a request for additional privileges, or even approval privileges that are more restrictive than requested represent NPDB-reportable actions if the decisions are based on the physician's competence or professional conduct.

Hospital Staff Privileging

The process for privileging of providers is similar and in fact complementary to the process of credentialing. Whereas credentialing represents an admission of a provider to the medical staff body, privileging defines what that provider may actually do. The CMS CoPs related to medical staff privileging are relate back to 42 CFR § 482.12 and § 482.22 which require "criteria for determining the privileges to be granted to individual practitioners and a procedure for applying the criteria to individuals requesting privileges." Additional CMS requirements for hospital medical staff privileging are outlined in a CMS letter [39] dated November 12, 2004, which requires the hospital's governing body to ensure "all patient care is provided by or in accordance with the orders of a practitioner who meets the Medical Staff criteria for the privileges granted; who has been granted privileges by the Governing Body in accordance with established procedures for applying those criteria; and who is working within the scope of those granted privileges." The letter goes on to outline limitations on the scope of practice or privileges stating that "the hospital's Medical Staff bylaws must state the duties and scope of privileges each category of practitioner may be granted. Specific privileges for each category must clearly and completely list the specific privileges or limitations for that category of practitioner. The specific privileges must reflect activities that the majority of practitioners in that category can do and that the hospital can support. It cannot be assumed that a practitioner can perform every task/activity/privilege listed/specified for the applicable category of practitioner." Privileges may be added usually through the attainment of additional certification, training, or experience; or privileges may be restricted as a result of performance or outcome review through an established peer review process.

Peer Review

The process of peer review refers to the evaluation, or reevaluation, of a professional practitioner's work by peers in the same profession. Peer review occurs uniformly across all healthcare professions including physicians, advanced practice providers, pharmacists, and nurses. The *Patrick* case, albeit about adverse peer review, nonetheless exemplified the widespread concern that without immunity, the potential exposure to litigation would have a chilling effect on effective peer review by hospitals and physicians. The HCQIA was enacted to address the concerns of those involved in credentialing, privileging, and peer review activities.

> The purpose of this legislation is to improve the quality of medical care by encouraging physicians to identify and discipline other physicians who are incompetent or who engage in unprofessional behavior. … Under this bill, hospitals and physicians that conduct peer review will be protected from damages in suits by physicians who lose their hospital privileges, provided the peer review actions meet the due process and other standards established in the bill. In addition, hospitals and physicians that discipline doctors will be required to report these disciplinary actions to the state medical boards. [40]

The first section of the HCQIA provides for a limited immunity for peer review participants if a professional review action, by a professional review body, meets all the procedural requirements. HCQIA immunity applies to (1) the professional review body, (2) any person acting as a member of or staff to the body, (3) any person under a contract or other formal agreement with the body, and (4) any person who participates with or assists the body with respect to the action [41]. In order for the immunity protections of the HCQIA to apply to a peer review entity, the professional review action must conform to specific standards, including (1) in the reasonable belief that the action was in the furtherance of quality healthcare, (2) after a reasonable effort to obtain the facts of the matter, (3) after adequate notice and hearing procedures are afforded to the physician involved or after such other procedures are fair to the physician under the circumstances, and (4) in the reasonable belief that the action was warranted by the facts known after such reasonable effort to obtain facts and after adequate notice and hearing procedures [42].

It is noteworthy that immunity under the HCQIA is with respect to damages, as illustrated by *Manion v. Evans* [43], but not from a lawsuit; thus, those involved in peer review remain exposed to the costs of defending a lawsuit. In the case of *Brader v. Allegheny General Hospital*, the court opined that under the provisions of the HCQIA, a physician challenging a peer review process "must prove, by a preponderance of the evidence, that the [peer] review process was unreasonable" [44] and that burden of proof rests with the plaintiff.

Peer review is largely, but not always, protected by statute. For example, the New York State peer review statute states in, part that:

> No person in attendance at a meeting when a medical or a quality assurance review or a medical and dental malpractice prevention program or an incident reporting function described herein was performed, including the investigation of an incident reported pursuant to section 29.29 of the mental hygiene law, shall be required to testify as to what transpired thereat. *The prohibition relating to discovery of testimony shall not apply to the statements made by any person in attendance at such a meeting who is a party to an action or proceeding the subject matter of which was reviewed at such meeting.* [45] (emphasis added)

Specifically, the NY statute may be construed to allow the discovery of statements made by those involved in the outcome(s) being addressed. Peer review and quality assurance data regarding a provider may also be subject to subpoena by state boards during disciplinary proceedings.

Peer review is often resolved through a process of informal resolution via departmental or administrative procedures. The most common outcome of an "informal action" is a warning, reprimand, or counseling with an internal performance improvement plan. In some circumstances, the provider will be required to complete a voluntary remediation. Providers who receive such an "informal" peer action, even if it not escalated to a more formal peer review, must be careful to clarify as to whether there are plans to report the "informal action" to NPDB.

The HCQIA specifies requirements of adequate notice and hearing procedures so as to conform with due process. In general, there are two types of due process: (1) substantive due process requires that a decision be neither arbitrary nor capricious; and (2) procedural due process requires that a practitioner receive a fair hearing, including a right to notice of the facts relied upon, a right to be heard, a right to present evidence and argument in opposition to the proposed action, a right to confront the accuser, and a right to be heard by an unbiased tribunal.

Thus, with respect to due process, the HCQIA requires that the provider under review must be provided with notice regarding the proposed action that includes (1) notice that a professional review action has been proposed, (2) the events or reasons for the proposed action, (3) notice of the right to request a hearing on the proposed action, (4) mention of any applicable time limits (to not be less than 30 days) within which to request such a hearing, and (5) a summary of the rights of the provider with respect to the proposed hearing [46]. If the provider under review then chooses to request a hearing, that hearing must also be duly noticed with respect to (1) place, time, and date, not be less than 30 days after the date of the notice, and (2) a list of the witnesses, if any, who are expected to testify at the hearing on behalf of the professional review body [47]. The term "fair hearing" is a term of art which refers to an administrative hearing or a private hearing in a hospital during the peer review process. If the provider avails himself or herself of the right to a fair hearing, then that hearing should be held before either (1) an arbitrator mutually acceptable to the provider and the healthcare entity, (2) a hearing officer who is appointed by the entity and who is not in direct economic competition with the provider involved, or (3) before a panel of individuals appointed by the entity and are not in direct economic competition with the physician involved [48]. The provider's rights at the hearing include the rights to (1) representation by an attorney or other person of the provider's choosing; (2) copies of the record of the proceedings; (3) call, examine, and cross-examine witnesses; (4) present evidence determined to be relevant by the hearing officer, regardless of its admissibility in a court of law; and (5) submit a written statement at the close of the hearing [49]. Finally, at the conclusion of the hearing, the provider under review has the rights to (1) receive the written recommendation of the arbitrator, officer, or panel, including a statement of the basis for the recommendations, and (2) receive a written decision of the healthcare entity, including a statement of the basis for the decision [50]. The peer review process must also operate exactly in accordance with the medical staff bylaws. Successful representation of providers under review often hinges on inadvertent violations of due process or hospital bylaws.

The National Practitioner Data Bank

An additional result of the HCQIA is that any disciplinary action taken against a physician must be reported to the NPDB. Once credentialing bodies determine, through the peer review process, that a provider's practice does not conform to standards, a duty arises to terminate or limit that provider's medical staff privileges and to report that action to the State Board of Health (OPMC) and/or the National Practitioner Data Bank (NPDB). The NPDB is a federal data repository which warehouses all adverse quality data regarding medical providers in the USA. The final regulations defining the NPDB were published in 1989 in the Federal Register at 45 CFR part 60; in 1990, the NPDB became operational. The NPDB was the result of a collaborative effort between the US Department of Health and Human Services (HHS), Health Resources and Services Administration (HRSA), and Bureau of Health Professions (BHPr), which begins developing the NPDB. In 1997, the HHS Office of Inspector General requested that the Division of Quality Assurance of the BHPr design, develop, and operate a Healthcare Integrity and

Protection Data Bank (HIPDB) which represented a database of healthcare fraud and abuse actions and to coordinate the operations of the NPDB and HIPDB.

> NPDB reporting aims to ensure that hospitals and state medical boards receive critical information about the physicians they employ and license. In Congress's judgment, any "professional review action ... related to professional competence or conduct" that adversely affects privileges for more than thirty days bears sufficiently on a physician's credentials to require reporting. [51]

Three categories of information must be reported to the NPDB: (1) malpractice payments made on behalf of any licensed healthcare practitioner, (2) sanctions by licensure boards, and (3) adverse credentialing actions which are (a) based on competence or professional conduct which affects conduct or could affect adversely the health or welfare of a patient or patients, (b) actions by a "professional review body" in the conduct of a "professional review activity," (c) acceptance of a surrender of clinical privileges by a provider while he or she "is under an investigation by the entity relating to possible incompetence or improper professional conduct" or in return for not conducting such an investigation, or (d) a professional society review action which adversely affects membership.

Appendix: Professional Misconduct as Defined By New York State

New York State defines professional misconduct in Education Law § 6530 and in the Rules of the Board of Regents § 29 ("unprofessional conduct"). Subsection references have been redacted for clarity.

New York State Education § 6530: Definitions of Professional Misconduct [53]

Each of the following is a professional misconduct:

1. Obtaining the license fraudulently;
2. Practicing the profession fraudulently or beyond its authorized scope;
3. Practicing the profession with negligence on more than one occasion;
4. Practicing the profession with gross negligence on a particular occasion;
5. Practicing the profession with incompetence on more than one occasion;
6. Practicing the profession with gross incompetence;
7. Practicing the profession while impaired by alcohol, drugs, physical disability, or mental disability;
8. Being a habitual abuser of alcohol, or being dependent on or a habitual user of narcotics, barbiturates, amphetamines, hallucinogens, or other drugs having similar effects, except for a licensee who is maintained on an approved therapeutic regimen which does not impair the ability to practice, or having a psychiatric condition which impairs the licensee's ability to practice;

9. (a) Being convicted of committing an act constituting a crime under:

    (i) New York state law or,
    (ii) federal law or,
    (iii) the law of another jurisdiction and which, if committed within this state, would have constituted a crime under New York state law;

   (b) Having been found guilty of improper professional practice or professional misconduct by a duly authorized professional disciplinary agency of another state where the conduct upon which the finding was based would, if committed in New York state, constitute professional misconduct under the laws of New York state;
   (c) Having been found guilty in an adjudicatory proceeding of violating a state or federal statute or regulation, pursuant to a final decision or determination, and when no appeal is pending, or after resolution of the proceeding by stipulation or agreement, and when the violation would constitute professional misconduct pursuant to this section;
   (d) Having his or her license to practice medicine revoked, suspended or having other disciplinary action taken, or having his or her application for a license refused, revoked or suspended or having voluntarily or otherwise surrendered his or her license after a disciplinary action was instituted by a duly authorized professional disciplinary agency of another state, where the conduct resulting in the revocation, suspension or other disciplinary action involving the license or refusal, revocation or suspension of an application for a license or the surrender of the license would, if committed in New York state, constitute professional misconduct under the laws of New York state;
   (e) …
10. Refusing to provide professional service to a person because of such person's race, creed, color or national origin;
11. Permitting, aiding or abetting an unlicensed person to perform activities requiring a license;
12. Practicing the profession while the license is suspended or inactive as defined in subdivision … of the public health law, or willfully failing to register or notify the department of education of any change of name or mailing address, or, if a professional service corporation, willfully failing to comply with … of the business corporation law or, if a university faculty practice corporation willfully failing to comply with … business corporation law;

…

16. A willful or grossly negligent failure to comply with substantial provisions of federal, state, or local laws, rules, or regulations governing the practice of medicine;
17. Exercising undue influence on the patient, including the promotion of the sale of services, goods, appliances, or drugs in such manner as to exploit the patient for the financial gain of the licensee or of a third party;
18. Directly or indirectly offering, giving, soliciting, or receiving or agreeing to receive, any fee or other consideration to or from a third party for the referral of a patient or in connection with the performance of professional services;
19. Permitting any person to share in the fees for professional services, other than: a partner, employee, associate in a professional firm or corporation, professional subcontractor or consultant authorized to practice medicine, or a legally authorized trainee practicing under the supervision of a licensee. This prohibition shall include any arrangement or agreement whereby the amount received in payment for furnishing space, facilities, equipment or personnel services used by a licensee constitutes a percentage of, or is otherwise dependent upon, the income or receipts of the licensee from such practice, except as otherwise provided by law with respect to a facility licensed pursuant to … public health law or … mental hygiene law;

20. Conduct in the practice of medicine which evidences moral unfitness to practice medicine;
21. Willfully making or filing a false report, or failing to file a report required by law or by the department of health or the education department, or willfully impeding or obstructing such filing, or inducing another person to do so;
22. Failing to make available to a patient, upon request, copies of documents in the possession or under the control of the licensee which have been prepared for and paid for by the patient or client;
23. Revealing of personally identifiable facts, data, or information obtained in a professional capacity without the prior consent of the patient, except as authorized or required by law;
24. Practicing or offering to practice beyond the scope permitted by law, or accepting and performing professional responsibilities which the licensee knows or has reason to know that he or she is not competent to perform, or performing without adequate supervision professional services which the licensee is authorized to perform only under the supervision of a licensed professional, except in an emergency situation where a person's life or health is in danger;
25. Delegating professional responsibilities to a person when the licensee delegating such responsibilities knows or has reason to know that such person is not qualified, by training, by experience, or by licensure, to perform them;

25-a. With respect to any non-emergency treatment, procedure or surgery which is expected to involve local or general anesthesia, failing to disclose to the patient the identities of all physicians, except medical residents in certified training programs, podiatrists and dentists, reasonably anticipated to be actively involved in such treatment, procedure or surgery and to obtain such patient's informed consent to said practitioners' participation;

26. Performing professional services which have not been duly authorized by the patient or his or her legal representative;
27. Advertising or soliciting for patronage that is not in the public interest.
    (a) Advertising or soliciting not in the public interest shall include, but not be limited to, advertising or soliciting that:
        (i) is false, fraudulent, deceptive, misleading, sensational, or flamboyant;
        (ii) represents intimidation or undue pressure;
        (iii) uses testimonials;
        (iv) guarantees any service;
        (v) makes any claim relating to professional services or products or the costs or price therefor which cannot be substantiated by the licensee, who shall have the burden of proof;
        (vi) makes claims of professional superiority which cannot be substantiated by the licensee, who shall have the burden of proof; or
        (vii) offers bonuses or inducements in any form other than a discount or reduction in an established fee or price for a professional service or product.
    (b) The following shall be deemed appropriate means of informing the public of the availability of professional services:
        (i) informational advertising not contrary to the foregoing prohibitions; and
        (ii) the advertising in a newspaper, periodical or professional directory or on radio or television of fixed prices, or a stated range of prices, for specified routine professional services, provided that if there is an additional charge for related services which are an integral part of the overall service being provided by the licensee, the advertisement shall so state, and provided further that the advertisement indicates the period of time for which the advertised prices shall be in effect.

(c) (i) All licensees placing advertisements shall maintain, or cause to be maintained, an exact copy of each advertisement, transcript, tape or video tape thereof as appropriate for the medium used, for a period of 1 year after its last appearance. This copy shall be made available for inspection upon demand of the department of health;

(ii) A licensee shall not compensate or give anything of value to representatives of the press, radio, television or other communications media i anticipation of or in return for professional publicity in a news item;

(d) No demonstrations, dramatizations or other portrayals of professional practice shall be permitted in advertising on radio or television;

28. Failing to respond within 30 days to written communications from the department of health and to make available any relevant records with respect to an inquiry or complaint about the licensee's professional misconduct. The period of 30 days shall commence on the date when such communication was delivered personally to the licensee. If the communication is sent from the department of health by registered or certified mail, with return receipt requested, to the address appearing in the last registration, the period of 30 days shall commence on the date of delivery to the licensee, as indicated by the return receipt;
29. Violating any term of probation or condition or limitation imposed on the licensee pursuant to … the public health law;
30. Abandoning or neglecting a patient under and in need of immediate professional care, without making reasonable arrangements for the continuation of such care, or abandoning a professional employment by a group practice, hospital, clinic or other health care facility, without reasonable notice and under circumstances which seriously impair the delivery of professional care to patients or clients;
31. Willfully harassing, abusing, or intimidating a patient either physically or verbally;
32. Failing to maintain a record for each patient which accurately reflects the evaluation and treatment of the patient, provided, however, that a physician who transfers an original mammogram to a medical institution, or to a physician or health care provider of the patient, or to the patient directly, as otherwise provided by law, shall have no obligation under this section to maintain the original or a copy thereof. Unless otherwise provided by law, all patient records must be retained for at least 6 years. Obstetrical records and records of minor patients must be retained for at least 6 years, and until 1 year after the minor patient reaches the age of 18 years;
33. Failing to exercise appropriate supervision over persons who are authorized to practice only under the supervision of the licensee;
34. Guaranteeing that satisfaction or a cure will result from the performance of professional services;
35. Ordering of excessive tests, treatment, or use of treatment facilities not warranted by the condition of the patient;
36. Claiming or using any secret or special method of treatment which the licensee refused to divulge to the department of health;
37. Failing to wear an identifying badge, which shall be conspicuously displayed and legible, indicating the practitioner's name and professional title authorized pursuant to this chapter, while practicing as an employee or operator of a hospital, clinic, group practice or multiprofessional facility, or at a commercial establishment offering health services to the public;
38. Entering into an arrangement or agreement with a pharmacy for the compounding and/or dispensing of coded or specially marked prescriptions;
39. With respect to all professional practices conducted under an assumed name, other than facilities licensed pursuant to article … failing to post conspicuously at the site of such

practice the name and licensure field of all of the principal professional licensees engaged in the practice at that site (i.e., principal partners, officers or principal shareholders);

40. Failing to provide access by qualified persons to patient information in accordance with the standards set forth …
41. Knowingly or willfully performing a complete or partial autopsy on a deceased person without lawful authority;
42. Failing to comply with a signed agreement to practice medicine in New York state in an area designated by the commissioner of education as having a shortage of physicians or refusing to repay medical education costs in lieu of such required service, or failing to comply with any provision of a written agreement with the state or any municipality within which the licensee has agreed to provide medical service, or refusing to repay funds in lieu of such service as consideration of awards made by the state or any municipality thereof for his or her professional education in medicine, or failing to comply with any agreement entered into to aid his or her medical education;
43. Failing to complete forms or reports required for the reimbursement of a patient by a third party. Reasonable fees may be charged for such forms or reports, but prior payment for the professional services to which such forms or reports relate may not be required as a condition for making such forms or reports available;
44. In the practice of psychiatry, (a) any physical contact of a sexual nature between licensee and patient except the use of films and/or other audiovisual aids with individuals or groups in the development of appropriate responses to overcome sexual dysfunction and (b) in therapy groups, activities which promote explicit physical sexual contact between group members during sessions; and
45. In the practice of ophthalmology, failing to provide a patient, upon request, with the patient's prescription including the name, address, and signature of the prescriber and the date of the prescription.
46. A violation of … public health law.
47. Failure to use scientifically accepted barrier precautions and infection control practices as established by the department of health pursuant to … public health law.
48. A violation of section … .

Rules of the Board of Regents: Part 29 – Unprofessional Conduct [54]

§ 29.1 General provisions.

a. Unprofessional conduct shall be the conduct prohibited by this section. The provisions of these rules applicable to a particular profession may define additional acts or omissions as unprofessional conduct and may establish exceptions to these general prohibitions.
b. Unprofessional conduct in the practice of any profession licensed, certified or registered pursuant to title VIII of the Education Law, except for cases involving those professions licensed, certified or registered pursuant to the provisions of Article 131 or 131-B of such law in which a statement of charges of professional misconduct was not served on or before July 26, 1991, the effective date of Chapter 606 of the Laws of 1991, shall include:

   1. willful or grossly negligent failure to comply with substantial provisions of Federal, State or local laws, rules or regulations governing the practice of the profession;

2. exercising undue influence on the patient or client, including the promotion of the sale of services, goods, appliances or drugs in such manner as to exploit the patient or client for the financial gain of the practitioner or of a third party;
3. directly or indirectly offering, giving, soliciting, or receiving or agreeing to receive, any fee or other consideration to or from a third party for the referral of a patient or client or in connection with the performance of professional services;
4. permitting any person to share in the fees for professional services, other than: a partner, employee, associate in a professional firm or corporation, professional subcontractor or consultant authorized to practice the same profession, or a legally authorized trainee practicing under the supervision of a licensed practitioner. This prohibition shall include any arrangement or agreement whereby the amount received in payment for furnishing space, facilities, equipment or personnel services used by a professional licensee constitutes a percentage of, or is otherwise dependent upon, the income or receipts of the licensee from such practice, except as otherwise provided by law with respect to a facility licensed pursuant to Article 28 of the Public Health Law or Article 13 of the Mental Hygiene Law;
5. conduct in the practice of a profession which evidences moral unfitness to practice the profession;
6. willfully making or filing a false report, or failing to file a report required by law or by the Education Department, or willfully impeding or obstructing such filing, or inducing another person to do so;
7. failing to make available to a patient or client, upon request, copies of documents in the possession or under the control of the licensee which have been prepared for and paid for by the patient or client;
8. revealing of personally identifiable facts, data or information obtained in a professional capacity without the prior consent of the patient or client, except as authorized or required by law;
9. practicing or offering to practice beyond the scope permitted by law, or accepting and performing professional responsibilities which the licensee knows or has reason to know that he or she is not competent to perform, or performing without adequate supervision professional services which the licensee is authorized to perform only under the supervision of a licensed professional, except in an emergency situation where a person's life or health is in danger;
10. delegating professional responsibilities to a person when the licensee delegating such responsibilities knows or has reason to know that such person is not qualified, by training, by experience or by licensure, to perform them;
11. performing professional services which have not been duly authorized by the patient or client or his or her legal representative;
12. advertising or soliciting for patronage that is not in the public interest:
    i. Advertising or soliciting not in the public interest shall include, but not be limited to, advertising or soliciting that:
        a. is false, fraudulent, deceptive or misleading;
        b. guarantees any service;
        c. makes any claim relating to professional services or products or the cost or price therefore which cannot be substantiated by the licensee, who shall have the burden of proof;
        d. makes claims of professional superiority which cannot be substantiated by the licensee, who shall have the burden of proof; or
        e. offers bonuses or inducements in any form other than a discount or reduction in an established fee or price for a professional service or product.
    ii. The following shall be deemed appropriate means of informing the public of the availability of professional services:
        a. informational advertising not contrary to the foregoing prohibitions; and
        b. the advertising in a newspaper, periodical or professional directory or on radio or television of fixed prices, or a stated range of prices, for specified routine profes-

sional services, provided that if there is an additional charge for related services which are an integral part of the overall service being provided by the licensee, the advertisement shall so state, and provided further that the advertisement indicates the period of time for which the advertised prices shall be in effect.

iii.

a. all licensees placing advertisements shall maintain, or cause to be maintained, an exact copy of each advertisement, transcript, tape or videotape thereof as appropriate for the medium used, for a period of 1 year after its last appearance. This copy shall be made available for inspection upon demand of the Education Department;
b. a licensee shall not compensate or give anything of value to representatives of the press, radio, television or other communications media in anticipation of or in return for professional publicity in a news item;

iv. Testimonials, demonstrations, dramatizations, or other portrayals of professional practice are permissible provided that they otherwise comply with the rules of professional conduct and further provided that the following conditions are satisfied:

a. the patient or client expressly authorizes the portrayal in writing;
b. appropriate disclosure is included to prevent any misleading information or imagery as to the identity of the patient or client;
c. reasonable disclaimers are included as to any statements made or results achieved in a particular matter;
d. the use of fictional situations or characters may be used if no testimonials are included; and
e. fictional client testimonials are not permitted;

13. failing to respond within 30 days to written communications from the Education Department or the Department of Health and to make available any relevant records with respect to an inquiry or complaint about the licensee's unprofessional conduct. The period of 30 days shall commence on the date when such communication was delivered personally to the licensee. If the communication is sent from either department by registered or certified mail, with return receipt requested, to the address appearing in the last registration, the period of 30 days shall commence on the date of delivery to the licensee, as indicated by the return receipt;
14. violating any term of probation or condition or limitation imposed on the licensee by the Board of Regents pursuant to Education Law, Section 6511.

§ 29.2 General provisions for health professions.

a. Unprofessional conduct shall also include, in the professions of: acupuncture athletic training audiology certified behavior analyst assistant certified dental assisting chiropractic creative arts therapy dental hygiene dentistry dietetics/nutrition licensed behavior analyst licensed pathologists' assistants licensed perfusionist licensed practical nursing marriage and family therapy massage therapy medicine mental health counseling midwifery occupational therapy occupational therapy assistant ophthalmic dispensing optometry pharmacy physical therapist assistant physical therapy physician assistant podiatry psychoanalysis psychology registered professional nursing respiratory therapy respiratory therapy technician social work specialist assistant speech-language pathology (except for cases involving those professions licensed, certified or registered pursuant to the provisions of article 131 or 131-B of the Education Law in which a statement of charges of professional misconduct was not served on or before July 26, 1991, the effective date of chapter 606 of the Laws of 1991):

1. abandoning or neglecting a patient or client under and in need of immediate professional care, without making reasonable arrangements for the continuation of such care, or abandoning a professional employment by a group practice, hospital, clinic or other health care facility, without reasonable notice and under circumstances which seriously impair the delivery of professional care to patients or clients;
2. willfully harassing, abusing or intimidating a patient either physically or verbally;

3. failing to maintain a record for each patient which accurately reflects the evaluation and treatment of the patient. Unless otherwise provided by law, all patient records must be retained for at least 6 years. Obstetrical records and records of minor patients must be retained for at least 6 years, and until 1 year after the minor patient reaches the age of 21 years;
4. using the word "Doctor" in offering to perform professional services without also indicating the profession in which the licensee holds a doctorate;
5. failing to exercise appropriate supervision over persons who are authorized to practice only under the supervision of the licensed professional;
6. guaranteeing that satisfaction or a cure will result from the performance of professional services;
7. ordering of excessive tests, treatment, or use of treatment facilities not warranted by the condition of the patient;
8. claiming or using any secret or special method of treatment which the licensee refuses to divulge to the State Board for the profession;
9. failing to wear an identifying badge, which shall be conspicuously displayed and legible, indicating the practitioner's name and professional title authorized pursuant to the Education Law, while practicing as an employee or operator of a hospital, clinic, group practice or multiprofessional facility, registered pharmacy, or at a commercial establishment offering health services to the public;
10. entering into an arrangement or agreement with a pharmacy for the compounding and/ or dispensing of coded or specially marked prescriptions;
11. with respect to all professional practices conducted under an assumed name, other than facilities licensed pursuant to article 28 of the Public Health Law or article 13 of the Mental Hygiene Law, failing to post conspicuously at the site of such practice the names and the licensure field of all of the principal professional licensees engaged in practice at that site (i.e., principal partners, officers or principal shareholders);
12. issuing prescriptions for drugs and devices which do not contain the following information: the date written, the prescriber's name, address, telephone number, profession and registration number, the patient's name, address and age, the name, strength and quantity of the prescribed drug or device, as well as the directions for use by the patient. In addition, all prescriptions for controlled substances shall meet the requirements of article 33 of the Public Health Law;
13. failing to use scientifically accepted infection prevention techniques appropriate to each profession for the cleaning and sterilization or disinfection of instruments, devices, materials and work surfaces, utilization of protective garb, use of covers for contamination-prone equipment and the handling of sharp instruments. Such techniques shall include but not be limited to:
    i. wearing of appropriate protective gloves at all times when touching blood, saliva, other body fluids or secretions, mucous membranes, nonintact skin, blood-soiled items or bodily fluid-soiled items, contaminated surfaces, and sterile body areas, and during instrument cleaning and decontamination procedures;
    ii. discarding gloves used following treatment of a patient and changing to new gloves if torn or damaged during treatment of a patient; washing hands and donning new gloves prior to performing services for another patient; and washing hands and other skin surfaces immediately if contaminated with blood or other body fluids;
    iii. wearing of appropriate masks, gowns or aprons, and protective eyewear or chin-length plastic face shields whenever splashing or spattering of blood or other body fluids is likely to occur;
    iv. sterilizing equipment and devices that enter the patient's vascular system or other normally sterile areas of the body;
    v. sterilizing equipment and devices that touch intact mucous membranes but do not penetrate the patient's body or using high-level disinfection for equipment and devices which cannot be sterilized prior to use for a patient;

vi. using appropriate agents, including but not limited to detergents for cleaning all equipment and devices prior a sterilization or disinfection;
vii. cleaning, by the use of appropriate agents, including but not limited to detergents, equipment and devices which do not touch the patient or that only touch the intact skin of the patient;
viii. maintaining equipment and devices used for sterilization according to the manufacturer's instructions;
ix. adequately monitoring the performance of all personnel, licensed or unlicensed, for whom the licensee is responsible regarding infection control techniques;
x. placing disposable used syringes, needles, scalpel blades, and other sharp instruments in appropriate puncture-resistant containers for disposal; and placing reusable needles, scalpel blades, and other sharp instruments in appropriate puncture-resistant containers until appropriately cleaned and sterilized;
xi. maintaining appropriate ventilation devices to minimize the need for emergency mouth-to-mouth resuscitation;
xii. refraining from all direct patient care and handling of patient care equipment when the health care professional has exudative lesions or weeping dermatitis and the condition has not been medically evaluated and determined to be safe or capable of being safely protected against in providing direct patient care or in handling patient care equipment; and
xiii. placing all specimens of blood and body fluids in well-constructed containers with secure lids to prevent leaking; and cleaning any spill of blood or other body fluid with an appropriate detergent and appropriate chemical germicide; and

14. failing to adhere to applicable practice guidelines, as determined by the commissioner, for the compounding of sterile drugs and products.

References

1. Carlson D, Thompson JN. The role of state medical boards. AMA J Ethics Virtual Mentor. 2005;7(4):311–4.
2. Interstate Medical Licensure Compact. Available online: https://www.imlcc.org/. See also: AMA. Resource Advocacy Center. 2020. Available online: https://www.ama-assn.org/system/files/2020-03/ama-arc-licensure-chart.pdf.
3. Hall MA. Law, medicine, and trust. J Nurs Law. 2003;9(1):33–84.
4. Furrow BR, Johnson SH, Jost TS, Schwartz RL. Health law: cases materials and problems. 2nd ed. St. Paul: West Publishing; 1991. p. 41.
5. Bang D. Nguyen v. The Department of Health, Medical Quality Assurance Commission, 144 Wn.2d 516, 29 P.3d 689 (2001).
6. Dent v West Virginia, 129 U.S. 114, 122 (1889).
7. Hawker v New York, 170 U.S. 189 (1898).
8. Board of Medical Quality Assurance v Andrews, 260 Cal.Rptr 113 (Cal.App.1989).
9. State v. Nelson. 317 \S.E.2d. 711 (N.C. App. 1984).
10. Brooks v. Tex. Med. Bd., 2015 Tex. App. LEXIS 6142 (Tex. App. June 18, 2015.
11. State v. Pac. Health Ctr., Inc., 135 Wn. App. 149 (Wash. Ct. App. 2006).
12. State Dep't of Health v. Hinze, 441 N.W.2d 593 (Neb. 1989).
13. Stetina v. State, 513 N.E.2d 1234 (Ind. Ct. App. 1987).
14. People v. Amber, 349 N.Y.S.2d 604 (N.Y. Sup. Ct. 1973).
15. Ohio State Attorney General. Opinion Number 99–044. August 31, 1999. Available online at: https://www.ohioattorneygeneral.gov/getattachment/8c6bc3d9-bb34-406f-aece-4231c6c30f03/1999-044.aspx.

16. Murphy v. Board of Medical Examiners of the State of Arizona, 949 P.2d 530 (Ariz. Ct. App. 1997).
17. Leigh v. Board of Registration in Nursing, 481 N.E.2d 1347 (mass.1985).
18. Morrison J, Wickersham P. Physicians disciplined by a state medical board. JAMA. 1998;279(23):1889–93.
19. Haley v. Medical disciplinary board, 818 P2d 1062, 1069 (Wash: Supreme Court 1991).
20. In re Kindschi, 52 Wash. 2d 8, 319 P.2d 824 (1958).
21. Dent *supra.*
22. Barsky v. Board of Regents of University of State of New York, 347 U.S. 442 (1954).
23. Federation of State Medical Boards of the United States. U.S. Medical Regulatory Trends and Actions 2018. Available online at: https://www.fsmb.org/siteassets/advocacy/publications/us-medical-regulatory-trends-actions.pdf.
24. Papadakis MA, Teherani A, Banach MA, et al. Disciplinary action by medical boards and prior behavior in medical school. N Engl J Med. 2005;353(25):2673–82.
25. Szalados, JE. Regulatory, legal, and liability issues pertaining to transesophageal echocardiography in Reich D.L., Fischer G.W. Perioperative transesophageal echocardiography. Elsevier. Philadelphia. 2014.
26. Dower C, Moore J, Langelier M. It is time to restructure health professions scope-of-practice regulations to remove barriers to care. Health Aff. 2013;32(11):1971–6.
27. Szalados, J.E. Medical staff credentialing pitfalls. Western New York Physician. 2012;3:21–2. Available online at: https://www.wnyphysician.com/PDF/MauerIssuevol32012FINALWeb.pdf.
28. Schloendorff v. The Society of the New York Hospital, 211 N.Y. 125, 105 N.E. 92 (1914).
29. Bing v. Thunig, 2 N.Y. 2d 656, 163 N.Y.S. 2d 3, 143 N.E. 2d 3 (1957).
30. Darling v. Charleston Community Mem'l. Hosp., 211 N.E.2d 253, 33 Ill. 2d 326 (Ill. 1965).
31. Mitchell J. Wiet Darling v. Charleston Community Memorial Hospital and Its Legacy, 14 Annals Health L. 399 (2005).
32. 15 U.S.C. § 1.
33. Oksanen v. Page Mem'l Hosp., 945 F.2d 696, 702 (4th Cir. 1991).
34. Copperweld Corp. v. Independence Tube Corp., 467 U.S. 752, 768–69 (1984).
35. See Muzquiz v. W.A. Foote Mem'l Hosp., Inc., 70 F.3d 422, 429 (6th Cir. 1995); Willman v. Heartland Hosp., 34 F.3d 605, 612 (8th Cir. 1994); Bolt v. Fairfax Hosp. Med. Ctr., 891 F.2d 810, 819 (11th Cir. 1990); Oksanen v. Page Mem'l Hosp., 945 F.2d 696, 706 (4th Cir. 1991).
36. Weiss v. York Hosp, 745 F.2d 786, 824 (3d Cir.1984).
37. Patrick v. Burget, 486 U.S. 94 (1988).
38. HCQIA. The Health Care Quality Improvement Act of 1986. Available online at: http://www.hcqia.net/.
39. CMS. Centers for Medicare & Medicaid Services (CMS) requirements for hospital medical staff privileging. S&C-05-04. November 12, 2004.
40. H.R. REP. NO. 99-903, at *2 (1986), 1986 WL 31972.
41. 42 U.S.C. § 11111(a)(1).
42. 42 U.S.C. § 11112(a).
43. *Manion v Evans*. 986 F.2d 1036 (6th Cir. 1993).
44. Brader v Allegheny General Hospital, 1999 U.S. App. LEXIS 2203, (3rd Cir. 1999).
45. N.Y. Educ. Law §6527 Special provisions.
46. 42 U.S.C. § 11112(b)(1).
47. 42 U.S.C. § 11112(b)(2).
48. 42 U.S.C. § 11112(b)(3)(A).
49. 42 U.S.C. § 11112(b)(3)(C).
50. 42 U.S.C. § 11112(b)(3)(D).
51. Anderson v. E. Conn. Health Network, Inc., No. 3:12-cv-00785, 2015 WL 4393552, at 1 (D. Conn. July 16, 2015).
52. U.S. Department of Health and Human Services. National practitioner databank. Available online at: https://www.npdb.hrsa.gov/hcorg/whatYouMustReportToTheDataBank.jsp.

53. NY State Department of Health. New York State Education § 6530 Definitions of professional misconduct. Available online at: https://www.health.ny.gov/professionals/office-based_surgery/law/6530.htm.
54. NY State Education Department. Office of the Professions. Rules of the board of regents. Part 29, unprofessional conduct. 2011. Available online at: http://www.op.nysed.gov/title8/part29.htm.

Chapter 7
Laws and Liability Relating to the Education and Supervision of Trainees and Allied Health Professionals

James E. Szalados

Medical Education

The History of Medical Education in the USA

The history of medical education is a gradual evolution of standardization and professionalization, a history that largely parallels the development of American medicine from a cottage industry to the modern model of academic medical centers and private health systems. The traditional purpose of education was the creation of a "learned gentleman." Thus, an education in medicine was the purview of aristocracy. At its infancy, the education of medical practitioners, both physicians and nurses, was largely through apprenticeship. In some cases, practitioners could establish their practices based on experience and reputation, skills honed in the battlefield, or within the community.

Medical schools in Europe, primarily in London, Oxford, Edinburgh, and Paris, began to attract students from the USA who desired a more formal education. In the latter part of the eighteenth century, the College of Philadelphia developed (1766) as an affiliation of physicians with the Pennsylvania Hospital, culminating in what is often referred to as the first US medical school intended not to replace but to supplement the apprenticeship model of American medical education. Subsequently, the medical department of Harvard College was established in Cambridge Massachusetts in 1783; the medical department of Dartmouth College was established in 1798; and the King's College in New York developed into the College of Physicians and Surgeons in 1807. These first US medical schools were

J. E. Szalados (✉)
Director, Surgical and Neurocritical Care Units, Rochester Regional Health System at Rochester General Hospital, Rochester, NY, USA

The Szalados Law Firm, Hilton, NY, USA
e-mail: james.szalados@rochesterregional.org; jszalados@aol.com

J. E. Szalados (ed.), *The Medical-Legal Aspects of Acute Care Medicine*,
https://doi.org/10.1007/978-3-030-68570-6_7

essentially proprietary, or private, business ventures by local physicians who presented didactic lectures supplemented by classes in anatomy. Formal requirements for acceptance to medical school, such as written exams and oral interviews, started to become accepted in the 1880s. A typical, but nonstandard, curriculum was generally 2 years in duration. At gradation, the matriculating physician achieved a de facto license to practice medicine, since, at the time, certifications and licensing boards had not yet been established. Specialization after graduation from medical school was largely based on experience and, again, through apprenticeship. William Osler was the first physician to establish a structured postgraduate residency training at Johns Hopkins Hospital. The American Medical Association (AMA) did not establish educational standards for internship programs until 1919. In the diverse stand-alone US medical schools, although the AMA developed regulations for medical education and postgraduate training, it nonetheless had a limited influence and lacked disciplinary oversight. In 1910, the Flexner Report criticized the US medical education system as a lax apprenticeship system established primarily for financial gain and which lacked educational goals and standards. The Flexner Report was the result of a study from the Johns Hopkins University Medical School which critically appraised the quality of educational facilities, entrance requirements, and the qualifications of faculty members at medical schools.

The duration of early medical postgraduate training was arbitrary; often determined by the institution, it became more standardized as national certifying bodies, and their certification examinations became established. In 1951, the US National Intern Matching Program was created in an attempt to regulate the placement of medical school graduates into accredited internship and residency program based jointly upon graduates' and hospitals' preferences. The Accreditation Council for Graduate Medical Education (ACGME) was established in 1981 with the mission of providing one powerful national body to oversee the diverse providers of graduate medical education with respect to the duration, content, and the qualifications of instructors and entities. In 2003, the ACGME moved to restrict the duty hours of residents and in 2011 established a ceiling of no more than 80 hours per week. The ACGME continues to add new areas of subspecializing to its oversight responsibilities as the science and technology of medicine continue to evolve.

Foreign medical graduates (FMGs), also referred to as international medical graduates (IMGs), are physicians who complete their medical education at a school outside the USA and are composed of both US citizens who chose to study abroad and citizens of other countries who immigrate to, and practice medicine, in the USA. American citizens who chose to study abroad may do so for a variety of reasons, including a desire for a cultural experience or to circumvent the very high costs of medical education or the limited number of positons available in medical schools in the USA and Canada. FMGs may complete their studies at universities in other countries or in "offshore" medical schools, such as those in the Caribbean. The challenges of a foreign medical education together with the challenges to integration within the US postgraduate training and licensing systems may be a testament to the drive and dedication of those who study abroad. Many argue that the availability of physicians lags with respect to the projected demand for physicians in the USA especially given the aging population and the prevalence of chronic disease. Thus, FMGs or IMGs represent an important segment of the US physician workforce; at present, approximately 33% of the US physician workforce is composed of foreign-trained graduates [1], from 25% in 2015 [2]. Foreign-trained graduates must pass high quality standards to ensure that their competency is comparable to that of American medical graduates; they must graduate from a school listed within the World Directory of Medical Schools, be certified by the Educational Commission for Foreign-Trained Medical Graduates (ECFMG); pass the same examinations taken by domestic graduates, and pass the US Medical Licensing Examination (USMLE). FMGs also compete increasingly effectively with US graduates of allopathic and osteopathic medical schools for postgraduate residency positions. In 2019, the graduates of US allopathic medical had a 93.9% match rate; graduates of US osteopathic medical schools had an 84.6% match rate, and US citizen international medical graduates had a match rate of 59% [3].

The US healthcare workforce enjoys a similar level of international diversity with respect to allied health providers. As of 2016, approximately 24% of dentists, 20% of pharmacists, and 16% of registered nurses are graduates of foreign educational programs [4]. Once healthcare professionals are duly certified and licensed, they are integrated into the US healthcare system.

Liability for Medical Students and Medical Student Liability

A key issue in medical education is the balance between classroom education which focuses on the basic and applied medical sciences and the need to train students in the basic practical skills of clinical patient care. Medical students are in a unique position; they need to learn and practice their provider-patient skills, physical examination skills, and even procedural skills on patients since the process of acquiring such skills is a process, not an occurrence. Of course, medical education during clinical training does not occur in a vacuum; rather it is, or should be, closely supervised, monitored, and assessed. However, the degree of oversight of medical students can vary greatly between hospitals, depending on the culture and the teaching orientation of the institution. For example, medical students may be supervised by interns, residents, advanced practice provides, attendings, or a combination of these at any one time. There is substantially more to a solid clinical rotation than allowing students to be present at rounds, conferences, and case discussions or even to observe procedures and surgery; an effective medical rotation must allow a degree of hand on experience. The degree of hands on experience can vary from listening to lung sounds, to checking a blood pressure, to holding retractors, and to indirectly "assisting" with procedures. In some institutions, medical students can even write notes and orders, which of course must be cosigned by a licensed provider to be meaningful or effective. Procedures performed by medical students are usually of a basic nature and, even so, should never be performed independently.

Since medical students must be supervised, the assessments they make or the orders they write are always of a preliminary nature; nothing a medical student does during a clinical rotation is considered final. Thus, medical student malpractice is rarely an issue; even in a situation where an assessment is incorrect or a procedure is poorly performed, it is the attending or the hospital that is held liable under the doctrine of negligent supervision. Since the student is not a licensed professional, he or she cannot personally held liable for medical errors, unless they willfully and negligently acted outside the scope of their position, misrepresented themselves as a licensed provider, or willfully disregarded rules and regulations. Medical students doing clinical rotations in the USA are required to carry medical professional liability insurance; such insurance is usually maintained either through their medical school or through the teaching hospital or both.

A more common issue implicating liability for medical students is that of informed consent, consent to interview, examine, and participate in procedures. Informed consent requires that the patient agrees to a provider's involvement in his or her care [5]; this is especially true when the relationship does not in fact medically *require* the presence of the student. Medical students are taught to introduce themselves as such, whoever data suggests that students may often avoid or disguise their actual roles either to (1) increase the probability of patient consent, (2) reassure patients of the near-professional status of the student [6], or (3) as a self-image perception where the perceived importance of conveying one's student status diminishes as medical students progress through medical school and near their internships [7]. Although only 37.5% of teaching hospitals specifically informed patients that students would be involved in care [8], the vast majority of patients will consent to procedures by a medical student even as most also felt that they should be informed of the student's status [9]. Leung and Patel argue that explicit informed consent is essential for theater-based teaching, even when students are simply acting as observers in the operating theater [10]. Students must also be educated regarding and also agree to be bound by the patient privacy rules of HIPAA. Mostly, such agreements occur as business associate agreements with medical schools.

Malpractice Liability in Graduate Medical Education

In general, medical malpractice is the principal legal risk facing residency training programs and their faculty. Both sponsoring hospitals and the educational institutions share liability for errors of commission or omission arising during the course of graduate medical education involving patient care. It is well recognized that residents may provide needed care to patients; however, they do so not as providers but as trainees. Hospitals receive federal funding and often stipends from the respective universities, for the supervision and training necessary to oversee the care provided by residents. Thus, teaching hospitals have a contractually created legal duties to both provide and supervise patient care [11] and are directly liable for any breaches. In general, lawsuits naming residents alone are rare; more likely the attending and the hospital will be the primary defendants in the lawsuit. Resident physicians, attending physicians, and graduate medical education (GME) institutions share a collective and shared responsibility to the patients they treat. Although the attending is legally responsible for the care provided by trainees under his or her supervision, residents and other trainees are commonly also named when they have been involved in the care provided.

Medical malpractice cases involve negligence liability, which is a fault-based system in tort law, whereby the plaintiff must establish that a defendant's conduct did not conform to the applicable standard of care. The standard of care in malpractice cases is established through expert witness testimony; however, the standard to which a graduate medical trainee, either intern, resident, or fellow, should be held remains less clear. In general, there are three views that courts have adopted regarding the standard of care that is applicable to graduate medical trainees.

In *Rush v. Akron General Hospital* [12], a first-year resident sutured a lacerated shoulder closed but failed to identify retained glass fragments; one piece measured 3–1/4 inches. The *Rush* ruling was the first case to address the standard of care for a first-year resident. The *Rush* court adopted a subjective rule that tied the standard to that which interns ordinarily possess under similar circumstances.

Another potential standard to which a physician-in-training may be held is that of general licensed physician or a general practitioner. The case of *Jenkins v. Clark* [13] overruled the standard of care described in *Rush*, holding instead that first-year residents should be held to the standard of "reasonably careful generalist physicians or hospital emergency room attendings, not that of interns." *Jenkins* is important since it ushered in a new standard, changing the standard of care from that of other interns similarly situated to that of a general practitioner attending working in an emergency department (ED). The standard of care, as articulated in *Jenkins*, required that the plaintiff proved that the resident physician "did or failed to do something" that a "physician or surgeon of ordinary skill, care, and diligence" would (or would not) have done under like or similar conditions or circumstances. The "general practitioner standard" thus became widely accepted. In the case of *McBride v. United States* [14], McBride, a retired naval officer, suffered a fatal heart attack, and his estate commenced a wrongful death action. McBride presented to the ED with complaints of pain in his lower chest after a hospitalization for the same complaints 3 days prior where a workup had revealed no evidence of heart disease. The resident on duty in the ED interpreted the electrocardiogram (EKG) and advised McBride that the pain was probably a result of a gastrointestinal disturbance and advised admission to the coronary care unit; McBride instead expressed a preference to return home where he died shortly afterward. At trial, the resident acknowledged that he had erroneously interpreted McBride's EKG as normal, although it in fact was abnormal. Plaintiff experts testified that a general practitioner with ordinary skill would have read the electrocardiogram accurately. The Chief of Cardiology testified that many interns and residents would not have recognized the abnormal tracings, and thus the misinterpretation did not demonstrate negligence in the context of the resident's lack of special training and experience. The American Law Institute has noted that the duty of care owed to the patient does not vary according to the doctor's individual knowledge or education and thus the normal standard will be altered only if the doctor represents to his patients that he possesses special skill. The court held that "McBride had the right to expect the quality of care usually found in the medical community and the hospital was obliged to provide physicians who could meet that standard," thus finding that the resident should be held to the standard of a general licensed physician staffing an ED. *Centman v. Cobb* [15] further affirmed *Jenkins* when it held that first-year residents are medical practitioners who must exercise the same standard of skill as a physician with an unlimited license to practice medicine.

Finally, an alternative approach is that of specialist standard of care. In the case of *Powers v. United States* [16], Powers, following a prior cervical laminectomy, was diagnosed with an instability of his cervical spine at C3–C4 and was referred for a posterior cervical facet fusion of C2 through C7 with a fibula bone graft. The operation was performed by four physicians: Raycroft, the senior attending supervising surgeon for this operation; assisted by Biondino, a first-year orthopedic resident; Cole a third-year orthopedic resident; and Romero, a first-year surgical resident. The operative report indicated that Dr. Biondino was the surgeon and indicates that while Drs. Raycroft and Romero operated on the leg to remove the fibula bone graft, Drs. Biondino and Cole operated on the neck at the fusion site. Powers had a complicated postoperative course during which time Biondino regularly assessed Powers; subsequently, Powers was discharged with weakness which was later found to be due to narrowing of the cervical spinal canal at C5 and C6 with cord impingement. Expert testimony later testified that "Powers suffered spinal cord impingement and nerve root compression because the excessive anterior angulation of the spine after the fusion brought the cord into constant contact with the preexisting bony ridges on Powers' vertebrae." The Court found "that the surgeons who performed the plaintiff's fusion failed to adequately take into account his unique, pre-fusion spinal condition, including his bone spurs and cervical subluxation. As a result, they fused the plaintiff's cervical spine at an excessive angulation for him and, in so doing, failed to exercise the good judgment required in each individual case by the standard of due care involved." The Court also stated that "the postoperative care which he received did not measure up to the standards of care ordinarily exercised in similar cases in Connecticut." Moreover, the "senior attending orthopedic surgeon for the operation, Dr. Raycroft, having been alerted to the problem by Dr. Biondino, failed to adequately monitor Powers' condition and he offered Dr. Biondino virtually no personal diagnostic supervision and assistance in correcting his postoperative condition." Here, the court held the resident to a standard of care expected of a specialist orthopedic surgeon performing a similar operation. In other words, the conduct was measured against that of an attending surgeon performing a cervical fusion, although the defendant was in training [17].

A similar case that reached a similar conclusion is *Gonzalez v. St John Hospital & Medical Center* [18] involved a third-year surgical resident who performed a colorectal surgery procedure that led to patient injury and litigation. The patient-plaintiff argued that a physician could be held to the standard of a specialist without being board-certified in the specialty, especially since the resident was receiving advanced surgical training at the time of the procedure. The Michigan court decided that residents who "limit their training to a particular branch of medicine or surgery and who can potentially become board-certified in that specialty are specialists" for standard of care purposes.

Alternatively, courts will deliberately avoid the legal issue with respect to the applicable standard of care that applies to physicians in training. In *National Bank of Commerce v. Quirk* [19], a medical malpractice action was commenced against several physicians, including two licensed residents. Here, plaintiff's expert stated the standard of care which would apply to an attending but admitted that he did not know the standard that would apply to a resident. The court ruled in favor of the resident defendants citing the uncertainty of the standard of care. The uncertainty of what standard to apply is reiterated in the case of *Mercil v. Mathers* [20]. In *Mercil*, a malpractice claim was brought by the estate of a woman who died shortly after childbirth. A first-year resident who assisted during the delivery was among the defendants. Although the court opined that an unlicensed, first-year resident is not immune from liability, the standard of care to which a first-year resident must be held is that "degree of skill and learning which is normally possessed and used by doctors in good standing in a similar practice."

In summary, the trend in verdicts and case law favors the view that graduate medical trainees, including interns who are in their first year of training, have to be generally held to a professional standard of care in medical malpractice case expected of a licensed nonspecialist, such as a general practitioner [21]. However, courts may hold resident physicians who are in a specialty training program to the same standard expected of the average specialist in that specific field [22]. Given the nature of medical training and the attendant supervision requirements mandated by evolving focus patient safety and public health, it would seem reasonable to hold physicians in training to that standard which applies to the supervising physician, since supervision is presumed by all parties.

Reviews of medical malpractice claims data suggests that trainees are named as defendants in 22% [23] to 27% [24] of malpractice claims. Medical malpractice cases involving surgical residents disproportionately involved junior residents and resulted in a median payout of $900,000 [25]. The payment of any claim against a provider, including a physician-in-training, must be reported to the National Practitioner Data Bank (NPDB). The Accreditation Council for Graduate Medical Education (ACGME) requires institutions that sponsor-accredited training programs provide physicians-in-training with professional liability insurance to cover claims arising from training [26]. Lawsuits can also produce stress and emotional distress; 95% of physicians sued for malpractice report emotional distress during the litigation process [27]. For a physician-in-training, such distress may add to the stresses of the training program and may produce lasting impact.

Physicians-in-training should seek supervision and attending physicians to provide such supervision. Supervision in itself does not diminish or detract from a training opportunity, rather it provides an opportunities to improve or hone skills, oversight, and rescue in the event of an evolving potential patient harm. Arguably, failure to properly supervise a technical procedure, other than routine procedures performed by experienced trainees, is a higher level of negligence. Certainly, at some point one must relinquish the scalpel, the needle, the drill, or the trocar;

however, that decision should be made after a careful risk assessment. Attending physicians face malpractice exposure not only for the care they themselves provide but also for the care they direct. In addition, attendings are likely to be held vicariously liable for the negligence of resident physicians working with them or directly liable for inadequate supervision. In cases such as those outlined above, the trainee, the supervisor, and the institution(s) are all potentially liable. Nonetheless, supervising physicians may, in addition to an allegation of malpractice, also be held liable under a separate and distinct cause of action that of negligent supervision, above and beyond malpractice. Thus, in addition to being named as a defendant through vicariously liability, attending may also have a direct liability based in negligent oversight or negligent supervision [28]. The precise parameters that legally define responsibility for supervision are not yet well defined in the case law; what exactly constitutes adequate supervision remains unsettled in the law [29].

In the case of *Lownsbury v. VanBuren* [30], an expectant mother was admitted for induction of labor; the on-call resident physicians instead ordered a contraction stress test, erroneously interpreted the test, and subsequently discharged the patient home. Later, the mother delivered a newborn with severe brain damage and filed suit against the on-call attending physician for negligent supervision. That on-call attending physician was not an employee of the hospital, but was under contract to provide on-call services in obstetrics. The on-call attending physician had neither seen the mother nor been contacted by the on-call resident physicians. Thus, the on-call physician argued that there was no patient-physician relationship and therefore he could not be found legally responsible. The court held that despite the lack of patient contact, or even a constructive actual knowledge of the circumstances, the on-call agreement was sufficient to indirectly construe the existence of a patient-physician relationship and a concomitant duty to supervise the residents.

In contrast, the case of *Prosise v. Foster* [31] involved a 4-year-old who presented to the ED with chicken pox and lethargy. The patient was examined by a first-year resident physician, who discussed the case with a third-year resident physician. The child was evolving pulmonary complications; the resident physicians failed to diagnose and instead treated her with intravenous fluids and discharged her home. The residents did not contact the ED attending physician, who was on-call at home. The child later died as a result of pulmonary complications. In this case the court held that the mere existence of an on-call relationship was an insufficient basis upon which impute a patient-physician relationship, and the court dismissed the dismissed claim of "failure to supervise."

Finally, in the case of *Mozingo v. Pitt County Memorial Hospital* [32], the court did not specifically opine on the issue of liability arising from an on-call relationship. *Mozingo* involved the case of a pregnant woman who presented to the ED in difficult labor. The resident physicians contacted the attending obstetrician who was on-call at home and who had no prior contact with the patient, but nonetheless came immediately to the hospital. When the attending arrived, the delivery had already occurred, but the child had sustained a shoulder dystocia, which led to severe permanent disability. The family brought suit against the attending physician for negligent supervision. Here, the existence of a patient-physician relationship and a concomitant duty to supervise were not in dispute, since the attending acknowledged his duties. Nonetheless, the plaintiff introduced expert testimony which rendered an opinion that the physician on-call physician would have called into the hospital during the evening to learn about potential cases that may require the presence of an attending physician; the defendant countered and introduced expert testimony that an on-call physician would not customarily do so. In its analysis, the court considered that "[m]edical professionals may be held accountable when they undertake to care for a patient and their actions do not meet the standard of care for such actions as established by expert testimony. Thus, in the increasingly complex modern delivery of health care, a physician who undertakes to provide on-call supervision of residents actually treating a patient may be held accountable to that patient, if the physician negligently supervises those residents and such negligent supervision proximately causes the patient's injuries." The trial court granted summary judgment for the physician. The appellate court reversed the trial court's summary judgment for the defendant concluding that "a contract providing for supervision of resident physicians in a manner which substantial evidence tends to show is negligent will not shield a supervising physician such as the defendant from legal liability for providing such negligent supervision, at least where, as here, the plaintiff patient was not a party to that contract." The appellate court here explicitly left open the possibility that merely being available to answer questions from home may not qualify as adequate supervision, but not decide that issue. The dissent by Justice Meyer in this case is important, reasoning that "contrary to the majority's conclusion, Dr. Kazior did not have a duty of general supervision of the residents. Pursuant to his employment with Eastern, Dr. Kazior merely assumed responsibility to provide limited supervision of the residents to remain at home when he was assigned on-call supervision and to make himself available by telephone for advice and assistance to the chief resident.... the cases relied upon by the majority do not support the conclusion that Dr. Kazior owed any duty beyond that which he voluntarily assumed pursuant to his employment agreement with Eastern... [t]o permit liability for negligent supervision to be imposed against Dr. Kazior, however, flies in the face of the cardinal principles of contract and tort law. We have long recognized that a physician may contractually limit the extent or scope of professional services to be rendered."

Therefore the case varies widely by jurisdiction and the specific circumstances. Nonetheless, case law does illustrate the fact that, at least in some instances, courts will hold a supervising physician liable to patients treated by their house staff, including patients with whom they have never had direct contact. The assignment of liability will depend on (1) the existence of a colorable patient-physician relationship through explicit agreement or implicit promises that allocates a duty beyond a supervisory responsibility, and (2) the threshold determination by the court of the adequacy of the supervision under the appropriate standard of care. Again, although that standard is unclear, the courts have not clearly ruled that passive supervision from home in itself rises to negligence, and court rulings have suggested willingness to look beyond prior customary practice in the interest of patient care and public policy.

Due Process in Medical Education and Discipline

Throughout the professional education process, from medical school, and through the postgraduate physician-in-training continuum, situation may arise, either based in academic performance or in behavior, which necessitate disciplinary sanctions such as remediation or dismissal. Moreover, through all stages of disciplinary action, policies and procedures, including due process, must be followed. Termination without due process can lead to litigation. In general, where there is a strict adherence to process, faculty and intuitional decisions are upheld by the courts. The US Supreme Court, in *Board of Curators, Univ. of Missouri v. Horowitz* [33], addressed this issue on point. In *Board of Curators*, the clinical performance of a medical student during a pediatrics rotation was determined unsatisfactory by the Medical School's Council of Evaluation who recommended that the student be advanced to her final year only on a probationary basis; after further faculty dissatisfaction with the student's clinical performance during that year, the Council reevaluated her progress and concluded that she should not be considered for and that, absent "radical improvement," she be dropped as a student in her final year of medical school. Following additional negative review, when a report on another rotation turned out to be negative, the Council recommended that the student be dismissed. The student then appealed to the provost, who, after review, sustained the decision of the Council. The student then brought suit under 42 USC § 1983, contending that she had not been accorded her due process rights prior to her dismissal.

42 US Code § 1983 provides the basis for civil action for deprivation of their constitutional rights. Such rights may include violations of due process rights or rights under the Fourth Amendment (searches) and Fifth Amendment (self-incrimination). 42 USC § 1983 states, in relevant part:

> Every person who, under color of any statute, ordinance, regulation, custom, or usage, of any State or Territory or the District of Columbia, subjects, or causes to be subjected, any citizen of the United States or other persons within the jurisdiction thereof to the deprivation of any rights, privileges, or immunities secured by the Constitution and laws, shall be liable to the party injured in an action at law, suit in equity, or other proper proceedings for redress, except that in any action brought against a judicial officer for an act or omission taken in such officer's judicial capacity, injunctive relief shall not be granted unless a declaratory decree was violated or declaratory relief was unavailable. …

The 14th Amendment makes the Due Process Clause of the Fifth Amendment [34] binding in the states. Furthermore, the 14th Amendment, Section 1, of to the US Constitution includes several clauses, such as the Citizenship Clause, Privileges or Immunities Clause, Due Process Clause, and Equal Protection Clause [35]. The 14th Amendment states, in relevant part:

> No State shall make or enforce any law which shall abridge the privileges or immunities of citizens of the United States; nor shall any State deprive any person of life, liberty, or property, without due process of law; nor deny to any person within its jurisdiction the equal protection of the laws.

The intent of due process is to provide procedural safeguards for the protection previous of individuals from arbitrary actions. Due process is implicated in hospital medical staff peer review actions, state medical board disciplinary actions, actions by state professional regulatory agencies [Chap. 6], and actions of federal agencies [Chap. 30]. Due process includes substantive and procedural components: procedural due process requires notice and an opportunity to be heard, whereas substantive due process mandates a showing of a legitimate basis for the action so as to overcome a claim that the action was arbitrary or capricious.

The US Supreme Court, in *Horowitz*, deferred to the University Council stating that "university faculties must have the widest range of discretion in making judgments as to the academic performance of students and their entitlement to promotion or graduation." Here, the Court also noted that:

> [t]he procedures leading to respondent's dismissal for academic deficiencies, under which respondent was fully informed of faculty dissatisfaction with her clinical progress and the consequent threat to respondent's graduation and continued enrollment, did not violate the Due Process Clause of the Fourteenth Amendment. Dismissals for academic (as opposed to disciplinary) cause do not necessitate a hearing before the school's decisionmaking body. (citing Goss v. Lopez, 419 US 565)
>
> *Horowitz*, 435 US 84–91

A similar case was again heard by the US Supreme Court regarding the dismissal of a medical student: *Regents of University of Michigan v. Ewing* [36]. Typically, at the University of Michigan, a student who successfully completed the requiremenents of the six-year Interflex program would, upon graduatioon, be awarded both undergraduate and doctorate of medical degrees. One requirement for progression through the Inrerflex program was a successful score on Part I of the National Board of Medical Examiners (NBME) examination test. In the case of *Ewing*, a student who was dismissed from the University after failing to pass the NMBE I (notably achieving the lowest examination score in the recorded history of the Interflex program), brought suit against the University alleging violation of his rights as guaranteed by the 14th Amendment. The US Supreme Court once again upheld the dismissal, holding that:

> Even if respondent's assumed property interest gave rise to a substantive right under the Due Process Clause to continue enrollment free from arbitrary state action, the facts of record disclose no such action. The record unmistakably demonstrates that the decision to dismiss respondent was made conscientiously and with careful deliberation, based on an evaluation of his entire academic career at the University, including his singularly low score on the NBME Part I examination. The narrow avenue for judicial review of the substance of academic decisions precludes any conclusion that such decision was such a substantial departure from accepted academic norms as to demonstrate that the faculty did not exercise professional judgment.

Thus, dismissals of students by Universities based on academic failures, when policies and procedures are followed, will generally be upheld by the courts, who accord broad deference to educational standards. In situations where a disciplinary action is based in aspects of character, such as professionalism, courts again will generally defer to educational institutions, as long as the policies and procedures and procedural due process are followed [37].

In general, the courts will treat physicians-in-training within programs of graduate medical education (GME) as students subject to the academic requirements as established by the program and as administered by the Program Director and/or GME Director. In the case of *Hernandez v. Overlook Hospital* [38], a resident in Internal Medicine had his contract terminated on the basis of observations and reports by peers, and on the the conclusion of the Program Director, that the resident had exhibited poor judgment, poor leadership qualities, and a lack of professonalism. Here, the Supreme Court of New Jersey opined that:

> [i]f academic termination hearings are transformed into legal proceedings that involve legal procedures, the academic hearing would become an adversarial and litigious contest. The panel of doctors would no longer be acting as academics reviewing medical decisions, but rather as judges, ruling on legal issues that they are not trained or qualified to evaluate.
> [149 N.J. 80]

> The court went further to state that:
> A graduate or professional school is, after all, the best judge of its students' academic performance and their ability to master the required curriculum. The presence of attorneys or the imposition of rigid [procedural] rules ... would serve no useful purpose, notwithstanding that the dismissal in question may be of permanent duration [39].

In conclusion, the process of peer review and discipline during the professional education process, from student to graduate trainee, is similar to the peer review and discipline which occurs during the medical staff credentialing process and the process of state professional licensing body oversight [Chap. 6]. Although litigation by students and trainees is not uncommon; the courts will generally defer to the assessments and evaluations of the educational system as long as polices and due process are followed [40].

Malpractice Liability in Nursing Education and Practice

Nursing students, whether they are nursing or advanced practice nursing students, are pursuing and completing a curriculum of professional study; that study will necessarily include didactic and clinical study in a manner analogous to that of medical education. The issues faced by nursing students with respect to educational evaluations and the risks of malpractice during patient contact in the course of their training are similar to that of medical students or physician assistant students. During the clinical portions of nursing study, student nurses begin to have direct patient contact under the supervision and direction of their nursing educators or preceptors. Preceptor liability is supervisory liability. Preceptor liability is a form of vicarious liability under the doctrine *of respondeat superior* where "even though a nurse has no direct patient contact, provides no direct patient care, or is not involved in direct patient teaching, if that nurse is responsible for another nurse providing direct care, any act or behavior done by the nurse providing direct care is still the responsibility of the supervising nurse" [41]. Students are held to the same professional standards for individuals in the profession for which they are training. Once again, the student and preceptor can be jointly and severally liable for malpractice arising from patient care.

The Captain of the Ship Doctrine

The "captain of the ship doctrine" was a legal principle created by the Pennsylvania Supreme Court in the 1949 case of *McConnell v. Williams* [42]. Here, Mrs. McConnell, an expectant mother, consulted her physician who determined that she would need a caesarian which was to be performed at the Jewish Hospital in Philadelphia. The Jewish Hospital was not a public hospital in the sense of being owned or operated by government, but it is a nonprofit, charitable institution, with both private-patient and ward service, its facilities being available to everyone in need. The operation was a difficult one, complicated by bleeding that required the physician's complete attention. Once the baby was delivered, it was turned over to the intern for the purpose of tying the cord and applying a solution of silver nitrate to the infant's eyes. Silver nitrate is an extremely caustic drug requiring careful dosage of one or two drops and proper technique; in this case, the intern "filled a syringe and squirted the solution once into the child's left eye and twice into its right eye, putting into the latter 'a great many drops'; moreover, he failed to irrigate the eyes." The eye was so badly burned that it had later to be excised, the child lost her sight and required a glass eye. Suit was brought, although the physician was not personally named since the operation he performed on Mrs. McConnell was entirely satisfactory and not subject to criticism. During trial, testimony substantiated a prima facie case of negligence against the intern, and the court was faced with the question of whether the doctrine of *respondeat superior* would apply. The surgeon testified that "he had complete control of the operating room and of every person within it while the operation was in progress." The court reasoned that:

> If, then, it be true that defendant had supervisory control and the right to give orders to the intern [sic] in regard to the very act in the performance of which the latter was negligent, it would follow, according to the classical test of agency hereinbefore stated, that a jury would be justified in concluding that the temporary relationship between defendant and the intern [sic] was that of master and servant, and that consequently defendant was legally liable for the harm caused by any negligence on the part of the intern [sic]. … Nor is it a tenable argument that defendant should be relieved from legal responsibility because the hospital furnished the services of an intern [sic] just as it furnished the silver nitrate solution and the facilities of its laboratory and just as it furnished Mrs. McConnell with a room and board upon her payment of the hospital charges.

Where one, under the control of another, commits a tort, such as negligence, then the responsibility is imputed to he or she in control; this is *respondeat superior*. Vicarious liability is an indirect legal responsibility for injury; liability arises based solely within the nature of the relationship between the parties. *Respondeat superior*, or "let the master answer," holds that an employer or principal may be held legally liable for the negligent acts of an employee or agent who is acting within the scope of their employment. The "borrowed servant doctrine" is a legal principle through which one in control is held liable for the actions of another servant, who is actually in the employ of another, but who becomes temporarily the employee or servant of that person in control. For example, an operating room nurse, under the doctrine, could be in the employ of the hospital; however during an operation, he or she comes under the control of the surgeon who directs the actions of the nurse and thus becomes his or her "special employer." The "captain of the ship doctrine" was a special form of the "borrowed servant doctrine," whereby the fact that the surgeon was in fact considered to be in full control of all those in the operating room, any negligence that occurred under his constructive control was his or hers alone, even absolving the hospital of liability. The "captain of the ship doctrine" has now been rejected in whole or part by most contemporary courts [43].

Scope of Practice

The term, "scope of practice" refers to state-specific legislative or state-specific statutory restrictions regarding the types of responsibilities or interventions that a healthcare practitioner may perform within his or her license. Scope-of-practice determinations are made by licensing boards and are generally based upon education, certification, and demonstrated competencies. Within healthcare, "scope of practice" applies to, for example, physician assistants (PAs), nurses, advanced practice nurses (NPs), emergency medical services (EMS), dietitians, respiratory therapists, physical therapists, occupational therapists, pharmacists, and dentists. The scope of practice for physicians is usually defined through an institution-specific privileging process, rather than by law. Most, if not all state laws, allow physicians to perform any of the duties associated with the practice of medicine, including those duties that would otherwise fall to allied health support staff. The "scope of practice" for unlicensed allied health workers is usually defined through a job hospital-specific description.

Scope of practice is important in all aspects of healthcare; however, in a team model of care, such as that found in hospitals, there is a general trend to collaboration within multidisciplinary practice. Thus, arguably the scope of practice may be more relevant in the nonhospital, or independent, practice settings. The scope of practice is a contentious issue wherein the scope of practice for nonphysician providers continues to expand, a change that is sometimes perceived to be threatening by physicians. The public policy aim of increasing access to healthcare is largely supported by scope of practice expansion. Three important recent developments have accelerated scope-of-practice expansion. First, the Triple Aim articulated by the Institute for Health which advocated (1) improvement of the patient experience of care, (2) improvement of the health of populations, and (3) reduction of the per capita cost of healthcare. Second, the Affordable Care Act which envisioned the transformation of the healthcare system to a patient-centered model based in the goals of (1) higher-quality, (2) safer, (3) more affordable, and (4) more accessible care. Finally, a report by the Institute of Medicine (IOM) published a report entitled "Future of Nursing" which made four recommendations to best align the profession of nursing with the ACA and the Triple Aim, namely, (1) that nurses should practice to the full extent of their education and training; (2) that nurses should achieve higher levels of education and training through a system that promotes seamless academic progression; (3) that nurses should be full partners, with physicians and other health professionals, in redesigning health care; and (4) that there is a need for more effective workforce planning and policy through data collection and information infrastructure. Nursing advocacy to "practice at the top of one's license" has come to mean that a healthcare team member (APRNs, RNs, LPNs, CNAs, and support staff) performs duties commensurate with the full extent of their education, training, and abilities, since the changes to legal scope of practice requires legislative and statutory revisions which are usually time-consuming with respect to legislative process and potentially adversarial [44].

All states require that PAs practice under the directions and supervision of a physician. The manner by which (a) scope of practice, (b) supervision requirements, and (c) prescriptive authority are determined for PAs varies by state and may be determined either (1) by the State Medical Board or (2) defined at the practice level. Most states have accepted that the training and specialization of PAs cannot be universally recognized within scope-of-practice legislation and have shifted to a practice-level determination model. PA practice parameters are also governed by the bylaws, policies, and procedures of licensed healthcare facilities through the privileging process. Anesthesiology Assistants (AAs) also allied health professionals who work within the anesthesia care team (ACT) exclusively under the direction of a licensed anesthesiologist. With respect to scope of practice and other regulations regarding clinical practice, AAs share many similarities to PAs; although AAs are not recognized by all US states. Although AAs and certified Nurse Anesthestists are both members of the ACT; there are numerous and often subtantial, differences with respect to background, training, licensure, and supervision requirements.

Advanced practice nurses (APNs) include nurse practitioners, certified nurse anesthetists, and nurse midwives. Once again, the scope of practice for advanced practice nurses is legislatively defined by each state for each category of advanced practice nurse, also subject to hospital bylaws, policies, and rules.

The scope of practice has a significant impact on liability. Where professionals practice under the direction or supervision of another, supervisory doctrines such as vicarious liability, *respondeat superior*, or agency may apply so that the supervisor is legally responsible for the acts of the supervised. Thus, if an APP (PA or APN) renders professional services outside their scope of practice and there is patient harm stemming from a violation of the standard of care, the medical malpractice liability will depend on whether the practitioner was acting in a supervised relationship; if so, the liability will likely impute to the supervisor, although the practitioner may also be held independently liable. On the other hand, where the practitioner is

Table 7.1 Nurse practitioner claims Analysis 1998–2008 (after CNA HealthPro 2019 [50])

During the 10-year period:
Average indemnity and expense payments increased
Adult/geriatric, family, and pediatric/neonatal specialties had the greatest number of claims
The medical care office was the location with the highest number of claims
Diagnosis-related allegations accounted for 39% of open and closed claims
Scope-of-practice-related allegations were relatively rare but had the highest average severity
Failure to order/obtain appropriate consultation/referral had the highest severity among treatment-related allegations
More than 80% of medication errors were prescription-related
Cardiac condition was associated with 22.1% of the closed claims that resulted in death and indemnity payment
Four closed claims during the time period that settled at the policy limit resulted from allegations of failure to diagnose or failure to properly asses

practicing independently, he or she will be fully liable for any verdict and damages related to the cause of action. Although data are sparse, because of out-of-court settlements and the relative infancy of the claims database, malpractice actions against NPs claims are increasing [Table 7.1].

In 2007, a Tampa, FL jury awarded the second-largest malpractice award in US history, $217 million, including $100 million in punitive damages on behalf of Navarro whose cerebellar stroke was misdiagnosed as sinusitis. The supervising ED physician testified that he assumed the PA who allegedly provided care to Navarro was licensed and credentialed where in actual fact, the "PA" was in effect a scribe, an unlicensed PA who had failed the state PA licensure examination four times [45].

Advance practice providers such as PAs, AA, and APN are also potentially liable for misrepresentation and/or failure to obtain an informed consent to treat if they do not properly identify themselves to a patient; this situation is similar to that of medical students and residents discussed above. Furthermore, misrepresentation and failure to obtain an informed consent have liability implications not only in tort (such as battery and malpractice) but also with respect to professional misconduct under the jurisdiction of state licensing boards [see Chap. 6].

Liability Issues Arising from Preceptorship and Proctoring

Clinical learning at all levels necessarily involves observation, supervised performance, and peer review. Similarly, the policies and bylaws of the medical staff will define each facility's process for the granting of privileges to a provider for a newly acquired skill requiring the credentialing body of a healthcare facility to review the provider's training and to document reasonable procedural competence, a process which then begins a continuous process of reevaluation through ongoing peer review. However, the nature of medical practice is such that, at times, skills previously learned but not used over long periods of time or new skills acquired during the course of practice in order to accommodate evolving developments in technology or procedures into one's practice becomes necessary. In such cases, "mature" practitioners, no longer within a program of training, must learn, demonstrate, competence, and become privileged to incorporate new skills into their practice; this occurs through the processes of preceptorship and/or proctoring.

Two situations arise where a more skilled observer is present during a procedure for the purposes of training and evaluation, respectively: (1) a preceptorship, wherein the preceptor is an instructor or teacher and is therefore responsible for the actions of the trainee, and (2) a proctorship, whereby the proctor is not teaching, but has assumed only the limited responsibility for assessment and documentation of the performance of another for the purposes of credentialing and/or privileging.

It is well settled that the preceptor, in the role of instructor, is fully liable for the actions of his or her trainee; this is analogous to the teaching or training relationships discussed above. However, the issue of the extent to which a proctor is liable for the actions of the provider whose performance is being assessed is more complex. There is little question that a proctor has an ethical duty to a patient in the situation that the procedure being proctored goes awry; some proctoring guidelines recommend that the proctor intervene in the event of a complication or emergency. In theory, Good Samaritan laws could immunize proctoring physicians when they intervene during an emergency; the legal criteria for protection under a Good Samaritan stature are, in general, (1) an action taken in good faith, (2) to provide emergency medical care, and (3) the absence of a preexisting duty to treat or to the affected person. However, it is not clear that an emergency arising during an elective operation will be viewed by the courts as an emergency under the Act. For example, the case of *Bryant v. Bakshandeh* [46] involves a case where a urologist was consulted following multiple attempts by the surgeon to insert a Foley catheter. Here, the patient was asleep but the operation had not started. The urologist was also unable to pass the catheter; the operation was then aborted, but the patient developed complications from the attempted catheterization and the patient sued. Although the urologist invoked the Good Samaritan statute as a defense, the court ruled against the defense holding that there was no "emergency" situation. In general, proctors are not held legally liable for injuries to a patient, by an otherwise qualified provider unless there is evidence that the proctor had established a professional relationship with the patient. Few cases have addressed the liability of proctors.

Liability in negligence is predicated in a legal duty to the patient; absent a legal duty, there can be no breach, and therefore there can be no liability. Proctors has been held to not be liable even if they witness gross malpractice and choose not to intervene. In the case of *Clarke v. Hoek* [47], an orthopedic surgeon who was proctoring an operation witnessed malpractice and chose not to intervene. In *Clarke*, the trial court dismissed on summary judgment finding that the surgeon had no legal duty to intervene. The verdict was appealed, where at trial the plaintiff's expert witness testified that it was a violation of the standard of care to not intervene, but the appellate court sustained the summary judgment holding that the "duty to treat" was not an issue of "standard of care" for expert opinion, rather the "duty to treat" was an issue of law: "absent a special relationship giving rise to a duty to act, a person is under no duty to take affirmative action to assist or protect another, no matter how great the danger in which the other is placed, or how easily he could be rescued."

In the case of *Zablocki v. Wilkin* [48], a plaintiff suffered a fractured right ankle and was referred to the care of Dr. Wilkin who was recently credentialed in podiatric surgery and was mandated to have a proctor present for his first five surgeries. Another surgeon was appointed to proctor, was not paid for proctoring services, did not scrub in, and was not present for the entire procedure; however he admitted to discussing the proposed procedure with Wilkin before the surgery. The proctor, Dr. Walkovich, testified that his "sole function as a proctor was to observe another doctor for purposes of determining if that doctor has demonstrated the skills necessary to justify an extension of privileges." Zablocki later filed a medical malpractice action against both surgeons, in which she alleged, inter alia, that Dr. Walkovich failed to properly supervise the procedure. The Ohio court dismissed the action as a matter of law, stating that a "physician who, on behalf of a hospital and without compensation, acts as a proctor in observing a surgical operation for the sole and express purpose of assessing and reporting on the competence of a candidate for membership of a hospital medical staff" does not owe a duty to a patient to "intervene in that surgery in order to prevent malpractice by the proctored surgeon."

Therefore, both preceptorship and proctorship create potential legal liabilities. Case law suggests that a physician-patient relationship might be implied if the patient is led to believe that the proctor will be "supervising" the procedure, if the proctor is named as member of the operating team on the consent form, if the proctor meets with the patient and suggests that he or she will be assisting in the procedure, or if the proctor actively participates in the procedure either by offering medical advice or procedural assistance. If the proctor "crosses the line" from observer to "participant," then an argument for co-defendant liability can be more convincingly made. Suggestions of active involvement even indirectly can lead to vicarious liability, active intervention may create liability as a surgical assistant, and offering advice may create liability as a consultant. Where a proctor, without invitation, intervenes on behalf of a patient, there are potential collateral liabilities not predicated in a theory of negligence; these may include a violation of the peer review process, bias, battery, unauthorized practice, or defamation of character. In some situations, out-of-state experts may be retained as proctors specifically for the purpose of attesting to competency; these proctors may neither be licensed to practice in the state nor credentialed to perform that procedure within the institution in which the proctoring occurs; in such cases, the active involvement of the proctor in the procedure may be construed to represent the unlicensed practice of medicine [49].

References

1. Mccullough M. Nearly 1 in 3 US physicians were born abroad. The Philadelphia Inquirer. 2018. Available online at: https://medicalxpress.com/news/2018-12-physicians-born.html.
2. Ranasinghe PD. International medical graduates in the US physician workforce. J Am Osteopath Assoc. 2015;115:236–41.
3. Murphy B. Inside the numbers behind the record-setting 2019 Match. AMA. 3 Mar 2020. Available online at: https://www.ama-assn.org/residents-students/match/inside-numbers-behind-record-setting-2019-match.
4. Rapaport L. U.S. relies heavily on foreign-born healthcare workers. Healthcare & Pharma. Reuters. 4 Dec 2018. Available online at: https://www.reuters.com/article/us-health-professions-us-noncitizens-idUSKBN1O32FR.
5. AMA. Code of Ethics. Code of Medical Ethics Opinion 2.1.1. Informed Consent. Available online at: https://www.ama-assn.org/delivering-care/ethics/informed-consent.
6. Carson-Stevens A, Davies MM, Jones R, Chik AD, Robbé IJ, Fiander AN. Framing patient consent for student involvement in pelvic examination: a dual model of autonomy. J Med Ethics. 2013;39(11):676–80.
7. Silver-Isenstadt A, Ubel PA. Erosion in medical students' attitudes about telling patients they are students. J Gen Intern Med. 1999;14(8):481–7.
8. Cohen DL, McCullough LB, Kessel, et al. J Med Edu. 1987;62:789–98.
9. Santen SA, Hemphill RR, Spanier CM, Fletcher ND. 'Sorry, it's my first time!' Will patients consent to medical students learning procedures? Med Educ. 2005;39(4):365–9.
10. Leung GK, Patil NG. Medical students as observers in theatre: is an explicit consent necessary? Clin Teach. 2011;8(2):122–5.
11. Felice v Valley Lab Inc, 520 So 2d 920 (La Ct App 1988).
12. Rush v Akron General Hospital 171 NE2d 378, 381 (Ohio Ct App 1957).
13. Jenkins v Clark, 454 NE2d 541; Ohio Ct App (1982).
14. McBride v. United States, 462 F.2d 72, 73 (9th Cir. 1972).
15. Centman v Cobb, 581 NE2d 1286 (Ind Ct App 1991).
16. Powers v United States, 589 F Supp 1084, 1099–1101 (D Conn 1984).
17. Wegman B, Stannard JP, Bal BS. Medical liability of the physician in training. Clin Orthop Relat Res. 2012;470(5):1379–85. https://doi.org/10.1007/s11999-012-2244-4.
18. Gonzalez v St John Hospital & Medical Center, 739 NW2d 392 (Mich Ct App 2007).
19. National Bank of Commerce v Quirk; 918 SW2d 138 (Ark 1996).
20. Mercil v Mathers; No C3–93-140, 1994 WL 1114 (Minn Ct App Jan 4, 1994), rev'd on other grounds, 517 NW2d 328 (Minn 1994).
21. McBride v United States , 462 F2d 72 (9th Cir 1972); St. Germain v Pfeifer , 637 NE2d 848 (Mass 1994); Jenkins v Clark, 454 NE2d 541 (Ohio Ct App 1982); Baccari v Donat , 741 A2d 262 (RI 1999).
22. Valentine v Kaiser Foundation Hospital, 15 Cal Rptr 26 (Cal Ct App 1961); Parmelee v Kline , 579 So2d 1008 (La Ct App 1991); Felice v Valleylab, Inc ., 520 So2d 920 (La Ct App 1988).
23. Bailey RA. Resident liability in medical malpractice. Ann Emerg Med. 2013;61(1):114–7.
24. Singh H, Thomas EJ, Petersen LA, Studdert DM. Medical errors involving trainees: a study of closed malpractice claims from 5 insurers. Arch Intern Med. 2007;167(19):2030–6.
25. Thiels CA, Choudhry AJ, Ray-Zack MD, et al. Medical malpractice lawsuits involving surgical residents. JAMA Surg. 2018;153(1):8–13.
26. American Academy of Pediatrics Committee on Medical Liability. Professional liability coverage for residents and fellows. Pediatrics. 2000;106:605–9.
27. Charles SC. Coping with a medical malpractice suit. West J Med. 2001;174(1):55–58.
28. McCullough v Hutzel Hospital, 276 NW2d 569 (Mich Ct App 1979); Morris v Francisco , 708 P2d 498 (Kan 1985); Cole v Tennessee, 1998 Tenn App LEXIS 485 (Tenn Ct App 1998).
29. Kachalia A, Studdert DM. Professional liability issues in graduate medical education. JAMA. 2004;292(9):1051–6.

30. Lownsbury v VanBuren, 762 NE2d 354 (Ohio 2001).
31. Prosise v Foster, 544 SE2d 331 (Va 2001).
32. Mozingo v Pitt County Memorial Hospital, 415 SE2d 341 (NC 1992).
33. Board of Curators of University of Missouri v Horowitz, 435 US 78 (1978).
34. US Constitution. amend V.
35. US Constitution. amend XIV, § 1.
36. Regents of University of Michigan v Ewing, 474 US 214 (1985).
37. Corso v Creighton University, 731 F2d 529 (8th Cir1984); *see also* Lee v University of Michigan-Dearborn, 2007 US LEXIS 72236 (WD Mich 2007).
38. *Hernandez v Overlook Hospital*, 149 NJ 68 (NJ 1997).
39. *Hernandez v Overlook Hospital, citing* [Board of Curators of the Univ. of Mo. v. Horowitz, 435 U.S. 78, 85 n. 2, 98 S.Ct. 948, 953 n. 2, 55 L.Ed.2d 124, 132 n. 2 (1978) (quoting Greenhill v. Bailey, 519 F.2d 5 (8th Cir.1975)).
40. Conran RM, Elzie CA, Knollmann-Ritschel BE, Domen RE, Powell SZ. Due process in medical education: legal considerations. Acad Pathol. 2018;5:2374289518807460. Published 2018 Nov 14. https://doi.org/10.1177/2374289518807460.
41. Ashley RC. The liability of preceptors. Crit Care Nurse. 2004;24(2):98–9.
42. McConnell v. Williams, 65 A.2d 243, 245 (Pa. 1949).
43. *See* Truhitte v. French Hosp., 128 Cal. App. 3d 332, 348, 180 Cal. Rptr. 152, 160 (1982) ("A theory that the surgeon directly controls all activities of whatever nature in the operating room certainly is not realistic in present day medical care.").
44. Szalados JE. Scope of practice in Szalados JE. Smith W., Wright W. Law and ethics in neurocritical care. Neurocritical Care Society. 2019, pp. 200–201.
45. Insurance Journal. Fla. Jury Awards $217M to Misdiagnosed stroke patient. October 10, 2006. Available online at: https://www.insurancejournal.com/news/southeast/2006/10/10/73064.htm.
46. *Bryant v. Bakshandeh* (226 Cal.App.3d 1241(1991)).
47. *Clarke v. Hoek* (California 174 Cal. App. 3d 208 (1985)).
48. Zablocki v. Wilkin (Ohio Com. Pl. 2003).
49. Szalados JE. Preceptorship and proctoring: what is my liability? Western New York Physician (5); 2014: 21–22.
50. CNA HealthPro. Nurse practitioners are at the forefront of a paradigm shift occurring in today's health industry. Understanding nurse practitioner liability. CNA healthpro nurse practitioner claims analysis 1998-2008. CNA. Available online at: https://international.aanp.org/Content/docs/UnderstandingNursePractitionerLiability.pdf.

Chapter 8
The Science of Teamwork in Healthcare: Importance to Patient Outcome

James E. Szalados

Introduction

The US healthcare delivery system is a complex network wherein providers from many specialties, nurses, and their support staff provide care to patients and their families at diverse points of care. The complexity of the subsystems and systems can create waste and error. Waste may occur through redundancy, over- and under-treatment, and medical diagnostic or treatment errors, generally categorized as errors of commission or omission.

Sir William Osler, a founding professor of Johns Hopkins Hospital and often referred to as the Father of Moderate Medicine, once commented that "errors in judgment must occur in the practice of an art which consists largely of balancing probabilities" [1]. Osler's observation has proved to be timeless and continues to highlight the uncertainties inherent in the treatment of complex diseases affecting even more complex individuals where decisions made urgently in real time, often in the absence of complete information, have critical ramifications on the lives of patients.

With the added recognition that many if not most of preventable medical errors are the result of system failures, focus has been redirected from blaming individuals to developing systems capable of detecting and preventing errors before these areas become capable of harming individual patients. Thus, although healthcare quality engineers continue to advocate for a "zero defects" approach to medical errors and

J. E. Szalados (✉)
Director, Surgical and Neurocritical Care Units, Rochester Regional Health System at Rochester General Hospital, Rochester, NY, USA

The Szalados Law Firm, Hilton, NY, USA
e-mail: james.szalados@rochesterregional.org; jszalados@aol.com

J. E. Szalados (ed.), *The Medical-Legal Aspects of Acute Care Medicine*,
https://doi.org/10.1007/978-3-030-68570-6_8

a "zero tolerance" for patient harm, the inherent variability and complexity of healthcare preclude absolute "zero defects." Instead, and more realistically, healthcare clinicians, leaders, and systems must maintain their commitment to excellence so as to continually progress toward a state of clinical and operational perfection. In the words of Vince Lombardi, "Perfection is not attainable, but if we chase perfection, we can catch excellence."

Individuals in healthcare often function within teams, which may be variably categorized as divisions, services, or departments. In many instances, teams may even assembled on short notice for the completion of a brief specific task, such as a surgery, a procedure, or a resuscitation. Teams have the potential to achieve more than any one person can achieve working alone; however, the concept of collaboration and teamwork sometimes remains elusive in a system founded upon a cottage industry model. In the words of Andrew Carnegie, "Teamwork is the ability to work together toward a common vision. The ability to direct individual accomplishments toward organizational objectives. It is the fuel that allows common people to attain uncommon results."

Patient safety programs have evolved from traditional quality assurance and quality improvement programs into more system-wide approaches to develop ingrained cultures of safety highlighting the importance of collaboration and teamwork to better achieve the shared cultural goal of optimal patient outcomes. In addition, the landmark publication *To Err Is Human* authored by the Institute of Medicine [2] not only highlighted the pervasive nature of medical errors but also underscored the opportunities for the healthcare system to improve patient safety through standardization, evidence-based medicine, collaboration, and communication. Although providers are conditioned to introspect and continually evaluate the outcomes of their practice patterns, because they strive to provide the best care possible to their patients, such introspection is limited because of perspective and bias. Thus, quality management is by its very nature a team endeavor. Teams facilitate situational awareness and "bias dilution."

The term *ethics* has its origin in the Greek *ethos* which is translated as "custom" or "habit" and is a branch of philosophy relating to the analysis and application of precepts regarding right and wrong and also interactions between people. Medical ethics refers to the systematic study of ethical or moral issues as applied to the practice of medicine. Traditionally, ethics is based in open discourse and discussion regarding issues for which there are frequently no clear-cut answers and therefore medical ethics often provides a framework for problem solving in highly complex clinical dilemmas in situations. Whereas medicine as practiced in industrialized countries is widely believed to be a science [3], others continue to highlight the human and humanistic elements inherent in medical practice [4]. The first chapters of *Cecil's Textbook of Medicine* represent with a discourse on the art of medicine, with its focus on the patient, and the importance of teaching and reinforcing provider respect for patients as persons, interpersonal skills with patients and within the team, professional attitude, and the importance of developing and better understanding of people as individuals so as to better communicate and foster caring. Therefore, in a sense, any discussion regarding patient harm and medical error must by necessity begin with discussions regarding values, conduct, and advocacy [5]. Safety and quality must be ingrained into organizational culture; these core values need to be driven and supported by the highest levels of organizational leadership, including the President, CEO, and the Board of Directors. In the words of Mark Sanborn, "In teamwork, silence isn't golden, it's deadly," and Peter F. Drucker "The most important thing in communication is to hear what isn't being said."

The Transformation of Healthcare: From Cottage Industry Artisans to Multidisciplinary Teams

The delivery of healthcare in America was characterized by a rapid transformation in the mid-twentieth century from a cottage industry model composed of independent and diverse practitioners into a corporate healthcare model now characterized by increasingly large and complex health systems, close ties with industry through technology development and material supplies, and continuously increasing regulatory oversight.

The original model of US healthcare, the cottage industry model, was one where individual office-based physicians fiercely and independently owned and managed the their practices, practiced alone, and in settings where prevailing training, technology, and resources were the primary determinants of patient outcomes. The rewards of early physician practice models included a stature in the community, a high barrier to entry for competitors, and a steady income base through a loosely structured fee-for-service model, all with little or no regulatory or legal oversight. Such a cottage industry network of small private practices remains in suburban and rural America but continues to decline. Berwick et al. argue that the present US healthcare system functionally remains a cottage industry of nonintegrated, dedicated artisans who eschew standardization, that services are often highly variable, performance remains largely unmeasured, care is customized to individual patients, and standardized processes are regarded with skepticism [6].

The evolutionary transformation of the American healthcare system was the combination of many factors, including scientific and technological advances, increasing complexity and cost, government regulation and third-party payers, national standards of care, tort law, and the rise of hospitals and hospital systems as the primary point of care for complex acute and chronic disease. Providers realized that better care outcomes could be achieved through consultation with specialists and the utilization of evolving technologies such as testing, medications, and monitoring which were beyond the capabilities of individual practices and practitioners. The first recognized importance of hospitals to communities lays within the ability of community physicians to refer to their patients to hospitals where increasingly complex patients could be treated by a safety net composed of medical specialists and nurses and where an increasing concentration of technical and technological support could help those patients who were previously considered untreatable when their care was limited to physician offices. Thus, the evolving scientific complexity of medicine led first to an ever-increasing interdependence of private physicians with hospitals and subsequently to the development of hospital-based medical staff [7].

Whereas the independent and autonomous private physicians who comprised the "country doctor" model simply "did the best they could" under the circumstances with little legal or regulatory oversight of their clinical outcome, quality and safety have assumed a pivotal role in modern healthcare. A fundamental impetus for the standardization of quality and safety was rooted in the legal tort system. Hospital liability under tort law forced an administrative oversight for the quality of care provided by private referring physicians. The court case of *Darling v. Charleston Community Memorial Hospital* established that a hospital may be liable for the negligence of its staff. In its opinion, the *Darling* court stated that:

> The conception that the hospital does not undertake to treat the patient, does not undertake to act through its doctors and nurses, but undertakes instead simply to procure them to act upon their own responsibility, no longer reflects the fact. Present-day hospitals, as their manner of operation plainly demonstrates, do far more than furnish facilities for treatment. They regularly employ on a salary basis a large staff of physicians, nurses and internes, as well as administrative and manual workers, and they charge patients for medical care and treatment, collecting for such services, if necessary, by legal action. Certainly, the person who avails himself of 'hospital facilities' expects that the hospital will attempt to cure him, not that its nurses or other employees will act on their own responsibility [8].

Subsequent to the court decision in *Darling*, a further series of medical negligence cases reaffirmed (a) that hospitals owed a duty to private patients to establish, publish, and enforce rules and regulations pertaining to patient care, the patient which could result in independent liability of the hospital, and (b) that vicarious liability could be imposed upon a hospital for the negligence of independent medical staff and personnel in the care of hospitalized patients under doctrines of either apparent authority or ostensible agency [9]. Thus, hospital liability provided the initial impetus for administrative oversight of hospital-based medical care. The initial hospital-based quality programs consisted of provider credentialing and privileging, peer review, and later as formal hospital quality assurance and hospital-based quality improvement programs. Subsequently, in 1951, the Joint Commission on Accreditation of Hospitals (JCAH) was established as a nonprofit organization designed to provide voluntary accreditation of hospitals based on defined minimum national quality standards. The Joint Commission continues its mission of continuous improvement of the safety and quality of care through standards, oversight, and accreditation.

Risk Management Versus Quality Assurance

Risk management in healthcare is the sum of a variety of clinical and administrative systems, processes, and reporting systems which all serve to detect, monitor, assess, mitigate, and prevent financial loss. Through the use of effective risk management, healthcare organizations can proactively and systematically improve patient safety and also safeguard the organization's assets, market share, accreditation, reimbursement levels, brand value, and community standing [10].

Optimally, a tight interface between a proactive risk management program and a quality assurance program is dynamic and can serve the legitimate interests of both, whereby opportunities identified through risk management can be directly and immediately channeled into system-wide opportunities for quality improvement. In its current more comprehensive role, enterprise risk management is composed of the assessment and management of risk across at least eight operational domains:

1. Operational
2. Clinical and patient safety
3. Strategic
4. Financial
5. Human capital
6. Legal and regulatory
7. Technological
8. Environmental- and Infrastructure-based hazards

Quality assurance (QA), or quality improvement (QI), in healthcare, as opposed to quality control in manufacturing and industrial models, relates to the identification and improvement of processes which minimize errors and improve outcomes. The Institute of Medicine defines healthcare quality as "the degree to which health care services for individuals and populations increase the likelihood of desired health outcomes and are consistent with current professional knowledge" [11]. A fundamental challenge to quality improvement in healthcare has always been and continues to be the practical definition of quality and identification of meaningful metrics by which quality can be quantified. Traditional patient-centered measures of quality were rooted in morbidity and mortality (M&M) conferences, peer review, and the tort litigation system. Deming argued the importance of data collection and analysis and asserted that meaningful quality improvement must be data-driven; improvement presupposed and mandated data collection and analysis. In addition, Deming articulated "14 key principles or Points on Quality Management," through the Deming Model of Quality Management, a core foundation for total quality management (TQM) which emphasized the standardization of processes, training, and infrastructure. TQM is characterized by the Plan-Do-Check-Act Cycle in which processes are analyzed, changes are instituted, effects are verified, and new processes and protocols are implemented. TQM has now evolved into the Lean Six Sigma philosophy which focused on continuously reducing the number of errors to the point where the error rate continues to decrease. In the 1990s, data revealed that medical care in the USA was characterized by large geographic variations in practice patterns which led to development of clinical guidelines. With the development of clinical guidelines, the focus of quality measurement became standardization – where performance measures could be more easily quantitatively measured as deviations from established norms.

TQM and General Systems Theory helped recognize that the quality or outcome of clinical care was very much a function of the environment and the support system, as well as the individual. With the evolution of systems theory, and its application to quality management, especially the work of Donabedian, it became increasingly apparent that many medical errors are more attributable to system or process failures rather than failure of any one individual. Through his model of systems thinking, Donabedian suggested that quality could be measured by assessing three domains: (a) structures, (b) processes, and (c) outcomes of care. Structure refers to the attributes of the environment, the individuals and the teams, and the organizational structure. Process describes the actual activities and the way in which they are carried out. Outcome refers to the impact and measureable end result. Therefore compromised leadership or organizational cultures, a poorly designed work environment, or dysfunctional teamwork may all undermine quality and safety. Nonetheless, a fundamental problem in healthcare, as opposed to other industries, is that safe care does not, in itself, translate into high-quality care.

General Systems Theory

The Austrian biologist, von Bertalanffy, is credited with the development of modern General Systems Theory, asserting that systems cannot be reduced to a series of parts functioning in isolation, but rather, to understand the whole, one must understand the interrelations between the parts [12]. Systems theory offers a framework for quality improvement (QI) in healthcare because systems theory supports "systems thinking" – a discipline that focuses on the system as a whole, and its interrelationships, rather than simply the isolated components. High-quality care is more likely to occur within systems where relationships and interrelationships are considered important, since effective communication, team building, conflict management, behavioral competencies and skill competencies, process management, and education all contribute to safe and effective outcomes [13]. Although systems theory had no practical application in the cottage industry model of healthcare, it has become largely intuitive to modern-day healthcare professionals.

The importance of systems theory to healthcare quality and teamwork rests in the assumption that most individuals strive to do good work but that the outcome is largely a function of the environment. Causal analysis based on systems theory asserts that, when errors occur, individual failings should not be the primary focus; rather, the inquiry should focus on the environment which failed to detect or mitigate the effects of the error. Systems theory shifted the QI approach from the traditional "name, blame, and shame" approach toward the creation of error-resistant and error-resilient environments where the system, teams, and individuals work together to achieve optimal outcomes.

A proponent of General Systems Theory is Peter Senge, who further proposed that organizations such as businesses and healthcare organizations are in fact complex systems which, similar to biological complex-adaptive systems, function optimally when they transform culturally to become "learning organizations." Senge identified five disciplines, or five capabilities, that an organization and its members must possess in order to become a learning organization: (1) systems thinking, (2) personal mastery, (3) mental models, (4) building-shared vision, and (5) team learning.

Culture and Safety in Healthcare

The relationship between an organizational culture of safety and good patient outcomes is well established [14]. It is now considered axiomatic that an organizational culture which supports cohesive and dedicated teamwork is essential to excellence in healthcare. When organizational leadership not only supports but also encourages a disciplined yet compassionate team approach to patient care, then the patient, family, care team, and institution can best succeed together [15]. The National Patient Safety Foundation (NPSF) now considers leadership support for a culture of safety to be the most important of its recommendations for optimizing patient safety [16].

A patient safety culture may perhaps be best conceptualized as a series of interventions which are rooted in principles of leadership, teamwork, and behavior change rather than a specific process, team, or technology [14]. The practical importance of Tom Peters' principle of "management by walking around" (MBWA) cannot be overstated. Executive walk rounds is an interventional strategy which engages organizational leadership directly with frontline care team members. Organizations which do not achieve optimal outcomes frequently lack the leadership engagement and commitment necessary to inspire and support the frontline team.

The Challenger space shuttle launch decision exemplifies the importance of organizational culture to outcomes and has significant applicability to the science of error management and safety in healthcare. The early National Aeronautics and Space Administration (NASA) was shaped by a team-based problem-solving culture with a spirited "can do" attitude. Later however, as NASA became structurally more complex and bureaucratic, it slowly transformed into more of a technical production system characterized by administrative hierarchy which increasingly focused on budgetary constraints, public perceptions, and production benchmarks. Simultaneously, corporate leadership stressed prior successes, and a work group culture evolved which began to accept and even normalize risk.

In *The Challenger Launch Decision: Risky Technology, Culture, and Deviance at NASA*, Diane Vaughan examined the series of events believed to have led to the ill-fated Challenger launch decision [17]. Vaughan posits that "incalculable risk" became normalized into a concept of "acceptable risk" which, in turn, was culturally internalized and progressively rationalized as a part of NASA's standard operating procedures. Rocket science was understood to be innately risky; however, NASA culture chose to marginalize risk given its history of "beating the odds" believing that its technical superiority and redundancies would continue to "beat the odds" going forward. Thus, NASA engineers built two O-rings into the shuttle rocket design as a redundancy and chose to accept the risk of O-ring failure even when test performance results deviated from design specifications. Reportedly, engineer Morton Thiokol concerned that the planned Challenger launch in the setting of forecasted cold temperatures in Florida could undermine O-ring performance, making a "no launch" recommendation for the Challenger; however, he was unable to persuade NASA leadership to postpone the launch. Thus, production pressure and a leadership culture in which negativism was frowned upon forced the Challenger launch which ended in catastrophe. Factors believed to have led to the Challenger launch decision include (1) perceived pressure, (2) rigid conformity to perceived role requirements, (3) questionable reasoning, (4) ambiguous communications, and (5) failure to ask important relevant questions [18].

Vaughan also identified three organizational factors which, in her opinion, resulted in the Challenger disaster: (1) the normalization of deviance, a belief in acceptable risk; (2) the culture of production whereby lunch schedules and budgetary pressures relegated safety behind cost and schedule imperative; and (3) the structural secrecy, wherein siloed information, coupled with poor communication and an attempt to avoid negativism, resulted in constrained information flow and inaccurate perceptions of the actual operating conditional and risks. Effective technical and group communication requires a sincere exchange of information in four dimensions: clarity, interrelatedness, centrality, and openness [19].

The relevance of the lessons learned from the Challenger launch decision to the safety culture in healthcare cannot be overstated. Repeatedly, studies have demonstrated that pressures which prioritize output over the safety produce conditions deleterious to patient safety. For example, Gaba et al. determined that production pressure and financial pressure are detrimental to team functionality and result in unsafe clinical decisions [20]. Moreover, leadership in the healthcare is often overly focused on optimism, confusing realism with negativism, and thereby fails to appreciate the potential deleterious impact of administrative directives on frontline performance and patient safety.

A "safety culture" refers to an organizational culture in which perceptions, beliefs, values, attitudes, and actions form the basis for a shared commitment to safety and an effort to minimize errors which may lead to patient harm. The notion of a "safety culture" originated in studies of high reliability organizations (HROs) which demonstrated a consistent ability to minimize adverse events while managing intrinsically complex and hazardous work. The importance of true and committed leadership involvement inpatient safety is exemplified in the high reliability organization.

The High Reliability Organization

The study of "high reliability" is rooted in the recognition that many organizations function very well under intrinsically hazardous and fast-paced conditions and yet manage highly complex systems in an essentially error-free manner and sustain exemplary safety records over extended periods of time [21]. Examples of HROs include commercial aviation, oilfield services, the nuclear power industry, and aircraft carriers. One important feature of HROs is that they are culturally preoccupied with a potential for failure and therefore resist temptations to simplify observations and experiences. The HRO mindset exemplifies the apparent failures at NASA which led to the Challenger launch decision. HROs train their teams to recognize that threats to safety can be complex and that the earliest indicators of potential threats usually and typically appear as almost imperceptible small events or variations [22].

HROs maintain their resilience even in the event of mishaps through a recognition that despite best efforts and past successes, errors will inevitably occur and safety may ultimately be compromised. HROs enhance that resilience through a deference to expertise within their team structure and preemptively identify individuals with relevant expertise. HROs value the perspectives of frontline team members and are culturally able to subordinate organizational hierarchy. Clear and efficient communication between leadership and "boots on the ground" team members is essential if potential threats to safety are to be efficiently and effectively identified and corrected.

Roberts and Rousseau identified eight characteristics of HROs: (1) hypercomplexity, (2) tightly coupled, (3) extreme hierarchical differentiation, (4) many decision-makers working in complex communication networks, (5) high degree of accountability, (6) frequent, immediate feedback regarding decisions, (7) compressed time factors, and (8) synchronized outcomes [23].

Hypercomplexity exists in HROs because of an innately high number and variety of subcomponents and subsystems each characterized by unique procedures, training routines, and command hierarchy. Thus, in order to successfully manage hypercomplexity, good communication between many individual teams and subsystems is essential to coordinate interrelated activities and even to efficiently monitor overall system performance. Hypercomplexity is intrinsic to healthcare since a multitude of subspecialties and disciplines, including support systems such as nursing, pharmacy, and technical support, all must focus their efforts on a clinical situation, such as a complex patient, to coordinate their activities in order to effect the optimal clinical outcome.

Tight coupling is defined in HROs as reciprocal task interdependence across many units and levels so that the effective performance of any given task is naturally dependent upon effective performance of a number of other preceding, concurrent, and subsequent tasks. In contrast to tight coupling, a loosely coupled system is one in which each of components either lacks or makes little use of knowledge regarding the state of other subsystems or components. Siloed systems are loosely coupled and therefore at high risk for dysfunction due to a lack of coordination. In a tightly coupled system, all the elements are "in tune" with each other to manage the overall progress toward the end goal. Tight coupling presupposes effective communication but also mutual support; it is coordination, communication, and unified focus. Tight coupling, as it applies to healthcare, describes real-time clinical decision-making, whereby effective decisions are based upon a myriad of streaming data points from many sources, which in turn requires timely, accurate, and reliable communication of information to minimize the possibility of error.

Extreme hierarchical differentiation in HROs refers to an organizational command structure in which levels and roles are clearly differentiated. Hierarchical differentiation characterizes the aviation industry and the armed forces and can be a source of both weakness and strength depending on the effectiveness of the leadership culture in the hierarchy. In an ineffective hierarchy, poor coordination and cohesiveness lead to dysfunctional communication, which in turn results in error-prone decision-making. On the other hand, in an effective hierarchy, leadership serves to unify, direct, and coordinate through the development and support of shared vision, responsibility, and direction. Well-led teams exhibit both assertiveness and mutual trust, which create an environment wherein all team members can assert their ideas and concerns to a higher-ranking team member without fear of criticism or reprisal. In a well-led team, the perspectives of all team members, especially frontline team members, are elicited and valued [this mindset is an essential element of Crew Resource Management; see below]. Therefore, HROs are characterized by a culture of "collective mindfulness," whereby every team member, irrespective of hierarchical status, is continuously and acutely aware that even small failures and safety protocols or processes can result in catastrophic adverse outcomes and therefore every member is fully committed and focused on finding, addressing, and correcting potential safety concerns at an early stage before a larger system failure can occur [24]. HROs maintain robust process improvement and also embrace that model of organizational culture which is now recognized as the "safety culture."

Teams in HROs are composed of many individual decision-makers with diverse backgrounds working in complex networks. For example, within healthcare, a specific team may include a physician, advanced practice provider, nurse, therapists, and technicians. Such diverse team members are each trained specifically within their respective professions with varying styles of communication depending on their role and hierarchical position. Since the ability to frame a critical communication is essential in a complex environment, the manner of communication is as important as the message. Communication theory recognizes seven major elements of communication process: (1) sender, (2) ideas, (3) encoding, (4) communication channel, (5) receiver, (6) decoding, and (7) feedback. In healthcare, new and emerging models of communication such as the Situation, Background, Assessment, Recommendation (SBAR) strategy have been used in healthcare to effectively overcome communication barriers.

HROs are also characterized by "immediate feedback" regarding decisions; there is an identifiable, measurable outcome metric associated with HRO team performance. In order to ensure effective feedback, feedback must be timely and specific and appropriately delivered. Optimally, feedback should be respectful, and every feedback should be recognized as a potential teaching/learning opportunity.

Major HRO activities often occur under compressed timelines; even routine procedures in healthcare can rapidly change and evolve into stressful, time-compressed situations, where minutes count in a medical emergency. Teams must be capable of changing pace based on the situation and rapidly reconfigure and adapt to urgencies and emergencies.

In the Roberts and Rousseau model, the eighth characteristic of HROs is that critical outcomes occur simultaneously; therefore, teams differ from groups or individuals working in isolation because of intra-dependency which creates a need for synchronization of activities.

Therefore, in summary, the key features of an HRO are:

1. Acknowledgment of the high-risk nature of an organization's activities and the determination to achieve consistently safe operations
2. A blame-free environment where individuals are able to report errors or near misses without fear of reprimand or punishment
3. Encouragement of collaboration across ranks and disciplines to seek solutions to patient safety problems
4. Organizational commitment of resources to address safety concerns [25]

HRO teamwork and the KSAs which comprise it are critical for successful performance, at the process and at organizational levels. KSA is an acronym for Knowledge, Skills, and Attitudes. The Joint Commission suggests that hospitals and healthcare organizations work to create a strong foundation to support their subsequent maturation into HROs. Foundational work for HRO development in healthcare includes a leadership commitment to zero-harm goals, establishment of a safety culture, and institution of a robust process improvement culture. The Joint Commission has developed and published tools and metrics to help with organizational culture development on the road to high reliability [26]. The IOM also issued recommendations designed to move healthcare institutions toward high reliability. Furthermore, the Agency for Healthcare Research and Quality (AHRQ) has assumed a lead role in supporting and implementing the recommendations of the IOM toward health system-wide HRO development.

Crew Resource Management (CRM) has emerged within HROs as an effective approach to training, developing, and sustaining essential team skills that facilitate safe and effective operations under critical situations. CRM is essential to effectively managing the hierarchical differentiation inherent in HROs.

Crew Resource Management

Healthcare delivery systems exemplify the paradigm of a complex organization – one that operates as a multidisciplinary team under high stakes in dynamic policy and regulatory environments. Therefore, the coordination and delivery of safe, high-quality care demand effective teamwork and collaboration within, as well as across, organizational, disciplinary, technical, and cultural boundaries. The concept of CRM was originally derived from safety training in aviation and has recently been successfully adapted to the healthcare sector [27].

Formal civil aviation Crew Resource Management (CRM) was first introduced in the USA as an aviation industry training competency in 1979 [28]. Nonetheless, the conceptual foundations for CRM can be traced to earlier human factors' performance research conducted by the US Army Air Corps and US Navy during World War II. Since 1979, the CRM concept has evolved through several iterations, each modified based on new human performance research as well as aviation safety perspectives derived from aviation mishap analyses conducted by the Federal Aviation Administration and Flight Safety International, the National Transportation Safety Board, and NASA, among others. Flawed decision-making, as exemplified by poor CRM, is considered as a root cause in the Challenger and Columbia Space Shuttle disasters, the loss of the Mars Climate Orbiter, and the Mars Polar Lander. In the most recent fifth generation of CRM, a major philosophical shift now assumes that human error is pervasive and cannot be totally eliminated and therefore must be effectively mitigated.

CRM theory was developed as a systemic response by the aviation industry to accident reconstructions, analysis of data from flight data recorders (FDRs), and data from cockpit voice recorders (CVRs). Data suggested that many aviation accidents were not a result of technical malfunctions, failure of aircraft handling skills, or a lack of technical knowledge, but rather a result of the inability of crews to collectively and appropriately respond to a rapidly evolving complex situation. Thus, CRM was developed as management system designed to optimize the use of available resources – equipment, procedures, and people – to promote operational safety and efficiency. CRM focuses on the cognitive and interpersonal skills needed to manage complex situations. To accomplish its goal, CRM employs team-based training which encompasses basic knowledge, skills and attitudes such as effective communication, promotion of situational awareness, crisis problem-solving, personal accountability, decision-making, and teamwork [29]. CRM represented an organizational culture shift in the traditional hierarchical differentiation of the airline industry to recognize the value of the team.

Human behaviors are recognized to be a product of knowledge and training, thought process, personality, attitude, and background. CRM views decision-making as a series of cognitive and behavioral events where the leader and team members work together to (1) plan a work process, (2) designate and brief members regarding roles and functions (3), monitor the process as it occurs (4), detect and report deviations from the plan (5), communicate corrections from the top down (6), adjust actions as needed, (7) debrief at important moments (at significant change or conclusion of work), and (8) learn to refine the human-machine interface.

The basic structure of traditional CRM addresses the elements of:

1. Communication
2. Workload management
3. Decision-making
4. Conflict resolution
5. Leadership
6. Team management
7. Stress management

Communication and decision-making skills are a core factor in CRM. Team members must accept that critical information or data which will subsequently affect decision-making must be requested, offered, or given freely in a timely way to permit accurate, effective decision-making.

Team building consists of two interrelated concepts: (a) leadership and (b) team management. The aviation industry has recognized that complex large aircraft is managed by teams and not by individual pilots. Teams facilitate the effective management of complexity and also provide redundancy. However, CRM also aims to reduce dysfunctions which can occur in teams such as bystander effect, social conformity, social loafing, and groupthink [30]. The bystander effect refers to a complacency which occurs when the presence of others discourages an individual from acting in an emergency situation; potential explanations include a perceived diffusion of responsibility and social signals promoting a sense of ambiguity. Conformity is a behavior resulting from social influence where behaviors change in order to fit in with group patterns or standards. Social loafing refers to a tendency of individual team members to exert less effort on a task than they would have if alone. Finally, groupthink is a similar behavior wherein group members refrain from stating facts expressing opinions out of a perceived need for conformity and consensus; groupthink frequently results in irrational or dysfunctional decisions. The interplay between leadership, teamwork, and communication is exemplified by the CRM focus on the value of individuals and individual perspectives within the team.

Workload management addresses the fact that errors and accidents are most likely to occur when workload demands exceed team capabilities. Excessive workload can compromise attention to details and response time. However, low workload can also compromise safety and promote errors by inducing states of boredom, complacency, and inattentiveness. The Yerkes-Dodson law defines an empirical relationship between arousal and performance such that higher levels of arousal improve an individual's performance to a point: the "optimal" state of arousal or stimulation. The relationship between stress and performance is also illustrated by the "inverted U" stress response curve where optimum stress, a point between boredom and overwhelming stress, correlates with enhanced performance. In order to manage workload and stress, the CRM element of workload management addresses concepts such as mission planning and briefing, stress management, and workload distribution to maximize the matching of workload and capacity.

Situational awareness is a fundamental element of CRM which refers to the development and maintenance of a dynamic awareness of one's surrounding and situational context through the accumulation of information from multiple sources. Situational awareness involves a conscious awareness regarding the relevant environment, a continuous perception of the implications of that information, and an assessment of the appropriateness of evolving responses. Appropriate situational assessment and awareness is the basis for critical decision-making and therefore optimal performance. Good situational awareness is based on good resource utilization, managing internal and external inputs, both from one's own sensory inputs and the information communicated by others. Loss of situational awareness can take many forms, all potentially mitigated by teamwork. For example, "target fixation" occurs where an individual becomes so intensely focused on one aspect of the environment that they compromise all other sensory inputs, where a fighter pilot focuses so closely on the target that he or she crashes the plane. Loss of situational awareness also occurs during "task saturation" where the workload exceeds the available time, tools, or resources and thus leads to an inability to focus on the essential issues.

The applicability of CRM to healthcare is obvious and natural. In 2001, Gaba developed Anesthesia Crisis Resource Management (ACRM) [31]. ACRM was first designed to help anesthesiologists effectively manage crisis situations through the recognition of the value of multidisciplinary teams including physicians, nurses, technicians, and other support staff. ACRM employed simulators to provide training in specific, technical, and generic teamwork skills. The team skills developed through ACRM included empowerment for inquiries and assertions; effective communication; the ability to give and receive feedback, appropriately exert leadership, and maintain a positive group and team climate; and the critique and reevaluation of events in debriefing.

An effective team structure has backup and redundancy which exemplified by the HRO and CRM models. Since most errors are the culmination of a series or preceding small mishaps, the primary advantage of a strong and highly functional team is to bolster the safety of a complex system by introducing multiple points where an error can be identified and its propagation stopped. The Swiss cheese model of error illustrates the capacity of teams to catch errors before they create harm. Errors, including latent conditions, latent failures, and active failures, can be trapped only if the "holes" are not aligned; that is, any one member of the team can stop an error from causing harm. Moreover, arguably, the optimal approach to error management involves the steps of error avoidance, error, entrapment, and error effect mitigation, whereby the effects of errors that cannot be stopped in the Swiss cheese model can be minimized.

Current understanding of team dynamics is partly the culmination of lessons learned from General Systems Theory, the safety culture, and Crew Resource Management. The Donabedian TQM quality model emphasized the importance of structure and process, which are attributes of the organization and the way that individuals in the organization interact. Another model of quality management, the Command Team Effectiveness (CTEF) model, refines the framework of analysis to be more relevant to healthcare, specifically surgical teams, which have unique attributes as action teams [32]. Examples of "action teams" are emergency medical, surgical, or anesthesia teams, air crews, and military command and control. Action teams are characterized by diverse specialized professionals that collaborate in the context of high-acuity, complex tasks, ad hoc team compositions, and time-pressured conditions. In the CTEF model, dimensions of activity include mission framework, task, organizational characteristics, leadership, and the characteristics of team members.

Subsequently, the importance of human factors as contributors to medical error has been increasingly recognized, especially since the publication of *To Err Is Human* [33] and subsequently within the WHO Curriculum for Patient Safety [34]. Human factors are defined in a systemic perspective as the sum of the interrelationships of the contextual environment, organizational and job factors, and individual characteristics which influence behavior. The field of human factors science addresses the manner in which a system, as the sum of its component parts, is committed to the prevention of accidental harms. Specifically, within the field of healthcare, human factors research would seek to optimize the environment in which the cognitive and physical elements of the work that healthcare professionals perform takes place; this in order to achieve the highest possible quality and safety in patient care. Thus, the interplay of leadership and teamwork within the healthcare system has now become a system-wide priority forcus.

Teamwork

We have established that effective teamwork is a mission critical in healthcare. Effective teamwork in healthcare builds a positive organizational culture and improves patient safety and the outcomes of care. Nonetheless, the creation of teams is infinitely more complex than the assembly of a group of individuals and the assignment of a task. The science of team dynamics studies the subconscious forces that influence the interactions between team members and leadership, between team members themselves, and the resulting behaviors and performance.

Groups are not teams. Groups are assemblies of two or more individuals merged through directives or social needs who are working toward individual goals; a team is a group of interdependent individuals who collaborate toward the achievement of a defined common purpose, goal, or mission. Healthcare teams are two or more people who interact interdependently with a common purpose, working toward measurable goals, such as patient safety, patient outcomes, or community health, for example. Teams are composed of individuals. Individuals who have a sense of commitment to the team will enthusiastically share their potentially unique fund of information, ideas, and perspectives for the good of the team and with a focus on goals and outcome. Intellectual capital is the term used to describe any one individual's intellectual storehouse – the knowledge, information, skills, and experience – which can be engaged to help create a winning team. Individuals sharing intellectual capital create a similar intellectual capital "account" for the team from which team leadership can "draw" to "invest" in goal-directed activities.

Successful teams are characterized by synergy, whereby the performance of the team as a whole exceeds that which the sum of its parts could accomplish. A growing trend in team science addresses cross-disciplinary interactions, whereby team members with diverse training and expertise from different fields work together to combine or integrate their perspectives in a single purposeful endeavor. In the words of Ken Blanchard, "None of us is as smart as all of us."

Individuals, however, are prone to biases. Biases are personal and unreasoned subconscious judgments. A cognitive bias can cause a systematic nonlogical error in the processing and interpretation of information. Cognitive biases are not the same as logical fallacies. A logical fallacy stems from an erroneous but superficially believable logical argument; on the other hand, a cognitive bias is the product of cognitive processing errors. Biases are one, but extremely important, form of loss of situational awareness. The sheer complexity and the amount of information in the environment prompt humans to subconsciously develop mental shortcuts, or "gut reflexes," known as heuristics. A large number of cognitive biases have been described; however, examples of the more common biases include:

- *Confirmation bias*: The tendency to search for, favor, or interpret information which confirms one's preconceptions while ignoring or discounting non-conforming evidence.
- *Framing*: The tendency to draw varying conclusions from identical data depending on the presentation of the information.
- *Availability heuristic*: The tendency to focus on the most recent or emotionally charged information.
- *Anchoring bias*: This is the tendency to rely too heavily on the first data element or the most pleasing data element encountered.

An understanding of potential biases by both leadership and team members, and their implications to group decision-making, is vital since biases can result in erroneous decisions. Biases may also be contagious in situations where the bias is introduced by leaders or influencers perpetuating a loss of situational awareness through groupthink or social conformity. Nonetheless, a major strength of teams, not previously described, is "bias dilution" – it is a term I use to describe the ability of effective teams to jointly overcome the biases of individual team members. As long as team members are encouraged to individually acquire information, communicate freely, and commit to the mission, there is a potential that team situational awareness can overcome individual biases. Bias dilution is a valuable characteristic of highly functional teams.

Woolley et al. studied the individual intelligence of team members and compared that to a collective intelligence factor, a latent factor describing a team's general ability to perform on a wide variety of tasks. When the collective intelligence score was calculated based on the team's performance on a set of tasks, researchers found that collective intelligence was only moderately related to the individual members' intelligence scores and that collective intelligence was more predictive of future team performance than was individual members' average intelligence score [36]. Thus, "smart teams" are not simply teams of smart people. Collective intelligence appears to be related to social perceptiveness of team members, or their ability to infer others' mental states, such as beliefs or feelings based on subtle cues. Collective intelligence is also related to a perceived freedom of communication, where a greater amount of participation, encouraged participation, and equal participation are all associated with higher collective intelligence in teams [37].

Since teams are composed of individuals, individuals have varying personalities. The Myers-Briggs Type Indicator (MBTI) is one frequently used personality assessment tool. The theory behind Myers-Briggs is that random variations in the behavior of individuals is in fact orderly and consistent and is a product of measurable differences in the ways individuals use perception and judgment. "Perception involves all the ways of becoming aware of things, people, happenings, or ideas. Judgment involves all the ways of coming to conclusions about what has been perceived. If people differ systematically in what they perceive and in how they reach conclusions, then it is only reasonable for them to differ correspondingly in their interests, reactions, values, motivations, and skills" [38]. In a very simplified fashion, Myers-Briggs identifies 16 basic personality types based in four domains:

- Favorite world: Environmental focus. Extraversion (E) versus Introversion (I).
- Information gathering style: A predisposition to focus on reality, facts, and information acquired through one's senses or rather a focus patterns and impressions and added meaning with a tendency for visualizing future possibilities and abstractions. Sensing (S) or Intuition (N).
- Decision-making: A focus on objective facts, logic, and consistency or focus on people, emotions, and circumstances. Thinking (T) or Feeling (F).
- Structure: A preference for structure and firm decisions or a tendency to see theings more openly, with a flexible and adaptable mindset. Judging (J) or Perceiving (P).

The 16 personality types are then classified by a four-letter code and a general descriptor of that personality profile:

Each personality type is then identified by its four-letter code:

- ISTJ – The Inspector
- ISTP – The Crafter
- ISFJ – The Protector
- ISFP – The Artist
- INFJ – The Advocate
- INFP – The Mediator
- INTJ – The Architect
- INTP – The Thinker
- ESTP – The Persuader
- ESTJ – The Director
- ESFP – The Performer
- ESFJ – The Caregiver
- ENFP – The Champion
- ENFJ – The Giver
- ENTP – The Debater
- ENTJ – The Commander

Teams represent the reservoir for potential creativity and innovation in organizations. Team strengths and dysfunctions may be a function of the personality types comprising the team, termed "team chemistry." The dominant personalities in a team can shape the outcome based on the way they perceive and process information. Personality types and biases can influence the outcome of a team's mission in subtle ways. A good mix of MBTI types can also further bias dilution, through consideration of diverse points of view. Where circumstances allow, and the mission of a team is predefined, the MBTI can help assemble a potentially more functional team by providing diversity and facilitating conflict management. Consideration to diversity in team selection and team management builds strength but can also cause dysfunction. Thus, understanding personalities can greatly increase team effectiveness. In the words of Tom Peters, "Stellar teams are invariably made up of quirky individuals who typically rub each other raw, but they figure out - with the spiritual help of a gifted leader - how to be their peculiar selves and how to win championships as a team...at the same time." There is no magic formula to create teamwork. Teams are groups of very diverse individuals unified by a mission and a sense of duty; missions succeed or fail because of team chemistry. In the words of Vince Lombardi, "Individual commitment to a group effort: That is what makes a teamwork, a company work, a society work, a civilization work."

A great deal has been written in the management sciences regarding teams, team building, and team leadership. In *The Wisdom of Teams*, Katzenbach and Smith [39] define a team as "a small number of people with complementary skills who are committed to a common purpose, performance goals, and approach for which they hold themselves mutually accountable." High-performance teams may be generally defined by a combination of purpose and goals, talent, skills, performance ethics, incentives and motivation, efficacy, leadership, conflict, communication, power and empowerment, and norms and standards [40]. There is no team without a performance challenge which is considered meaningful to all team members. Leaders can best foster team performance through strong performance ethics rather than team promotion. In an effective team, the manner of communication, freedom, and frequency directly determine the effectiveness of the team.

Extensive research suggests that teamwork is defined by a set of interrelated KSAs that facilitate coordinated, adaptive performance [41]. Within teams, members' behaviors can be categorized in terms of both taskwork and teamwork processes; taskwork is what teams are doing, whereas teamwork describes "how they are doing it with each other" [42]. Team dynamics represent the unconscious, psychological forces which influence a team's behavior and performance, created by and a function of the nature of the team's work, the personalities within the team, their working relationships with other people, and the environment in which the team works. Collins [43] argues that the road from goodness to greatness within a system requires disciplined people, disciplined thought, and disciplined action. *Disciplined people* is about building the right team with the right members and keeping them focused on excellence. Getting the right people takes precedence over strategy and vision. The importance of an effective team cannot be overstated. In an effective team, people are not the most valuable asset; instead, the right people are. *Disciplined thought* refers to honesty and commitment. *Disciplined action* is about focus. Collins also defines "Level 5 Leaders" as those who embody a powerful mixture of personal humility and indomitable will. The characteristic behaviors of such leaders include the following: (1) *paradox*: ambition for the organizational rather than personal success, (2) *driven* to the point of obsession to produce exceptional results on a sustainable basis, (3) understanding the need to *build successors*, (4) a realization of the importance of *sharing praise*, (5) the ability to take blame when things go wrong, (6) are normal people without larger-than-life personalities, and they (7) come from within the organization because their greatness comes from quiet hard work, rather than heroic acts.

Studies of military and aviation teams identified team/collective orientation, mission analysis and planning, mutual performance monitoring, backup behavior, adaptability, and leadership as critical teamwork competencies. The Institute of Medicine Committee on the Health Professions Education Summit legitimized teamwork competencies as a standard component of graduate and continuing professional education in the health professions; its report identified the capacity to "work in interdisciplinary teams … to cooperate, collaborate, communicate, and integrate care in teams to ensure that care is continuous and reliable" as a core competency that all clinicians should possess regardless of discipline [44]. For example, it is recognized that the inclusion of a pharmacist as a team member during intensive care unit (ICU) rounds can reduce prescribing orders by as much as 66% because needed expertise about medication indications, doses, and interactions is made available to the team [45]. Nonetheless, role boundary conflicts may emerge as team, dysfunctions in instances where teamwork is poor, where hierarchy or leadership is compromised, or where team members overstep professional boundaries through poor communication [46].

Teamwork and quality are inextricably linked. Failures of interprofessional teamwork and communication lead directly to compromised patient care, staff distress, tension, and inefficiency [47], make a substantial contribution to medical error [48], and are a contributory factor in 61% of sentinel events [49]. Studies confirm the importance of communication and coordination of teamwork. Observational studies in surgical services indicate that approximately 30% of team interactions include a communication failure of some type and that patients receiving care with poor teamwork are almost five times as likely to experience complications or death [50]. An Australian study found preventable patient deaths were twice as likely to be caused by a communication failure as an error of technical competence [51]. ICUs with a "team-oriented culture" have shorter lengths of stay, lower nursing turnover, and higher quality of care and can better meet family members' needs [52]. The quality of teamwork is also directly associated with patient's perceptions regarding the quality of their care and satisfaction with their care [53].

Research has shown that teamwork and organizational culture scores are inversely related to adverse events, with areas related to handoffs and transitions of care, teamwork within units, and teamwork across units having the strongest relationship [54]. Simply said, the better the teamwork, the better the outcomes. Communication failures are both an independent cause of preventable patient harm. Transitions of care or handoffs in acute care settings represent significant risks for communication failures which contribute to medical errors and preventable patient harm. Transition or handoffs represent high-risk interactions wherein critical information about patient history, status, and plan of care can be miscommunicated, and therefore transitions are recolonized to be directly associated with 28% of surgical adverse events [55].

With respect to the theory and models for teamwork competencies in healthcare, many programs have been developed: the nomenclature varies, but the core concepts are almost identical. Application of the principles of CRM to teamwork in healthcare has led to Team Resource Integration Management (TRIM). TRIM adapts CRM principles with three goals: to avoid, trap, and mitigate the consequences of decision-making errors. TRIM also employs four steps of CRM: problem recognition, problem definition, identification of probable solutions, and the implementation of appropriate action. The notion of "integration" is applies to TRIM related to the importance of successful integration of the entire team's KSA into an effective solution. TRIM also stands for terms that emphasize communication:

- Talk with each other.
- Respect each other.
- Initiate action.
- Monitor results [56].

TeamSTEPPS is another evidence-based toolkit developed jointly by the Agency for Healthcare Research and Quality (AHRQ) and Department of Defense (DoD) designed to strengthen teamwork competencies. TeamSTEPPS is based in five key principles which are composed of team structure plus four teachable-learnable skills: (1) leadership, (2) communication, (3) situation monitoring, and (4) mutual support.

Situation monitoring refers to a process of continually scanning and assessing the relevant environment to maintain situation awareness (STEP = status of the patient, team members, environment, progress toward goal). Similar to CRM, situation monitoring, or awareness, represents continuous and conscious perception of those factors in the environment which might pose either threats or opportunities. Effective communication is communication which is complete, clear, brief, and timely. Shared mental models result from the combined and shared individual situation awareness of each team member. Cross-monitoring refers to an error reduction strategy, similar to that in HROs, whereby team members monitor the actions of other team members to provide a safety net for and within the team. Mutual support refers to task assistance, whereby the team protects its members from work overload situations, frames offers and requests for assistance in the context of patient safety, and fosters a work climate where assistance will be actively sought and offered.

TeamSTEPPS recognizes two types of leaders: (a) designated and (b) situational. High-functioning teams recognize that in complex situations the leadership role can shift to the member with the skills to best manage the particular situation. An effective TeamSTEPPS team leader (a) organizes the team, (b) articulates clear goals, (c) makes decisions through collective input of members, (d) empowers members to speak up and challenge, (e) actively promotes and facilitates good teamwork, and (f) fairly resolves conflicts.

Teams have a great potential; however, as the Challenger disaster illustrates, even high- performing teams are prone to fatal dysfunctions:

- Absence of trust – avoidance of being perceived vulnerable

- Fear of conflict – the need for artificial harmony over constructive passionate debate
- Lack of commitment – false buy-in for group decisions
- Avoidance of accountability – avoidance of responsibility
- Inattention to results – a prioritization of personal success, status, and ego before team success [57]

Team dysfunction can be avoided or minimized by embracing common sense with uncommon levels of discipline and persistence. In effective teams, members of the team respect and trust each other in order to give and receive feedback on their performance, must have good communication skills to accurately convey information, and must have a shared mental model [58]. Shared mental models are critical for effective teamwork in general and specifically in healthcare. Shared mental models lead to a common understanding of the situation, the plan for treatment, and the roles and tasks of the individuals in the team. Without a shared mental model, the different members of the team cannot fully contribute to problem-solving and decision-making [59].

Once again, groupthink is an important dysfunction of teams. Groupthink is a situation where otherwise engaged team members will make irrational or suboptimal decisions; in a sense it is "going along to get along." Groupthink is especially prone to occur where team leadership urges conformity, marginalizes inquisitiveness, or discourages participation or dissent. Premature or frankly erroneous consensus may be driven by a particular agenda, an imposed sense of urgency, or simply a culture of complacency where group members are encouraged to value harmony and coherence above discourse.

Team decision-making is also prone to the "Risky Shift Phenomenon" where a group, or team, may be more likely to make a riskier decision than any individual team member would make alone. Such a tendency for shift in risk perception is also sometimes called "choice shift." The psychology underlying the "risky shift" remains unclear; however dilution of individual accountability, desensitization to risk through repetition, and a shared sense of power that is associated with risk-taking behavior may all play a role.

Studies which explore the effects of group discussion on attitudes, jury decisions, ethical decisions, judgments, person perceptions, negotiations, and risk-taking are also generally consistent with a "group polarization" hypothesis, derived from the risky shift. Group polarization is defined as a phenomenon when "members of a deliberating group move toward a more extreme point in whatever direction is indicted by the members' pre-deliberation tendency" [60]. In the "Group Polarization Phenomenon," team members tend to take more extreme positions with respect to their decisions. Group polarization can be a result of social comparison or normative influence, where team members change opinions when in a group in order to fit in or to be accepted or informational influence which occurs when members are unsure of their positions and although they enter a discussion with an open mind, they change opinion favoring the side which is more likeable, persuasive, or passionate.

Thus, the quality of care at the bedside, in any situation, unit, or system, is a direct reflection of team effectiveness and therefore team culture. Therefore, it is axiomatic that teamwork dynamics and the quality of the results achieved are inextricably linked.

The Importance of Leadership

There is no single definition of leadership. Although positions of leadership are often conferred, leadership is not strictly about a title or position in a team hierarchy. Leadership also is not the same as management; managers manage the mission while leaders lead with vision. *Forbes* has defined leadership as "a process of social influence, which maximizes the efforts of others, towards the achievement of a goal" [61]. Invariably, leadership is an ability to accomplish a mission through talent and skill. Leaders create meaning for the mission. Leadership is not just about personality; rather, leadership *is* about behavior and it is about vision and courage.

Leadership attributes variably include (a) decisiveness, (b) awareness, (c) focus, (d) accountability, (e) empathy, (f) confidence, (g) optimism, (h) honesty, and (i) inspiration [62]. Leadership is adaptive and flexible, changing style, but not substance, with circumstances. Good leadership empowers others and inspires confidence and self-esteem to inspire commitment and create meaningful contribution. Leadership involves not only task coordination and planning but also development of the team, as well as team motivation and the establishment of a "can do" culture. Leadership is critical for effective teamwork. Again, leadership is often about envisioning and realizing change.

However, mission and vision statements are not enough. In the words of Peter Drucker, "Culture eats strategy for breakfast." In any system, there are two cultures: the leadership culture and the organizational culture. Leadership culture is the set of beliefs, practices, patterns, and behaviors, especially by designated leaders; that culture will explicitly and implicitly define the way that people interact, make decisions, and influence others. Leadership culture shapes organizational culture by creating and nurturing the environment which supports the success or the failure of a mission. Organizational culture refers to the underlying beliefs, assumptions, values, and ways of interacting that contribute to the unique social and psychological environment of an organization. The pervasiveness of organizational culture into every aspect of a system mandates that leaders recognize and understand its impact on the way people think, speak, and act. Leadership and organizational culture together drive everything in the organization from job satisfaction, organizational commitment, patient or client satisfaction, and ultimately both outcomes and performance. Leaders define organizational culture through their attitudes, words, and actions. It is incumbent upon leadership to align the leadership and organizational cultures.

Organizational leadership is about leading an organization into the future. In a sense, organizations are networks of teams. Leaders must empower teams to set their goals and make decisions within the context of an overarching strategy or business plan; that strategy derives from leadership. Empowerment requires some level of transparency. In addition, leadership is, in a sense, the strategy and operations nerve center which identifies connections between the activities of various teams through transparency. Leaders replace silos with information and transparency, organize teams around specific goals or mission, encourage team learning and development of new skills, and support cross-team collaboration and migration as needed. Senior leaders assume roles that are focused on planning, strategy, vision, culture, and cross-team communication. The transformational theory of leadership emphasizes that in order to achieve a shared sense of mission, leaders must clearly communicate their vision. Thus, leadership must support their teams, because engaged and supported teams contribute intellectual capital toward a goal or mission, and through leadership and teamwork, the organization gains or maintains its competitive edge.

Inspirational leaders will find an opportunity for the team to learn from every challenge, thereby developing capabilities and resilience. Thus, one way to develop and support a culture of excellence is through shared learning. Peter Senge [63] defined "learning organizations" as "…organizations where people continually expand their capacity to create the results they truly desire, where new and expansive patterns of thinking are nurtured, where collective aspiration is set free, and where people are continually learning to see the whole together." Senge's premise is that in situations of rapid change, only those organizations that are flexible, adaptive, and productive will survive. Senge defined five leadership learning disciplines: (a) shared vision, (b) mental models, (c) personal mastery, (d) team learning, and (e) systems thinking.

Shared vision is about creating and realizing a vision as a team. Shared vison is not about the vision statement; it is a creation of genuine inspiration. Senge posits that leadership inspires through a capacity to develop and share a mental picture of a future the leader and the team seek to create. The development of a shared vison requires crucial conversations to build common understanding and commitment and explore aspirations and reservations. Leaders use tools such as "positive visioning," "concept-shifting," and "values alignment" to create a shared vision, forge common meaning, and develop strategies to meet benchmarks toward the realization of the goals.

Mental models refer to the beliefs, values, mindsets, and assumptions that define the challenges which must be overcome in order to reframe the mission into an action plan. The ability to develop mental models requires an ability to carry on "learningful" introspective conversations that balance inquiry and advocacy. Leaders use tools such as the "ladder of inference" and "reflective inquiry" to clarify mental models and challenge assumptions in order to build shared vision.

Personal mastery represents self-awareness as a path to fulfilling a personal calling. Those who have developed personal mastery live in a continual learning mode, as a lifelong discipline. Those who have developed personal mastery never "arrive." "Organizations learn only through individuals who learn. Individual learning does not guarantee organizational learning; but without it no true organizational learning occurs. Personal mastery is the discipline of continually clarifying and deepening our personal vision, of focusing our energies, of developing patience, and of seeing reality objectively." Personal mastery is essential to leadership since it provides the insight necessary to manage change and communicate values in an authentic and principled fashion. Leaders with a high level of personal mastery are acutely aware of their ignorance and their incompetence, and yet they are deeply self-confident. Leaders use tools such as "perceptual positions" and "reframing" to enhance the quality of interaction and relationship in and outside their teams.

Team learning occurs when teams share experiences, insights, collective knowledge, and skills. Effective teams develop their skills in reflection, inquiry, and discussion to form the basis for a shared vision of change and deciding on common commitments to action. Leaders use tools such as the "action learning cycle" and "dialogue" to develop critical reflection and communication skills.

Systems thinking is a framework for seeing interrelationships that underlie complex situations and interactions and enables teams to see hidden influences and leverage points and the potentially intended and unintended consequences of envisioned change. Leaders learn to use "systems thinking maps" and "archetypes" to map situations, events, problems, and possible courses of action to reach potentially more optimal solutions.

The many models of leadership all share common themes, which quickly become obvious. Perhaps the most important tasks of leadership are to define and communicate the vision and mission, develop the energy and the synergy, engage and support the team, actively lead through presence and mentorship, and then share the credit or take responsibility for failure. It is not enough for leadership to envision, inspire, communicate, or motivate. Leaders succeed or fail based on their ability to operationalize and execute the vision. Successful leaders facilitate and create a sense of ownership in the team. In the words of Ronald Reagan, 40th President of the USA, "The greatest leader is not necessarily the one who does the greatest things. He is the one that gets the people to do the greatest things."

Kouzes and Posner [64] offer an alternate, but well-regarded, functional leadership model in the "leader-as-hero" tradition which largely contradicts notions about sharing leadership and define five leadership principles: (a) model the way, (b) inspire a shared vision, (c) challenge the process, (d) enable others to act, and (e) encourage the heart [65].

In order to *model the way*, leaders must establish principles, create standards, and set an example. To *inspire a shared vision*, leaders must passionately believe that they can make a difference. By creating and inspiring a vision, leaders persuade others to see possibilities for a new future. Leaders also *challenge the process* and in doing so seek innovative opportunities to change the status quo and improve the organization. Leaders *enable others to act* by fostering collaboration and teamwork, through the creation of an atmosphere of trust and empowerment. Finally, leaders *encourage the heart*, recognize contributions, reward the efforts of their teams, and create a sense of pride in the collective accomplishments.

Kouzes and Posner [66] argue that "leadership is a reciprocal relationship between those who choose to lead and those who decide to follow" and that such reciprocity is achieved only when leaders earn and maintain credibility. Credibility is the foundation of leadership. If leaders hope others follow you, they must believe that a leader's words can be trusted, that he or she has the knowledge and skill necessary to lead, and that he or she is genuinely excited and enthusiastic about his or her vison for the future. Thus, "credibility, like reputation, is something that is earned over time. It does not come automatically with the job or the title." Kouzes and Posner posit four personality traits which define leaders: honest, forward-looking, inspiring, and competent. Three of the four characteristics – honest, competent, and inspiring – correspond to how social scientists define personal "credibility." Notably, these personality traits resemble the Aristotelian model of *ethos* (honesty, trustworthiness), *pathos* (forward-looking, inspiring, dynamic), and *logos* (competence, expertise).

Kouzes and Posner list six disciplines that lead to the development of these three currencies: (a) discovering yourself, (b) appreciating your constituents, (c) affirming shared values, (d) developing capacity, (e) serving a purpose, and (f) sustaining hope.

Discover your self refers to the concept that, in order to be credible as a leader, one must first clarify the values that guide your decisions and actions and the standards by which one lives life. The need to *appreciate constituents* is about fostering dialogue, not monologue, and thereby building strong relationships premised in mutual understanding. The importance of *affirm(ing) shared values* is about finding common ground and uniting the team toward a common cause. The need to *develop capacity* is about continuous development of skills and knowledge. Credible leaders know that leadership is about *serv(ing) a purpose* and reinforcing that commitment through visible actions. Finally leaders know the importance of *sustain(ing) hope* because team members with high hope can sustain higher aspirations and higher levels of performance.

Parenthetically, in looking at leadership traits, self-awareness, enthusiasm, credibility, and resilience are common themes. Daniel Goleman defines "emotional intelligence" (EQ) [67] as the ability to identify, assess, and control one's own emotions, the emotions of others, and that of groups. Goleman posits that EQ operates in five realms: awareness of one's own emotions; being able to shake off negative emotions such as anxiety, gloom, and irritability; motivating oneself; feeling empathy; and interacting smoothly with others. Leaders must be self-aware, since they are "always on stage" and thus have the power to set or change mindsets. Where leadership is shared, all members must understand that attitudes are contagious and that behaviors are a result of attitude.

Summary and Conclusions

Modern healthcare delivery is often characterized by rapid-fire decisions in the absence of complete information. In the words of Phil Jackson, "The strength of the team is each individual member. The strength of each member is the team." When the power of the team is effectively leveraged, it results in the best medical care possible under the circumstances.

References

1. Woods D. The Quotable Osler. BMJ. 2003;326(326):289.
2. Kohn LT, Corrigan JM, Donaldson MS. To err is human: building a safer health system. Washington, DC: National Academies Press; 2000.
3. Glymour C, Stalker D. Engineers, cranks, physicians, magicians. N Engl J Med. 1983;308:960–4.
4. Wyngaarden JB, Smith LH. Cecil textbook of medicine. Phuiladelphia: Saunders; 1985.
5. Szalados JE. Complications and risk management. In: Barasch P, Cullen B, Cahalan M, Ortega R, Sharar S, Stock C, editors. Foundations of clinical anesthesia. Phildelphia: Wolters-Kluwer; 2015.
6. Swensen SJ, Meyer GS, Nelson EC, et al. Cottage industry to postindustrial care: the revolution in health care delivery. N Engl J Med. 2010;362(5):e12. https://doi.org/10.1056/NEJMp0911199. Epub 2010 Jan 20.ew England Journal of Medicine. 2010 Jan 20.
7. Starr P. The social transformation of American medicine. New York: Basic Books; 1982.
8. Darling v. Charleston Community Memorial Hospital, 33 Ill. 2d 326, 211 N.E.2d 253, 1965 Ill. LEXIS 250, 14 A.L.R.3d 860 (Ill. 1965).
9. *See* University of Louisville v. Hammock, 127 Ky. 564, 106 SW 219, 220 (1907) noting that "the sick leave their homes and antrum hospitals because of the superior treatment there promised them" and, *see also* Williams v. St. Claire Medical Center 657 S.W.2d 590 (1983) holding that "when a hospital has received a patient, under whatever circumstance, and has undertaken treatment, that patient is owed a duty by the hospital through its employees and staff, including independent staff personnel, to exercise appropriate care to provide for the patient's well-being and to promote his cure. A breach of this duty may expose the hospital to liability in tort. Any lesser rule would be insensible to the true role of a hospital as an institution in present day society."
10. What is risk management in healthcare? NEJM Catalyst. April 25, 2018. Online at: https://catalyst.nejm.org/what-is-risk-management-in-healthcare/.
11. Institute of Medicine. Crossing the quality chasm: a new health system for the 21st Century Committee on Quality of Health Care in America. Washington, DC: N.A. Press; 2001.
12. von Bertalanffy L. General system theory; foundations, development, applications. New York: G. Braziller; 1969.
13. Petula S. Can applying systems theory improve quality in healthcare systems? J Healthcare Qual. Web Exclusive. 2005;27(6):W6-2–6. Online at: http://citeseerx.ist.psu.edu/viewdoc/download?doi=10.1.1.470.9969&rep=rep1&type=pdf.
14. Weaver SJ, Lubomksi LH, Wilson RF, Pfoh ER, Martinez KA, Dy SM. Promoting a culture of safety as a patient safety strategy: a systematic review. Ann Intern Med. 2013;158(5 Pt 2):369–74.
15. Szalados JE. Developing and leading a sustainable high reliability high-performance unit: series of quality, teamwork, medical error, and patient safety. In: Szalados JE, editor. Ethics and law for neurosciences clinicians: foundations and evolving challenges. New Brunswick: Rutgers University Press; 2019. p. 116–29. ISBN: 978-0-8135-9388-3.

16. Institute for Healthcare Improvement. Patient safety essentials toolkit. Online at: http://www.ihi.org/resources/Pages/Tools/Patient-Safety-Essentials-Toolkit.aspx.
17. Vaughan D. The challenger launch decision: risky technology, culture, and deviance at NASA. Chicago/London: University of Chicago Press; 1996.
18. Gouran DS, Hirokawa RY, Martz AE. A critical analysis of factors related to decisional processes involved in the challenger disaster. Commun Stud. 1986;37(3):118–35.
19. Pace RC. Technical communication, group differentiation, and the decision to launch the space shuttle challenger. J Tech Writ Commun. 1988;18(3):207–20.
20. Gaba DM, Howard SK, Jump B. Production pressure in the work environment. California anesthesiologists' attitudes and experiences. Anesthesiology. 1994 Aug;81(2):488–500.
21. Roberts KH. Some characteristics of high reliability organizations. Organ Sci. 1990b;1:160–77.
22. Weick KE, Sutcliffe KM. Managing the unexpected. 2nd ed. San Francisco: Jossey-Bass; 2007.
23. Roberts KH, Rousseau DM. Research in nearly failure-free, high-reliability organizations: having the bubble. IEEE Trans Eng Manag. 1989;36:132–9.
24. Weick KE, Sutcliffe KM. Managing the unexpected: resilient performance in an age of uncertainty. 2nd ed. San Francisco (CA): Jossey-Bass; 2007.
25. Agency for Healthcare Research and Quality. PSNet. Culture of safety. January 2019. Online at: https://psnet.ahrq.gov/primers/primer/5/safety-culture.
26. Chassin MR, Loeb JM. High-reliability health care: getting there from here. Milbank Q. 2013;91(3):459–90. Available online at: https://www.jointcommission.org/assets/1/6/Chassin_and_Loeb_0913_final.pdf.
27. Gaba D, Fish K, Howard S. Crisis management in anesthesiology. New York: Churchill Livingstone; 1994.
28. Helmreich RL, Merritt AC, Wilhelm JA. The evolution of crew resource management training in commercial aviation. Int J Aviat Psychol. 1999;9:19–32.
29. Leadership and crew resource management in high-reliability organizations: a competency framework for measuring behaviors. Available from: https://www.researchgate.net/publication/317053301_Leadership_and_Crew_Resource_Management_in_High-Reliability_Organizations_A_Competency_Framework_for_Measuring_Behaviors. Accessed 12 Aug 2019.
30. Jensen RS. Pilot judgement and crew resource management. Aldershot: Ashgate Publishing Limited; 1995.
31. Gaba DM, Howard SK, Fish KJ, et al. Simulation-based training in anesthesia crisis resource management (ACRM): a decade of experience. Simul Games. 2001;32(2):175–93.
32. Sundstrom E, De Meuse KP, Futrell D. Work teams: applications and effectiveness. Am Psychol. 1990;45:120.
33. Kohn LT, Corrigan JM, Donaldson MS, editors. To err is human: building a safer health system, vol. 6. Washington, DC: National Academies Press; 1999.
34. World Health Organization. Patient safety curriculum guide: multi-professional edition. Geneva: World Health Organization; 2011.
35. Russ AL, Fairbanks RJ, Karsh B-T, et al. The science of human factors: separating fact from fiction. BMJ Qual Saf. 2013;22:802–8.
36. Woolley AW, Chabris CF, Pentland A, Hashmi N, Malone TW. Evidence for a collective intelligence factor in the performance of human groups. Science. 2010;330(6004):686–8.
37. Woolley AW, Aggarwal I, Malone TW. Collective intelligence and group performance. Curr Dir Psychol Sci. 2015;24(6):420–4.
38. MBTI® Basics. The Myers & Briggs Foundation. Online at: https://www.myersbriggs.org/my-mbti-personality-type/mbti-basics/home.htm?bhcp=1.
39. Katzenbach JR, Smith DK. The wisdom of teams. Boston: Harvard Business School Press; 1993.
40. Developing and Sustaining High-Performance Work Teams. https://www.shrm.org/resourcesandtools/tools-and-samples/toolkits/pages/developingandsustaininghighperformanceworkteams.aspx.
41. Holzman RS, Cooper JB, Gaba DM, Philip JH, Small SD, Feinstein D. Anesthesia crisis resource management: real-life simulation training in operating room crises. J Clin Anesth. 1995;7:675–87.

42. Marks MA, Mathieu JE, Zaccaro SJ. A temporally based framework and taxonomy of team processes. Acad Manag Rev. 2001;26(3):356–76. at 357.
43. Collins JC. Good to great: why some companies make the leap ... and others don't. New York: HarperBusiness; 2001.
44. Institute of Medicine Committee on the Health Professions Education Summit. The core competencies needed for health care professionals. In: Greiner AC, Knebel E, editors. Health professions education: a bridge to quality. Washington, DC: National Academies Press; 2003. p. 45–74.
45. Leape LL, Cullen DJ, Clapp MD, Burdick E, Demonaco HJ, Erickson JI, Bates DW. Pharmacist participation on physician rounds and adverse drug events in the intensive care unit. J Am Med Assoc. 1999;282:267–70.
46. Kvarnström S. Difficulties in collaboration: a critical incident study of interprofessional healthcare teamwork. J Interprof Care. 2008;22:191–203.
47. Pronovost PJ, Berenholtz S, Dorman T, et al. Improving communication in the ICU using daily goals. Crit Care. 2003;18:71–5.
48. Reason J. Human error. 1st ed. Cambridge, UK: Cambridge University Press; 1990.
49. JCAHO. Sentinel Event Data 2012.
50. Mazzocco K, Petitti DB, Fong KT, Bonacum D, Brookey J, Graham S, Thomas EJ. Surgical team behaviors and patient outcomes. Am J Surg. 2009;197:678–85.
51. Wilson R, Runciman W, Gibbard R, Harrison B, Newby L, Hamilton J. The quality in Australian health care study. Med J Aust. 1995;163:458–71.
52. Stockwell DC, Slonim AD. Quality and safety in the intensive care unit. J Intensive Care Med. 2006;21:199–210.
53. Lyu H, Wick EC, Housman M, Freischlag JA, Makary MA. Patient satisfaction as a possible indicator of quality surgical care. J Am Med Assoc Surg. 2013;148:362–7.
54. Mardon RE, Khanna K, Sorra J, Dyer N, Famolaro T. Exploring relationships between hospital patient safety culture and adverse events. J Patient Saf. 2010;6:226–32.
55. Gawande AA, Zinner MJ, Studdert DM, Brennan TA. Analysis of errors reported by surgeons at three teaching hospitals. Surgery. 2003;133:614–21. https://doi.org/10.1067/msy.2003.169.
56. Jerry Mulenburg. Crew resource management improves decision making. INSIGHT|ASK MAGAZINE|11. Online at https://www.nasa.gov/pdf/546130main_42i_crew_resource_management.pdf.
57. Lencioni P. The five dysfunctions of a team: a leadership fable. San Francisco: Jossey-Bass; 2002.
58. Salas E, Sims DE, Burke CS. Is there a "Big Five" in teamwork? Small Group Res. 2005;36:555–99.
59. Stout RJ, Cannon-Bower JA, Salas E, et al. Planning, shared mental models, and coordinated performance: an empirical link is established. Hum Factors. 1999;41:61.
60. Cass R. Sunstein, "The law of group polarization" (John M. Olin program in law and economics. Working Paper No. 91, 1999).
61. Kevin Kruse. What is leadership. Forbes. 2019 Forbes Media LLC. https://www.forbes.com/sites/kevinkruse/2013/04/09/what-is-leadership/#71e0c7015b 90.
62. Sammi Caramela. 4 ways to define leadership.Business News Daily. 2017. https://www.businessnewsdaily.com/3647-leadership-definition.html.
63. Senge PM. The fifth discipline: the art & practice of the learning organization. New York: Doubleday; 1990.
64. Kouzes JM, Posner BZ. The leadership challenge. San Francisco, CA: Jossey-Bass; 2007.
65. Kouzes JM, Posner BZ. The five practices of exemplary leadership. Hoboken, NJ: Pfeiffer; 2011.
66. James M. Kouzes and Barry Z. Posner, credibility: how leaders gain and lose it, why people demand it. Revised Edition. Jossey-Bass; 2003.
67. Goleman D. Emotional intelligence: why it can matter more than IQ. New York: Bantam Books; 1995.

Chapter 9
Medical Error, Quality Management, and the Evolving Culture of Safety

James E. Szalados

Medical Error

Physicians, providers, and other healthcare practitioners are, for the most part, by nature competitive and driven perfectionists. Thus, although most physicians and providers hold themselves to high standards, it is also unfair to hold physicians and providers to a standard of perfection. Where providers practice honestly and diligently and nonetheless commit an error in judgment, which may not in itself rise to the level of medical malpractice or medical negligence, that error may or may not result in harm to a patient. It is likely that the number of unappreciated medical errors that occur each day but remain unrecognized because they do not result in harm is very substantial. In addition, since medical malpractice requires showing of compensable damages, medical errors in themselves are not legally actionable.

In general, medical experience, or knowledge; or, when there is a demonstrable element of carelessness or lack of due diligence. The legal standard for reaching a conclusion that malpractice has occured, is proof that the provider deviated from the generally accepted standards or care. Since medical error generally involves little or no moral or ethical culpability, a punitive legal response, in itself, is most probably unlikely to prevent a recurrence. Rather, a transparent examination of the underlying design, structure, and process failures is perhaps more likely to result in a less error-prone system.

J. E. Szalados (✉)
Director, Surgical and Neurocritical Care Units, Rochester Regional Health System at Rochester General Hospital, Rochester, NY, USA

The Szalados Law Firm, Hilton, NY, USA
e-mail: james.szalados@rochesterregional.org; jszalados@aol.com

J. E. Szalados (ed.), *The Medical-Legal Aspects of Acute Care Medicine*,
https://doi.org/10.1007/978-3-030-68570-6_9

Historical Perspectives on Medical Errors

Hippocratic writings note that some medical errors arise due to "misfortune" and that "a physician should not be blamed for things that resulted from the nature of the disease and its course" [1]. Furthermore, Hippocrates espoused the principle of *primum non nocere* [2], translated to "first, do no harm" and which has become a pillar of medical ethics now recognized as the principle of nonmaleficence. Sir William Osler (1849–1919), perhaps the greatest contemporary physician, noted that "errors in judgment must occur in the practice of an art which consists largely of balancing probabilities" [3]. In the 1950s, medical errors were described as "diseases of medical progress" [4] and dismissed as "the price we pay for modern diagnosis and therapy" [5]. Schimmel reported that 20% of patients admitted to a university hospital medical service suffered from iatrogenic injury and asserted that the "assessment of all untoward reactions, regardless of severity, is essential to determine their total incidence and to indicate the cumulative risk assumed by the patient exposed to the many drugs and procedures used in his care" and defined the term "noxious episode" as a surrogate term for medical error to encompass all the untoward events, complications, and mishaps that resulted from otherwise acceptable diagnostic or therapeutic measures in a hospital [6].

In the 1990s, a view of medical errors as adverse events *caused by*, rather than being events *incident to*, the process of medical care emerged. The Harvard Medical Practice Study defined medical errors as "unintended injury to patients caused by medical management (rather than the underlying condition of the patient) that results in measurable disability, prolonged hospitalization, or both" [7]. The Institute of Medicine (IOM) in 2000 published *To Err is Human: Building a Safer Health System* in which it purported that medical errors accounted for at least 98,000 inpatient deaths annually, or at least 270 deaths daily.

Nonetheless, physicians and providers remain preoccupied with medical errors; and a substantial body of empirical research on the nature of human error, the cognitive processes by which errors occur, and potential safety models have been published. The design of a medical system in which errors are eliminated is the goal of the patient safety initiative; patients are safer and receive more optimal care in a system in which errors do not occur. It is very likely that medical errors will continue to occur as an inevitable consequence of human fallibility and system complexity.

Definitions of Medical Error

By nature and by definition, an error is unintentional. Nonetheless, there is no standard definition of a "medical error"; instead, studies discuss the conditions under which errors occur and surrogate measures of error that largely depend on the type of adverse patient outcomes or injury caused by errors. Reason has defined medical errors as "the failure of a planned action to be completed as intended (an error of execution) or the use of a wrong plan to achieve an aim (an error of planning)" [8]. The "reason" definition has become widely accepted with the caveat that errors of omission may be equally important. The definition of error that reason posited is both process-dependent and outcome-independent. Leape recognized that both acts of commission (action) and acts of omission (inaction) contribute to medical errors. Reason has argued that errors occur from the convergence of multiple and complex contributing factors and has stress the importance of a systems approach to medical error prevention (see Chap. 8). Rasmussen classified human errors as either skill-based, rule-based, or knowledge-based [9, 10].

Legal Implications of Medical Error

Although adverse patient events may occur as a result of medical error, not all medical errors cause adverse events; and not all adverse patient outcomes are the result of error. These concepts are important in arguments of legal syllogism, since persuasion through advocacy can convince triers of fact of negligence, where there is in fact no negligence or malpractice (see Chap. 18). Leape noted in 1994 that "[g]iven the complex nature of medical practice and the multitude of interventions that each patient receives, a high error rate is perhaps not surprising" [11]. Liability risks that stem from new procedures, drugs, and technology impact providers and also researchers, manufacturers, distributors, and those involved in marketing of new technology. These new technologies may allow access to certain elements of care that were previously out of reach for many; these patients may now be candidates for treatment exactly because of new technology. The term "too sick" (or too young or old for surgery) is largely only of historical interest. Nonetheless, with increasing complexity, there comes a smaller margin of error and greater risk of an adverse outcome. The paradox is that technology brings both opportunities for treatment and also risk and litigation. The relevance of such technological risk has a broader social importance since medical innovation is important to individual health, the health of communities, and the economic viability of hospitals and the medical research and innovation pipeline. Moreover, the incidence of malpractice litigation within a cohort is often used a surrogate for quality within medical staff credentialing and in public reporting of the purposes of comparisons.

US Courts have long recognized that the practice of medicine involves drugs and treatments which are "unavoidably unsafe" [12]. The Restatement of Torts discusses unavoidably unsafe products:

> … which, in the present state of human knowledge, are quite incapable of being made safe for their intended and ordinary use. These are especially common in the field of drugs. … Such a product, properly prepared, and accompanied by proper directions and warning, is not defective, nor is it unreasonably dangerous…. It is also true in particular of many new or experimental drugs as to which, because of lack of time and opportunity for sufficient medical experience, there can be no assurance of safety, or perhaps even of purity of

ingredients, but such experience as there is justifies the marketing and use of the drug notwithstanding a medically recognizable risk.

Restatement of Torts (Second), Section 402A, Comment k

Iatrogenic injury refers to unintentional injuries caused by medical care. Negligent adverse events, caused by a deviation from accepted standards of care, represent a subset of preventable adverse events that may rise to a level of medical negligence. Quality management paradigms stress a definition of quality as a variation or a deviation from standards. Thus, some have argued that variation in medical practice may in itself constitute a subtle form of medical error [13].

Modern medical malpractice liability law is best understood as "regulation by litigation," not merely the private resolution of individual actions [14]. The regulatory role of the tort legal system is thus potentially composed of three independent elements of a "malpractice system" (1): the legal-judicial tort litigation system addresses private controversies regarding quality of care and rules on the validity of the claims; (2) liability insurance indemnifies providers and compensates for victim's injuries; and (3) risk management and providers define new standards and modify behaviors to decrease future risk. An additional well-recognized direct effect of medical malpractice litigation is the notion of defensive medicine; however, the ways in which defensive medicine impacts patient care can be subtle. The most commonly discussed type of defensive medicine is that of providers "over-utilizing" services such as laboratory testing, consultations, and imaging [15]. However, there are other insidious types of defensive medicine that can involve "cherry picking" of patients to maximize indicators of outcome and quality or the legitimizing and rationing risky interventions in order to minimize the risk of an apparent error of commission.

In general terms, the goals of medical malpractice tort litigation are based upon the principles of corrective justice, distributive justice, and prevention or deterrence [16]. The intent of the medical liability system is to serve three functions (1): compensate patients injured by negligence, (2) promote corrective justice by providing a mechanism to rectify wrongful losses caused by defendants, and (3) deter negligence [17]. Although deterrence leads to a clinical calibration of safety measures so that the costs do not exceed the benefits, a related phenomenon, defensive medicine, reflects responses that are costly and provide little or no clinical benefit [18]. Mello et al. reviewed 37 studies of malpractice deterrence and found that malpractice liability risk may not be effective in preventing substandard care.

Medical errors have broad sweeping ramifications. The term "error" is associated with a stigma; the term connotes inadequacy and perpetuates a culture of blame [19] (see Chap. 36). An accusation of medical error creates significant emotional distress for physicians, a distress influenced by prior beliefs, perfectionism, and competitiveness engendered by medical training [20].

Responding to an Adverse Event That Causes Patient Harm

In the event that an adverse event occurs that results in patient harm, all involved should be familiar with some model response protocol. Institutions generally lack such protocols. A standardized, or protocolized, response to an adverse event will facilitate after event reviews, system safety initiatives, and potentially help in the defense of a litigation. In general, it is difficult to improve something that is not measured or defined; recollections obtained days or weeks after the event have only limited value in quality and safety improvement. Incident reporting is essential to incident management; likewise, incident analysis is essential to future planning to avoid and better manage similar events in the future.

The US military has developed the "after-action review" (AAR) to support continuous improvement efforts. Learning organizations (see Chap. 8) recognize that "organizational learning requires that teams continuously assess their performance to identify and learn from successes and failures" [21]. The military conducts AARs on successes as well as failures with the intent of identifying both successful strategies and potential pitfalls, or near misses. As is often the case with quality paradigms, the AAR does not extrapolate to the healthcare environment in a perfect fashion; however, the *importance of some model of AAR following a critical incident in healthcare cannot be overstated.*

The Anesthesia Patient Safety Foundation (APSF) has developed an Adverse Event Protocol (AEP) to facilitate an effective, efficient, and coordinated response to a perioperative adverse event. The AEP represents a "standard operating procedure" and a standardized reasonable best practice that eliminates variability through improvisation. The APSF AEP is divided into a series of actions: (1) communication and coordination which is designated to an incident commander who assumes administrative direction and control over the event and coordinates the involvement of consultants and the notification of departmental leadership, administrators, and family members; (2) preservation of evidence which is designed to sequester drugs and equipment to subsequently rule out contamination or malfunction in such a way as to provide credibly unspoiled evidence for later review; (3) debriefing and documentation support which promotes clear, complete, factual, and objective memorialization of the events for the medical record; and (4) subsequent peer review [22].

Numerous methods have been devised by which to analyze a reported incident to reveal the fundamental cause(s) and/or contain potential further adverse effects. Prevention and Recovery Information System for Monitoring and Analysis (PRISMA) represents traditional root cause analysis; it was originally designed for the chemical industry but was effectively applied to incidents arising in healthcare in 1997 [23]. PRISMA, or RCA, develops a causal tree which seeks to work backward from the adverse event to identify a single root cause. One of the limitations of PRISMA, or RCA, in healthcare is that there is rarely one single root cause or latent failure, and thus the RCA can inappropriately assign blame to one of the many potential contributing failures. The "Systemic Incident Reconstruction and

Evaluation" (SIRE) is a Dutch prototype method of root cause analysis that offers multiple modalities for critical incident analysis including reconstructions of timeline, processes, and obstacles. SIRE was developed by the National Center for Patient Safety of the Department of Veterans Affairs. The Ishikawa (fishbone) diagram is also a RCA tool that devises a diagram of the outcome, establishing the key contributing causes and the sub-causes. The functional resonance analysis method (FRAM) represents a more rigid control chart method that looks at variations from standard practices. In general, regardless of the method used to retrospectively analyze the adverse event, it must be contemporaneous, tangible, reliable, evidence-based, and transparent.

The verbal, written, and behavioral responses of involved providers after a perioperative incident have potentially enormous legal ramifications: (1) statements made to peers and support staff are discoverable and may be later admitted into evidence against the provider unless they occur in a protected setting; (2) written documentation which is not objective can later be scrutinized and found to be misleading or self-serving; and (3) "cleaning up" may either result in loss of important evidence (i.e., turning off monitors can wipe temporary electronic memory) or be construed as spoliation (intentional loss or destruction) of evidence [24].

Quality Management

Donabedian, in 1966, published "Evaluating the Quality of Medical Care" as a landmark article in which he divided healthcare quality measures into structure, process, and outcome as a framework for conceptualizing and classifying the matrix of quality inputs which impacted outcome in healthcare. Donabedian considered structure as the sum of available resources including facilities, equipment, and personnel, process as all the supportive and direct activities related to patient care, and outcomes as the end results of care including outcome and also satisfaction [25]. Donabedian divided the available resources into two primary domains: technical and interpersonal. Donabedian further defined "technical care" as the application of science and technology that was necessary to the management of a personal health problem and the "interpersonal" aspect of care as the social and psychological interactions between patient and practitioner. Donabedian's domains have subsequently been referred to as the science and the art of medicine, respectively. The norms of the scientific aspect are governed by the available technical resources, whereas the norms of the personal aspect of medicine are governed by moral and ethical principles of interpersonal relationships or normative behaviors.

In 1974, The Joint Commission first mandated that hospitals implement internal quality audit as a condition of accreditation. Early quality assessment programs were based upon a process of criteria mapping, using implict subjective criteria to review the outcomes stemming from the care rendered to any one particular patient. Service-level quality management programs were largely physician- or group-focused discussions of outcome and potential changes in approach and/or group educational efforts. This early quality assurance model was that of departmental or hospital-level peer review. In fact, departmental quality assurance programs were often used primarily as a teaching mechanism; this approach led to two potential sub-optimal outcomes (1): powerful figures were not criticized; and (2) quality assurance could be weaponized against less influential peers. Although such peer review was mandated by regulatory bodies, the process was neither standardized, comprehensive, nor data-driven. The widely recognized failure of peer review as an effective quality management tool was highlighted by publications in the lay, legal, and medical literature alleging a medical conspiracy of silence.

Quality management in healthcare underwent a rapid evolution and growth in the 1980s and 1990s with the convergence of innovation in managerial science, organizational culture, social psychology, human factors, and safety science and the demonstrable value of quality management programs imported from the non-healthcare industry sectors. The 1980s were also characterized by concerns regarding cost of care and outcomes. The extrapolation of quality improvement and quality management paradigms from diverse industries to healthcare in the 1990s led to widespread recognition that traditional models of service-level quality measures were largely inadequate. Deming espoused the Plan, Do, Check, Act (PDSA) cycle as a model of continuous quality improvement change implementation [26]. Juran adapted the industrial model of total quality management based on the assumption that quality was an organizational, rather than a personnel, issue [27]. Based upon the pioneering and cumulative works of Donabedian, Deming, and Juran, an emerging consensus formed within healthcare regulation and governance that, in order to implement the empirical, theoretical, and methodological foundations to clinical medicine necessary to advance the study of quality and safety, a multidisciplinary approach, beyond that of clinical medicine, was necessary.

A fundamental problem with quality improvement is that healthcare, as a system, has yet to define quality in an objective manner. Crude quality-of-care indicators such as mortality, disciplinary actions, malpractice actions or awards, or patient satisfaction may be more situational and less actionable as indicators of quality. For example, mortality needs to be case mix index; malpractice and patient satisfaction may be related to personalities or motivations.

Quality programs continue to evolve and are becoming increasingly complex with advances in the sciences of data analysis and systems engineering. Nonetheless, despite a relatively robust commitment of resources to quality management programs at the institutional, accreditation, and governmental levels, errors continue to occur, and many indicators of quality do not seem to reflect the impact of the resources expended. More recently, healthcare systems are looking at the dollar costs of quality improvement activities in the form of a rerurn on investment (ROI). Costs associated with qality programs include staffing, data collection, and meetings; these may be significant to a healthcare entity and may, in fact, only marginally affect, or reflect, overall clinical outcomes [28].

Patient Safety

The National Patient Safety Foundation (NPSF) notes that "patient safety is related to 'quality of care', but the two concepts are not synonymous. Safety is an important subset of quality" [29]. Patient safety generally relates to the prevention and mitigation of adverse outcomes that stem from the processes of healthcare. The NPSF addresses patient safety in the context of defining characteristics. Patient safety has to do primarily with the avoidance, prevention, and amelioration of adverse outcomes or injuries stemming from the processes of healthcare itself. Thus, the NPSF considers "errors and deviations," "dangerous situations," "near misses," and accidents as elements of patient safety. Nonetheless, patient safety is the result of interactions of the components of the system; it is more than the absence of adverse outcomes and more than the avoidance of identifiable "preventable" errors or occurrences (Table 9.1) [29].

The medical model for team coordination has its origins in the aviation industry which developed the "crew resource management" (CRM) paradigm in 1978 (see Chap. 8). CRM focuses on building and sustaining an organizational culture that encourages all team members to respectfully question authority while preserving authority and chain of command; it encompasses knowledge, skills, and attitudes including communications, situational awareness, problem-solving, decision-making, and teamwork. Thus, there is a general similarity between the Donabedian model of structure, process, and outcome and CRM; the holistic and team approach of CRM seeks to make the best use of all available resources including equipment, procedures, and people in order to promote safety and enhance operational efficiency. CRM has permeated healthcare in the form of a "safety culture" which universally establishes safety as an organizational priority by fostering teamwork, patient involvement, transparency, and accountability. The fundamental importance of teamwork is further exemplified in the high-reliability organization (HRO). A high-reliability organization (HRO) is one that has succeeded in avoiding catastrophes despite a high level of risk and complexity [24]. The optimal approach to patient safety in healthcare remains controversial and uncertain. Chassin and Loeb

Table 9.1 NPSF agenda for patient safety research

Incident reporting system
Medication error
Safety culture
Patient handoffs and discontinuities in care
Missed diagnosis
Misdiagnosis
Medical device design
Coordination of medical work
Understanding of the nature of expertise
Analyses of technical work

[30] determined that the methodology through which HROs generate and maintain high levels of safety cannot be directly extrapolated to the healthcare environment; rather, incremental changes can be identified through which healthcare systems may progress toward high reliability. These incremental changes include (1) a leadership's commitment to zero harm, (2) a functional culture of safety throughout the organization, and (3) the widespread deployment of highly effective process improvement tools. In summary, patient safety is best accomplished through a combination of individual personnel commitment to, and an organizational culture that unconditionally supports, patient safety. It is likely that no single "model" will provide a better solution than a shared commitment to excellence.

Conclusions

Despite the existence of a single American healthcare system, there is extreme variability in the availability and the quality of care within the individual components of that system. Providers have varying levels of skill, experience, and knowledge; and practitioners, as humans, have differing work ethic, priorities, and standards. Similarly, there is a wide variability in the type of services which are available in different office, clinical, and hospital settings; diagnostic and treatment services that are commonplace in a tertiary or quaternary medical center may not even be contemplated in rural community or critical access hospitals. Thus, universal or national constructs of health quality can best be described as efforts to provide the most appropriate, timely, and best care under the circumstances. Similarly, by extrapolation, discussions of access to healthcare are meaningless unless that access refers to a basic but uniform quality of healthcare. Finally, as the cost of healthcare undergoes increasingly greater scrutiny, that care which demonstrably and repeatedly does not conform to quality standards may be classified as waste. The goal of the tort legal system is not the truth but justice; therefore, malpractice litigation is also a suboptimal mechanism to improve the quality of healthcare.

References

1. Papavramidou N, Voultsos P. Medical malpractice cases in Hippocratic collection: a review and today's perspective. Hippokratia. 2019;23(3):99–105.
2. Nightingale F. Notes on hospitals. London: Longman; 1863.
3. Silverman ME, Murray TJ, Bryan CS, editors. The quotable Osler. Philadelphia: American College of Physician Press; 2008.
4. Moser RH. Diseases of medical progress. N Engl J Med. 1956;255(13):606–14.
5. Barr DP. Hazards of modern diagnosis and therapy: the price we pay. JAMA. 1955;159(15):1452–6.
6. Schimmel EM. The hazards of hospitalization. Ann Intern Med. 1964;60:100–10.
7. Leape LL, Brennan TA, Laird N, et al. The nature of adverse events in hospitalized patients. Results of the Harvard Medical Practice Study II. N Engl J Med. 1991;324(6):377–84.

8. Reason J. Human error. Cambridge: Cambridge University Press; 1990.
9. Embrey D. Understanding human behaviour and error. Available online at: http://www.human-reliability.com/downloads/Understanding-Human-Behaviour-and-Error.pdf.
10. Rasmussen J. Skills, rules and knowledge: signals, signs and symbols and other distinctions in human performance models. IEEE Trans Syst Man Cybern. 1983;13:257–66.
11. Leape LL. Error in medicine. JAMA. 1994;272(23):1851–7.
12. Restatement (Second) of Torts § 402A cmt. k (Am. Law Inst. 1965).
13. McPherson K, Wennberg JE, Hovind OB, Clifford P. Small-area variations in the use of common surgical procedures: an international comparison of New England, England, and Norway. N Engl J Med. 1982;307:1310–4.
14. Viscusi WK, editor. Regulation through litigation. Washington: AEI-Brookings Joint Center for Regulatory Studies; 2002.
15. Black L. Effects of malpractice law on the practice of medicine. Virtual Mentor. 2007;9(6):437–40.
16. Watson K, Kottenhagen R. Patients' rights, medical error and harmonisation of compensation mechanisms in Europe. Eur J Health Law. 2018;25(1):1–23.
17. Keeton WP, Dobbs DB, Keeton RE, Owen DC. Prosser and Keeton on the law of torts. 5th ed. West Group: St Paul; 1984.
18. Mello MM, Frakes MD, Blumenkranz E, et al. Malpractice liability and health care quality a review. JAMA. 2020;323(4):352–66.
19. Holloway RG, Panzer RJ. Lawyers, litigation, and liability: can they make patients safer? Neurology. 2001;56(8):991–3.
20. Christensen JF, Levinson W, Dunn PM. The heart of darkness: the impact of perceived mistakes on physicians. J Gen Intern Med. 1992;7(4):424–31.
21. Salem-Schatz S, Ordin D, Mittman B. Guide to the after action review. Available online at: https://www.cebma.org/wp-content/uploads/Guide-to-the-after_action_review.pdf.
22. Cooper JB, Cullen DJ, Eichhorn JH, Philip JH, Holzman RS. Administrative guidelines for response to an adverse anesthesia event. The Risk Management Committee of the Harvard Medical School's Department of Anaesthesia. J Clin Anesth. 1993;5(1):79–84.
23. van der Schaaf TW, Habraken MMP. PRISMA-medical a brief description. Eindhoven: Eindhoven University of Technology, Faculty of Technology Management, Patient Safety Systems; 2005.
24. Szalados JE. Complications and risk management. In: Barasch P, Cullen B, Cahalan M, Ortega R, Sharar S, Stock C, editors. Foundations of clinical anesthesia. Philadelphia: Wolters-Kluwer; 2015.
25. Ayanian JZ, Markel H. Donabedian's lasting framework for health care quality. N Engl J Med. 2016;375:205–7.
26. Graham NO. Quality in health care: theory, application, and evolution. Gaithersburg: Aspen; 1995.
27. Goonan KJ. Juran prescription: clinical quality management. 1st ed. San Francisco: Jossey-Bass; 1995.
28. Chen J, Patel MM. Costs of quality measurement. JAMA. 2018;319(6):615.
29. National Patient Safety Foundation. Agenda for research and development in patient safety. Available online at: https://cdn.ymaws.com/www.npsf.org/resource/collection/4B2E552F-48FA-4DCF-8BD8-574EE15EFD99/Agenda_for_RD_in_Patient_Safety.pdf.
30. Chassin MR, Loeb JM. High-reliability health care: getting there from here. Milbank Q. 2013;91(3):459–90.

Chapter 10
Laws Pertaining to Insurance and Risk Management

James E. Szalados

Definitions and History of Insurance in the USA

A general dictionary definition of insurance is coverage by contract whereby one party undertakes to indemnify or guarantee another against loss by a specified contingency or peril; whereby it provides a legal definition of insurance as "coverage by contract, whereby for an agreed upon payment of a premium, one party agrees to indemnify or guarantee the other against loss by a specified contingency or peril" [2].

The party purchasing coverage is "the insured" is generally seeking insurance against financial loss. Furthermore, the "named insured" is the specific individual defined as the insured in the policy contract. The named insured may or may not be the beneficiary of the insurance. The "beneficiary" is a named individual who may become eligible to receive an insurance payout. The insured may be the beneficiary. However, in the case of a "third-party beneficiary," the beneficiary is the one who, through designation by either contract or assignment, steps into the shoes of the insured to receive the benefits of the insurance. The financial loss the insured is seeking protection from can be secondary to illness, disability, or unexpected death; loss of property because of theft, loss, or destruction; or lawsuit. In general, anything that can be legally insured can be considered for insurance. Under contract, the insured makes payments, for a predetermined amount, at agreed-upon intervals; these payments are known as "the premium." The contract of insurance is known as

J. E. Szalados (✉)
Director, Surgical and Neurocritical Care Units, Rochester Regional Health System at Rochester General Hospital, Rochester, NY, USA

The Szalados Law Firm, Hilton, NY, USA
e-mail: james.szalados@rochesterregional.org; jszalados@aol.com

J. E. Szalados (ed.), *The Medical-Legal Aspects of Acute Care Medicine*,
https://doi.org/10.1007/978-3-030-68570-6_10

the “policy” which is the written contract that ratifies the legality of an insurance contract or agreement.

The insurer, as a business, expects to collect money in excess of its payouts to insured, thereby making a corporate profit. The amount of a premium is not arbitrary; premiums are based on actuarial data. Actuaries use accepted methods based on mathematical and statistical science to assess the statistical degree of risk and to help insurers set economically responsible but profitable premiums. An insurer’s “loss ratio” is the relationship between incurred losses and earned premiums, expressed as a percentage. To calculate the loss ratio, incurred losses (actual paid claims plus loss reserves) are divided by earned premiums (the portion earned of the total premiums allocated over the life of the policy). Loss reserves are financial liabilities from known losses which remain to be paid to insureds paid by the insurer. The loss ratio is important to both the insurer and the insured. Insurers with high loss ratios are risking losses and insolvency and may need to reevaluate the risks they take or raise premiums. Insurers with low loss ratios are overcharging for coverage under their policies and risk losing market share in an open market.

The “combined ratio” or “the combined ratio after policyholder dividends ratio,” is one measure of an insurer’s profitability, and is the mathematical sum of incurred losses and expenses divided by the earned premium. The insurer’s “expense ratio” similar to that of any operating entity looks at the percentage of premiums (operating revenue) used to pay costs of acquiring, writing, and servicing insurance and reinsurance.

The party which guarantees to pay for another’s loss is the “insurer.” An “insurer” as an entity must be authorized to write insurance under the laws of any state. Nonetheless, insurers also reinsure themselves against catastrophic losses, so that they minimize the risk of default, or non-payment, to their insureds. Reinsurance represents a contract between a primary insurer a reinsurer where the reinsurer guarantees to cover all or part of the losses of the primary insurer. Reinsurance allows the risk of loss to be underwritten by another company, the “underwriter.” Insurance underwriters establish their own premiums for accepted insurable risks.

Insurance operates under the legal principle of “indemnity” which is a defining characteristic of insurance, whereby the insured recovering under an insurance policy should be restored to the approximate financial position it was in prior to the loss without rewarding or penalizing the insured for its loss, or to the limits of the policy coverage. The term “under-insured” refers to insureds who either have chosen to purchase coverage insufficient to indemnify them in the event of a loss or, for any of a number of reasons, cannot qualify for the appropriate amount of coverage. Where a person or entity is under-insured, losses in excess of policy coverage will need to be managed at an individual level.

Furthermore, in order to be considered “insurance” under a legal definition, a contract must have two elements: (1) risk distribution (2) among a substantial number of members, through an insurer engaged primarily in the business of insurance [3]. Insurers must be licensed in the state(s) in which they operate. Regulation of insurance and insurers occurs at the state level. Each state has a “state insurance department” under the state commissioner of insurance who is empowered under the laws of a state to oversee the business of insurance within that state. The power of the states over regulation of insurers is based on the notions that insurance was not interstate commerce and that insurance is an industry established in the public interest. Thus, states grant regulatory and enforcement powers to insurance commissioners and their offices which include (1) the approval of insurance premium rates; (2) the authority to conduct periodic financial audits of insurers; (3) the oversight authority over the licensing of insurance companies, agencies, agents, and brokers; and (4) the monitoring and regulation of the processes for the handling of claims.

The McCarran-Ferguson Act of 1945 delegates regulation of the business of insurance to the individual states. States generally approve and regulate the insurers their states through the state's Commissioner of Insurance. An insurance company that is licensed and regulated by any state's Department of Insurance is referred to as an "admitted" carrier in that particular state. The "admitted" status confers protection to an insurer's policy holders through the admitting state's "guarantee fund" which gives policyholders a degree of protection in the event that the insurance company becomes "insolvent." The financial state of insurance companies is reflected in ratings conferred by AM Best, the most widely recognized insurer ratings company: an AM Best rating of "A-" or better reflects good financial standing.

In 1869, the US Supreme Court decision in *Paul v. Virginia* [4] decided that insurance was not interstate commerce subject to the Commerce Clause in the US Constitution, and as a result, the regulation of insurance was referred to the individual states until 1944. In 1944, the Supreme Court overturned its earlier decision in its ruling in the case of *United States v. South-Eastern Underwriters Association* [5] where it then determined that insurance was indeed a matter interstate commerce and therefore subject to federal jurisdiction under the Commerce Clause. The resulting uncertainty prompted the McCarran-Ferguson Act of 1945 [6] which was signed into law by President Franklin D. Roosevelt. The Act states "that the continued regulation and taxation by the several States of the business of insurance is in the public interest, and that silence on the part of the Congress shall not be construed to impose any barrier to the regulation or taxation of such business by the several states." The Act also limited application of antitrust laws to the business of insurance only as long as and to the extent that states enacted state-specific laws and assumed responsibility for the regulation of the business; otherwise, federal antitrust laws such as the Sherman Antitrust Act, Clayton Antitrust Act, and Federal Trade Commission Act would resume responsibility. Nonetheless, states continue to differ on the extent that they regulate their insurers. Regardless of variability in the regulations between states, universal principles apply: (1) insurance policy premiums must be sufficient to maintain insurance company solvency, (2) but not so excessive as to allow for unreasonable profits, and (3) the policy premiums must not be discriminatory so that premiums reflect expected loss ratios.

The National Association of Insurance Commissioners (NAIC) [7] was established in 1999 as a non-governmental not-for-profit organization created and governed by the chief insurance regulators from the 50 states, the District of Columbia, and the 5 US territories. NAIC was established with the goal of setting standards and best practices, conducting peer review, and coordinating their regulatory oversight over the US state-based insurance system.

The Law of Insurance

Insurance law refers to that concentration of law which focuses on the relevant federal and state regulatory laws and the relevant corporate and business laws relating to insurance, the law of torts, and the contractual interactions between insurers and insureds.

Insurance usually begins with the identification of a need to insure an insurable interest. An individual has an insurable interest when that individual derives financial benefit from the preservation of the subject matter or is at risk for a pecuniary loss from the loss, compromise, or destruction of that subject matter. For example, an insured interest might include a life, a home, or a car but may also include business continuity or protection from potential liability.

Once the desire or need for insurance is identified, the next step is to locate an admitted insurer who is willing to provide insurance for that interest, often with the aid of an insurance broker and an insurance agent. An insurance broker represents consumers; he or she has a fiduciary duty to the client. The insurance broker does not work for, represent, or have a responsibility to any one insurance company. The insurance broker typically helps a client identify their specific needs and resources; works with the client to research appropriate and acceptable types of coverage, terms, conditions, and cost; and will then recommend one or more insurers and/or policies which best fit the client's needs and resources. An insurance agent, on the other hand, sells insurance on behalf of one or more insurers; a captive agent represents one insurance company, whereas an independent agent may represent more than one insurance company. The important distinction between a broker and an agent is that the broker works to represent the client and recommends, whereas the agent works for the insurance company, usually on commission, and sells policies.

Once a decision is reached regarding a potential type of policy and a potential insurer, the client must complete an application for insurance. The process of application and the format must meet specific requirements which have legal implications. The completed and submitted application for insurance represents an offer to enter into a binding contract; that offer is subject to the prospective insurer's acceptance or rejection. A blank application form does not in itself represent such an offer.

Insurance is a contract whereby one party promises to pay, or indemnify, another in the event that the other sustains a covered loss. A contract is an agreement with legal purpose that is enforceable by law. Insurance contracts have important distinguishing features:

1. Insurance contracts are aleatory, which means that insurance implies an element of chance and therefore a potential for unequal exchange of value or consideration for both parties. Thus, the insured may suffer a loss soon after entering into

the contract and thereby benefit at the insurer's expense; or the insured may pay significant premiums and not suffer a loss, in which case the insurer makes a profit.

2. Insurance contracts are unilateral, which means that the only party with an enforceable obligation is the insurer, since the insurer promises to indemnify if a specific event occurs; however, the insurer cannot require payment of the premium. Nonetheless, the insurer has the right to cancel the policy in the event of non-payment of premiums.
3. Insurance contracts are conditional, which means that the insurer's obligation to pay benefits is dependent on the occurrence of a specified event.
4. Insurance contracts are considered to be contracts of utmost good faith, which means that both the insured and the insurer are legally entitled to a full, fair, and honest disclosure of all material facts and relevant information prior to the formation of the contract. Terminologies pertinent to the notion of utmost good faith include warranties, representations, and concealment.

Since insurance contracts are considered to be contracts of utmost good faith, all statements of fact within the application must be honest and true. Misrepresentations or omissions within the application for insurance that are either fraudulent or material may be grounds for subsequent rejection of the application or later prevent recovery under the policy. A misrepresentation of fact is a false statement which influences the decisions of another. Only facts can be misrepresented, misrepresentation to not apply to opinions. Misrepresentations typically fall into one of four categories: (a) innocent misrepresentations are are false statements regarding a material fact, for which the party who made the statement, was unaware that the statemnent was unture, at the time the statement was made; (b) a negligent misrepresentation is a statement regarding a material fact, which the party making the statement did not attempt to verify as to its veracity; (c) a fraudulent misrepresentation is a statement made either with knowledge that was false or made recklessly so as to induce the other party to act in reliance of that statement; or (d) an omission whereby one fails to disclose known material facts.

A material fact is a fact that is reasonably important to the outcome of a certain decision. The term "material" is used in contradistinction to a detail which is insignificant, unimportant, or trivial and therefore has no reasonable bearing on the making of a given decision. Where one party, such as the insurer, justifiably relies on a misrepresentation of material fact, in a subsequent analysis or dispute, the contract may be cancelled, voided, or sued upon for damages, or the insurer can refuse payment.

The insurer has the right to accept or reject the application for insurance; in addition, either party may explicitly impose additional conditions or negotiate premiums, in essence imposing a counteroffer. Nonetheless, assuming no changes or additional conditions are required, the signing and delivery of the policy contract by the insurer creates a binding agreement, although the details here can vary by state. For example, in some cases, a policy signed by the insurer may subsequently require the insured's signature to show his or her acceptance of the insurer's written offer. Furthermore, the acceptance by an insurer of the application may be conditional, conditioned, for example, upon the insured's receipt of the policy or payment of the first premium by the insured.

A binder or binding receipt is evidence of temporary insurance until the permanent policy is issued or disapproved, or some other condition is satisfied. A binder is only valid for a certain period of time, often defined either by statute and/or the insurer, usually no more than 90 days, although written extensions may be possible. An insurance binder serves as proof of insurance and will usually specify (1) what is insured, (2) the amount of liability coverage, (3) deductibles and coverage limits, (4) the named insured, (5) the insurer/insurance company and type of coverage, (6) the term including the effective date and the date of expiration, and (7) the insurance agent who authorized the binder. The exact requirements for insurance binders may be defined by statute.

The final contract of insurance may include various elements potentially including the policy, riders, endorsements, referenced statutes, and other relevant materials which the parties may deem necessary and relevant. Where the contents of an insurance policy are regulated by statute, such statutory requirements may be deemed to be incorporated either specifically or by reference. The actual insurance policy defines the rights and obligations of the parties involved in the insurance agreement. The policy will usually include a declarations page, attached to the standard policy form, which specifies the name of the insured, the policy period, the limits coverage, the covered risk, the limits of liability, and the premium. In any policy, there are provisions; mostly these are standard and statutorily or legislatively required.

Exclusion clauses eliminate coverage for one or more specific events, which, but for the exclusion clause, would have been covered by the initial coverage. The purpose of an exclusion may be to eliminate coverage for situations or events that create risks of loss greater than those normally associated with the hazard. An ambiguous exclusion is usually construed against the insurer. Common exclusions in professional liability or medical malpractice policies can include (a) sexual misconduct, (b) fraudulent acts such as false claims violations, (c) claims arising under the Health Insurance Portability and Accountability Act (HIPAA) or similar actions relating to medical records privacy, (d) administrative work, (e) expert witness work, (f) supervision and/or teaching, or (g) exclusions pertaining to specific scope of practice or procedural restrictions.

Insurance policy conditions can shift the risk of loss if certain conditions are not met or complied with, or if certain conditions become operative. Conditions are enumerated and defined within the policy. Of extreme importance are the "Duties in Event of an Occurrence or Loss" or similar clause, which outlines the procedures an insured must follow in the event of a loss or claim; moreover, in certain polices such as professional liability policies, the relevant duty may also extend to anticipated losses or claims. The duty of notification varies by policy, but in effect, it represents the duty of the insured to notify the insurer of circumstances which may give rise to a claim as soon as practical after the insured becomes aware of a situation which could potentially trigger a claim. It is important to know the exact circumstances which trigger the duty of notification applicable to any particular insurance policy, since failure to timely notify the insurer as soon as reasonably possible can result in the rejection of a claim. Another potential condition relates to limitation of an insurer's liability in the circumstance where the insured owns other applicable insurance coverage.

Increasingly, insurance policies and other contracts are being written in plain langauge, so that there are no legal terms of art which may be ambiguous to laypersons. When faced with questions of contract interpretation, courts commonly begin with the principle that "[t]he primary goal in interpreting contracts is to determine and enforce the parties' intent" [8]. The general rule regarding contract interpretation is that except as otherwise dictated by statute or public policy, insurance policies are interpreted in a similar manner as ordinary business contracts between individuals, subject to the same general principles of construction [9]. The interpretation of ambiguous contract terms follows a general algorithm: (a) if the policy contract expressly defines a term, courts will apply that definition; (b) if the term at issue is not defined in the policy, the court looks to the plain meaning of the term; (c) if the term or the language are ambiguous (when reasonably intelligent persons reading the language would honestly differ on its meaning), then the ambiguous terms or language are generally construed in favor of an insured.

A contract of insurance generally ceases to be in effect when it is cancelled or terminated. Cancellation is the termination of a policy before its expiration; however, cancellation is usually a right which must be reserved explicitly within the contract. A policy can be cancelled by the insurer for cause such as misrepresentation, non-payment of premiums, or materially changed circumstances. On the other hand, the insured can usually cancel the contract at any time. Termination refers to the ending of a policy through the ending of the stated policy period.

Types of Professional Liability Insurance

Professional liability insurance (PLI) is insurance that protects professionals such as physicians, accountants, and lawyers against claims of professional negligence. PLI is also referred to as malpractice insurance, professional indemnity insurance, and, less commonly, as errors and omissions insurance. PLI helps protect professionals, who offer professional advice and perform professional services, from financial liabilities arising out of claims of malpractice or professional negligence. Claims of professional negligence may be brought by patients, families, or other clients against professionals for errors or omissions arising through statements and acts by the professional. Professional negligence arises in situation where a professional renders opinions or performs services of a highly technical nature upon which the client reasonably relies, and, subsequently, questions as to the professional's reasonable judgment will inevitably often arise. Claims of professional negligence are brought in civil courts under tort law and are expensive to defend, and direct financial liability takes the form of a monetary award for damages. General liability insurance policies do not confer protection against claims arising out professional negligence or malpractice. Thus, the insurer who provides a professional liability insurance policy typically assumes the dual duties to (1) defend and (2) indemnify. The insurer's duty to defend relates to the retention and reimbursement of legal counsel to defend the insured, whereas the duty to indemnify relates to the insurer's duty to pay the judgment award in the event that the plaintiff prevails.

State licensing boards may require that medical professionals maintain PLI coverage; in addition, hospital bylaws and rules and health insurance plans may require that providers carry PLI in order to provide services in the hospital and/or related medical facilities. The minimum state-mandated levels of PLI vary greatly between states, ranging from $100,000 to $1 million in coverage per claim and from $300,000 to $3 million in coverage total each year. Coverage typically includes attorney and court costs, costs of arbitration or mediation, settlements, and verdicts. PLI may be obtained in the form of an individual policy, a group policy, or an employer-based program and may be purchased from a traditional insurer or a risk retention group. Frequently, PLI coverage is paid on the behalf of an employed provider by the group or hospital which employs that provider. Where facilities cover providers through an employer-based policy, personal coverage confers potential advantages in the event that the individual provider's interests diverge from that of the facility. States may also have created legislatively enacted programs designed to aid physicians to minimize liability arising out of claims; such state programs can include limitations (or "caps") on claims or on specified elements of claims (such as "pain and suffering"), patient compensation funds (e.g., neurological claims arising out of birth-related injuries), or supplemental levels of coverage to help protect against catastrophic verdicts. The cost of medical malpractice premiums generally vary by state, practice location, specialty, provider experience, the provider's claims history, the limits of the specific policy, and procedures performed.

Non-physician medical providers and staff such as physician-assistants, advanced practice nurses (nurse-anesthetists, nurse-midwives, and nurse practitioners), therapists, and registered nurses also may carry PLI coverage. Although nurses are often covered for claims by the facility they work for, once again, personal coverage may confer advantages in the event that the individual's interests diverge from that of the facility.

Liability coverage is also classified as either (a) direct liability coverage, which insures provider for the medical services that they personally provide, or (b) vicarious liability coverage which insures the provider for the services provided by others for whom the provider is legally responsible such as advanced practice providers, employees, students, or volunteers.

An important consideration to medical malpractice PLI is the relevant statute of limitations governing claims for medical malpractice in the state in which the policy is in effect. The statute of limitations refers to the statutorily, or legislatively, defined maximum period of time that may pass after an event within which legal proceedings may be initiated (filed). State statutes of limitations vary between individual states; however, in all cases, the statute of limitations will exceed at least 1 year. Therefore, and in general, a provider may first become aware that a lawsuit has been filed against him or her, many years after a contested issue occurs. In general, with the exception of situational modifications, medical malpractice PLI will take the form of either:

1. *A "claims-made" policy* which provides coverage if and only if the policy is in effect both when the treatment took place and when a lawsuit is filed. The claims-made policy excludes events which occurred before and after the term of the policy and excludes coverage for claims which arise from events that occurred during the term of the policy but where litigation was not commenced until after the term of the policy expired (Table 10.1 and Fig. 10.1).

   Claims-made policies are offered at lower premiums than are occurrence policies. The premiums are also further discounted through the initial years of the policy. However, with each additional year of coverage, and as the corresponding statistical likelihood of a lawsuit increases, the premium increases incrementally (the "step factor") until a "mature" rate is reached. The mature rate may increase based on claims history.

Table 10.1 A comparison of claims-made versus occurrence of medical professional liability insurance policies [18]

Policy details	Claims-made policy	Occurrence policy
Covered acts	The insured is indemnified for any and all covered acts arising during the period which the policy is in effect *as long as* both acts occur and notice of the claim during the active term of the policy	The insured covered for any and all covered acts which occur during the term of the policy
Key distinction: indemnification for potential causes of action	If a medical malpractice claim is brought against the insured after the policy has expired or was terminated, even though provider was insured under the policy at the time that the cause of action accrued, the insured is not covered under that policy, and insurer is not liable for coverage (unless there is tail coverage)	The insurer is responsible for the coverage for all medical malpractice causes of action which accrue during the coverage period, regardless of when the claim is brought against the provider
Extended reporting period/"tail" coverage	Extended reporting coverage, if in effect, will cover any and all covered acts which occurred during the term of the policy even if the provider was first on notice of the claim after the policy expired or was terminated	Extended reporting coverage is not necessary since claims resulting from any and all covered acts are covered by the insurer regardless of when the claim is brought against the insured
Prior acts ("nose") or retroactive coverage	Available	Available
Cost of insurance	Insurance premium costs are generally lower than occurrence policies Premiums are generally subject to an incremental increase over the first years in proportion to the insured's claim history, after which a mature premium level is reached barring annual rate adjustments	Insurance premium costs are higher than claims-made policies; however, the insured's financial exposure for claims brought after the term of the policy is more clearly defined

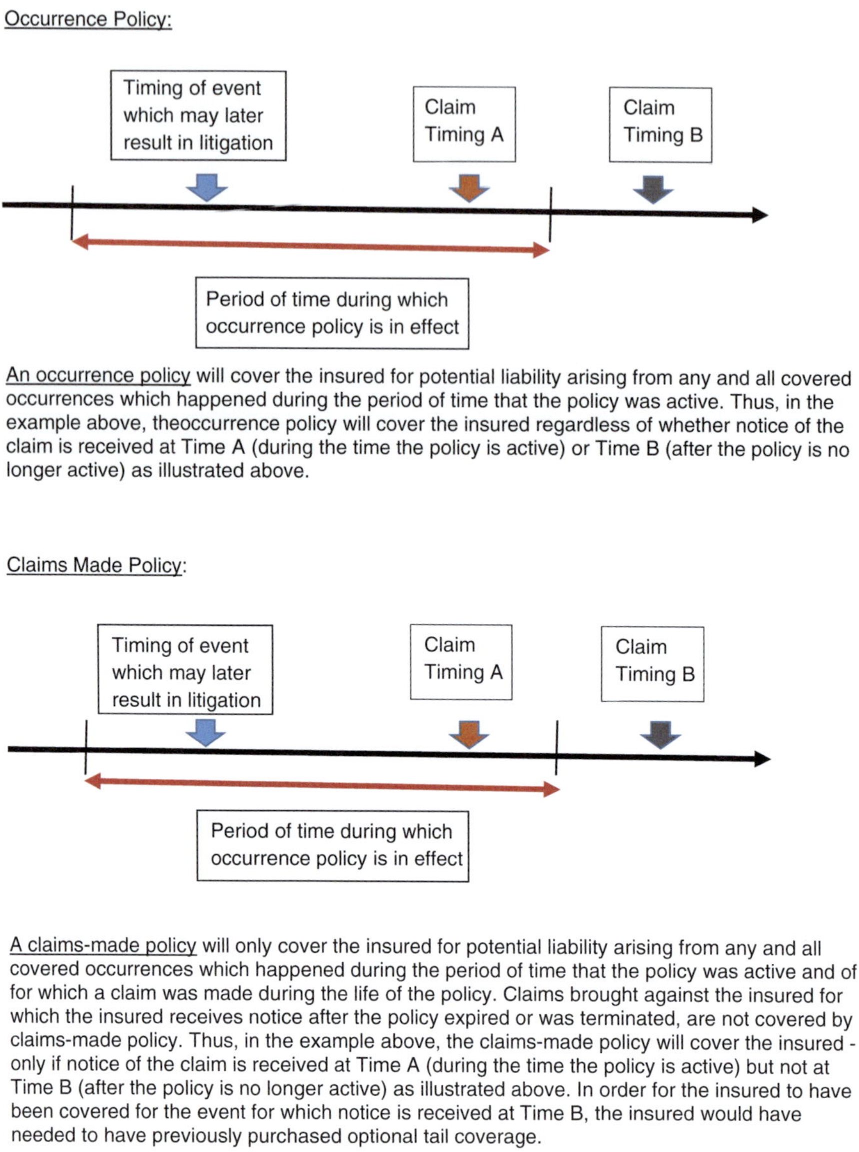

Fig. 10.1 Visual comparison of occurrence and claims-made policies

Claims-made policies typically generate issues when a provider moves between practices or retires, since that provider is longer insured for events which took place while the claims-made policy was in effect. In order to continue to be insured for events which occurred during the term of a prior claims-made policy, the provider can chose to purchase optional "tail" or "extended reporting" coverage, or endorsement. Claims-made policies may contain provisions within the contract regarding the extended reporting period. Tail coverage should ideally extend from the last date that the provider practiced under the claims-made policy through the maximum applicable state statute of limitations (allowing for potential extensions, tolls, and special circumstances such as pediatrics). Depending on the provider's risk profile, the cost of a tail can be substantial. Instead of purchasing a tail, an alternative option may be to purchase prior acts coverage with the new claims-made policy (see below).

Claims-made policies may, under some circumstances, provide extended reporting coverage at no additional cost in the event of retirement, death, or permanent disability.

2. *A "modified claims-made" policy* provides a prepaid indefinite tail coverage on a claims-made basis. For the insured, the modified claims-made policy is functionally equivalent to an occurrence policy. Coverage is triggered in the same manner as in claims-made coverage; however, a modified claims-made policy automatically triggers and provides tail coverage after the policy terms expire.
3. *An "occurrence" policy* provides coverage for any claim regarding any event which took place ("occurred") during the period ('term') of coverage. Thus, an occurrence policy will fully indemnify the provider even if the claim is filed by a plaintiff after the term of the policy has expired or lapsed. The actuarial uncertainty involved in the prediction of the cost of future claims has made occurrence policies expensive and/or difficult to obtain. The higher premium cost of an occurrence policy is, in essence, a prepaid tail, since the cost of the tail is built into the premiums of an occurrence policy. Providers insured under occurrence policies therefore do not need to purchase tail coverage (Table 10.1 and Fig. 10.1).
4. *Retroactively dated coverage* ("prior acts" or "nose") is an option which provides coverage for services provided before the effective date of the policy. "Prior acts" coverage transfers the retroactive date for an old policy to a new insurance carrier—eliminating the need to purchase tail coverage from the last carrier. Nose coverage is frequently less costly than the option of purchasing tail coverage from the prior carrier.

Clause Caveats in Professional Liability Insurance

The law of insurance applies to PLI; it is prudent to review one's policy carefully to understand and recognize issues such as conditions, exclusions, coverage, specific clauses, and the required duties of the insured provider. Examples of such language in policies include the following:

Misrepresentations

Misrepresentations or omissions on applications for insurance can render a policy void. A misrepresentation may take the form of either a false affirmative statement or a failure to disclose. In the case of applications for insurance, misrepresentations usually pertain to prior acts, prior coverage denials, restrictions in medical staff privileges, or exclusion from payer panels or will be as regards education, training, credentialing, or licensure. In some cases, such misrepresentations may take the form of misunderstandings; however, every effort must be made to understand the specific details requested before submitting the application. Claims of misrepresentation must demonstrably distinguish between innocent, negligent, and fraudulent misrepresentation. Misrepresentations which are "material" are those where the insurer had prior knowledge before issuing the policy and would have triggered a refusal to contract. Misrepresentations which are material can result in a rescission of the policy, declaration of the policy as void, or even a disclaimer or denial of coverage [10].

During the PLI application process, questions regarding "awareness" of "any circumstances" might give rise to a claim. Misrepresentation in this circumstance can trigger the "Known Claims or Circumstances" exclusion regarding both claims reported to a prior insurer and claims which *should have been* reported to a prior insurer.

All-Risk Policies

Medical malpractice PLI policies are written on an "all-risk" basis and generally provide coverage for all claims arising out of *professional activities*, except as noted. All-risk policies are typically broad in the scope of coverage and may moonlighting include supervisory roles or administrative duties; however, the exceptions must be examined and understood.

Exclusions

Exclusions refer to acts or activities which are not covered within the policy. Insurers and policies may differ with respect to enumerated exclusions. In fact, not all types of medical errors and omissions may be covered. State statutes pertaining to insurance vary and define the legality of specific exclusions within insurance contracts, either as a matter of law or as a matter of public policy.

Medical malpractice PLI policies will exclude coverage for actions deemed to be reckless or wanton, or those which are deemed to be indifferent, willful, and intentional. In medical malpractice claims, attorneys will often combine claims based on ordinary negligence together with claims based on gross negligence. Ordinary negligence refers to the failure to exercise reasonable care to adhere to the applicable standards of care under the circumstances. Gross negligence generally requires that the plaintiff demonstrate (a) knowing or intentional disregard of an unreasonable risk and (b) a risk which is associated with a high degree of probability of causing substantial harm. Gross negligence is often used as a basis to justify punitive damages in a medical malpractice action to increase the recovery for an injured plaintiff; however, these allegations and ensuing allegations may not be covered under a medical malpractice PLI.

Most medical malpractice PLI policies will also exclude coverage for criminal acts, sexual misconduct, false and fraudulent insurance claims, and spoliation of medical records. In some cases, the PLI may exclude high-risk procedures and/or the prescription of drugs for non-FDA-approved uses. Where a provider's professional activities occasionally or regularly include extracurricular but colorable work-related activities such as EMS supervision, medical care at community or sports events, or providing legally required medical examinations, clarification and disclosure of such activities to the insurer are important to assure a mutual understanding regarding coverage in such circumstances.

A potentially important exclusion to consider is an exclusion for either "moonlighting" or services provided at satellite locations; providers will need to verify that they are in fact covered for all the services they provide at all locations at which they practice. Medical malpractice PLI policies may specifically exclude administrative duties such as medical director duties.

An important exclusion is that pertaining to allegations of professional misconduct. Professional misconduct investigations are typically brought by State Departments of Health or similar licensing and oversight boards and result not in malpractice litigation but rather in administrative sanctions, restriction, or revocation of licensure. The costs of defense for a professional misconduct hearing are substantial, and the typical malpractice PLI does not cover such circumstances. Increasingly, insurers are providing additional insurance, or optional riders, to cover such circumstances. In New York State, such an optional rider is referred to as a "legal defense cost coverage" rider which provides optional supplementary insurance coverage for the costs of defending state or federal administrative actions such as either professional misconduct (NY OPMC) or a Medicare or Medicaid False Claims Act allegation.

Duty-to-Cooperate Clause

Medical malpractice PLI policies customarily include a clause requiring the insured's "cooperation" with the insurer's efforts to defend the insured against a claim. A duty to cooperate may include providing timely notice of a claim to the insurer, testifying capably in one's defense at deposition or trial, assisting one's assigned defense attorney with case preparation, and avoiding statements which amount to an admission of liability. The duty-to-cooperate clause is important in instances where a provider meets with families regarding apologies and disclosure of medical errors.

Consent-to-Settle Clause

A "consent-to-settle" clause in a PLI policy (sometimes referred to as a "pride clause") requires that the insurer seek and obtain the consent of the insured prior to settling a medical malpractice claim. "Consent to settle" may be considered important to providers since malpractice claims have not only financial but also reputational ("pride") and regulatory implications. Where there is a consent-to-settle clause, and the insured and insurer work together, not only can the insurer not settle a claim without the insured's consent, but the collaboration may actually decrease payments in the case of nuisance lawsuits.

In the event that a provider exercises his or her "consent-to-settle clause" and he or she prevails, avoiding either settlement or judgment, then that particular case of alleged malpractice does not become a part of his or her permanent claims history. Providers should remember that the best interests of the hospital, groups, or insurance company may not be the same as the best interests of the particular provider.

The "Hammer Clause"

Although a consent-to-settle clause may benefit both the insured and the insurer, some policies contain a "hammer clause" whereby if the insured does not approve the insurer's recommendation to settle, or the amount of the settlement, a typical consent to settlement clause will nullify the insurer's further liabilities to defend or indemnify the provider beyond the amount of the proposed settlement. For example, if a plaintiff offers to settle a claim for $100,000 and the insured refuses to settle despite the insurer's advice to do so, under the "hammer clause," the insured provider will assume personal liability for any judgment or awards in excess of $100,000. Ignoring a hammer clause opens you up to a serious financial risk. In general, most insurers will offer a "consent to settle" without a hammer clause.

Defense Costs

Most malpractice insurance PLI policies typically assume the risk of the costs of both defense and indemnification; however, some polices are now distinguishing and separating the two costs. Where "defense within" is specified within or in conjunction with the policy limits clause, the costs of defense erode the amount of coverage available to pay indemnity.

A clause specifying "ultimate net loss coverage" will generally pay attorney fees and defense costs in addition to any awards, whereas a clause specifying "pure loss coverage" will generally pay only the settlement or judgment amount. Ultimate net loss coverage will also confer the flexibility to retain one's defense counsel in addition to the hospital, group, or carrier's attorney, which may be important if one's interests need to be represented separately from those of the others named in the suit.

Thus, where applicable, the phrase "defense in addition" is financially more desirable than is "defense within." For example, assuming that a provider carries a policy with limits of $1,000,000 per occurrence/$3,000,000 annual aggregate, and the policy specifies "defense costs in addition," then, if the verdict or judgment in a specific action reaches $1,000,000, the provider will be liable for the costs of defense which may be substantial. The average cost of defending a malpractice claim is approximately $30,000; this figure includes attorney's fees, costs for medical records, expert witness fees, court costs, and incidental fees; however, depending on the location and the type of claim, the costs of defense may be higher. An alternate view would be that where the policy specifies "defense within" in the event of a $1,000,000 judgment or verdict and $30,000 defense costs, the actual amount available to pay the judgment is decreased to $970,000.

Incident Reporting/Duty to Notify

The duty to notify an insurer regarding an actual or potential claim is a condition precedent to the insurer's obligation to defend and indemnify the insured. The definition of a "claim" varies by policy and insurer. The exact circumstances which trigger the duty to report will almost certainly be contractually defined. Timely reporting of an incident before it actually becomes a claim can potentially allow the implementation of risk management interventions which may then prevent a lawsuit or help the insurer prepare for anticipated loss. Some insurers require the insured to report any and all incidents which may reasonably be expected to lead to claims.

In some cases, insurers require only that formal claims be reported on receipt of notice. A "claim" is a demand served upon the insured by a plaintiff; in most cases, the first formal notice of a lawsuit occurs on receipt of the summons and complaint. This requirement is commonly referred to as a "written demand for damages" requirement. In such cases, the provider must be formally served with a lawsuit sued before the claim will be recognized by the insurer.

Typically, occurrence policies are more likely to encourage early notice of potential claims so that they can potentially encumber, or make available, funds to settle or litigate if needed. On the other hand, claims-made policies are more likely to require receipt of a written demand, or actual notice, of a lawsuit before acknowledging a claim, since a provider may migrate practices before a claim is made, thus shifting potential liability to another insurer.

Once a provider-defendant is formally served with notice of a claim, a strict legally operative timeline becomes operative. Specifically, failure to answer the claim (i.e., the notice and complaint) within a statutorily defined time period will result in a default judgment against the defendant, and that defendant loses the opportunity to defend the lawsuit. Insurers may thus deny coverage based on late notice to instances where the insurer can prove that it was adversely affected, or prejudiced, by the delay.

The National Practitioner Data Bank

If a malpractice claim against the insured is settled, even if that claim is otherwise perceived by the insured as frivolous or non-meritorious, the settlement will be reported against the provider in the National Practitioner Data Bank (NPDB).

The NPDB is a data repository, or confidential data clearinghouse, mandated under federal statute [11] which maintains records of malpractice claims, disciplinary actions, state licensing actions, and adverse privileging restrictions involving healthcare practitioners. Specifically, all payments are made by or on behalf of a healthcare practitioner, in satisfaction (in whole or in part) of a claim or judgment (including out-of-court settlement payments). In 2010, under the authority of Section 1921 of the Social Security Act, the HHS expanded the scope reporting for the NPDB to include reports of actions not just against physicians but against all healthcare practitioners.

Data remains within the NPDB permanently unless modified or removed by the reporting entity. A "query" is a search of the NPDB database performed for the purpose of due diligence during credentialing and recredentialing of a healthcare practitioner. Mandatory queries are those which are mandated by federal or state law; or by regulatory agencies such as The Joint Commission, when practitioners apply for clinical privileges and seek to expand existing privileges every 2 years during the recredentialing process. The NPDB is also regularly accessed for use in employment, affiliation, or licensure decisions. Nonetheless, medical liability carriers, private accreditation organizations, professional societies with peer review functions, and federal agencies such as the DEA and the HHS are prohibited from submitting queries [12].

There are potential "loopholes" to NPDB reporting; however, these should be considered only on the advice of an attorney.

The "corporate shield loophole" takes advantage of the fact that the reporting statute requires reporting only in those instances where a provider or practitioner is a named defendant to the action at the time of the payment. Thus, if a provider or practitioner is dismissed without a duty of payment before a settlement or verdict is finalized, the provider is potentially exempt from the reporting statute. Dismissals of named defendants generally occur in those lawsuits where a large group or hospital is named alongside with numerous providers also individually named and where one or more providers may be dismissed during stages of litigation. In such cases, providers should specifically and individually verify that their names have indeed been deleted from the settlement or judgment document.

The "personal fund loophole" takes advantage of the fact that the reporting statute mandates reporting to the NPDB where a payment is made on behalf of a provider or practitioner by another party. The corollary is that payment made by an individual provider or practitioner on his or her own behalf is therefore not reportable.

In the event that a practitioner is reported to the NPDB, the practitioner and the reporting entity are accorded a 60-day period to contest the report or its wording. If a satisfactory dispute resolution regarding the report cannot be achieved, the practitioner who is the subject of a report may submit a written explanatory statement on his or her own behalf, containing 4000 words or less, to supplement the report.

Alternatives to Traditional Insurance Providers

Traditional commercial insurance companies are typically owned by shareholders, issue stock which is traded in public exchanges, and pay dividends to shareholders based on financial performance.

Nontraditional insurance companies may include (a) physician-owned insurers, (b) risk retention groups, (c) risk purchasing groups or captive entities, (d) mutual insurance companies, or combination entities. Nontraditional insurance entities may enjoy financial incentives since they may not be subject to the level of the regulatory and administrative oversight as are as traditional insurers. However, conversely, those insured by nontraditional insurers may not have access to state guaranty funds in the event of insolvency of such insurers.

A captive insurer is usually formed to insure a specific group of providers such as a hospital system or a coalition of academic medical centers. A similar concept of self-insurance allows an entity to establish and administer its own insurance fund without specifically forming a company.

A risk retention group ("RRG") is an insuring entity formed under the federal Liability Risk Retention Act of 1986 and is similar to a captive insurance company in that it is formed for a specific entity or to cover groups with a relatively homogeneous risk. In a risk retention group, the policyholders are also its members and owners. Once a RRG meets and complies with state licensing requirements as an insurer in any one of the 50 states, it may then operate nationwide in any other or all other states without having to meet those individual other states' licensing rules. Although risk retention groups must adhere to the insurance laws of the state in which they are domiciled, they are not admitted insurance carriers, and member policyholders are thus not eligible for any state guaranty funds. Thus, RRGs are exempt from the requirements to be licensed in each state in which they operate, are exempt from contribution requirement imposed on insurance companies by which insurers must contribute to state guaranty funds, are less subject to regulation by the states' insurance commissioners, and are generally operated as mutual companies. Policies issued by RRGs must inform potential insureds, through a federally mandated warning, which states that the policy is neither regulated nor guaranteed in the same way as other insurance [13].

Medical Malpractice Insurance Limits and Excess Verdicts

The policy limits of liability are specified and defined within the policy contract, as discussed above. Where state laws mandate liability policy limits, the limits generally vary between states because some states have enacted caps on damages or have enacted "Patient Compensation Funds" which allow providers to maintain lower levels of coverage. Minimum liability limits may also be established under hospital bylaws or terms of employment.

A typical policy might provide coverage for $1 million per occurrence and $3 million per year; settlements or verdicts below these limits are covered by the insurer, as discussed above. However, where either a single settlement or verdict exceeds the per-occurrence coverage, or where the annual aggregate exceeds the annual aggregate limit, the provider is liable. For example, if, given the limits above, there are two judgments or settlements in 1 year for $2 million each, the insurer would pay each occurrence to the policy limit of $1 million, and the provider would be responsible for $1 million for each of the suits. On the other hand, if, given the limits above, there are five judgments for $50,000, the insurer would fully pay each claim. Finally, if there are eight lawsuits for $40,000, then the provider would be liable for the excess over the annual limit, or $200,000.

Although trends may suggest a decline in malpractice cases brought to litigation, there also appears to be a trend toward larger verdicts. The large majority of medical malpractice claims are either discontinued ("dropped") by the plaintiff, judicially dismissed for lack of merit, or settled prior to trial usually for an amount within the defendant's policy limits; of those cases which proceed to trial, the majority of verdicts favor the defense. Catastrophic verdicts are rare against individual providers and are more commonly seen where groups or institutions with "deep pockets" are also named in the suit. Catastrophic verdicts, or "mega-awards," most frequently involve debilitating nerve injury and permanent incapacitation requiring great lifetime financial costs for medical and custodial care of the injured. It is sometimes argued that "jury sympathy" may sometimes drive verdicts against providers and hospitals, based not so much on a finding of actual negligence but rather because the jurors perceive that well-insured providers and hospitals have the ability to pay large awards to an injured plaintiff [14].

Furthermore, the larger the verdict, the more likely is an appeal, which delays or risks loss of potential compensation to the injured plaintiff. Moreover, judgments in excess of a provider's policy limits, which would require a provider to liquidate personal assets to satisfy the judgment, are generally avoided.

The formation of a corporate or professional limited liability company (or partnership) is often employed as an attempt to shield personal assets in the event of litigation. The laws regulating the formation of professional corporations or professional service corporations vary by state. Providers or practitioners contemplating the formation of a corporate entity as a shield against personal liability in the event of a large malpractice settlement or verdict should do so only on the advice of their attorney. In general, professional corporations may limit the personal liability of the owners in the event of business debts and claims. For example, a corporate entity, and not the individual owners, may be liable for a non-professional employee's actions, assuming the corporate entity carries insurance against such events. However, in general, courts are likely to readily "pierce the corporate veil" in the event of medical malpractice, thereby removing that protection of limited liability.

Umbrella Insurance Policies

Umbrella insurance policies are policies which provide excess coverage in the event of home, renters, personal, or personal property damage. Umbrella policies are usually either personal or commercial.

Personal umbrella policy will almost uniformly contain an exclusion clause specifically excluding coverage for liabilities arising from business activities. Thus, a typical exclusion clause within an umbrella policy will stipulate exclusion of coverage for "personal injury or property damage arising out of the rendering or failing to render professional services."

Commercial general liability policies are intended to insure against potential liabilities arising out of usual business activities. However, commercial general liability policies also generally exclude professional liability—however, there are umbrella policies available which are designed to supplement commercial general liability policies, and some of these umbrella policies will provide additional coverage for professional liability.

Officers' and Directors' Insurance

Physician executives who assume administrative or medical director roles, or healthcare administrators in general, are potentially liable for the non-medical decision-making they may make in professional executive capacities. Personal liability for healthcare executives can result from decisions they make, or decisions they fail to make, stemming from actions as participants on committees, workgroups, or boards of directors. In general, organizations will purchase "Directors' and Officers'" or "D&O" insurance policies to protect both the organization and its executives. Under most but not all circumstances, the "D&O" policy will indemnify against both losses and also legal costs.

Administrative liability is distinct and separate from medical malpractice liability. The types of healthcare facilities where administrative risks can arise are varied and may include medical practices and groups, ambulatory surgical centers, hospitals and clinics, urgent care facilities, pain treatment centers, community health centers, nursing homes or assisted living facilities, hospice facilities, rehabilitation facilities, psychiatric or drug rehabilitation facilities, medical laboratories, foundations supporting healthcare, and various structures of managed care organizations. The types of liability associated with administrative decision-making can range from fraud and false claims, health information privacy violations, claims based in contract, human resources liability such as potential employee discrimination or unfair employment practices including toxic workplace or wrongful termination, antitrust violations, or the Federal Trade Commission, tax, or financial issues such as loans and debts, income tax claims, dividend or profit sharing, or asset acquisition, use, or disbursement.

In general, as long as executives understand and maintain their fiduciary obligations, the law accords broad discretion decision-making to corporate officers under the legal doctrine known as the "business judgment rule." The business judgment rule is a legal principle that immunizes officers, directors, managers, and other agents of a corporation or other business entity from liability to the corporation or its shareholders in the event that the corporation incurs losses stemming from decisions made by corporate directors or officers in "good faith." The rule has its origins in the case of *Otis & Co. v. Pennsylvania R. Co.* [15], where the court reasoned that "mistakes or errors in the exercise of honest business judgment do not subject the officers and directors to liability for Negligence in the discharge of their appointed duties." However, courts have also ruled that the fiduciary duty of executives to their shareholders requires more than simply the avoidance of bad faith and rather includes affirmative obligations to obtain, consider, and review information relevant to the making of sound business decisions [16] and that the business judgment rule will apply only when the executives abide by fiduciary principles and remain disinterested and independent in their decision-making [17].

References

1. Szalados JE. Insurance law. Chapter 36. In: Szalados JE, Smith W, Wright W, editors. Law and Ethics in Neurocritical Care. Neurocritical Care Society. Chicago, IL; 2019. p. 94–5.
2. Merriam-Webster Dictionary. Insurance. Available online at https://www.merriam-webster.com/dictionary/insurance. Verified October 11, 2020.
3. Dobbyn JF. Insurance law in a nutshell. 3rd ed. St Paul: West Publishing Company; 1996.
4. Paul v. Virginia, 75 U.S. 168 (1869).
5. United States v. South-Eastern Underwriters, 322 U.S. 533 (1944).
6. The McCarran-Ferguson Act of 1945. 15 U.S.C.A. § 1011 *et seq.*
7. The National Association of Insurance Commissioners. *See ie.* Online at: https://content.naic.org/. Verified October 11, 2020.
8. Old Kent Bank v. Sobczak, 243 Mich. App. 57, 63 (2000); *see also* AIU Ins. Co. v. Superior Court, 51 Cal. 3d 807, 821 (1990); *and see* Greenfield v. Philles Records, Inc., 98 N.Y.2d 562, 569 (2002).
9. 1A Couch on Insurance §11.1 et seq. (3d ed 1995 & Supp 2011).

10. Szalados JE. Using malpractice insurance. In: Szalados JE, Smith W, Wright W, editors. Law and ethics in neurocritical care. Neurocritical Care Society. Chicago, IL; 2019. p. 100–1.
11. Title IV of Public Law 99–660, the Health Care Quality Improvement Act of 1986. Codified at 45 CFR Part 60.
12. Szalados JE. National practitioner databank. In: Szalados JE. Smith W, Wright W, editors. Law and ethics in neurocritical care. Neurocritical Care Society. Chicago, IL; 2019. p. 193–4.
13. Szalados, JE. Malpractice insurance basics. In: Szalados JE, Smith W, Wright W, editors. Law and ethics in neurocritical Care. Neurocritical Care Society; 2019. p. 96–9.
14. Vidmar N. Juries and medical malpractice claims: empirical facts versus myths. Clin Orthop Relat Res. 2009;467(2):367–75. https://doi.org/10.1007/s11999-008-0608-6.
15. *Otis & Co. v. Pennsylvania R. Co.,* 61 F. Supp. 905 (D.C. Pa. 1945).
16. Smith v. Van Gorkom, 488 a.2d 858 (Del. 1985).
17. Aronson v. Lewis, 473 A.2d 805 [Del. 1984]).
18. Modified from Szalados JE. Civil law and liability. In: Ethics and law for neurosciences clinicians: foundations and evolving challenges. Newark: Rutgers University Press; 2019.

Chapter 11
Overview of the Claims Submission, Medical Billing, and Revenue Cycle Management Processes

Joette Derricks

Claim Submission

The process of submitting claims to billing an insurance company, including Medicare and Medicaid, is difficult to summarize because so much of it depends on variables. These variables include things like the patient's insurance plan, the insurance payer's guidelines for claim submission, the provider's contract with the insurance company, and the type of practice management (PM) software the practice is using. Tips and best practices for managing these variables are provided in this chapter.

There are hundreds of different PM systems in the market today and most of them have a companion electronic medical record (EMR) system to capture the physician's documentation of the patient's visit. An integrated PM and EMR systems allow the physician to document the visit diagnosis, treatment, and other pertinent information in the EMR and automatically transfer the billing diagnosis and procedure code information to the PM system. In some cases, there is little intervention by a medical coder or biller to send the claims. With other systems, a medical coder or biller enters the specific information required on the claim form into the PM system.

Some physician practices may decide to outsource their medical billing to a billing service. According to a Black Book 2016 Physician Revenue Cycle Management Survey, the outsourcing of comprehensive medical business office services is staged to grow 30% from practices of less than 25 doctors in the next few years [1]. There are pros and cons for outsourcing part or the entire RCM function. Regardless, to protect the practice, they must control the outsourcing process, including issuing a request for proposal (RFP), performing due diligence, and negotiating terms and pricing that benefit the practice. See more on this subject in section "The Medical Billing and Revenue Cycle Management Processes."

J. Derricks (✉)
Derricks Consulting, LLC, Hunt Valley, MD, USA
e-mail: jderricks@derricksconsulting.com

J. E. Szalados (ed.), *The Medical-Legal Aspects of Acute Care Medicine*,
https://doi.org/10.1007/978-3-030-68570-6_11

Until the passage of the Health Insurance Portability and Accountability Act (HIPAA), most practices sent paper claims or used an electronic system accepted by the insurance company. Each payer may have had their own submission protocols. With HIPAA, the government adopted national standards for electronic transactions to improve the efficiency and effectiveness of the nation's health care system. A transaction is an electronic data interchange (EDI) of information between two parties to carry out financial or administrative activities related to health care. For example, a health care provider will send a claim to a health plan to request payment for medical services.

These standards apply to all HIPAA-covered entities:

- Health plans
- Health care clearinghouses
- Health care providers who conduct electronic transactions, not just those who accept Medicare or Medicaid

Whether the practice sends their electronic claims directly, or use a billing company, or through a clearinghouse vendor, any provider who accepts payment from any health plan or other insurance company must comply with HIPAA if they conduct the adopted transactions electronically. These providers must also have written agreements in place to ensure business associates follow HIPAA. Examples of business associates include clearinghouses and independent medical scribe services.

The HIPAA-adopted standard transactions for the electronic exchange of health care data include the following:

- Claims and encounter information
- Payment and remittance advice
- Claims status
- Eligibility
- Enrollment and disenrollment
- Referrals and authorizations
- Coordination of benefits
- Premium payment [2]

Under HIPAA, the government also adopted specific code sets for diagnoses and procedures used in all transactions (Table 11.1).

Finally, HIPAA establishes and requires unique identifiers for the following:

Table 11.1 Code sets

<table>
<tr><th>Code set classification</th><th>Required code sets</th></tr>
<tr><td>Diagnoses</td><td>International Classification of Diseases, 10th edition (ICD-10-CM)</td></tr>
<tr><td>Procedures</td><td rowspan="4">Health Care Common Procedure Coding System (HCPCS)
Current Procedure Terminology (CPT)
Code on Dental Procedures and Nomenclature (CDT)
National Drug Codes (NDC)</td></tr>
<tr><td>Diagnostic tests</td></tr>
<tr><td>Treatments</td></tr>
<tr><td>Equipment and supplies</td></tr>
</table>

- Health plans – Health Plan Identifier (HPID) is a standard, unique identifier for health plans.
- Employers – Employer Identification Number (EIN) is issued by the Internal Revenue Service and is used to identify employers in electronic transactions.
- Providers – National Provider Identifier (NPI) is a unique 10-digit number used to identify health care providers.
- Patients – There is no adopted standard to identify patients.

NPIs and EINs must be used on all HIPAA transactions. However, there is currently an enforcement discretion period for HPID until further notice, which went into effect on October 31, 2014 [3].

In addition to the HIPAA electronic transaction standards, code set standards, and unique identifier requirements for correct claim submission, other uniform claim standards are set by the National Uniform Claim Committee (NUCC). HIPAA named the NUCC in the administrative simplification section of the Act to have an authoritative voice about national standard content and data definitions for non-institutional health care claims in the United States. The NUCC is a voluntary organization chaired by the American Medical Association (AMA), with the Centers for Medicare and Medicaid Services (CMS) as a critical partner [4].

For example, the NUCC provides definitions to distinguish on the claim form between the rendering, ordering, and supervising physicians.

- The Referring Provider is the individual who directed the patient for care to the provider rendering the services being reported. Examples include, but are not limited to, primary care provider referring to a specialist; orthodontist referring to an oral and maxillofacial surgeon; physician referring to a physical therapist; and provider referring to a home health agency.
- The Ordering Provider is the individual who requested the services or items being reported on this service line. Examples include, but are not limited to, provider ordering diagnostic tests and medical equipment or supplies.
- The Supervising Provider is the individual who provided oversight of the Rendering Provider and the care being reported. An example includes, but is not limited to, supervision of a resident physician or an advanced care practitioner (ACP) providing services under CMS' "incident-to" requirements [5].

CMS and many other payers claim submission guidelines require the completion of block 17 of the CMS Form 1500. Per the NUCC 1500 Health Insurance Claim Form Reference Instruction Manual for Form Version 02/12, item number 17 requires [6] the following:

ITEM NUMBER 17

17. NAME OF REFERRING PROVIDER OR OTHER SOURCE

TITLE: Name of Referring Provider or Other Source

INSTRUCTIONS: Enter the name (First Name, Middle Initial, Last Name) followed by the credentials of the professional who referred or ordered the service(s) or supply(ies) on the claim.

If multiple providers are involved, enter one provider using the following priority order:

1. Referring Provider
2. Ordering Provider
3. Supervising Provider

Do not use periods or commas. A hyphen can be used for hyphenated names.

Enter the applicable qualifier to identify which provider is being reported.

DN	Referring Provider
DK	Ordering Provider
DQ	Supervising Provider

Enter the qualifier to the left of the vertical, dotted line.

DESCRIPTION: The name entered is the referring provider, ordering provider, or supervising provider who referred, ordered, or supervised the service(s) or supply(ies) on the claim. The qualifier indicates the role of the provider being reported.

FIELD SPECIFICATION: This field allows for the entry of 2 characters to the left of the vertical, dotted line and 24 characters to the right of the dotted line.

EXAMPLE:

17. NAME OF REFERRING PROVIDER OR OTHER SOURCE
DN Jane A Smith MD

The NUCC, AMA, and CMS set other standard codes like the place-of-service codes (POS). These codes should be used on professional claims to specify the entity where service(s) were rendered. CMS advises physicians to check with individual payers (e.g., Medicare, Medicaid, and other commercial insurance) for reimbursement policies regarding these codes [7]. Since the reimbursement amount by a payer may vary depending on where the service is rendered, it is important that physicians report the correct POS. The complete list of POS is found at https://www.cms.gov/Medicare/Coding/place-of-service-codes/Place_of_Service_Code_Set.html.

In sum, today's claims submissions by practices are electronic claims transactions using the Accredited Standards Committee Electronic Data Interchange (ASC X12N) [8]. The ASC standards explicitly parallel the paper claim form known as the CMS Form 1500. See Fig. 11.1 for CMS Form 1500. For instructions regarding completion, see, http://nucc.org/images/stories/PDF/1500_claim_form_instruction_manual_2012_02-v6.pdf. The NUCC, CMS, or individual insurance payers may establish specific coverage and reimbursement policies associated with information sent on CMS Form 1500. Some PM and EMR systems have modules to help the practice track and bill the correct code set information required by a specific

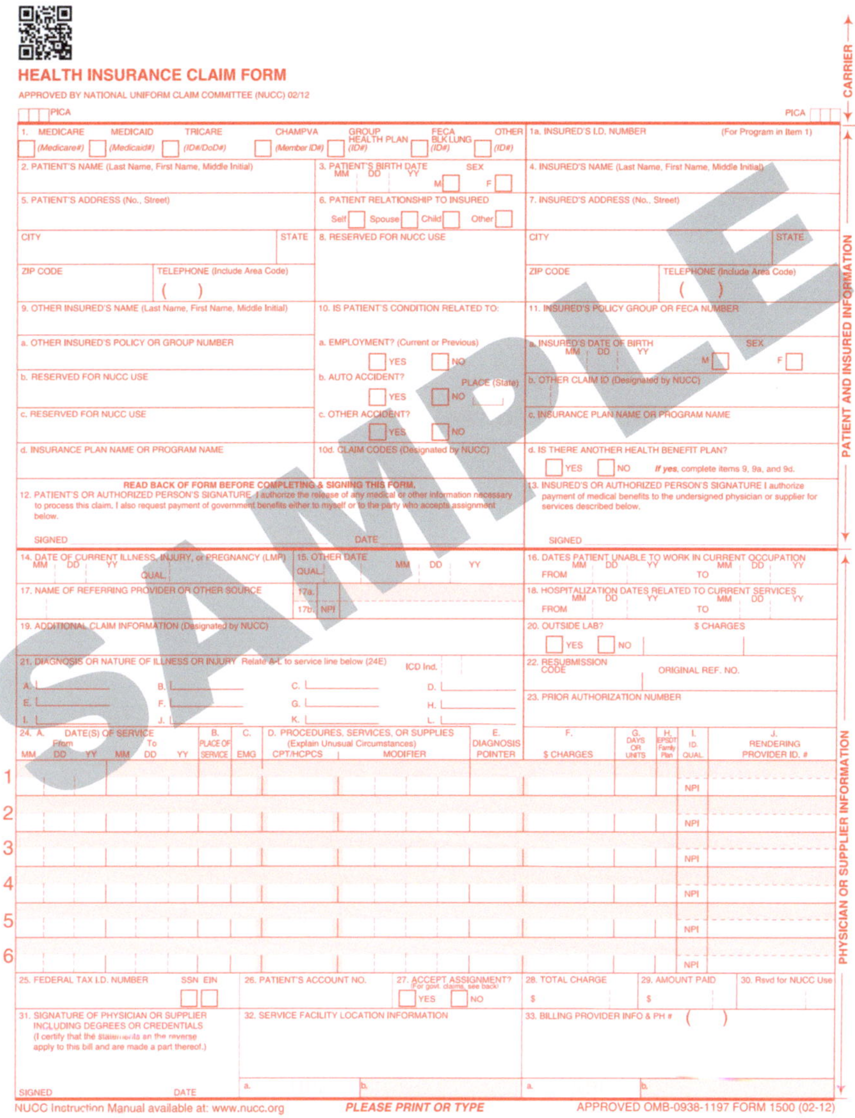

HEALTH INSURANCE CLAIM FORM

APPROVED BY NATIONAL UNIFORM CLAIM COMMITTEE (NUCC) 02/12

PICA PICA

CARRIER

1. MEDICARE (Medicare#) MEDICAID (Medicaid#) TRICARE (ID#/DoD#) CHAMPVA (Member ID#) GROUP HEALTH PLAN (ID#) FECA BLK LUNG (ID#) OTHER (ID#)

1a. INSURED'S I.D. NUMBER (For Program in Item 1)

2. PATIENT'S NAME (Last Name, First Name, Middle Initial)

3. PATIENT'S BIRTH DATE MM DD YY SEX M F

4. INSURED'S NAME (Last Name, First Name, Middle Initial)

5. PATIENT'S ADDRESS (No., Street)

6. PATIENT RELATIONSHIP TO INSURED Self Spouse Child Other

7. INSURED'S ADDRESS (No., Street)

CITY STATE

8. RESERVED FOR NUCC USE

CITY STATE

ZIP CODE TELEPHONE (Include Area Code) ( )

ZIP CODE TELEPHONE (Include Area Code) ( )

9. OTHER INSURED'S NAME (Last Name, First Name, Middle Initial)

10. IS PATIENT'S CONDITION RELATED TO:

11. INSURED'S POLICY GROUP OR FECA NUMBER

a. OTHER INSURED'S POLICY OR GROUP NUMBER

a. EMPLOYMENT? (Current or Previous) YES NO

a. INSURED'S DATE OF BIRTH MM DD YY SEX M F

b. RESERVED FOR NUCC USE

b. AUTO ACCIDENT? PLACE (State) YES NO

b. OTHER CLAIM ID (Designated by NUCC)

c. RESERVED FOR NUCC USE

c. OTHER ACCIDENT? YES NO

c. INSURANCE PLAN NAME OR PROGRAM NAME

d. INSURANCE PLAN NAME OR PROGRAM NAME

10d. CLAIM CODES (Designated by NUCC)

d. IS THERE ANOTHER HEALTH BENEFIT PLAN? YES NO *If yes*, complete items 9, 9a, and 9d.

READ BACK OF FORM BEFORE COMPLETING & SIGNING THIS FORM.

12. PATIENT'S OR AUTHORIZED PERSON'S SIGNATURE I authorize the release of any medical or other information necessary to process this claim. I also request payment of government benefits either to myself or to the party who accepts assignment below.

SIGNED DATE

13. INSURED'S OR AUTHORIZED PERSON'S SIGNATURE I authorize payment of medical benefits to the undersigned physician or supplier for services described below.

SIGNED

PATIENT AND INSURED INFORMATION

14. DATE OF CURRENT ILLNESS, INJURY, or PREGNANCY (LMP) MM DD YY QUAL.

15. OTHER DATE QUAL. MM DD YY

16. DATES PATIENT UNABLE TO WORK IN CURRENT OCCUPATION FROM MM DD YY TO MM DD YY

17. NAME OF REFERRING PROVIDER OR OTHER SOURCE 17a. 17b. NPI

18. HOSPITALIZATION DATES RELATED TO CURRENT SERVICES FROM MM DD YY TO MM DD YY

19. ADDITIONAL CLAIM INFORMATION (Designated by NUCC)

20. OUTSIDE LAB? YES NO $ CHARGES

21. DIAGNOSIS OR NATURE OF ILLNESS OR INJURY Relate A-L to service line below (24E) ICD Ind.

A. B. C. D. E. F. G. H. I. J. K. L.

22. RESUBMISSION CODE ORIGINAL REF. NO.

23. PRIOR AUTHORIZATION NUMBER

24. A. DATE(S) OF SERVICE From MM DD YY To MM DD YY | B. PLACE OF SERVICE | C. EMG | D. PROCEDURES, SERVICES, OR SUPPLIES (Explain Unusual Circumstances) CPT/HCPCS MODIFIER | E. DIAGNOSIS POINTER | F. $ CHARGES | G. DAYS OR UNITS | H. EPSDT Family Plan | I. ID. QUAL. | J. RENDERING PROVIDER ID. #

1 NPI
2 NPI
3 NPI
4 NPI
5 NPI
6 NPI

PHYSICIAN OR SUPPLIER INFORMATION

25. FEDERAL TAX I.D. NUMBER SSN EIN

26. PATIENT'S ACCOUNT NO.

27. ACCEPT ASSIGNMENT? (For govt. claims, see back) YES NO

28. TOTAL CHARGE $

29. AMOUNT PAID $

30. Rsvd for NUCC Use

31. SIGNATURE OF PHYSICIAN OR SUPPLIER INCLUDING DEGREES OR CREDENTIALS (I certify that the statements on the reverse apply to this bill and are made a part thereof.)

SIGNED DATE

32. SERVICE FACILITY LOCATION INFORMATION a. b.

33. BILLING PROVIDER INFO & PH # ( ) a. b.

NUCC Instruction Manual available at: www.nucc.org PLEASE PRINT OR TYPE APPROVED OMB-0938-1197 FORM 1500 (02-12)

SAMPLE

Fig. 11.1 CMS Form 1500

payer (see section 11.3. 2. regarding HCPCS/CPT Coding). Software tools or the medical billing procedures and workflow help physicians and their staff to manage these diverse guidelines. Larger practices and hospital-employed physicians rely on dedicated RCM teams to use the PM software and billing procedures to send the claim right the first time. If the claim is not properly adjudicated by the payer, they employ extensive denial management and appeal processes.

When everything on the claim form is correct, the practice may expect payment between 14 and 30 days from the date of submission.[1] When there is a problem with the patient's eligibility, the provider's credentialing with the insurance company, the submission of incomplete claim data, incorrect claim data (e.g., CPT billing code or ICD-10-CM diagnosis code) or another problem, payment may take months to complete. Resolving the problems takes direct, clear communication with the insurance company. Merely resubmitting the service without understanding and correcting the root problem for the delay in payment or a denial of payment is unproductive and may result in a loss of revenue. The next section elaborates on the medical billing workflow and the entire RCM processes.

The Medical Billing and Revenue Cycle Management Processes

Using whatever proprietary software, all medical providers need to perform the same industry-wide standard billing workflow that encompasses the RCM processes as shown in Fig. 11.2.

Patient Scheduling, Registration, and Insurance Verification

Years ago, the billing process began with the patient's visit. Today, the practice's billing workflow should kick-in several steps prior to when the patient walks in the door for their visit. Incorporating these steps help ensure that the claim is sent to the right insurance company. These steps are:

1. Patient scheduling and registration
2. Insurance verification

When a patient calls to schedules an appointment, a best practice is to verify the patient's demographic information including their insurance status. It is also advisable to ask about the reason for the visit. This is important as some insurance coverage guidelines have specific time guidelines between when the patient may be seen for the same diagnoses or the same treatment protocol. Some payers have frequency or utilization guidelines only covering a certain number of treatments in a year. Asking pertinent questions in the scheduling and registration process also allows the

[1] Medicare requires clean claims to be paid following a fourteen-day period. A clean claim is one that is complete based on claims processing guidelines including patient's eligibility, provider credentialing, correct claim data and meets medical necessity. If the claim is denied due to insufficient information, it may be released back to the provider prior to the end of the fourteen-day hold period. Private payers may process the claim in as few as 5 days.

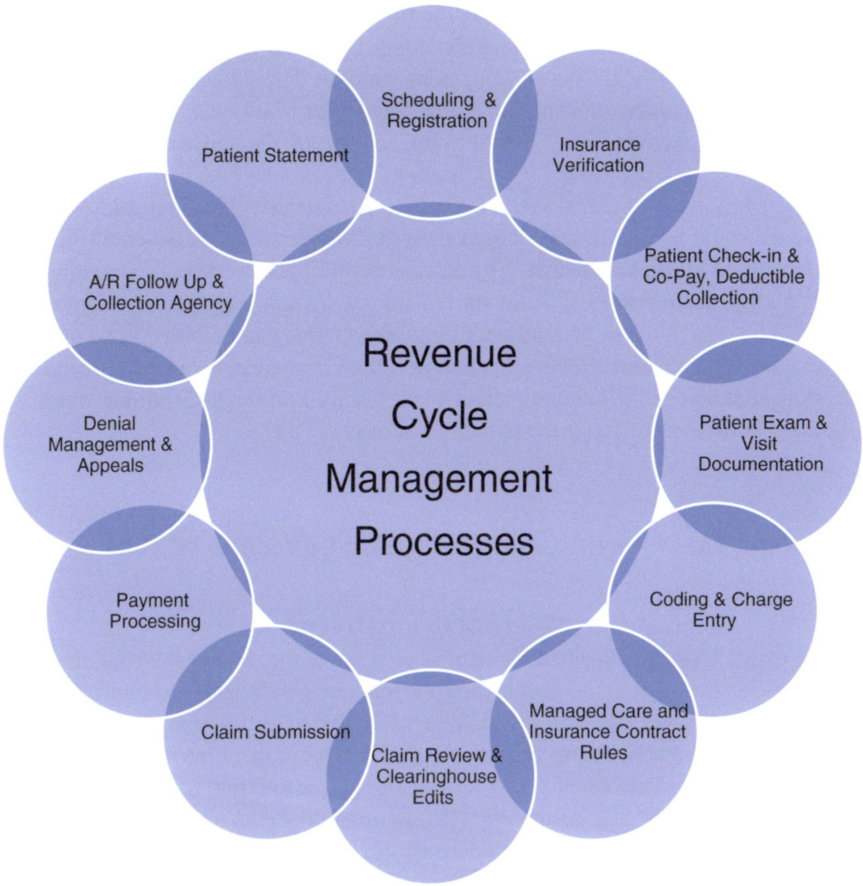

Fig. 11.2 The medical billing workflow and revenue cycle management system

scheduler to allocate the right amount of time for the visit based on the practice's standards of care for different types of presenting problems or procedures.

While pre-visit insurance verification of eligibility and coverage is available by calling the payer, using the payer's website, or by sending an electronic transaction, some practices still ignore these options and enter whatever information the patient presents without any verification. If the practice is using a billing service, they copy the patient's insurance card and send the copy to the billing company along with the patient's demographic information. Depending on the practice's contract with the billing company, when they receive the practice's information, they may electronically send an EDI 270 and receive an EDI 271 transaction to verify the patient's eligibility and coverage status. By using the EDI 270/271 transaction, a practice or a billing company bills the right insurance company the first time resulting in fewer eligibility denials, thus reducing related costs and protecting revenue by sending the claim to the right place the first time. Due to payers' short, prompt billing guidelines (e.g., claims must be filed within a specific timeframe as short as 30 days or as long as 365 days from the date of service), sending the claim to the wrong insurer can result in missing the right payer's payment window. The 270/271 transactions are industry-wide accepted standards that any practice or billing company should routinely use as claim eligibility denials rank as one of the top denial reasons for all payers.

Gary Marlow, Vice President of Finance for Beverly Hospital and Addison Gilbert Hospital, spoke in 2015 about their RCM operations as a seven-time 100 Top Hospital. Marlow said that "[F]rom a revenue cycle perspective, getting the most accurate information up front starts with patient scheduling and patient registration. That provides the groundwork by which claims can be billed and collected in the most efficient and effective manner possible. If you can do a clean claim from the start, that helps alleviate the patient's and family's anxiety. I would attribute all of this to helping to improve the patient's experience" [9].

Check-In, Co-payments, and Deductible Collection at Time of Service

A best practice process is when the patient presents at the time of the visit, the front desk checks the patient in, reconfirms the patient's demographic and insurance information, and collects any deductible or co-payment amount. By telling the patient during the scheduling process that a deductible or co-payment is due, the patient is not surprised when asked for the amount at the time of the service. This process is important due to the growth of high-end deductible insurance plans. According to a Kaiser Family Foundation report, an increasing proportion of insured working enrollees are paying more out-of-pocket for healthcare. For example, in the 10 years from 2006 to 2016, deductibles increased from $303 on average to over $1200 [10].

Patient Exam and Physician Documentation

The physician documents the visit information in the patient's EMR summarizing the diagnosis, treatment, and any other pertinent information. The EMR can be a benefit or a determent to the practice depending on the software they have and the workflow procedures. Some EMRs allow for a great deal of customization and the development of well-designed templates to aid the physician in documenting the service appropriately without excessive clicks or output that is not relevant to the patient's condition or treatment, etc. Others are "out-of-the box" and may not work well with the practice's existing workflow. Physicians who actively take part in the EMR decision and implementation process and have access to personalized training are more satisfied with their EMR software than those that do not [11].

As previously discussed, the EMR may automatically transfer billing information such as the patient's diagnosis and CPT procedure code directly to the PM system. In integrated systems where the documentation, coding, and billing links are properly working, the practice may save valuable time and reduced labor costs. However, the practice must verify the claims accuracy through the pre- and post-submission process and perform a periodic audit to ensure that the software is generating the proper ICD-10-CM and HCPCS/CPT codes. Often practices find that a certified coder accuracy is better than the software. Yet, as the software improves, so will the accuracy.

Coding and Charge Entry

The Medicare Claims Processing Manual states that proper coding is necessary on Medicare claims because codes are generally used in determining coverage and payment amounts. Proper coding includes the actual use of codes to define procedures, units of service, and application of modifiers. The CMS, as well as many third-party payers, have adopted the HCPCS/CPT coding system for use by physicians and others to describe services rendered [12].

The relationship between the HCPCS/CPT and ICD-10-CM codes is important to meet the insurer's medical necessity requirements for the procedure or service. The HCPCS/CPT code stands for the procedure or service that was provided at the patient's encounter. The ICD-10-CM code supports why the procedure or service is medically necessary for the patient. Most EMR/PM systems load these files either in their entirety or partially based on the physician's specialty. Since both sets of codes change each year (HCPCS/CPT are effective from January 1 each year and ICD-10-CM are effective from October 1 each year), the practice needs to either have a support agreement with the software vendor or have an internal information technology group to keep the files up-to-date.

ICD-10-CM Coding

As mentioned in section 11.3.3, the EMR system may push an ICD-10-CM code to the PM system. When the practice has this configuration, the physician or a staff member is still responsible for finding the right ICD-10-CM code in the EMR system. Most EMR systems have a physician "pick list" which keeps a brief list of the most often used ICD-10-CM codes. A problem with a pick list is when the primary ICD-10-CM file is updated, the physician may have to reset the pick list or risk billing outdated codes.

Selecting the right ICD-10-CM code is based on understanding the ICD-10-CM-CM Official Guidelines for Coding and Reporting [13]. Updated each year, effective with the ICD-10-CM October 1 update, few physicians are aware or understand the guidelines and their impact on their revenue. Physicians should take the time to review section IV. Diagnostic Coding and Reporting Guidelines for Outpatient Services are in use by hospitals/providers in coding and reporting hospital-based outpatient services and physician office visits [13]. Several key guidelines from section IV are as follows:

- IV. D. Codes that describe symptoms and signs: Codes that describe symptoms and signs, as opposed to diagnoses, are acceptable for reporting purposes when a diagnosis has not been established (confirmed) by the provider. Chap. 18 of ICD-10-CM-CM, Symptoms, Signs, and Abnormal Clinical and Laboratory Findings Not Elsewhere Classified (codes R00-R99) contain many, but not all codes for, symptoms.
- IV.F. Level of Detail in Coding 1. ICD-10-CM-CM codes with 3, 4, 5, 6, or 7 characters: ICD-10-CM-CM is composed of codes with 3, 4, 5, 6, or 7 characters. Codes with three characters are included in ICD-10-CM-CM as the heading of a category of codes that may be further subdivided by the use of fourth, fifth, sixth, or seventh characters to provide greater specificity.
- IV.G. ICD-10-CM-CM code for the diagnosis, condition, problem, or other reason for encounter/visit: List first the ICD-10-CM-CM code for the diagnosis, condition, problem, or other reason for encounter/visit shown in the medical record to be chiefly responsible for the services provided. List additional codes that describe any co-existing conditions. In some cases, the first-listed diagnosis may be a symptom when a diagnosis has not been established (confirmed) by the physician.
- IV.H. Uncertain diagnosis: Do not code diagnoses documented as "probable," "suspected," "questionable," "rule out," or "working diagnosis" or other similar terms indicating uncertainty. Rather, code the condition(s) to the highest degree of certainty for that encounter/visit, such as symptoms, signs, abnormal test results, or other reason for the visit. Please note: This differs from the coding practices used by short-term, acute care, long-term care, and psychiatric hospitals.
- IV. J. Code all documented conditions that co-exist: Code all documented conditions that co-exist at the time of the encounter/visit and require or affect patient care, treatment or management. Do not code conditions that were previously treated and no longer exist. However, history codes (categories Z80-Z87) may be used as secondary codes if the historical condition or family history has an impact on current care or influences treatment [13].

The EMR also uses the ICD-10-CM code for the patient's problem list. According to a 2011 AHIMA report on Problem List Guidance in the EMR, a "well-designed problem lists provide important information for patient care and support meaningful use requirements and health information exchange. There are many approaches to a well-designed problem list. The key is to define clear policies and procedures that support the organization's objectives in using the information contained in a problem list" [14]. Although the AHIMA paper is from 2011, it remains a good reference on how to functionally design the electronic record to auto-record problem list data, to maintain the accuracy of the data, and to implement problem list standards within the system.

HCPCS/CPT Coding

HCPCS means HCFA Common Procedure Coding System. HCFA stands for the Health Care Finance Administration now known as CMS. Developed in 1983, the HCPCS coding system allows providers and medical suppliers to report professional services, procedures, and supplies to meet the operational needs of the Medicare and Medicaid programs. There are two levels of HCPCS codes:

- Level I – CPT-4 (Current Procedural Terminology, 4th Edition © AMA)
- Level II – HCPCS/National codes [15]

The AMA develops and maintains the CPT-4 coding system. First developed in 1966, it is updated annually by the AMA, effective from January 1 of each year. CPT codes are a list of descriptive terms, guidelines, and identifying codes for reporting medical services and procedures. The purpose of CPT is to provide a uniform language that describes medical, surgical, and diagnostic services. There are more than 7000 service codes, plus descriptors, and modifiers, in the Level I or CPT section of HCPCS. CPT code descriptions include coding conventions, modifier instructions, coding guidelines, and other logic. There are six major sections within CPT-4:

1. Evaluation and Management (E/M) (99201-99499)
2. Anesthesiology (00100-01999)
3. Surgery (10040-69990)
4. Radiology (70010-79999)
5. Pathology and Laboratory (80048-89399)
6. Medicine (90281-99199 and 99500-99999)

Within each section, there are subsections according to body areas, service, or procedure description. Also included in the CPT-4 are various appendixes:

- Appendix A – Modifiers
- Appendix B – Summary of Additions, Deletions, and Revisions
- Appendix C – Clinical Examples
- Appendix D – Summary of CPT Add-On Codes
- Appendix E – Summary of CPT Codes Exempt from Modifier – 51
- Appendix F – Summary of CPT Codes Exempt from Modifier – 63
- Appendix G – Summary of CPT Codes That Include Moderate (Conscious) Sedation
- Appendix H – Alphabetical Clinical Topics Listing
- Appendix I – Genetic Testing Code Modifiers
- Appendix J – Electrodiagnostic Medicine Listing of Sensory, Motor, and Mixed Nerves

- Appendix K – Product Pending FDA Approval
- Appendix L – Vascular Families
- Appendix M – Remembered CPT Codes-Citations Crosswalk
- Appendix N – Summary of Resequenced CPT Codes
- Appendix O – Multianalyte Assays with Algorithmic Analyses
- Appendix P – CPT Codes That May be Used for Synchronous Telemedicine Services [16]

Level II HCPCS codes are the second level of codes and were developed because CPT does not have all the codes needed to report medical services and supplies to Medicare, Medicaid, or other third-party payers. These codes always begin with a single letter (A through V) followed by 4 numeric digits. Grouped by the type of service or supply they are as follows:

- A codes – transportation services including ambulance (A0000-A0999), medical and surgical supplies (A4000-A8999), administrative, miscellaneous, and investigational (A9000-A9999)
- B codes – enteral and parenteral therapy
- C codes – Outpatient Prospective Payment System (OPPS) codes – supply items that insurers may pay in addition to normal supply charges; some codes required by Medicare
- D codes – dental procedures and supplies
- E codes – durable medical equipment (DME)
- G codes – temporary procedures and professional services; once CPT codes are assigned, the G codes are removed
- H codes – rehabilitative services
- J codes – drugs administered other than oral method (J0000-J8999), chemotherapy drugs (J9000-J9999)
- K codes – temporary codes for DME regional carriers
- L codes – orthotics procedures and devices (L0000-L4999), prosthetic procedures, and devices (L5000-L9999)
- M codes – medical services
- P codes – pathology and laboratory services
- Q codes – temporary procedures, services, and supplies – once CPT codes are assigned, the Q codes are removed
- R codes – diagnostic radiology services
- S codes – private payer codes
- V codes – vision services (V0000-V2999), hearing services (V5000-V5999) [15]

Modifiers identify circumstances that alter or enhance the description of a service or supply. Some modifiers have an impact on reimbursement by either reducing or increasing the allowed amount for the code that it is modifying. There are two levels of modifiers – one for each level of HCPCS codes.

1. Level I CPT modifiers are two numeric digits appended to the five-digit CPT code. The AMA also maintains and updates them annually. Some commonly used modifiers are as follows:

- 26 Professional Component: Represents the professional (provider) component of a global service or procedure and includes the provider's work, associated overhead and professional liability insurance costs [17].
- TC Technical Component: Modifier TC is used when only the technical component of a procedure is being billed when certain services combine both the professional and technical portions in one procedure code. Use modifier TC when the physician performs the test but does not do the interpretation [17].
- 25 Separate, Distinct E/M Service: Identifies a significant, separately identifiable evaluation and management (E/M) service. It should be used when the E/M service is above and beyond the usual pre- and postoperative work of a procedure with a global fee period performed on the same day as the E/M service. Different diagnoses are not required for reporting the E/M service on the same date as the procedure or other service with a global fee period. Modifier 25 is added to the E/M code on the claim. Both the medically necessary E/M service and the procedure must be appropriately and sufficiently documented by the physician or qualified NPP in the patient's medical record to support the need for Modifier 25 on the claim for these services, even though the documentation is not required to be submitted with the claim [18].
- 59 Distinct Procedural Service: Under certain circumstances, it may be necessary to indicate that a procedure or service was distinct or independent from other non-E/M services performed on the same day. Modifier 59 is used to identify procedures/services, other than E/M services, that are not normally reported together, but are appropriate under the circumstances. Documentation must support a different session, different procedure or surgery, different site or organ system, separate incision/excision, separate lesion, or separate injury (or area of injury in extensive injuries) not ordinarily encountered or performed on the same day by the same individual. However, when another already established modifier is appropriate, it should be used rather than modifier 59. Only if no more descriptive modifier is available, and the use of modifier 59 best explains the circumstances, should modifier 59 be used. Note: Modifier 59 should not be appended to an E/M service. To report a separate and distinct E/M service with a non-E/M service performed on the same date, see modifier 25 [19].

All four of these modifiers have a high level of incorrect use. The Health and Human Services (HHS) Office of Inspector General (OIG) has released several reports on the abuse of these modifiers. They include the following:

- OIG Evaluation & Inspection Report: Use of Modifier 25 (OEI-07-03-00470; 11/05)
- Use of Modifier 59 to Bypass Medicare's National Correct Coding Initiative Edits (OEI-03-02-00771; 11/05) [20]

Physicians and their billing staff should review the CPT and payers' guidelines on how to properly report all modifiers.

2. Level II HCPCS modifiers are two alphabetic digits (AA-VP) appended to the alpha/numeric HCPCS code. CMS and many payers recognize them. CMS maintains and updates the level II modifiers annually [15].

Physicians should familiarize themselves with the HCPCS and CPT codes and modifiers that they often use. According to the *Instructions for Use of the CPT Codebook*, physicians are instructed

> To select the name of the procedure or service that accurately identifies the service performed. Do not select a CPT code that merely approximates the service provided. If no such specific code exists, then report the service using the appropriate unlisted procedure or service code [21].

Unfortunately, selecting the right HCPCS code is not as easy as implied in the CPT Codebook instructions. This is due to payers, including CMS Medicare and Medicaid, having their own coding requirements. For example, designed as temporary codes, HCPCS G or Q codes are to only be used until a CPT is approved. However, many G and Q codes have been in place for years and sometimes have corresponding CPT codes. The G or Q code remain due to CMS's payment rules rather than correct coding rules. HCPCS S codes are also problematic. Private payers may want an S codes even when there is a CPT code available. Regrettably, sending a CPT code when Medicare wants a G code or vice versa may result in a rejection, thus requiring the procedure or service to be rebilled. When a payer suspects deliberate abuse of the coding system, they may levy potential fines, paybacks, or charges of fraudulent billing. In short, wrong codes impact reimbursement.

Capturing All Services and Physician Fees

Charge capture means billing for all services and procedures provided to a patient. Even in the age of automation, physicians still record some charge information on post-it notes, cafeteria napkins, hospital day lists, etc. Physicians sacrifice revenue every time they forget about one of these charges. Some EMR and PM software work with the physician's smartphone or a small tablet making it easier to capture all charges. Nevertheless, what the physician bills may under-represent the actual procedures or services given.

Automated checks and balances between the daily schedule and billed services help to find missing charges. The PM software should have reporting functionalities that will identify unbilled charges. The reports can help with determining if an encounter has been created but not billed, or an appointment is created but not kept (which could be an appointment not kept or an appointment that was kept but not registered properly).

Many times, the practice's schedule only reflects procedures or services performed in the office. Out-of-office services such as inpatient consults or nursing home visits may not be in the schedule. Unfortunately, without a means to reconcile out-of-the office procedures or services, the practice may be overlooking them.

Even when an EMR pushes billing information to the PM system, it is not failproof. The EMR can only push services that the physician documents. A charge capture audit will show services that are falling through scheduling, documentation template, or other workflow gaps. The audit can be as detailed or simple as desired. A charge capture audit may be for a whole week's worth of schedules or random days. The most important thing is to do them periodically.

Physicians may set their charges at whatever amount they wish. Most physicians keep one charge schedule to bill services to all payers and patients. If the patient does not have health insurance, that charge amount is billable to the patient. A 2014 working paper by Clemens and Gottlieb at the National Bureau of Economic Research found that private physician payment charges follow the Medicare fee schedule allowances at an average of 130 percent [22]. Some physicians may set their charges at 200 or 300 percent of the Medicare allowed amount.

Each payer has their own payment fee schedule, often called the allowed amount, which may change annually or at a different time. The practice's contract with the payer needs to outline the reimbursement provisions, including how the fees are set, their term, and update process. Many private payers use the Medicare physician fee schedule as a reference point for the establishment of their network physician payment schedule using relative value units (RVUs) and a conversion factor. Some payers' physician contracts will apply a specific multiplier to the Medicare physician fee schedule to determine their fees or allowed amounts. See section 11.3.5 for more on payer contracts.

A best practice is to store the physician's practice charges and the payer's fee schedules allowances for the client's top payers. Most store the allowed amounts in the PM system based on the Pareto principle, that is, entering enough payer allowances to cover at least 80 percent of all services. This allows the practice or billing company to detect underpayments. According to MGMA studies, insurers underpay practices in the United States by an average of 7–11 percent [23]. Unless the expected allowed amount is in the PM system, the practice or the billing company cannot routinely find the underpayments. If the practice or billing company does not verify the expected insurance payment to the actual payment, they are forfeiting the practice's revenue.

Managed Care and Insurance Contract Rules

It is not unusual for a practice to have many payer contracts. Often the practice agrees to participate without performing adequate due diligence on the contract terms and fees. Sometimes the contracts are outdated. Years ago, plan representatives were plentiful and available to remind practices that renewal dates were approaching. Now, most contracts are "evergreen," meaning they will automatically renew unless the practice or the health plan takes other action. As a result, a practice may find out sometime later that they had missed the window to negotiate terms or payment schedules. This lack of control over the contract process results in potentially unacceptable terms and a practice receiving lower than reasonable reimbursement rates.

The PM system should be able to house the allowed amounts for the practice's major procedures or services by the major payers. In addition to the allowed amounts, the practice's PM system may have an integrated payer contract module to help management to readily find unique contract coverage, eligibility, coding, reimbursement, and appeals processes. If the module is not part of the PM system, the practice should develop their own database of this critical information. They may use a simple excel spreadsheet or a contract management software tool that houses all critical data, including the renewal date on each payer's contract, to ensure that a contract does not fall through the gap. Scanning the complete contract into a secure database also helps when the physician or administrator wants to verify key contract language.

A few key questions to ask to evaluate contracts are:

- How old is the original contract?
- Is the contract held together via amendments?
- When was the last time rates changed?
- Is it based on Medicare and is that an old fixed year? (e.g., 2017 Medicare rates)
- Have providers materially changed?
- Have services or volumes materially changed?
- Is the structure of the contract outdated?

It is important that a practice be aware of what they are signing and how it may affect their practice now and in successive years. Often, in contract negotiations, the practice's focus is on the reimbursement rates; however, the other contract terms may be more important overall. If the practice does not feel confident to handle the negotiation process, they may want to seek legal counsel or other professional advice.

Claim Review and Clearinghouse Edits

All PM system and billing company's software should have routine claim entry edits. At claims entry, these consistency and validation alert edits identify basic problems. For example, entering a date of service prior to the current date would generate an alert. Entering an invalid HCPCS/CPT or entering inconsistent data based on the patient's sex or age likewise triggers an alert. More advanced information technology claim scrubbers go beyond basic validation edits to ensure that all the required claim data is present and meets national or payer-specific correct coding edits.

The correct coding imitative edits (CCI) are available electronically to all practices and billing companies. Applying the CCI edits prior to the claim submission allows the claim to be sent correctly rather than being rejected by the payer. By prescreening the claim data and verifying that the claim is complete and meets correct coding requirements, the practice or billing company is reducing downstream rejections for missing information, coding, or medical necessity issues. If the practice or billing company does not apply these readily available and industry-wide claim edits prior to claim submission, the practice's A/R and denial rates will increase. A best practice is to build custom edits based on payer's medical policies to verify that the diagnosis/treatment information meets insurer's coverage guidelines for the service. When the service may be questionable, certified coders may then check the patient's medical record to see if supplemental information is available to allow the claim to be adjudicated.

Most practices employ a clearinghouse to scrub claims prior to sending the claims to the payer. The clearinghouse will send on the claims that are "clean" and return questionable claims to the practice or billing company. The goal is to submit 95 percent of clean claims. Most practices average a 75–85 percent clean claim rate [24]. A pre-claims scrubbing should include edits for National Coding Determinations (NCD) Local Coding Determinations (LCD), CCI, CPT-4/HCPCS, and specific payer edits. Some common edits include:

- CPT codes incompatible with age or gender
- Add-on codes requiring primary CPT code
- Deleted CPT and diagnosis codes
- Diagnosis code specificity or medical necessity issues
- Improper unbundling
- Invalid modifiers

When Medicare or another payer receives the physician professional claims (1500/837P), they will apply all types of validation, consistency, and payment edits. As far as the payer is concerned, if your claim does not make it past the clearinghouse and payer edits to be accepted into the adjudication system, the claim does not exist. The practice needs to know their clean claim rate to make improvements in their workflow to improve future clean claim rates. The clearinghouse should provide two different clean claims rates:

1. First Pass Acceptance Rate (FPAR)

$$\frac{\text{Number of Claims Submitted} - \text{Number of Claims Rejected}}{\text{Number of Claims Submitted}}$$

Front-end rejections are often the most preventable issues impacting your clean claims rate. Best practice is for the PM system to alert billers when entering the claim data and eliminating most, if not all, of the FPAR errors. If the same type of FPAR errors are occurring, the PM system is not working to the best interest of the practice. Still, it is better to have the defective claim stopped by the clearinghouse so that it may be worked rather than send it to the payer and receive a rejection.

2. First Pass Resolution Rate (FPRR)

$$\frac{\text{Number of Claims Resolved Upon First Submission}}{\text{Number of Claims Submitted}}$$

"Resolved" claims are either paid or transferred to patient responsibility by the payer. Thus, it is best to do it right in the PM system to avoid a rejection or denial. See section 11.3.9 regarding denials.

Claim Submission

The next step in the medical billing process is to send the claim to the proper insurance company using an ANSI 837 file. For more information, see section "Claims Submission."

Payment Posting

All payers sent back electronic payment and rejection information in the form of an Explanation of Benefits (EOB) or Electronic Remittance Advice (ERA). The practice or billing company's PM software allows the EOB/ERA information to automatically post the payments to the patient's account and to automatically generate any secondary insurance or patient billing required due to deductible or co-insurance amounts being outstanding.

The ERA files provide itemized information for each claim and/or line to enable the physician's billing team to associate the adjudication decisions with the original claims/lines. The ERA gives the reason for each adjustment and the value of each adjustment. The adjustment reasons are standard codes. For any line or claim-level adjustment, the ERA uses three sets of codes:

1. Claim Adjustment Group Code (Group Code)
2. Claim Adjustment Reason Code (CARC)
3. Remittance Advice Remark Code (RARC)

Group Codes assign financial responsibility for the unpaid part of the claim balance (e.g., CO (Contractual Obligation) assigns responsibility to the provider and PR (Patient Responsibility) assigns responsibility to the patient). A patient statement goes out for Group Code PR (see section 11.3.11 on Patient Statements). CARCs provide an overall explanation for the financial adjustment and may offer more specific explanation using the RARC denial reason codes, so the biller can quickly access what is or is not being denied for what reason.

In short, the practice or billing company must review any rejection codes and messages, make corrections, and resubmit the claim. This process may occur several times, until the practice gets a payment or a final adjudication decision.

Denial Management and Appeals

Denial management is the process of working all rejections. Industry-wide data shows that the typical practice will have a denial rate of 5–10 percent.[2] A medical practice with a 15 percent denial rate stands to lose as much as $250,000 in annual revenue, that is, if they are among those who fail to correct and resubmit 65 percent of their claim denials, which is the national standard according to the MGMA [25].

The top denial reasons are:

- Eligibility
- Duplicate claims
- Missing information
- Payer-specific coding/billing rules

Industry data supports that 90 percent of all denials are preventable by using rule-based billing and available electronic technology [26]. Better PM systems and billing companies have a high-tech information platform to quickly find denials and denial trends. They use data analytics to find the root causes and set up automatic rules to prevent recurring issues with denials. Finally, they prioritize workflow to resolve denials promptly, so the claims do not age out of the payer's prompt payment or appeal guidelines. The results of a well-designed denial management system are reduced AR days, elimination of future denials by preventing the same type of error, an acceleration of cash flow, and an increase in net collections.

Detailed denial management reports include:

- Percentage of claims denied due to front-end edits vs. coding oversights
- Percentage of claims denied due to authorization/referral, insurance information, or eligibility oversights
- Percentage of claims denied overall, and by payer
- Percentage of no-response claims overall, and by payer
- Denials by category (over time, a larger percentage should be due to payer error and/or request for further information, not due to practice mistakes)

Practices need to be able to slice and dice denials by payer, by provider, by service or procedure, by expected allowance, by date of service (DOS), by payer payment timelines, etc., to find trends quickly and to work denials promptly and effectively.

Many practices only appeal a denied claim to the first level of appeal. Medicare claims and most third-party payers have more appeal levels that are available and should be used by the practice. The Medicare appeal process has five levels. Those levels are as follows:

[2] Quantify denial rates for smooth revenue cycle management, by Jacqueline DiChiara, RevCycleIntelligence.com, March 30, 2015. To calculate the practice's denial rate, add the total dollar amount of claims denied by payers within a given period and divide by the total dollar amount of claims submitted within the given period.

- First Level of Appeal: Redetermination by a Medicare Administrative Contractor (MAC)
- Second Level of Appeal: Reconsideration by a Qualified Independent Contractor (QIC)
- Third Level of Appeal: Decision by the Office of Medicare Hearings and Appeals (OMHA)
- Fourth Level of Appeal: Review by the Medicare Appeals Council
- Fifth Level of Appeal: Judicial Review in Federal District Court

For detailed information about each level of appeal, see https://www.cms.gov/Medicare/Appeals-and-Grievances/OrgMedFFSAppeals/index.html. For other payers, check their respective website or your payer contract.

A/R Follow-Up and Collections

Accounts receivable (A/R) follow-up is a process the practice or billing company should be continuously checking to determine why a claim is outstanding. A good indicator of how well a practice is doing with collecting on accounts is to calculate the number of days it takes to collect on the practice's A/R. Industry data shows that the national average for all practices is 45–50 days from the DOS to the payment date. The following figures are industry-wide benchmarks for medical billing and collections:

- 30 days or less is a high performing practice.
- 40–50 days is average performance.
- 60 days or more means the performance is below average [27].

As a best practice, when office visits generate most of the revenue, the metric should be less than 30 days. For surgical groups or other types of practices with a larger concentration of hospital-based services, the metric should be between 30 and 40 days. If a practice's metric is above 50 days, it is a sign that there are major billing and collection issues [28].

Once a claim is greater than 90 days old, its dollar value to collect rapidly decreases. Often, claims over 120 days are classified as uncollectable and transferred to an external collection agency that takes 35 to 50 percent of the recovered amount as their fee. Only 5 percent of patients with accounts over 90 days past due will ever pay voluntarily [29]. Better practices work diligently to meet industry-wide accepted AR standards as claims outstanding over 90 days are worth between 15 percent and 50 percent of their original worth to the practice [29].

The most unwanted scenario would be when the AR is 120 days old. This means that a mistake has been committed either by the billing company or by the insurance company. Practices with 10 percent or more of their claims aged over 120 days have significant billing problems [28].

The practice or billing company must run financial reports at least monthly to show the status of the practice's claims. Reviewing a daily dashboard of key performance indicators is a better practice. Standard A/R monthly reports slice and dice the data in different ways to help find patterns or trends that are the root cause of the outstanding A/R.

The Medical Group Management Association (MGMA) is a premier organization for physician benchmarking data and statistics. Figure 11.3 shows the following comparative benchmarks based on data from the 2017 MGMA DataDive Cost and Revenue survey for non-surgical practices:

- Mean percentage of AR in specified classifications (0–30 days, 31–60 days, 61–90 days, 91–120 days, over 120 days)
- Median days gross fee-for-service (FFS) charges in AR
- Median days adjusted FFS charges in AR [30]

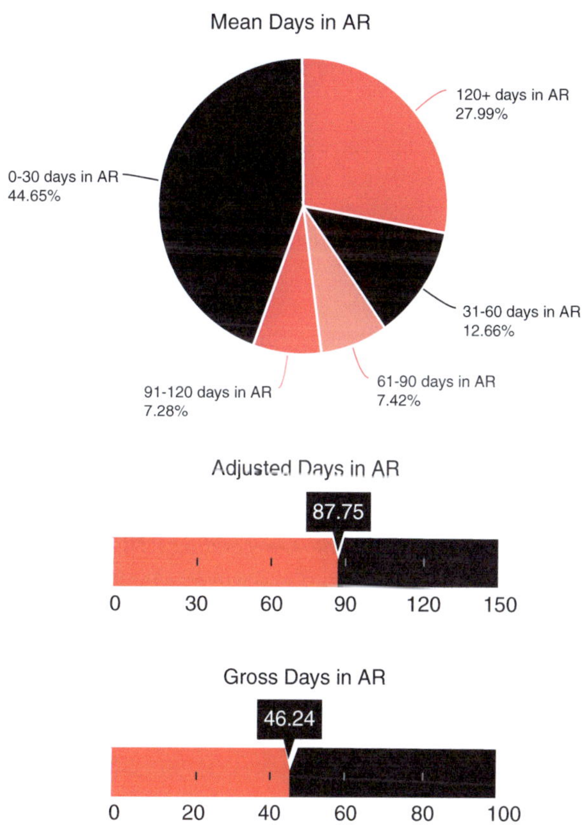

Fig. 11.3 Key AR Data (Source: 2017 MGMA DataDive Cost and Revenue, based on 2016 data. Used with permission from MGMA, 104 Inverness Terrace East, Englewood, Colorado 80112. 877.272.6462. www.mgma.com. Copyright 2017)

Patient Statements

Most PM software vendors will provide access to print-houses that have the ability to automatically print and mail patient statements to your patients. Keep in mind that much like printing claims in your office, the estimated cost of printing a patient statement includes the human labor cost of printing each statement, getting those statements off the printer, putting them in envelopes, licking the envelopes, and putting stamps on them. Then, there is also the cost of the raw materials such as toner cartridges, envelopes, stamps, and paper. According to Nicholas Fabrizio, principal with MGMA Health Care Consulting Group, "All told, it costs $11– $12 to send out a statement." According to Fabrizio, "If you don't collect a $25 copay, you've lost half your net revenue." Many PM vendors will pull the statement data for you and print/stuff/mail the statement for a fraction of the in-house cost [31]. Practices should consider using a reliable statement company as a means of better turnaround and cost savings.

RCM Optimization

Ineffective and inefficient revenue cycle operations can take its toll on the practice by increasing:

- Incidents of data entry errors, workflow delays, and billing mistakes
- Manual intervention and processing
- Call and work volumes and reduced productivity
- Reliance on third parties, e.g., collections and temporary staffing

Revenue cycle optimization principles focus on several key areas:

1. Quality and Key Performance Indicators (KPIs) – the principle that "You cannot manage what you do not measure" is a key focus. Practices should have automated and simple means of sorting, analyzing, and reporting on their data. Further, for metrics to be useful, they must be timely, transparent, and actionable. By actionable, someone or a team in the practice is performing a deep dive into the data to improve future KPIs. Here are four important metrics to monitor:

   (a) Days in Receivable Outstanding (DRO)

   DRO indicates the average amount of time required to collect a day's worth of gross charges from the financially responsible parties. To calculate DRO, total current receivables (net of credits) are divided by the average daily charge amount. The average daily charge amount equals the total gross charges for the past year divided by 365 days. Ideally, your DRO should be less than 35 days. Anything over 50 days is cause for serious concern.

   (b) Percentage of Receivables 60, 90, 120 Days

This metric assesses your practice's ability to collect on a timely basis and, perhaps, your ability to collect at all. To calculate the percentage of receivables over a certain day, total receivables that are over that bucket due (net of credits) are divided by your total receivables (net of credits).

(c) Net Collection Rate

Net collection rate shows how effective the practice is at collecting all allowable reimbursement based on contractual obligations. The rate is computed by dividing payments (net of credits) by charges (net of approved contractual adjustments) for a selected time period — say, 6 months — and then multiplying by 100.

(d) Denial Rate

The denial rate is the percentage of claims that are rejected by payers. The figure reflects the efficiency and accuracy of your claim submission processes and directly affects cash flow. Calculate this rate by dividing the dollar value of denied claims by the total amount of claims submitted for a specific period, such as 3 months.

2. Elimination of DOWNTIME – DOWNTIME is a lean tool acronym to help find unproductive tasks within an organization. Downtime stands for:

- *D*efects (e.g., poor documentation, weak processes, missing data)
- *O*verproduction (e.g., poor designed processes, long-time to do task)
- *W*aiting (e.g., unbalanced workloads, unplanned downtime, insufficient staffing)
- *N*ot utilizing talent (e.g., poor communication, lack of teamwork or training)
- *T*ransportation (e.g., poor office layout, misaligned process flow)
- *I*nventory excess (e.g., poor monitoring systems, management, and processes)
- *M*otion waste (e.g., poor workstation layout, shared computers, and equipment)
- *E*xcess processing (e.g., re-entering data and duplicated data, excessive meetings) [32]

A few simple tools can help the practice find recurring rejections and take steps to eliminate the most common rejections. Better PM systems have automated report systems, but a simple spreadsheet can provide valuable insight into trends and the most frequent rejections. By identifying reasons for rejections, the practice can focus on high priorities to end the most frequent or most costly rejections.

3. Maximize Workflow – Empowering staff to own the processes and workflow. Too often worthless tasks have been carried forward under the "that's the way we have always done it" philosophy. By looking at each step in the workflow and flowcharting employees movements in a "spaghetti chart," one can readily see the waste by the intersecting lines to accomplish a task. When the flowchart looks like a plate of spaghetti, it is time to reengineer the processes.

Outsourcing RCM

According to Black Book data, outsourcing RCM is a growing trend. According to Black Book surveys, more than half of healthcare organization CFOs (54 percent) believe that outsourcing RCM functions would improve efficiency and their organizations' financial health [33]. Outsourcing the billing or entire RCM function is becoming popular due to increased billing complexity, labor market restraints, sophisticated technology needs, and privacy and security compliance issues. While outsourcing can solve many issues, it raises new ones.

How do you know if the vendor is HIPAA compliant? Is there performance on par with the contractual provisions? Do they provide the level of expertise promised? The only way to know is to evaluate what the practice's needs are to outsource either certain functions (e.g., coding and denials) or the entire RCM process. Once the practice knows what they needs are, they should develop an RFP with a pre-agreed to evaluation system for determining the best vendor. The RFP needs to outline the staffing requirements credentials and experience for the job duties, address vendor staffing turnover, security, and, if the arrangement does not work out, the termination provisions. Price, while a consideration, should never be the sole determining factor. Some outsourcing vendors oversell their expertise and stability. The practice must go beyond what the vendor's sales representative said and find out what is in place. An on-site visit, including having the vendor run a "billing cycle test" with practice monitors following the test claims through the vendor's workflow, may be insightful. The key is to know what your requirements are and do in-depth due diligence of the vendors. Once a decision is made, make sure you, as the client, have an equal say in the contract terms and pricing. Involving your legal counsel and other professional advisors protects the practice.

Tips for Successful Claim Submission and Overall RCM

1. Submit insurance claims same day.
2. Reconcile appointments and claims daily, including out-of-office procedures and services.
3. Use real-time insurance eligibility verifications.
4. Understand payer contract provisions on timely billing, coverage, and reimbursement.
5. Work clearinghouse edits daily.
6. Rebill rejected electronic claims same day.
7. Post payments using automatic ERA.
8. Work AR and denials by slicing and dicing the data.
9. Submit appeals timely.
10. Submit patient statements automatically with a statements partner.

References

1. Accelerating number of physicians select outsourced RCM services to align clinical & financial outcomes, shows black book survey on value-based care prep, Sep 29, 2016, https://www.prnewswire.com/news-releases/accelerating-number-of-physicians-select-outsourced-rcm-services-to-align-clinical%2D%2Dfinancial-outcomes-shows-black-book-survey-on-value-based-care-prep-300336641.html.
2. https://www.cms.gov/Regulations-and-Guidance/Administrative-Simplification/Transactions/TransactionsOverview.html.
3. Health Insurance Portability and Accountability Act of 1996, Public Law 104-191, https://aspe.hhs.gov/report/health-insurance-portability-and-accountability-act-1996.
4. http://www.nucc.org/index.php. Who are we?
5. http://www.nucc.org/index.php/definitions-mainmenu-37.
6. 1500 health insurance claim form reference instruction manual for form version 02/12, see http://www.nucc.org/images/stories/PDF/1500_claim_form_instruction_manual_2012_02-v6.pdf.
7. https://www.cms.gov/Medicare/Coding/place-of-service-codes/Place_of_Service_Code_Set.html.
8. 42 U.S. Code § 1320d–2. Standards for information transactions and data elements.
9. DiChiara J, How Beverly Hospital succeeds at revenue cycle management. https://revcycleintelligence.com/news/how-beverly-hospital-succeeds-at-revenue-cycle-management.
10. Claxton G, Levitt L, Rae M, Sawyer B, Increases in cost-sharing payments continue to outpace wage growth, Kaiser Family Foundation, June 15, 2018. https://www.healthsystemtracker.org/brief/increases-in-cost-sharing-payments-have-far-outpaced-wage-growth/#item-start.
11. Castellucci M. One-on-one EHR training improves physician satisfaction, saves time, Modern Healthcare September 15, 2018.
12. Medicare Claims Processing Manual, Chapter 12, 30 - Correct coding policy (Rev. 1, 10–01-03) https://www.cms.gov/Regulations-and-Guidance/Guidance/Manuals/Downloads/clm104c12.pdf.
13. ICD-10-CM-CM official guidelines for coding and reporting FY 2019 (October 1, 2018 - September 30, 2019), found at https://www.cdc.gov/nchs/icd/data/10cmguidelines-FY2019-final.pdf.
14. AHIMA Work Group. Problem list guidance in the EHR. J AHIMA. 2011;82(9):52–8. Found at: http://library.ahima.org/doc?oid=104997#.XNc1uHdFx00.
15. Healthcare Common Procedure Coding System (HCPCS) Level II coding procedures. https://www.cms.gov/Medicare/Coding/MedHCPCSGenInfo/Downloads/2018-11-30-HCPCS-Level2-Coding-Procedure.pdf.
16. CPT Professional 2019, Contents, p ix ff.
17. CPT Professional, 2019.
18. MLN Matters Number: MM5025 Related Change Request (CR) #: 5025 Related CR Release Date: May 19, 2006. https://www.cms.gov/Outreach-and-Education/Medicare-Learning-Network-MLN/MLNMattersArticles/downloads/MM5025.pdf.
19. CMS https://www.cms.gov/Medicare/Coding/NationalCorrectCodInitEd/Downloads/modifier59.pdf.
20. https://oig.hhs.gov/reports-and-publications/.
21. CPT Professional 2019, Instructions for use of the CPT codebook, p xii.
22. Clemens J, Gottlieb J. Bargaining in the shadow of a giant: Medicare's influence on private payment systems. NBER Working Paper No. 19503. Cambridge, MA: National Bureau of Economic Research; October 2013. http://www.nber.org/papers/w19503.pdf. Cited July 26, 2015.
23. https://www.mgma.com/data.
24. How to improve your clean claims, Mary Guarino, October 19, 2010. https://www.himss.org/news/how-improve-your-clean-claims-rates.

25. https://www.mgma.com/resources/revenue-cycle/you-might-be-losing-thousands-of-dollars-per-month.
26. An ounce of prevention pays off: 90percent of denials are preventable, December 11, 2014 by Morgan Haines https://www.advisory.com/research/financial-leadership-council/at-the-margins/2014/12/denials-management.
27. https://www.foxgrp.com/assessment-benchmarks/medical-accounts-receivable-monitoring-and-measuring-performance/.
28. Medical billing best practices: metrics and key performance indicators. http://pacificmds.com/medical-billing/medical-billing-best-practices-metrics-and-key-performance-indicators/.
29. The ROI of IT: best billing practices, Rosemarie Nelson MGMA Healthcare Consulting Group.
30. MGMA data represents over 3,800 practices in healthcare. To learn more about data from this dataset see: https://www.mgma.com/data/calculators/accounts-receivable-dashboard.
31. How much does it really cost to send out a statement? Part Deux, September 18, 2010 by Brandon. https://pediatricinc.wordpress.com/2010/09/18/how-much-does-it-really-cost-to-send-out-a-statement-part-deux/.
32. https://asq.org/quality-resources/lean. What is DOWNTIME?
33. https://blackbookmarketresearch.com/finance-revenue-cycle-management.

Chapter 12
Regulations and Regulatory Compliance: False Claims Act, Kickback and Stark Laws, and HIPAA

James E. Szalados

Introduction

A free market is an economic system that is governed by the principles of supply and demand economics and in which there is minimal extrinsic or government control. Free markets are characterized by private, uncoerced, voluntary transactions based on each party's relative perceived value of the available goods or services. Supply and demand create competition, through which suppliers compete for market share. However, just as laws define norms of conduct for transactions between individuals, some degree of government regulation is arguably essential to set parameters and norms of conduct in the public marketplace. Therefore, freed markets are almost universally constrained by at least some regulation. Arguably, regulation is most important in those markets where there is an imbalance of power between the supplier and the consumer. Therefore, through regulations, the government ostensibly steps in to protect the interests of the public [1]. Subsequently, healthcare is among the most regulated of industries in the USA.

Legislation refers to law created by a legislative body. "Acts" and "statutes" represent legislation, that is, laws which are created by the federal legislation in Congress. Congress is legally empowered to delegate legislative power to administrative agencies by enacting statutes referred to as "enabling acts." Administrative agencies are created to oversee a specific area of commercial endeavor, such as energy, intelligence, food and drugs, or healthcare. Since agencies are specialized, they have or will develop specialized expertise and experience in their area. Enabling

J. E. Szalados (✉)
Director, Surgical and Neurocritical Care Units, Rochester Regional Health System at Rochester General Hospital, Rochester, NY, USA

The Szalados Law Firm, Hilton, NY, USA
e-mail: james.szalados@rochesterregional.org; jszalados@aol.com

J. E. Szalados (ed.), *The Medical-Legal Aspects of Acute Care Medicine*,
https://doi.org/10.1007/978-3-030-68570-6_12

acts define the scope of an agency's power, objectives, and the areas or subjects over which any particular agency will have jurisdiction.

Regulatory agencies or regulatory boards act through regulations. A "regulation" is defined as a "rule or order issued by an executive authority or regulatory agency of a government and having the force of law" [2]. "Regulations, also called administrative laws or rules, are the primary mechanism whereby governments implement laws; they are specific standards or instructions concerning what individuals, businesses, and other organizations can or cannot do" [3]. Once created, agencies are also further empowered to interpret and enforce such intent of the enabling act which created that particular agency in accordance with the principles of administrative law and procedures. Thus, administrative agencies have two major functions: (1) rulemaking and (2) enforcement (adjudication).

The law relating to regulations is known as administrative law; it is the branch of law which relates to the creation, operation, and oversight of administrative agencies and the procedures whereby rules and regulations are created and enforced. The Administrative Procedure Act (APA) [4] enacted in 1946 is the US federal statute which governs the way in which federal administrative agencies may create and enforce their regulations.[1] A "rule" is defined to mean "the whole or a part of an agency statement of general or particular applicability and future effect designed to implement, interpret, or prescribe law or policy or describing the organization, procedure, or practice requirements of an agency" [5]. Federal statutes also define rulemaking requirements, hearing procedures, adjudicatory standards, and enforcement procedures by which agencies must operate [5]. The Federal Register defines the process by which agencies may enact rules and regulations [6]. When enacting rules and regulations, agencies follow a prescribed stepwise process: (1) agencies survey their area of legal responsibility, decide on whether a new or revised rule or regulation is needed to achieve a policy or regulatory outcome, and then consult with stakeholders, including interested parties and the public; (2) publish a proposal to create a rule in the Federal Register ("notice of proposed rulemaking"); (3) accompanied by a defined 30-day period during which there is public notice and an opportunity for comments, the "notice-and-comment period" now managed electronically via "regulations.gov"; (4) publish a draft rule in the Federal Register, accompanied by a statement of purpose and a cost-benefit analysis 30 days before it is scheduled to take effect; and (5) if there are no objections, the rule then takes effect with the force of law. Thus, laws created by agencies are published in the (1) Federal Register, where federal rules and regulations are first individually published, and (2) the Code of Federal Regulations (CFR), which is a complete codification of those rules and regulations.

[1] For example, the Massachusetts Administrative Procedure Act ("Act") is found in Part I, Title III, Chapter 30A of the Annotated Laws of Massachusetts; the New York State Administrative Procedures Act ('SAPA) can be found at NY CLS St Admin P Act § 102 *et seq*. (2019); and the Connecticut Uniform Administrative Procedure Act (UAPA) (Chapter 54, CGS § 4-166 et seq.). Moreover, cities may also have Administrative Procedure Acts.

When controversies arise between private parties and administrative agencies, these cases are heard and adjudicated by administrative law; therefore, the judiciary provides a mechanism for review of agency decisions. However, courts are generally deferential to government agencies, since agencies and their staff are presumed to have specialized knowledge regarding the often highly technical issues that they oversee [7]. First, always, is the question whether the Congress has directly spoken to the precise question at issue. If the intent of the Congress is clear, that is the end of the matter, for the court, as well as the agency, must give effect to the unambiguously expressed intent of the Congress. If, however, the court determines the Congress has not directly addressed the precise question at issue, the court does not simply impose its own construction on the statute. Rather, if the statute is silent or ambiguous with respect to the specific issue, the question for the court is whether the agency's answer is based on a permissible construction of the statute [8]. Through precedent, the US Supreme Court established three different standards for judicial review of agency decisions: (1) under *Chevron v. NRDC* [9], courts deferred to agency interpretations of enabling statutes unless they are unreasonable on their face; (2) under *Auer v. Robbins* [10], courts deferred to the agency's interpretations of its own ambiguous regulations; and (3) under *Skidmore v. Swift* [11], courts did not give a binding deference to the agency's interpretations but gave a varying amount of deference in accordance with the agency's expertise in a specific matter. The classic legal test for determining whether to grant deference to a government agency's interpretation of a statute that it administers lies with *Chevron*, which gave rise to the two-part framework for reviewing court's analysis of agency decision-making.

Agencies operate simultaneously at two levels: federal and state. In a fashion similar to the creation and empowerment of agencies by the US Congress, state legislatures, under the authority of the state governor, may authorize the creation of state administrative agencies. States also have parallel administrative procedure acts, which govern their rule-making and rule enforcement practices; these acts are generally based upon the 1961 Model State Administrative Procedure Act and as subsequently amended [12]. In the Tenth Amendment to the US Constitution, powers not delegated to the federal government are reserved to the states or to the people [13]. States may regulate areas of law not addressed by the federal government or may regulate in parallel to the federal government with some important exceptions. The doctrine of preemption within the Supremacy Clause [14] of the US Constitution (Article VI) establishes that state laws are subordinate to, or preempted by, federal laws and regulations. Where a state law is in explicit conflict with federal law, the federal law generally prevails [15]. Preemption itself is classified as either express preemption or implied preemption: express preemption occurs when the Congress explicitly directs state law will be preempted; implied preemption occurs where a federal statute is either silent or ambiguous; courts may infer a congressional intent to preempt under the subcategories of conflict preemption or field preemption. Conflict preemption occurs when a state law conflicts with federal law in such a way that it is impossible to comply with both or when the state law impedes the purposes and objectives of the Congress [16]. Field preemption occurs when the Congress has chosen to dominate the regulation of a substantive field, thereby precluding state regulation within that field [17]. Floor preemption occurs where a higher (i.e., federal) level of government passes a law that establishes a minimum set of requirements but yet expressly allows lower (i.e., state) levels of government to enact legislation which impose more rigorous requirements. Thus, in a sense, in many cases, federal law "provides a floor, not a ceiling" for state regulation [18].

The US DHHS administers healthcare in the USA. DHHS is led by the Secretary of Health and Human Services, who is appointed by the President of the USA. The principal administrative bodies within DHHS include the Centers for Medicare & Medicaid Services (CMS, formerly Health Care Financing Administration [HCFA]), the Centers for Disease Control and Prevention (CDC), the National Institutes of Health (NIH), the Food and Drug Administration (FDA), the Health Resources and Services Administration (HRSA), and the Agency for Healthcare Research and Quality (AHRQ).

DHHS also administers the Office of the Inspector General (OIG), an investigative arm of DHHS established in 1976 that is primarily charged with enforcing compliance with Medicare and Medicaid rules and regulations and investigations regarding violations of the Federal False Claims Act, the Stark Law, and the Anti-Kickback Statute (AKS). Thus, the federal agencies charged with enforcing healthcare compliance mandates include the Department of Justice (DOJ), the Federal Bureau of Investigation (FBI), the Department of Health & Human Services Office of Inspector General (OIG), and the Centers for Medicare & Medicaid Services (CMS). Where claims are submitted through the mail, the US Postal Inspection Service may also have jurisdiction under the mail fraud statutes.

To more effectively investigate and prosecute Medicare and Medicaid fraud and abuse, including Anti-Kickback violations, the HHS, together with the DOJ, created the Health Care Fraud Prevention and Enforcement Action Team (HEAT) in 2009. Of note, the "Office of Inspector General"s (OIG) is a generic term and refers to the investigative and enforcement arm of any federal or state agency. Thus, at present, there are 73 federal Offices of Inspector General [19]. The Health Care Fraud and Abuse Control Program now utilizes artificial intelligence-enhanced data analysis capabilities including predictive analytics, trend evaluation, and modeling approaches to recognize and target patterns of abuse and fraud and calculate ratios of individual provider's charges, number of encounters, and outcomes, in comparison to regional and national averages.

The federal fraud and abuse laws that apply to healthcare providers are (1) the False Claims Act, (2) the Anti-Kickback Statute, (3) the Physician Self-Referral Law (Stark Law), (4) the Civil Monetary Penalties Law, and (5) the exclusion authorities.

Medicare Fraud and Abuse in General

Medicare "fraud" is broadly defined to include violations of the FFCA (knowingly submitting false or fraudulent claims for payment to a federal program), the AKS (knowingly soliciting, receiving, offering, or paying remuneration induce or reward referrals for goods or services reimbursed by a federal program), and the Stark Law (the making of prohibited referrals for certain designated health services). Medicare fraud exposes providers and entities to criminal, civil, and administrative liability punishable by imprisonment, fines, and penalties. The potential liability to providers, physicians, medical groups, and healthcare institutions under the FFCA cannot be understated.

Whereas fraud as it pertains to healthcare is fairly well-defined, the exact definition of "abuse" has been more nebulous; however, it can nonetheless expose providers and entities to equally severe criminal and civil liability. Medicare "abuse" generally refers to clinical or administrative practices which may directly or indirectly result in unnecessary costs to the Medicare program. Examples of abuse may range from incorrect coding mistakes to inefficiencies such as the ordering of excessive diagnostic testing or performance of unnecessary procedures. Similarly, "waste," which also represents fraud and abuse, is broadly defined to include actions which incur unnecessary costs as a result of deficient management, practices, or controls.

There are a number of practical implications to providers and practices where Medicare fraud and abuse is alleged: (1) although discussions of fraud and abuse generally relate to Medicare, the discussion applies equally to all federally funded payment programs, as well as state Medicaid programs which receive federal funds; (2) private insurers are increasingly monitoring clinical and billing practices and may cooperate and share data with government agencies to minimize fraud in both the private and government sectors; (3) providers must be aware that prosecutions by either federal or state governments, under the respective federal or state statutes respectively, are typically neither defended or indemnified by medical liability ("medical malpractice") insurance policies and the costs associated with the defense and retribution of such claims can be extremely expensive; (4) under the Exclusion Statute, exclusion is essentially equivalent to loss of the ability to practice medicine unless one's practice is limited to an office-based self-pay population; and (5) a criminal conviction can effectively translate into a loss of state medical licensure. In addition to the civil FCA, there also is a criminal FCA which imposes criminal penalties that may include imprisonment and criminal fines [20] (Table 12.1).The Civil Monetary Penalties Law (CMPL) states, in relevant part, that [21], "any person (including an organization, agency, or other entity ... that—

(1) knowingly presents or causes to be presented to an officer, employee, or agent of the United States, or of any department or agency thereof, or of any State agency ... a claim that the Secretary determines—

(A) is for a medical or other item or service that the person knows or should know was not provided as claimed, including any person who engages in a pattern or practice of presenting or causing to be presented a claim for an item or service that is based on a code

Table 12.1 Potential liability under the FFCA

Civil monetary penalties
Restitution
Exclusion from all federally funded payer programs
Criminal penalties under the FFCA (18 U.S.C. § 287)
Loss of licensure and DEA certification
Medical staff exclusion (loss of privileges)

that the person knows or should know will result in a greater payment to the person than the code the person knows or should know is applicable to the item or service actually provided,

(B) is for a medical or other item or service and the person knows or should know the claim is false or fraudulent,

…

(D) is for a medical or other item or service furnished during a period in which the person was excluded from the Federal health care program

(E) is for a pattern of medical or other items or services that a person knows or should know are not medically necessary;

…

(3) knowingly gives or causes to be given to any person, with respect to coverage under subchapter XVIII of inpatient hospital services subject to the provisions of section 1395ww of this title, information that he knows or should know is false or misleading, and that could reasonably be expected to influence the decision when to discharge such person or another individual from the hospital;

…

(5) offers to or transfers remuneration to any individual eligible for benefits…

…

(10) knows of an overpayment … and does not report and return the overpayment in accordance with such section; …

shall be subject, in addition to any other penalties that may be prescribed by law, to a civil money penalty…".

Therefore, the CMPL authorizes the Secretary of DHHS to impose civil money penalties on providers. Providers are individually liable; however, a healthcare institution can be also held liable based on its own negligence and the negligence of its provider employees. Proof of intent to defraud is not required. The burden of evidence must be sufficient only to prove liability by a "preponderance of the evidence.".

Under the Exclusion Statute [22], the OIG is statutorily required to exclude providers who convicted of criminal violation of the FFA, including violations of the Anti-Kickback Statute (AKS; see below) from participation in any and all federally funded healthcare programs including Medicare, Medicaid, Children's Health Insurance Program (CHIP), TRICARE, and the Veterans Health Administration. Providers, practices, clinics, and institutions who employ others are individually responsible to ensure that they do not employ or contract with excluded individuals or entities; to facilitate compliance with this mandate, the OIG maintains an online database [23] which must be accessed and verified prior to an offer of employment [24]. The exclusion statute applies even if the employed or contracting provider is not submitting claims on his or her own but rather is doing so through a non-excluded practice or provider.

Institutional Compliance and Compliance Plans

Compliance refers to the processes whereby individuals or organizations meet legal and regulatory standards. Compliance with rules and regulations has become increasingly complex so as to have evolved into a legal or quasi-legal administrative subspecialty. Every sector of the economy must comply with specific laws and regulations relating to their business practices; banking, aviation, finance, pharmaceuticals, and insurance are examples of sectors other than healthcare which face significant regulatory oversight and therefore regulatory compliance requirements. Healthcare is one of the most regulated sectors of the US economy. The laws and regulations affecting healthcare compliance are not static and are constantly evolving or changing. New regulations, updated regulations, special fraud alerts, advisory bulletins, and advisory opinions constantly modify the legal landscape of compliance and therefore require continuous monitoring and modification of business practices in order to remain in compliance with relevant laws and regulations (Table 12.2).

In healthcare, compliance is required of all healthcare providers, whether they practice as a solo practitioner, member of a group practice, or an affiliate or employee of a healthcare institution or system. Liability for breaches can be individual or shared, depending upon the specific circumstances. Compliance requirements in healthcare arise from federal, state, and local regulations and involve often overlapping jurisdictional requirements. Thus, although federal law applies in all states, state healthcare laws and regulations may differ but must nonetheless be understood and adhered to. Examples of federal regulations applicable to healthcare involve Fraud and Abuse; HIPAA and HiTECH as they pertain, for example, to health information privacy and security; the Drug Enforcement Administration (DEA), the Food and Drug Administration (FDA); the Equal Employment Opportunity Commission (EEOC); the Occupational Health and Safety Administration (OSHA); and the Emergency Medical Treatment and Active Labor Act (EMTALA) among others. Compliance is not voluntary and is not informal; regulatory compliance is achieved through a detailed corporate compliance plan which is administered through a corporate compliance office which reports to the governing body of the organization. Larger practices and institutions will have a Corporate Compliance Office, led by a chief compliance officer or compliance committee, which reports directly to the CEO or Board of Directors.

Not only must providers have a compliance plan, but that plan must be demonstrably effective with the authority to enforce regulatory standards within the

Table 12.2 Examples of healthcare compliance risk areas

Failure to implement an effective compliance plan
Coding, billing, and claims submission compliance and audits
Documentation requirements for procedures and evaluation/management (E/M)
Consent
Medical necessity
Medical direction or medical supervision
Diagnosis and procedural coding
Medical records of confidentiality, release, and retention
Safe medication practices
Patient rights
Conflicts of interest
Self-referral, professional courtesy, research, Sunshine Act, etc.
Employee safety, rights, and obligations
Family and Medical Leave Act, non-discrimination, code of conduct, etc.
Environmental safety
Hazardous waste disposal, personal protective equipment, etc.

practice or institution. An effective compliance plan outlines processes, policies, and procedures to monitor the regulatory environment, educate and train staff, and subsequently monitor and guide behavior. Ideally, practices and healthcare organizations develop a culture of accountability whereby adherence to standards, laws, and regulations becomes ingrained.

In the event of a government investigation at a practice or institution which may potentially be in breach of regulatory requirements, one of the first things investigators will request will be the organizational compliance plan; failure to produce such a plan will be an immediate red flag. The Office of Inspector General (OIG) of the Department of Health and Human Services (HHS) has published comprehensive guidance for healthcare providers and organizations regarding essential elements of an effective healthcare compliance program [25].

Compliance with laws relating to "fraud and abuse" requires that all providers develop and maintain an effective compliance plan. Federal law requires that all healthcare practices develop and implement a compliance plan [26]. Section 6401 of the Patient Protection and Affordable Care Act (ACA) of 2010 mandated compliance plans by stipulating that individuals and practices and institutions formalize compliance programs as a condition of enrollment in federally funded programs [27]. In general, an effective compliance program is regarded as the first line of a practice's defense against fraud and abuse. Failure to implement an effective voluntary compliance program can result in (1) increased risk of false claims violations, (2) increased risk for kickbacks and/or self-referral violations, (3) presumptive evidence against a practice of "deliberate ignorance," and (4) increased risk that the OIG will mandate a corporate integrity agreement.

The broad purposes of a compliance plan are (1) as an aspirational statement of an intent to conduct ethical business practices, (2) to meet the legal obligations imposed by federal requirements, (3) to provide a venue for education and training, (4) to promote early detection of potential compliance problems, (5) to develop a response plan in the event of an audit, and (6) to present on demand to government investigators in the event of an audit or investigation.

The OIG has outlined seven fundamental elements of an effective compliance program [28]:

1. The implementation of written policies, procedures, and standards of conduct
2. The designation of a compliance officer and compliance committee
3. Conduct of effective training and education
4. The development of effective lines of communication
5. Conduct of internal monitoring and auditing
6. The enforcement of standards through well-publicized disciplinary guidelines
7. The prompt response to detected offenses with corrective action [29]

In addition to a compliance plan against fraud and abuse, practices must have in place an effective HIPAA Compliance Plan. HIPAA required the Secretary of the US DHHS to develop regulations protecting the privacy and security of certain health information, requirements which resulted in definitions inherent in the HIPAA Privacy Rule and the HIPAA Security Rule. The Privacy Rule, or Standards for Privacy of Individually Identifiable Health Information, established national standards for the protection of health information, whereas the Security Standards for the Protection of Electronic Protected Health Information (Security Rule) established a national set of security standards for protecting health information that is held or transferred in electronic form. The Security Rule operationalized the Privacy Rule by defining technical and nontechnical safeguards which "covered entities" must put in place. Specifically, covered entities must (1) ensure the confidentiality, integrity, and availability of all e-PHI they create, receive, maintain, or transmit; (2) identify and protect against reasonably anticipated threats to the security or integrity of the information; (3) protect against reasonably anticipated, impermissible uses or disclosures; and (4) ensure compliance by their workforce members (Table 12.3).

Table 12.3 OIG guidance regarding elements of an effective healthcare compliance plan [88]

Standards, policies, and procedures
Compliance program administration
Screening and evaluation of employees, physicians, vendors, and other agents
Communication, education, and training on compliance issues
Monitoring, auditing, and internal reporting systems
Discipline for non-compliance
Investigations and remedial measures

Documentation

The medical record is a living document which serves medical, legal, and business purposes; it is an ongoing record and is necessary to record and communicate the circumstances of patient care to other providers, to substantiate and justify the medical reasoning involved in reaching a diagnosis and determining a plan of care, and to support a claim for reimbursement [30]. Documentation in the medical record is a professional work product which reflects the care that a provider rendered. Accurate clinical documentation is the basis for accurate coding. Claims and requests for reimbursement from federal healthcare programs must be supported by complete and accurate documentation that reflects the reasonable and necessary services ordered and performed by a participating licensed medical professional [31]. Clinical documentation must be accurate and timely and reflect the necessity for and the particulars of specific services provided to a patient.

Clinical documentation improvement (CDI) programs [32] aim to facilitate the accurate representation of a patient's clinical status, thereby optimizing medical documentation to maximize claims of reimbursement and revenue [33]. CMS has published guidelines regarding documentation in Evaluation and Management (E/M) Services in which it states that payers of healthcare may require that the medical records contain reasonable documentation to reflect that services provided and claimed are consistent with the patient's insurance coverage and which validate:

- The site of service.
- The medical necessity and appropriateness of the diagnostic and/or therapeutic services provided.
- That the services provided are reported accurately.
- The medical record should be complete and legible.

Furthermore, CMS has published expectations regarding general principles for good medical record documentation which would apply to medical records in both medical and surgical services provided in all clinical settings. The documentation of each patient encounter should include:

- Reason for the encounter and relevant history, physical examination findings, and prior diagnostic test results.
- Assessment, clinical impression, or diagnosis.
- Medical plan of care.
- Date and legible identity of the observer.
- If the rationale for ordering diagnostic and other ancillary services is not documented, it should be easily inferred.
- Past and present diagnoses should be accessible to the treating and/or consulting physician.
- Appropriate health risk factors should be identified.
- The patient's progress, response to and changes in treatment, and revision of diagnosis should be documented.

- The diagnosis and treatment codes reported on the health insurance claim form or billing statement should be supported by documentation in the medical record.
- To maintain an acuurate business and medical record; to document services rendered during an encounter (or as soon as practicable after the encounter) [34].

The regulatory oversight of clinical documentation remains contentious and controversial. Opponents of clinical documentation guidelines argue that "E&M guidelines were devised, at least initially, with the support of organized medicine as a response to the lack of an externally verifiable measure of cognitive services. These guidelines largely redefined cognitive services as not what was done but rather what was documented. They created a complex system of rules that further specified format requirements. This has created an imbalance of values, with coding and compliance trumping clarity and conciseness, as well as a harshly negative "gotcha" mentality that saps the professionalism out of physicians" [35].

Physician profiling based upon electronic review of electronically searchable medical records within the Medicare claims database is emerging as an adjunct potential method of cost and fraud control based on utilization and documentation practices. The Medicare claims database can potentially be analyzed to develop profiles of individual providers based on their practice patterns, quality of care, and billing patterns [36]. Electronic data interchange (EDI) refers to the transfer of electronic data which is then stored in searchable electronic databases. The Physician and Other Supplier Public Use File (Physician and Other Supplier PUF) provides information on services and procedures provided to Medicare beneficiaries by physicians and other healthcare professionals. The Physician and Other Supplier PUF contains information on utilization, payment, and submitted charges organized by the National Provider Identifier (NPI), Healthcare Common Procedure Coding System (HCPCS) code, and place of service. This PUF is based on information from CMS administrative claims data for Medicare beneficiaries enrolled in the fee-for-service program [37]. Moreover, the Medicare-Medicaid Data Integration (MMDI) program is another initiative jointly sponsored by the Centers for Medicare & Medicaid Services (CMS) Medicare-Medicaid Coordination Office (MMCO) and the Center for Medicaid and CHIP Services (CMCS) which further combines federal and state-level claims and quality data regarding providers. The volume of electronically searchable data regarding any provider is enormous but allows for temporal, site of service, and peer-to-peer comparisons which may help identify outliers in performance or billing patterns. The 2013 Office of Inspector General ("OIG") Work Plan first listed EHR abuse as an area of focus for OIG investigation in potential false claims actions and has since evolved to consider issues such as the use of "cut and paste," "carry forward," and cloning in consideration of large volumes of pasted information to facilitate an artificial inflation of billing codes, use of speech recognition and dictation, the accuracy and quality of the record, and patient safety.

The Federal False Claims Act

The Federal False Claims Act (FFCA), sometimes referred to as either the "Lincoln Law" or informally as the "'Fraud and Abuse Law," was enacted by the Congress on March 2, 1863, during the Civil War in response to profiteering merchants who fraudulently supplied the Union Army. The legal impact of the FFCA was minimal until, in 1986, amendments reduced procedural barriers to enforcement, funded the enforcement program, and increased financial incentives and protections for whistleblowers. Arguably, since the 1986 FFCA amendments were enacted, the FFCA has become the government's most effective program against fraud and abuse, as well as waste, in all spending sectors including energy, defense, housing, and healthcare. In fiscal year 2018, the Justice Department (DOJ) recovered more than $2.8 billion through the prosecution of False Claims Act Cases; in the ninth consecutive year, the Department's civil healthcare fraud settlements and judgments have exceeded $2 billion. The enormous significance to the FFCA to healthcare providers is in the government's real-time review of the coding and billing practices of both individual providers and institutions and the associated penalties.

From an ethical and moral standpoint, the societal benefit of combating "fraud, waste, and abuse" as a means of maintaining access restoring money to the federal treasury is important to maintain law and order and quality of services and to ensure the common good. Theft or waste of precious resources compromises access to such resources and violates principles of distributive justice. However, the equally important imperative is the progressive depletion of the Medicare Trust Fund and the enactment of initiatives designed to recoup expenditures. From the point of view of justice, instances of fraud must be actionable with punishment tailored to the wrongdoing; however, errors of compliance are often insidious and unintentional. At present, there is no bright line test to separate instances of intentional fraud and unintentional errors under the False Claims Act. The return on investment (ROI) to the federal government from enforcement actions predicated in the FFCA is presently approximately $7.20 for every dollar expended [38]. Although, the overwhelming majority of FCA recoveries come from the healthcare industry, from the perspective of total dollars recovered, the largest settlements and enforcement actions tend to be in the realm of the pharmaceutical and medical device manufacturer market. Healthcare fraud accounted for $2.5 billion in fraud recoveries for the federal government in 2018, and the sum total of recoveries, since 1986, total more than $59 billion.The FFCA [39] is defined, in relevant past, in 31 US Code § 3729 *et seq.* as follows:

(a) Liability for Certain Acts.—
(1) In general.—Subject to paragraph (2), any person who—
(A) knowingly presents, or causes to be presented, a false or fraudulent claim for payment or approval;
(B) knowingly makes, uses, or causes to be made or used, a false record or statement material to a false or fraudulent claim;
(C) conspires to commit a violation of subparagraph (A), (B), (D), (E), (F), or (G);
...

(G) knowingly makes, uses, or causes to be made or used, a false record or statement material to an obligation to pay or transmit money or property to the Government, or knowingly conceals or knowingly and improperly avoids or decreases an obligation to pay or transmit money or property to the Government,

is liable to the United States Government for a civil penalty of not less than $5,000 and not more than $10,000, as adjusted by the Federal Civil Penalties Inflation Adjustment Act of 1990 (28 U.S.C. 2461 note; Public Law 104–410 [1]), plus 3 times the amount of damages which the Government sustains because of the act of that person.

…

(3) Costs of civil actions.—

A person violating this subsection shall also be liable to the US government for the costs of a civil action brought to recover any such penalty or damages.

In general terms, FFCA §§ (1)(A) and (B) establish liability for anyone who knowingly submits a false claim to the government or causes another to submit a false claim to the government or knowingly makes a false record or statement to get a false claim paid by the government. This means that any practitioner who knowingly falsifies documentation, coding, or billing, either personally or through a hospital or other contracted claims service, is liable under the FFCA. It is important to note that no specific intent to defraud is required to violate the civil FCA. Each and every provider is liable for the integrity of all claims for payment submitted under his or her National Provider Identification (NPI) number.

The terms "knowing" and "knowingly" are statutorily defined in § (b)(1)(A) to "mean that a person … (i) has actual knowledge of the information; (ii) acts in deliberate ignorance of the truth or falsity of the information; or, (iii) acts in reckless disregard of the truth or falsity of the information; and requires no proof of a specific intent to defraud." Thus, there is no intent requirement necessary to establish liability.

A submission of a claim for services purporting to be higher than those actually provided represents "upcoding," whereas submission of a claim for services purporting to be lower than those actually performed represents "downcoding"; both represent miscoding and are all illegal under the FFCA (Table 12.4).

Table 12.4 Examples of False Claims Act violations [89]

Submission of claims for services not rendered
Submission of claim without documentation of services rendered
Submission of claims for services for patients who never actually existed ("ghost patients")
Submission of claims for services billed at a higher level than actually performed ("upcoding")
Submission of claims for individual services when some or all of those services should be bundled, or are in a global fee, per Medicare regulations ("unbundling")
Billing services performed by an improperly supervised or unqualified employee
Billing services performed by an employee excluded from participation in the federal healthcare programs
Billing for medically unnecessary services
Anti-kickback statute violations
Stark Law violations
Part of a previously submitted claim
Billing services of such low quality are virtually worthless

"Unbundling" refers to the practice of charging separately for procedures which were otherwise combined into a single charge and is similarly illegal. For example, where an E/M code includes a variety of components, procedures, or interpretations, the billing for each of these components separately constitutes unbundling.

Medical necessity is increasingly important as a potential liability under abuse. Government scrutiny of medical necessity has become an increasingly important basis for FCA prosecutions. In 2015, Cincinnati-based West Chester Hospital/UC Health paid a $4.1 million settlement after the OIG alleged violations of the FCA through claims submitted to federal healthcare programs for medically unnecessary spine surgeries performed between 2009 and 2013. The US Attorney Carter M. Stewart of the Southern District of Ohio noted that "[f]ederal health care programs cover only those procedures that are medically necessary" [40].

Institutional liability under the FFCA can occur in any one of a multitude of ways. Each hospital that participates in Medicare Part A must submit an annual cost report to HHS which details, for example, the diagnosis-related groups (DRGs) of the procedures performed at the hospital, the costs of pharmaceuticals, devices and equipment, charges, revenue, profits, and charge-to-cost ratios. Integral to this annual cost report is a mandatory certification by which the hospital certifies its compliance with applicable laws and regulations, including the FFCA, which specifically incudes the statement: "if services identified in this report were provided or procured through the payment directly or indirectly of a kickback or were otherwise illegal, criminal, civil and administrative action, fines and/or imprisonment may result" [41]. Areas of potential risk to hospitals include (1) knowing inflation of costs itemized in cost reports; (2) knowing mischaracterization of non-reimbursable costs as reimbursable; (3) knowing manipulation of patient admissions or treatments to inflate costs of; (4) providing kickbacks to physicians or providers in order to influence referral patterns; (5) false certification of services characterized as medically necessary were actually performed and were performed in accordance with all applicable rules and regulations, when they were not; (6) red-lining or discrimination practices which discourage treatment of patients deemed to be higher risk for length of stay and cost; (7) Medicare Part D Fraud; and (8) Research Grant Fraud.

Section (1)(G), referred to as the "reverse false claims section," establishes liability for failure to avoid payments or repayments. The reverse false claims section applies to situations where a practice received overpayments and failed to return them. The FFCA obligates providers to report and return any overpayment within 60 days after "the date on which the overpayment is identified." Legally, there is an overpayment "if the person fails to exercise reasonable diligence and the person in fact received an overpayment."

In the case of *United States v. Continuum Health Partners, Inc., et al.* [42], a health system (Continuum Health Partners, Inc., comprised of Beth Israel Medical Center and St. Luke's-Roosevelt Hospital in New York) received notice of approximately 900 potential overpayments and hired a consultant to investigate; the system subsequently fired the consultant who then became a whistleblower. The system settled the case for $2.95 million, which included the overpayment of approximately $850,000 and $2.1 million in civil penalties. Compliance plans should include policies and procedures regarding the collection and review of potential overpayments and the subsequent processes for their resolution.

The CMP has recently been adjusted upward in accordance with inflation. The CMPL has been amended to make future upward adjustments in the CMP mandatory. If found liable under the FFCA, that party is liable to a civil monetary penalty (CMP) of a base penalty, which has continued to be adjusted upward, presently $10,781 to $22,927 (for year 2019), plus three times the amount of the false claim, for each false claim.

Thus, assume *arguendo* the following scenario: a provider submits ten claims to Medicare, each upcoded to a higher level of service than is justified, each consisting of a $100 overbilling the government. The government investigates and alleges fraud. The potential liability to the practitioner for the ten claims is calculated as follows: 10 claims × $100 = 1000 × treble damages = $3000, plus the base penalty resulting in a potential penalty range of $13,781 to $25, 927. In addition, the government will also most likely review all claims from that provider for up to the prior 6 years and assess additional fines, in accordance with the formula above, apply the Exclusion Statute and effectively terminate the provider's ability to practice, and potentially assess criminal charges with jail time. Although this example is probably an unrealistically harsh one, it does exemplify the risks inherent to practitioners through the FFCA.

In response to a successful prosecution arising from any of the civil false claims statutes, the OIG may negotiate a corporate integrity agreement (CIA) as part of the settlement. Through the CIA, providers or entities agree to perform specific obligations, and in exchange, OIG agrees not to seek their exclusion from participation in Medicare, Medicaid, or other Federal healthcare programs. A comprehensive CIA typically lasts 5 years and is characterized by close governmental oversight of a provider or practice [43].

The statute of limitations for either the government or a private party to bring action under the FFCA is the later of either (1) 6 years from the date of the FFCA violation or (2) 3 years after the government knows or should have known about the violation, but in no event greater than 10 years after the FFCA violation. The standard of proof in civil FFCA cases is the "preponderance of the evidence."

The FFCA as applied to healthcare became a widely publicized compliance imperative in 1993 when the Secretary of DHHS initiated a program, the Physicians at Teaching Hospitals ("PATH") program, to review Medicare Part B billings by teaching hospitals with the intent of recovering past overpayments for services rendered. Following a PATH audit of the billings submitted by the University of Pennsylvania Health System, a settlement of over $30 million was made to the government for Medicare claims submitted between 1989 and 1994. A challenge to the PATH program by the American Association of Medical Colleges was dismissed in federal court. The key findings in the University of Pennsylvania PATH audit were (1) a lack of documentation showing the physical presence of the teaching physician during a service performed by a resident and subsequently billed for payment under Medicare Part B and (2) "upcoding" or billing for a more complex level of care than that which was provided. According to the government, services performed by a resident may be billed to Medicare Part B by a teaching physician only if that physician was present during the performance of the service [44].

The PATH audit was a result of an investigation by the OIG to determine compliance with "teaching rules" at major US teaching hospitals. Compliance with CMS billing and coding requirements in the teaching hospital setting appears to require that the attending physician must be physically present and immediately available in order to submit a claim for reimbursement to CMS. For Medicare purposes, a teaching physician is defined to be a physician (other than another resident) who involves residents in the care of his or her patients. Supervision of interns and residents is reimbursed to hospitals under Medicare Part A through Graduate Medical Education (GME) payments. Medicare payments to hospitals and hospital-based providers for the costs of approved GME also include residents' salaries and benefits and other GME program costs which are intended in part to cover teaching physicians' salaries related to the time they spend teaching residents. Through GME funding, teaching physicians are paid for taking responsibility for the hospital's oversight physicians in training. Medicare also makes payments to teaching hospitals under the prospective payment system for the higher indirect operating costs hospitals incur by having GME programs and supports GME programs in teaching hospitals through claims submitted for the services of attending physicians who involve residents in the care of their patients under Medicare Part B [45]. Thus, a service provided by a resident alone cannot be billed to Medicare Part B since that represents a "double reimbursement" [46].

CMS generally defines the requirements of a teaching physician to include documentation that "[i]f a resident participates in a service furnished in a teaching setting, physician fee schedule payment is made only if a teaching physician is present during the key portion of any service or procedure for which payment is sought. In the case of surgical, high-risk, or other complex procedures, the teaching physician must be present during all critical portions of the procedure and immediately available to furnish services during the entire service or procedure…. In the case of evaluation and management services, the teaching physician must be present during the portion of the service that determines the level of service billed….[T]he medical records must document that the teaching physician was present at the time the service is furnished. The presence of the teaching physician during procedures may be demonstrated by the notes in the medical records made by a physician, resident, or nurse. In the case of evaluation and management procedures, the teaching physician must personally document his or her participation in the service in the medical records" [47].

Although compliance with CMS teaching rule requirements may be variably defined by individual Institutional Compliance Policies, the teaching rule has been most conservatively interpreted to require the teaching physician to be fully present, gowned and gloved if so required, at the bedside, although other interpretations exist. Residents who have been credentials as technically proficient to perform independently may, under some hospital rules, perform procedures in the absence of supervision; however, in these instances, the teaching requirement is not met, and claims may not be submitted for procedural reimbursement. Note that inadequate supervision may represent negligence as well as a false claim action. Also, time spent in the teaching of residence cannot be claimed toward CCM time unless the physician and resident are together both directly engaged in patient care.

The Deficit Reduction Act of 2005 ("DRA") Section 6032 *et seq* requires all entities which receive Medicaid payments of $5 million or more annually ("covered entities") to provide written education and policies to all their employees, contractors, and agents about the Federal False Claims Act [48]. Although the DRA requirement is a federal law, it also is a requirement that is extended onto individual states by virtue of their respective participation in the Medicaid program. Through the DRA, the Congress authorized the creation of a Medicaid Integrity Program with specific contractors to monitor fraud and abuse in various state Medicaid programs and provides states with a monetary incentive to develop and implement state-specific false claims which ideally would mirror the requirements of the FFCA. Thus, if there is a state-based false claims action against a provider under Medicaid, the state is entitled to receive 10% of the federal government's share of any recovery. Medicaid fraud is jointly prosecuted by state Medicaid Fraud Control Units (MFCUs) with federal oversight. Forty-nine states and the District of Columbia have based within each state's Attorney General's office. Similar to OIG investigations, MFCU investigations may involve simultaneous criminal charges and civil lawsuits, referred to as "parallel proceedings" and simultaneous state and federal proceedings.

Many states [49] have successfully enacted state False Claims Acts, enforced by the offices of the respective State Attorney General.[2] The OIG has articulated four guiding principles to be considered in determining whether a state FCA statute will qualify for bonus recovery:

> The law must establish liability to the state for false or fraudulent claims described in 31 U.S.C. § 3729 with respect to any expenditure described in section 1903(a) of the Act;
>
> The law must contain provisions that are at least as effective in rewarding and facilitating qui tam actions for false or fraudulent claims as those described in 31 U.S.C. §§ 3730-3732;
>
> The law must contain a requirement for filing an action under seal for 60 days with review by the state's Attorney General; and
>
> The law must contain a civil penalty that is not less than the amount of the civil penalty authorized under 31 U.S.C. § 3729 [51].

The FFCA allows private citizens ("whistleblowers") who have evidence of fraud against federal programs to bring actions premised on the FFCA on behalf of the US government; these are known as *qui tam* actions, and the person bringing the action is referred to as a *qui tam* "relator" [52] *Qui tam* is the abbreviation for the Latin phrase *qui tam pro domino rege quam pro se ipso in hac parte sequitur*, which

[2] For example, see [50].

roughly means "he who brings an action for the king as well as for himself." The *qui tam* complaint must be filed with the court and served on the US Attorney for the relevant judicial district as well as on the US Attorney General. If the government or another private party has already filed a *qui tam* lawsuit based on the same evidence, that relator's suit is barred. Once initiated, a *qui tam* action may not be discontinued without government consent. If the government chooses to intervene, it then assumes responsibility for prosecution. If the government prosecutes the *qui tam* action, the relator is entitled to receive between 15% and 25% of the amount recovered, whereas if the government declines to prosecute, but the realtor continues the lawsuit, his or her share of the recovery is increased to 25% to 30% plus legal fees and expenses. In fiscal year 2018, more than $2.1 billion of the total $2.8 billion in settlements and judgments recouped by the US government stemmed from lawsuits filed by *qui tam* relators.

The potential defendant who is to be named in *qui tam* FCA suits is not served with a complaint until the case is unsealed, which generally occurs after a period of preliminary investigation known as "discovery" conducted by the OIG/DOJ, at which time the OIG informs the court whether it intends to intervene and pursue the case or if it will step aside, leaving the whistleblower with the option to potentially litigate privately. The existence of a whistleblower complaint is intended to be a secret until a federal judge orders the case unsealed for litigation.

Whistleblower protections protect any person who is discharged, demoted, suspended, harassed, threatened, or otherwise discriminated against because he or she brought a qui tam suit against his or her employer and include (1) reinstatement with seniority, (2) double back pay, (3) interest on back pay, (4) compensation for any costs or special damages such as the costs of litigation and reasonable attorneys' fees, and (5) compensation for discriminatory treatment. Witnesses who provide testimony or assistance in an FFCA proceeding likewise are legally protected from retaliation.

It is important to note that the FFCA has since been strengthened by amendments under the Fraud Enforcement and Recovery Act of 2009 [53], the Patient Protection and Affordable Care Act of 2010 [54], and the Dodd-Frank Wall Street Reform and Consumer Protection Act of 2010 [55], which, individually and together, expanded liability under the FFCA and also expanded the rights and protections afforded to whistleblowers.

Although, the False Claims Act addresses claims for payment for services rendered to Medicare and Medicaid patients, there is a trend for private insurers to also monitor and enforce coding and billing. Furthermore, CMS contracts with local and national private insurers to process claims for Medicare and Medicaid patients on behalf of CMS; in such instances, non-compliant claims submitted to such private insurers are likely to be immediately reported for potential enforcement action [56].

Recent Examples of FEFCA Enforcement Actions

In 2014, the Department of Justice announced that Community Health Systems ("CHS") agreed to pay $98.15 million to settle nine whistleblower lawsuits alleging that the company violated the False Claims Act. The whistleblowers alleged that CHS knowingly billed Medicare, Medicaid, and TRICARE for medically unnecessary inpatient admissions at 119 hospitals that should have been billed as outpatient or observation services. According to the whistleblowers' complaints, CHS routinely admitted Medicare patients from their emergency rooms that did not require admission so that it could bill Medicare at the inpatient rates rather than the lower outpatient rates. To drive these valuable inpatient admissions, CHS allegedly established daily quotas for Medicare and Medicaid admissions through emergency rooms without regard to medical necessity or patient safety. CHS supposedly enforced those benchmarks by incentivizing and pressuring emergency department physicians and administrators to meet them. Physicians and administrators who failed to meet CHS's benchmarks were threatened with termination, and some were allegedly fired. Among a number of allegations, management at CHS's Heartland Regional Center in Marion, Illinois, purportedly held daily meetings in the emergency room where personnel were required to explain the release of any Medicare or Medicaid patient treated in the ER [57].

In 2016, the US DOJ reached a FCA settlement under the FFCA with an anesthesiology provider "Sweet Dreams Nurse Anesthesiology" ("Sweet Dreams") based in Alpharetta, Georgia, for $1.1 million dollars [58]. The suit was brought via a *qui tam* whistleblower action to resolve allegations that Sweet Dreams submitted false claims to both Medicare and Georgia's Medicaid programs. The whistleblower who filed suit claimed that Sweet Dreams used "underqualified" professionals to perform anesthesia, was "up-charging" the government, and used "kickbacks." The whistleblower alleged that Sweet Dreams provided anesthesiology services to medical facilities including podiatry centers by Certified Registered Nurse Anesthetists ("CRNAs"). In Georgia, CRNAs may not provide anesthesia services unless under the direction or responsibility of a duly licensed physician; CRNAs may not administer general anesthesia when under the direction of a podiatrist. In addition, Sweet Dreams provided free anesthesia drugs to ambulatory surgery centers (ASCs) in exchange for those ASCs granting Sweet Dreams an exclusive contract to provide anesthesia services at those ASCs; and an affiliate of Sweet Dreams agreed to fund the construction of an ASC in Marietta, Georgia, in exchange for contracts for selection by that facility of Sweet Dreams as the exclusive anesthesia provider at that facility and a number of other podiatry-based ASCs affiliated with the Marietta ASC. This investigation was the result of a qui tam action filed by Adam Nauss jointly under the whistleblower provisions of the False Claims Act and the False Medicaid Claims Act.

Recovery Audit Contractors

The Medicare Fee for Service (FFS) Recovery Audit Program was created through the Medicare Prescription Drug, Improvement and Modernization Act of 2003 (MMA) §306 and the Tax Relief and Healthcare Act of 2006, §302, with the mission of identifying and recovering improper Medicare payments through the review of claims on a post-payment basis (Table 12.5). The Recovery Audit Contractor (RAC) program is in demonstration project phase from March 2005 through March 2008 in order to determine if RAC auditors could effectively identify improper claims; however, the Social Security Act has authorized the program expansion nationwide by January 1, 2010, and has expanded the scope of RAC jurisdiction to include Medicare Parts A, B, C, and D. Under the Patient Protection and Affordable Care Act of 2009 (ACA), the RAC program was expanded to include claims submitted to Medicaid. The CMS report detailing the effectiveness of the demonstration project revealed that 96% of improper payments identified by RACs were overpayments, and 4% were underpayments; the majority (85%) of overpayments were to inpatient hospital providers, 6% to inpatient rehabilitation facilities, and 4% from outpatient hospital providers. The majority of recovered funds resulted from audits of hospitals and other Part A entities [59].

RACs utilize proprietary software programs to identify potential payment errors in areas such as duplicate payments, fiscal intermediaries' mistakes, medical necessity, and coding. RACs conduct reviews of claims through systematic and concurrent operating processes based upon algorithms within proprietary software programs; however, RACs will also conduct reviews of medical records. RAC teams include, by legislative mandate, nurses, therapists, certified coders, and a physician medical director. RACs will audit any and all providers or suppliers who submit claims to Medicare and include providers, hospitals, physician practices, suppliers of durable medical equipment (DME), and home health agencies. RACs are reimbursed by HHS through a contingency fee structure.

Table 12.5 Designated health services under the Stark/physician self-referral law

Clinical laboratory services
Physical therapy, occupational therapy, and outpatient speech-language pathology services
Radiology and imaging services
Radiation therapy services and supplies
DME and supplies
Parenteral and enteral nutrients, equipment, and supplies
Prosthetics, orthotics, and prosthetic devices and supplies
Home health services
Outpatient prescription drugs
Inpatient and outpatient hospital services

Anti-Kickback and Stark

Early Congressional legislative attempts to address Medicare fraud included the 1972 Medicare Penalties Provision, section 1877(b) of the Social Security Amendments [60], which established provisions making it illegal for any individual to use Medicare funds in a manner that constituted either a bribe, kickback, or rebate. Thus, false claims and fraud and abuse laws not only include the federal and state FCA statutes but are closely interrelated with the Anti-Kickback Statute (AKS) and the Physician Self-Referral Law (Stark). From the point of view of justice, kickbacks in the healthcare industry may lead to unfair economic competition, corruption of decision-making, and unjust distribution of healthcare resources.

The AKS [61] is a criminal statute which prohibits the "knowing and willful" payment of "remuneration" to induce or reward patient referrals or the generation of business involving any item or service payable by the federal healthcare programs. The AKS, in relevant part [62], states:

> (1) Whoever knowingly and willfully solicits or receives any remuneration (including any kickback, bribe, or rebate) directly or indirectly, overtly or covertly, in cash or in kind—
> (A) in return for referring an individual to a person for the furnishing or arranging for the furnishing of any item or service for which payment may be made in whole or in part under a Federal health care program, or
> (B) in return for purchasing, leasing, ordering, or arranging for or recommending purchasing, leasing, or ordering any good, facility, service, or item for which payment may be made in whole or in part under a Federal health care program,
> shall be guilty of a felony and upon conviction thereof, shall be fined not more than $25,000 or imprisoned for not more than five years, or both.
> (2) Whoever knowingly and willfully offers or pays any remuneration (including any kickback, bribe, or rebate) directly or indirectly, overtly or covertly, in cash or in kind to any person to induce such person—
> (A) to refer an individual to a person for the furnishing or arranging for the furnishing of any item or service for which payment may be made in whole or in part under a Federal health care program, or
> (B) to purchase, lease, order, or arrange for or recommend purchasing, leasing, or ordering any good, facility, service, or item for which payment may be made in whole or in part under a Federal health care program,
> shall be guilty of a felony and upon conviction thereof, shall be fined not more than $25,000 or imprisoned for not more than five years, or both.

"Remuneration" refers to *anything* of value including cash, allowances, benefits, gifts, incentives, or excessive compensation for medical directorships or consultancies. Criminal penalties and administrative sanctions for convictions for violation of the AKS include monetary fines, jail terms, and exclusion from participation in the federal healthcare programs; in addition, under the Civil Monetary Penalties Law (CMPL), physicians who pay or accept kickbacks also face penalties of up to $100,000 (for year 2018) per kickback plus 3x the dollar amount of the remuneration. The AKS statute and the penalties apply simultaneously to both those who offer or pay remuneration as kickbacks and simultaneously to the solicitors or recipients of kickbacks [63]. The Patient Protection and Affordable Care Act of 2010 expanded the liability of the False Claims Act to definitively include AKS claims as grounds for FFCA violation. Thus, violations of the AKS will generally also constitute violations of the FFCA, so that Anti-Kickback investigations can implicate liability under both statutes simultaneously. In fact, at this time, prosecutions under the AKS and Stark Law constitute the majority of all cases brought by the government under the FFCA.

Thus, by way of example, assume *arguendo* that a physician is engaged as a medical director at say perhaps an ambulatory surgery center, or a pharmaceutical manufacturing company, without clear administrative responsibilities but is retained primarily because of an ability to exert influence with respect to referrals of patients covered by a federal healthcare program either for services or goods, as applicable in the scenario above. Practicing physicians may be offered opportunities as consultants or promotional speakers for the drug or device manufacturers. The medical director salary is $50,000 per year. The government investigates and prosecutes for fraud and abuse. The potential CMP liability is calculated as $100,000 base penalty +3 times $50,000 = $250,000, plus potential exclusion and potential criminal prosecution and imprisonment.

Obviously, not all medical director arrangements are in violation of Stark; however, where the contracts are not supported by documentation of performance requirements, or where payments are in excess of fair market value (FMV) for similar services, there are in fact potential compliance concerns. In order to comply with Stark Law requirements, for example, and at a minimum, the agreement must be in writing and signed by both parties for a term of at least 1 year; the agreement must specify what services will be provided in exchange for compensation; the services must be commercially reasonable and cannot involve counseling or promotion of a business; compensation must meet requirements both for a demonstration of FMV; and compensation must not be based on volume or value of referrals known as "per click" remuneration.

A 2006 Office of the Inspector General (OIG) report entitled "An Open Letter to Health Care Providers" [64] provided insight regarding the OIG's position regarding provider/physician compliance with the Anti-Kickback Statute (AKS), the Physician Self-Referral Law (Stark Law), and the False Claims Act (FCA), wherein the OIG emphasized its plans for increased scrutiny and enforcement actions surrounding questionable medical directorships and other similar arrangements. Contracts with consultants and medical directors have become a central compliance issue to healthcare providers.

In 2009, the University of Medicine and Dentistry of New Jersey (UMDNJ) settled with the OIG for $8.3 million after the US District Court for New Jersey found clinical assistant professorship agreements with several community-based cardiologists in exchange for compensation as teaching stipends ranging from $50,000 to $180,000 per year. The USA argued that the primary purpose for the agreements was to induce referrals of patients from the private practice for services to the hospital, and there was little indication that the teaching services were in fact performed. The court thus determined that the arrangement violated Stark Law, because they failed the fair market value and also commercial reasonableness requirements [65].

Applicable tests for the appropriateness of physician consulting and directorship agreements will include (1) the demonstrable actual need for contracted for outside services; (2) the compensation structure in terms of fair market value, commercial reasonableness, and appropriateness; and (3) potential or actual referral opportunities.

There are complex exceptions to the AKS, known as "safe harbors" which are embedded within the statute; these may include (i) referrals made as part of an employment or professional services arrangement, (ii) payments made for the lease of equipment or of office space, and (iii) certain payments made for the purposes of health practitioner recruitment.

The 1985 landmark case of *United States v. Greber* [66] established that payments made to physicians to refer patients to use a specific laboratory's services, even if the remuneration was in part compensation for professional services, constituted a violation of the AKS and therefore deemed illegal. *Greber* made it clear that no payment of any kind, either gratuitous or compensatory in nature, can be used to secure a referral.

Routine waiver of copays could implicate the AKS, although individual determinations to waive copays based on an individual patient's ability to pay or non-enforcement of bad debt collections in cases of economic hardship are generally deemed allowable.

The Beneficiary Inducement Statute (42 USC § 1320a-7a(a)(5)) imposes CMP penalties on providers who offer remuneration to Medicare and Medicaid beneficiaries as inducements to utilize their practices or services.

The Physician Self-Referral Law, also known as the Stark Law [67], prohibits physicians from referring Medicare or Medicaid beneficiaries for "designated health services" to provider entities with which the physician or an immediate family member has a financial relationship; such financial relationships may include ownership/investment interests and also compensation arrangements. The Stark Law is exclusively a civil enforcement statute and does not include provisions for criminal liability (Table 12.6).

The Physician Self-Referral Law states in relevant part [68]:

(a) Prohibition of certain referrals

(1) In general

Except as provided in subsection (b) of this section, if a physician (or an immediate family member of such physician) has a financial relationship with an entity specified in paragraph (2), then—

(A) the physician may not make a referral to the entity for the furnishing of designated health services for which payment otherwise may be made under this subchapter, and

(B) the entity may not present or cause to be presented a claim under this subchapter or bill to any individual, third party payor, or other entity for designated health services furnished pursuant to a referral prohibited under subparagraph (A).

(2) Financial relationship specified

For purposes of this section, a financial relationship of a physician (or an immediate family member of such physician) with an entity specified in this paragraph is—

Table 12.6 Comparison of the Anti-Kickback Statute and Stark Law

	Anti-Kickback Statute	Stark Law
Authority	42 USC § 1320a–7b(b)	42 USC § 1395nn
Prohibitions	Remuneration (the offering, paying, soliciting, or receiving anything of value) in exchange to induce or reward referrals to a federal healthcare program	A physician from referring Medicare patients for designated health services to an entity with which he or she, or an immediate family member, has a financial relationship, unless an exception applies The submission of claims to Medicare by a designated health services entity for services stemming from a prohibited referral
Applicable referrals	Anyone	Physician
Applicable to	Any goods or services	Designated health services
Intent requirement	Showing of intent required (knowing and willful)	No intent standard (strict liability) Intent is required to impose CMP
Exceptions	Voluntary safe harbors	Mandatory exceptions
Applicable Healthcare Programs	All federal	Medicare/Medicaid
Penalties	*Criminal* Fines up to $25,000 per violation Up to a 5-year prison term per violation *Civil/administrative* False Claims Act liability Civil monetary penalties and program exclusion Potential $50,000 CMP per violation Civil assessment of up to three times amount of kickback	*Civil* Overpayment/refund obligation False Claims Act liability Civil monetary penalties and program exclusion for knowing violations Potential $15,000 CMP for each service Civil assessment of up to three times the amount claimed

(A) except as provided in subsections (c) and (d) of this section, an ownership or investment interest in the entity, or

(B) except as provided in subsection (e) of this section, a compensation arrangement (as defined in subsection (h)

(1) of this section) between the physician (or an immediate family member of such physician) and the entity.

With respect to prohibited self-referrals, the federal government is concerned that excessive or medically unnecessary referrals waste federal resources and may also expose patients to harm. Physician investors who have financial interests in business ventures to which they may refer patients for goods or services may potentially be unduly influenced by financial motivations as a basis for such referrals.

Under appropriate circumstances, hospitals and health systems may legitimately provide physician recruitment incentives to induce geographic relocation and employment, obtain medical staff privileges, or establish a practice designed to serve community needs. However, in competitive markets, hospitals may also develop relationships with community physicians and established practices and offer potentially illegal incentives, such as an electronic medical record, to loosely affiliate with a hospital and, in return, change referral practices. Such incentives may fall with a safe harbor provision; however, such incentives must be structured to comply with the very specific parameters of the AKS and Stark Law.

The Physician Self-Referral Law is a strict liability statute, which means proof of specific intent to violate the law is not required in order to sustain culpability. Penalty violations include fines and exclusion from participation in the federally funded healthcare programs.

Thus, by way of example, assume *arguendo* that a physician has an ownership interest in an outpatient radiologic imaging center and refers patients to that center for imaging services. Over the course of a year, 100 patients are referred and receive their imaging at that center. The government investigates and prosecutes for fraud and abuse. The potential CMP liability is calculated as $24,478 (in 2018) for each service or $24,478 × 100 = $2,447,800 + repayment of the dollar value of the claims submitted, plus potential exclusion.

Recent Examples of AKS and Stark Enforcement Actions

In 2015, three surgeons, including orthopedic and neurosurgeons, were indicted by the OIG for their alleged roles in a $580 million kickback scheme. OIG Investigators alleged that surgeons accepted kickbacks and bribes in order to direct or perform spine surgeons at Pacific Hospital of Long Beach (California). The conspirators allegedly paid a kickback of $15,000 for each lumbar fusion surgery and $10,000 for each cervical fusion surgery. The conspirators allegedly concealed the kickback payments by entering into fraudulent contracts to cover for the doctors, chiropractors, and others who received illegal payments. In total, five individuals were indicted as part of the scheme that allegedly occurred over 8 years. The owner of Pacific Hospital pleaded guilty to charges of conspiracy and paying illegal kickbacks and was sentenced to more than 5 years in prison. The case was jointly investigated by the FBI, IRS Criminal Investigation, California Department of Insurance, the US Postal Service, and OIG [69].

In 2018, William Beaumont Hospital, based in the Detroit Michigan area, settled with the DOJ for the sum of $84.5 million to resolve allegations under the False Claims Act of improper relationships with eight referring physicians, resulting in the submission of false claims to the Medicare, Medicaid, and TRICARE programs. The settlement was made to resolve allegations that Beaumont provided compensation substantially in excess of fair market value and free or below-fair market value office space and employees to certain physicians to secure their referrals of patients in violation of the Anti-Kickback Statute and the Stark Law and then submitted claims for services provided to these illegally referred patients, in violation of the False Claims Act. The alleged activity occurred between 2004 and 2012. Their settlement was initiated by a *qui tam* whistleblower action. In addition, the settlement also served to resolve alleged misrepresentation by Beaumont that a CT radiology center qualified as an outpatient department of Beaumont in claims to federal healthcare programs. In its report, the DOJ noted that:

> [t]he Anti-Kickback Statute prohibits offering, paying, soliciting, or receiving remuneration to induce referrals of items or services covered by Medicare, Medicaid, and other federally funded programs. The Physician Self-Referral Law, commonly known as the Stark Law, prohibits a hospital from billing Medicare for certain services referred by physicians with whom the hospital has an improper financial arrangement, including the payment of compensation that exceeds the fair market value of the services actually provided by the physician and the provision of free or below-market rent and office staff. Both the Anti-Kickback Statute and the Stark Law are intended to ensure that physicians' medical judgments are not compromised by improper financial incentives and instead are based on the best interests of their patients. [70]

Also in 2018, Detroit-based William Beaumont Hospital paid $84.5 million to resolve kickback allegations leveled by four former employees in whistleblower lawsuits. Prosecutors alleged that, between 2004 and 2012, Beaumont hospitals in Royal Oak, Troy, and Grosse Pointe compensated eight physicians with free or substantially discounted office space and employees in exchange for patient referrals, violating the Anti-Kickback Statute and Stark Law.

Privacy of Protected Health Information: HIPAA

It is a well-established principle of common medical practice, medical ethics, and health law that medical information obtained through the course of evaluation and treatment is strictly confidential except as required for the purposes of consultations, referrals, or quality reviews, or legal actions. Professional respect for each individual's privacy is integral within the principle of autonomy, whereby each individuals' right to bodily and psychological integrity is paramount. With the absence of the element of trust, trust in the belief that one's rights will be respected, there can be no effective patient-provider relationship. The duty of physicians regarding confidentiality of medical information dates at least to the Hippocratic Oath which reads "[w]hat I may see or hear in the course of the treatment or even outside of the treatment in regard to the life of men, which on no account one must spread abroad, I will keep to myself, holding such things shameful to be spoken about." Numerous other medical codes, oaths, and treatises reaffirm the obligation of confidentiality. The AMA Code of Ethics states that "information disclosed to physician during the course of the relationship between physician and patient is confidential to the greatest possible degree. … The physician should not reveal confidential communications or information without the express consent of the patient unless required to do so by law" [71]. The Federal Privacy Act of 1974 recognized an impending threat to the privacy of medical information as increasingly large amounts of personal medical data were being stored in computerized databanks; however, the Act was limited in both scope and effect. Thus, in the absence of effective federal legislation regulating the privacy of health information, the regulation of health information privacy fell under the legislative and regulatory purview of the individual states through the state regulation of the practice of medicine and civil laws regulation privacy [72].

A medical record contains an enormous amount of potentially sensitive personal information including family history; lifestyle and social history; past and present medical, surgical, and psychiatric diagnoses and treatments; laboratory, imaging, and pathology results; medication histories; payment or insurance data; and moreover subjective impressions of the healthcare team. The medical record is legally the work product of the therapeutic encounter. Unlike sensitive data from other sources, such as credit or financial records, the health history cannot be cancelled, expunged, or rewritten—health history is unique, essential, and therefore of potentially great intelligence value to anyone with unauthorized access.

Therefore, in response to rapid evolution of digital technology applications in medicine, such as EDI and the EMR, the Congress enacted the Health Insurance Portability and Accountability Act (HIPPA) [73] in 1996. The broad stated goals of HIPAA were to (1) increase the efficiency of electronic healthcare transactions, (2) ensure the continuity of employee's health insurance coverage after leaving an employer in the process of changing jobs (portability), and (3) mandate widespread uniform adoption of privacy protection measures for ensuring the security of individually identifiable health information. Accordingly, the rules and mandates within the structure of HIPAA were divided into three interrelated parts: (1) Administrative Simplification provisions which mandated standard data sets and electronic transaction forms for electronic data interchange (EDI), (2) the Privacy Rule which mandated security standards and policies for the management of personally identifiable health information (PHI), and (3) the Security Rule which governed the secure storage of digital health information and also the exchange of confidential medical information between business partners.

Through the Administrative Simplification provisions, HHS implemented six standards governing electronic exchange of health information: (1) standards for transactions and the data elements comprising such transactions; (2) unique health identifiers for each individual, employer, health plan, and healthcare provider; (3) code sets for the data elements for the transactions; (4) standards for security; (5) standards for electronic signatures; and (6) standards to facilitate the transfer of data elements.

The Privacy Rule regulated the process by which "covered entities" acquire, store, and disclose individually identifiable health information or protected health information (PHI) regardless of the form of the data. HIPAA protects PHI in both electronic (electronic protected health information (EPHI)) as well as non-electronic form. HIPAA defined the term "health information" to mean "any information, whether oral or recorded in any form or medium, that - (a) is created or received by a health care provider, health plan, public health authority, employer, life insurer, school or university, or health care clearinghouse; and (b) relates to the past, present, or future physical or mental health or condition of an individual, the provision of health care to an individual, or the past, present, or future payment for the provision of health care to individual." HIPAA privacy regulations strictly protect only that health information which is individually identifiable. The general rule states that "covered entities" "may not disclose PHI except as explicitly authorized by the individual patient or their legal representative. Safeguards to maintain privacy are divided into (1) administrative; (2) physical; and (3) technical safeguards. "Administrative safeguards" are defined as "administrative actions, and policies and procedures by which the selection, development, implementation, and maintenance of security measures is managed to protect EHPI" [74]. A final Privacy Rule published by HHS in 2000 is subsequently modified in August 2002.

HIPAA *requires* disclosures of PHI under two circumstances: (a) to individuals (or their personal representatives) specifically when they request access to, or an accounting of disclosures of, their protected health information and (b) to HHS when it is undertaking a compliance investigation or review or enforcement action.

In addition to required disclosures of PHI, HIPAA allows for permitted disclosures under specific circumstances, such as (1) treatment, payment, and healthcare operations; (2) as required by law (including by statute, regulation, or court orders) [75], public health activities such as to public health authorities authorized by law to collect or receive information for preventing or controlling disease, injury, or disability and to public health or other government authorities authorized to receive reports of child abuse and neglect, individuals who may have contracted or been exposed to a communicable disease when notification is authorized by law, and employers, regarding employees as needed by the employer to comply with the Occupational Safety and Health Administration (OHSA); (3) government authorities regarding victims of abuse, neglect, or domestic violence; (4) in response to court order, subpoena, or other lawful process; (5) law enforcement officials for law enforcement purposes under the following six specific circumstances subject to specified conditions [76]; and (6) cadaveric organ, eye, or tissue donation, for example.

Administrative safeguards under HIPAA consist of four mandatory specifications: risk analysis, risk management, sanction policy, and information system activity review. Risk analysis requires accurate, regular, and thorough assessments of potential risks and vulnerabilities to the confidentiality, integrity, and availability of electronic protected health information held by the covered entity. Risk management required the implementation of security measures sufficient to reduce risks and vulnerabilities to a reasonable and appropriate level. Sanction policies publicize and enforce sanctions against workforce team members who fail to comply with or violate security policies and procedures. Information system activity reviews mandate a regular review information system activity records such as audit logs, access reports, and security incident tracking reports. Measures by which an entity might mitigate administrative risks might include (1) dissemination of security updates and reminders; (2) developing and implementing procedures and protocols for guarding against, detecting, and reporting malicious software; (3) devising a program for the monitoring of log-in attempts and a regular report of discrepancies; and (4) enacting policies and procedures for the creation, changing, and safeguarding of passwords. Finally, under the administrative safeguards, the "covered entity" must protect the integrity of EPHI by establishing a contingency plan to access data in the event of a catastrophe. The contingency plan requirements include a (1) data backup plan which creates and maintains retrievable copies of EHPI, (2) a disaster recovery plan which addresses procedures for the restoration of any lost data, and (3) an emergency mode operation plan which enables continuation of critical business processes for protection of the security of electronic protected health information while operating in emergency mode.

Physical safeguards are intended to protect EPHI from unauthorized disclosure, modification, or destruction. Therefore, (1) the facility and its equipment should be safe from unauthorized physical access, tampering, and theft; (2) the organization should implement procedures to control and validate each person's access to facility and its internal areas based on their individual role or function, including visitors; and (3) document repairs and modifications to the physical components of a facility are related to security.

Technical safeguards require "covered entities" to implement technical policies and procedures for access control and include (1) unique user identification to identify and track the identity of each system use and (2) procedures for obtaining necessary electronic protected health information during a system emergency.

The HIPAA Breach Notification Rule [77] requires covered entities and their business associates to provide notification to potentially exposed individuals, the HHS, and, in some cases, the media. Such notifications must be provided without unreasonable delay and no later than 60 days following discovery of the data breach by the covered entity.

HIPAA rules apply to "covered entities." "Covered entities" are defined as health plans, healthcare clearinghouses, healthcare providers, and their "business associates" who use and transmit health information in electronic form. The Security Rule requires a "chain of trust partner agreement," now referred to as a "Business Associate agreement" between parties exchanging data electronically; this is also an element of the Privacy Rule. In business relationships in which third parties create, receive, maintain, or transmit EPHI on the covered entity's behalf, the Security Rule requires the "business associate" to (1) implement administrative, physical, and technical safeguards that reasonably and appropriately protect the confidentiality, integrity, and availability of the covered entity's EHPI; (2) ensure that its agents, and subcontractors, to whom it provides EHPI, agree to implement reasonable and appropriate safeguards to protect it; (3) report to the covered entity any security incident of which it becomes aware; and (4) ensure that the contract authorizes unilateral termination of the agreement if the business associate has violated a material contractual term.

HIPAA permits the disclosures of PHI without authorization in instances where the PHI disclosure (1) is required by federal, state, or local laws; (2) is requested by authorized public health individuals; (3) is used for healthcare research following a waiver obtained from an institutional review or privacy board; (4) is used to report abuse, neglect, or domestic violence; (5) is required by law enforcement pursuant to a court order, subpoena, or other legal orders relating to a crime; (6) is required by judicial or administrative proceedings; (7) is used to facilitate organ procurement or cadaveric organ transplantation; (8) is required for authorized health oversight activities; and (9) is work-related health information and must be disclosed to the extent necessary to comply with workers' compensation programs.

The American Recovery and Reinvestment Act of 2009 (ARRA) later established a tiered civil penalty structure for HIPAA violations and also defined the Health Information Technology for Economic and Clinical Health Act (HITECH). The HITECH Act focused primarily on incentivizing the adoption of electronic health records (EHRs) but also made the HIPAA Privacy Rule and the HIPAA Security Rule critical issues for healthcare providers because breach of HIPAA became punishable not only by civil and criminal penalties but also loss of financial incentives associated with EHR adoption and use. HITECH also specifically mandated that HIPAA-covered entities and their business associates provide notifications following any breach of unsecured protected health information—a provision known as the Breach Notification Rule. HITECH's timeframe requires providers notify those affected by a data breach within 60 days of the event.

The Patient Protection and Affordable Care Act of 2010 (ACA) further broadened liability and increased civil and criminal penalties under HIPAA and HITECH. The civil monetary penalties under HIPAA are based on the level of knowledge that violators are presumed to have had at the time of the breach, ranging from fines for (1) individuals who did not reasonably know they violated HIPAA begin at $100 per violation with an annual maximum of $25,000, ranging to violations by individuals with "willful neglect" fined at $10,000–$50,000 per violation with an annual maximum of $1.5 million. The Department of Justice (DOJ) imposes criminal liability for "knowing" breach or disclosure of PHI ranging from a criminal fine of up to $50,000 with imprisonment up to 1 year, through fines of $250,000 and imprisonment for up to 10 years in cases of malicious breach associated with personal gain. "Knowingly" for the purposes of criminal liability requires only a general knowledge that a breach could constitute an offense. Furthermore, civil and criminal penalties can extend to any or all business associates.

The Office for Civil Rights (OCR) has been authorized to investigate and enforce HIPAA violations. In addition to federal enforcement of HIPAA by the OCR and the DOJ, individual states are free to enact their own state-specific privacy laws under the jurisdiction of the State Attorney General, potentially resulting in both a federal and a separate state-level prosecution. Physicians must realize that civil prosecutions under HIPAA and HITECH may be associated with exclusion from federally funded payment programs, and such exclusions can rapidly escalate to include state and private funded insurers. In addition, criminal prosecutions must be reported to the Department of Health and consequently result in loss of medical licensure. Finally, depending on the physician's liability insurance policy, it is likely that neither prosecution is covered under traditional "malpractice insurance" [78]. Since the compliance date of the Privacy Rule in April 2003 and through May 31, 2019, OCR received over 208,797 HIPAA complaints and resolved 98% of these cases and imposed civil money penalties resulting in a total recovery of $102 million. However, HHS collected a record $28.7 million from healthcare providers and insurers in 2018.

CMPs imposed by the OCR for HIPAA violations are based on a tiered civil penalty structure (Table 12.7).

Table 12.7 Civil monetary penalties for HIPAA violations [90]

Unknowing
Minimum penalty: $100 per violation, with an annual maximum of $25,000 for repeat violations
Maximum penalty: $50,000 per violation, with an annual maximum of $1.5 million
Reasonable cause
Minimum penalty: $1000 per violation, with an annual maximum of $100,000 for repeat violations
Maximum penalty: $50,000 per violation, with an annual maximum of $1.5 million
Willful neglect but violation is corrected within the required time period
Minimum penalty: $10,000 per violation, with an annual maximum of $250,000 for repeat violations
Maximum penalty: $50,000 per violation, with an annual maximum of $1.5 million
Willful neglect and is not corrected within required time period
Minimum penalty: $50,000 per violation, with an annual maximum of $1.5 million
Maximum penalty: $50,000 per violation, with an annual maximum of $1.5 million

Recent Examples of HIPAA Enforcement Actions

In 2011, Cignet Health of Prince George's County was fined a $4.3 M Civil Money Penalty for HIPAA Privacy Rule Violations after the OCR found that Cignet violated 41 patients' rights by denying them access to their medical records [79]. Under the Privacy Rule, a covered entity must comply with a patient's request for a copy of their medical records within 30 (and no later than 60) days [80].

CardioNet, a wireless health service provider (remote mobile monitoring), settled a CMP of $2.5 million after an unencrypted laptop containing the ePHI of 1391 individuals was stolen from an employee's vehicle. The investigation revealed insufficient risk analysis and risk management processes and a lack of a HIPAA Compliance Plan or similar policies and procedures [81].

In 2018, Anthem settled a CMP of $16 million in response to a data breach. Cyberattackers gained access to the Anthem IT system via an undetected continuous and targeted cyberattack for the apparent purpose of extracting data, otherwise known as an advanced persistent threat attack, through spear phishing emails wherein hackers stole the names, birth dates, social security numbers, ePHI, home addresses, and other personal information of approximately 79 million individuals in 2015. The Anthem agreement represents the largest settlement reached by HHS' OCR for a HIPAA breach. OCR's investigation revealed that Anthem failed to conduct an enterprise-wide risk analysis, had insufficient procedures to regularly review information system activity, failed to identify and respond to suspected or known security incidents, and failed to implement adequate minimum access controls to prevent the cyberattackers from accessing sensitive ePHI [82]. Of note, a separate class action lawsuit against Anthem for the same breach was resolved by Anthem in the courts for $115 million [83].

Security of Electronic Health Information: The HITECH Act

The Health Information Technology for Economic and Clinical Health Act (HITECH) is part of the American Recovery and Reinvestment Act of 2009 (ARRA) and was signed into law as economic stimulus bill in anticipation of further expansion of ePHI exchange. ARRA included economic incentives designed to facilitate the creation of a national healthcare infrastructure and accelerate the adoption of EHR and supporting technology by providers. EMR adoption under HITECH was supported by the "Meaningful Use" program (EHR-MU), under the auspices of CMS and the Office of the National Coordinator for Health IT (ONC), whereby eligible professionals were eligible for financial incentives if they purchased and implemented certified EHR technology (certified by an Authorized Testing and Certification Body (ATCB)) in compliance with staged criteria for meaningful use. Meaningful Use is defined by the use of certified EHR technology in a meaningful manner, as defined in the regulations. CMS/ONC published the final rules as it related to meaningful use in the context of objectives and measures and standards, implementation, and vocabulary, respectively, in 2010 [84]. Through meaningful use, HITECH is widely considered to be a powerful opportunity to improve public health through population health initiatives.

Substantial incentive payments were available to healthcare professionals from 2011 through 2015; however, after 2015, a failure demonstrating meaningful use of EHRs was penalized by progressive reductions in Medicare and Medicaid reimbursement [85]. In general, meaningful use criteria included activity such as disease management criteria, implementation of clinical decision support, medication management support, patient access, and communication between providers to facilitate transitions in care and the measurement and reporting quality metrics.

In 2015, CMS released the final rule on Stage 3 Modifications to Meaningful Use which specified mandatory requirements necessary to qualify for further Medicare and Medicaid electronic health record (EHR) incentive payments and avoid downward payment adjustments under the Medicare EHR Incentive Program [86].

HITECH also increased the scope of privacy and security requirements which had been mandated under HIPAA and increased enforcement and created additional legal liability for non-compliance with regulatory mandates.

HITECH imposed mandatory penalties for privacy violations constituting "willful neglect." HITECH revised the Social Security Act by establishing (a) four-tiered categories of violations proportionate to levels of culpability, (b) four corresponding tiers of monetary penalty levels which significantly increased the minimum penalty amount for each violation over HIPAA, and (c) a maximum CMP of $1.5 million for all violations of an identical provision of HITECH. Furthermore, HITECH abolished the provision under HIPAA which imposed a bar on penalties if the covered entity "did not know and with the exercise of reasonable diligence would not have known of the violation" and added a prohibition on penalties for violations corrected within a 30-day time period, as long as that violation was not due to willful neglect [87].

The absence of a Privacy and Security Compliance Plan may now be considered de facto evidence of willful neglect. HITECH further formalized the requirement for comprehensive business associate agreements and breach notification protocols and also increased the monetary amount of CMP imposed for willful neglect. HITECH compliance also mandates patient access to their electronically stored PHI in a digital format.

Regulations regarding health information management (HIM) and health information technology (health IT) continue to evolve. And this is an area of significant legislative and regulatory flux. For example, the twenty-first century Cures Act aims to improve the flow and exchange of electronic PHI through rules relating to interoperability, accessibility, and privacy and security. The Medicare Access and CHIP Reauthorization Act of 2015 (MACRA) not only ended CMS reliance on the Sustainable Growth Rate formula which formed the basis for annual provider payment calculations but also introduced Advanced Alternative Payment Models (APMs) and Merit-Based Incentive Payment System (MIPS) which provided a performance-based payment adjustment for the electronic reporting of EMR meaningful use data.

Conclusion

The legal complexities inherent in these statutes, together with the evolving enforcement landscape, should immediately signal risk to healthcare organizations and providers who are strongly advised to proactively consult legal counsel to develop a risk assessment and mitigation plan and to immediately consult legal counsel in the event of a signaled or imminent government investigation.

References

1. Shleifer A. Understanding regulation. Eur Finan Manag. 2005;11(4):439–51. Available online at https://scholar.harvard.edu/files/shleifer/files/02_eufm00121.pdf. Verified 11 Oct 2020.
2. Merriam-Webster Dictionary. Available online at https://www.merriam-webster.com/dictionary/regulation.
3. Susan ED, Jerry B. Regulation: a primer. 2nd ed. Mercatus Center. George Mason University. 2012. p. 1. Available online at https://www.mercatus.org/system/files/RegulatoryPrimer_DudleyBrito_0.pdf. Verified 11 Oct 2020.
4. Administrative Procedure Act, 5 U.S.C. § 551 et seq. (2019).
5. Administrative Procedure Act (APA). 5 U.S.C. §551(4) (2019).
6. A Guide to the Rulemaking Process. Prepared by the Office of the Federal Register. Available online at: https://www.federalregister.gov/uploads/2011/01/the_rulemaking_process.pdf. Verified 11 Oct 2020.
7. Szalados JE. Regulatory law and the clinical practice of the neurosciences. In: Szalados JE, editor. Ethics and law for neurosciences clinicians: foundations and evolving challenges: Rutgers University Press. p. 81–103.

8. Chevron U.S.A. v. NRDC, 467 U.S. 837, 842–43 (1984).
9. Chevron U.S.A., Inc. v. Natural Resources Defense Council, 467 U.S. 837 (1984).
10. Auer v. Robbins, 519 U.S. 452 (1997).
11. Skidmore v. Swift, 323 U.S. 134 (1944).
12. Administrative Procedure Act, Report of the House Judiciary Committee, No. 1989, 79th Congress, 1946. See also Revised Model State Administrative Procedure Act. Drafted by the National Conference Of Commissioners On Uniform State Laws. 2010. Available online at https://www.uniformlaws.org/HigherLogic/System/DownloadDocumentFile.ashx?DocumentFileKey=3ab796d4-9636-d856-48e5-b638021eb54d&forceDialog=0. Verified 11 Oct 2020.
13. U.S. Const. U.S. CONST. AMEND. X.
14. U.S. Const., ART. VI, cl. 2.
15. Gade v. Nat'l Solid Waste Mgmt. Ass'n, 505 U.S. 88, 108 (1992) ("[U]nder the Supremacy Clause, from which our pre-emption doctrine is derived, any state law, however clearly within a State's acknowledged power, which interferes with or is contrary to federal law, must yield.").
16. Florida Lime & Avocado Growers, Inc. v. Paul, 373 U.S. 132, 142–143 (1963).
17. Rice v. Santa Fe Elevator Corp., 331 U.S. 218, 230 (1947); *see also* English v. General Electric Co., 496 U.S. 72, 79 (1990).
18. Wyeth v. Levine. 555 U.S. 555 (2009).
19. OIGs created under the auspices of The Inspector General Act of 1978 (92 Stat. 1101 §2).
20. False, fictitious or fraudulent claims. 18 U.S.C. § 287.
21. Civil Monetary Penalties. 42 U.S. Code § 1320a–7a.
22. Exclusion Statute [42 U.S.C. § 1320a-7].
23. Available online at: https://exclusions.oig.hhs.gov/. Verified 11 Oct 2020.
24. OIG Special Advisory Bulletin. The Effect of Exclusion From Participation in Federal Health Care Programs. September 1999. Available online at: https://oig.hhs.gov/fraud/docs/alertsandbulletins/effected.htm. Verified 11 Oct 2020.
25. Health and Human Services Office of the Inspector General. Compliance Resource Portal. See online at: https://oig.hhs.gov/compliance/compliance-resource-portal/index.asp. Verified 11 Oct 2020.
26. Patient Protection and Affordable Care Act, 42 U.S.C. § 18001 et seq. (2010).
27. Compliance Guidance. Office of Inspector General, U.S. department of Health and Human Services. Available online https://www.oig.hhs.gov/compliance/compliance-guidance/index.asp. Verified 11 Oct 2020.
28. United States Sentencing Commission. 2015 Guidelines manual (Effective November 1, 2015) §8B2.1. Effective Compliance and Ethics Program. Online at https://www.ussc.gov/guidelines/2015-guidelines-manual/2015-chapter-8#NaN. Verified 11 Oct 2020.
29. Health Care Compliance Program Tips. The Seven Fundamental Elements of an Effective Compliance Program. Available online at https://oig.hhs.gov/compliance/provider-compliance-training/files/Compliance101tips508.pdf. Verified 11 Oct 2020.
30. Szalados JE. Complications and risk management. In: Barasch P, Cullen B, Cahalan M, Ortega R, Sharar S, Stock C, editors. Foundations of clinical anesthesia: Wolters-Kluwer, Philadelphia; 2015.
31. https://oig.hhs.gov/fraud/docs/complianceguidance/012705HospSupplementalGuidance.pdf. Verified 11 Oct 2020.
32. Hicks TA, Gentleman CA. Improving physician documentation through a clinical documentation management program. Nurs Adm Q. 2003;27(4):285–9.
33. Aiello FA, Judelson DR, Durgin JM, et al. A physician-led initiative to improve clinical documentation results in improved health care documentation, case mix index, and increased contribution margin. J Vasc Surg. 2018;68(5):1524–32.
34. Evaluation and Management Services. Department of Health and Human services. Centers for Medicare & Medicaid Services. Available online at: https://www.cms.gov/Outreach-and-Education/Medicare-Learning-Network-MLN/MLNProducts/Downloads/eval-mgmt-serv-guide-ICN006764.pdf. Verified 11 Oct 2020.

35. Medical Informatics Committee of the American College of Physicians (ACP). Clinical documentation in the 21st century: executive summary of a policy position paper from the American College of Physicians. Ann Intern Med. 2015;162(4):301–3.
36. John C, Tom M. Medicare records reveal troubling trail of surgeries. Wall St J. 29 March 2011. Available online at https://www.wsj.com/articles/SB10001424052748703858404576214642193925996. Verified 11 Oct 2020.
37. Medicare Provider Utilization and Payment Data: Physician and Other Supplier. Centers for Medicare and Medicaid Services. https://www.cms.gov/Research-Statistics-Data-and-Systems/Statistics-Trends-and-Reports/Medicare-Provider-Charge-Data/Physician-and-Other-Supplier.html. Verified 11 Oct 2020.
38. Kelly K., $4.1B recovered in fight against health care fraud. USA Today. Feb. 14, 2012.
39. 31 U.S.C. §§ 3729–3733. *Also codified at* Pub. L. 97–258, Sept. 13, 1982, 96 Stat. 978; Pub. L. 99–562, § 2, Oct. 27, 1986, 100 Stat. 3153; Pub. L. 103–272, § 4(f)(1)(O), July 5, 1994, 108 Stat. 1362; Pub. L. 111–21, § 4(a), May 20, 2009, 123 Stat. 1621.
40. U.S. D.O.J. Ohio Hospital to Pay $4.1 Million to Resolve False Claims Act Allegations. Friday, October 9, 2015. *Available online at*: https://www.justice.gov/opa/pr/ohio-hospital-pay-41-million-resolve-false-claims-act-allegations. Verified 11 Oct 2020.
41. U.S. Dep't of Health & Human Services, Ctrs. for Medicare & Medicaid Services, CMS 2552–96, Hospital and Hospital Care Complex Cost Report.
42. U.S. ex rel Kane v. Healthfirst Inc et al, U.S. District Court, Southern District of New York, No. 11-02325 (2105). Available online at https://www.justice.gov/sites/default/files/usao-sdny/legacy/2015/03/25/Continuum%20HealthPartners%2C%20Inc.%2C%20et%20al.%20Complaint%20in%20Intervention.pdf. Verified 11 Oct 2020.
43. Health and Human Services Office of the Inspector General. Corporate Integrity Agreements. Avaiable online at: https://oig.hhs.gov/compliance/corporate-integrity-agreements/index.asp. Verified 11 Oct 2020.
44. Association of Am. Med. Colleges v. United States, 217 F.3d 770, 774 (9th Cir. 2000).
45. United States ex rel. Schuhardt v. Wash. Univ., 228 F. Supp. 2d 1018 (D. Mo. 2002).
46. United States ex rel. Schuhardt v. Wash. Univ., 361 F. Supp. 2d 992 (D. Mo. 2003).
47. Physician fee schedule. 42 C.F.R. 415.172(2006).
48. Deficit Reduction Act. Pub. L. 109-171, §§ 6031-33 (2006) codified at 42 U.S.C. § 1396h(a).
49. As of this writing: State Laws Reviews by OIG include: California, Florida, Georgia, Hawaii, Illinois, Indiana, Louisiana, Massachusetts, Michigan, Nevada, New Hampshire, New Jersey, New Mexico, New York, Oklahoma Rhode Island, Tennessee, Texas, Virginia, Wisconsin. *See online:* https://oig.hhs.gov/compliance/state-false-claims-act-reviews/index.asp.
50. N.Y. State Fin. Law § 194, the New York State False Claims Act. Available online at: https://ag.ny.gov/tpb/procedural-regulations-false-claims-act. Verified 11 Oct 2020.
51. Publication of OIG's Guidelines for Evaluating State False Claims Acts, 71 Fed. Reg. 48,552, 48,553 (Aug. 21, 2006).
52. Civil actions for false claims. 31 U.S. C. § 3730.
53. The Fraud Enforcement and Recovery Act of 2009. Pub. L. 111-21 (2009).
54. Pub. L. 111-148 (2010).
55. Pub. L. 111-203 (2010).
56. Szalados JE. Legal issues in the practice of critical care medicine: a practical approach. Crit Care Med. 2007;35(2 suppl):S44–58.
57. Daniel M. One of the country's largest hospital organizations to pay $98.15 million settlement on false claims act allegations. Online at https://www.beneschlaw.com/resources/one-of-the-country-s-largest-hospital-organizations-to-pay-98-15-million-settlement-on-false-claims-act-allegations.html. Verified 11 Oct 2020.
58. Sweet Dreams Nurse Anesthesia Group Pays More Than $1 Million to Resolve Kickback Allegations. Department of Justice, U.S. Attorney's Office, Middle District of Georgia. Friday, August 5, 2016. https://www.justice.gov/usao-mdga/pr/sweet-dreams-nurse-anesthesia-group-pays-more-1-million-resolve-kickback-allegations. Verified 11 Oct 2020.

59. Medicare Recovery Audit Contracting Lessons Learned to Address Improper Payments and Improve Contractor Coordination and Oversight. Statement of Kathleen M. King, Director Health Care and Statement of Kay L. Daly, Director Financial Management and Assurance. United States Government Accountability Office. Online at https://www.gao.gov/assets/130/124986.pdf. *See also* The Medicare Recovery Audit Contractor (RAC) Program: An Evaluation of the 3-Year Demonstration. June 2008. American Health information management Association. *Available online at*: http://bok.ahima.org/PdfView?oid=93598. Verified 11 Oct 2020.
60. Medicare Penalties Provision of the Social Security Amendments. 42 U.S.C. § 1395nn(b).
61. Anti-Kickback Statute [42 U.S.C. § 1320a-7b(b)].
62. 42 U.S.C.§ 1320(b).
63. https://oig.hhs.gov/compliance/physician-education/01laws.asp. Verified 11 Oct 2020.
64. DHHS Office of Inspector General: An Open Letter to Health Care Providers, April 24, 2006. Available at http://1.usa.gov/1gkYhy3. Verified 11 Oct 2020.
65. United States v. Campbell, 2011 U.S. Dist. LEXIS 1207 (D.N.J. Jan. 4, 2011).
66. United States v. Greber, 760 F.2d 68 (3d Cir. Pa. 1985). cert. denied, 106 S. Ct. 396 (1985).
67. Physician Self-Referral Law [42 U.S.C. § 1395nn].
68. 42 U.S.C. §1395nn (a) – (b).
69. Five Individuals, Including Two Doctors, Charged in Kickback Schemes Involving nearly $600 Million in Fraudulent Claims by Southern California Hospitals. Department of Justice. Tuesday, November 24, 2015. https://www.justice.gov/opa/pr/five-individuals-including-two-doctors-charged-kickback-schemes-involving-nearly-600-million. Verified 11 Oct 2020.
70. Detroit Area Hospital System to Pay $84.5 Million to Settle False Claims Act Allegations Arising From Improper Payments to Referring Physicians. Department of Justice. Thursday, August 2, 2018. Online at: https://www.justice.gov/opa/pr/detroit-area-hospital-system-pay-845-million-settle-false-claims-act-allegations-arising. Verified 11 Oct 2020.
71. American Medical Association. Code of medical ethics, Chicago. 1997.
72. Szalados JE. Health information privacy and HIPPA: the health insurance portability and accountability act. Curr Rev Clin Anesth. 2004;25(1):3–14.
73. Health Insurance Portability and Accountability Act of 1996. Pub. L. No. 104-191, 100 Stat. 1396; as codified at 45 CFR § 160 et seq. (2000); and amended.
74. Administrative Safeguards § 164.308.
75. 45 C.F.R. § 164.512(a).
76. 45 C.F.R. § 164.512(f).
77. Breach Notification Rule. 45 CFR §§ 164.400-414.
78. Szalados JE. HIPAA and HiTECH. Chapter 25. In: Szalados JE, Rihht W, Smith W, editors. Legal and ethical issues in neurocritical care. Chicago: The Neurocritical Care Society; 2019. p. 61–3.
79. Notice of final determination. February 4, 2011. https://www.hhs.gov/sites/default/files/ocr/privacy/hipaa/enforcement/examples/cignetpenaltyletter.pdf. Verified 11 Oct 2020.
80. Cignet Health Fined a $4.3M Civil Money Penalty for HIPAA Privacy Rule Violations. Online at https://www.hhs.gov/hipaa/for-professionals/compliance-enforcement/examples/cignet-health/index.html. Verified 11 Oct 2020.
81. $2.5 million settlement shows that not understanding HIPAA requirements creates risk. HHS Press Office. April 24, 2017. https://www.hhs.gov/about/news/2017/04/24/2-5-million-settlement-shows-not-understanding-hipaa-requirements-creates-risk.html. Verified 11 Oct 2020.
82. Anthem Pays OCR $16 Million in Record HIPAA Settlement Following Largest U.S. Health Data Breach in History. HHS Press Office October 15, 2018. https://www.hhs.gov/about/news/2018/10/15/anthem-pays-ocr-16-million-record-hipaa-settlement-following-largest-health-data-breach-history.html. Verified 11 Oct 2020.

83. In re Anthem, Inc. Data Breach Litigation. U.S.D.C. So CA, San Jose Division. Case No. 15-MD-02617-LHK. Online at https://www.databreach-settlement.com/pdf/AAB%20-%20Order%20re%20Atty%20Fees.pdf.
84. Medicare and Medicaid Programs; Electronic Health Record Incentive Program. 75 FR 44313. July 28, 2010. Online at https://www.federalregister.gov/documents/2010/07/28/2010-17207/medicare-and-medicaid-programs-electronic-health-record-incentive-program. Verified 11 Oct 2020.
85. HITECH Act of 2009, 42 USC sec 139w-4(0)(2) (February 2009), sec 13301, subtitle B: Incentives for the Use of Health Information Technology.
86. Medicare and Medicaid Programs; Electronic Health Record Incentive Program—Stage 3 and Modifications to Meaningful Use in 2015 Through 2017. 80 F.R. 62762. October 16, 2015.
87. HITECH Act of 2009, 42 USC sec 139w-4(0)(2) (February 2009), subtitle D, part 1, sec 13402(d): Tiered increase in amount of civil monetary penalties.
88. HCCA-OIG Compliance Effectiveness Roundtable, Roundtable Meeting, January 17, 2017, Washington DC. Available online at https://oig.hhs.gov/compliance/compliance-resource-portal/files/HCCA-OIG-Resource-Guide.pdf. Verified 11 Oct 2020.
89. U.S. Centers for Medicare & Medicaid Services. https://www.cms.gov/Outreach-and-Education/Medicare-Learning-Network-MLN/MLNProducts/Fast-Facts/False-Claims.html. Verified 11 Oct 2020.
90. Modifications to the HIPAA Privacy, Security, Enforcement, and Breach Notification Rules Under the Health Information Technology for Economic and Clinical Health Act and the Genetic Information Nondiscrimination Act; Other Modifications to the HIPAA Rules. Health and Human Services Department on 01/25/2013. 45 CFR Parts 160 and 164. Fed. Reg. Vol. 78, No. 17/Friday, January 25, 2013 / Rules and Regulations.

Chapter 13
Medical Records and Confidentiality: Evolving Liability Issues Inherent in the Electronic Health Record, HIPAA, and Cybersecurity

James E. Szalados

The Legal Basis of Privacy Protections

Privacy is defined simply as "freedom from unauthorized intrusion" [1] – in general, a person's right to be free from unwanted publicity and scrutiny without their consent. The right to privacy is also defined as the "right of a person to be free from intrusion into or publicity concerning matters of a personal nature" [2]. Privacy enables individuals to create boundaries and insulate themselves from unwarranted interference. The notion of a right to control one's self is universally understood, and generally recognized, because that right is rooted in principles of personal property, liberty, autonomy, and personhood. Privacy, then, is widely held to be a fundamental human right and is the foundation for the respect for human dignity.

Although the right to privacy is a fundamental human right recognized in the United Nations Declaration of Human Rights, by the constitutions of most countries, and by the majority of world courts, it is not universally conferred. Historically, Plato argued that the complete life of the individual was to be determined by the state and its aims, and consequently there was no place for individual freedom and autonomy. Furthermore, the natural philosophers, including Mill and Locke, did not see privacy right as a societal value; rather, they viewed the individual as a member of the larger community. The right to one's privacy is similar to other fundamental human rights and can be subjugated to competing interests or authoritarianism and

J. E. Szalados (✉)
Director, Surgical and Neurocritical Care Units, Rochester Regional Health System at Rochester General Hospital, Rochester, NY, USA

The Szalados Law Firm, Hilton, NY, USA
e-mail: james.szalados@rochesterregional.org; jszalados@aol.com

J. E. Szalados (ed.), *The Medical-Legal Aspects of Acute Care Medicine*,
https://doi.org/10.1007/978-3-030-68570-6_13

can easily also be either involuntarily or voluntarily surrendered. Indeed, through technology, individuals are surrendering privacy rights in an unprecedented manner.

The American legal definition of privacy is rooted in American culture, although privacy is not an express individual right in the US Constitution. In fact, the US Supreme Court first recognized a right to privacy in the case of *Griswold v. Connecticut*, where, the Court, in its ruling in a case challenging a statute which had criminalized contraception, derived, or extrapolated, a right to privacy through penumbras otherwise inferred from explicitly stated constitutional protections. The *Griswold* court held that an implied right to marital privacy could be reasonably inferred from individual rights explicit within the First, Third, Fourth, Fifth, and Ninth Amendments, so that when the inherent penumbras are taken together, the Constitution can reasonably create a "zone of privacy." [3]

Thus, aspects of The Bill of Rights may reasonably be construed to suggest a right to aspects of privacy, for example:

1. The First Amendment, addressing the privacy of beliefs ("Congress shall make no law respecting an establishment of religion…")
2. The Third Amendment, addressing a right to privacy within the home ("No Soldier shall, in time of peace be quartered in any house, without the consent of the Owner…")
3. The Fourth Amendment, addressing a right to privacy of person and possessions ("The right of the people to be secure in their persons, houses, papers, and effects, against unreasonable searches and seizures, shall not be violated…")
4. The Ninth Amendment, addressing a general right to privacy ("The enumeration in the Constitution, of certain rights, shall not be construed to deny or disparage others retained by the people.")
5. The reiteration of the importance of personal liberty within the 14th Amendment ("No State shall... deprive any person of life, liberty, or property, without due process of law.")

Although many will find it remarkable that there is no clearly articulated right to personal privacy within the Constitution, the Constitution does articulate, perhaps more so than any other founding document in the history of civilization, deep respect for property, liberty, autonomy, and personhood. Nonetheless, despite past judicial rulings, the right to privacy in the United States remains open to debate and to future court interpretation.

Perhaps the strongest formal articulation regarding the importance of privacy is found not within the constitution but rather in early American jurisprudence. Justice Brandeis stated, somewhat presciently, within a ruling dissent in 1928 that:

> Moreover, 'in the application of a Constitution, our contemplation cannot be only of what has been, but of what may be.' The progress of science in furnishing the government with means of espionage is not likely to stop with wire tapping. Ways may some day be developed by which the government, without removing papers from secret drawers, can reproduce them in court, and by which it will be enabled to expose to a jury the most intimate occurrences of the home…

> The principles laid down in this opinion affect the very essence of constitutional liberty and security. They reach farther than the concrete form of the case there before the court, with its adventitious circumstances; they apply to all invasions on the part of the government and its employees of the sanctities of a man's home and the privacies of life. It is not the breaking of his doors, and the rummaging of his drawers, that constitutes the essence of the offense; but it is the invasion of his indefeasible right of personal security, personal liberty and private property…
>
> The protection guaranteed by the amendments is much broader in scope. The makers of our Constitution undertook to secure conditions favorable to the pursuit of happiness. They recognized the significance of man's spiritual nature, of his feelings and of his intellect. They knew that only a part of the pain, pleasure and satisfactions of life are to be found in material things. They sought to protect Americans in their beliefs, their thoughts, their emotions and their sensations. They conferred, as against the government, the right to be let alone-the most comprehensive of rights and the right most valued by civilized men. To protect, that right, every unjustifiable intrusion by the government upon the privacy of the individual, whatever the means employed, must be deemed a violation of the Fourth Amendment. Justice Brandeis's dissent in Olmstead v. U. S. [4] (1928)

Although Brandeis, in *Olmstead,* referred specifically to a right to privacy from governmental intrusion, he continued to explore the importance of personal privacy within society as a whole, within the context of "political, social and economic changes" [5]. Following the publication of "The Right to Privacy," Warren and Brandeis were largely credited with establishing the invasion of privacy tort into American jurisprudence.

Contemporary state tort laws widely recognize a cause of action for "invasion of privacy" in settings and situations where a "reasonable expectation of privacy" would apply. Invasion of privacy constitutes an intentional tort, thus requiring proof of an intent to intrude upon the affairs of another, where there would otherwise be a reasonable expectation to be left alone. Prosser classifies invasion of privacy [6] claims into four general types:

(1) Intrusion of Solitude: "consists solely of an intentional interference with his interest in solitude or seclusion, either as to his person or as to his private affairs or concerns, of a kind that would be highly offensive to a reasonable man" [7].
(2) Appropriation of Name or Likeness: "the interest of the individual in the exclusive use of his own identity, in so far as it is represented by his name or likeness, and in so far as the use may be of benefit to him or to others" [8].
(3) Public Disclosure of Private Facts: "one who gives publicity to a matter concerning the private life of another is subject to liability to the other for invasion of his privacy, if the matter publicized is of a kind that (a) would be highly offensive to a reasonable person, and (b) is not of legitimate concern to the public" [9].
(4) False Light: the protection of one's reputation [10].

Brandeis and Warren recognized in 1890 that privacy was an important personal right and that new and evolving technology could and would alter our individual relationships with the matter we would hold private. The technologies which Brandeis and Warren saw in evolution, at the time they considered the impact of technology, were telephone, telegraph communications, and cameras. With the subsequent development of computer technology, the ability to store and transmit large volumes of information electronically supported a widespread perception that technology could further jeopardize privacy, resulting in a slow promulgation of legal and regulatory safeguards [11].

Nonetheless, over the course of the past decade, the personal importance of individual privacy is arguably fading whereas a new perception of privacy as a norm that regulates and structures social life (the social dimension of privacy) is gaining ever-increasing importance in legislation, law, relationship, popular culture, and commerce [12]. Some would argue that in the age of social media and the Internet, despite the inherent risks, many of the things that Americans previously considered to be inviolably private are increasingly accepted as reasonably pubic [13].

A Distinction Between Privacy and Confidentiality

Privacy is an expectation based on autonomy; to a large degree it is a right, a right controlled by the holder, and therefore surrendered at will. Confidentiality on the other hand is a duty owed to another, restricting the use and dissemination of private information; the duty of confidentiality is ethical and legal. Confidentiality is a key element of the fiduciary relationship between professionals and their clients/patients. Privacy is a quasi-right rooted in common law, whereas confidentiality is an ethical and/or legal duty. Confidentiality refers to the protection of privileged information. Therefore, from a legal point of view, privacy and confidentiality have distinctly different meanings.

Reasonable expectations of privacy attach to certain places, things, and activities, for example, your home, your bedroom, your mail, your telephone calls or text messages, public bathrooms. Duties of confidentiality, on the other hand, apply to information shared, with the expectation that it be held in confidence, on the behalf of another, and shared only if and when appropriate authorization has been provided by the one to whom the duty of confidentiality is owed. Examples of confidentiality include information held on one's behalf by those legally empowered to do so; banks or federal or state agencies; health information privacy in the custody of healthcare providers; confidentiality mandated by contract such as confidentiality or nondisclosure agreements; or confidentiality dated by privilege, such as the attorney-client privilege, the patient-physician privilege, spousal privilege, and the priest-parishioner privilege. Privileged communications and information represent the highest level of civilian privacy and confidentiality; privileged communication refers to the exchange of, and the information exchanged between, two parties in which the law recognizes a private, protected relationship where the communication is protected by law.

In legally recognized protected relationships wherein the communication is expected to be in private and where a duty of privilege applies, the rights for protection for the communication belong to the client, patient, or penitent. The recipient of the information must keep the communication private, unless the privilege is waived by the discloser of the information, in other words, the holder of the privilege. Confidentiality is a duty; privilege is a rule of evidence by which confidentiality is protected.

The attorney-client privilege is the oldest privilege recognized by western jurisprudence, with its beginnings in the Roman Republic, subsequently established in English law as early as the reign of Elizabeth I in the sixteenth century [14]. The privilege afforded to confidential communications between client and attorney was recognized at common law and is now well established in the US Federal Courts [15]. At the most basic level, the attorney-client privilege is essential to justice. The court in *United States v. Grand Jury* Investigation noted that:

> … although the law strives to ascertain the truth, there exists a countervailing policy of insuring the right of every person to freely and fully confer with and confide in a person having knowledge of the law and skilled in its practice, so that adequate advice may be received and proper defenses asserted. Such assistance can be given only when the client is free from the consequences of apprehension or disclosure by reason of the subsequent statements of his own skilled lawyer. [16]

Thus, the attorney-client privilege, firmly grounded in the confidential nature of the relationship, allows for honest and complete disclosure of the relevant facts and impressions by a client to his or her legal counsel. Since the client can rest secure in the knowledge that his or her statements cannot be construed against his or her interest, that candid and open communication will then allow the attorney to provide accurate and well-reasoned professional advice based on a complete understanding of all the facts and issues at hand. The privilege in effect creates a legally protected "zone of privacy" essential to the relationship [17]. The rules regarding attorney-client privilege will vary between jurisdictions. However, in general the scope of privilege is defined:

> (1) Where legal advice of any kind is sought (2) from a professional legal adviser in his capacity as such, (3) the communications relating to that purpose,
> (4) made in confidence (5) by the client, (6) are at his instance permanently protected (7) from disclosure by himself or by the legal adviser, (8) except the protection be waived. [18]
>
> Wigmore on Evidence. 1961.

An attorney-client privilege exists when there is an attorney-client relationship; and the meaning of "relationship" is broadly construed. The attorney-client relationship presupposes a "reasonable belief" that an attorney-client relationship indeed exists. An express contract is not necessary to form an attorney-client relationship; the relationship may be implied from the conduct of the parties. The court opinion in *Togstad v. Vesely* extended the definition of the attorney-client relationship to non-clients if: (1) the non-client seeks legal advice, (2) then the non-client reasonably relies on that advice as legal advice, and (3) the attorney does not attempt to dissuade the non-client from relying on the advice [19].

Nonetheless, the simple act of communicating information to an attorney does not render the information, itself, confidential. Where the information communicated is public, known to or in the possession of another, then the underlying information itself is not privileged [20]. Communications with an attorney, even if stipulated that they be in confidence, will not prevent the underlying facts from compelled disclosure, if that information can be found in the public domain or discovered from a non-privileged source [21].

Privilege applies only to private information that is communicated in confidence. In addition, the privilege belongs to the client, who is the "holder" of the privilege, and the client has the authority either to assert the privilege or waive it. The mere presence of a third party compromises confidentiality and can negate the creation of an attorney-client privilege; similarly the privilege may be destroyed or waived by a careless, unintentional, or inadvertent disclosure. Where the privilege is waived, intentionally or inadvertently by the client, the confidential nature of the information is destroyed; on the other hand, where the attorney, either deliberately or negligently, discloses privileged information, then he or she may be found liable for legal malpractice.

Privacy and Confidentiality Within the Healthcare Context

The privacy and confidentiality of medical records is a well-established principle of both medical ethics and health law; and the confidentiality of communications in the healthcare context is the basis for the patient-physician privilege. Once again, privacy refers to the nature of the information conveyed, confidentiality refers to the duty to hold the private information securely and in confidence, and privilege refers to the rule of evidence that protects the confidential communication from a compelled disclosure.

In the same manner that honest, thorough, and candid communications between attorney and client are essential to promote the interests of justice, during the therapeutic encounter, the private communications between patient and physician serve to promote the best medical interests of the patient. Without trust, patients will not freely reveal their personal health information, and the scope and quality of the medical encounter are subsequently jeopardized.

The importance of confidentiality to the relationship between the patient and their health care provider has been repeatedly affirmed as a professional responsibility of physicians since antiquity and is exemplified by the professional oaths of medicine. The Classical Version of the Oath of Hippocrates states:

> ...Whatever, in connection with my professional service, or not in connection with it, I see or hear, in the life of men, which ought not to be spoken of abroad, I will not divulge, as reckoning that all such should be kept secret. While I continue to keep this Oath unviolated, may it be granted to me to enjoy life and the practice of the art, respected by all men, in all times. But should I trespass and violate this Oath, may the reverse be my lot. [22]

Therefore, as professionals, physicians and providers are obligated by a fiduciary duty to protect the privacy and confidentiality of their patients, their health information, and the relevant confidential communications. A "fiduciary duty" is one which a professional owes to a beneficiary by virtue of his position of trust, within the setting of inequality of knowledge, training, and/or experience. Thus, fiduciary principles impose a heightened duty of loyalty, integrity, and devotion on physicians. A breach of the duty confidentiality also fundamentally undermines the expectation of confidentiality and the presumption of compete trust inherent in the physician-patient relationship.

> There is no real doubt, of course, that the relationship between a doctor and his patient is one in which the patient normally reposes a great deal of trust and confidence in the doctor, accepting his recommendations without question. … The relation of physician and patient has its foundation on the theory that the former is learned, skilled, and experienced in those subjects about which the latter ordinarily knows little or nothing, but which are of the most vital importance and interest to him, since upon them may depend the health, or even life, of himself or family; therefore the patient must necessarily place great reliance, faith, and confidence in the professional word, advice, and acts of the physician. [23]
> Witherell v. Weimer (1981)

The ethical foundations of the patient-physician confidentiality extend to well-established legal ramifications; these include, but not limited to, breaches of privacy, confidentiality, loyalty, and contract. Disclosure of confidential medical information to outsiders may have associated "damages" and can lead to severe emotional, social, or economic injury as well as humiliation, social stigma, loss of reputation, job, insurance, or marital relationship. Confidential communications during psychiatric treatment or psychotherapy are afforded a heightened level of privacy protection; even where consent is obtained for the release of medical records, psychiatric and psychological treatment information must be redacted and separated from the disclosure; and separate consent is generally required for the release of such sensitive records.

Until recently, there was no single pervasive body of US legislation which uniformly and comprehensively covered the protection of private and personal health information; instead, the confidentiality of health information was afforded some protection through a myriad of federal and state laws and case law.

The Federal Privacy Act of 1974 established standard information practices to address the collection, maintenance, use, and dissemination of information about individuals that is maintained in systems of records by federal agencies [24]. Although the act did not apply to private sector healthcare facilities, it was nonetheless important because it was among the first legislation enacted which recognized the threat to privacy resulting from the accumulation of large amounts of personal information in computerized databanks or government files. The act is considered limited in application because it was limited by vagueness and imprecision [25]. The Joint Commission, in its 1990 standards, required that medical records be accurate, accessible, authenticated, organized, confidential, secure, current, legible, and complete [26].

The duty to maintain confidentiality has always been balanced against the duty to breach confidentiality under some circumstances. For example, mandatory reporting laws regarding transmissible diseases, injuries related to crimes, or cases of abuse, neglect, or exploitation require disclosure of relevant health information to authorities, even in the absence of patient consent. The first American public health laws addressing surveillance regulations were enacted in Rhode Island in 1741; the law required tavern keepers to report persons with infectious diseases to local health officials [27]. Public health exceptions to privacy have historically presented a dichotomous challenge to clinical ethics and the patient-physician relationship.

The primary analysis of clinical ethics relates to the resolution of ethical and moral dilemmas between healthcare providers and their individual patients during the process of clinical care. On the other hand, the relevant analysis for public health, where the focus is population and community well-being, the community rather than the individual is the patient. The dominance of individual autonomy despite prima facie equivalence in clinical ethics is incompatible with the population-centered focus of public health [28].

The California Supreme Court, in *Tarasoff v. Regents of California*, imposed an affirmative duty on physicians to breach the confidentiality of the patient-physician relationship. The California Supreme Court heard the case twice, and the subsequent legal doctrine is based upon the outcome of two rulings: Tarasoff I (1974) and Tarasoff II (1976). In brief, the case involves a man named Prosenjit Poddar, then a student at the University of California at Berkeley, and a woman named Tatiana Tarasoff who met at a dance class in 1968. Poddar took a liking to Tarasoff; however, she did not reciprocate. Poddar developed a mental conflict stemming from the failed relationship and sought help from a counselor at Cowell Memorial Hospital to whom he disclosed that he was going to kill Tarasoff. The psychiatrist, Dr. Moore notified the campus police who interviewed Poddar and then released him. Upon learning of the circumstances, the then director of psychiatry, Dr. Powelson, demanded the destruction of all clinical notes as well as the letter which was sent to the campus police by Dr. Moore regarding Poddar. Poddar then went to the home of Tarasoff, where he shot her with a pellet gun and stabbed her numerous times, killing her. Tarasoff's parents filed suit against the University of California, resulting in the 1974 Tarasoff I decision [29] and in the "duty to warn" or "Tarasoff doctrine," which required mental health providers to warn potential victims. In its decision, the court relied on

> the Principles of Medical Ethics of the American Medical Association (1957) section 9: "A physician may not reveal the confidences entrusted to him in the course of medical attendance . unless he is required to do so by law or unless it becomes necessary in order to protect the welfare of the individual or of the community." (Emphasis added.) We conclude that the public policy favoring protection of the confidential character of patient-psychotherapist communications must yield in instances in which disclosure is essential to avert danger to others. The protective privilege ends where the public peril begins. … For the reasons stated, we conclude that plaintiffs can assert the elements essential to a cause of action for breach of a duty to warn. … The majority's opinion correctly holds that when a psychiatrist, in terminating treatment to a patient, increases the risk of his violence, the psychiatrist must warn the potential victim.
>
> Tarasoff v. Regents of California, 1974.

The court heard the case again in 1976, where, in Tarasoff II [30], the ruling was extended from a "duty to warn" potential victims but also to take reasonable precautions to protect potential victims from known dangers by patients. Nonetheless, the

Table 13.1 Civil Monetary Penalties (CMP) under HIPAA [62]

Tier	OCR penalty discretion	OCR penalty discretion	Minimum penalty per violation	Maximum penalty per violation	Annual aggregate limit for identical violations
Tier 1	No knowledge	Waive or reduce	$ 100	$ 50,000	$ 25,000
Tier 2	Reasonable cause	Waive or reduce	$ 1000	$ 50,000	$ 100,000
Tier 3	Willful neglect corrected	Penalty mandatory	$ 10,000	$ 50,000	$ 250,000
Tier 4	Willful neglect Not corrected	Penalty mandatory	$ 50,000	$ 50,000	$ 1,500,000

California *Tarasoff* ruling, notwithstanding, states different states have taken different points of view regarding the duty to warn or the duty to protect (Table 13.1). Since the *Tarasoff* rulings were in California State Court, they are at best persuasive; at present 23 states have enacted statutes mandating reporting; 11 states maintain a permissive posture; and others have established neither precedent nor statute to guide clinicians. The laws change, and it is incumbent on providers to be familiar with the exact nature of the laws of the state in which they practice. Furthermore, a recent review of court decisions involving Tarasoff issues, even states with existing statutes did not uniformly rely on them in their decisions underscoring the importance of clinical and ethical judgment [31] and perhaps institutional protocols.

The Medical Record

The medical record is a repository of a vast amount of a patient's personal information; it includes information on lifestyle choices, social history, past and current medications, past and present medical, surgical and psychiatric diagnoses, treatments, physical examination findings, responses, laboratory and radiologic data, and photographs. In addition, the medical record also includes assessments of medical necessity and the subjective impressions and opinions of providers, making the medical record, in a sense, a "work product." A variety of providers and clinicians enter documentation into the medical record, for example, therapists, nurses, and social workers. Since the medical record is continually updated and modified, it is, in a sense, a living document. In terms of function, the medical record facilitates communication between providers, supports claims for reimbursement, and documents medical reasoning in the event of litigation, peer review, or medical board inquiry [32]. Thus, the medical record is simultaneously a medical, administrative, and legal document. The basic requirements for documentation in the medical record are generally prescribed by numerous entities including, but limited to, the Centers for Medicare & Medicaid Services (CMS) [33], the National Committee for

Quality Assurance (NCQA) [34], the Joint Commission [35], state statutes,[1] and also, hospital policies and medical staff bylaws.

The ownership of the patient's medical records is divided between the provider and the patient: the provider has ownership (or custody) of the physical patient records and chart, whereas the patient has ownership of the information contained therein. Thus, the safety and the integrity of the medical record is the responsibility of the custodian, institution, or provider. The minimum record retention rules for medical records is mandated by federal [37] and state laws, and also multiple regulatory agencies [38]. Clinicians must know, understand, and follow all applicable laws and regulations.

The Health Insurance Portability NAND Accountability Act of 1996 (HIPAA)

Overview of HIPAA

US Congress began to address concerns regarding the portability and renewability of health insurance in the 1970s starting with legislation such as the Employee Retirement Income Security Act (ERISA) of 1974 and the Consolidated Omnibus Reconciliation Act of 1985 (COBRA). The Federal Privacy Act of 1974 exemplified concerns regarding the inevitability of computerized information management and the associated security concerns associated with storage and transmission of sensitive information.

The Health Insurance Portability and Accountability Act (HIPAA) was enacted by Congress in 1996 [39]. Broadly stated, the goals of HIPAA were to (1) increase the efficiency of electronic healthcare transactions; (2) ensure the continuity of employee's health insurance coverage after leaving an employer in the process of changing jobs; and (3) mandate widespread uniform adoption of privacy protection measures for ensuring the security of individually identifiable health information. Thus, HIPAA is a complex framework of regulations intended to facilitate portability of health data; reduce administrative costs by increasing efficiency through information technology (IT); maintain the integrity of electronically stored health data; and mandate the confidentiality of health information.

HIPAA is divided into five titles:

- Title I: HIPAA Health Insurance Reform/Access, Portability, and Renewability
  Requires employers and health plans to allow a medical insurance coverage to remain continuous despite pre-existing conditions; protects health insurance coverage for workers and their families when they change employment.
- Title II: HIPAA Administrative Simplification/Healthcare Fraud and Abuse

[1] See, for example, [36].

Requires the Department of Health and Human Services (HHS) to establish national standards for electronic healthcare transactions and national identifiers for providers (the National Provider Identifier; NPI), health plans (the Standard Unique Health Plan Identifier; HPID), and employers (the Standard Unique Employer Identifier; (EIN). It also addresses the security and privacy of health data. Adopting these standards will improve the efficiency and effectiveness of the nation's healthcare system by encouraging the widespread use of electronic data interchange in health care. Title II also addresses the security and privacy of health data and intended to prevent healthcare fraud and abuse.

- Title III: HIPAA Tax-Related Health Provisions

  Provides changes to health insurance laws and deductions for medical insurance and guidelines for pre-tax medical spending accounts.
- Title IV: Application and Enforcement of Group Health Plan Requirements

  Specifies conditions for group health plans regarding coverage of persons with preexisting conditions and modifies the continuation of coverage requirements.
- Title V: Revenue Offsets

  Includes provisions related to taxes affecting company-owned life insurance and to the treatment of individuals without US citizenship.

In the Federal Privacy Act, the federal government articulated the increasing importance and also the vulnerability of electronic data interchange (EDI) between business partners. Throughout the early stages of EDI, there was tremendous heterogeneity in the electronic and coding languages used, the information technology platforms, and the means of transmission. In healthcare, that lack of standardization was an obstacle to the evolution of the electronic medical record, access to health information, and the portability of health records. The Administrative Simplification provisions of HIPAA mandated the development of transaction and code sets to standardize the format of health information for storage, use, and EDI. HIPAA represented a uniform starting point for industry standardization of health information management and set the stage for the development of the electronic health/medical record (the EHR or EMR). The Institute of Medicine, in its 2001 report, "Crossing Quality Chasm: A New System for the 21st Century," [40] called for the creation of a national information infrastructure and for the increased adoption of information technology within the healthcare industry to facilitate access and to optimize quality and cost management, as well as quality and cost comparisons. Thus, HIPAA also sets the stage for a standardized data architecture, and information technology infrastructure allows the warehousing of healthcare data which would then facilitate quality comparisons, improve the quality of medical care, and facilitate the development of cost reduction strategies across the US healthcare system.

HIPAA privacy standards represent a national set of minimum basic protections. Noncompliance with the HIPAA Administrative Simplification regulations is enforced by the Centers for Medicare and Medicaid Services (CMS). Thus, in general, state laws contrary to HIPAA are preempted. "Contrary" means that it would be impossible for a covered entity to comply with both the state and federal requirements or that the provision of state law is an obstacle to accomplishing the full purposes and objectives of the Administrative Simplification provisions of HIPAA. Therefore, HIPAA will preempt any contrary provision of any state law relating to written or electronic records. However, preemption may not apply if the state law: (a) is necessary to prevent fraud and abuse related to the provision of or payment for health care, (b) is necessary to ensure appropriate State regulation of insurance and health plans to the extent expressly authorized by statute or regulation; (c) is necessary for state reporting on healthcare delivery or costs and is necessary for purposes of serving a compelling public health, safety, or welfare need and if a privacy rule provision is at issue and if the secretary determines that the intrusion into privacy is warranted when balanced against the need to be served; or, (d) has as its principal purpose the regulation of the manufacture, registration, distribution, dispensing, or other control of any controlled substances (as defined in 21 U.S.C. 802) or that is deemed a controlled substance by state law [41].

HIPAA was divided into three interrelated parts: (1) the privacy rule provisions which set security standards and policies for the way in which providers manage personally identifiable health information (PHI); (2) the security rule which governs relationships between healthcare business associates who necessarily exchange confidential medical information; and, (3) the enforcement rule which provides for the enforcement of all the Administrative Simplification rules.

The HIPAA Privacy Rule

The HIPAA Privacy Rule addresses the process by which covered entities acquire, store, and disclose individually identifiable health information. The Privacy Rule was published in 2000 and was subsequently modified in 2002.

The Privacy Rule [42] delineates national standards for the protection of individuals' medical records and other personal health information (PHI) regardless of the format; it applies to health plans, healthcare clearinghouses, and healthcare providers who conduct healthcare transactions electronically. The Privacy Rule mandates safeguards to protect the privacy of personal health information and sets limits and conditions on the uses and disclosures of such information. The Privacy Rule was designed to (1) increase the level of patient control over the use of their medical records, (2) balance public health needs and responsibilities against information confidentiality, and (3) establish procedural safeguards to protect health information privacy. An individual's control over their PHI under HIPAA requires providers to (a) notify individual patients regarding the privacy rights and how their PHI is used through a process of adequate notice, (b) allow individuals the right to inspect and copy their medical records, (c) allow individuals to request amendments to their PHI record set, (d) receive an accounting of certain types of disclosures of their PHI, and (e) request the placement of restrictions on specific uses or disclosures of their PHI, with the exception of emergency treatment situations. Under HIPAA, patients also have a right to obtain and review a covered entity's "notice of privacy practices." Individually identifiable health information includes many common identifiers such as name, address, birth date, and social security number. The Privacy Rule excludes employment records maintained by employers and educational institutions and other records subject to, or defined in, the Family Educational Rights and Privacy Act [43].

Definitions in HIPAA are essential since they represent legal terms of art (see Chap. 28: Anatomy of Healthcare Contracts: Pitfalls and Avoidance of Liability).

HIPAA defines the terms [44]:

- "Covered entity" to mean "(1) a health plan; (2) a health care clearinghouse; or, (3) a health care provider who transmits any health information in electronic form in connection with a transaction covered by this subchapter."
- "Healthcare provider" to mean "a provider of services (as defined in section 1861(u) of the Act, 42 U.S.C. 1395x(u)), a provider of medical or health services (as defined in section 1861(s) of the Act, 42 U.S.C. 1395x(s)), and any other person or organization who furnishes, bills, or is paid for health care in the normal course of business."
- "Health care" to mean "care, services, or supplies related to the health of an individual. Health care includes, but is not limited to, the following: (1) Preventive, diagnostic, therapeutic, rehabilitative, maintenance, or palliative care, and counseling, service, assessment, or procedure with respect to the physical or mental condition, or functional status, of an individual or that affects the structure or function of the body; and (2) Sale or dispensing of a drug, device, equipment, or other item in accordance with a prescription."
- "Health information" to mean "any information, whether oral or recorded in any form or medium, that - (a) is created or received by a health care provider, health plan, public health authority, employer, life insurer, school or university, or health care clearinghouse; and (b) relates to the past, present, or future physical or mental health or condition of an individual, the provision of health care to an individual, or the past, present, or future payment for the provision of health care to individual."
- "Protected health information" to mean "individually identifiable health information: (1) Except as provided in paragraph (2) of this definition, that is: (i) Transmitted by electronic media; (ii) Maintained in electronic media; or (iii) Transmitted or maintained in any other form or medium (2). Protected health information excludes individually identifiable health information: (i) In education records covered by the Family Educational Rights and Privacy Act, as amended, 20 U.S.C. 1232 g; (ii) In records described at 20 U.S.C. 1232 g(a) (4)(B)(iv); (iii) In employment records held by a covered entity in its role as employer; and (iv) Regarding a person who has been deceased for more than 50 years."
- "Individually identifiable health information" to mean "information that is a subset of health information, including demographic information collected from an individual, and: (1) Is created or received by a health care provider, health plan, employer, or health care clearinghouse; and (2) Relates to the past, present, or

future physical or mental health or condition of an individual; the provision of health care to an individual; or the past, present, or future payment for the provision of health care to an individual; and (i) That identifies the individual; or(ii) With respect to which there is a reasonable basis to believe the information can be used to identify the individual."

- "Disclosure" to mean "the release, transfer, provision of access to, or divulging in any manner of information outside the entity holding the information."
- "Electronic media" to mean:
  - (1) Electronic storage material on which data is or may be recorded electronically, including, for example, devices in computers (hard drives) and any removable/transportable digital memory medium, such as magnetic tape or disk, optical disk, or digital memory card;
  - (2) Transmission media used to exchange information already in electronic storage media. Transmission media include, for example, the Internet, extranet or intranet, leased lines, dial-up lines, private networks, and the physical movement of removable/transportable electronic storage media. Certain transmissions, including of paper, via facsimile, and of voice, via telephone, are not considered to be transmissions via electronic media if the information being exchanged did not exist in electronic form immediately before the transmission.
- "Business associate" to mean:
  - (1) Except as provided in paragraph (4) of this definition, business associate means, with respect to a covered entity, a person who:
    - (i) On behalf of such covered entity or of an organized health care arrangement (as defined in this section) in which the covered entity participates, but other than in the capacity of a member of the workforce of such covered entity or arrangement, creates, receives, maintains, or transmits protected health information for a function or activity regulated by this subchapter, including claims processing or administration, data analysis, processing or administration, utilization review, quality assurance, patient safety activities listed at 42 CFR 3.20, billing, benefit management, practice management, and repricing;
    - (ii) or (ii) Provides, other than in the capacity of a member of the workforce of such covered entity, legal, actuarial, accounting, consulting, data aggregation (as defined in §164.501 of this subchapter), management, administrative, accreditation, or financial services to or for such covered entity, or to or for an organized health care arrangement in which the covered entity participates, where the provision of the service involves the disclosure of protected health information from such covered entity or arrangement, or from another business associate of such covered entity or arrangement, to the person.
  - (2) A covered entity may be a business associate of another covered entity.

- (3) Business associate includes:
  - (i) A Health Information Organization, E-prescribing Gateway, or other person that provides data transmission services with respect to protected health information to a covered entity and that requires access on a routine basis to such protected health information.
  - (ii) A person that offers a personal health record to one or more individuals on behalf of a covered entity.
  - (iii) A subcontractor that creates, receives, maintains, or transmits protected health information on behalf of the business associate.
- (4) Business associate does not include:
  - (i) A health care provider, with respect to disclosures by a covered entity to the health care provider concerning the treatment of the individual.
  - (ii) A plan sponsor, with respect to disclosures by a group health plan (or by a health insurance issuer or HMO with respect to a group health plan) to the plan sponsor, to the extent that the requirements of §164.504(f) of this subchapter apply and are met.
  - (iii) A government agency, with respect to determining eligibility for, or enrollment in, a government health plan that provides public benefits and is administered by another government agency, or collecting protected health information for such purposes, to the extent such activities are authorized by law.
  - (iv) A covered entity participating in an organized health care arrangement that performs a function or activity as described by paragraph (1)(i) of this definition for or on behalf of such organized health care arrangement, or that provides a service as described in paragraph (1)(ii) of this definition to or for such organized health care arrangement by virtue of such activities or services.

Health information is considered to be used when it is "shared" within a healthcare entity, and it is considered to be "disclosed" when it is shared outside that entity. Disclosure of confidential health information may be either required or permitted. A covered entity must disclose PHI (a) to individuals (or their personal representatives) specifically when they request access to, or an accounting of disclosures of, their PHI and (b) to HHS in the event of compliance investigation or review or enforcement action [45] (*see* Chap. 12, The Implications of False Claims, Stark, and Anti-Kickback Laws). Covered entities are permitted, but not required, to disclose PHI, even absent an individual's authorization, in the following instances [46]:

(1) To the individual
(2) Treatment, payment, and healthcare operations:

Treatment is defined as "the provision, coordination, or management of health care and related services for an individual by one or more health care providers, including consultation between providers regarding a patient and referral of a patient by one provider to another." [47] *Payment* is defined to address the "activities of a health plan to obtain premiums, determine or fulfill responsibilities for coverage and provision of benefits, and furnish or obtain reimbursement for health care delivered to an individual and activities of a health care provider to obtain payment or be reimbursed for the provision of health care to an individual." [47] *Healthcare operations* are defined to include any of the following activities: (a) quality assessment and improvement activities, including case management and care coordination; (b) competency assurance activities, including provider or health plan performance evaluation, credentialing, and accreditation; (c) conducting or arranging for medical reviews, audits, or legal services, including fraud and abuse detection and compliance programs; (d) specified insurance functions, such as underwriting, risk rating, and reinsuring risk; (e) business planning, development, management, and administration; and (f) business management and general administrative activities of the entity, including but not limited to de-identifying protected health information, creating a limited data set, and certain fundraising for the benefit of the covered entity [47].

(3) Opportunity to agree or object:

Informal permission is obtained either explicitly, or through the operation of, circumstances that clearly give the individual the opportunity to agree, acquiesce, or object. These situations will occur in the case of facility directories, wherein healthcare facilities will maintain a directory of patients and their contact information. In such cases the facility or provider inquire about the individual by name, and providers may also disclose religious affiliation to clergy [48].

(4) Incident to an otherwise permitted use and disclosure

(5) Public interest and benefit activities:

The Privacy Rule permits use and disclosure of PHI, without an individual's authorization or permission, for 12 "national priority" purposes [49]:

(a) *Required by Law*: such as by statute, regulation, or court order [50].
(b) *Public Health Activities*: in the event of "(1) public health authorities authorized by law to collect or receive such information for preventing or controlling disease, injury, or disability and to public health or other government authorities authorized to receive reports of child abuse and neglect; (2) entities subject to FDA regulation regarding FDA regulated products or activities for purposes such as adverse event reporting, tracking of products, product recalls, and postmarketing surveillance; (3) individuals who may have contracted or been exposed to a communicable disease when notification is authorized by law; and (4) employers, regarding employees, when requested by employers, for information concerning a work-related illness or injury or workplace related medical surveillance, because such information is needed by the employer to comply with the Occupational Safety and Health Administration (OHSA), the Mine Safety and Health Administration (MHSA), or similar state law" [51].
(c) *Victims of Abuse, Neglect, or Domestic Violence*.

(d) *Health Oversight Activities*: "such as audits and investigations necessary for oversight of the health care system and government benefit programs" [52].
(e) *Judicial and Administrative Proceedings*: "if the request for the information is through an order from a court or administrative tribunal. Such information may also be disclosed in response to a subpoena or other lawful process if certain assurances regarding notice to the individual or a protective order are provided" [53].
(f) *Law Enforcement Purposes*: Covered entities may disclose protected health information to law enforcement officials for law enforcement purposes under the following six circumstances and subject to specified conditions:

   i. "as required by law (including court orders, court-ordered warrants, subpoenas) and administrative requests;
   ii. to identify or locate a suspect, fugitive, material witness, or missing person;
   iii. in response to a law enforcement official's request for information about a victim or suspected victim of a crime;
   iv. to alert law enforcement of a person's death, if the covered entity suspects that criminal activity caused the death;
   v. when a covered entity believes that protected health information is evidence of a crime that occurred on its premises; and,
   vi. by a covered health care provider in a medical emergency not occurring on its premises, when necessary to inform law enforcement about the commission and nature of a crime, the location of the crime or crime victims, and the perpetrator of the crime" [54].

   Furthermore, the authorization to use or disclose psychotherapy notes must be specific with some specific exceptions, including, "to avert a serious and imminent threat to public health or safety…" [55].

(6) Limited data set for the purposes of research, public health, or healthcare operations: used and disclosed for research, healthcare operations, and public health purposes, provided the recipient enters into a data use agreement promising specified safeguards for the protected health information within the limited data set. HIPPA makes exceptions regarding the use of PHI for research. HIPAA defines "research" as "a systematic investigation, including research development, testing, and evaluation, designed to develop or contribute to generalizable knowledge" [47]. HIPAA regulations protect only that health information which is individually identifiable (PHI). Generally, appropriately de-identified patient data can be used or shared without restrictions in situations such as clinical research, organizational strategic planning, and epidemiologic research. De-identified data refers to aggregate statistical data stripped of individual identifiers.

In addition, even the use of PHI may be used internally within institutions (covered entities) to facilitate or optimize healthcare operations, provided that the information is not disseminated. Thus, PHI may generally be used internally within organizations, without authorization, in the course of operational, financial, or strategic planning, competency assurance, credentialing and accreditation, medical reviews, or legal services and to manage compliance programs.

HIPAA also differentiates between the terms "consent" which refers to a broad general permission that is granted by the individual to a "covered entity" to use or disclose PHI for treatment, payment, or healthcare operations and "authorization" which refers to more specific and detailed permission to share PHI. The request and the consent and authorization to release individually identifiable health information for any purpose must therefore be to express, in plain language and specify the information to be disclosed, the person(s) disclosing and those receiving the information, the expiration of the consent to disclose, and the right to revoke in writing. Authorization for the release of PHI must be documented in writing. A sample authorization form is included at the end of this chapter.

Arguably, HIPAA makes allowances for professional ethics and best judgment may guide the permissive uses and disclosures of PHI. Clinicians must often access PHI medical in critical and emergency treatment situations where a documented consent cannot be obtained in a timely fashion. In such cases, the provider must nonetheless obtain consent as soon as it is reasonably possible to do so. Thus, the Privacy Rule does not absolutely mandate that information not be shared without consent in all circumstances; rather, that disclosure of information should be "incident to" medical justification. Permissible reasonable use or disclosure of PHI therefore permitted in degrees, as long as the provider uses reasonable safeguards to inappropriate disclosure, and that information shared is limited to the "minimum necessary" information necessary under the clinical circumstances, often referred to as the "minimum necessary" standard for PHI disclosure.

The HIPAA Security Rule

The HIPAA Security Rule, published in 2003, mandates administrative, physical, and technical safeguards to ensure the confidentiality, integrity, and security of electronic PHI (ePHI). Thus, the Security Rule specifically applies to and protects a subset of medical record information that is covered in the Privacy Rule; the Security Rule applies to individually identifiable health information that a covered entity creates, receives, maintains, or transmits in electronic form. The Security Rule defines "confidentiality" to mean that e-PHI is not made available or disclosed to unauthorized persons. The Security Rule applies to health plans, healthcare clearinghouses, and to any healthcare provider who transmits health information in electronic form in connection with a transaction for which the Secretary of HHS has adopted standards under HIPAA (the "covered entities"); the HITECH Act of 2009 (see below) expanded the responsibilities of "business associates" under the HIPAA Security Rule. Failure to meet security standards risks both civil and criminal penalties under HIPAA but also incurs potential civil liability under private causes of action initiated by plaintiffs, or their representatives, under state tort, privacy contract, and consumer protection laws and also under state heath oversight statutes.

A key mandate of the HIPAA Security Rule is the mandate for a program of ongoing risk analysis and a program for risk management. Ideally, the risk analysis and management program of any institutions should be included in its HIPAA compliance plan. An entity's security and compliance program are subject to federal scrutiny, on demand, at any time. The risk analysis process should include, at least, (a) an assessment and evaluation of the likelihood and impact of potential risks to e-PHI; (b) the implementation of appropriate security measures to address the risks identified in the risk analysis; (c) documentation of the rationale for choosing the security measures adopted; and (d) a program of continuous, reasonable, and appropriate security assessment [56]. Under the Security Rule, the requisite safeguards to ensure the integrity of ePHI are (1) administrative safeguards; (2) physical safeguards; and (3) technical safeguards.

Administrative safeguards are those administrative actions and policies and procedures which are enacted to protect eHPI. These safeguards focus on the policies and procedures designed to prevent, detect, contain, and correct security violations. The general elements of administrative safeguards, under HIPAA, are (1) the designation of a security official who is responsible for developing and implementing its security policies and procedures; (2) access management through policies and procedures for authorizing "role-based access" within an entity; (3) workforce training and management through authorization and supervision, and policies for sanctions against workforce members who fail to comply with, or violate, security policies and procedures; and (4) periodic assessment of the efficacy of existing security policies and procedures [57]; these may include, for example, audit logs, access reports, and security incident tracking reports.

The Security Rule also includes a contingency plan as a standard under administrative safeguards. Entities must protect the integrity of ePHI through contingency plans designed to maintain access to potentially critical ePHI required for medical care in the event of a catastrophe. Contingency planning is often managed under business continuity planning (BCP) and disaster recovery planning (DRP) which are the overall processes to ensure data backup, disaster recovery, emergency operations [58]. Additionally, entities must develop and implement (1) procedures and policies regarding periodic testing and revision of contingency plans and (2) an assessment of the relative criticality of specific data management applications.

Physical safeguards include (1) limitation of physical access to the facilities while ensuring authorized access as needed and (2) training, education, and policies and procedures which specify proper use of and access to workstations and electronic media. Covered entities must also develop and implement policies and procedures regarding the transfer, removal, disposal, and re-use of electronic media [59]. Entities must also be able to timely identify and respond to suspected or known security incidents, mitigate the potential harm of known security, and develop a system to document the nature of security incidents and their impact. In addition, good monitoring of the efficacy of physical safeguards might include (a) regular updates, education, and reminders; (b) procedures for guarding against, detecting, and reporting malicious software such as malware, hacking, Trojan horses, or viruses; (c) continuous monitoring of failed log-in attempts and password discrepancies; and (d) policies and schedules for creating, changing, and safeguarding passwords.

Technical safeguards include (1) technical policies and procedures for the restriction of access to authorized persons; (2) audit controls; (3) integrity controls; and (4) transmission security while e-PHI is transmitted over an electronic network [60].

The HIPAA Enforcement Rule

Enforcement of the Privacy Rule became effective in 2003; and the enforcement of the Security Rule became effective in 2005. The Office for Civil Rights (OCR), within HHS, is responsible for investigating and enforcing the Privacy and Security Rules; and OCR refers to cases and may collaborate with the Department of Justice (DOJ) to investigate criminal violations of HIPAA. In general, the OCR investigates complaints; however, the OCR may also conduct random compliance reviews to review compliance plans. A complaint must allege an activity which, if proven, would violate the Privacy or Security Rule. Such complaints must be filed within 180 days of when the person submitting the complaint knew or should have known about the alleged violation of the Privacy or Security Rule.

In general, a HIPAA violation occurs when a HIPAA-covered entity fails to adhere to, or violates, one or more of provisions of the HIPAA Privacy, Security, or Breach Notification Rules. CMPs for HIPAA violations are assessed based on a tiered civil penalty structure (Table 13.1):

- Tier 1: The covered entity was unaware of the HIPAA violation and, through reasonable due diligence, could not have known of a HIPAA violation.
- Tier 2: Through the exercise of its reasonable due diligence, the covered entity knew or reasonably should have known of, but could not have reasonably prevented a HIPAA violation.
- Tier 3: Willful neglect of HIPAA Rules with correction of the violation within 30 days of discovery.
- Tier 4: Willful neglect of HIPAA Rules, where no efforts have been made to correct the violation within 30 days of discovery.

For the purposes of HIPAA violations, the following definitions apply:

1. "Reasonable cause" is defined as "an act or omission in which a covered entity or business associate knew, or by exercising reasonable diligence would have known, that the act or omission violated an administrative simplification provision, but in which the covered entity or business associate did not act with willful neglect."
2. "Reasonable diligence" is defined as "the business care and prudence expected from a person seeking to satisfy a legal requirement under similar circumstances."
3. 'Willful neglect' is defined to mean "conscious, intentional failure or reckless indifference to the obligation to comply with the administrative simplification provision violated" [61].

Table 13.2 Criminal penalties under HIPAA

Culpability category	Penalty
Knowingly	$ 50,000 + 1 year prison
False pretenses	Up to $ 50,000 + 5 years prison
Intent for monetary gain	Restitution + up to $ 250,000 + 10 years prison

In addition to CMPs, HHS has the authority to exclude entities and/or providers from participation in federally funded payment programs, such as Medicare and potentially Medicaid.

Criminal actions for HIPAA violations are investigated and prosecuted by the DOJ. For the purposes of criminal prosecutions under HIPAA, the term "knowingly" requires only that the entity has knowledge of the actions that constitute an offense; there is no requirement that the entity actually or specifically know that the actions are in violation of the HIPAA statute.

There are three tiers of criminal penalties for HIPAA (Table 13.2):

- Tier 1: Reasonable cause or no knowledge of violation – a maximum of 1 year in jail
- Tier 2: Obtaining PHI under false pretenses – a maximum of 5 years in jail
- Tier 3: Obtaining PHI for personal gain or with malicious intent – a maximum of 10 years in jail

In addition to HIPAA violations through the unauthorized disclosure of ePHI, the OCR may impose CMPs for HIPAA noncompliance, in instances where no breach of PHI occurred but the entity has failed to develop and implement a compliance program. Key compliance program risks are (1) failure to complete a comprehensive, organization-wide risk assessment and (2) failure to execute business associate agreements (BAAs).

Health Information Technology for Economic and Clinical Health Act of 2009 (HITECH)

The Health Information Technology for Economic and Clinical Health (HITECH) Act of 2009 [63] was enacted as part of the American Recovery and Reinvestment Act of 2009 (ARRA) [64]. HITECH built upon the foundation of HIPAA to expand the adoption of, and the leverage of information (as opposed to data entry) capabilities of EHRs, together with enhanced access, privacy, and security provisions for PHI management (Table 13.3).

Within the HHS, two agencies, the CMS and the Office of the National Coordinator for Health Information Technology (ONC), collaborated to coordinate the operationalization of the HITECH Act, together defining meaningful use criteria and EHR certification criteria. EHR certification criteria (defined by the ONC) specified the requisite functional (the what) criteria for a certified EMR, whereas the meaningful use criteria (defined by CMS) specified the operational (the how) criteria of a certified EHR system.

Table 13.3 Key provisions of the HITECH Act relating to HIPAA privacy and security provisions

Area of regulation	Provision
Civil monetary penalties	Increase in the minimum penalty for each violation of HIPAA rules; increasing to up to $50,000 per violation and a maximum of $1.5 million for all annual repeat violation of the same provision
Use and disclosure of PHI	Prohibits the sale of PHI without a signed authorization
Breach notification	Mandatory HIPAA/PHI breach notification requirements imposed on covered entities and business associates
Business associate liability	Application of HIPAA compliance requirements to business associates
Meaningful use	

HITECH Breach Reporting Requirement

The first rule within HITECH, published by the HHS OCR in 2009, addressed notification requirements in the event of a breach of unsecured PHI and mandated the notification of affected individuals in the event that a security breach when "unsecure PHI" is disclosed or used for an unauthorized purpose [65]. A breach is defined as an impermissible use or disclosure under the Privacy Rule that compromises the security or privacy of the protected health information. The breach reporting requirement requires healthcare providers and other HIPAA covered entities to promptly notify affected individuals of a breach, as well as the HHS secretary and prominent media outlets, in the form of a press release, to media serving the state or jurisdiction in cases where a breach affects more than 500 individuals [66].

There are three exceptions to the definition of "breach":

(1) The unintentional acquisition, access, or use of protected health information by a workforce member or person acting under the authority of a covered entity or business associate, if such acquisition, access, or use was made in good faith and within the scope of authority.
(2) The inadvertent disclosure of protected health information by a person authorized to access protected health information at a covered entity or business associate to another person authorized to access protected health information at the covered entity or business associate or organized healthcare arrangement in which the covered entity participates. In both cases, the information cannot be further used or disclosed in a manner not permitted by the Privacy Rule.
(3) If the covered entity or business associate has a good faith belief that the unauthorized person to whom the impermissible disclosure was made, would not have been able to retain the information [67].

Under HITECH, "unsecured PHI" essentially means "unencrypted PHI."

Meaningful Use

The second rule, published by the HHS CMS in 2009, addressed incentive payments available under the Medicare and Medicaid programs for hospitals, physicians, and other healthcare providers who qualified as "meaningful users" of EHRs [68]. HITECH provided financial incentives to "eligible professionals" for the meaningful use of certified qualified electronic health records (EHRs) beginning in 2011 and penalties for failure to achieve meaningful use after 2015 [69].

Through focusing on the effective use of EHRs with certain capabilities, the HITECH Act makes clear that the adoption of records is not a goal in itself: it is the use of EHRs to achieve health and efficiency goals that matter. HITECH's incentives and assistance programs seek to improve the health of Americans and the performance of their healthcare system through "meaningful use" of EHRs to achieve five health care goals:

- To improve the quality, safety, and efficiency of care while reducing disparities
- To engage patients and families in their care
- To promote public and population health
- To improve care coordination
- To promote the privacy and security of EHRs [70]

"Meaningful Use" incentive payments were conditioned by CMS upon the demonstration of the (1) use of certified EHR technology in a demonstrably meaningful manner, for example, e-prescribing; (2) the use of certified EHR technology so as to facilitate the exchange of electronic health data and information so as to improve the quality of healthcare, such as promoting care coordination; and (3) the use of certified EHR technology to report clinical quality measures (CQM) and other measures selected by the HHS secretary [71]. The Meaningful Use program consisted of three stages:

- Stage 1 Meaningful Use established basic requirements for the electronic capture of clinical data, including providing patients with electronic copies of their PHI.
- Stage 2 Meaningful Use expanded on Stage 1 criteria with a focus on advancing clinical processes and ensuring that the meaningful use of EHRs supported the aims and priorities of the national quality strategy. Stage 2 criteria encouraged the use of CEHRT for continuous quality improvement at the point of care and the exchange of information in the most structured format possible.
- Stage 3 Meaningful Use established in 2017, focused on using CEHRT to improve health outcomes [72].

In order to comply with meaningful use of certified EHR technology as defined by CMS, providers must report on a combination of required core objectives, objectives selected from a menu set, and reporting of CQMs as specified by HHS [73]. In 2018, eligible healthcare professionals (EPs) or eligible clinicians (ECs) who had been participating in the Medicare Promoting Interoperability Program (MPIP) were required to report using the quality payment program (QPP) measures; also in 2018, CMS renamed the EHR incentive programs as the promoting interoperability programs.

Certification Criteria for EHR Technology

The third rule, published by the HHS ONC, developed certification criteria for EHR technology. The ONC is charged with the development and coordination of a nationwide health information technology (HIT) strategy and policy and the promotion of a nationwide HIT infrastructure for the management of electronic health information. The ONC was created by the HITECH Act and is a division HHS was created by Executive Order in 2004.

The third rule identified the functional and technical capabilities that the EHR technology and systems must possess:

> ...certification criteria establish the required capabilities and specify the related standards and implementation specifications that serve as an electronic health record (EHR) technology will need to include to, at a minimum, support the achievement of meaningful use Stage 1 by eligible professionals, eligible hospitals, and/or critical access hospitals...under the Medicare and Medicaid EHRs Incentive Programs. [74]

The following definitions were applied to certified EHR technology:

(1) A Complete EHR that meets the requirements included in the definition of a Qualified EHR and has been tested and certified in accordance with the certification program established by the National Coordinator as having met all applicable certification criteria adopted by the Secretary; or
(2) A combination of EHR Modules in which each constituent EHR Module of the combination has been tested and certified in accordance with the certification program established by the National Coordinator as having met all applicable certification criteria adopted by the Secretary, and the resultant combination also meets the requirements included in the definition of a Qualified EHR.

Where a "Complete EHR means EHR technology that has been developed to meet, at a minimum, all applicable certification criteria adopted by the Secretary" [74].

Business Associates and the Privacy and Security Provisions of HITECH

The privacy and security provisions of HIPPA were directly applicable to "covered entities," defined in HIPAA as healthcare payers, providers, and clearinghouses; business associates were indirectly, but not directly, bound to the HIPAA provisions. In HIPAA, the Privacy Rule required nonemployee "business associates" whose relationships with "covered entities" required the sharing of PHI to establish a "chain of trust partner agreement" now referred to as a "business associate agreement." HIPAA required the "business associate" to:

(1) Implement administrative, physical, and technical safeguards that reasonably and appropriately protect the confidentiality, integrity, and availability of the "covered entity's EHPI
(2) Ensure that its agents, and subcontractors, to whom it provides EHPI agree to implement reasonable and appropriate safeguards to protect it
(3) Report to the covered entity any security incident of which it becomes aware
(4) Ensure that the contract authorizes unilateral termination of the agreement if the business associate has violated a material contractual term

Although the BAA was less prominent in HIPAAA, the HITECH Act directly applied HIPAA provisions directly to business associates, mandating that covered entities establish contractual agreements with every business associate, known as business associate agreements (BAAs). Failure to have BAAs is considered a serious compliance violation under HITECH and cause for OCR disciplinary proceedings.

HIPAA Violation Fines Can Also Be Issued by State Attorneys General

Under the HITECH Act as of 2009, state attorneys general (SAGs) are empowered to hold HIPAA-covered entities accountable for the exposure of the PHI of state residents and initiate separate civil actions for PHI disclosure violations [75]. HITECH extends HIPAA violation fines to the states with a minimum fine of $100 per violation to a maximum level of $25,000 per violation category, per calendar year. Furthermore, a covered entity that sustains a data breach affecting residents of multiple states may be fined for HIPAA violation penalties by SAGs in multiple states. OCR developed HIPAA enforcement training in order to educate and train SAG and their staff enforce the HIPAA Privacy and Security Rules. Enhanced collaboration and enforcement coordination between the OCR and the SAGs will allow the OCR to assist SAG in the exercise of this new enforcement authority through the sharing of breach information regarding pending or concluded OCR actions against covered entities or business associates related to SAG investigations, and the OCR will also provide SAGs guidance regarding the HIPAA statute, the HITECH Act, and the HIPAA Privacy, Security, and Enforcement Rules as well as the Breach Notification Rule as needed to effectively prosecute these cases on a state level. The implication to providers is that the HITECH Act increases the potential liability for healthcare information privacy breaches by an additional layer, above and beyond the HIPAA and HITECH CMP fines, state disciplinary procedures, and private civil causes of action, potential criminal liability, and potential CMS exclusion.

References

1. Merriam-Webster Dictionary. Available online at: https://www.merriam-webster.com/dictionary/privacy.
2. Merriam-Webster Dictionary. Available online at: https://www.merriam-webster.com/legal/right%20of%20privacy.
3. Griswold v. Connecticut. 381 U.S. 479. (1965).
4. Olmstead v. U. S. 277 U.S. 438. (1928). Justice Brandeis's dissent at 61, 72, and 73.
5. Warren S, Brandeis LD. The right to privacy. Harvard Law Rev. 1890;4(193)
6. Prosser Restatement of the Law, Second, Torts, § 652. The American Law Institute. 1977.
7. Prosser, *supra* at § 652B Intrusion Upon Seclusion.
8. Prosser, *supra* at § 652C Appropriation of Name or Likeness.
9. Prosser, supra at § 652D Publicity Given to Private Life.
10. Bruce A. McKenna, False Light: Invasion of Privacy, 15 Tulsa L. J. 113 (2013).
11. Urs Gasser. Recoding privacy law: reflections on the future relationship among law, technology, and privacy. Harvard Law Rev. 2016;130(2)
12. Becker M. Privacy in the digital age: comparing and contrasting individual versus social approaches towards privacy. Ethics Inform Technol. 2019;21:307–17.
13. Szalados JE. Digital distraction and legal risk. In: Bertman S, Papadakos PJ, editors. Distracted doctoring: returning to patient-centered care in the digital age. Cham: Springer; 2017.
14. Edna Selan Epstein. The attorney-client privilege and the work-product doctrine. American Bar Association, Section of Litigation. Chicago. 2017.
15. Prichard v. United States, 181 F.2d 326 (6th Cir. 1950), aff'd 339 U.S. 974, 70 S. Ct. 1029, 94 L. Ed. 1380 (1950).
16. United States v. Grand Jury Investigation, 401 F. Supp. 361 (W.D. Pa. 1975).
17. Cathryn MS. The application of the attorney-client privilege to communications between lawyers within the same firm: Evaluating United States v. Rowe, 30 ARIZ. ST. L. J. 859, 859. 1998.
18. 8 Wigmore on Evidence §2292, at 554 (McNaughton ed. 1961).
19. Togstad v. Vesely, 291 N.W.2d 686 (1980).
20. Upjohn Co. v. United States, 449 U.S. 383, 389 (1981).
21. Paul RR. Attorney-client privilege: continuing confusion about attorney communications, drafts, pre-existing documents, and the source of the facts communicated, 48 AM. U. L. REV. 967, 969–70. 1999.
22. The Editors of Encyclopaedia Britannica. Hippocratic oath. Available online at: https://www.britannica.com/topic/Hippocratic-oath.
23. Witherell v. Weimer, 421 NE2d 869 (1981).
24. The Privacy Act of 1974 (Pub.L. 93–579, 88 Stat. 1896, enacted December 31, 1974. 5 U.S.C. § 552a.
25. U.S. Department of Justice. Office of Privacy and Civil Liberties. Overview of the Privacy Act of 1974. Online at: https://www.justice.gov/opcl/introduction.
26. Joint Commission on Accreditation of Healthcare Organizations. Medical Record Services (MR). Accreditation Manual for Hospitals. Chicago; 1990.
27. Thacker SB. Historical development. In: Lee LM, Teutsch SM, Thacker SB, St. Louis ME, editors. Principles and practice of public health surveillance. 3rd ed. New York: Oxford University Press; 2010. p. 1–17.
28. Lee LM, Heilig CM, White A. Ethical justification for conducting public health surveillance without patient consent. Am J Public Health. 2012;102(1):38–44.
29. Tarasoff v. Regents of the University of California. S.F. 23042. December 23, 1974.
30. Tarasoff v. Regents of University of California (1976) 17 Cal.3d 425,434–436, 131 Cal.Rptr. 14, 551 P.2d 334.
31. Kachigian C, Felthous AR. Court responses to Tarasoff statutes. J Am Acad Psychiatry Law. 2004;32(3):263–73.

32. Szalados JE. Health information privacy and HIPPA: the health insurance portability and accountability act. Curr Rev Clin Anesth. 2004;25(1):3–14.
33. CMS. Complying with Medical Record Documentation Requirements. Available online at: https://www.cms.gov/Outreach-and-Education/Medicare-Learning-Network-MLN/MLNProducts/Downloads/CERTMedRecDoc-FactSheet-ICN909160.pdf.
34. NCQA. Guidelines for Medical Record Documentation. Available online at: https://www.ncqa.org/wp-content/uploads/2018/07/20180110_Guidelines_Medical_Record_Documentation.pdf.
35. HCPro. Know the JCAHO's ongoing records review requirements. Available online at: https://www.hcpro.com/HIM-53615-865/Know-the-JCAHOs-ongoing-records-review-requirements.html.
36. New York Codes, Rules and Regulations. Title 10, Chapter V, Subchapter A, Article 2, Part 405, Section 405.10 - Medical records. Available online at: https://regs.health.ny.gov/content/section-40510-medical-records. 42 CFR § 485.638.
37. Condition of participation: Medical record services. 42 CFR § 482.24(b)(1) and 42 CFR § 485.638(c); Conditions of participation: Clinical records. 42 CFR § 485.638.
38. *See, for example*, American Health Information Management Association, Retention and Destruction of Health Information. Available online at: https://library.ahima.org/PB/RetentionDestruction#.XvDx6mhKiUk.
39. Health Insurance Portability and Accountability Act of 1996. Pub. L. No. 104–191, 100 Stat. 1396; as codified at 45 CFR § 160 et seq. (2000); and as amended.
40. Institute of Medicine. Crossing the quality chasm: a new system for the 21st century. Washington DC: National Academy Press; 2001.
41. HIPAA. 45 C.F.R. § 160.203; and 45 C.F.R. § 160.202.
42. HIPAA. 45 CFR Part 160 and Subparts A and E of Part 164. The Privacy Rule; and as updated; *See also* US Department of Health and Human Services, HHS. The HIPAA Privacy Rule. Available online at: https://www.hhs.gov/hipaa/for-professionals/privacy/index.html.
43. Family Educational Rights and Privacy Act 20 U.S.C. §1232g.
44. HIPAA. 45 CFR §160.103. See supra. Definitions. "Health Information".
45. HIPAA. 45 C.F.R. § 164.502(a)(2).
46. HIPAA. 45 C.F.R. § 164.502(a)(1).
47. HIPAA. 45 C.F.R. § 164.501.
48. HIPAA 45 C.F.R. § 164.510(a).
49. HIPAA. See 45 C.F.R. § 164.512.
50. HIPAA. 45 C.F.R. § 164.512(a).
51. HIPAA. 45 C.F.R. § 164.512(b).
52. HIPPA. 45 C.F.R. § 164.512(d).
53. HIPAA. 45 C.F.R. § 164.512(e).
54. HIPPA. 45 C.F.R. § 164.512(f).
55. HIPAA. 45 C.F.R. § 164.501. "Psychotherapy notes" means notes recorded (in any medium) by a health care provider who is a mental health professional documenting or analyzing the contents of conversation during a private counseling session or a group, joint, or family counseling session and that are separated from the rest of the of the individual's medical record. Psychotherapy notes excludes medication prescription and monitoring, counseling session start and stop times, the modalities and frequencies of treatment furnished, results of clinical tests, and any summary of the following items: diagnosis, functional status, the treatment plan, symptoms, prognosis, and progress to date. See also HIPAA. 45 C.F.R. § 164.508(a)(2).
56. HIPAA [8] 45 C.F.R. § 164.306(b)(iv); 45 C.F.R. § 164.308(a)(1)(ii)(B); 45 C.F.R. § 164.306(d)(3)(ii)(B)(1); 45 C.F.R. § 164.316(b)(1); and 45 C.F.R. § 164.306(e).
57. HIPAA. 45 C.F.R. § 164.308(a)(2); 45 C.F.R. § 164.308(a)(4)(i); 45 C.F.R. § 164.308(a)(3) & (4); 45 C.F.R. § 164.308(a)(5)(i); 45 C.F.R. § 164..308(a)(1)(ii)(C); and 45 C.F.R. § 164.308(a)(8).
58. HIPAA. 164.308(a)(7)(i); 164.308(a)(7)(ii)(A)-(E).

59. HIPAA. 45 C.F.R. § 164.310(a); 45 C.F.R. §§ 164.310(b) & (c); and 45 C.F.R. § 164.310(d).
60. HIPAA. 45 C.F.R. § 164.312(a); 45 C.F.R. § 164.312(b); 45 C.F.R. § 164.312(c); 45 C.F.R. § 164.312(e).
61. HIPAA 45 CFR §160.401 Definitions.
62. HIPAA. 45 CFR §160.404 Amount of a civil money penalty.
63. Health Information Technology for Economic and Clinical Health (HITECH) Act, Title XIII of Division A and Title IV of Division B of the American Recovery and Reinvestment Act of 2009 (ARRA), Pub. L. No. 111-5, 123 Stat. 226 (Feb. 17, 2009) (full-text), codified at 42 U.S.C. §§300jj et seq.; §§17901 et seq.
64. American Recovery and Reinvestment Act (ARRA) of 2009, Pub. L. No. 111-5, 123 Stat. 115, 516 (Feb. 19, 2009).
65. U.S. Department of Health and Human Services, Breach Notification for Unsecured Protected Health Information, Interim final rule with request for comments. 45 CFR Parts 160 and 164, Federal Register 74, August 24, 2009; p. 42740.
66. HHS. HITECH Breach Notification Interim Final Rule. 2013. Available online at: https://www.hhs.gov/hipaa/for-professionals/breach-notification/laws-regulations/final-rule-update/hitech/index.html.
67. HIPAA Breach Notification Rule, 45 CFR §§ 164.400-414. See also, Breach Notification Rule. HHS. Available online at: https://www.hhs.gov/hipaa/for-professionals/breach-notification/index.html.
68. Medicare and Medicaid Programs: Electronic Health Record Incentive Program. Federal Register 75, January 13, 2010; p. 1844. The proposed regulations will be located mainly at new part 495 of title 42 of the Code of Federal Regulations. Amendments are also proposed for parts 412, 413, and 422 of title 42.
69. HITECH Act of 2009, 42 USC sec 139w-4(0)(2) (February 2009), sec 13301, subtitle B: Incentives for the Use of Health Information Technology.
70. CMS. Newsroom. CMS and ONC final regulations define meaningful use and set standards for electronic health record incentive program. 2010. Available online at: https://www.cms.gov/newsroom/fact-sheets/cms-and-onc-final-regulations-define-meaningful-use-and-set-standards-electronic-health-record.
71. ARRA Title IV Subtitle A § 4101(a) (adding new section 1848(o)(2)(A) to the Social Security Act), 42 U.S.C.A. § 1395w-4 (West, Westlaw through March 2010).
72. Centers for Disease Control and Prevention. CDC. Public Health and Promoting Interoperability Programs (formerly, known as Electronic Health Records Meaningful Use). 2019. Available online at: https://www.cdc.gov/ehrmeaningfuluse/introduction.html.
73. Centers for Medicare and Medicaid services. Medicare and Medicaid EHR incentive program: Meaningful use stage 1 requirements overview. 2010. Available online at: https://www.cms.gov/EHRIncentivePrograms/Downloads/MU_Stage1_ReqOverview.pdf.
74. Health information technology: initial set of standards, implementation specifications, and certification criteria for electronic health record technology. Final rule. Office of the National Coordinator for Health Information Technology (ONC), Department of Health and Human Services. Fed Regist. 2010; 75(144):44589–654.
75. HITECH Act (Section 13410(e) (1)).

Chapter 14
The Legal and Regulatory Components of Tele-ICU Care

Mario V. Fusaro, Christian Becker, Daniel Miller, Zohair Ahmed Al Aseri, and Corey Scurlock

Introduction

Intensive care physician staffing will continue to decline relative to the population over the next decade [1]. Combating this shortfall in intensive care unit (ICU) staffing will require both training of new physicians and increased efficiency with which ICU services are delivered. Telemedicine services have increased over the past decade with Tele-ICU being one of the most important. As of 2011, more than 40 Tele-ICU central modules have been started [2]. Since its inception, Tele-ICU services have expanded physician coverage throughout the United States. The effect on mortality [3], length of stay, ICU-related complications [4–7], and costs [2, 8, 9] have been extensively reported [10, 11]. Once implemented, a multitude of centers have reported substantial decreases in costs per ICU case as well increased case contribution margins [12]. Additionally, Tele-ICU can affect the frequency of

M. V. Fusaro (✉) · C. Becker · D. Miller
eHealth Center, Westchester Medical Center Health Network, Taylor Pavilion, Valhalla, NY, USA

Department of Medicine, Division of Pulmonary, Critical Care and Sleep Medicine, Westchester Medical Center and New York Medical College, Valhalla, NY, USA
e-mail: Mario.Fusaro@wmchealth.org

Z. A. Al Aseri
Departments of Emergency Medicine and Critical Care, College of Medicine, King Saud University, Riyadh, Saudi Arabia

C. Scurlock
eHealth Center, Westchester Medical Center Health Network, Taylor Pavilion, Valhalla, NY, USA

Department of Medicine, Division of Pulmonary, Critical Care and Sleep Medicine, Westchester Medical Center and New York Medical College, Valhalla, NY, USA

Department of Anesthesiology, Westchester Medical Center and New York Medical College, Valhalla, NY, USA

J. E. Szalados (ed.), *The Medical-Legal Aspects of Acute Care Medicine*,
https://doi.org/10.1007/978-3-030-68570-6_14

interhospital transfers [13]. Infrequently discussed are the potential effects on other important clinical, reputational, and financial endpoints from a medical-legal standpoint. Becker et al. have recently published a two-part series examining several important legal aspects of Tele-ICU care [14, 15].

Reimbursement

The reported implementation costs of a Tele-ICU core facility and ICU bed installation ranges from $1,000,000 to $7,000,000 with yearly operating costs ranging between $3,100,000 and $3,400,000 [3]. These figures require a robust business plan be in place to ensure financial survival and maximize institutional benefit. In the past, Tele-ICU programs have been largely justified in a financial sense by reducing the cost of ICU operations [16, 17]. This has included reductions in length of stay, pharmacy spending, radiology use, staffing, and complications. As more studies have been published, Tele-ICU has been noted to safely reduce hospital transfers allowing smaller institutions to keep more reimbursement [13, 18]. In addition to reducing expenses, increases in contribution margins have also been noted by both improvements in billing capture as well as increased volumes with increased ICU coordination in the form of command centers [19]. The financial benefits in these instances are secondary in nature and not the result of direct billing. Medicare, Medicaid, and other third-party payers are beginning to reimburse for more telemedicine services each year (Table 14.1).

Medicare

The guidelines for Medicare reimbursement as they relate to telemedicine are described by The Centers for Medicare and Medicaid Services (CMS). For services to be considered a substitution for an in-person encounter and thus billable under

Table 14.1 Telemedicine reimbursement overview

Medicare	The overall structure requires an "originating site," "distant site practitioners," an audiovisual communication platform, and a specific set of billable codes
Medicaid	CMS allows the individual states to describe and institute their respective laws governing Medicaid reimbursement. Additionally, physicians can utilize stored audiovisual transmissions as well as real-time feeds as qualifying visits. A separate originating location fee is payable for real-time encounters in some states
Private payers	Similar to Medicaid rules, each state has different laws governing the reimbursement of telemedicine services. Each insurer can create their own policies within the context of the law to dictate reimbursement. Telemedicine parity laws dictate whether an insurance company needs to cover telemedicine as in-person visits

Medicare, certain prerequisite conditions must be met. These guidelines are updated yearly to reflect needs and current practices. The overall structure requires an "originating site," "distant site practitioners," an audiovisual communication platform, and a specific set of billable codes [20].

An "originating site" is defined by US law as a site where a Medicare beneficiary goes to get their healthcare services in either a Health Professional Shortage Area (HPSA) or outside of a metropolitan statistical area (MSA). A HPSA is a location (zip code) designated by the Health Resources and Services Administration (HRSA) as a place where a shortage of healthcare provider services relative to the overall population exists. Authorized originating sites include traditional hospitals, critical access hospitals, physician offices, and many other outpatient sites. The site may also be eligible for a separate facility fee. Patients cannot use their home as an originating site in most cases. The provider need not be in a specific location as long as the provider type is physician, nurse practitioner, physician assistant, clinical nurse specialists, and nurse anesthetist, among other roles. An audiovisual platform must be used to facilitate real-time communication with the patient and provider.

As of 2019, 51 clinical services have codes reimbursed by Medicare. ICU-related services include "Telehealth consultations, emergency department or initial inpatient," "Follow-up inpatient telehealth consultations furnished to beneficiaries in hospitals or SNFs," "Individual and group medical nutrition therapy," "|Telehealth Consultation, Critical Care, initial, physicians typically spend 60 minutes communicating with the patient and providers via telehealth," "Telehealth Consultation, Critical Care, subsequent, physicians typically spend 50 minutes communicating with the patient and providers via telehealth" [20].

Medicaid

CMS allows the individual states to describe and institute their respective laws governing Medicaid reimbursement and so a detailed analysis is out of the scope of this chapter. A comprehensive review of each states' treatment of telehealth reimbursement can be found at The Centers for Connected Health Policy. As an example to illustrate some differences in Medicaid reimbursement, California will allow Medicaid eligible patients to be seen in a Medicare-type "originating location" or at their home. Additionally, physicians can utilize stored audiovisual transmissions as well as real-time feeds as qualifying visits. A separate originating location fee is payable for real-time encounters [21].

New York State will also allow for reimbursement of real-time video encounters for Medicaid eligible patients but not most stored interactions of billable services. This is with the caveat that telemedicine be used in the setting of geographic separation and not solely for the convenience of a provider. A facility fee will not be reimbursed for most episodes of care in New York State. Texas will reimburse for both real-time telemedicine as well as stored transmissions; however only a specific list of services are eligible for reimbursement as are facility fees. Although the backbone of each states' telemedicine-related Medicaid reimbursement is defined, certain idiosyncratic differences are noted [21].

Private Insurance

Similar to Medicaid rules, each state has different laws governing the reimbursement of telemedicine services. To further complicate the issue, each insurer can create their own policies within the context of the law to dictate reimbursement. The Centers for Connected Health Policy also provide an overview of how each respective state interprets the law with regard to private payer reimbursement. One concept which pervades the rules of private payer telemedicine reimbursement is the parity law. Parity laws require that private payers reimburse Telemedicine services as though they were in-person. In California, private payers cannot require that an in-person visit be a prerequisite to reimbursement but leaves further detail of each plan to their respective hospital contract. New York State parity laws require that a private insurer reimburse a provider for services provided via telemedicine if they are required to reimburse them in-person. Texas law states that private payers must establish a telemedicine payment schedule which is available online. They are not required to list payment prices and are not required to reimburse for services provided by audio communication only [21]. Although private insurers may be required to cover in-person and telemedicine encounters, they may not be required to compensate them equally.

Tele-ICU Regulation

Tele-ICU as a care delivery modality has been around for longer than 20 years; however specific regulation is still evolving. Although most individual states have well-defined Tele-ICU regulations, this clinical care model will often be conducted across multiple states simultaneously making regulation less clear. To best ensure compliance with legal regulations, the Tele-ICU leadership team should pay close attention to their respective states, licensing requirements, privacy protection, governing body mandates, and institutional bylaws.

Licensing

For physicians medical licensing requirements can vary by state; however they will usually require that the physician be licensed both in the state in which the physician practices and the state in which the patient is seen [22]. To further streamline the process, several states have started issuing telemedicine-specific licenses to reduce the licensure burden [21]. In an effort to further streamline medical licensing regulation overall, at least 29 states have entered into the Interstate Medical Licensure Compact (IMLC) which provides a voluntary uniform license where qualifying physicians would be issued a common license to practice in multiple states [23]. The Drug Enforcement Agency (DEA) is in the process of further clarifying the requirements for prescribing controlled substances. The latest interpretation states the practitioner should hold a DEA license in the state of the patient and where the physician is practicing [24]. Nursing regulations are also evolving, and an interstate compact similar to the IMLC was approved allowing nurses to be licensed for telemedicine in up to 29 states if they meet certain prerequisites [25].

Governing Body Oversight

Similar to beginning practice at a new hospital, providers will need to be credentialed and given privileges with the hospital in which they will provide Tele-ICU care as directed by The Joint Commission. Because the process for credentialing and privileging can be onerous, a modified acceptance by proxy pathway might be considered, whereby the credentials and privileges of a site hospital with the provider can be used at the distant hospital where the patient is located [26]. Specific rules and regulations are governed by the states involved and hospitals participating. At present no specific board requirement is available for the practice of Tele-ICU. Many physicians will be board certified or eligible in critical care; however the requirement is ultimately up to the hospital credentialing body.

More governing bodies are also developing regulations within their respective purviews as telemedicine use expands. The Federal Drug Administration is increasingly regulating mobile health devices as well as Tele-ICU platforms to ensure public safety [27]. The Federal Communications Commission has been identifying physician shortage areas and capacity for broadband connectivity expansion [28]. The Federal Trade Commission tasked with protecting consumers has been involved with regulations related to telemedicine board licensure and antitrust suits related to telemedicine practice [29].

Privacy Protection

As the world migrates more and more to digital platforms and cloud computing, consumer data will be more accessible but also more at risk. Increasing the use of electronic medical records (EMR) in patient care settings has led to the recording of enormous stores of patient data. As the volume of data grows, so has concern over measures to safeguard the privacy and integrity of the patient data. Federal regulations have been in place for decades to safeguard patient care records in the form of Health Insurance Portability and Accountability Act (HIPAA) and the Health Information for Economics and Critical Health Act (HITECH). Hospital regulations regarding privacy become more complicated across systems and state lines.

To fulfill the privacy obligations required with patient contact, platforms and audiovisual equipment must be secure digitally. As cyberattacks rise, having a qualified information technology department and secure software platforms is of paramount importance. In addition to these technical obligations, the American Telemedicine Association (ATA) recommends privacy safeguards for when visitors from outside of the Tele-ICU are present on visits or tours. Additionally, the ATA recommends an explanation of Tele-ICU services and information on how the patient's and family's privacy will be maintained. Informed consent is required for telemedicine practice in over 38 states and so local regulations will need to be integrated into workflows [22].

Medical-Legal Risk

The practice of medicine is one of fulfillment, stress, satisfaction but at times, concern. The specter of medical malpractice is a common concern and can affect physician practice patterns [30]. Tele-ICU and telemedicine in general have led to concerns about the risk for medical liability in the event of an unintended patient outcome. One theory holds that telemedicine may make providers feel particularly vulnerable as they are not physically at the bedside [31]. Although this may be a concern for some, the use of telephone communications to direct care is widespread and does not lead to a significant number of malpractice claims [31]. For a provider to be at risk for malpractice, the law requires that the following conditions are met: a physician-patient relationship exists, a duty to act on behalf of the patient exists, the care provided deviated from the standard of care, and the patient sustained harm with ascertainable damages [32]. As it relates to telemedicine, what defines patient relationships and standard of care is constantly evolving.

The relative novelty of Tele-ICU and telemedicine in general results in a dearth of specific examples of case law. Between 1992 and 2014 an estimated 280,368 medical malpractice claims were paid in the United States [33]. The rate of telemedicine-related malpractice claims appears low with zero found in a report over a very short duration and 0.05% of claims paid in another report over a 10-year period [15]. These figures incorporate direct telemedicine involvement; however data are not granular enough to comment on Tele-ICU specifically. Although objective data are still being compiled, the very nature of Tele-ICU augmented care suggests a mitigating effect toward malpractice could exist.

The fundamental mandate of Tele-ICU care is to act as a "second set of eyes" and another layer of patient safety. Tele-ICU can be differentiated into two dominant subtypes including continuous and episodic care [34]. Episodic care can be most likened to a virtual second opinion by either a bedside nurse, physician assistant, nurse practitioner, or physician. The Tele-ICU physician will have access to the medical record and radiology data as well as the ability to have audiovisual communication with the distant Tele-ICU site. In the episodic model, the flow of information is on demand and not continuous. As the name suggests, the continuous

Tele-ICU model will have a constant flow of bedside labs, vitals, allergies, medications, radiology to the Tele-ICU EMR, and platform which is constantly monitored by nursing, clinical alerts, and support algorithms. In both cases, an on-demand expert will be available when called or proactively in the continuous model. The potential for risk mitigation is inherent with the addition of Tele-ICU support.

The most compelling data for medical malpractice risk reduction from Tele-ICU comes from a report of two hospital systems comparing both the number of ICU claims and amount paid per claim before Tele-ICU implementation and afterward. The Tele-ICU was a continuous model monitoring over 450 beds throughout five states. The first ICU noted a reduction from over 60 claims per year to less than 40 claims per year at an original cost of greater than $6 million per claim to less than $1 million dollars per claim. The second institution had not noted a single malpractice claim over a 5-year period of Tele-ICU implementation [31]. Although these data are promising, these results must be taken cautiously as the details of the report are not given. Additionally, malpractice claims can take several years to be available, and the sample size is rather limited.

Conclusions

Tele-ICU is a growing branch of medicine that allows intensivists to reach patients in understaffed locations or during periods of low-intensity staffing. The technology has been associated with improvements in mortality, length of stay, financial endpoints, and patient/staffing satisfaction. In order to implement these systems, especially across state lines, multiple regulatory considerations must be pursued including physician licensing, credentialing, privileging, as well as obtaining malpractice insurance. At present, the risk of malpractice liability appears low and might be reduced further with Tele-ICU support. The majority of financial benefit is realized with reductions in costs of care, improved case volume, and resultant case contribution margin. With time, CMS and private payers have begun direct reimbursement for specific Tele-ICU patient encounters.

Conflict of Interest The authors confirm to have read BioMed Central's guidance on competing interests. All authors declare not to have any competing interests in the manuscript.

References

1. Dill MJ SE. The complexities of physician supply and demand: projections through 2025. . 2008.
2. Ries M. Evaluating tele-ICU cost--an imperfect science. Crit Care Med. 2016;44(2):441–2. https://doi.org/10.1097/CCM.0000000000001506.
3. Fusaro MV, Becker C, Scurlock C. Evaluating tele-ICU implementation based on observed and predicted ICU mortality: a systematic review and meta-analysis. Crit Care Med. 2019;47(4):501–7. https://doi.org/10.1097/CCM.0000000000003627.

4. Lilly CM, Cody S, Zhao H, et al. Hospital mortality, length of stay, and preventable complications among critically ill patients before and after tele-ICU reengineering of critical care processes. JAMA. 2011;305(21):2175–83. https://doi.org/10.1001/jama.2011.697.
5. Lilly CM, McLaughlin JM, Zhao H, et al. A multicenter study of ICU telemedicine reengineering of adult critical care. Chest. 2014;145(3):500–7. https://doi.org/10.1378/chest.13-1973.
6. Thomas EJ, Lucke JF, Wueste L, Weavind L, Patel B. Association of telemedicine for remote monitoring of intensive care patients with mortality, complications, and length of stay. JAMA. 2009;302(24):2671–8. https://doi.org/10.1001/jama.2009.1902.
7. Young LB, Chan PS, Lu X, Nallamothu BK, Sasson C, Cram PM. Impact of telemedicine intensive care unit coverage on patient outcomes: a systematic review and meta-analysis. Arch Intern Med. 2011;171(6):498–506. https://doi.org/10.1001/archinternmed.2011.61.
8. Kruklitis RJ, Tracy JA, McCambridge MM. Clinical and financial considerations for implementing an ICU telemedicine program. Chest. 2014;145(6):1392–6. https://doi.org/10.1378/chest.13-0868.
9. Franzini L, Sail KR, Thomas EJ, Wueste L. Costs and cost-effectiveness of a telemedicine intensive care unit program in 6 intensive care units in a large health care system. J Crit Care. 2011;26(3):329.e1–6. https://doi.org/10.1016/j.jcrc.2010.12.004.
10. Scurlock C, D'Ambrosio C. Telemedicine in the intensive care unit: state of the art. Crit Care Clin. 2015;31(2):187–95. https://doi.org/10.1016/j.ccc.2014.12.001.
11. Carlson RW, Scurlock C. Telemedicine in the ICU. Crit Care Clin. 2015;31(2):ix–x. https://doi.org/10.1016/j.ccc.2015.01.001.
12. Willmitch B, Golembeski S, Kim SS, Nelson LD, Gidel L. Clinical outcomes after telemedicine intensive care unit implementation. Crit Care Med. 2012;40(2):450–4. https://doi.org/10.1097/CCM.0b013e318232d694.
13. Fortis S, Sarrazin MV, Beck BF, Panos RJ, Reisinger HS. ICU telemedicine reduces interhospital ICU transfers in the veterans health administration. Chest. 2018;154(1):69–76. doi: S0012-3692(18)30636-6 [pii]
14. Becker CD, Dandy K, Gaujean M, Fusaro M, Scurlock C. Legal perspectives on telemedicine part 1: legal and regulatory issues. Perm J. 2019;23 https://doi.org/10.7812/TPP/18-293. Epub 2019 Jun 7.
15. Becker CD, Dandy K, Gaujean M, Fusaro M, Scurlock C. Legal perspectives on telemedicine part 2: telemedicine in the intensive care unit and medicolegal risk. Perm J. 2019;23 https://doi.org/10.7812/TPP/18.294. Epub 2019 Aug 29.
16. Breslow MJ, Rosenfeld BA, Doerfler M, et al. Effect of a multiple-site intensive care unit telemedicine program on clinical and economic outcomes: an alternative paradigm for intensivist staffing. Crit Care Med. 2004;32(1):31–8. https://doi.org/10.1097/01.CCM.0000104204.61296.41.
17. Rosenfeld BA, Dorman T, Breslow MJ, et al. Intensive care unit telemedicine: alternate paradigm for providing continuous intensivist care. Crit Care Med. 2000;28(12):3925–31.
18. Marcin JP, Nesbitt TS, Struve S, Traugott C, Dimand RJ. Financial benefits of a pediatric intensive care unit-based telemedicine program to a rural adult intensive care unit: impact of keeping acutely ill and injured children in their local community. Telemed J E Health. 2004;10(Suppl 2):S-1-5.
19. Lilly CM, Motzkus C, Rincon T, et al. ICU telemedicine program financial outcomes. Chest. 2017;151(2):286–97. doi: S0012-3692(16)62552-7 [pii]
20. CMS. The medicare learning network: telehealth services. 2019:1–12.
21. The Centers for Connected Health Policy. Current state laws & reimbursement policies. Current State Laws & Reimbursement Policies Web site. https://www.cchpca.org/telehealth-policy/current-state-laws-and-reimbursement-policies?jurisdiction=All&category=All&topic=All. Published 10/19/2019. Updated 2019.
22. Davis TM, Barden C, Dean S, et al. American telemedicine association guidelines for TeleICU operations. Telemed J E Health. 2016;22(12):971–80. https://doi.org/10.1089/tmj.2016.0065.

23. IMLC. The interstate medical licensure compact. https://imlcc.org/. Updated 2020. Accessed 02/05. 2020.
24. Drug Enforcement Administration. Use of telemedicine while providing medication assisted treatment (MAT). 2018:1–2.
25. NCSBN. Nurse licensure compact. https://www.ncsbn.org/nurse-licensure-compact.htm. Updated 202002/05/2020.
26. Centers for Connected Health Policy. National policy: credentialing and privileging. https://www.cchpca.org/telehealth-policy/credentialing-and-privileging. Updated 2019. Accessed 2/5. 2020.
27. FDA. Digital health. https://www.fda.gov/medical-devices/digital-health. Updated 2020. Accessed 02/05. 2020.
28. FCC. FCC health IT actions and activities timeline. https://www.fcc.gov/general/fcc-health-it-actions-and-activities-timeline. Updated 2018. Accessed 02/05. 2002.
29. Centers for Connected Health Policy. National policy: the federal trade commission and professional licensure boards. https://www.cchpca.org/telehealth-policy/federal-trade-commission-and-professional-licensure-boards. Updated 2019. Accessed 02/05. 2020.
30. Lyu H, Xu T, Brotman D, et al. Overtreatment in the united states. PLoS One. 2017;12(9):e0181970. https://doi.org/10.1371/journal.pone.0181970.
31. Lilly CM, Zubrow MT, Kempner KM, et al. Critical care telemedicine: evolution and state of the art. Crit Care Med. 2014;42(11):2429–36. https://doi.org/10.1097/CCM.0000000000000539.
32. Kuszler PC. Telemedicine and integrated health care delivery: compounding malpractice liability. Am J Law Med. 1999;25(2–3):297–326.
33. Schaffer AC, Jena AB, Seabury SA, Singh H, Chalasani V, Kachalia A. Rates and characteristics of paid malpractice claims among US physicians by specialty, 1992–2014. JAMA Intern Med. 2017;177(5):710–8. https://doi.org/10.1001/jamainternmed.2017.0311.
34. Ramnath VR, Ho L, Maggio LA, Khazeni N. Centralized monitoring and virtual consultant models of tele-ICU care: a systematic review. Telemed J E Health. 2014;20(10):936–61. https://doi.org/10.1089/tmj.2013.0352.

Chapter 15
Digital Technologies in Healthcare: Opportunities and Risk for Health Systems and Providers

Peter J. Papadakos and Tiffany M. Ingham

Technology is a fact of everyday life. Personal electronic devices (PEDs) are portable, lightweight devices including smartphones, tablets, laptops, and computers. These devices are now ubiquitous in American society. Everywhere one looks, one sees people of all ages and backgrounds looking at their cell phones; this includes physicians and other healthcare providers, as well as patients. Younger adults, the "millennial generation" in particular, are digitally savvy and maintain a high social media presence and interaction. This chapter will explore the both benefits and risks that PEDs and the web-connected age present professionals in the healthcare setting.

The case of an anesthesiologist in Dallas illustrates how PED use can prove guilt in a malpractice case. In this case, the anesthesiologist was alleged to be on his PED while managing a patient under anesthesia and failed to notice the patient had love blood oxygen levels which resulted in the death of that patient [1]. The smartphone records were part of the discovery in this case and his documented use affected the outcome of the case. While it would seem difficult to successfully litigate a medical malpractice case solely on the allegation a physician was distracted by their PED in such a manner as to be the proximate cause of the patient injury, it could certainly be cited as a substantial contributing factor. Electronic discovery first was first used in distracted driving cases and is now a common practice. PED records can be subpoenaed and reveal whom an individual was texting at what exact time as well as the nature of the conversation. The same records can also reveal Internet browser use including which websites were visited, at exactly what time, and for how long. While PEDs offer a convenience to access specialized information helpful in clinical decision-making, thereby enhancing patient care, that same ease of access can

P. J. Papadakos (✉)
Critical Care Medicine, Anesthesiology, Surgery, Neurology, and Neurosurgery, University of Rochester, University of Rochester School of Medicine and Dentistry, Rochester, NY, USA
e-mail: peter_papadakos@urmc.rochester.edu

T. M. Ingham
Envision Physician Services, Houston, TX, USA

J. E. Szalados (ed.), *The Medical-Legal Aspects of Acute Care Medicine*,
https://doi.org/10.1007/978-3-030-68570-6_15

be used to imply distraction or, worse, incompetence and indifference. Even the most innocuously intended communications, assumed to be private, may come back to haunt a practitioner for years into the future.

Other high-reliability organizations, such as aviation, have embraced practices to minimize PED distraction. For example, the aviation industry has embraced the concept of the "sterile cockpit." This means that during critical portions of flight that are both high risk and high mental workload such as taxi, takeoff, and landing, cockpit communications are limited to only those necessary for the operation of the plane [1]. Moreover, personal PED use is forbidden. It seems both reasonable and intuitive that this concept would translate, although imperfectly, to the healthcare setting. Some healthcare institutions have followed suit by instituting their own versions of these practices. For example, the University of Rochester Medical Center (URMC) has established guidelines for the appropriate use of PEDs during rounds, when important and sometimes critical information is discussed and disseminated among members of the healthcare team. A summary of the guidelines employed by URMC is shown in Fig. 15.1. In addition to this, all staff receive a mandatory education program during initial onboarding and orientation and annually thereafter in order to maintain hospital credentials. Other healthcare organizations have taken up such guidelines. Many medical schools and postgraduate medical education training programs have developed curriculums to educate medical students and residents. While thoughtful policies and continuing education prudent and necessary, there is a lack of consensus regarding the specifics these policies and guidelines should encompass [2]. It is important stakeholders adopt guidelines to meet the needs of specific departments.

Cameras and audio recording devices are constantly present. In the wake of the September 11th attacks on the World Trade Center and the Pentagon, the American society became willing to accept these devices as part of the effort to identify and stop terrorist activity. Closed-circuit cameras exist in most public places in metropolitan areas. Facial recognition technology has advanced substantially and is now commonly used to identify individuals.

Most people own a PED and use it for several hours daily. According to a Pew Research Center Mobile Fact Sheet dated June 2019, 96% of Americans own a cellphone of some kind [3]. Another study conducted by the Pew Research Center in January 2018 found 26% of American adults now report that they go online "almost constantly" [4]. In mobile Internet users, those using a smartphone, tablet, or other mobile devices, 83% of Americans surveyed used the Internet at least occasionally, and of that 83%, 89% go online daily, and 31% go online almost constantly [4]. The same surgery revealed that among younger adults, 39% of 18–29-year-olds now go online almost constantly, and 49% go online multiple times per day [4]. As PEDs have become increasingly common, people have become more interested in their effects on the brain. Studies of the brain have shown the technology to have addictive qualities through the modulation of dopamine receptors [5].

Our smartphones and tablets make it possible communicating with others anywhere and anytime, nearly instantaneously. They can be used it to convey important information via voice or text; this applies to healthcare providers as well. Most

SMH CLINICAL PRACTICE GUIDELINE

Code of eConduct at the University of Rochester Medical Center

Purpose

1. To promote safe patient care through minimizing the distractions of eDevices (e.g. IPhone, Blackberry, IPad, Laptops) in the workplace while allowing for optimal use of electronic support in the care and treatment of patients and families.
2. Promote professionalism and the positive perception that patients and families have of clinicians at SMH.
3. Ensure confidentiality of protected health information
4. Clarify the expectations for all staff so that they can monitor themselves and their colleagues regarding eDevices conduct and provide constructive feedback/enforcement of the Standard Practices in order to promote ICARE PFCC values and objectives.

A. Minimal Standard Practice for use of eDevices:

- All devices, including but not limited to Smart phones and cell phones, other than hospital issued pager/urgent on-call communication devices should be in "silent" mode whenever in a patient room or discussing patient information with the patient/family
- Clinicians will refrain from using computers and eDevices at clinical work stations to conduct personal business. Use of computers and eDevices for necessary personal use is allowable in break room/break areas out of view of patients and families. (Please refer to the SMH electronic device use policy)
- Use of personal and business eDevices in the clinical setting for collection and transmission of protected health information will be done through approved, secure networks in accordance with University of Rochester Medical Center HIPAA policies[i]. Protected health information (PHI) transmitted through or to secured business eDevices will not be stored on personal eDevices.

B. Optimal Practice for use of eDevices:

- Rounding: Departments should create guidelines that provide clear delineation of roles for clinicians when rounding, including use of eDevices.
- The Senior most rounding clinician (Round Leader) is in the primary role of communicating with the patient and teaching others during rounding. As such, the leader should refrain from computer and/or eDevice use while in patient rooms with the exception of using eDevices during the course of teaching or explaining to the patient and family their diagnosis and plan of care.
- Clinicians should introduce the function and use of eDevices for medical management to patients and families upon admission and when first introducing themselves to the patient and family.
- Clinicians should have a separate eDevice or device with the technology that allows for the separation of work related and personal communication. Work issued phones/blackberries, computers and "smart" devices, etc. should not be used for personal use in patient care and clinical work areas.

History:

7/12 Developed by team led by Chief Quality Officer
8/12 Approved by Clinical Council

SMH HIPAA Privacy Policies: OP 29, OS 2, OS 8, OS 9
SMH Policy 6.2
Papadakos PJ. Electronic Distraction: Unmeasured Variable in Modern Medicine. *Anesthesiology News*, 2011;27:11.
Smith T, Darling E, Searles B. 2010 Survey on cell phone use while performing cardiopulmonary bypass. *Perfusion*, 2011:26(5);375-380.
Halamka J. Order interrupted by text: Multitasking mishap. AHRQ Agency for Health Care Research and Quality US Department of Health and Human Services. Web M+M, December 2011
Westbrook JI, Woods A, Rob MI, Dunsmuir WT, Day RO. Association of interruptions with an increased risk and severity of medication administration errors. Arch Intern Med. 2010;170:683-690.
American College of Surgeons [ST-59]. Statement on use of cell phones in the operating room. Bulletin of the American College of Surgeons. Vol. 93, No. 9, September 2008.

Guidelines are intended to be flexible. They serve as reference points or recommendations, not rigid criteria. Guidelines should be followed in most cases, but there is an understanding that, depending on the patient, the setting, the circumstances, or other factors, guidelines can and should be tailored to fit individual needs.

Reviewed: 8/12

Fig. 15.1 URMC guideline

healthcare providers are responsible for the clinical care for many patients simultaneously, and part of maturing in practice is to learn to prioritize which tasks for which patients are most urgent and attend to those first. PEDs can be a useful tool for communicating with colleagues who are in different clinical locations. For example, when a physician texts colleagues about current patient status shortly before beginning a sterile procedure (and unavailable during that time), it allows the colleague to prepare to temporarily assume care of one's patients, thereby maintaining efficient continuity of care. This is particularly important in information-dense locations like the intensive care unit (ICU) and the operating room (OR) where patients are high acuity and conditions are constantly changing. It is a highly convenient, even essential way to keep all the players on the healthcare team updated, thereby aiding in patient cross-coverage, particularly in information-dense locations (the ICU, the OR). Furthermore, PEDs can provide instant answers about the most current information to guide clinical decision making through the use of medical applications like UpToDate, which you can then share with colleagues with the intent of enhancing patient care. PEDs allow both physicians and patients to access electronic medical records from anywhere at any time.

But like so many things in life, PEDs present a mixed blessing in healthcare. The spread of information intended to be helpful can turn into a barrage from disparate sources (nursing staff, pharmacy, transfer centers, hospital operator, the ED, radiology, etc.) about different patients, often all at once. This creates a higher-level challenge to prioritize clinical urgency and act accordingly. In an age where communication is near instantaneous, there is an underlying expectation to receive an immediate answer to a text or phone call, and if that is not forthcoming, for whatever reason, it may create confusion, lead to disgruntled feelings, and place a strain on working relationships. The cumulative effect is a risk of creating an environment where healthcare providers are burdened with the expectation to always be "on," which may lead to feelings of overwhelm and frustration, a precursor for professional burnout. Ironically, this may lead to increase usage of PEDs as a distraction, providing a mental break for the user, and may or may not impact patient care [1]. Another risk to consider is when protected health information (PHI) is accessed or communicated using PEDs, it creates a vulnerability for the unintended release of that information. While the intent may have been to provide better patient care, if that information inadvertently is seen by someone who has no need to see it without the consent of the patient, it is still a Healthcare Information and Portability and Accountability Act (HIPAA) violation, for which the healthcare provider is liable. Examples of unintended, unauthorized disclosure include when the sender mistypes the intended recipient's number and the information goes to a random number or if, unbeknown to the sender, an outside party is able to observe information via hacking or spyware.

Most if not all cell phones contain an integrated microphone and speaker and a recording application pre-installed at the factory. There are many free or low-cost applications of varying sophistication designed for recording. This technology makes it very easy for anyone in possession of a smartphone to make recordings. While conversations in the healthcare setting were once reasonably considered private and confidential, given the ubiquitous nature of PEDs with recording capabilities, that is no longer the case. In one case in Virginia, a patient (who was a lawyer) while under general anesthesia with a natural airway used the recording application on his cell phone (which he activated prior to entering the patient care area) to record the conversations of the healthcare team before, during, and after his procedure without the knowledge or consent of the healthcare team. He recorded the conversations of the procedure room staff without their consent, and since he was unable to give consent while under anesthesia, thus essentially made secret recording of a third-party conversation, which would appear to be in violation of federal and state wiretapping laws. The patient later successfully litigated a malpractice suit against the healthcare team members, not because the medical care was substandard in any way (there was no adverse outcome for the patient). As the patient was not expected to be a participant in a conversation, and awareness under general anesthesia is a very rare event, the healthcare team appeared to have a reasonable expectation of privacy. Further, there was no proof other than the plaintiff's word that the recording was not altered; nonetheless the recording was allowed into evidence. Finally, if the patient is the original owner of the recording, there is nothing preventing him/her from publicly releasing recordings which may subsequently find their way into social media or other websites, for example, physician rating sites, as well as other wide-reaching publication modalities (television, print newspapers). Operating from the baseline assumption that you are being recorded (and the recording may be published for consumption by the public) will help develop a higher level of mindfulness in choosing one's words and actions. This problem may be compounded if information regarding other patients is inadvertently captured on a recording or even later released publicly. This release could be construed as a HIPAA violation on an entirely different patient.

Physicians and other healthcare providers are bound ethically and legally to maintain patient confidentiality. The 1996 Health Insurance Portability and Accountability Act (HIPAA) is legislation prohibiting unauthorized disclosure of protected health information (PHI). However, there are no such constraints on patients; they are free to share their own PHI at any time with whomever they wish and may even do so in a highly public forum such as social media accounts.

The legality of secretly recording conversations with others varies widely from state to state. Many states have one-party consent laws, meaning so long as one person (the recorder) in a conversation consents to making the recording, it is legal, even if the other party is unaware of and does not consent to the recording [2, 6]. The only legal requirement is that one person, the recorder, must give consent to the recording (one-party consent). Only a few states, such as Florida, require both parties to agree to recording a conversation (two-party consent). According to the Digital Media Law Project, "regardless of whether state or federal law governs the situation, it is almost always illegal to record a phone call or private conversation to which you are not a party, do not have consent from at least one party, and could not naturally overhear" [6].

While many healthcare facilities and offices have policies banning the use of PEDs in clinical areas, and post signs forbidding recordings in these areas, because

PEDs are small and easily hidden, these are difficult to enforce. Some suggest these policies and signs may even encourage covert recordings [2, 7]. A suggested potential advantage of recording a clinical encounter is that it may help patients improve compliance and better adhere to treatment plans through relistening to the recording at a later time. Knowing one is or may be recorded makes many uncomfortable and has the potential to not only alter but degrade the patient-physician relationship by damaging trust and creating a barrier to open honest communication between both parties. Physicians may quite understandably question the motives of a patient for making such a recording, especially a secret one. The physician may start to question their clinical decision making and order more tests as a strategy to practice "defensive medicine," ultimately driving up healthcare costs [7].

In the age of Press-Ganey scores, healthcare systems are constantly trying to improve and maintain a positive public image, including online. Many scholarly articles exist which attempt to quantify factors which influence patient selection and loyalty of patients to healthcare providers and facilities. The theory of perceived quality, discussed in business and retail literature, would seem to now apply to healthcare. In essence, this theory suggests perceived quality is a measure of the consumer belief, and one can then infer perceived healthcare quality is directly related to patient perception and beliefs. For better or worse, healthcare is now, at least in part, a marketplace. Given the competitive nature of this marketplace, and its impact on profit, there is tremendous fear of receiving or even being associated with "bad publicity." With the use of PEDs, everyday personal and private conversations can be perceived in ways that create varying patient perceptions, the impact of which can be exponentially increased by publication online. Accurate or not, once out on the Internet, it is nearly impossible to remove. In the everyday healthcare work environment, patient perceptions are likely affected by the disclosure of conversations about medical information or casual conversations with others.

The phrase "freedom of speech" in the first amendment of the constitution generally means citizens have a guaranteed right to speak openly without government interference or reprisal. It does not, however, guarantee any words uttered will be without consequences. In fact, there can be severe impacts in other areas of life, particularly in today's environment of rapid, even near instantaneous communications via the Internet. For example, losing one's job and one's employability may result. Public shaming practices, like public stocks, fell out of favor in the eighteenth century, labeled as cruel and unusual punishment. Yet with the rapid growth of the Internet and social media, humiliation tactics have experienced a digital revival. Many authors have written on this topic; Jon Ronson gives several detailed examples of this in his book entitled *So You've Been Publicly Shamed.*

Multiple forums exist online where the public can publicly voice their opinion on physicians. From Google to dedicated rating websites such as vitals.com and healthgrades.com, any person can write nearly anything about a physician. The quality and accuracy of these websites vary greatly. In many cases, "reviews" are not reviewed by the site administrators at all, and further these website administrators are under no legal obligation to do so. The Communications Decency Act, enacted in 1996, is legislation intended to restrict free speech on the Internet, with particular regard to pornography. Section 230 of the act provides immunity from liability to Internet service providers, website hosts, and bloggers for posting third-party comments. While Congress intended for these entities to police their sites for criminal activity, there is no legal incentive to do so, and no legal consequences for allowing comments, even ones that are false or constitute a crime on their websites. Such ratings may be anonymous, and in some cases the "reviewer" does not need to provide any user information such as name, email address, or contact information, nor is the user required. The website hosts are under no obligation to ensure the information posted is truthful. The situation becomes even more complicated for physicians who are constrained by HIPAA obligations. A physician cannot even respond to negative or false comments because of privacy concerns, nor is it professional to engage in an argument in a public forum. Unfortunately, the general public has no way to verify truthfulness or accuracy and may well believe what's written, even if false. With the viral nature of the Internet, a single post can be reposted in multiple places and spread exponentially.

There is very little recourse for a physician to not only have these comments removed but to identify and punish the perpetrator. Typically, these sites will publish a user agreement that, in general, says the user agrees to write truthful information based on personal experience with the physician rated and further agrees not to post defamatory information or otherwise act in an illegal fashion. But again, since the website is not liable for what other people post, there is no incentive to verify the accuracy of information. Contacting the website administrators with a request for removal may be successful and should be the first move of a physician who finds themselves in this position. To identify an anonymous user is more difficult and most likely would require a lengthy and expensive legal procedure, and may or may not be successful. Social media and websites are sometimes used to harass individuals (cyber-harassment and cyberbullying), and physicians are no exception. Cyber-harassment may spill over into reality, creating a threat to personal safety, particularly for women. The social, reputational and professional, psychological, and financial impacts (loss of employment and employability, legal costs) of negative publicity can be devastating and last for years.

The healthcare landscape is constantly changing, and it is clear PEDs are well entrenched in our professional lives. Navigating this new landscape presents significant challenges. With the ubiquitous availability of personal recording and video devices integrated into nearly every aspect of personal and professional life, it becomes increasingly complicated to successfully navigate between the personal privacy of the patients and healthcare providers. As technology and social media advances, there is a lack of understanding of the implications of the public perceptions on healthcare providers. Healthcare providers are bound by distinct laws pertaining to confidentiality and the disclosure of patient information, specifically HIPAA laws, yet patients, their families, and other non-physicians with access are not, nor do they have any training or education in the consequences of their actions. Family members posting pictures from inside the ICU, including pictures of staff members without permission, even when the intent is benign intrudes upon the privacy of the staff and the patient. It is a slippery slope; staff members posting to social media pictures of themselves with families, even when the intent is innocuous, risks disclosing information that may be used to identify a patient. PEDs create a unique and murky environment that leaves the clinician and the patient at risk for loss of privacy. Whether it is a private conversation between staff members regarding a patient and their care within a closed, private work environment or a recording of clinical conversations with patients and their families of direct patient care, there is high risk for damage to personal privacy all around. In recent years, healthcare entities have begun to issue policies on electronic etiquette with the goal of preventing distraction that may be detrimental to patient care and to prevent problems related to recordings/videos/photos published online for the world to view. The clinician must be cognizant and understand how PEDs create an environment that can quickly become a quagmire with regard to patient and personal privacy.

We make the following recommendations for both clinicians and healthcare organizations to consider incorporating into their practices:

1. Use good situational awareness. Understanding there is always the potential to become distracted or to be recorded is the first step in minimizing this problem. Always speak and act as if you are being recorded for widespread public broadcast. Considering ahead of time the consequences of how one's words and actions may be perceived, misunderstood, or taken out of context, compounded by how quickly this misperception (accurate or not) can spread and remain public forever may seem dramatic but will help one choose to speak in and act in a disciplined fashion.
2. Avoid the temptation to text other healthcare team members on one's personal smartphone. While it is a highly convenient, and in some ways even an essential way to keep all members of the healthcare team updated, this puts the user at risk for inadvertent disclosure of PHI. Safer options include using a hospital-issued device, ideally secured by the information technology (IT) department. Another safer option is to use only encrypted applications approved by and installed on one's personal PED by the hospital IT department. The safest option is to not use one's personal PED at all to access PHI and to avoid using it in clinical areas.
3. Healthcare organizations should continue to institute policies outlining *disciplined* electronic etiquette with the goals of preventing distraction detrimental to patient care and preventing problems related to unauthorized recordings and/or their inappropriate disclosure. Organization-wide policies may necessarily be general, and efforts should be made by the department leadership to tailor policies and address the specific needs of their clinical locations as these needs may be significantly different (i.e., what is useful in a primary care office may be impossible in the ICU). The curriculum must be geared toward professionals from all aspects of healthcare (physicians, nurses, therapists, technologists, etc.) and should occur at the time of initial clinical orientation and be continually updated on at least an annual basis. This could be done in the form of a continuing medical education lecture or an online computer-based training.
4. Regardless of potential advantages, the best course of action is to prohibit any recordings of clinical encounters by patients. If a patient asks to record a conver-

sation, an alternative is offering the patient paper and pen to use for notes and then at the end of the encounter going over those notes together to ensure correct understanding [8]. Another alternative, if the physician is comfortable with it, is to allow the patient to record a specific portion of the conversation in which the physician addresses the instructions the patient wishes to reference in the future [8]. This fosters open and honest communication between both parties while avoiding negative feelings that damage the clinical relationship.

References

1. Saran JS, Papadakos PJ. Electronic distraction in the operating room: a major safety issue. ORNAC J. 2018;36(2):12–8.
2. King M. Docs on candid camera: patients recording clinical encounters. https://www.magmutual.com/learning/article/docs-candid-camera-patients-recording-clinical-encounters/. Accessed 17 Feb 2020.
3. Mobile Fact Sheet. https://www.pewresearch.org/internet/fact-sheet/mobile/. Accessed 17 Feb 2020.
4. Perrin A, Jiang J. About a quarter of U.S. adults say they are 'almost constantly' online. https://www.pewresearch.org/fact-tank/2019/07/25/americans-going-online-almost-constantly/. Accessed 17 Feb 2020.
5. Papadakos PJ. The rise of electronic distraction in healthcare is addiction to devices contributing. J Anesthe Clin Res. 2013;4:e112.
6. Recording Phone Calls and Conversations. http://www.dmlp.org/legal-guide/recording-phone-calls-conversations-meetings-and-hearings. Accessed 17 Feb 2020.
7. Rodriguez M, Morrow J, Seifi A. Ethical implications of patients and families secretly recording conversations with physicians. JAMA. 2015;313(16):1615–6.
8. Are Your Patients Recording Doctors' Office Visits. https://www.remindercall.com/patients-are-recording-doctors/. Accessed 17 Feb 2020.
9. Papadakos PJ, Ingham T. Electronic distraction in medicine. In: Szalados J, editor. Legal and ethical issues in neurocritical care: Society of Neurocritical Care in Press; 2019.

Chapter 16
The Laws of Professional Negligence: What Is Malpractice – And How Does Litigation Work?

James E. Szalados

Introduction

A "tort" is an English Common Law term for a civil wrong whereby an act or omission gives causes injury or harm to another and for which the courts will impose liability. "Tort" is the old Norman word for a "wrong." Torts include, for example, negligence, trespass, defamation, invasion of privacy, assault, battery, false imprisonment, conversion, product liability, and negligent or intentional infliction of emotional distress. The notion of torts is founded in principles of ethics and morality and therefore based on philosophies of normative behavior addressing issues such as justice, rights, and duties. The aim of the legal system, in addressing a tort, is to compensate the injured party, impose civil liability on those responsible, and deter others from committing similar actions. Torts, by definition, require that the plaintiff demonstrate a compensable harm, for which the judicial system can provide relief through compensation. Since torts are civil causes of action, they are differentiated from criminal actions, or crimes, which are governed by criminal statutes and where the judicial system can impose more than monetary compensation.

Thus, medical malpractice lawsuits are generally filed in state courts and are governed by state statutes and, generally, state case law (precedent). Nonetheless, federal courts may have jurisdiction if (1) there is a diversity of citizenship (between states) as between the parties; or (2) the Federal Torts Claims Act applies. The Federal Torts Claim Act (FTCA) [1] applied to medical malpractice lawsuits can be

J. E. Szalados (✉)
Director, Surgical and Neurocritical Care Units, Rochester Regional Health System at Rochester General Hospital, Rochester, NY, USA

The Szalados Law Firm, Hilton, NY, USA
e-mail: james.szalados@rochesterregional.org; jszalados@aol.com

J. E. Szalados (ed.), *The Medical-Legal Aspects of Acute Care Medicine*,
https://doi.org/10.1007/978-3-030-68570-6_16

filed against physicians working at medical facilities operated by the federal government including, for example, the Veterans Administration. Through the FTCA, eligible Health Resource Services Administration (HRSA)-supported health centers may be granted medical malpractice liability protection with the federal government acting as their primary insurer; employees and eligible contractors are considered federal employees and are immune from lawsuits for medical malpractice, and the plaintiff must bring suit against the US Government. Nonetheless, even where the care is filed in federal court, substantive issues of law including the applicable standard of care are governed by state law.

Unintentional torts are differentiated from (a) intentional torts and (b) strict liability torts such as product liability. The civil laws relating to negligence are based on the statutes and case law; these laws may be similar but also can vary substantially and substantively between the states. "Negligence" is the most common form of unintentional tort in which an actor fails to "behave with the level of care that someone of ordinary prudence would have exercised under the same circumstances" [2]. Thus, "reasonable care" is fundamental to the concept of negligence, since notions such as "reasonableness" and "ordinary prudence" can be verified through either testimony and/or judgment of one's of peers. A negligent act may be either one of affirmative commissions of an act or failure to act when there is a duty or obligation to do so. The concept of duty represents a legal conclusion pertaining to relationships between individuals and determined by the specific circumstances under consideration [3]. Fundamental to the concept of duty is a foreseeability of harm. If there is a foreseeability that one's action (or inaction) may result in harm, then one owes a "duty of reasonable care." Not all risks are reasonably foreseeable; for example, "when determining whether a danger is foreseeable, we 'look at whether the specific danger was objectively reasonable to expect, not simply whether it was within the realm of any conceivable possibility'" [4].

In general negligence, the issue is then a general duty to act in such a way to reasonably prevent reasonably foreseeable harm to others; however, in the case of professional negligence, the duty is imposed by virtue of professional standing and fiduciary relationship.

A profession is an "occupation whose core element is work based upon the mastery of a complex body of knowledge and skills. It is a vocation in which knowledge of some department of science or learning or the practice of an art founded upon it is used in the service of others. Its members are governed by codes of ethics and profess a commitment to competence, integrity and morality, altruism, and the promotion of the public good within their domain. These commitments form the basis of a social contract between a profession and society, which in return grants the profession a monopoly over the use of its knowledge base, the right to considerable autonomy in practice and the privilege of self-regulation. Professions and their members are accountable to those served and to society." [5] Thus, a profession is grounded on knowledge that generally is acquired through prolonged specialized education and training, accompanied by a certification of formal qualifications, and is held by society to maintain the highest standards of fiduciary obligations towards clients or patients.

Where the unintentional tort of negligence involves professionals engaged in the exercise of professional conduct, a negligent act is referred to as "professional negligence" or, more commonly "professional malpractice." Where the profession at issue is medicine, the professional negligence is referred to as medical malpractice.

A claim of medical malpractice can be predicated on various theories: (1) departure from the standard of medical care; (2) absence of informed consent; (3) responsibility for the actions of others under one's supervision and control (vicarious liability; *respondeat superior*; or negligent supervision); or (4) patient abandonment. Once again, the laws relating to medical malpractice are based in statutes and case law; these laws may be similar but also can vary substantially and substantively between the states [6].

The Requisite Elements of a Cause of Action for Medical Malpractice

The term "prima facie" refers to the Latin term "at first sight" and is used in the legal context to denote circumstances, which at first blush, or initial examination, seems to support a rebuttable basis for a cause of action. A rebuttable presumption is one which appears to be true and sufficient on its face to support a conclusion but is nonetheless subject to offers of proof which may contradict or disprove it. Thus, "since a presumption is an assumption of fact accepted by the court until disproved, all presumptions are rebuttable" [7]. A cause of action is a set of legal facts upon which a legal action may properly be initiated and, at least preliminarily, sustained. A civil cause of action can arise from an act, an omission, a failure to perform a legal obligation such as a contracted duty, a breach of duty, or an interference with another's right. The cause of action is the grounds for a complaint, and therefore, the basis for a legal right to initiate a lawsuit. Initiation of causes of action requires that each of the elements upon which that cause of action is predicted be alleged as true buy one who brings the action (the "plaintiff") against another (the "defendant"). In some circumstances, the facts or circumstances which entitle a plaintiff to seek judicial relief may create more than one cause of action.

Legal redress for a cause of action is through a lawsuit. A lawsuit is initiated through a formal presentation of legal papers ("pleadings") filed in court by the plaintiff, alleging that he or she was harmed, through the cause of action, and requesting judicial intervention to provide relief. Pleadings serve to (1) describe the alleged facts which support the cause of action; (2) give notice to the defendant regarding a pending lawsuit; (3) specify the relief that is being sought; and (4) facilitate the efficiency of the legal process. Traditionally, the summons and complaint are considered as the initial pleadings; however pleadings also include every other supporting legal document filed in a lawsuit including motions, petitions, answers, demurrers, and memoranda of law.

A summons and complaint are together one type of pleading which is filed in the court of jurisdiction and which both initiates the lawsuit and also informs the defendant of the lawsuit, containing, in general, (1) the legal basis for the court's jurisdiction over the matter and the defendant; (2) the cause of action from which the claim or claims are derived; (3) a concise description of the claim or claims of the claim itself; (4) the relief being sought; (5) the person claiming relief; (6) and a demand for judgment, or a "prayer for relief." Technically, the compliant initiates the lawsuit, and the summons provides notice of service and specifies a date for a court appearance. The format for the service of pleadings varies by jurisdiction; in most jurisdictions the two documents are served together, although this is not always the case. An important purpose of the complaint is to provide the defendant with notice so that he or she can initiate the process of defending against the claim. For example, under contracts for medical malpractice insurance, the insurer must be immediately informed of the receipt of pleadings, so that timely answers to the allegations can be formulated and formally submitted in defense of the complaint. The time period in which the answers to a summons and complaint are due, vary by jurisdiction and by circumstance, but may be as short as 20 days. In the event that the defendant does not file an answer to a summons and complaint with the court in the statutorily defined time period, a summary default judgment may be entered against the defendant who has thus lost the right to defend his or her case in court.

The manner in which a defendant receives his or her "notice" through delivery and receipt of the summons and/or complaint ("service of process") is extremely important and can have a significant bearing on the validity of the subsequent lawsuit. Proper notice regarding a lawsuit is required by constitutional due process and governed by federal and state rules and regulations. Potential defendants should keep track of the exact circumstances surrounding the service of process since these may later help in defense of the lawsuit.

A lawsuit alleging medical malpractice must be filed with the court within a statutorily prescribed time period, the statute of limitations. Each type of civil cause, and some criminal actions, is governed by a specified statute of limitations. The statute of limitations begins to run at the time that the cause of action occurred and runs until the pleadings seeking relief for such action are properly filed in court. If a lawsuit is filed ("commenced") after the statute of limitations has fully run ("run out"), the lawsuit is considered "time-barred," and the court no longer has jurisdiction over the matter. Failure to timely commence or file a lawsuit is potentially professional legal malpractice attributable to the plaintiff's attorney.

In general, the elements required to support a prima facie cause of action alleging medical malpractice are as follows: (1) the professional duty owed to the patient; (2) the breach of such duty; (3) injury caused proximally by the breach of duty; and (4) monetary damages (Table 16.1). "If the circumstances supporting a theory of negligence are of greater weight than the evidence supporting the theory of no negligence, then it becomes a question of fact for the jury to determine whether or not the cause of the injury was the negligence alleged" [8].

Table 16.1 Elements of medical malpractice

Duty
Breach
Proximate causation
Damages

Duty

There are many ways in which a provider or health system owes a legal duty to the patient. First, there is a fiduciary duty arising by virtue of an established patient-provider relationship. Fiduciary duties arise from the inequality of knowledge, training, and experience that the professional applies to his or her services on behalf of the patient; because of the provider's standing as a professional and the inequality of understanding, the patient must place his or her trust in the provider. The usual fiduciary duties involve (1) the duty of loyalty and (2) the duty of care. There can be no duty in the absence of a demonstrable patient-provider relationship; however, such a relationship has been increasingly broadened.

In the 1901 case of *Hurley v. Eddingfield*, the Supreme Court of Indiana opined that "the State does not require, and the [medical] licensee does not engage, that he will practice at all or on other terms than he may choose to accept" [9], thereby finding that a patient-provider relationship exists only when both parties consent to and accept their obligations and roles within the therapeutic relationship. A provider has no obligation to treat all comers, unless the provider meets certain criteria such as an employed provider or on-call provider treating emergencies.

On the other hand, in *Mead v. Adler*, a patient presented to an emergency department where an on-call neurosurgeon was consulted for the patient's possibly evolving *cauda equina* syndrome, the neurosurgeon examined the patient and recommended that she be admitted but determined that surgery was not needed; in the interval between the initial presentation and the subsequent deterioration, the neurosurgeon did not re-examine the patient since he did not believe that a patient-provider relationship had been formed. The issue in *Mead v. Adler* was whether the circumstances of that communication gave rise to a physician-patient relationship between the defendant and plaintiff. The court opined that "in the absence of an express agreement by the physician to treat a patient, a physician's assent to a physician-patient relationship can be inferred when the physician takes an affirmative action with regard to the care of the patient" [10].

Thus, opinions rendered, even without other interventions, may create a relationship; such is also the issue with informal curbside consultations (also known as "sidewalk," "elevator," or "hallway" consults which are informal consultations between often sharing thoughts on complex cases and sometimes even seeking informal suggestions regarding patient management). The general rule has long been that "a physician who gives an 'informal opinion,' however, at the request of a treating physician, does not owe a duty to the patient because no physician-patient relationship is created" [11].

However, in the 2019 case of *Warren v Dinter*, a patient, Susan Warren, was evaluated by a nurse practitioner (NP) in the outpatient facility of the Essentia healthcare system in Minnesota where the NP determined that the patient probably had a serious infection and should be admitted to the hospital and by following a standard procedure called a hospitalist Fairview Hospital. The hospitalist never examined the patient, accessed the patient's medical record, or charged for the consult but determined that the patient did not need hospitalization. The NP accepted the recommendation of the hospitalist and sent the patient home where she died 3 days later of sepsis caused by an untreated staphylococcal infection. At trial, the trial court granted summary judgment to the hospitalist, opining that a patient-provider relationship had not been established. The court of appeals affirmed. The case was then further appealed to the Minnesota Supreme Court which reversed the lower courts' decisions, noting that a physician-patient relationship is not a necessary element of a claim for professional negligence, holding that (1) a physician owes a duty of care to a third party when the physician acts in a professional capacity and it is reasonably foreseeable that the third party will rely on the physician's acts and be harmed by a breach of the standard of care and (2) it was reasonably foreseeable that the patient in this case would rely on the hospitalist's acts and be harmed by a breach of the standard of care [12]. Thus, at least in a minority of states, informally consulted clinicians may be liable for negligent advice. The American Medical Association has issued a memorandum calling out the *Dintner* case "abusive litigation against physicians" and "very unfavorable" [13].

Where a patient-physician relationship is established, the physician has an ethical and legal duty to continue care. In general, "abandonment" occurs when the relationship between physician and patient is terminated either (1) at an unreasonable time or (2) without affording the patient time to find a qualified replacement [14]. Patient abandonment is often actionable not only under malpractice laws but also under state disciplinary statutes governing the practice of medicine.

The second element of duty is the "duty of reasonable professional care to the patient" or "duty to practice in accordance with prevailing standards of care." The definition of the standard of care is complex and varies by jurisdiction. In the 1860 case of *Richie v West*, then defense attorney Abraham Lincoln defended a physician and in which the court stated that "[w]hen a person assumes the profession of physician and surgeon, he must…be held to employ a reasonable amount of skill and care" [15]. The traditional standard of care for physicians is to exercise "the degree of care and skill that a physician or surgeon of the same medical specialty would use under similar circumstances" [16]. The standard of reasonable professional care is generally that of a "reasonably prudent" physician [17].

Medical malpractice is a legal fault by a physician arising from a failure to provide the quality of care required by law. When a physician undertakes to treat a patient, he or she assumes an obligation, contract, or duty, enforceable at law, to use minimally sound medical judgment and render minimally competent care during the course of the provision of care. Physicians do not guarantee recovery or success. If a patient sustains an injury because of a physician's failure to perform that duty, the physician may be liable for damages. A competent physician is not liable per se for a mere error of judgment, mistaken diagnosis, or the occurrence of an undesirable outcome or result [18].

Traditionally, when defining the applicable standard of care, courts would rely on the standard established in the case of *Small v. Howard*, that the standard to be applied in a particular case was that prevailing within the particular locality where the alleged tortious act took place: the "locality rule" [19]. Specifically, the "locality rule" recognizes "as a rule of substantive law that a physician is bound to bestow to each patient such reasonable and ordinary care, skill, and diligence and to exercise such good medical judgment as physicians and surgeons in good standing in the same neighborhood or locality, in the same general line of practice, ordinarily have and exercise in like cases" [20].

Through the rise of national medical organizations and national board certification bodies and in accordance with increased mobility of physicians and their practices throughout the United States, physicians became responsible for adhering to a national standard of care as applicable to their specialty and/or subspecialty. Although the majority of jurisdictions have abandoned the "locality rule," the states of Arizona [21], Idaho [22], New York [23], Tennessee, Virginia [24], and Washington [25] continue to rely on the locality rule. In all, 29 states and the District of Columbia have adopted a national standard of care, whereas 21 states maintain a version of the locality rule, in which the standard of care by which a physician is judged is the standard of care in a particular locality [26]. The State of Louisiana uses a "modified locality rule," whereby general practitioners are held to a community standard and whereby specialists are held to a national standard of care. A normative approach to defining the standard of care requires a formal definition of how a reasonable physician would have done under the circumstances.

One problem with the locality rule is that where malpractice is alleged within a small community, the expert witnesses necessary to establish the prevailing local standard of care would need to come from the accused physician's community peers [27], potentially or practically immunizing any physician in that community from liability [28]. Thus, the locality rule may jeopardize the application of basic principles of justice on behalf of patients who are harmed as a result of suboptimal local care standards.

Nonetheless, a core validity to the concept of local standards of care may rest within the notion of resource availability, based on the circumstances and the availability of resources, treatment options, and equipment. In such cases, the determination of the standard of care may need to include an analysis of the feasibility and options for the transfer of patients to a "higher level of care."

On the other hand, under a competence-based national standard of care, physicians "may with reason and fairness be expected to possess or have reasonable access to such medical knowledge as is commonly possessed or reasonably available to minimally competent physicians in the same specialty or general field of practice throughout the United States, to have a realistic understanding of the limitations on his or her knowledge or competence, and, in general, to exercise minimally adequate medical judgment. Beyond that, each physician has a duty to have a practical working knowledge of the facilities, equipment, resources (including personnel in health related fields and their general level of knowledge and competence), and options … reasonably available to him or her as well as the practical limitations on same" [29].

In 1923, the landmark case of *Frye v. United States* [30] established that the admissibility of scientific evidence required "general acceptance" in the scientific community, leading to the possible use of medical treatises under this condition of admissibility. Frequently the issue of admissibility of treatises, textbooks, journal articles, or other published material arises when discussing the standard of care; in general, such material, in itself, is generally not admissible to prove the standard of care, under the hearsay rule of evidence, since the author is not usually present to verify the statements directly. Nonetheless, clinical practice guidelines (CPGs), including algorithms, statements, and protocols, are increasingly considered by many to represent persuasive outlines of "best practices" to be at least considered during individualized clinical decision-making [31]. Electronic medical records are also increasingly incorporating decision support. In general, although guidelines are frequently referred to as "standards" they are not in themselves considered to represent legal "standards of care, since, arguably, it is individualized medical judgment rather than 'cookbook medicine" that drives individualized clinical decision-making. In addition, guidelines are frequently updated or revised; and, different societies within the same specialty may publish conflicting guidelines. Finally, CPGs may be authored for nonmedical reasons such as utilization review or claims management and therefore are designed to meet the needs of a drafting organization, rather than defining a true clinical standard of care [32].

Nonetheless, in some circumstances, guidelines may be, and have been, introduced as "learned treatises" and bypass the hearsay rule. Thus, CPGs may be used to bolster the testimony of an expert witness, impeach an expert witness, defend a physician for following the document as the standard of care or to suggest physician deviance from the document as deviance from the standard of care [33]. Arguably, CPGs have had a greater effect by the plaintiff's bar for inculpatory evidence than by the defense as an exculpatory standard [34]. Treatises such as CPGs may also be admissible as demonstrative evidence if defendant physicians relied on such guidelines when rendering medical treatment.

In 2006, the New York Court of Appeals decided *Hinlicky v. Dreyfuss* [35], a case in which a patient underwent a successful carotid endarterectomy but suffered a postoperative myocardial infarction and died 25 days later. The plaintiff's cardiology expert witness asserted that as a "mandatory minimum," the patient should have had a preoperative cardiac stress test. At trial, the defendant anesthesiologist testified at length regarding his deliberate adherence to the American Heart Association (AHA)/American College of Cardiology (ACC) guidelines which represented an algorithm ("a link in the chain of data") on which he relied for his decisions regarding preoperative cardiac testing. The value of the AHA/ACC exhibit was underscored when all defense experts agreed that the algorithm not only "represented the standard of care' but actually represented the "state of the art." The court subsequently ruled in favor of the physician; however, the case was subsequently appealed to New York's highest Court of Appeals. The verdict for the defense was upheld where the court recognized that clinical practice guidelines represented "systematically developed statements to assist practitioner and patient decisions about appropriate health care for specific clinical circumstances" and as "standardized specifications for care, either for using a procedure or for managing a particular clinical problem" [36]. The Court of Appeals ruled that it had been appropriate for the lower court to admit the guidelines into evidence, not for the purposes of defining the standard of care but to illustrate (for the jury and the court) the process of clinical decision-making used by the defendant physician in the care of the patient.

Medical judgment involves a careful balancing of factors that are both intuitive and data-based. Medical judgment embodies the art, training, and experience which become critical when complex decisions are made in clinical settings where data is incomplete or inconsistent. An error in judgment is, in itself, insufficient to sustain liability. The "error in judgment rule" maintains that malpractice cannot be predicated solely on an error in judgment in choosing among different therapeutic approaches or in diagnosing a condition [37]. Physicians and other providers who choose between two reasonable alternatives (e.g., diagnoses, therapies, procedures) may be not liable where the documentation supports good medical care. "The art of healing frequently calls for a balancing of risks and dangers to a patient" [38]. The Canadian physician and one of the four founding professors of Johns Hopkins Hospital, Sir William Osler, expressed the uncertainty of medical practice stating both that "Medicine is a science of uncertainty and an art of probability" [39] and that "Errors in judgment must occur in the practi8ce of an art which consists largely of balancing probabilities" [40]. Nonetheless, the "error in judgment" and the "respectful minority" rules are increasingly being challenged [41]. The outcome of litigation in such cases will depend heavily on the documentation, and specifically the clinical reasoning memorialized in the medical record to support the reasonable weighing of alternatives at the time of decision-making.

Breach

An allegation of medical malpractice will hinge on whether there was a deviation from the standard of care; such a deviation represents a breach (Table 16.2.)

Since a definition of the standard of care is outside the realm of knowledge possessed by laypersons, it must be established through the testimony of medical professionals with expertise regarding the subject matters or expert witnesses. In a legal proceeding alleging medical malpractice, as in any civil action, the plaintiff had the burden of proof to establish the prima facie elements of the cause of action. In order to maintain a case through its initial stages (or withstand a motion for a directed verdict), the plaintiff must first qualify its medical witness as an expert; demonstrate to the court that the witness will assist the jury or judge in weighing the evidence; and, present the expert opinions in accordance with the rules of evidence. On the issue of breach, expert witnesses are called upon to offer proof regarding two issues: (1) opinion as to the relevant standard of care and (2) opinion as to the failure of the

Table 16.2 Examples of breaches of the standard of care

Failure to treat
Failure to diagnose, or misdiagnosis
Failure to timely diagnose or treat
Misreading or ignoring laboratory results
Unnecessary surgery
Surgical errors or wrong site surgery
Improper medication, route, or dosage
Poor follow-up or aftercare
Premature or unsafe discharge
Disregarding or not taking reasonable patient history
Failure to order proper testing
Failure to note symptoms
Failure to document allergies
Failure to warn

defendant physician to conform to the standard of care. The plaintiff's expert need not explicitly render an opinion as to whether the defendant physician actually committed "malpractice."

The expert physician will be examined directly by the plaintiff's attorney, during which time he or she will educate the court on the medical issues by answering open-ended questions at length, showing models or illustrations, and translating the medical terms and evidence into plain English. The expert will then under a cross-examination by the physicians' defending attorney who will attempt to undercut the assumptions, credibility, substance, or reliability of the expert.

Causation

Causation is the third element of a prima facie case of medical malpractice. In order to establish medical malpractice, it is necessary to prove, on a balance of probabilities, that the breach of duty is directly caused by the alleged harm or injury. Legal proof of medical malpractice will next hinge on whether the deviation from the standard of care, or breach, directly caused the alleged injury. Causation is often more difficult to prove than is the breach in the standard of care. Proof of causation generally requires expert testimony. Causation may be proximate or actual. However, "To establish causation, the tortfeasor's conduct must be both the cause in fact and the proximate, or legal, cause of the plaintiff's injury" [42]. Causation is an issue to be determined by the jury.

Cause in fact, or factual causation, refers to injuries which would not have occurred "but for" the defendant's actions. The "but for" test of causation requires the plaintiff to show that '"but for" the defendant's negligent act, the injury would not have occurred.' In other words, had the provider not been negligent, the patient would not have been harmed. "In all but those rare cases where two independent forces concur to cause an injury, causation, in fact, is evaluated through the familiar "but for" test; that is, it must be shown that, but for the tortfeasor's conduct, the injured party would not have been damaged" [43].

Some jurisdictions use the "substantial factor" test, as opposed to the "but for" test to establish factual causation. Under the substantial factor test, the court considers whether a defendant's actions or omissions represent a substantial factor, or material factor, in causing injury [44].

The second facet of causation is proximate cause, which is often described as a limitation on liability, absolving those actors whom it would be "unfair" to punish because of the attenuated relation which their conduct bears to the plaintiff's injury. Proximate cause is also referred to as "legal causation." Here, if the court determines that a particular cause is an actual cause, the inquiry turns to whether that cause is also the proximate cause [45]. Proximate cause is a legal limitation on causation that basically indicates the defendant's actions are the most likely cause of the plaintiff's damages, requiring that the breach of duty be the primary cause of the injury. Legal causation is an essential element in the proof of negligence. Thus, even if a defendant's action is established through the "but for" test as the cause of an injury, liability the defendant might not be liable for damages if the actions were not the proximate cause of the injuries.

Proximate or legal causation requires that the injuries be "foreseeable." A defendant in a negligence case can only be liable for those injuries which could have been foreseen to be a consequence of one's actions. A breach may not be an initial action that results in an injury; similarly it may not be the last event that immediately precedes an injury. The proximate cause is a breach of duty with foreseeable consequences.

The classic case illustrating the importance of distinguishing between actual causation and proximate causation is *Palsgraf v. Long Island Railroad Co.*, where a plaintiff standing on a railroad platform purchasing a ticket, was injured when the defendant dropped a package containing fireworks fell and the contents exploded. In brief, the facts of the case relate that the plaintiff, Mrs. Palsgraf, was standing at the end of a train platform waiting for a train at the Long Island Railroad Station when at the other end of the same platform, a man raced to board a departing train carrying a box of fireworks. That man jumped onboard the moving train but lost his balance and was assisted by railroad employees, both on the train and on the platform, who both pushed and pulled at the man, to help him get on the train, during which time he dropped his package of fireworks which exploded. The noise of the exploding fireworks startled the crowd on the platform, causing one person to tip over a set of scales, which then landed on Mrs. Palsgraf, injuring her. Mrs. Palsgraf sued the railroad, claiming that the workers were at fault for her injury, by being negligent in their handling of the man who was clearly holding a package of fireworks. The case went to the Court of Appeals of New York which reversed the rulings of the lower courts finding that although there was evidence for the actual cause, there could be no legal cause the railroad workers could not have possibly foreseen, that any passerby, in particular Mrs. Palsgraf, would be hurt as a result of their helped another train passenger board a train. Therefore, without proximate cause there could be no negligence [46].

The causal chain of causation can also be affected by intervening or superseding events and such events may affect a defendant's liability. Jurisdictions vary as to whether they use the interning cause or the superseding cause. An "intervening cause" is a "separate act or omission that breaks the direct connection between the defendant's actions and an injury or loss to another person, and may relieve the defendant of liability for the injury or loss" [47]. Similarly, in those jurisdictions using superseding cause, the "superseding cause relieves from responsibility (liability) the party whose act started the series of events which led to the accident, since the original negligence is no longer the proximate cause" [48].

Res Ipsa Loquitur

Breach of duty is generally demonstrated by expert testimony because knowledge of both the standard of care and a practitioner's deviation from it are not generally known to the laypersons of a jury. However, there are instances in medical practice trials where expert testimony about the standard of care is not required. Courts may waive the need for expert witness testimony where negligence may reasonably be *inferred* from facts which laypersons may understand based on common experience.

Res ipsa loquitur is a Latin phrase meaning either "the thing itself speaks" or "the thing speaks for itself." The phrase *res ipsa loquitur* is merely a form of circumstantial evidence which depends upon the common understandings of mankind for its application. It has been said that the doctrine is properly applicable in those situations which "contain within themselves a sufficient basis for an inference of negligence" [49]. Courts may also use the doctrine of *res ipsa loquitur* in the analysis of cases where the actual negligent act cannot be proved, but it is clear that the injury was caused by negligence. Thus, the doctrine of *res ipsa loquitur* is a rule of evidence [50], which creates a legal foundation through which negligence can be inferred in situations in which there is no direct evidence of negligence or wrongdoing (Table 16.3).

Table 16.3 Examples of *res ipsa* medical malpractice cases

Unintentionally retained foreign object after surgery or other invasive procedure
Intraoperative burns to a patient during a surgical procedure or operation
Operation performed on the wrong body part
Positioning injuries
Intraoperative burn injury (or burn in a sedated patient)
Fall out of bed in an anesthetized or sedated patient

In the general negligence context, the doctrine of *res ipsa loquitur* has its origins in the 1863 British case of *Byrne v Boadle*, a case arising when a barrel of flour that fell out of the defendant's shop window struck the plaintiff [51]. Medical application of *res ipsa loquitur* doctrine was developed through the 1944 court case of *Ybarra v Spangard* wherein Ybarra developed appendicitis and presented for an appendectomy. During anesthesia and surgery, Ybarra was allegedly positioned in such a way that his upper back was rested against two hard objects, about an inch below his neck. Following the operation, Ybarra could not move his arm and was diagnosed with a permanent neurologic injury to his brachial plexus. Since Ybarra was unconscious under anesthesia during the surgery, he could not determine who had positioned him improperly; the operative team also could not determine the person who had done the positioning. Thus, the court proceeded by shifting the burden of proof to the defendants, citing the *res ipsa loquitur* doctrine and held that "where a plaintiff receives unusual injuries while unconscious and in the course of medical treatment, all those defendants who had any control over his body or the instrumentalities which might have caused the injuries may properly be called upon to meet the inference of negligence by giving an explanation of their conduct" [52].

Res ipsa allows a jury to *infer* negligence, *if* the preponderance of the evidence supports that "(1) the defendant had exclusive control of the instrumentality causing the occurrence, (2) that the circumstances were such that in the ordinary course of events the incident would not have occurred if the defendant had exercised reasonable care and (3) plaintiff's voluntary act or negligence did not contribute to the occurrence" [53]. In short, *res ipsa loquitur* requires the plaintiff to demonstrate that the alleged injury cannot ordinarily occur unless there is medical negligence and that the circumstances which caused the injury were at all times always under the exclusive control of the defendant and the plaintiff could not have contributed to his or her injuries.

Res ipsa is difficult to apply in cases of misdiagnosis, rare complications [54], or poor outcomes [55]. Furthermore, the inference of negligence is not mandatory but is rather permissible. Thus, the *res ipsa* doctrine is not synonymous with liability. *Res ipsa* creates a rebuttable presumption of negligence; the presumption can be nullified by a convincing defense argument.

The Loss-of-Chance Doctrine

In a negligence action, such as medical malpractice, the plaintiff has the burden to prove to the trier of fact, either the judge or the jury, that (1) the defendant physician was negligent by deviating from the standard of care and that (2) the injuries were "more likely than not" a direct result of that negligence. "More likely than not" defines the "preponderance of the evidence" standard necessary to prove liability in a civil case and means that the probability of negligence must be greater than 50%; if it is not, the plaintiff loses and recovers nothing [56].

In cases where there is a treatable pre-existing condition, and a provider negligently fails to the condition from spreading or worsening, through a delay in proper diagnosis or treatment, the plaintiff can be compensated for the extent by which the defendant's negligence reduced the plaintiff's chance of survival or a potentially more favorable outcome. The "loss-of-chance doctrine" or the "lost chance doctrine" is a legal principle which permits a plaintiff to recover damages from a defendant if that plaintiff was exposed to a heightened risk of death or injury; even if the plaintiff cannot prove the defendant's negligence by a preponderance of the evidence. It is very important that providers understand the "lost chance doctrine" and its implications.

The doctrine is premised on the theory that a plaintiff should be compensated for the loss of potentially achieving a more favorable outcome [57]. The loss of chance doctrine is not uniformly accepted by all state courts in the United States. In New York, courts generally require the plaintiff to prove that negligence deprived him or her of a "substantial possibility" of recovering from the underlying ailment [58]. Furthermore, in some states, such as South Dakota, the legislature has expressly prohibited the use of the doctrine [59].

Thus, the relaxed standard of causation inherent in the doctrine makes it possible for a plaintiff to recover when the defendant's actions have substantially harmed the plaintiff by decreasing his chance for survival, even if the actual probability of negligence is less than 50%. The doctrine allows a plaintiff to be compensated in direct proportion to the probability of a more successful outcome if the opportunity had not been lost. For example, if it can be shown that a defendant physician deprived the plaintiff of a 30% chance of a more successful recovery and plaintiff's ultimate injury would otherwise be compensated with a $100,000 verdict, the plaintiff's award would be $30,000.

The doctrine is most often applied in cases where there is a failure to diagnose; for example, breast cancer spreads after a prior mammogram was read as "normal"; a treatable lung cancer spreads after a prior nodule was missed on radiology reading, or a treatable infection is misdiagnosed. For example, in the case of *Cudone v. Gehret*, the United States District Court for the District of Delaware permitted recovery on the basis of a "lost chance" claim where there was an alleged delay in the timely diagnosis of Ms. Cudone's breast cancer. Plaintiffs' experts testified that based on a reasonable medical probability, Ms. Cudone's breast cancer would not have metastasized if there had been an earlier diagnosis. The experts also testified that based on a reasonable medical probability, the defendant's negligence resulted in the progression of Ms. Cudone's cancer from a "stage I" lesion to a "stage II" lesion with a concomitant increase in the chance that Ms. Cudone will experience a recurrence of her cancer. Although the court reasoned that it could not be stated with a reasonable medical probability that the physician's negligence was the cause of the patient's death, the plaintiff should nonetheless be compensated proportionately for the increased risk of death attributable to the delayed diagnosis.

The Iowa Supreme Court case of *DeBurkarte v. Louvar* addressed the issue of a plaintiff who claimed a failure to diagnose palpable breast cancer at an early stage. Elaine DeBurkarte "found a lump in her left breast. Because her sister died of breast cancer, she made an appointment the next day with Dr. Louvar, who examined her and ordered a mammogram, an x-ray of the breast. The results of the mammogram were negative." The lump did not go away, and Elaine DeBurkarte returned to Dr. Louvar, less than a month later where he assured her the lump was only a cyst, and not cancerous. He advised her to perform self-examinations, and not to return for a year. When Ms. DeBurkarte discovered another lump in her breast, Dr. Louvar referred her to a surgeon, Dr. Robert Brimmer who performed a biopsy the following day, and test results indicated the lumps were cancerous. Elaine subsequently underwent a mastectomy and later underwent oophorectomy. The DeBurkartes then brought suit, alleging Dr. Louvar has failed to diagnose her cancer at a stage when removal of the lump could have arrested the cancer; claiming damages for disfigurement, past and future pain and suffering, emotional distress, medical expenses, shortening her life, and death; and, her husband claimed damages for the lost consortium. Relying on expert testimony regarding relative survival probabilities of lesions resected early versus late, the plaintiff recovered under Iowa's lost chance of survival statute [60].

This "loss-of-chance" theory of recovery is being increasingly applied in medical malpractice cases involving reduced life expectancy or increased risk of future harm. "Lost chance" is mostly invoked where a plaintiff suffers from a pre-existing condition sufficiently grave as to undermine the causal chain of events necessary to prove negligence. In *Hicks v. United States*, a physician, following a 10-minute physical examination, diagnosed the decedent with gastroenteritis and discharged her home where she died later the same day of a small bowel obstruction. The United States Court of Appeals for the Fourth Circuit stated that "[w]hen a defendant's negligent action or inaction has effectively terminated a person's chance of survival, it does not lie in the defendant's mouth to raise conjectures as to the measure of the chances that he has put beyond the possibility of realization. If there was any substantial possibility of survival and the defendant has destroyed it, he is answerable." Thus, the court opined that the physicians' negligence nullified whatever chance of recovery the decedent would have had and therefore the misdiagnosis represented the proximate cause of her death [61].

In *King v. St. Barnabas Hospital*, a man at a gym playing basketball suffered a cardiac arrest. Upon the arrival of medical personnel, the patient's cardiac rhythm was found to be a mixture of asystole and ventricular fibrillation which the defendants attempted to defibrillate unsuccessfully. The plaintiff's estate sued on a theory of medical negligence alleging that it was a departure from ACLS protocols to defibrillate a patient who was in asystole and that defendants failed to timely administer epinephrine and atropine; the defendants argued that their actions could not be proven to have a detrimental effect on the outcome. The trial court agreed noting that even under "the best circumstances, plaintiff's expert cannot predict whether [plaintiff] could have been saved or if cardiac function could have been restored." The first department, however, reversed on appeal stating that New York permits claims for negligent resuscitation efforts to the extent the defendants departed from life support protocols and deprived the plaintiff of "any possibility of survival." According to the court, "the very fact that advanced life support protocols exist for patients in asystole means that adherence to the protocols afford a chance of reviving the patient, notwithstanding the grave nature of the condition. It necessarily follows that failure to follow the protocols reduces the chances of reviving the patient." [62]

Therefore, under the "loss-of chance" doctrine, a provider could be liable in damages if even a 1% reduction of a patient's optimal outcome can be proven. Relaxing the standard of causation increases the plaintiff's odds of a favorable outcome in two possible ways: (1) a plaintiff is more likely to present the case to a jury; and (2) it reduces the plaintiff's burden of persuasion, requiring the plaintiff to establish only that the act or omission was "more likely than not" a "substantial factor."

Damages

Civil lawsuits seek to compensate a plaintiffs for a wrong that is committed against them. The intent of compensation in a civil lawsuit is to make the plaintiff "whole", understanding that monetary compensation may never compensate adequately for physical or emotional injuries. The amount of the compensation, claimed or awarded, is referred to as "damages." Damages compensation may be for economic or noneconomic damages or both. The pleadings served at the onset of a lawsuit as the "complaint" will usually outline the nature of the damages sought.

Economic damages, or special damages, seek to reimburse a victim for financial costs related to the injury; these may include, for example, past, present, and future medical expenses; lost wages; costs of therapy, rehabilitation, or custodial care; and medical equipment or renovations to a home to ensure access. Economic damages are fairly quantifiable.

Noneconomic damages, or general damages, seek to compensate a plaintiff for pain and suffering, loss of enjoyment of life; loss of spousal companionship or consortium; and earning capacity. Noneconomic damages are distinguished by a speculative and extrapolative nature such that they are not easily amenable to a definitive mathematical accounting. A foundation for a noneconomic damages claim may be based on pain, mental anguish, disfigurement, aggravation of a pre-existing condition, and an inability to participate in the enjoyment of life.

Punitive damages seek to punish actions that the court finds to be egregious. The intention of a plaintiff to pursue punitive damages may sometimes be evident in the use of words such as "wanton," "reckless," or "intentional" within the complaint. The intent of punitive damages awards is to both punish the defendant and deter future potential defendants.

Proof of damages also requires expert testimony. In order to quantify damages, the experts may be both medical, such as physiatrists, therapists, psychologists, and rehabilitation specialists, and nonmedical such as accountants, actuaries, and financial experts.

Defense of Medical Malpractice

The defense of a medical malpractice cause of action will involve a skilled and experienced litigator, who, in collaboration with the defendant and experts in support of the defendant, will seek to establish that the care provided was either (1) not a departure from accepted medical standards of care; (2) an unforeseeable event; (3) a known complication for which the defendant gave informed consent; or (4) that the plaintiff was contributorily negligent. In addition, there are a number of procedural, or affirmative, defenses, such as the statute of limitations, for example. Contributory negligence can be important in cases where the plaintiff failed to disclose an element of his or her history such as substance abuse, ingestion of food on the morning of surgery despite instructions to the contrary, or noncompliance with prescribed treatment, medications, or instructions. The issue of causation, especially in cases where there are multiple providers over a period of time, or where supervening or intervening causes can be established, can be used by the defense to argue on behalf of the defendant.

One of the most important elements in a malpractice defense is good and thorough documentation in the medical record, especially with respect to medical judgment [63]. It is important to note that the plaintiff has the burden of proof; the defendant is innocent until proven guilty.

References

1. Federal Tort Claims Act (August 2, 1946, ch.646, Title IV, 60 Stat. 812, 28 U.S.C. Part VI, Chapter 171 and 28 U.S.C. § 1346).
2. Negligence. Legal information institute. Cornell Law School. Online at https://www.law.cornell.edu/wex/negligence. Verified October 11, 2020.
3. W. Prosser & W. Keeton, Torts (5 th Ed. 1984) § 53, p. 358. See also, Jaworski v. Kiernan, 241 Conn. 399, 405 (1997) ("the threshold inquiry has always been whether the specific harm alleged by the plaintiff was foreseeable to the defendant").
4. Foss v Kincade, 766 N.W.2d 317, 322 (Minn. 2009) (*quoting* Whiteford ex rel. Whiteford v. Yamaha Motor Corp., U.S.A., 582 N.W.2d 916, 918 (Minn. 1998)).
5. Cruess SR, Johnston S, Cruess RL. "Profession": a working definition for medical educators. Teach Learn Med. 2004;16(1):74–6. https://doi.org/10.1207/s15328015tlm1601_15.
6. Szalados JE. Legal issues in the practice of critical care medicine: a practical approach. Crit Care Med. 2007;35:S44–58.
7. West's Encyclopedia of American Law, edition 2. 2008.
8. Whetstine v. Moravec, 291 N.W. 425 (Iowa 1940).
9. Hurley v Eddingfield, 156 Ind 416, 59 NE 1058 (Ind 1901).
10. Mead v Adler, 231 Or App 451, 220 P3d 118 (Or 2009).
11. Irvin v. Smith, 31 P.3d 934, 941 (Kan. 2001).
12. Warren v. Dinter, 926 N.W.2d 370 (Minn. 2019).
13. American Medical Association. Warren v. Dinter, 926 N.W.2d 370 (Minn. 2019). 2018. Available online at: https://searchltf.ama-assn.org/case/documentDownload?uri=/unstructured/binary/case/Case-Summary_Warren-v-Dinter.pdf.
14. Byrd v WCW, 868 SW2d 767 (Tex 1994).

15. Richie v. West, 23 III. 329 (1860).
16. Garner BA. Black's law dictionary. 8th ed. Eagan: Thomson West Publishing; 2004.
17. Sanabria v. City of New York 42 A.D.2d 615 (N.Y. App. Div. 1973).
18. Furrow, Barry R., Johnson, Sandra H.,, Jost, Timothy S. ,Schwartz, Robert L. Health Law: cases, materials and problems. 2nd ed. West Publishing. St Paul. Minn. 1991, *at 126.*
19. Small v. Howard. In: 128 mass 131; 1880.
20. Hill v. Stewart, 209 So. 2d 809, 812 (Miss. 1968).
21. Ariz Rev Stat §12-563 (2019).
22. Idaho Code §6-1012 (2019).
23. Nestorowich v Ricotta, 97 NY2d 393, 767 NE2d 125 (2019).
24. Va Code Ann §8.01-581.20 (2019).
25. Wash Rev Code §7.70.040 (2019).
26. Lewis MH, Gohagan JK, Merenstein DJ. The locality rule and the physician's dilemma: local medical practices vs the national standard of care. JAMA. 2007;297(23):2633–7.
27. Waltz JR. The rise and gradual fall of the locality rule in medical malpractice litigation. DePaul L Rev. 1969;18:408.
28. Trull v Long, 621 So2d 1278 (Ala 1993).
29. Hall v. Hilbun. 466 So. 2d 856. 1985.
30. Frye v United States, 293 F1013 (DC Cir 1923).
31. Szalados JE. Policies, protocols, and guidelines. In: Szalados JE, Smith W, Wright W, editors. Law and ethics in neurocritical care: Neurocritical Care Society; 2019. p. 206–7.
32. Mello MM. Of swords and shields: the role of clinical practice guidelines in medical malpractice litigation. Univ of Penn Law Rev. 2001;149(3):645–710.
33. Moffett P, Moore G. The standard of care: legal history and definitions: the bad and good news. West J Emerg Med. 2011;12(1):109–12.
34. Moses RE, Feld AD. Legal risks of clinical practice guidelines. Am J Gastroenterol. 2008;103(1):7–11.
35. Hinlicky v. Dreyfuss 18 A.D.3d 18. 2005.
36. Hinlicky v. Dreyfuss 6 N.Y.3d 636. 2006.
37. Papke v. Harbert, 738 N.W.2d 510, 517 (S.D. 2007).
38. Perlmutter v. Beth David Hosp. 308 N.Y. 100 (N.Y. 1954)
39. Bean WB. Sir William Osler: aphorisms from his bedside teachings and writings. Springfield: Charles C. Thomas Publisher; 1961, at 129
40. Osler W. Teacher and Student, in Aequanimitas With Other Addresses to Medical Students, Nurses and Practitioners of Medicine. PA, USA: H K Lewis, 190, at 38.
41. Pringle v. Rapaport, 980 A.2d 159 (Pa.Super. 2009).
42. Callahan v. Cardinal Glennon Hospital, 863 S.W.2d 852 (Mo. banc 1993).
43. Callahan at 860-61.
44. Lester R. The "substantial factor test" for causation: Juedeman v. Montana Deaconess Medical Center. In: 48 Mont. L. Rev; 1987.
45. Callahan at 865.
46. Palsgraf v. Long Island R. Co., 162 N.E. 99, 248 N.Y. 339, 1928 N.Y. LEXIS 1269, 59 A.L.R. 1253 (N.Y. 1928).
47. Superseding intervening cause. (n.d.) West's Encyclopedia of American Law, edition 2. (2008). Retrieved June 7 2020 from https://legal-dictionary.thefreedictionary.com/Superseding+intervening+cause.
48. Superseding cause. (n.d.) TheFreeDictionary.com. (2020). Retrieved June 7 2020 from https://legal-dictionary.thefreedictionary.com/Superseding+cause. Verified October 11, 2020.
49. Aaron J. Broder, Res Ipsa Loquitur in Medical Malpractice Cases, 18 DePaul L. Rev. 421 (1969) *citing* Foltis v. City of New York, 287 N.Y. 108, 38 N.E.2d 455 (1948).
50. Haddock v. Arnspiger, 793 S.W.2d 948, 950 (Tex. 1990).
51. Byrne v Boadle, 2 H & C. 772, 159 Eng. Rep. 299, 300 (Ex. 1863).
52. Ybarra v. Spangard , 25 Cal.2d 486 (1944).

53. State of New Jersey. Civil Model Jury Charge 5.10D RES IPSA LOQUITUR. 2015. Available online at https://civiljury.blogspot.com/2015/03/510d-res-ipsa-loquitur-model-jury-charge.html. Verified October 11, 2020.
54. George v. City of New York, 22 A.D.2d 70. 1964.
55. Rosen HM. Defense against res Ipsa in medical malpractice. 13 Clev.-Marshall L Rev. 1964;128
56. Szalados JE. Lost chance doctrine. In: Szalados JE, Smith W, Wright W, editors. Law and ethics in neurocritical care: Neurocritical Care Society; 2019. p. 28–9.
57. King JH. "Reduction of likelihood" reformulation and other retrofitting of the loss-of-A-chance doctrine, 28 U. Mem L Rev. 1998;491:492.
58. Kallenberg v. Beth Israel Hosp, 45 A.D.2d 177 (N.Y. App. Div. 1974).
59. South Dakota Legislature, Codified Law § 20-9-1.1 (2013).
60. DeBurkarte v. Louvar, 393 N.W.2d 131, 132 (Iowa 1986).
61. Hicks v. United States – 368 F.2d 626 (4th Cir. 1966).
62. King v St. Barnabas Hosp. 2011 NY Slip Op 05641.
63. Szalados JE. Civil law and liability. In: Szalados JE, editor. Ethics and law for neurosciences clinicians: foundations and evolving challenges. New Brunswick: Rutgers University Press; 2019. p. 50–1.

Chapter 17
Legal Reasoning: Why the Law and Its Application Are Confusing to Medical Providers

James E. Szalados

Scientific Facts Versus Legal Facts

Scientific facts are data elements that are characterized by objective repeatedly verifiable observation and therefore reproducibility. Since the validity scientific facts depend only on the method by which they are acquired, not on the person acquiring them, they are accepted as being true as to what they represent. Scientific facts may also be referred to as empirical evidence. Examples of scientific fact may include, for example, the speed of light or the molecular weight of oxygen. Clinical facts are similar; for example, the concentrations of sodium or potassium in a blood sample, the size, and the reactivity of a human pupil measured by a pupilometer at one point in time or a patient's oxygen level measured by a pulse oximeter at a point in time under one set of circumstances. Clinical facts are accepted as empirically accurate and valid by clinicians, who rely upon the data to draw conclusions (diagnoses) and implement pans of action (treatment plans) in real time. Clinicians view data points as facts, even though there is an uneasy understanding that data is not perfectly accurate and may be in flux at the time it was obtained. For example, a clinician understands that the limits of clinical laboratory technology may introduce an error of almost 10% to many clinical laboratory results. Nonetheless, imperfect, but largely reproducible, data points are nonetheless facts to clinicians. Clinicians may obtain both subjective and objective data; when the story and the data do not match, clinicians will generally discount subjective data and rely on objective data for their

J. E. Szalados (✉)
Director, Surgical and Neurocritical Care Units, Rochester Regional Health System at Rochester General Hospital, Rochester, NY, USA

The Szalados Law Firm, Hilton, NY, USA
e-mail: james.szalados@rochesterregional.org; jszalados@aol.com

J. E. Szalados (ed.), *The Medical-Legal Aspects of Acute Care Medicine*,
https://doi.org/10.1007/978-3-030-68570-6_17

diagnosis and treatment. For example, a patient who presents as though they may be having a heart attack (ischemic epiphenomena) but who denies chest pain will still be diagnosed as having a myocardial infarction by electrocardiography and serum enzyme levels.

On the other hand, legal facts represent any and all of the individual elements of evidence introduced in the prosecution or defense of a case in controversy. Although legal facts will often include scientific facts and similar objective data such as photographs and recording, legal facts will also include the allegations of the parties, recollections and testimony of witnesses, and expert opinion. Legal facts may include data points that are highly subjective, such as matter of perception, judgment, interpretation, and understanding and recollection. Thus, the testimony of a witness, even though controverted by that of another witness, is nonetheless a legal fact. Moreover, questions of degree (e.g., more or less likely), questions of standard (e.g., reasonable versus unreasonable behavior), and even the meanings of an ordinary words may be admitted into evidence as legal facts [1]. For the clinician to whom a fact is an objectively verifiable and reproducible data point, the notion that purely subjective and unverifiable assertions could be represented as fact is confusing and almost objectionable.

Scientific Proof Versus Legal Proof

Legal proof may be construed to be similar to scientific proof in that it is based in rational logic and analysis. In science, as in law, facts are used to support or controvert a theory. Inductive reasoning is a form of logical thinking that uses related data points to develop a general conclusion. Life scientists such as biologists generate observations and record them, and, from many observations, the scientist can infer conclusions (inductions) based on the data. Inductive reasoning involves formulating conclusions inferred from careful observation and the analysis of a large amount of data.

In the clinical sciences, clinical facts are accumulated to support one or more potential theories, such as a differential diagnosis, and the weight of the facts supports one differential over another. Legal proof has little to do with whether the facts are accurate or inaccurate and everything to do with logic. Thus, legal proof is based in logic games, occurs in retrospect, and makes conclusions based on narrow interpretations of circumstances, stories, and opinions. Clinical proof occurs based on accumulating data, in real time, and, at least under optimal conditions, is not accumulated to support a foregone conclusion. Clinical scientists are trained in the process of scientific reasoning and develop their theories in real time objectively based on the available facts.

Both clinical and legal reasoning and logic will at times use inductive or deductive logic in reaching conclusions. However, there is a difference: in the clinical sciences, the data is not compiled to support the conclusion; clinicians, especially experienced and unbiased clinicians, will accumulate and analyze all available data before reaching a conclusion. In clinical medicine, there are often multiple possible competing theories to explain the problem at hand. The data leads to a pattern and the pattern in turn leads to a conclusion; this is inductive logic. The measure of the strength of an inductive argument is known as an inductive probability, which is a measure of how probable the conclusion is if the premises are true [2].

Legal reasoning is more of a deductive logic approach. Legal reasoning is a method of thought and argument used by lawyers and judges when applying legal rules to specific interactions among legal persons. Opposing counsel take positions a priori, based on the parties they represent. During their research, they develop a theory of the case, which they will then support with facts intended to prove their argument to the trier of fact. Legal counsel must take an undisciplined mass of information, the evidence, and reshape it into a persuasive tool, the argument. The argument must be presented in such a way so as to convert even the most skeptical decision-maker to support the counsel's point of view [3]. Effective and persuasive legal argument will take an indistinct subject and present it in such a way so as to make it seem mathematical through a process known as syllogistic argument which provides the requisite element of apparent certainty [3]. A classic syllogism is the derivation of the mortality of Socrates: (1) all men are mortal; (2) Socrates is a man; and therefore (3) Socrates is mortal. Here, the conclusion follows from the premises and the mind will reach a conclusion without prompting. In clinical medicine, clinicians are trained to be cautious of syllogisms since syllogisms represent a type of bias, confirmation bias, and can be harmful.

The trier of fact may be either the judge or the jury or both. Witnesses are chosen to testify so as to support each side's theory of the case, through evidence offered as proof of that theory. A deductive argument is valid if and only if it is logically impossible that its conclusion is false if the premises are accepted as true. In developing a legal argument, the logic pattern is more of a deductive style, since the line of legal reasoning begins with a theory and the point of view is supported by syllogisms intended to persuade.

The trier of fact, in a legal argument, will weigh the merits of the evidence offered by each side of opposing counsel. The role of the trier of fact is to weigh the evidence offered in proof and reach a conclusion based on a subjective probability. The weight of the evidence may be a result of impressions such as the credibility of the witnesses or the believability of the story, emotion such as the psychological impact of some of the evidence, or to subjective internal theories or biases [4].

Legal Terms of Art

A term of art is a word or phrase that has a particular meaning within a specific context. Terms of art are part of the vocabulary of many professions, since, as a type of shorthand, terms of art can convey complex concepts in simple terms or phrases. Legal terms of art are everyday words and phrases that take on special and specific meanings. The special meanings of terms of art may not be intuitively obvious to otherwise well-educated non-attorneys. Terms of art are often embedded within legal documents without a corresponding warning or reference. Contracts are one such type of document which contains terms of art; however, similar terms of art may appear, for example, in a summons and complaint. Thus the language of law can produce traps for the unwary.

Examples of legal terms of art include, for example, the notion of employee, which is a legal concept defined differently by various state laws. In addition, word such as "should," "must," and "shall" have different meanings as defined by the context in which they appear.

The Burdens of Proof, Production, and Persuasion

The burden of proof is the affirmative duty imposed upon one party in a controversy to prove or disprove a disputed fact. In the USA, the accused defendant is presumed innocent until he or she is proven guilty. Thus, it is the burden of the plaintiff, or prosecution, to establish the guilt of the defendant. The defendant does not need to establish his or her innocence or non-culpability; rather the defendant needs to only successfully rebut the argument of the plaintiff. Thus, the burden of proof may be shifted at times during the course of a trial so that where the prosecution or plaintiff has made out a sound legal case, the prima facie case, then the burden will shift to the defense to disprove the facts by establishing doubt as to the facts, as evidence, that the plaintiff had introduced.

The burden of proof is associated with an at least de minimis threshold showing that the facts or circumstances show that the argument to be presented has merit and the threshold facts, supported by additional facts, can support a case in controversy. Thus, one of the first challenges to a civil lawsuit is the "motion to dismiss" which is raised by the defense soon after the case is filed, often as part of the answer.

The burden of proof is associated with a burden of production; the prosecution or the plaintiff must present evidence to substantiate his or her allegations. Data, or evidence, must be produced to substantiate the claim which is the basis of the lawsuit. When the burden of production is satisfied, then a prima facie case is considered to have been established. The modem Greek equivalent of "prima facie" literally translated means "on/at first viewing." Prima facie derives from the Latin term, meaning that which is sufficient to establish a fact or raise a presumption unless disproved or rebutted. Thus, if a case is considered to be prima facie, then the plaintiff or prosecution is, subject to a convincing counter-argument, entitled to prevail on his or her cause of action. In more common usage, however, prima facie simply refers to the fact that a party has met their burden of production [5].

When evidence is submitted, that evidence must be of a type which is legally admissible under the Rules of Evidence [6]. The Federal Rules of Evidence (FRE) govern the admissibility of evidence in federal courts; state rules of evidence are largely similar to and frequently modeled after the federal rules. In general, there are four main types of evidence: (1) real evidence (usually a tangible thing), (2) demonstrative (a reconstruction, model, or schematic), (3) documentary (a document), and (4) testimonial (testimony provided by witnesses). Furthermore, circumstantial evidence refers to circumstances that support a reasonable inference, and corroborating evidence refers to separate and different evidence, which supports or strengthens other evidence. Hearsay is a type of evidence that is offered as a truth but which has been independently verified. The FRE, in conjunction with the Federal Rules of Civil Procedure [7], represent a substantial component of the body of procedural (as opposed to substantive) law.

The "burden of persuasion" refers to a specific level of proof, or weight of evidence, that is necessary to meet the legally applicable evidentiary standard in support of a legal conclusion. In general there are three levels of persuasion required by law. In criminal trials, the requisite burden of persuasion is the "beyond a reasonable doubt" standard. "Beyond a reasonable doubt" means that there is no other reasonable explanation or conclusion that can be reached from the evidence presented that there is a virtual certainty.

The burden of persuasion in civil trials, the level of persuasion, is the "preponderance of the evidence" standard; this means that it's more likely than not that a claim is true. The "preponderance of the evidence" refers to a balancing of scales, with one side being of even very slightly greater weight; statistically this may be a 50.01% probability.

In administrative law courts, the third level of persuasion is the "clear and convincing" standard, which is an intermediate standard that represents a higher level of persuasion than "preponderance of the evidence" but is less stringent than the "beyond reasonable doubt." In *Colorado v New Mexico* [8], the US Supreme Court defined clear and convincing to mean that the evidence is *highly and substantially more likely* to be true than untrue. In general, the types of cases in which a clear and convincing evidence standard is likely to apply may include cases of testamentary challenges and issues such as Wills and cases of fraud. Healthcare providers will also realize that the "clear and convincing standard is the standard that applies to the determination of a patient's preferences for life-sustaining treatment." Furthermore, New York courts will use the clear and convincing evidence standard when determining whether to involuntarily hospitalize a mentally ill patient.

The Adversarial System of Justice

The adversarial system of justice consists of advocates who represent the parties each side of a controversy and who advocate, or argue their cases, on behalf of their clients to an impartial judge or jury (the triers of fact). In an adversarial system, counsel present the facts in such a way as to portray their clients in the best possible light, in an effort to convince the trier of fact of the merits of their cases, and thus prevail in the verdict or judgment. Since the adversarial system is by definition confrontational, plaintiff and defendant will witness or provide testimony that is often emotional which would seem to attack their integrity, character, and veracity. It is important that defendants maintain their objectivity and do their best to retain their professional demeanor since loss of control can result in poorly chosen words, maybe interpreted by the jury as hostility, and provoke undue stress. In addition, it is important for parties to understand the role of their counsel and to the greatest extent possible trust in the training, experience, and knowledge of counsel – a position similar to that of a patient and physician.

Precedent: Case Law

Legal process is premised on procedural law, which defines the operating rules by which the law operates. Legal process determines every aspect of a lawsuit from the service of process, the elements of pleadings (summons and complaint), the deadlines for and the requisite elements of the answer, the motions, and the presentation of evidence, for example. Procedural law is the body of legal rules that govern the process.

Substantive law is the "black letter" law that is found, for example, in legislation, statutes, ordinances, regulations, and also precedent. Thus, substantive law includes not only the rules and regulations which define normal rules of behavior but also establish causes of action and precedent. Precedent is established by prior court decisions which addressed similar or identical facts and similar or the same legal issues. Precedent refers to "a court decision that is considered as authority for deciding subsequent cases involving identical or similar facts, or similar legal issues. Precedent is incorporated into the doctrine of stare decisis and requires courts to apply the law in the same manner to cases with the same facts" [9]. The strength of a precedent case depends on (1) the similarity of the issues and facts in the prior case to the case being litigated, (2) the level of court issuing the ruling that is cited as precedent, and (3) the jurisdiction. Rarely will cases be identical; this in itself does not disallow a precedent. However, if the facts or issues in a previous case are substantially different, the previous case cannot be used precedent without distinguishing the differences to maximize transparency. Thus, precedent can be either binding or persuasive based on its characteristics.

Binding precedents are rulings on the same or very similar fact pattern, which are delivered by courts of higher authority applicable to that jurisdiction. For example, rulings from the US Supreme Court on similar facts are binding on all courts in the USA. Therefore a ruling by the US Supreme Court is binding on all courts in the US federal and state. Within the federal courts, circuit courts will be bound by from decisions previously issued within that circuit, and district courts that are under the jurisdiction of a circuit court will be bound by rulings of the circuit court. Within a jurisdiction a ruling by an appellate court, on similar facts, must be followed by lower courts within that jurisdiction. Decisions of federal courts are binding on state courts when the case involves an issue of federal law.

In cases such a medical malpractice, state laws will be similar but may also differ slightly based on both state statutes and local precedent. Nonetheless, similar cases from other jurisdictions may be introduced to illustrate situations in which there is no prior ruling on point within a state or jurisdiction. In such cases, the precedent is not controlling, or binding, but may be reasonably introduced to the court, or cited, as non-binding precedent or a relevant persuasive authority. The court rules and procedure for introducing non-binding but persuasive precedent must be carefully followed and accompanied by relevant explanations as to why the court should recognize such precedent.

Successfully Coping with a Medical Malpractice Lawsuit

The second victim syndrome (see Chap. 32) in the course of a medical malpractice lawsuit refers to the healthcare providers "who commit an error and are traumatized by the event manifesting psychological (shame, guilt, anxiety, grief, and depression), cognitive (compassion dissatisfaction, burnout, secondary traumatic stress), and/or physical reactions that have a personal negative impact" [10]. The psychological impact of a professional negligence lawsuit on a medical provider has been characterized as a type of post-traumatic stress disorder which may impact not only the professional identity but also the personal and spiritual well-being of affected providers [11]. Providers tend to be self-critical, especially in retrospect, and therefore have a tendency to reconstruct and re-evaluate the events of a bad outcome. Providers will forget that decisions were made in real time and often without all the information that subsequently is uncovered at trial. Therefore, providers will retrospectively judge themselves as guilty, develop self-doubt, and lose self-confidence. Providers have a tendency to see an accusation of malpractice, a deviation from the standard of care, as an accusation that they are incompetent. The emotional turmoil associated with an accusation is subsequently compounded by the sense of loss of control and further sense of incompetence brought on by the legal process and proceedings, which are foreign to most providers. Each provider that must defend an allegation of medical malpractice will have challenges that are unique, based on the circumstances, their support system, and their own sense of preparedness. General strategies for survival are outlined in Tables 17.1 and 17.2.

Table 17.1 Strategies for prevailing in your medical malpractice lawsuit

Notify your carrier, department, or hospital risk managers immediately when you are served
Do not discuss the case with anyone (except as in Table 17.2) outside the boundaries of privilege
Do not alter, hide, or destroy anything that might be evidence
Find an expert and experienced attorney you are comfortable with: choose your own if needed
Do not talk with the plaintiff, their family, friends, or plaintiff's counsel about the case without your attorney
Work with your attorney to *actively prepare your case*
Know the standards of care
Participate in selection of experts on your behalf
Review everyone's depositions (objectively)
Learn about the legal process and learn about the law: go watch a trial
Consider training in communication or media skills
Prepare for depositions and trial: materially and psychologically
Do not educate plaintiff's counsel
Answer honestly but completely
Refresh your memory if needed
Do not argue with plaintiff's counsel
Do not lose your emotional balance
Talk to (not down to) the jury
Project humanity, trustworthiness, likeability, and professionalism

Table 17.2 Strategies for psychological survival during a medical malpractice lawsuit

Do not take the accusation personally: bad outcomes are not necessarily malpractice
Resist thinking that you are being judged (by your peers, friends, family, patients) or that your competence as a provider is on trial
Maintain social support and relationships: resist isolation
Maintain life balance: be kind to yourself
Seek counseling if needed
Return to work when you are ready

Conclusions

A principal intention of this text is to educate providers about how the legal system works and its language, its logic, and its process. Louis Pasteur noted that "chance favors the prepared mind," and in the context of litigation, nothing could be truer. For attorneys, litigation is natural; conflict, strategy, and argumentation are basic aspects of the profession. There are motivations other than justice for which persons may argue. The goal of the legal system is less about truth than it is about justice. Thus, the understanding of the legal system and its rules can make one's involvement in a lawsuit a little less emotionally taxing.

References

1. Szalados JE. Legal reasoning: legal process, legal proof and why it is confusing to clinical scientists. In: Szalados JE, editor. Ethics and law for neurosciences clinicians: foundations and evolving challenges. NJ: Rutgers University Press; 2019.
2. Kaye DH. Proof in law and science. Jurimetrics. 1992;32:313.
3. Gardener JA. Legal argument: the structure and language of effective advocacy. Charlottesville, LexisNexis: The Michie Company; 1993.
4. Berch MA, Berch RW, Sprizer RS. Introduction to legal method and process. 2nd ed. St Paul: West Group; 1992.
5. Georg Nils Herlitz, The Meaning of the Term "Prima Facie", 55 La. L. Rev. (1994).
6. Federal Rules of Evidence. 2020 Edition. Online at: https://www.rulesofevidence.org/. Okay to.
7. Federal Rules of Civil Procedure. Available online at: https://www.uscourts.gov/rules-policies/current-rules-practice-procedure/federal-rules-civil-procedure.
8. Colorado v. New Mexico, 467 U.S. 310 (1984).
9. Cornell Legal Information Institute. Precedent. Available online at: https://www.law.cornell.edu/wex/precedent#:~:text=Precedent%20refers%20to%20a%20court,cases%20with%20the%20same%20facts.
10. Wu AW. Medical error: the second victim. The doctor who makes the mistake needs help too. BMJ. 2000;320(7237):726–7.
11. Baas MAM, Scheepstra KWF, Stramrood CAI, Evers R, Dijksman LM, van Pampus MG. Work-related adverse events leaving their mark: a cross-sectional study among Dutch gynecologists. BMC Psychiatry. 2018;18(1):73.

Chapter 18
Ethical Conflicts and Legal Liability in Professional Nursing

Taylor Hughes

The Professionalization of Nursing

The field of nursing has evolved dramatically since its organized formation in the mid-nineteenth century. Prior to this, nursing was considered more of a vocation than a profession, and nurses were thought to be an extension of mothers and wives rather than clinicians [60]. The practice of "nursing" was less of an occupation and more of a household responsibility for women, with knowledge being passed on generationally rather than through formal education [53]. In fact, women could be appointed as nurses without any formal training whatsoever [53]. In a paternalistic society, it was believed that the benevolent nature of women would afford them the disposition for this task. It was not until the 1850s, when Florence Nightingale introduced female nurses into a combat zone during the Crimean War, that nursing became recognized as an employable position that required training [48]. This role, however, was still vastly different from that of nurses today.

Although nursing had become a career, the job description of the nurse retained many of the antiquated qualities of its previous years. Early training programs in the United States modeled their educational content after Nightingale's work, only permitting female applicants with good moral conduct, the majority of them being from Caucasian descent [33]. Nurses were considered distinctly separate from physicians with a role focused on the duty of caring. The Nightingale-era scope of nursing practice generally included spending time with patients, dressing their wounds, making their beds, feeding them meals, and maintaining sanitation [33]. Nightingale was a staunch proponent for the division of labor, saying that "the Matron must look to the Medical Officer for professional instructions which she is to obey; but for nothing else [44]." Due to an absence of interdisciplinary collaboration between the various roles in the medical field, nurses were expected to follow physician orders

T. Hughes (✉)
Surgical Intensive Care Unit, Rochester General Hospital, Rochester Regional Health System, St. John Fisher College AGACNP Candidate, Rochester, NY, USA

J. E. Szalados (ed.), *The Medical-Legal Aspects of Acute Care Medicine*,
https://doi.org/10.1007/978-3-030-68570-6_18

without question or input. These limitations to the role of early nurses were compounded by cultural assumptions regarding gender characteristics, in turn leading to the division between physicians and nurses [53].

Formal education for nurses in the United States began in 1862, with hospitals setting up nurse training programs specific to their facilities. It wasn't until the 1920s that the education process moved away from small, employer-sponsored training to a more formal and rigorous university-based system [33]. Reform of the nursing practice was met with conflict, and there were widely differing public opinions on increasing the educational standards for nurses [53]. A small group of reformers, now understood to be the origins of the American Nurses Association, argued that educational restructuring was imperative to the professionalization of nursing and that it would lead to clinical improvements. The opposition believed that increasing the training requirements for nurses would exacerbate the ever-present nursing shortage and push current nurses out of the profession [53]. Many nurses expressed the desire to continue practicing with skills determined by "womanly virtue" rather than professional autonomy [53].

However, practice standards began to change after World War II, when North American nurses led the movement to professionalize the nursing practice [53]. The United States was thriving in the postwar era, and the 1950s brought increased hospital development, the expansion of private health insurance, and an increase in the birth rate (now known as the baby boomer generation). Clinical research became necessary for all medical providers, and many nurses pursued advanced degrees in order to keep in line with practice standards.

Today, professionalism is one of the major components of nursing practice and is highly valued by medical institutions throughout the healthcare system. With an increasing acuity among patients, nursing responsibilities have evolved to include critical thinking, interdisciplinary collaboration, advanced assessment skills, and leadership. Nurses are now seen as essential clinical resources that complement physicians rather than as an adjunct. With the implementation of the Affordable Care Act in 2010, healthcare experienced one of its largest overhauls of the past century. In order to prepare for this transition, the Robert Wood Johnson Foundation and the Institute of Medicine began a 2-year study (2008–2010) of the nursing profession and its potential for growth.

Considering that nurses constitute the largest percentage of healthcare professionals, the IOM and the RWJF advocated for nursing partnership and leadership, stating that the delivery of high-quality care was impossible without a strong nursing workforce. The Future of Nursing Initiative intended to find ways to standardize practice and increase nursing efficiency in order to eliminate present barriers to patient care. The RWJF created a committee staffed with experts in health policy, business, academia, and healthcare delivery. Members were appointed in order to examine the current role of nursing, staff shortages, nursing education, and future nurse recruitment [24].

At the conclusion of their study, the committee produced a detailed report that was 642 pages in length and supported 4 main recommendations. Although this report refers to advanced practice nurses, licensed practical nurses, and registered nurses, we will focus on registered nurses for the purpose of this chapter. First, it was determined that nurses should be practicing to the full extent of their education and training [24]. Although many nurses receive the same education, their scope of practice is defined by their state of residence. While some states strictly outline their professional standards, others are less clear about staff expectations. Standardizing the scope of practice would eliminate the ambiguity of professional standards across state lines, creating an easily definable job description.

The second recommendation was the promotion of growth in nursing leadership and interdisciplinary collaboration [24]. With their constant presence at the bedside, nurses can offer an informed, real-time, patient assessment, a luxury that physicians and advanced practice providers do not have. It is believed that increased interdisciplinary collaboration can provide a potentially vital system of checks and balances, as enabling nurses to openly communicate with physicians and APPs about care planning could potentially prevent or correct medical errors before they occur. In the committee's report, nurses were encouraged to share their assessment, and interdisciplinary collaboration was proven to be essential in promoting high-quality care. As such, healthcare organizations were additionally advised to engage nursing staff and assist them in developing improved patient care models to leverage these benefits.

In order to help promote these recommendations, nursing education was reformed to include courses in leadership, while clinical practice was designed in such a way that nursing students were given the ability to develop their leadership skills. Once employed, nurses were encouraged to seek out leadership opportunities and strive for professional growth within their careers. It was further suggested that employers offer leadership development and mentoring programs in order to assist their nursing staff.

The third recommendation was the improvement of data collection in order to enhance workforce planning and policy development [24]. Considering that the nursing shortage is only expected to become more severe, the IOM and RWJF suggest that the National Health Care Workforce Commission, the Health Resources and Services Administration, and the Department of Labor should collaborate in order to identify healthcare workforce needs and create a plan to increase the number of nurses for future employment [24]. The committee believed that by utilizing predictive analytic techniques that the data collected could be used to optimize planning for future workforce requirements.

The last, and most emphasized, recommendation from the committee was to increase the educational requirements for nurses due to increasing patient acuity and the varying responsibilities of the profession [24]. The IOM and RWJF agreed that a bachelor's degree was the preferred level of education for registered nurses and aimed to increase the percentage of baccalaureate-prepared nurses from 50% to 80% by 2020. They stated that healthcare facilities should offer incentives for continuing education such as tuition reimbursement and competitive salary benefits for their associate degree nurses. In addition, student loan forgiveness and grants should be made available for those with nursing degrees.

In addition to increasing the proportion of baccalaureate nurses, the committee also emphasizes the need for nurses to partake in lifelong learning while employed. Although it is true that nurses learn daily while on the job, the IOM and RWJF argue that mandated continuing education should be an additional requirement. Continuing education can come in the form of lectures, journal article readings, or participatory certifications. Nurses are also required to complete annual competencies in order to ensure they are up to date with their current facility policies and requirements on how to use the equipment. Some states have already implemented these suggestions, requiring nurses to prove a certain number of continuing education hours when reapplying for their RN license.

With the professionalization of practice, many nurses were experiencing dramatic developments in their clinical roles. Becoming more of a prominent medical liaison at the patient's bedside began to shed light on additional changes that needed to happen within our healthcare system; one being the lack of ethical care that patients were receiving. In the next section, we will discuss some of the most common ethical considerations nurses face in their day-to-day roles.

Ethical Conflicts in Professional Nursing

Historically speaking, ethical care as we know it was not always a priority of medical treatment. The 1950s and 1960s saw rapidly advancing medical technology virtually reshape the culture of healthcare. Hospital staff were practicing within the ethical concepts of beneficence and nonmaleficence when treating patients [50], while new equipment had created the philosophy of "preserve life at all costs [50]." In other words, medical personnel were expected to do no harm and act in their patients' best interests, while simultaneously extending the human body past its corporeal existence. It was not until the 1980s and 1990s that the ideas of patient autonomy and advanced directives became the prominent determinants of care planning [32, 43]. Nursing has played a pivotal role in this paradigm shift, and that role is expanding due to the professionalization of the nursing practice [29].

Albeit morbid, life and death decisions are made daily in intensive care units around the world. As such, it is crucial for physicians and advanced practice providers to be explicit when providing information on care options to patients and families—as seen with the practice of informed consent. Nurses are often an additional resource that is able to supplement the information being provided. As the primary point of contact, nurses have the potential to develop a trusting relationship with patients and families. Through this relationship nurses are able to have discussions about autonomy, goals of care, and quality of life. Nurses then have the ability to articulate discussed directives to the medical team in ways that the patient and/or proxy may not.

Communication is arguably the critical care nurse's most useful tool. In an environment in which multiple team members from various disciplines are constantly circulating through the unit's milieu, it is often the nurse's responsibility to gather and relay information. The intensive care unit can be intimidating to the layman because it is a high-stress area where patients and their families are required to make substantial decisions involving their care. There are many instances in which patients are unable to speak for themselves, and medical decisions become the responsibility of their surrogate, also known as next of kin. Said surrogate is charged with making decisions that they believe to be in line with the patient's wishes; however, that is not always the case. For example, according to the New York State Attorney General's Office, next of kin has the power to rescind a do not resuscitate order on a mentally incapacitated patient [2], even though the process may not be in line with the patient's wishes.

While the patient remains the main focus of nursing attention, the practice of holistic care is leading family members to become more involved throughout the hospitalization. Although a familial presence can be valuable to the critically ill patient in many ways, it can also lead to an array of ethical conflicts for medical staff requiring oversight through hospital ethics committees.

Ethics Committees and Litigation

Critical care nurses have the ability to voice their ethical opinions among the medical team, but because of their legal limitations as a restricted diagnostician without ordering privileges, their opinions can often be overlooked. One example of this can be the overall limitations of bedside nurses within formal ethical and legal hospital agencies. Many hospitals appoint ethics committees that are responsible for reviewing patient cases within their administration and then assisting the care team by reporting their assessment of the situation. Ethics committees are consulted for many reasons, but they are commonly involved in situations pertaining to medical futility. One study in the Midwest United States found that there was an average of two nurses on hospital ethics committees, and those nurses were serving the hospital in managerial or administrative roles [49]. Although these nurses were formally educated in ethics, many of them lacked familiarity with the patient's experience while in the hospital and did not directly participate in patient care [49]. In contrast, other hospitals have ethics committees that involve nurses with backgrounds in administration, floor nursing, and critical care nursing [21]. While it is vital to have an unbiased committee presiding over potentially life-sustaining ethical treatments, it could be beneficial to bring in witnesses with bedside contact—in the same way that physicians and nurses can be expert witnesses during legal proceedings in court. In this way, ethics committees can gain testimonials from those directly responsible for the care being questioned.

In an effort to become more involved in ethical discussions, nurses formed parallel nurse ethics committees in which all members were from a nursing background. The first NEC was formed in Omaha, Nebraska, in 1984 [28]. In addition, the early 1990s saw both the Joint Commission on Accreditation of Healthcare Organizations and the American Nurses Association require institutions to have standards in place that allowed nurses to partake in ethical discussions [28]. It is thought that a nurse-based ethics committee would help empower nurses and familiarize them with ethical situations. This would, in turn, assist them in becoming more involved in hospital ethics committees and more ethically minded providers [61].

Although not infallible, ethics committees have been shown to resolve many conflicts before they reach formal legal proceedings. A study conducted by Baylor University Medical Center showed that 98% of conflicts in medical futility cases were resolved by ethics consultations prior to litigious action being taken [16]. Unfortunately, there are times when involved parties cannot come to an amicable conclusion, and those situations are frequently involving the end of life [42]. Even though nurses may not be directly involved with the litigious side of medicine, nurses are largely impacted by the decisions that lead to judicial intervention.

There are many legal cases that involve medical futility and end-of-life decisions. For example, Baby L, *Gilgunn V. MGH*, *In re Wanglie*, and *In re Baby K* all involved patients that physicians believed no longer benefitted from aggressive medical care due to their insurmountable comorbidities [42]. Said physicians wished to withdraw care on the patients, but the family members insisted on the continuation of care and, in the cases of Helga Wanglie and Baby K, ended up pursuing legal action [42]. Litigious proceedings can be time-consuming for all involved. Throughout that time, nurses are at the bedside, continuing to take care of a critically ill patient along with their grief-stricken family regardless of their professional opinions on the care they are being required to provide. This direct exposure to the effects of medical futility is one of the primary causes of staff burnout, a serious and pervasive dilemma within the field of nursing that we will discuss in the next section.

Medical Futility

It has been shown that critical care nurses experience high levels of moral distress when carrying out families' wishes that they (the nurses) believe to be unethical towards the patient. Unsurprisingly, many studies have referenced the most pervasive cause of moral distress to be in cases where the critical care nurses believe there to be an unnecessary prolongation of life insisted upon by the patient's loved ones [20]. At times, critical care nurses have even felt that the family can be a hindrance to patient care [55]. Repeatedly referenced high-stress situations in the intensive care unit often involve patients' loved ones opting for the continuation of aggressive medical treatment that the nurses see as causing the patient undue suffering without providing any tangible medical benefits [12, 19, 20, 36]. Critical care nurses often believe these efforts to be a futile attempt of prolonging life.

Futility is a relatively new concept in medicine. Since the term "medically futile" is heavily subjective and therefore undefinable, groups like the American Thoracic Society have suggested using terminology like "potentially inappropriate treatment" instead [50]. Defined by Kon et al., inappropriate treatment is "when there is no reasonable expectation that the patient will improve sufficiently to survive outside of the acute care setting, or when there is no reasonable expectation that the patient's neurologic function will improve sufficiently to allow the patient to perceive the benefits of treatment" [29]. The entire medical team is responsible for establishing realistic goals and expectations for patient care, and their constant presence at the bedside allows nurses to play a vital role in care planning. It is possible that frequent time spent at the patient's bedside will allow the nurse to develop insight about the patient and family's wishes.

It is often argued that ethical situations involving end-of-life care are exacerbated by the rapid evolution of medical technology. With the continued advancement of medical equipment, there are higher expectations for positive outcomes among patients, families, and medical professionals, alike. Some nurses interviewed in one study had generally positive opinions about technology within intensive care units [38]. In contrast, others have the opinion that technology has placed them in a precarious position [38]. Many nurses felt that technology had left them responsible "to implement heroic caring for dying patients, while decisions failed to be made on what technology realistically had to offer" [38]. Being employed in departments with life-sustaining equipment, critical care nurses often question their ethical and moral beliefs during advanced patient care. There are many occasions in which critical care nurses are repeatedly exposed to morally distressing situations involving their patients, an experience that is beginning to take a significant emotional and psychological toll on nurses globally.

Staff Burnout and Moral Distress

The continual attention required to care for a grieving, anxious family in addition to an acutely ill patient is a compounding emotional stressor that is increasingly plaguing critical care nurses around the world. As a self-defense mechanism, critical care nurses have been known to emotionally detach from situations that they do not agree with in order to continue providing patient care [19, 36]. After repeated exposure to such stressors, it is possible for nursing staff to become cynical and burnt out [19, 36]. Phrases such as "burnout" and "compassion fatigue" have been topics of conversation among hospital staff for decades, and academics are beginning to take notice.

Staff burnout was first introduced by H.J. Freudenberger in 1974, where he published information about workplace stress in the *Journal of Social Issues* [51]. Initially defined as "a state of fatigue or frustration that resulted from professional relationships that failed to produce the expected rewards" [17], the topic of burnout has since gained much attention from medical providers and researchers, alike.

The definition of burnout evolved in 1982 when psychologist Christina Maslach described it as "a psychological syndrome involving emotional exhaustion, depersonalization, and a diminished sense of personal accomplishment that occurred among various professionals who work with other people in challenging situations"

[34, 51]. Through her extensive research, Maslach was able to create a conceptual model, dubbed the Maslach Burnout Inventory, which helps quantify burnout. Drawing from common themes such as cynicism, detachment, emotional exhaustion, and personal inefficacy [14, 35], the MBI has three main domains: emotional exhaustion, depersonalization, and personal accomplishment [51]. Each domain has a various number of questions that ask participants to describe their feelings on a 7-point scale, ranging from never experiencing said feelings to experiencing them multiple times per week [51]. The higher the combined scoring, the more likely the interviewee is to be at risk. Although there are many tools to measure staff burnout, the Maslach Burnout Inventory is the most widely adopted tracking method across numerous professional disciplines [51].

A 2009 study researched the reliability of the MBI in evaluating staff burnout among nurses in adult general hospitals [51]. The sample size was 54,738 nurses working in 646 hospitals across 8 different countries. Using confirmatory and exploratory factor analyses, Poghosyan, Aiken, and Sloane determined that the MBI was validated and performed "relatively similarly" across all eight countries [51]. Using the MBI has allowed many institutions to determine the main causes of burnout among nurses, especially those within critical care.

Nurses working in high-stress fields are more likely to experience burnout from their careers [13, 52]. To quote McFeely, "[burnout] is so pervasive in the ICU that it almost has become a part of the background noise" [37]. Although all medical providers in critical care experience work-related stress, it has been shown that nurses experience increased levels of burnout due to their continual close contact with patients [6, 31]. Moreover, critical care nurses are caring for patients at the height of their illness; progression and improvement are not always witnessed by the healthcare team, increasing their risk of burnout due to emotional exhaustion [5, 6, 31]. As a result critical care nurses often develop coping strategies, such as depersonalization, in order to best care for their patients. Feelings of emotional attachment have the potential to cloud judgment and distract nurses at times when attention to detail is paramount [55]. While this self-preservation tactic can improve care and efficiency in high-stress situations, it presents a conundrum to ICUs given that, according to Maslach, increased feelings of depersonalization and detachment are likely causes of staff burnout. This presents nurses with the unenviable predicament of having to choose between maximizing patient care and protecting their own mental health.

For those working in critical care, another frequent cause of workplace burnout is moral distress. Moral distress takes place when one is unable to act within their moral or ethical code [14, 19]. Critical care nurses, although heavily involved with interdisciplinary collaboration, rarely have control over the prescribed orders and final decisions related to their patients. Due to this lack of control, critical care nurses have been shown to be more vulnerable to moral distress than physicians [6, 20, 31]. Ultimately, the act of accepting and fulfilling physician orders (within reason), whether or not said decisions are in line with the nurse's morals, is the leading cause for this distinction [31].

In addition to discrepancies between medical professional's ethical opinions, critical care nurses are prone to emotional distress when interacting with patient family members. Nurses are often the link between patients, family, and the rest of the medical team. Because of this, it is not uncommon for them to develop emotional attachments to patients and their families. Although nurses recognize the significance of this relationship, it has been shown to cause increased levels of emotional exhaustion among staff [55]. This can lead to a phenomenon called compassion fatigue. Defined by McHolm, compassion fatigue is "the emotional, physical, social, and spiritual exhaustion that overtakes a person and causes a pervasive decline in his or her desire, ability, and energy to feel and care for others" [39]. Compassion fatigue in the intensive care unit often results from constant involvement with critically ill patients and their families compounded by the high-stress environment. It is often argued that the combination of compassion fatigue and moral distress is responsible for high rates of staff turnover among nurses, particularly in critical care units.

Staff Turnover

As professionals, it is easy to diminish the significant amount of emotional distress experienced in the workplace. However, evidence shows that burnout in nursing is associated with poor patient outcomes and increased turnover among nursing staff [40, 41, 58]. A study conducted by Hiler et al. used the Moral Distress Scale-Revised (MDS-R) and the Practice Environment Scale of the Nursing Work Index (PES-NWI) to poll critical care nurses on their levels of moral distress and perceived job satisfaction [23]. While the MDS-R is a survey used to gauge moral distress, the PES-NWI is a survey designed to measure the nurses' overall sense of fulfillment and work productivity. Using these survey methods, Hiler et al. had the intention of studying the relationship between moral distress and nurse turnover. The sample size included 328 nurses employed in intensive care units across the United States, ranging from 1 to >10 years of experience. Although the majority of respondents (59%) echoed job satisfaction, 73% had contemplated leaving their position within the past 6 months [23]. It was found that the nurse's desire to leave their position was significantly correlated to their levels of moral distress [23]. Another study directed by Corely showed that 13% of critical care nurses left their jobs because of moral distress and 5% abandoned the field of nursing entirely [11].

In a profession that is already considered grossly understaffed, the continued loss of nurses due to burnout can be crippling to healthcare institutions. Considering the current statistics of the workforce, the demand for nurses will increase up to 30% by 2020 due to the retirement and aging of the baby boomer generation [3]. Although the nursing profession eagerly welcomes new members, the lack of veteran nurses is becoming evident. A study conducted by Buerhaus et al. revealed that nursing had lost 1.7 million "experience years" to retirement in 2015 and is expected to lose an additional 2 million "experience years" by 2020 [9].

Due to the positive correlation between nurse burnout and years of work experience [54], institutions are beginning to spend more time on nurse retention [3]. Some hospitals are developing employee assistance programs that provide counseling and coping strategies for stressful situations [5]. Others are encouraging off-campus retreats that combine education on mindfulness with scheduled periods of relaxation and self-reflection [7, 30]. Many survey-based studies show that nurses believe they are reducing their levels of burnout by practicing self-care [22].

Legal Liability in Professional Nursing

As with most professions, there are regulatory bodies that dictate standard policy, licensing, and regulation within nursing. The American Nurses Association (ANA) was a pioneer during the early days of nursing. Formed in 1896, the Nurses' Associated Alumnae of the United States and Canada (now known as the ANA) was responsible for setting professional standards and defining the scope of nursing practice [27]. Becoming licensed as a registered nurse is a relatively new concept for the profession. In the early 1900s, some states implemented optional licensure programs for nurses, but many states did not require their nurses to be licensed whatsoever. Optional licensure had spread nationwide in the 1920s, with state boards of nursing being implemented to distribute and monitor said licenses. Each state would have its own licensing exam, which often varied widely from other state's exams. In turn, the scope of nursing practice across state lines often had substantial differences [27].

The ANA formed the National Council of State Boards of Nursing, or NCSBN, after World War II in an attempt to standardize licensing and testing for nurses [27]. The NCSBN was, and still is, a federal agency that is comprised of 59 sub-boards belonging to each state and territory within the United States [1]. Board of Nursing (BON) officials are often elected or appointed, many of whom have experience in patient care from their designated state [45]. One of the key early achievements of the NCSBN was in spearheading the practice of mandatory licensure for registered nurses in the United States by advocating for professional reform. As a result, by the 1950s, US nurses were required to be licensed, each applicant having to take a standardized national exam in order to obtain their license. This national exam helped shape the current National Council Licensure Examination, or NCLEX-RN, required of students today [27].

In an effort to standardize practices and ideologies, the NCSBN also designed a Model Nurse Practice Act, which is meant to be a guide for state and territorial Board of Nursing regulations. The Model Nurse Practice Act outlines licensure qualifications, nursing accreditations and titles, scope of practice, and disciplinary actions resulting from breaking the aforementioned regulations [45]. The NCSBN has tasked each jurisdiction to form their own Nurse Practice Act, which would then be interpreted as the standard regulation governing said jurisdiction's nurses. We will discuss the nurse practice act further in the legal liability section.

Although state BONs base their regulations from the national standards of the NCSBN, states and hospitals are able to more specifically define the current scope of nursing practice should they see fit. According to the American Nurses Association, the scope of nursing practice is determined by a combination of Nurse Practice Acts, JCAHO regulations, the nursing code of ethics, organizational standards, and institution policy and procedure manuals [18]. As such, there are often instances in which the nursing scope of practice varies among different states, or even different hospitals within a single state.

To become a licensed professional, current standards require nursing students to first graduate from an accredited educational institution. Accredited institutions can be verified by transcript work, a diploma, or a letter from the program's dean [27]. Once a student's education is verified, they are then given the authorization to take the NCLEX-RN. With proof of a successful exam result, student nurses can then apply for licensure with their state board of nursing and pay applicable fees. It is the responsibility of individual states and territories to issue licenses to nurses within their region and to further monitor their adherence to prescribed laws based on that state's nursing policies. The applicant must be at least 18 years of age and does not have to be a US citizen [45]. Once approved, permission is granted to practice as a registered nurse in that state. If a nurse wishes to practice in another state, they must apply for licensure through said state's board of nursing. Additionally, some states participate in compact licensure programs. Further, many states also require continuing education in order to maintain licensure. Every time a nurse wishes to renew their license, often every 2–3 years, they must have proof of continuing education that meets their jurisdiction requirements. Most areas require between 20 and 40 hours of continuing education over the 2–3 year period [27].

In order to obtain a registered nurse license, many states require the applicant to display "good moral character as determined by the department" [45]. Licensure application may inquire if the candidate has ever been found guilty of a felony or misdemeanor, if there are any criminal charges pending against them or if they have been accused of professional misconduct [46]. State boards of nursing have outlined extensive definitions of professional misconduct. Some examples may include revealing protected health information, negligence, false reporting or failing to report, practicing beyond the scope of nursing, delegating to unlicensed personnel outside of their scope, treating without consent, or guaranteeing that success will result from medical treatment [47]. As one would expect, these are some of the most common areas in which nurses can experience legal liability within the scope of their practice.

Statutory Law

Throughout the history of medicine, nurses were not commonly considered to be medical professionals that were subject to litigation. The professionalization of nursing has led to increased autonomy and responsibility among nurses, which has in turn led to the development of numerous laws to help regulate the nursing practice and protect staff. Nursing laws are created by the federal government, states, and hospital policy and procedure manuals, resulting in varying legal implications depending on the location. It is the responsibility of the nurse to know the law; ignorance will not dismiss a legal deposition. Violations of nursing law can leave the accused subject liable for potential monetary fines, suspension or loss of license, and even possible imprisonment [27].

The determinants of nursing law can be broadly divided into two categories: statutory law and common law. First, we will explore examples of statutory law. Statutory law refers to laws that are created by legislative bodies such as Congress or state boards of nursing [27]. Federal statutes are responsible for defining the minimal standards of care for hospital personnel in all facilities that receive federal funds, whereas state statutes deal with more specific legislation, unique to the jurisdiction in which they are applicable.

There are four main federal laws that most greatly impact nurses [27]. First is the Emergency Medical Treatment and Active Labor Law, or EMTALA. Enacted in 1986, EMTALA was put in place to protect uninsured and/or financially vulnerable patients from being refused treatment by emergency departments due to their insurance status [27]. Second is the Americans with Disabilities Act of 1990, with an intent on ensuring that disabled persons receive equal, unbiased healthcare. This law requires institutions to provide assistive devices to accommodate a patient's disability in order to maintain an equitable standard of care [27]. 1990 also saw the implementation of the Patient Self Determination Act, our third federal law, which supported the patient to express preferences of treatment and participate in their healthcare. This law was also pivotal in informing patients about their ability to accept and/or refuse treatment and introduced advanced care directives [27]. The final, and probably most familiar, federal statute is the Health Insurance Portability and Accountability Act of 1996, also known as HIPAA. The primary directive of HIPAA is to ensure the confidentiality of patient protected health information [27].

State statutes are largely determined by nurse practice acts. As we have discussed, nurse practice acts are state-specific pieces of legislation that are designed to protect the public and define nursing responsibilities [27]. Nurse practice acts will generally define the term of registered nurse, outline standards and scope of practice, and give examples of behaviors that are prohibited by registered nurses. Examples of illegal nursing activity may include, but are not limited to, diverting medications, being impaired by drugs and/or alcohol while at work, treating outside of the scope of practice, falsifying records, and physical and/or sexual abuse of a patient [59]. Each state board of nursing has the ability to investigate any deviance from prescribed policies. It is the responsibility of the nurse to understand the policies designated by their state of practice as well as their state's nurse practice act. Failure to comply with one's state nurse practice act can lead to the revocation of professional licensure [59].

Common Law

In contrast to statutory law, common law comes from judicial decisions during medical litigation cases. Once a medical case has been brought to state or federal court and a judge has made a ruling, said ruling is incorporated into the standards of professional nursing conduct [57]. These standards of conduct will partially contribute to the evolution of the nursing scope of practice over time. One prominent example of a legal case determining the expected conduct of nursing was that of *Utter v. United Hospital Center, Inc.*, in which a jury determined that nurses were required to exercise judgment independent of physicians, if necessary, in order to prevent harm to the patient [57].

Plaintiff Garth R. Utter had fallen from a ladder and had sustained injuries to his right wrist, elbow, and back, injuries that were revealed to be a "comminuted compound fracture of the right wrist, a posterior dislocation of the right elbow, and a compression fracture of the second lumbar vertebra," respectively [57]. His right arm was casted by a physician, and he was admitted to United Hospital Center for monitoring. About 48 hours into his hospital stay, the patient began to show symptoms of compartment syndrome in his right arm and from then on rapidly deteriorated. These complications eventually led to his right arm being amputated. Documentation showed that staff nurses had reported the patient's condition to the overseeing physician, but that the physician did not escalate care. Since the nurses did not activate the physician chain of command, they were indicted with negligence. The reason this was considered to be a landmark case is because this was the first time that nurses were seen as legally independent medical professionals, and therefore liable to litigation [27]. Since it had been established that nurses could be subject to litigation as a direct result of their actions or inactions, further education was required on how instances of civil or criminal law could apply to nurses, specifically.

Tort Law: Unintentional Torts

There are many examples of civil lawsuits that fall under the legal umbrella of torts. A tort can either be intentional, as in cases of assault and/or battery, or unintentional, as with issues involving negligence or malpractice. In order for something to be considered a tort, it must be proven that there was a civil wrong committed by one party against another party that violates the legal duties determined by their personal relationship [26]. Reasonableness and social expectations determine whether or not the breach of duty between parties is considered a tort.

In addition to reasonable behavior, professionals are judged against standards of practice; if there is a violation in either of these categories, the practitioner is defined as negligent [56]. Negligence committed by professionals is otherwise referred to as malpractice [27]. Therefore, when considering its application to nurses, the terms can be used interchangeably. In other words, the nurse-patient relationship is a legally binding personal and professional contract. If the nurse wrongs the patient, whether intentionally or unintentionally, the nurse can be subject to litigation if he/she did not reasonably conform to the standards of nursing practice during the incident.

In order to prove malpractice, the plaintiff must prove that five specific circumstances had occurred. First, it must be proven that the nurse had a duty to the plaintiff. This can be determined by something as simple as the nurse's daily patient assignment. Second, if the nurse-patient relationship was proven, the plaintiff must then define the appropriate standard of care for the nurse in question [4]. The appropriate standard of care is defined as the general degree of skill, knowledge, and care that is ordinarily possessed by a practitioner in good standing within their profession [18]. Nurse practice acts, hospital policy, procedure manuals, and federal regulations all define the general standard of care.

Once the standard of care is determined, thirdly, the plaintiff must prove that the nurse had deviated from the standard of care. Juries test the standard of care by asking whether or not a prudent nurse with the same level of experience would have performed similarly under said circumstances [18]. For example, a critical care nurse with 15 years of experience will not be held to the same standard of care as an outpatient urgent care nurse with 15 years of experience. Additionally, a critical care nurse with 1 year of experience will not be held to the same standard of care as a critical care nurse with 15 years of experience. Next, if a breach in the standard of nursing practice has been identified, the plaintiff must then prove that their injury was a direct result of said breach. Finally, the plaintiff must then prove that said breach had resulted in damages [4].

Critical care nurses are held to the same level of legal liability as floor nurses. However, the standard of care is vastly different for a critical care nurse than that of a floor nurse. The scope of practice is heavily influenced by unit protocols and educational standards, and it is often more fluid and technical than in floor nursing [26]. As an example, the responsibilities of advanced practice providers relative to nurses often falls within a gray area precisely because critical care nurses are expected to interpret clinical signs and symptoms and act upon them immediately. This added level of responsibility over floor nurses crucially differentiates the necessary regulatory treatment between the two roles.

In many hospitals, critical care nurses have standing orders. For example, say a cardiac ICU nurses were to notice that her patient was having premature ventricular contractions and then drew a set of labs and replaced electrolytes per standing orders. Even though there are standing orders telling her to do so, she is technically making the medical diagnosis of PVCs caused by electrolyte imbalances. Legally, diagnosing within the context of nursing practice is significantly different than a medical diagnosis. In fact, if a nurse were to diagnose as a physician does, it would be seen as a breach of the scope of practice. Instead, nursing diagnoses are more related to physical and physiological signs that nurses observe as part of their clinical judgment [45]. This conundrum frequently presents itself in intensive care units and is part of the reason behind the immense level of continuing education required to be a critical care nurse.

Juries refer to many sources when determining the standard of care for nurses. Some examples of useful bodies of evidence are nurse practice acts, professional organizations such as the American Nurses Association or The Joint Commission on Accreditation of Healthcare Organizations (JCAHO), employee job descriptions, practice standards related to the nurse's specialty, and hospital policy and procedure manuals [56]. In addition to performing within the prescribed standard of care, nurses must also practice using the nursing process. If a nurse is able to demonstrate reasonable execution of assessment, planning, implementation, and evaluation, then they are considered to be practicing within the reasonable standards of care for their profession. If, however, any one of these methods is proven to be insufficient, the nurse may be liable for malpractice [56]. These cases are commonly referred to as the "failure to" cases; failure to assess, failure to evaluate, failure to document, failure to rescue, and failure to report are some examples.

A significant example of a legal case where nurses were subpoenaed for negligence was *Brandon HMA, Inc. v. Bradshaw* [8]. Dawn Bradshaw alleged that the treatment received from the nursing staff was negligent and did not meet the standard of care, said treatment resulting in her permanent disability from brain damage after cardiac arrest. Bradshaw was admitted to Rankin Medical Center on February 17, 1997, with the diagnosis of bacterial pneumonia. On February 21, 1997, a chest tube was inserted for fluid drainage on the affected left lung. Two nurses taking care of Bradshaw periodically took her vital signs and noted no distress after the chest tube insertion.

At 2300, Alex Lewis, LPN, assumed care of Bradshaw. Lewis was assigned to the patient and supervised by charge nurse Pam Nail, RN. Around midnight, Lewis performed his first assessment of Bradshaw, and a set of vital signs were normal other than a slightly elevated heart rate. The chart reflected that Bradshaw was complaining of pain on her left side. Throughout the night, Bradshaw continued to complain of increasing pain on her left side. Lewis did not take another set of vital signs; rather, Bradshaw was medicated with Tylenol for pain and Ativan for anxiety. At 0240, Lewis rounded on Bradshaw to find her sitting up in bed, complaining of significant pain, and with rapid, shallow breathing. Lewis medicated Bradshaw with the narcotic Lorcet Plus and did not take her vital signs. At 0330 Bradshaw was found to be disoriented, diaphoretic, and not following commands. Lewis then checked vital signs and left the room to notify Nail. When both Nail and Lewis returned to Bradshaw's room, she was found cyanotic, apneic, and pulseless. A code was called and CPR was initiated, Bradshaw was transferred to the ICU. While in intensive care, MRIs of the brain revealed that Bradshaw had extensive brain damage as a result of a lack of oxygen.

Bradshaw survived but was left permanently disabled as a result of her brain injury. She was unable to independently perform activities of daily living and requires assistance with mobility. She also requires continual administration of antispasmodic drugs to alleviate her frequent muscle spasms. Bradshaw stated that the negligence of the nursing staff was the direct cause of her injury. The standard of care would have required Lewis and/or Nail to take vital signs and notify the physician during her continued complaints of pain. The expert witnesses, judge, and jury agreed with Bradshaw and awarded her $9 million in damages.

Tort Law: Intentional Torts

In comparison to unintentional torts, intentional torts are defined as civil wrongs that directly violate a person's legal rights [27]. In respect to nursing, the offensive act of the nurse was intentional, although harm of the patient may not have been the intended result. Some examples of intentional torts are assault, battery, and false imprisonment [27]. Unlike with malpractice cases, intentional torts do not have to be proven by the plaintiff as being a divergence from the standard of care in order for them to be legally processed. Penalties for intentional torts vary based on the type of tort, but fines and punitive damages are often involved [27].

While the terms assault and battery are often grouped together within the realm of intentional tort law, they each have a distinct definition. Assault occurs when the plaintiff claims an intentional act had created reasonable discontent and fear of physical contact from the assailant [56]. It is important to note that physical contact is not required in order to determine an occurrence of assault. Battery, on the other hand, is defined by an intentional act that brings unauthorized or harmful contact to a person [27]. Although the definitions remain consistent across all types of law, the terms assault and battery are not always portrayed in the same way in medicine as they are within society. For example, nurses can face charges of assault for threatening to restrain a patient. Nurses could also be charged with battery for giving a patient a medication that they have refused. In most cases, nurses mold their treatment plan from the ethical principles of beneficence and nonmaleficence, and patient harm is not the intention of their actions. However, they can still be prosecuted if they do not practice within the legal limits of their profession.

As previously mentioned, the Patient Self Determination Act determined that the mentally competent patient has the right to refuse any treatment plan prescribed by healthcare professionals. If a patient is deemed capable of making their own decisions, they are legally able to refuse any treatment that had been previously agreed to. If a nurse were to prevent, either physically or verbally, the patient from acting on their wishes it would be considered false imprisonment [27]. It is important to note that physical restraint is not required for a charge of false imprisonment. Although not commonly seen in critical care, this issue often presents itself when a patient wishes to leave the hospital against medical advice, or AMA. The nurse does not have the authority to prevent the patient's departure and is legally required to let the patient leave. The nurse must simultaneously contact the provider and notify them of the patient's desire to leave AMA [27]. Many facilities have forms that exempt them from some legal liability if the patient's condition were to deteriorate after leaving the hospital against medical advice. Said forms detail the dangers of leaving the facility prior to medical readiness and require a patient signature.

An example of false imprisonment more commonly found in critical care is the application of physical restraints. Patients in intensive care are commonly supported with a multitude of machines. It is not uncommon for patients to have endotracheal tubes, feeding tubes, urinary catheters, and central intravenous access lines simultaneously, many of which are providing life-sustaining treatment. In addition to this, these patients can be taking medications that affect their mental capacity, such as sedatives or potent analgesics. Therefore, it is often difficult to assess the mental competency of an ICU patient. Since the assessment of mental capacity can be subjective, it is sometimes the case that nurses are at risk of prosecution when restraining patients.

The grey area arises when determining whether or not a patient's mental capacity is lacking to the point of warranting restraint application. Patients can often be alert, but it is difficult to discern whether or not they are completely oriented, which could lead to potential safety complications. Due to these circumstances, many critical care nurses often apply "medical restraints." Unlike forensic restraints, medical restraints are applied when patients are believed to be a safety risk or at risk to their medical progression. Confusion and attempts to dislodge medical devices are examples of determinants for the application of medical restraints. Restraints can be physical, such as soft wrist restraints or elbow immobilizers, or they can be chemical, such as sedatives.

Since restraint application is a serious consideration, organizations such as JCAHO and individual medical facilities have protocols involving restraint alternatives, restraint application requirements, and assessment requirements for patients in restraints. The Joint Commission states that nurses are responsible for preemptively identifying behaviors that could lead to restraint application and treating them as necessary. If less restrictive alternatives have failed, the nurse applying the restraints must be able to prove that other alternatives were attempted to maintain patient safety prior to restraint application [26].

Electronic Medical Records (or EMRs) Electronic Medical Records and Their Legal Implications

The use of is on the rise within healthcare systems across the globe. Designed to increase efficiency, safety, and productivity, electronic record keeping has the ability to provide innumerable benefits. With an increased utilization of electronic health records, and the benefits that come with it, healthcare institutions have also encountered significant pitfalls. The risks of patient data becoming public, increased time spent documenting, and lack of communication between different EMR systems are all significant problems that remain to be addressed with this new technology.

Nurses, in particular, are largely affected by the implementation and ongoing requirements of electronic documentation, both positively and negatively. One positive result of the technology is that electronic systems help documentation more accurately reflect the present condition of the patient. For example, nurses are able to chart on important aspects of patient care as they occur, such as vital signs or fluid output. Electronic monitors often have the capability to transmit some information directly into the chart, therefore reducing possible transcription errors. Once charted on, these numbers become available to all members of the healthcare team, making the distribution of information more efficient. Another benefit is that EMRs also allow for information to be easily located within the chart, especially if a patient has a complex medical history involving multiple hospitalizations.

Along with organizing the distribution of patient information across various health systems, electronic medical records are also being implemented by healthcare institutions with the intention of decreasing medical errors. Electronic order sets reduce prescribing time for providers but also eliminate the need for physically writing out orders. This is seen as particularly beneficial because eliminating illegible handwriting has enormous potential to decrease risk during medication administration and treatment. Additionally, barcode scanning technology provides a second check when nurses are administering medications. Nurses are taught to always scan the patient and the medication before administration, along with checking the "five rights" of medication administration. These safety protocols, both technological and practical, are crucial in reducing instances of medication and dosage errors.

An example of the importance of medication scanning and the rights of medication administration can be seen in the case *Farmer v. Willis-Knighton Medical Center* [15]. This case centered around the disputed events of Ms. Martin's unexplained death. Ms. Virginia Martin presented to the Willis-Knighton emergency room complaining of abdominal pain, vomiting, and diarrhea. After some initial lab work and imaging, Ms. Martin was given the diagnosis of gastroenteritis from Dr. John Reeves. After reviewing Ms. Martin's lab work, Dr. Reeves ordered Demerol for pain, Phenergan for nausea, and potassium for hypokalemia. Nurse Hansen, assigned to Ms. Martin, was responsible for medication administration. The chart reflected the following events: after medication administration at 2140, Ms. Martin's IV infiltrated, at 2144 Ms. Martin's face was mottled, and she had a decreased level of consciousness, and at 2147 a code was called. Resuscitation was attempted for 30 minutes and was unsuccessful. The cause of death was determined to be an acute cardiac arrhythmia and arteriosclerotic heart disease.

Two family members that were in the room during the medication administration, Ms. Farmer and Dr. Johnson, stated that they saw Nurse Hansen draw up three IV medications in similarly sized syringes and administer them all via IV push. It is important to note that, while Phenergan and Demerol can be administered IV push, potassium cannot. Both family members testify that almost immediately after the medication administration, the patient was writhing in pain and screaming that her IV arm was burning. As noted by the chart, that IV had infiltrated. The patient then became unresponsive and cardiac arrested. Both family members testify that Nurse Hansen administered the potassium IV push, which was the direct cause of Ms. Martin's death.

Expert witness Dr. Walter Simmons agreed that the immediate symptoms up to Ms. Martin's cardiac arrest would be seen with undiluted potassium administration and noted that there was a lack of charting supporting Nurse Hansen's actions. Expert witness JoAnne Gongora, RN, agreed that the charting did not meet the standard of care and noted that times were changed and written over in many places throughout the chart. Willis-Knighton Medical Center argued that Ms. Martin's IV had infiltrated during her contrast CT, prior to the medication administration, and therefore she could not have been given IV push potassium. The court eventually sided with the plaintiffs, awarding $60,000 to each of Ms. Martin's 13 children for wrongful death damages, $250,000 in survival damages, and $6833.72 in funeral expenses [15]. If Nurse Hansen had properly utilized the barcode scanning system and reviewed the medication administration order, Ms. Martin's life could have been saved.

Risk management is an essential component of healthcare. Electronic systems have recently developed "best practice advisories," or BPAs. A BPA is triggered when a patient meets certain criteria based on what the nurse has charted; once said criteria are met, nurses are prompted to reflect on their recent charting and assess the results further. For example, many systems have a SIRS BPA. When a patient has vital signs that may represent a potential cause of systemic inflammatory response syndrome (SIRS), a BPA is triggered, and the electronic charting system notifies the nurse to verify the vital signs. The nurse is then further required to chart whether or not the vitals have been addressed by his/herself and the primary care team.

From a legal standpoint, nursing documentation is usually the most referenced part of the chart during litigation. Due to its ability to paint a vivid picture of the patient in "real time," the attorney, judge, and jury depend on nursing documentation to make their decisions [25]. Expert witnesses are often able to ascertain whether or not the standard of care was maintained by assessing nursing documentation. Thanks to electronic prompts, EMRs are able to maintain facility and state charting standards in ways that paper charting could not. By requiring vital checks and manual acknowledgment after a predefined set of warning signs, EMRs ensure that documentation standards are more thoroughly being met. In addition, nurses are responsible for charting on almost every aspect of patient care, meaning their assessment dominates the majority of the electronic record. Accurate documentation is essential in order to protect nurses and hospitals from litigation.

Although there are many positive changes associated with electronic medical records, there are some shortcomings as well. The main concern with EMRs is the maintenance of HIPAA and the security of protected health information. Within the hospital, open computer screens or scraps of paper documentation left at the bedside could be accessed by anybody—potentially risking the privacy of the patient. Many facilities have developed paperless shift handoff systems and auto-locking computer screens in order to reduce these problems. Additionally, when PHI files are shared between departments and healthcare facilities, files must be encrypted if transmitted via email [4]. If the information is being faxed, face sheets are now required to precede any sensitive medical information. All of these protective measures aim to ensure that institutions can implement these highly beneficial EMRs while still maintaining HIPAA compliance.

Another concern with EMRs is the accessibility of charts. Although records have been shown to be easy to navigate in their electronic form, the same cannot be said for when electronic records are printed out. When an EMR is printed, it is typically a long and cumbersome document, lacking any sense of cohesion. Such documents can be a nightmare to navigate effectively. In some instances, when the electronic chart is not functioning or is getting updated (also known as downtime), nurses are forced to return to paper charting. Younger nurses typically have little to no experience with paper charting, creating a steep learning curve with relatively brief preparation and training.

Skeptics of EMRs also argue that they have made healthcare documentation more cumbersome and time-consuming. Several studies have shown that 30 minutes of patient care now requires 30–60 minutes of documentation for many US nurses [10]. In order to reduce time spent charting, some nurses utilize the "copy and paste" functionality of EMRs. Copying and pasting past nurses' documentation can lead to errors in transcription and inaccurate charting [25]. As such, nursing staff often find themselves balancing practical time constraints to their charting with the risks of transcription errors when copying and pasting. As is the case with any powerful new technology, EMR systems come with numerous benefits to the global healthcare industry but also substantial drawbacks.

Summary

The nursing profession has developed vastly since its original formation in the mid-1800s, so much so that it would be arguably unrecognizable to its founders. From Nightingale's early memorandums on sanitation to current global research partnerships and foundations, nurses are continuing to push the boundaries of their career limitations. While providing new platforms for medical research and treatment, nurses simultaneously uphold the original qualities of beneficence and nonmaleficence when treating patients. Although it is becoming difficult to navigate the sea of growing ethical and legal challenges in the workplace, nurses view this as just another challenge that they will adapt to and conquer.

References

1. About U.S. boards of nursing. In: NCSBN. https://www.ncsbn.org/about-boards-of-nursing.htm. Accessed 25 Jan 2019.
2. Advanced directives: making your wishes known and honored. In: New York state attorney general. 2019. https://ag.ny.gov/sites/default/files/advancedirectives.pdf. Accessed 2 Feb 2019.
3. Andrews DR, Dziegielewski SF. The nurse manager: job satisfaction, the nursing shortage and retention. J Nurs Manag. 2005;13(4):286–95.

4. Ashley RC. Understanding negligence. Crit Care Nurse. 2003;23(5):72–3.
5. Aycock N, Boyle D. Interventions to manage compassion fatigue in oncology nursing. Clin J Oncol Nurs. 2009;13(2):183.
6. Bakker AB, Le Blanc PM, Schaufeli WB. Burnout contagion among intensive care nurses. J Adv Nurs. 2005;51(3):276–87.
7. Bauer-Wu S. Seeds of hope, blossoms of meaning. Oncol Nurs Forum. 2006;33(4):K927. Oncology Nursing Society.
8. Brandon HMA, Inc. v. Bradshaw, 809 So. 2d 611 (Miss. 2001).
9. Buerhaus PI, Skinner LE, Auerbach DI, Staiger DO. Four challenges facing the nursing workforce in the United States. J Nurs Regul. 2017;8(2):40–6.
10. Clynch N, Kellett J. Medical documentation: part of the solution, or part of the problem? A narrative review of the literature on the time spent on and value of medical documentation. Int J Med Inform. 2015;84(4):221–8.
11. Corley MC. Moral distress of critical care nurses. Am J Crit Care. 1995;4(4):280–5.
12. Elpern EH, Covert B, Kleinpell R. Moral distress of staff nurses in a medical intensive care unit. Am J Crit Care. 2005;14(6):523–30.
13. Embriaco N, Papazian L, Kentish-Barnes N, Pochard F, Azoulay E. Burnout syndrome among critical care healthcare workers. Curr Opin Crit Care. 2007;13(5):482–8.
14. Epp K. Burnout in critical care nurses: a literature review. Dynamics. 2012;23(4):25–31.
15. Farmer v. Willis-Knighton Medical Center, 109 So. 3d 15 (La. Ct. App. 2012).
16. Fine RL. Point: the Texas advance directives act effectively and ethically resolves disputes about medical futility. Chest. 2009;136(4):963–7.
17. Freudenberger HJ. Staff burn-out. J Soc Issues. 1974;30(1):159–65.
18. Gilson S, Salicco S. Starting the movement and spreading the word: legal risks in critical care. The american association of critical care nurses: NTI recorded session C60M373. 2019. https://www.aacn.org/education/ce-activities/nti17373/starting-the-movement-and-spreading-the-word-legal-risks-in-critical-care . Accessed 4 Feb 2019.
19. Gutierrez KM. Critical care nurses' perceptions of and responses to moral distress. Dimens Crit Care Nurs. 2005;24(5):229–41.
20. Hamric AB, Blackhall LJ. Nurse-physician perspectives on the care of dying patients in intensive care units: collaboration, moral distress, and ethical climate. Crit Care Med. 2007;35(2):422–9.
21. Heitman E. Institutional ethics committees: local perspectives on ethical issues in medicine. In: Society's choices: social and ethical decision making in biomedicine. Washington, DC: The National Academies Press; 1995. p. 409–542.
22. Henry BJ. Nursing burnout interventions. Clin J Oncol Nurs. 2014;18(2):211.
23. Hiler CA, Hickman RL, Reimer AP, Wilson K. Predictors of moral distress in a us sample of critical care nurses. Am J Crit Care. 2018;27(1):59–66.
24. Institute of Medicine. The future of nursing: leading change, advancing health: The National Academies Press; 2014. https://www.nap.edu/read/12956/chapter/1#xvii. Accessed 16 Feb 2019.
25. Iyer P, Levin B, Ashton K, Powell V. Nursing malpractice: volume I: foundations of nursing practice claims. 4th ed. Tucson: Lawyers & Judges Publishing; 2011.
26. Iyer P, Levin B, Ashton K, Powell V. Nursing malpractice: volume II: roots of nursing malpractice. 4th ed. Tucson: Lawyers & Judges Publishing; 2011.
27. Jacob SR. Nursing licensure and certification. In: Contemporary nursing: issues, trends, and management. 6th ed. St. Louis: Elsevier; 2013. p. 62–73.
28. Kohlen H. Caring about Care in the Hospital Arena and Nurses' voices in hospital ethics committees: three decades of experiences. In: Care in healthcare. Cham: Palgrave Macmillan; 2018. p. 237–63.
29. Kon AA, Shepard EK, Sederstrom NO, Swoboda SM, Marshall MF, Birriel B, Rincon F. Defining futile and potentially inappropriate interventions: a policy statement from the Society of Critical Care Medicine Ethics Committee. Crit Care Med. 2016;44(9):1769–74.

30. Lambert N, Steward N. Staff retreat: a journey to team building. Oncol Nurs Forum. 2007;34(2):501.
31. Lederer W, Kinzl JF, Traweger C, Dosch J, Sumann G. Fully developed burnout and burnout risk in intensive care personnel at a university hospital. Anaesth Intensive Care. 2008;36(2):208–13.
32. Luce JM. A history of resolving conflicts over end-of-life care in intensive care units in the United States. Crit Care Med. 2010;38(8):1623–9.
33. Lundy KS, Masters K. A history of healthcare and nursing. In: 5th, editor. Role development in professional nursing practice. Burlington: Jones & Bartlett Learning; 2018. p. 3–47.
34. Maslach C. Burnout: the cost of caring. Englewood Cliffs: Prentice Hall; 1982. p. 37.
35. Maslach C, Schaufeli WB, Leiter MP. Job burnout. Annu Rev Psychol. 2001;52(1):397–422.
36. McClendon H, Buckner EB. Distressing situations in the intensive care unit: a descriptive study of nurses' responses. Dimens Crit Care Nurs. 2007;26(5):199–206.
37. McFeely JE. Burnout syndrome in the ICU. Critical care alert. 2007;15(5):37–9.
38. McGrath M. The challenges of caring in a technological environment: critical care nurses' experiences. J Clin Nurs. 2008;17(8):1096–104.
39. McHolm F. Rx for compassion fatigue. J Christ Nurs. 2006;23(4):12–9.
40. Mealer M, Jones J, Newman J, McFann KK, Rothbaum B, Moss M. The presence of resilience is associated with a healthier psychological profile in intensive care unit (ICU) nurses: results of a national survey. Int J Nurs Stud. 2012;49(3):292–9.
41. Milliken TF, Clements PT, Tillman HJ. The impact of stress management on nurse productivity and retention. Nurs Econ. 2007;25(4):203–12.
42. Moore P. An end-of-life quandary in need of a statutory response: when patients demand life-sustaining treatment that physicians are unwilling to provide. BCL Rev. 2007. http://lawdigitalcommons.bc.edu/bclr/vol48/iss2/4. Accessed 14 Jan 2019.
43. Moratti S. The development of "medical futility": towards a procedural approach based on the role of the medical profession. J Med Ethics. 2009;35(6):369–72.
44. Nightingale F. Extending Nightingale nursing in hospitals. In: McDonald L, editor. Florence Nightingale extending nursing: collected works of Florence Nightingale. Waterloo: Wilfrid Laurier University Press; 2009. p. 435.
45. NYS nursing: laws, rules & regulations: article 139. In: Office of the professions. 2018. http://www.op.nysed.gov/prof/nurse/article139.htm. Accessed 25 Jan 2019.
46. NYS nursing: laws, rules & regulations: article 139. In: Office of the professions. 2018. http://www.op.nysed.gov/prof/nurse/nurse-licensefaq.htm. Accessed 25 Jan 2019.
47. NYS nursing: laws, rules & regulations: article 139. In: Office of the professions. 2018. http://www.op.nysed.gov/title8/part29.htm#nurse. Accessed 25 Jan 2019.
48. O'Brien PD. The legacy of domesticity. Nursing in early nineteenth-century America. Nurs History Rev. 1993;1:229–46.
49. Oddi LF, Cassidy VR. Participation and perception of nurse members in the hospital ethics committee. West J Nurs Res. 1990;12(3):307–17.
50. Olmstead JA, Dahnke MD. The need for an effective process to resolve conflicts over medical futility: a case study and analysis. Crit Care Nurse. 2016;36(6):13–23.
51. Poghosyan L, Aiken LH, Sloane DM. Factor structure of the Maslach burnout inventory: an analysis of data from large scale cross-sectional surveys of nurses from eight countries. Int J Nurs Stud. 2009;46(7):894–902.
52. Poncet MC, Toullic P, Papazian L, Kentish-Barnes N, Timsit JF, Pochard F, Chevret S, Schlemmer B, Azoulay E. Burnout syndrome in critical care nursing staff. Am J Respir Crit Care Med. 2007;175(7):698–704.
53. Reverby S. A caring dilemma: womanhood and nursing in historical perspective. In: Hein EC, editor. Nursing issues in the twenty-first century: perspectives from the literature. Philadelphia: Lippincott; 2001. p. 10–25.
54. Rushton CH, Batcheller J, Schroeder K, Donohue P. Burnout and resilience among nurses practicing in high-intensity settings. Am J Crit Care. 2015;24(5):412–20.

55. Stayt LC. Nurses' experiences of caring for families with relatives in intensive care units. J Adv Nurs. 2007;57(6):623–30.
56. Urden LD, Stacy KM, Lough ME. Critical care nursing, diagnosis and management, 7: critical care nursing: Elsevier Health Sciences; 2013.
57. Utter v. United Hospital Center, Inc., 236 SE 2d 213 (W.Va, 1977).
58. Vahey DC, Aiken LH, Sloane DM, Clarke SP, Vargas D. Nurse burnout and patient satisfaction. Med Care. 2004;42(2 Suppl):II57.
59. What every nurse needs to know about state and territorial boards of nursing. In: National council of state boards of nursing. 2018. https://www.ncsbn.org/What_Every_Nurse_Needs_to_Know.pdf. Accessed 2 Jan 2019.
60. Yam BM. From vocation to profession: the quest for professionalization of nursing. Br J Nurs. 2004;13(16):978–82.
61. Zink MR, Titus L. Nursing ethics committees-where are they? Nurs Manag. 1994;25(6):70.

Chapter 19
Criminal Statutes Affecting Medical Providers

James E. Szalados

Introduction to Criminal Law

Criminal law is the body of law that relates to criminal prosecutions and defense. Crime is variably defined through social and humanistic lenses as "behavior against order," "behavior against public feelings and emotions," and "behavior incongruent with social conscience and common sense [1]." Crime, from a sociological viewpoint, relates to human behavior incongruent with the common norms and values of a society [2]. Merriam-Webster defines "crime" as an illegal act for which someone can be punished by the government or a grave offense especially against morality [3]. The gravity of criminal behavior, and therefore its punishment, is that, unlike civil actions, crimes may be punishable by fines (monetary loss), incarceration (loss of liberty), lifelong criminal records (loss of certain freedoms), and/or death (loss of life).

Crimes can be defined by federal or state statutes, and the jurisdiction for criminal prosecution may be federal, state, or both; therefore, a number of overlapping laws define crime and its punishment in America. Federal criminal law is governed entirely by statute; there are no federal common law crimes. States variably retain common law crimes. Criminal jurisdiction refers to both the authority to create or legislate substantive criminal laws and the authority of a court to enforce laws as a matter of criminal procedure. The "police powers" of states are derived from the Tenth Amendment to the US Constitution which gives states the rights and powers

J. E. Szalados (✉)
Director, Surgical and Neurocritical Care Units, Rochester Regional Health System at Rochester General Hospital, Rochester, NY, USA

The Szalados Law Firm, Hilton, NY, USA
e-mail: james.szalados@rochesterregional.org; jszalados@aol.com

J. E. Szalados (ed.), *The Medical-Legal Aspects of Acute Care Medicine*,
https://doi.org/10.1007/978-3-030-68570-6_19

"not delegated to the United States" [4], thereby giving the states the power to establish and enforce laws protecting the welfare, safety, and health of the public. The US Constitution prohibits federal and state governments from enacting ex post facto laws [5]. An ex post facto law is one which (1) makes criminal an act that was innocent when done, (2) aggravates a crime or increases the punishment thereof, (3) changes the rules of evidence to the detriment of a defendant, or (4) alters the rules of criminal procedure which may deprive defendants of their substantive rights.

A person accused of a crime is generally charged in a formal accusation called an indictment (for felonies or serious crimes) or information (for misdemeanors). Criminal cases are not brought privately but rather by the government, on behalf of the people of the USA, prosecuting the case either through the US Attorney's Office in the case of a federal crime or through the state's attorney's office ("District Attorney") in the case of state crimes. The Fifth Amendment to the US Constitution, as a provision of the Bill of Rights, enumerates protections for those accused of federal crimes including (1) protection from prosecution for crimes unless indicted by a grand jury, (2) protection from "double jeopardy" or being prosecuted more than once for the same criminal act, (3) protection from "self-incrimination" during testimony, and (4) protection against being deprived of life, liberty, or property without "due process of law" [6]. The right to grand jury indictment under the US Constitution is not binding on the states.

Crimes may be classified by Congress or the states as either a misdemeanor or a felony. Infractions are not considered crimes, although they may be punishable by fines. Classification of a crime as a misdemeanor or a felony depends on its maximum potential punishment, which is specific to the criminal code for a jurisdiction. Behavior that may constitute a misdemeanor in one state may be considered a felony in another. In some jurisdictions, a crime may result in either a misdemeanor or felony charge, to be determined at the discretion of the prosecutor. Also, repeated offenses for a misdemeanor offence may be prosecuted subsequently as felonies. The crime of "driving under the influence" or DUI may be classified as a misdemeanor or a felony, depending on the circumstances.

A misdemeanor is a crime for which the punishment is usually a fine and/or up to 1 year in a county jail. In a sense, a misdemeanor is a class defined by exclusion; it is a crime that is not a felony. Thus, a criminal act that is less serious than a felony is considered to be a misdemeanor. In general, there are four classes of misdemeanors (1–4 or A–D), although Class 4/D misdemeanors are often referred to as "unclassified" misdemeanors, prosecuted and sentenced primarily on the basis of discretion. A Class A or Class 1 misdemeanor refers to the most serious misdemeanors and may include assault causing bodily injury, DUI without bodily injury, resisting arrest, perjury, unlawful possession of a controlled substance, or the violation of a restraining order. A Class B or Class 2 misdemeanor may include criminal trespass, indecent exposure, or property theft of a worth greater than $50 but less than $500. Finally, a Class C or Class 3 misdemeanor are minor offences for which punishment may, but does not usually, include jail time, for example, disorderly conduct, criminal mischief, or reckless damage or destruction.

A felony is a crime punishable by at least 1 year in prison but may also include fines and a penalty or death. Felonies are further classified as violent and nonviolent felonies. Common laws and statutes in most states further classify felonies into degrees, 1–4 or A–D felonies, each associated with greater penalties, as specifically outlined in a state's criminal code. Federal felonies are classified differently and range A–E, where, in contradistinction to state felonies, Class A federal felonies are the gravest and associated with the harshest penalties.

Moral turpitude is defined vaguely as "a legal concept that refers to any conduct that is believed to be contrary to the community standards of honesty, justice, or good moral values. While there is no one exact definition of acts that are considered under moral turpitude, they are typically described as any acts of vileness or depravity, or of sexual immorality, whether in a private or social context" [7]. US law designates "moral turpitude" as a reason to restrict the licensing of professionals, including, but not limited to, doctors and lawyers, and also as a criterion for denial of admission to the US Black's Law Dictionary which defines the phrase "good moral character," in part, as:

> [a] pattern of behavior that is consistent with the community's current ethical standards and that shows an absence of deceit or morally reprehensible conduct .... A pattern of behavior conforming to a profession's ethical standards and showing an absence of moral turpitude. Good moral character is usu[ally] a requirement of persons applying to practice a profession such as law or medicine. [8]

A conviction involving a crime of moral turpitude may have significant implications regarding professional licensing, medical staff credentialing, or other certifications. Moral turpitude has been used by the American Bar Association (ABA) and in medical licensing as a reason for disbarment or licensure revocation. In 1983, the ABA removed the term because it was too broad and vague. Many licensure applications require that the applicant answer "have you been convicted of a misdemeanor involving moral turpitude?" Arguably, although any misdemeanor, by definition, involves the breach of a social duty that man owes to his fellow man or to society in general, the specific legal issue is whether the misdemeanor translates in conduct that constitutes baseness, vileness, or depravity.

In 1992 an Ohio physician, Lawrence J. Rossiter, failed to file one of his employee's quarterly federal tax returns, a misdemeanor, and in 1995 he failed to pay estimated taxes of about $160,000, a felony; in 1998 he pled guilty in federal court and paid, in addition to restitution, a $2000 fine and served 6 months of monitored home confinement, but subsequently in 2000, the Ohio board of medical licensure suspended his license for 90 days based on the interpretation of the law that the misdemeanor crime involved "moral turpitude." The physician challenged the decision of the medical board in court, but the court affirmed the board's license suspension [9]. The physician then appealed the trial court's decision, and, in 2002, an Ohio court of appeals reversed the trial court's decision opining "We believe appellant's misdemeanor offense under the circumstances of the present case did not rise to the level of baseness, vileness, or the depravity in private and social duties which man owes to his fellow man, or to society in general." The appeals court made a request to the licensing board to review the case; however the board reaffirmed the suspension [10].

The Elements of a Crime

In order to prove culpability under criminal law, the prosecution is required to prove specific elements: (1) "actus reus" (guilty action) which refers to a voluntary physical act or omission, (2) accompanied by (2) "mens rea" (guilty mind) which refers to a state of mind at the time of the act, (3) concurrence in time of "actus reus" and "mens rea," and (4) a harmful result caused both factually and proximately by the defendant's action(s). Strict liability crimes, such as statutory rape, do not require a proof of a mens rea; in this circumstance the law does not require that the prosecution shows that defendants have actual factual knowledge of the child's age.

The Model Penal Code and most state statutes require a showing of "purposely," "knowingly," or "recklessly" for most crimes. Providers should be aware that these terms, frequently included in a medical malpractice compliant, do not generally, but still may, impute criminal liability. Rather, the term "reckless" in terms of medical malpractice or personal injury refers to the proposition that a person knew or should have known that a certain conduct would likely cause harm, thus alleging a greater level of liability than pure negligence, which is a failure to exercise reasonable care resulting in the injury of another person. These terms in a medical malpractice complaint are mostly intended as a basis for supporting an award for punitive damages.

A finding of guilt for any given crime also requires that the prosecution proves each element of a crime, as defined by jurisdiction. For example:

- False imprisonment: (a) unlawful, (b) confinement of a person, and (c) without valid consent
- Larceny: (a) a taking, (b) and carrying away (asportation), (c) of tangible property, (d) of another, by trespass, (e) with the intent to permanently deprive another person of his interest in that property
- Assault: (a) an act intended to cause apprehension of harmful or offensive contact and (b) apprehension in the victim that harmful or offensive contact would occur
- Fraud: (a) a making of a false statement, (b) with knowledge that the statement is false or with reckless disregard as to whether or not the statement is false or true, (c) with the intent that the listener rely on the statement, (d) with the result that the listener relies on the statement, and (e) with the result that the listener is harmed
- Conspiracy: (a) an agreement between two or more persons, (b) with an intent to enter into an agreement, and (c) an intent to achieve the objective of the agreement (noting that most states now also require an overt act in furtherance of the conspiracy in addition to mere preparation)

Basics of Criminal Procedure

The US Constitution guarantees specific rights of individuals faced with criminal prosecution. Specifically, Amendments IV, V, VI, and VIII have important provisions regarding the rights of accuseds. The Fourth Amendment [11] includes both the prohibition against unreasonable searches and seizures and the exclusionary rule which prohibits the introduction of evidence obtained in violation of a defendant's Fourth, Fifth, or Sixth Amendment rights. The admissibility of evidence is governed by a preponderance of the evidence test. The Due Process Clause of the US Constitution provides that guilt in a criminal trial must be established by jury, finding the defendant "guilty beyond a shadow of a doubt" [12].

Evidentiary searches and seizures must be reasonable under the Fourth Amendment; a Fourth Amendment rights arises when (a) there is governmental conduct, (b) where the defendant has a reasonable expectation of privacy, and either a warrant is served or there is a valid warrantless search and seizure. Where a warrant is served, in order to be valid, it must (a) be issued by a neutral and detached magistrate [13], (b) be based in probable cause [14] based in facts obtained under oath or affirmation [15], and (c) describe with particularity the premises [16]. Only the police and not private citizens may execute a warrant; the presence of third parties, such as private citizens or the media, who are not critical to the warrant's execution, renders the search unreasonable. There are exceptions to the requirements for a warrant, such as a search incidental to a lawful arrest, items in plain view, automobiles, or consent.

The Fifth Amendment, applicable to the states through the Fourteenth Amendment, provides, in part, that no person will be compelled to give self-incriminating testimony [17]. The case of *Miranda v. Arizona* [18] defined the basis for the admissibility of a confession based on the Fifth Amendment rights. The Miranda Court opined that police interrogation as conceived and practiced at the time was inherently coercive and the resulting intimidation, though informal and without legal sanction, was contrary to constitutional protections. There are several elements to Miranda, including the following: (1) Miranda warnings must be given prior to "questioning initiated by law enforcement officers after a person has been taken into custody or otherwise deprived of his freedom of action in any significant way" [19]; (2) Miranda warnings must precede custodial interrogation; (3) prior to interrogation of a suspect in custody, he or she must be given full warnings, or the equivalent, of his rights; and (4) once a suspect who has been appraised of his or her rights asserts the *right to silence* and requests *counsel*, the police must respect that assertion [19]. Once an accused invokes his right to counsel, all questioning must cease until the accused is provided with attorney representation. Miranda rights may be waived; that waiver must be knowing, voluntary, and intelligent [20].

The Sixth Amendment right to a jury trial applies to the states. The defendant has a right to counsel under the Fifth and Sixth Amendments, which applies at all critical stages of a criminal prosecution after formal criminal proceedings are initiated.

The Sixth Amendment also grants a defendant in a criminal proceeding a right to confront his or her accuser and also to confront adverse witnesses.

There are four main insanity defenses in a criminal proceeding: (a) M'Naghten, (b) irresistible impulse, (c) substantial capacity, and (d) Durham. The M'Naghten insanity defense, created in England in 1843 [21], is the most common insanity defense in the USA. M'Naghten is a cognitive test which focuses on the defendant's awareness, rather than the ability to control his or her conduct. There are two elements of M'Naghten: (a) First, the defendant must be suffering from a mental defect at the time he or she commits the criminal act. (b) Second, the trier of fact must find that because of the mental defect, the defendant did not know either the nature and quality of the criminal act or that the act was wrong. The "substantial capacity test" is a defense created by the Model Penal Code and states that "a person is not responsible for criminal conduct if at the time of such conduct as a result of mental disease or defect he lacks substantial capacity either to appreciate the criminality [wrongfulness] of his conduct or to conform his conduct to the requirements of law" [22]. The Durham insanity defense [23] is used only in the state of New Hampshire.

Accomplice Liability

At common law there are potentially four types of parties to a felony: (1) the principal in the first degree, (2) a principal in the second degree (those who command, aid, or encourage and are present at the crime), (3) accessories before the fact (person(s) who aid, abet or encourage but are not present at the crime), and (4) accessories after the fact (who may assist the principal after the crime is committed). Modern statutes have combined the principal in the second degree with the accessories before the fact, leaving (1) the principal, accomplices, and accessories after the fact. The principal is the one who with the requisite mental state actually engages in the act or omission which results in the criminal act. The accomplice is the one who, with the requisite intent for a crime to be committed, knowingly, voluntarily, or intentionally aids, counsels, or encourages the principal before or during the commission of a crime. The accessory after the fact is the one who assists another, knowing that he or she has committed a felony, with the intent of helping to escape arrest, trial, or conviction.

An accomplice is criminally liable to the same extent as the principal. The accomplice is liable for complicity, the act of helping or encouraging another individual to commit a crime or failed to prevent it. The elements of proof necessary to establish complicity vary by state but generally include (1) the commission of a crime by another; (2) the accomplice "aided, counseled, commanded, or encouraged" the other person in the commission of the crime; and (3) the accomplice acted with the requisite mental state (as defined within the jurisdiction) to assist in commission of the crime. Furthermore the accomplice is liable for additional separate and subsequent crimes, resulting from the initial crime, as long as the subsequent crimes were probable or foreseeable.

Burden of Proof and Presentation of Evidence

There is a presumption of innocence as a component of a fair trial [24]. The Due Process Clause of the Constitution requires that the state proves guilt "beyond a reasonable doubt." Thus, the level of proof required in criminal cases is substantially greater than that required in civil cases, where the degree of proof is "by a preponderance of the evidence." The prosecution must prove all elements of the crime. In addition, the prosecution must meet the burden of proof to overcome any affirmative defenses.

Guilty Pleas and Plea Bargaining

A guilty plea is "more than a confession which admits that the accused did various acts"; it is a "stipulation that no proof by the prosecutor need be advanced" [25]. "A guilty plea is the 'legal equivalent' of a 'verdict' and is 'tantamount' to a 'finding'" of guilt [26]. A plea of guilty results in a waiver of the Sixth Amendment right to a jury trial for criminal cases. The judge must advise the accused personally [27] regarding the nature of the charge for which a plea is offered [28], the maximum penalty and any applicable mandatory minimum sentences, and the right to not plead guilty. If the court accepts the plea, the case proceeds to sentencing.

The laws regarding plea bargains vary between jurisdictions. California makes a distinction between "(1) a conditional plea, where a plea is conditioned upon receiving a particular disposition, and (2) an unconditional or open plea" [29]. In general, a plea bargain is an agreement between a defendant and a prosecutor, in which the defendant agrees to plead guilty or "no contest" ("nolo contendere") in exchange for the use of prosecutorial discretion to drop one or more charges, reclassify the crime to one of a less serious nature (and penalty), or recommend lenience in sentencing to the presiding judge. In general, plea bargains represent enforceable contracts as between defendant and prosecutor; however, the judge is neither bound by the agreement nor required to accept the plea. Nonetheless, although a court is not bound to a plea bargain until it sentences the defendant, it also must allow the defendant to withdraw the plea if it refuses to sentence the defendant according to the agreement [30].

Federal Criminal Statutes with Risks to Medical Providers

Medical liability in the setting of usual clinical medical practice is rare. For the most part, criminal liability in medicine occurs as a result of administrative activities such as billing and coding, inappropriate contractual relationships, or nonclinical activities with patients or staff. Nonetheless, providers must realize that recent high-profile medical malpractice cases have resulted in felony manslaughter convictions.

Criminal Prosecution for Medical Malpractice

The elements of proof necessary to sustain an allegation of medical malpractice under civil law are (1) duty, (2) breach, (3) causation, and (4) damages (see Chap. 17). In order for medical malpractice to rise to a criminal cause of action, a fifth element must be established, that is, "mens rea" – the state of mind. Once again, mens rea would require proof, beyond a shadow of a doubt, that the provider acted "purposely," "knowingly," or "recklessly." Thus, in order to demonstrate criminal negligence, there must be a gross and unjustifiable deviation from the standard of care, and in addition the provider must also be shown to have had a criminally culpable state of mind at the time that the malpractice occurred. Moreover, the departure from the duty of ordinary standard of care in a criminal malpractice setting requires the prosecution to show that the departure was objectively unjustifiable and the risk was substantial. Filkins has suggested that particular patterns of physician conduct generally influence a prosecutor's decision to file criminal charges against a physician and that the same patterns influence the jury in their verdict. The patterns of conduct which triggered a sense of criminal culpability included (a) recurrences of identical issues, (2) a failure to act in a timely manner, and (3) an appearance of improper motive such as "practicing outside of one's area of expertise" or "attempting to cover up a clinical mistake" [31]. Filkins' research suggested that a jury might find an accused physician criminally guilty "even if the prosecution fails to establish causation or the standard of care" so long as the jury finds that the physician was "irresponsible or indifferent" [31]. The court in *United States v. MacKay* [32] opined that:

> [T]he case presented the jury with the .. even more difficult task of deciding whether such behavior constituted a kind of medical malpractice, which, although negligent, is not criminal, or whether the doctor had knowingly and intentionally left the field of medicine…
> *United States v. MacKay* at 1297

Perhaps the best known, well-publicized case of a physician accused of criminal medical negligence was that of Dr. Conrad Murray, the personal physician of performer Michael Jackson [33]. Murray was arrested and charged with involuntary manslaughter in the death of Jackson after he administered propofol, an intravenous anesthetic to Jackson, following a prior ingestion of lorazepam, a benzodiazepine, outside the hospital setting, at Jackson's residence. Jackson died June 25, 2009; jury selection began on September 8, 2011; the trial began on September 27, 2011; and on November 7, following 8 hours of deliberation, Murray was found guilty of involuntary manslaughter and was sentenced to 4 years in prison. Murray was released after two serving years.

Criminal prosecution of healthcare professionals is not limited to just physicians, and both the Department of Justice and state attorney general have begun to also indict nurses and nursing assistants with criminal charges for alleged neglect or abuse of resident patients in nursing homes. The concern and justification for criminal prosecution is the protection of the vulnerable adult population in nursing homes. In 2009, prosecutors filed charges for second-degree criminal mistreatment against Virginia Munger, a CNA employed by HomeWell Senior Care in Seattle, WA, after prosecutors concluded that Munger failed to provide appropriate medical interventions for an elderly patient she was responsible for [34]. Also in 2009, California Attorney General charged Kern Valley Hospital administrators with eight felony counts of elder abuse based on allegation that they allowed staff to forcibly administer psychotropic medications to patients for convenience, rather than for their patients' therapeutic interests purportedly resulting in deaths of three of the nursing home residents [35]. In 2017, The Broward State Attorney's Office filed charges of "aggravated manslaughter of an elderly person or disabled adult" as against four staff members of a Hollywood Hills nursing home where several residents died after the air-conditioning system failed following Hurricane Irma in September 2017 [36].

In 2017, a Dallas neurosurgeon, Christopher Duntsch, was convicted of five felony counts of aggravated assault of serious bodily injury and sentenced to life in prison [37]. Apparently, Duntsch, a trained and licensed neurosurgeon, operated on 38 patients, leaving 31 paralyzed, seriously injured, or dead from surgical complications, over a span of 2 years [38]. The prosecution argued that Duntsch was not only incompetent but carried malice toward his patients and intentionally that put them in grave danger.

In 2019, Dr. William Husel was charged in the death of 25 critical care patients at hospitals in and around Columbus, Ohio, through prescribing fatal doses of fentanyl, a powerful opioid [39]. Husel has pleaded not guilty to 25 counts of murder in the deaths of the patients arguing that he was providing comfort care for dying patients rather than intentionally to kill them. Husel has brought suit against the Columbus-area Mount Carmel Health System and its parent organization, Trinity Health Corp. for defamation, with the claim that he did not deviate from hospital policy on end-of-life care [40]. The trial date has been moved to April 2021 [41].

The issue of opiate prescriptions for the management of pain is and will likely continue to be a public policy, regulatory, and legal risk for providers. The US Drug Enforcement Agency (DEA) enforces controlled substances law, and the federal Food and Drug Administration ("FDA") is responsible for standards of protection of the public in drug use through the Federal Food, Drug, and Cosmetic Act [42]. The Department of Justice enforces the Controlled Substances Act (CSA), which is a federal criminal drug law that prohibits illegal drug manufacturing and distribution. Providers may be charged with violations of the CSA for misprescribing and violations of the FDCA for misbranding or adulterating a drug sold in interstate commerce. The subsequent penalties may range from civil monetary penalties to criminal misdemeanors or felonies, on a legal theory that the provider did not issue a valid prescription (pursuant to legitimate medical practice) and therefore introduced a "prescription only" drug into the market without a prescription, rendering it misbranded [43]. Misprescribers, under the CSA, may face state or federal criminal charges. For liability to attach to physicians, they must prescribe controlled substances (1) knowingly, (2) without a legitimate medical purpose, and (3) outside the course of professional practice [44]. The challenge faced by prosecutors in criminal medical liability cases is a complex assessment of (1) the point at which a medical indication becomes illegitimate, (2) a determination of the boundaries of standard of care, and (3) the extent at which crossing those boundaries warrants criminal liability [45].

Harassment and Criminal Harassment

Harassment can occur in the workplace, potentially creating a hostile workplace environment, which may be actionable under various civil laws including federal statutes. Harassment in the workplace usually takes one of two forms: (1) discriminatory offensive conduct directed against a protected class or "quid pro quo" harassment, which occurs in cases in which employment decisions or treatment are based on submission to or rejection of unwelcome conduct, typically conduct of a sexual nature. Discriminatory harassment may be based in race, gender, religion, disability, sexual orientation, or age. Nondiscriminatory workplace harassment is usually based in workplace roles or positions of power. Workplace harassment may violate Title VII of the Civil Rights Act of 1964, the Age Discrimination in Employment Act of 1967 (ADEA), and the Americans with Disabilities Act of 1990 (ADA); such types of harassment are investigated and enforced by the US Equal Employment Opportunity Commission. In the context of noncriminal harassment, the aggrieved party may also bring a private civil suit.

Criminal harassment differs workplace or discriminatory harassment; criminal harassment is defined and governed by individual state laws. Here, harassment generally refers to unwanted, unwelcomed, and uninvited verbal or physical conduct directed against a person or persons which demeans, intimidates, threatens, or offends the victim and results in a hostile environment or puts a person in fear of their safety. Harassment encompasses "bullying." Harassment can take many forms including verbal, physical, stalking, or a display or signage. In such cases, a variety of state statutes may interplay regarding the form through which harassment is communicated. Harassment can occur through the use of the mail or electronic devices such as a phone or computer which are forms of cyberbullying or cyberstalking. In general, state laws require some showing of a credible threat to one's safety. The form, duration, or intensity of the behavior affects the potential criminal harassment charge, which can range from a misdemeanor to a high-level felony charges.

The following examples illustrate the criminal statutes of one state, New York, as they apply to criminal harassment (readers should consult the applicable laws of their own state). For example, New York's harassment law defines the offense of harassment as follows: (1) the accused makes a communication likely to cause annoyance or alarm; (2) the accused threatens to strike, kick, or shove another individual; and (3) the accused participates in any course of alarming conduct or repeated committed acts with the intention to alarm or significantly alarm another individual. The crimes of menacing, harassment, and aggravated harassment are similar; the circumstances and the discretion of the prosecution will determine the severity of the penalty sought.

New York State Penal Law § 120.13 defines "Menacing in the First Degree" which in New York is classified as a Class E felony as:

> A person is guilty of menacing in the first degree when he or she commits the crime of menacing in the second degree and has been previously convicted of the crime of menacing in the second degree or the crime of menacing a police officer or peace officer within the preceding ten years.

New York State Penal Law § 120.14 defines "Menacing in the Second Degree" which in New York is classified as a Class A misdemeanor as:

A person is guilty of *menacing in the second degree* when:

1. He or she intentionally places or attempts to place another person in reasonable fear of physical injury, serious physical injury or death by displaying a deadly weapon, dangerous instrument or what appears to be a pistol, revolver, rifle, shotgun, machine gun or other firearms; or
2. He or she repeatedly follows a person or engages in a course of conduct or repeatedly commits acts over a period of time intentionally placing or attempting to place another person in reasonable fear of physical injury, serious physical injury or death; or
3. He or she commits the crime of menacing in the third degree in violation of that part of a duly served order of protection, or such order which the defendant has actual knowledge of because he or she was present in court when such order was issued, pursuant to article eight of the family court act, section 530.12 of the criminal procedure law, or an order of protection issued by a court of competent jurisdiction in another state, territorial or tribal jurisdiction, which directed the respondent or defendant to stay away from the person or persons on whose behalf the order was issued.

New York State Penal Law § 120.15 defines "Menacing in the Third Degree" which in New York is classified as a Class B misdemeanor as:

> A person is guilty of menacing in the third degree when, by physical menace, he or she intentionally places or attempts to place another person in fear of death, imminent serious physical injury or physical injury.

New York State Penal Law § 240.25 defines "Harassment in the First Degree" which in New York is classified as a Class B misdemeanor as:

> A person is guilty of harassment in the first degree when he or she intentionally and repeatedly harasses another person by following such person in or about a public place or places or by engaging in a course of conduct or by repeatedly committing acts which places such person in reasonable fear of physical injury....

New York State Penal Law § 240.26 defines "Harassment in the Second Degree" which in New York is classified as a violation as:

> A person is guilty of harassment in the second degree when, with intent to harass, annoy or alarm another person:

1. He or she strikes, shoves, kicks or otherwise subjects such other person to physical contact, or attempts or threatens to do the same; or
2. He or she follows a person in or about a public place or places; or
3. He or she engages in a course of conduct or repeatedly commits acts which alarm or seriously annoy such other person and which serve no legitimate purpose…

New York State criminal law further distinguishes "harassment" from "aggravated harassment" which is a felony. New York State Penal Law § 240.31 defines "Aggravated Harassment in the First Degree" a Class E felony as:

> A person is guilty of aggravated harassment in the first degree when with intent to harass, annoy, threaten or alarm another person, because of a belief or perception regarding such person's race, color, national origin, ancestry, gender, religion, religious practice, age, disability or sexual orientation, regardless of whether the belief or perception is correct, he or she:

1. Damages premises primarily used for religious purposes, or acquired pursuant to section six of the religious corporation law and maintained for purposes of religious instruction, and the damage to the premises exceeds fifty dollars; or
2. Commits the crime of aggravated harassment in the second degree in the manner proscribed by the provisions of subdivision three of section 240.30 of this article and has been previously convicted of the crime of aggravated harassment in the second degree for the commission of conduct proscribed by the provisions of subdivision three of section 240.30 or he or she has been previously convicted of the crime of aggravated harassment in the first degree within the preceding ten years; or
3. Etches, paints, draws upon or otherwise places a swastika, commonly exhibited as the emblem of Nazi Germany, on any building or other real property, public or private, owned by any person, firm or corporation or any public agency or instrumentality, without express permission of the owner or operator of such building or real property;
4. Sets on fire a cross in public view; or
5. Etches, paints, draws upon or otherwise places or displays a noose, commonly exhibited as a symbol of racism and intimidation, on any building or other real property, public or private, owned by any person, firm or corporation or any public agency or instrumentality, without express permission of the owner or operator of such building or real property.

New York State Penal Law § 240.30 defines "Aggravated Harassment in the Second Degree" a Class A misdemeanor:

> A person is guilty of aggravated harassment in the second degree when:

1. With intent to harass another person, the actor either:
   (a) communicates, anonymously or otherwise, by telephone, by computer or any other electronic means, or by mail, or by transmitting or delivering any other form of communication, a threat to cause physical harm to, or unlawful harm to the property of, such person, or a member of such person's same family or household as defined in subdivision one of section 530.11 of the criminal procedure law , and the actor knows or reasonably should know that such communication will cause such person to reasonably fear harm to such person's physical safety or property, or to the physical safety or property of a member of such person's same family or household; or
   (b) causes a communication to be initiated anonymously or otherwise, by telephone, by computer or any other electronic means, or by mail, or by transmitting or delivering any other form of communication, a threat to cause physical harm to, or unlawful harm to the property of, such person, a member of such person's same family or household as defined in subdivision one of section 530.11 of the criminal procedure law , and the actor knows or reasonably should know that such communication will

cause such person to reasonably fear harm to such person's physical safety or property, or to the physical safety or property of a member of such person's same family or household; or

2. With intent to harass or threaten another person, he or she makes a telephone call, whether or not a conversation ensues, with no purpose of legitimate communication; or
3. With the intent to harass, annoy, threaten or alarm another person, he or she strikes, shoves, kicks, or otherwise subjects another person to physical contact, or attempts or threatens to do the same because of a belief or perception regarding such person's race, color, national origin, ancestry, gender, religion, religious practice, age, disability or sexual orientation, regardless of whether the belief or perception is correct; or
4. With the intent to harass, annoy, threaten or alarm another person, he or she strikes, shoves, kicks or otherwise subjects another person to physical contact thereby causing physical injury to such person or to a family or household member of such person as defined in section 530.11 of the criminal procedure law ; or
5. He or she commits the crime of harassment in the first degree and has previously been convicted of the crime of harassment in the first degree as defined by section 240.25 of this article within the preceding ten years.

Within the medical practice setting, harassment behavior may be on the part of the provider but may also be engaged in by patients, friends, or families. Furthermore, workplace harassment, or disruptive behavior, may escalate to the point of harassment. Thus, providers should be aware of not only their rights but also their duties and the attendant legal risks.

Assault/Battery

The definition of "assault" varies by jurisdiction; however, in general, the elements of "assault" is generally defined as (1) an action, (2) with the intent to cause reasonable apprehension of an imminent harmful or offensive contact in another, and (3) the defendant's action causes the victim to reasonably apprehend such a contact. Assault requires an overt or direct act that would put a "reasonable person" in fear for their safety. The standard for a "reasonable person" is the jury or trier of fact. No actual physical contact is necessary for an assault to occur; however, spoken words alone are not sufficient to constitute an assault unless the defendant also engages in an act in furtherance of the spoken words. The "intent" sufficient to constitute assault is a "general intent" such that intentional actions which would be considered dangerous by reasonable people are sufficient to sustain a charge of assault.

The definition of "battery" varies by jurisdiction; however, the elements of "battery" is generally defined as (1) intentional touching, (2) which must be either harmful or offensive, and (3) without the victim's consent. Battery generally does not require the intent to harm the victim, only the intent to cause a physical contact. Battery also does not require that the victim is harmed by the physical contact, as long as an intentional offensive contact actually occurs. The standard for the determination of whether a contact was in fact offensive is evaluated from the perspective of the "ordinary person" or the jury or trier of fact. There are both civil and criminal liabilities for battery, and a defendant may face both civil and criminal liabilities for the same act. Not all states have actions for criminal battery; for example, New York does not prosecute criminal battery and rather combines battery into the crime of assault. Consent is a defense to the crime of battery. Informed consent is a basic requirement for medical care, unless certain specific exceptions apply.

For medical treatment or procedural interventions without a patient's consent or in the case of an informed refusal, the patient may have a legitimate legal claim for a cause of medical battery, even in the absence of the provider's intent to cause harm. In a medical battery claim, there is generally no need to prove injury or negligence. However, as in all battery cases, it is necessary to prove that the medical personnel was engaged in unauthorized touching, contact, or handling of the victim. Medical battery is not the same as medical malpractice and therefore is unlikely to be covered under standard medical malpractice liability policies. Medical battery, similar to all crimes, is also likely to be investigated by the State Department of Health and be a basis for potential professional licensure sanctions.

In the 1993 case of *Craig L. Miller v. Rhode Island Hospital*, Miller et al. became intoxicated and was involved in a serious motor vehicle accident. Miller was transported to Rhode Island Hospital where his blood alcohol level was found to be 0.233. Based on the level of Miller's intoxication and the nature of the accident, physicians decided to perform a diagnostic peritoneal lavage which Miller refused. Miller was physically restrained, and the procedure was performed anyway. Subsequently, it was determined that Miller was not competent to make a decision based on his level of intoxication, and he later brought suit for battery [46].

In the 2014 case of *Shuler v. Garrett*, PLLC LLC, Pauline Sloan Shuler died in the intensive care unit of Baptist Memorial Hospital-Memphis on June 23, 2011, allegedly from an allergic reaction to heparin injections that had been administered despite her objections and despite that she wore a medical bracelet noting her heparin allergy and her medical records also documenting the allergy. The Tennessee Court noted that "[p]erformance of an unauthorized procedure constitutes a medical battery" [47] and that "[m]edical battery is also distinct from, although closely related to, a tort arising from a doctor's failure to obtain informed consent. Whereas the threshold question in an informed consent case is whether the patient's lack of information negated her consent, the question in a medical battery case is much simpler: Did the patient consent at all?" [47].

Criminal Federal Fraud and Abuse Laws

Although alleged violations of the federal "fraud and abuse" statutes, such as the federal False Claims Act or the Anti-Kickback Statute, are managed by the Office of the Inspector General (OIG), the enforcement of these statutes is through the Department of Justice and therefore the Federal Bureau of Investigation (FBI).

Potential fraud and abuse violations may come to the attention of the OIG through digital database analysis, Recovery Audit Contractors ("RACS"), Medicaid data, private insurers, whistleblowers, or patients and families. Once a complaint or a pattern is discovered, preliminary examination, based on all available data under the provider's Medicare National Provider Identification Number, is culled and confirmed. Medicare investigators will almost certainly work through the office of US Attorney General (USAG), with the collaboration of the Office of the Medicaid Inspector General at the state level and with the local oversight of the local Assistant US Attorney (AUSA). The provider is unlikely to be aware that such preliminary investigations are underway. If there is sufficient preliminary evidence to support further prosecution, the next step are the service of search warrants for the physician's office and home and initiation of grand jury subpoenas. The search warrants are likely to be executed unannounced by many armed FBI and other federal agents with the objective of securing potentially evanescent incriminating evidence. Providers should be advised that cooperation in such settings is essential and that any interference with the execution of the search warrant is grounds for further liability and criminal charges; however, the provider should not make statements to the agents and immediately seek legal counsel.

Where the investigating agency serves a grand jury subpoena upon the provider, the objective is to obtain additional evidence in support of an indictment. Defense counsel is not permitted at the grand jury proceeding. The grand jury is likely to be followed by a formal pre-indictment conference, with the intent of explaining the charges and the evidence and potentially securing a plea, or to begin negotiations. Any criminal conviction, or plea of nolo contendere, involving any offense related to the practice of medicine is ground for denial or revocation of licensure.

Criminal False Claims Statute

The federal False Claims Act ("FFCA") statutorily prohibits provider conduct involving the submission of false claims to the government and also the knowing and improper retention of overpayments of government funds (see Chap. 12). The FFCA has been effectively used to prosecute healthcare providers for the (a) billing for services or supplies not actually provided, (b) billing for non-reimbursable services, (c) using false diagnoses to justify claims, and (d) misrepresentations on government performance evaluations.

> The criminal False Claims Statute, 18 U.S.C. § 287 provides that:
>
> Whoever makes or presents to any person or officer in the civil, military, or naval service of the United States, or to any department or agency thereof, any claim upon or against the United States, or any department or agency thereof, knowing such claim to be false, fictitious, or fraudulent, shall be imprisoned not more than five years and shall be subject to a fine in the amount provided in this title.

In order to prove guilt under 18 USC § 287, the government prosecution must establish that the defendant (1) made or presented a false, fictitious, or fraudulent claim to a department of the USA; (2) knew such claim was false, fictitious, or fraudulent; and (3) did so with the specific intent to violate the law or with a consciousness that what he was doing was wrong [48]. In contradistinction to the Civil False Claims

Act [49], there may not be a requirement that the statements or claims be material or that specific intent to defraud is required [50]. Here, presentation of a claim is considered to represent more than an intention to make a claim [51]. Under the criminal FCA, individuals found guilty of knowingly presenting a false may be sentenced to a maximum prison sentence of 5 years in addition to criminal fines for each submitted claim.

Related statutes for 18 USC § 287 False Claims Act under which additional liability may be imposed include:

- 18 U.S.C. § 285 – Taking or using papers related to claims
- 18 U.S.C. § 286 – Conspiracy to defraud Government with claims
- 18 U.S.C. § 288 – False claims through postal service
- 18 U.S.C. § 289 – False claims for pensions payments
- 18 U.S.C. § 290 – Discharge papers withheld by claim agent
- 18 U.S.C. § 291 – Purchasing claims for fees by court officials
- 18 U.S.C. § 292 – Solicitation of employment and receiving unapproved fees
- 18 U.S.C. §§1341 - Federal Mail Fraud
- 18 U.S.C. §§1343 - Federal Wire Fraud
- 18 U.S.C. § 201 - Bribery
- 42 U.S.C. § 132Oa-7b(a) - Social Security Act False Claims
- 42 U.S.C. 132Oa-7b(b) - Social Security Act "anti-kickback" provision

Federal statutes can overlap with a number of other federal criminal statutes. An important intersection of the FFCA occurs with the federal mail and wire fraud statutes, which proscribe (1) causing the use of the mail or wire communications, including email; (2) in conjunction with a scheme to intentionally defraud another of money or property; and (3) by means of a material deception. The actual offenses, as well as attempts or conspiracies to commit them, carry a potential term of imprisonment of up to 30 years.

Criminal Anti-Kickback Statute (AKS)

The Medicare Anti-Kickback Statute [52] "provides criminal penalties for individuals or entities that knowingly and willfully offer, pay, solicit or receive remuneration in order to induce business reimbursed under the Medicare or State health care programs. The offense is classified as a felony, and is punishable by fines of up to $25,000 and imprisonment for up to 5 years" (see Chap. 12). In effect the AKS prohibits the receipt anything of value (including nonmonetary items such as free or below market value rent, below free market value exchanges, excessive compensation for medical directorships, excessive relocation agreements) to induce or reward referrals or otherwise generate income through reimbursements from any federal healthcare programs such as Medicare, Medicaid, and Tricare.

Criminal State Fraud and Abuse Laws

Medicaid Fraud Control Units (MFCUs) investigate and prosecute Medicaid provider fraud as well as patient abuse or neglect in healthcare facilities and board and care facilities. The MFCUs operate in 50 states, the District of Columbia, Puerto Rico, and the US Virgin Islands generally under the authority of the State Attorney General's Office [53]. The MCFUs will collaborate with the Office of the State Attorney General, and also the federal OIG, to appropriately investigate and potentially secure civil or criminal penalties.

Federal Sentencing Guidelines

The Federal Sentencing Guidelines were developed and authored by an independent government agency, the US Sentencing Commission. The Federal Sentencing Guidelines [54] are non-binding rules that set out an advisory guideline sentencing range for defendants. The Guidelines provide for "very precise calibration of sentences, depending upon a number of factors. These factors relate both to the subjective guilt of the defendant and to the harm caused by his facts" [55]. Since the Guidelines may result in a sentence based on facts that were not proven beyond a reasonable doubt to a jury, in violation of the Sixth Amendment, they are not mandatory [56]. Nonetheless, judges must consider the Guidelines when determining a criminal defendant's sentence, and if and where there is a departure, the judge must explain the basis for the discretion and discuss the factors he or she used in his or her determination.

The guidelines assign federal crimes to 43 "offense levels" and assign offenders to one of six "criminal history categories." The combination of the scores within the Commission's sentencing table provides a guideline range for sentencing the defendant.

Conclusions

The risk of a medical provider facing a criminal prosecution during his or her career is increasing; where historically the primary legal risk to providers was that of medical negligence or malpractice, federal statutes and state prosecutions under alternative theories of liability are increasing. Criminal convictions can result in fines, jail time, loss or medical staff privileges, loss of licensure, exclusion from payer panels, adjunct civil or regulatory sanctions, and a lifelong criminal record. Medical professionals faced with any criminal-level allegation should immediately seek attorney counsel. Furthermore, in the event of even lower level prior misdemeanor convictions, providers should seek legal counsel and guidance when completing any applications for employment, privileges, medical staff membership, or professional licensure or renewal.

References

1. Quick O. Prosecuting 'gross' medical negligence: manslaughter, discretion, and the crown prosecution service. J Law Soc. 2006;33:421–50.
2. Fathi MJ. Examination of crime and similar concepts in the medical law. J Med Ethics Hist Med. 2016;9:4.
3. Merriam-Webster. Crime. *Available online at*: https://www.merriam-webster.com/dictionary/crime.
4. U.S. Constitution. Amendment X.
5. U.S. Constitution Art I, §10, cl. 1.
6. U.S. Constitution. Amendment V. ("No person shall be held to answer for a capital, or otherwise infamous crime, unless on a presentment or indictment of a Grand Jury, except in cases arising in the land or naval forces, or in the Militia, when in actual service in time of War or public danger; nor shall any person be subject for the same offence to be twice put in jeopardy of life or limb; nor shall be compelled in any criminal case to be a witness against himself, nor be deprived of life, liberty, or property, without due process of law; nor shall private property be taken for public use, without just compensation."
7. Legal Dictionary. Moral turpitude. Online at: https://legaldictionary.net/moral-turpitude/
8. Black's law dictionary 714 (8th ed. 2000).
9. Rakatansky H. Criminal convictions and medical licensure. AMA J Ethics, *in*, Virtual Mentor. 2011;13(10):712–7. https://doi.org/10.1001/virtualmentor.2011.13.10.pfor1-1110.
10. *Rossiter v State Med Board of Ohio*. 155 Ohio App 3d 689, 802 NE2d 1149 (Ohio St Ct App 2004).
11. U.S. Constitution. Amendment IV.("The right of the people to be secure in their persons, houses, papers and effects against unreasonable searches and seizures shall not be violated, and no warrants shall issue but upon probable cause, supported by oath or affirmation, and particularly describing the place to be searched, and the persons or things to be seized.")
12. U.S. Constitution Amendments V and XIV. See also *In re Winship*, 397 U.S. 358 (1970).
13. *California v. Acevedo*, 500 U.S. 565 (1991).
14. *Carroll v. United States*, 267 U.S. 132 (1925).
15. *Aguilar v. Texas*, 378 U.S. 108 (1964).
16. *Stanford v. Texas*, 379 U.S. 476 (1965).
17. U.S. Constitution. Amendment V. ("No person shall be held to answer for a capital, or otherwise infamous crime, unless on a presentment or indictment of a grand jury, except in cases arising in the land or naval forces, or in the militia, when in actual service in time of war or public danger; nor shall any person be subject for the same offense to be twice put in jeopardy of life or limb; nor shall be compelled in any criminal case to be a witness against himself, nor be deprived of life, liberty, or property, without due process of law; nor shall private property be taken for public use, without just compensation.")
18. *Miranda v. Arizona*, 384 U.S. 436 (1966).
19. *Miranda* at 444.
20. Colorado v. Spring, 479 U.S. 564 (1987).
21. *R v McNaughton* (sic) (1843) 10 Cl & Fin 200; 8 ER 718. *See also*, M'Naghten's Case (1843) 10 Clark and Finnelly 200, (1843) 8 ER 718, [1843-60] All ER Rep 229.

22. American Law Institute. Model Penal Code: Official Draft and Explanatory Notes: Complete Text of Model Penal Code as Adopted at the 1962 Annual Meeting of the American Law Institute at Washington, D.C., May 24, 1962. Philadelphia: The Institute, 1985, § 4.01(1).
23. *Durham v. United States*. 214 F.2d 862 (1954).
24. Kentucky v. Whorton, 441 U.S. 786 (1979).
25. Boykin v. Alabama, 395 U.S. 238 (1969).
26. People v. Statum. 28 Cal.4th 682, 122 Cal.Rptr.2d 572, 50 P.3d 355 (2002).
27. McCarthy v. United States, 394 U.S. 459 (1969).
28. Henderson v. Morgan, 426 U.S. 637 (1976).
29. People v. Holmes (2004) 32 Cal.4th 432, 435.
30. People v. Cruz (1988) 44 Cal.3d 1247, 1250-1253; *See also, In re* Jermaine B. (1999) 59Cal. App.4th 634).
31. Filkins JA, With No Evil Intent: The Criminal Prosecution of Physicians for Medical Negligence, 22 J. Legal Med. 467, 472 (2001) at 509.
32. United States v. MacKay, 20 F. Supp. 3d 1287 (D. Utah 2014).
33. People of the State of California v. Conrad Robert Murray. Superior Court of Los Angeles County. November 7, 2011.
34. Nursing Home Law Center, LLC. Nurse Faces Criminal Charges After She Fails to Obtain Medical Treatment for Bedsore Patient, online at: https://www.nursinghomelawcenter.org/nurse-faces-criminal-charges-after-she-fails-to-obtain-medical-t.html. *See also*: Levi Pulkkinen, Bedsores contributed to woman's death; caregiver charged. SeattlePI Updated 10:00 pm PDT, Tuesday, October 13, 2009. Available online at: https://www.seattlepi.com/local/article/Bedsores-contributed-to-woman-s-death-caregiver-888460.php.
35. Xavier Becerra. Attorney General. State of California Department of Justice. Brown Files Criminal Charges Against Former Nursing Home Administrator in Kern Valley Elder Abuse Case. Posted Tuesday, September 8, 2009. Available online at: https://oag.ca.gov/news/press-releases/brown-files-criminal-charges-against-former-nursing-home-administrator-kern.
36. CBS News. Criminal Charges Filed In Hollywood Nursing Home Deaths Case. Posted September 16, 2019 at 6:18 pm. Online at: https://miami.cbslocal.com/2019/09/16/criminal-charges-filed-in-hollywood-nursing-home-deaths-case/.
37. Goodman M. Ex-Neurosurgeon Christopher Duntsch Sentenced to Life. FRONTBURNER posted February 20, 2017 4:59 PM. Online at: https://www.dmagazine.com/frontburner/2017/02/ex-neurosurgeon-christopher-duntsch-sentenced-to-life/. See also CBS News. Former Neurosurgeon sentenced to life in prison for maiming patients. Posted February 20, 2017 5:25 PM. Online at: https://dfw.cbslocal.com/2017/02/20/former-neurosurgeon-sentenced-to-life-in-prison-for-maiming-patients/.
38. Dyer O. US neurosurgeon deliberately botched spine operations, prosecutors allege. BMJ. 2015;351:h4739. Published 2015 Sep 4. https://doi.org/10.1136/bmj.h4739.
39. Braine T. Ohio doctor who over-prescribed fentanyl indicted on 25 counts of murder. Daily News. Posted JUN 05, 2019 AT 11:24 PM. Available online at: https://www.nydailynews.com/news/crime/ny-20190606-diz5v3yh6bhejgibckgbwjuomy-story.html.
40. NBC News. Ohio doctor charged with 25 murders sues hospital for defamation. The Associated Press. Posted Dec. 29, 2019, 9:43 AM EST. Online at: https://www.nbcnews.com/news/us-news/ohio-doctor-charged-25-murders-sues-hospital-defamation-n1108291.
41. NBC News. Husel murder trial moved to 2021. NBC4 Staff, The Associated Press. Posted: Apr 20, 2020 / 06:11 PM EDT / Updated: Apr 20, 2020 / 11:09 PM EDT. Online at: https://www.nbc4i.com/news/local-news/husel-investigation/husel-murder-trial-moved-to-2021/.
42. Federal Food, Drug, & Cosmetic Act, Pub. L. No. 75-717, 52 Stat. 1040 (1938) (codified as amended at 21 U.S.C. §301 et seq.) (2014).
43. Federal Food, Drug, & Cosmetic Act 21 U.S.C. § 353(b). *See also*, United States v. Nazir, 211 F. Supp. 2d 1372, 1377 (S.D. Fla. 2002) ("[T]he word 'prescription' cannot be defined as mere piece of paper signed by a doctor for drugs, no matter how fraudulent.")

44. Drug Enforcement Administration, Department of Justice. Prescriptions 21 C.F.R. § 1306.04 (2015).
45. Dineen KK, DuBois JM. Between a rock and a hard place: can physicians prescribe opioids to treat pain adequately while avoiding legal sanction? Am J Law Med. 2016;42(1):7–52. https://doi.org/10.1177/0098858816644712.
46. *Miller v Rhode Island Hospital*, 625 A2d 778 (R.I. 1993).
47. *Blanchard v. Kellum*, 975 S.W.2d 522, 524 (Tenn.1998).
48. United States v. Slocum, 708 F.2d 587, 596 (11th Cir. 1983)(citing United States v. Computer Sciences Corp., 511 F. Supp. 1125, 1134 (E.D. Va. 1981), rev'd on other grounds, 689 F.2d 1181 (4th Cir. 1982)).
49. False Claims Act. 31 U.S.C. § 3729 et seq.
50. 42 U.S. Code § 1320a–7b - Criminal penalties for acts involving Federal health care programs.
51. U.S. DOJ Archives. 922. Elements of 18 U.S.C. § 287. Online at: https://www.justice.gov/archives/jm/criminal-resource-manual-922-elements-18-usc-287.
52. Section 1128B(b) of the Social Security Act (42 U.S.C. 1320a-7b(b.
53. Medicaid Fraud Control Units (MFCUs). 42 CFR Part 1007, Revisions to State Medicaid Fraud Control Units Rules. *See also*, 84 FR 10700, March 22, 2019.
54. United States Sentencing Commission. 2018 Guidelines Manual Annotated. Online at: https://www.ussc.gov/guidelines/2018-guidelines-manual-annotated.
55. Payne v. Tennessee, 501 U.S. 808, 820 (1991).
56. United States v. Booker, 543 U.S. 20 (2005).

Chapter 20
Ethical and Legal Issues in Contemporary Pharmacy Practice: Scope of Practice, Drug Use Stewardship, Medical Error Management, and Teamwork

James E. Szalados

Federal Regulation of Pharmacy Practice

The federal government regulates the development, approval, and marketing of drugs, including biologics, generics, over-the-counter (OTC) drugs, and other medicinal products and compounds through the Food, Drug, and Cosmetic Act (FDCA) as amended (see Chap. 30). Prior to the FDCA, which authorized the Food and Drug Administration (FDA), untested and often unsafe substances were sold indiscriminately as "medicinal compounds" by unregulated merchants. In 1937, a mass public poisoning occurred when the S. E. Massengill Company sold a new liquid formulation of elixir of sulfanilamide, an antibacterial agent, which contained used diethylene glycol (DEG) as an excipient. Prior to 1937, toxicity studies were not required of medicinal compounds marketed to the public. Massengill successfully argued that that could not be held liable since the effects of DEG were unforeseen, no applicable regulation was violated, and, ultimately, the court did not hold Massengill legally responsible. In 1938, the FDCA was passed with the important consequence of requiring drug developers and manufacturers to perform efficacy and safety studies prior to submitting a new drug application (NDA) for FDA approval.

The FDCA also regulates drugs, and pharmacy practice, thro ugh regulations that apply to adulteration and misbranding. In general, adulteration occurs when a drug is contaminated in any way prior to sale or its strength differs from, or its quality or

J. E. Szalados (✉)
Director, Surgical and Neurocritical Care Units, Rochester Regional Health System at Rochester General Hospital, Rochester, NY, USA

The Szalados Law Firm, Hilton, NY, USA
e-mail: james.szalados@rochesterregional.org; jszalados@aol.com

J. E. Szalados (ed.), *The Medical-Legal Aspects of Acute Care Medicine*,
https://doi.org/10.1007/978-3-030-68570-6_20

purity falls below, the standard set forth in an official compendium [1]. The FDCA considers a drug to be misbranded if its labeling is false or misleading [2]. Changes in the formulation of a drug, manufacturers, or pharmacists who compound products cannot legally make such alterations so as to create an unregulated "new drug." The FDCA also regulates pharmacist dispensing of prescription medication, such that the dispensing of a prescription medication without valid authorization (the prescription) is a violation of the FDCA. Misbranding may also occur if a pharmacy receives, holds for sale, or sells a counterfeit drug. Thus, the pharmacy and pharmacist must maintain strict standards in their relationship with wholesalers and vendors to ensure that their products are not in violation.

The Comprehensive Drug Abuse Prevention and Control Act of 1970, also known as the Controlled Substances Act (CSA) requires registration and specific record keeping and imposes rules regarding the dispensing of controlled substances. The CSA classified drugs based on categories [3] or schedules which are Schedule I–V (Table 20.1). Schedule I drugs may not be handled by pharmacies, and a pharmacy found to be in possession of a Schedule I drug is in violation of the CSA, even if the scheduling of that drug was recently changed. For example, methaqualone (Quaalude) is a synthetic, barbiturate-like, central nervous system depressant that was a popular recreational drug in the USA from the 1960s through the 1980s and was a Schedule II drug, until 1984, when the US Drug Enforcement Agency (DEA) placed methaqualone into Federal Schedule I, making methaqualone no longer legally available in the USA. On the effective date of the reclassification of methaqualone, all pharmacies in possession of methaqualone were required to immediately and properly dispose of any drug they had in stock or face violation of the CSA.

Pharmacies are required to take inventory of controlled substances every 2 years. The inventory of Schedule II controlled substances must represent an actual physical count, and it must be kept separate from those of other controlled substances. The regulations regarding inventories of drugs are highly specific, and compliance is essential; inventory records must be available for inspection by the DEA at any time. The DEA allows the transfer of original prescription information between pharmacies for Schedule III, IV, and V controlled substances for the purpose of refill dispensing on a one-time basis.

The Poison Prevention Packaging Act (PPPA) [4] of 1970 was enacted in response to child poisonings by pharmaceuticals. The PPPA mandated packaging for drugs to be designed or constructed so as to be significantly difficult for children under 5 years of age to open within a reasonable time and not difficult for normal adults to use properly. In the case that the drugs are those commonly found on store shelves and are purchased for the use of elderly or disabled persons who might have difficulty with such packaging, the Act provides that the regulated product may be packaged in one noncompliant fashion as long as the product was accompanied with a warning stating that the packaging was not recommended for use in households with children. In addition, regulated prescription drugs may be also dispensed in non-child-resistant packaging upon the specific request of the prescribing doctor or the patient. Failure to comply with PPPA packaging requirements is considered a misbranding violation under the FDCA, and a pharmacist in violation of the

Table 20.1 Controlled substance act schedules

Classification	Description	Examples
Schedule I	Substances or chemicals with no currently accepted medical use and a high potential for abuse	Heroin, lysergic acid diethylamide (LSD), marijuana (cannabis), 3,4-methylenedioxymethamphetamine (ecstasy), methaqualone, and peyote
Schedule II	Substances or chemicals with a high potential for abuse, with use potentially leading to severe psychological or physical dependence. These drugs are also considered dangerous	Combination products with less than 15 mg of hydrocodone per dosage unit (Vicodin), cocaine, methamphetamine, methadone, hydromorphone (Dilaudid), meperidine (Demerol), oxycodone (OxyContin), fentanyl, Dexedrine, Adderall, and Ritalin
Schedule III	Substances or chemicals with a moderate to low potential for physical and psychological dependence	Products containing less than 90 mg of codeine per dosage unit (Tylenol with codeine), ketamine, anabolic steroids, testosterone
Schedule IV	Schedule IV drugs, substances, or chemicals with a low potential for abuse and low risk of dependence	Xanax, Soma, Darvon, Darvocet, Valium, Ativan, Talwin, Ambien, Tramadol
Schedule V	Substances or chemicals with lower potential for abuse than Schedule IV and consist of preparations containing limited quantities of certain narcotics. Schedule V drugs are generally used for antidiarrheal, antitussive, and analgesic purposes	Cough preparations with less than 200 mg of codeine or per 100 ml (Robitussin AC), Lomotil, Motofen, Lyrica, Parepectolin

regulations is subject to prosecution and imprisonment for not more than 1 year or sentenced to pay a fine of not more than $1000, or both.

The Prescription Drug Marketing Act (PDMA) of 1987 [5] was enacted with the intent to (1) ensure that drug products purchased by consumers are safe and effective and (2) avoid risk associated with counterfeit, adulterated, misbranded, subpotent, or expired drugs. The PDMA became a part of the FDCA as an amendment in 1988. The PDMA also addressed the practice whereby free samples, and deeply discounted drugs, were provided to hospitals, which in essence constituted a secondary gray market for drug distribution and which also potentially facilitated a drug diversion market that provides a portal through which lower-quality drugs were provided to patients. The PDMA requires that drug samples that are delivered by mail or common carrier must be directed to (1) a licensed prescriber or (2) a healthcare entity's pharmacy (i.e., not a retail pharmacy). The person receiving a drug sample must also complete and sign a written receipt, which must be returned to the manufacturer or distributor of record. The PDMA imposes criminal penalties for noncompliance: the act of, or an offer to, knowingly sell, purchase, or trade a prescription drug sample is punishable by a fine of up to $250,000 and up to 10 years' imprisonment; furthermore, there is a "whistleblower" clause in the PDMA providing up to $125,000 for individuals who provide information leading to the conviction of a violator of this portion of the PDMA. The PDMA also prohibits the resale by a pharmacist of any prescription drug that had previously been purchased by a hospital or other "healthcare entity" and banned the reimportation of drugs previously exported out of the USA.

The Omnibus Budget Reconciliation Act of 1990 (OBRA-90) included a number of mandates affecting pharmacists including new record-keeping mandates, Prospective Drug Utilization Review (ProDUR) requirements, and pharmacist counseling obligations. The ProDUR required state Medicaid provider pharmacists to review each Medicaid patient entire drug profile before filling their prescription(s). Table 20.2 outlines pharmacist screening requirements under ProDUR. In addition, pharmacists must offer and provide counseling to discuss the unique drug therapy regimen of each patient. Finally, under ProDUR, the pharmacist must make reasonable efforts to obtain, record, and maintain applicable medical information regarding the patients to whom prescriptions are dispensed.

The privacy and security provisions of the Health Insurance Portability and Accountability Act of 1996 (HIPAA) are directly applicable to pharmacies and pharmacists who maintain personally identifiable patient information (PHI) in electronic format or that conduct financial and administrative transactions electronically which are subject to both HIPAA and HiTECH. The privacy rules attach to computer patient profiles, paper prescription orders, telephone conversations with a physician, and patient counseling (see Chap. 13). HIPAA compliance requires the adoption and compliance with policies and procedures regarding the use of PHI and a conspicuous public notice of privacy practices and security provisions which implement reasonable administrative, physical, and technical safeguards to protect the confidentiality, integrity, and availability of PHI.

The scope of practice for pharmacists is established by state legislatures and regulated by a board or agency, most commonly the State Boards of Pharmacy. In general, pharmacy scope of practice include assessments of health and wellness testing, chronic disease management, antibiotic and medication stewardship in hospitals, hospital readmission management and performing medication management,

Table 20.2 Pharmacist screening requirements under the ProDUR

Therapeutic duplication
Drug-disease contraindications
Drug-drug interactions
Incorrect drug dosage
Incorrect duration of treatment
Drug-allergy interactions
Clinical abuse/misuse of medication

counseling patients with respect to their medications and potential interactions, and the administration of immunizations. In some states, pharmacists may enter into collaborative practice agreements with physicians to initiate, monitor, and modify a patient's pharmacologic regimen. Pharmacists may be entitled to order and interpret lab tests in 31 of the states. In general, the dispensing of medications is restricted by state laws. However, with respect to prescriptions for controlled substances, it may only be filled by a pharmacist, acting in the usual course of his professional practice and either registered individually or employed in a registered pharmacy, a registered central fill pharmacy, or registered institutional practitioner [6].

State Regulation of Pharmacy Practice

The practice of pharmacy as a profession, is regulated by federal and state laws and regulations. Although the FDA, DEA, DOJ, and other federal agencies play a significant role in the regulation of pharmacy practice at a national level, the practice of pharmacy is closely regulated by state regulations and laws. In general, the requirements of licensure as a pharmacist in any state requires (1) graduation from accredited or recognized school of pharmacy; (2) successful completion of the NAPLEX and associated law exam, most often the MPJE (except in California which requires a state-specific version known as the CPJE); and (3) a set minimum hours of clinical experience. Similar to other professions, the pathways to licensure include (1) initial state licensure; (2) score transfer; and, (3) reciprocity. Score transfer is a process whereby NAPLEX scores can be transferred to another state during the first 89 days of taking the examination. Licensure in another state through reciprocity requires at least a minimum of 1-year experience and completion of the MPJE in the other qualifying state.

The NAPLEX is the North American Pharmacist Licensure Examination which was created by the National Association of Boards of Pharmacy (NABP) as a standardized competency examination, the successful completion of which is a prerequisite to licensure. The importance of jurisprudence to the practice of pharmacy is underscored by the requirement that pharmacist applying for state licensure successfully complete the MPJE, the Multistate Pharmacy Jurisprudence Examination. The MPJE tests the candidate's understanding of the federal and state laws relevant to the practice of pharmacy. The purpose of the MPJE is to assess a licensure candidate's knowledge regarding pharmacy practice, including topics such as store and record-keeping requirements, dispensing, dispensing of pharmaceuticals and for the care of patients, licensure, registration, certification, and other legalities and operational requirements within the state in which licensure is sought. State laws differ as to pharmacy regulations.

State regulation of pharmacy practice is complex. Adams reviewed the different state regulations pertaining to pharmacy practice and found that in comparison to medicine and nursing, pharmacy laws are wordier, contain more restrictions, and have been amended more frequently [7]. The laws regarding pharmacy practice vary between the states, and therefore cases regarding statutory violations and even case law can be very state-specific with respect to pharmacist liability.

Laws regarding the authority of a pharmacist to substitute generic drugs in a prescription are one example of state-specific pharmacy law. Here, the dichotomy in the law is that some states require mandatory generic substitution, whereas others permit it based in pharmacist discretion. Nonetheless, in both situations, the patient/purchaser may overrule the substitution [8]. Another area of state variation in pharmacy laws involves the authority of a pharmacist to administer vaccines; the variations include the need for a prescription, the age of the vaccine, and the type of vaccine administered [9]. A similar area of expanding scope of practice is that of independent prescribing [10].

Thirty-one states require pharmacists to use the FDA's Orange Book, a guide for therapeutic equivalency, to determine generic substitution. Of the other states, 15 provide a state drug formulary which determines drugs deemed equivalent or interchangeable, and 5 states provide a list of drugs that are not equivalent and therefore not interchangeable. States have also enacted unique interchange laws regarding narrow therapeutic index (NTI) drugs where the consent of both the practitioner and patient is required prior to a pharmacist's substitution. The state boards of pharmacy for the states of Kentucky, North Carolina, and Pennsylvania maintain lists of NTI drugs which may not to be substituted.

Thirty-six states mandate that a non-controlled prescription is considered to be expired after 1 year from the date of issue. Eight states, including Alabama, California, Massachusetts, and New York, have no defined expiration limit. At the pharmacist and insurance company's discretion, a non-controlled prescription can be legally dispensed in these states almost indefinitely.

Electronic prescribing requirements are not uniform between the states. E-prescribing for controlled substances (EPCS) laws are also state-specific. New York State was the first to mandate EPCS in 2016 and followed suit in 2019, and Arizona, Iowa, Massachusetts, North Carolina, Oklahoma, and Rhode Island mandated SPCS in 2020. Pharmacists must also verify the prescriptive authority of the person submitting the prescription; this varies by state law and by provider type.

Pharmacists work with pharmacy technicians in collaborative practice model. The importance of training and education is important as the roles and responsibilities of the pharmacy technician evolve. Most, but not all, states regulate pharmacy technicians. The Pharmacy Technician Certification Board (PTCB) notes that, as of 2019, (1) 24 states and DC regulate pharmacy technicians and require national certification as part of state regulations; (2) of the remaining states, 22 states have enacted regulations regarding pharmacy technicians, but national certification is not required; and (3) some states do not regulate pharmacy technicians (Hawaii, New York, Pennsylvania, and Wisconsin) [11]. The relationship of pharmacist and technician may be employer-employee and/or supervisory in nature, each leading to different legal considerations and liabilities (see Chaps. 6 and 27). Pharmacist liability for the actions of their technicians is usually under *respondeat superior*; however, pharmacists may also be liable under negligence per se, a legal doctrine which states when a statute or regulation is violated, the plaintiff needs only to prove causation and damages in order to prevail, and there is no requisite showing of a standard of care violation. The laws of some states specifically state that a pharmacist is responsible for the actions of a technician; in such a case, negligence per se can prevail and impute the pharmacist regardless of intent, involvement, or knowledge.

Provider Self-Prescription

It remains a generally unsettled question of law as to whether or not licensed providers in the US may legally self-prescribe non-narcotics and Schedule IV and V medications. The federal laws, including the FDCA and CSA, do not specifically prohibit from self-prescribing or prescribing for friends and family of such medications. On the other hand, Opinion 8.19 of the AMA Code of Medical Ethics, "physicians generally should not treat themselves or members of their immediate families." The AMA cites the following reasons:

(a) Professional objectivity may be compromised when an immediate family member or the physician is the patient; the physician's personal feelings may unduly influence his or her professional medical judgment.
(b) Physicians may fail to probe sensitive areas when taking the medical history or may fail to perform intimate parts of the physical examination. Similarly, patients may feel uncomfortable disclosing sensitive information or undergoing an intimate examination when the physician is an immediate family member.
(c) When treating themselves or immediate family members, physicians may be inclined to treat problems that are beyond their expertise or training.
(d) Family members may be reluctant to state their preference for another physician or decline a recommendation for fear of offending the physician. In particular, minor children will generally not feel free to refuse care from their parents. Likewise, physicians may feel obligated to provide care to immediate family members even if they feel uncomfortable providing care.

Although AMA ethical guidelines are important, state law must be followed in every instance. In some states, statutes disallow prescriptions written outside the course of medical practice or require a documented patient-physician relationship in order to submit a prescription.

Antibiotic Stewardship

Pharmacists are directly integrated into multidisciplinary, or inter-professional, medical teams; this is especially true in modern medical centers where the complexity of care requires the special training and expertise of clinical pharmacist. Optimal management of antimicrobial agents requires a thorough understanding of (1) the hospital antibiograms which define optimal sensitivity and potential resistance patterns unique to the hospital; (2) the pharmacodynamics and pharmacokinetics of antimicrobial agents in patients with altered organ function and volumes of distribution; (3) and side effect profiles of antibiotics in acute illness. Antibiotics stewardship programs may range from education, consultation, or the control of antibiotic use. The goals of antibiotic stewardship programs include (1) cost control; (2) reductions in total or targeted antimicrobial use; (3) optimization of appropriate drug use; and (4) improvement in hospital susceptibility profiles for pathogens [12]. In a multidisciplinary care model, the importance of antibiotic, as well as overall drug stewardship, cannot be understated. In fact, professional societies for infectious diseases, public health agencies, and healthcare regulatory agencies increasingly endorse call for antibiotic stewardship programs.

Nonetheless, antibiotic stewardship programs are not without potential liability [13]. Specifically, pharmacists must practice within their scope of practice as defined by state regulations, as well as hospital bylaws. Where a pharmacist initiates a therapeutic relationship, he or she becomes potentially jointly liable for the outcome of care in that case, especially where providers "reasonably relied" on the advice and recommendations of the pharmacist.

Compounding

In general, a compounding pharmacy is a facility wherein drugs and other ingredients are mixed, prepared in customized dosages, or prepared in specific individualized formulations where these preparations are not otherwise commercially available. For example, situations arise where a specific dose or concentration is required, or a patient may be allergic or sensitive to an ingredient in a commercially available preparation. The International Academy of Compounding Pharmacists (IACP) estimates that there are approximately 56,000 community-based pharmacies in the USA. Compounding may be classified as either "sterile" or "non-sterile." Sterile compounded drugs include "intravenously administered fluids and injectable drug," and these present a heightened risk of injury or death in the event of error. Compounding was traditionally regulated by the FDA in the FDCA and by state laws.

The oversight of compounding pharmacies evolved rapidly after, in 2012, the New England Compounding Center (NECC) prepared injectable methylprednisolone acetate (MPA) in a compounding facility in Framingham, MA. Clinicians at Vanderbilt University noticed and notified the Tennessee Department of Health. The Mycotic Diseases Branch Laboratory at CDC later confirmed that three lots of MPA were contaminated by fungus/mold of the species *Exserohilum rostratum*, a plant pathogen and environmental mold [14]. Subsequently, 793 people in 20 states became infected, and 64 people died, although a greater number of infections, from an additional 17,675 vials comprising 29,641 mL of the implicated MPA lots, were averted through prompt recognition and action [15].

In December 2018, a jury convicted the majority shareholder of NECC, Doug Conigliaro, and the NECC Director of Operations, Sharon Carter, of conspiracy to defraud the US Food and Drug Administration (FDA) in violation of 18 US C.§371 which states that it is a felony to conspire "to defraud the United States, or any agency thereof in any manner or for any purpose" and either he or one of his co-conspirators performs "any act to effect the object of the conspiracy" [16] commonly known as a Klein conspiracy. The basis for the prosecution under §371 was that, prior to the fungal outbreak, NECC had represented itself as a conventional pharmacy regulated only by Massachusetts state law rather than a drug manufacturer that would have been subject to FDA oversight. The FDA, in conjunction with the FDA, also prosecuted the case, and the former supervisory pharmacist of NECC, Glenn Chin, was sentenced by the US District Court of Massachusetts, on January 31, 2019, to 8 years in prison, 2 years of supervised release, and forfeiture and restitution in an amount to be determined [17]. As a response to the NECC case, the Compounding Quality Act (Title I of the Drug Quality and Security Act (DSQA)) [18] was enacted by Congress as an amendment to the FDCA in 2013. Compounding facilities must now be registered and comply with Current Good Manufacturing Practices, and these facilities are subject to federal and state inspections.

Case Law in Pharmacy Practice

Pharmacists are legally liable in a way analogous to other healthcare providers and practitioners, for causes of action based, for example, in federal or state statutes, regulations established by state licensing bodies, and professional malpractice [19]. Pharmacists are increasingly involved in lawsuits based in the care they provided to patients. Pharmacists are implicated in hospital-based medical errors, medication errors after discharge, and community-based prescriber issues. A 2019 study by Healthcare Providers Service Organization (HPSO), in collaboration with CNA Insurance and the American Pharmacy Association, found that hospital and compounding specialty locations account for the highest average total liability claims incurred of all pharmacy types; (2) average of the pharmacy closed claims was $124,407, an increase of 22.8% increase since 2013; (3) independent or individually owned and compounding specialty locations had the highest distribution of closed claims of all pharmacy types; (4) incorrect drug and incorrect dose continued to account for the greatest number distribution of closed claims; (4) eye injury or vision loss had an average claim more than four times the overall average total incurred of all professional liability closed claims fort pharmacists; and (5) gastro-intestinal distress, infection/abscess, and death accounted for the greatest number of closed claims [20].

In-patient pharmacies have significant responsibilities which are compounded by the sheer volume of medications dispensed in a busy healthcare institution. In addition, medication errors, such as dose or route errors which are potentially prescribed by trainees, need to be verified and/or corrected. Hospital-based medical error cases are, unfortunately, not uncommon and are generally due to a series of errors which culminate in a bad outcome (see Chaps. 5 and 9). In 2017, a woman with an intracranial hematoma was admitted to a neuro-ICU at Vanderbilt University Medical Center. Subsequently, the patient, who had been alert and oriented in the neuro stepdown unit awaiting transfer to a medical floor, was taken to Radiology for a PET scan where a provider ordered midazolam (Versed) 2 mg IV for sedation to treat her claustrophobia. Here a nurse reportedly opened the automatic dispensing cabinet (ADC) and instead of midazolam (Versed), she pulled and administered vecuronium, a neuromuscular blocking agent (NMBA). The patient subsequently received a lethal dose of the paralyzing anesthetic, and it was later found that no one in the radiology department was monitoring the patient as she went into cardiac arrest [21]. A pharmacist was not involved in this case; however, analysis of the events suggests a multidisciplinary role to facilitate error prevention [22].

The Vanderbilt case is not unique; SMP National Medication Errors Reporting Program (ISMP MERP) suggests that medication errors involving NMBAs are not uncommon [23]. The causes are many and include, for example, (1) look-alike packaging and labeling; (2) unsafe mnemonics; (3) unlabeled and mislabeled syringes; (4) orders entered into the incorrect electronic health record; and (5) syringe swaps [24].

In the case of a 34-year-old man with acute bronchitis who presented to an ED with increasing shortness of breath, worsening cough, and chest pain who was treated with nebulizers and prednisone, he was then admitted to the hospital with a diagnosis of "asthma exacerbation." The next day the patient complained of chest pain with breathing and an order was entered by a provider for ketorolac 30 mg IV, which was electronically signed for by a pharmacist; within 14 minutes of administration, the patient suffered a severe bronchospasm, a "code blue" was called, and the patient remained intubated and ventilated in the ICU where he remained until his death 1 week later. Retrospective review revealed that available literature supported a risk of "severe respiratory compromise in patients who are reactive to NSAIDs: the package insert warned about the risk, and the hospital's intranet pharmacology literature contraindicated the use of ketorolac in patients with asthma." In addition:

> An expert pharmacist (JTOD) opined that the standard of care, state pharmacy law (Drug Utilization Review [DUR] regulations), American Society of Health-System Pharmacists' (ASHP) Best Practices,1 American Pharmacists Association Standards of Practice, 2 and the defendant hospital's own policies and procedures required the pharmacist to prospectively review and assess the patient's medication orders in relation to his diagnosis, and pertinent clinical information, before the first dose of medication was administered, and that a deviation from this requirement had occurred, resulting in the patient's death. Briefly, the standard of care required the pharmacist to provide a warning or an alert regarding a possible adverse drug event (ADE) associated with the use of toradol in a patient experiencing asthma exacerbation. Hospital policies dictated that the pharmacist review all orders and perform a DUR for allergies and drug–disease interactions [25].

Here, standards, best practices, pharmacy law, and hospital policies were each essential to prove that a departure from standard of care had occurred and negligence on the part of the pharmacist.

In the case of *Carl Oyler,* et al. vs. *Oyler v Hy-Vee, Inc.* [26], the survivors of Joyce Oyler brought a wrongful death lawsuit against Hy-Vee, Inc., a pharmacy alleged to have negligently misfilled a prescription with an incorrect medication causing the death of Joyce Oyler. In brief, Oyler was hospitalized with fluid buildup in her lungs and at her discharge was ordered a phoned-in prescription for multiple medications to the Hy-Vee pharmacy, of these medications was metolazone. A pharmacy technician at Hy-Vee, Pecora, who had no formal pharmacy training or education accepted the phone-in prescription order for Ms. Oyler. Pecora made numerous errors transcribing Ms. Oyler's prescriptions, including an error in the dosage for an albuterol inhaler at ten times the correct dose; however, most significantly, Pecora recorded an order for a daily dose of methotrexate, rather than the metolazone. The technicians at Hy-Vee used a dropdown menu to identify medications and doses. Hy-Vee pharmacist Kyle Long approved the methotrexate prescription, at a daily dose, rather than the more usual frequency of once weekly, or potentially twice weekly. An expert for the plaintiff testified at trial that Hy-Vee lacked a sufficient safety system for "high-alert" medications like methotrexate. When Ms. Oyler's prescriptions were picked by her husband at the pharmacy, an employee asked Mr. Oyler if he had any questions about Ms. Oyler's medications, he did not. The pharmacy employee then provided no further counseling or warning about any of the medications although Hy-Vee's Pharmacy Quality Commitment Manual ("PQC Manual") "strongly recommended" that all patients with new prescriptions receive patient counseling, even if not required by the laws of the state in which the pharmacy operates. Plaintiff's expert also testified that such counseling should be provided, at the least, when it comes to "high-alert" drugs like methotrexate. Hy-Vee admitted negligence at trial, and the jury returned a verdict for the Oylers of $2 million, but the trial court reduced the award to $125,000 as a result of a damages cap; the Oylers appealed. The appeals court considered: (1) Hy-Vee's corporate policy stated that "a pharmacist must independently use his or her professional judgment to ensure the prescriptions are safe"; (2) National Pharmacy Technician Training Program materials stated that "only pharmacists can receive oral prescriptions from prescribers or prescribers' authorized designees"; (3) The PQC Manual employed by Hy-Vee stated that "The laws of states vary; however, even if the law requires only an offer of counseling be made to patients, it is strongly recommended that all patients with new prescriptions or any changes in prescriptions receive patient counseling unless extraordinary circumstances prevent counseling." The Missouri Court of Appeals then concluded that the circuit court erred in directing a verdict for Hy-Vee on the Oylers' claim for aggravating circumstances damages and remanded the case, which at present has yet to be decided.

Pharmacists can be held vicariously liable for the actions of their employees. In the case of *Sternberg v. California State Board of Pharmacy* [27], a pharmacist was held strictly liable for employee's repeated thefts of a controlled substance. Sternberg served as pharmacist-in-charge of a Target Pharmacy, where, during a

2-year period, a pharmacy technician stole at least 216,630 tablets of hydrocodone/acetaminophen (Norco). The technician, Hurtado, placed orders for up to 3000 tablets (6 bottles × 500 tablets per bottle) of Norco to be delivered to the pharmacy on a day she was scheduled to work; as often as three times a week. The Target Pharmacy did not normally dispense Norco. When the medications arrived and when orders arrived, she took and hid the bottles, ultimately taking them to her car while on break. Hurtado's theft was discovered when Sternberg found a bottle of the Norco tablets in the storeroom and notified management; a loss prevention investigation ensued Hurtado was recaptured on surveillance and arrested with 3000 Norco tablets. The California State Board of Pharmacy initiated an administrative hearing against Sternberg on charges of "(1) failing to maintain complete and accurate drug records; (2) failing to maintain complete acquisition and disposition records; (3) allowing a non-pharmacist to order and receive controlled substances; (4) failing to properly supervise pharmacy staff; (5) failing to maintain security of the pharmacy; and (6) failing to maintain security of controlled substances." The Board found Sternberg liable on all grounds, revoking his pharmacist's license but staying the revocation on 3 years' probation. Sternberg challenged the Board's decision and order through a petition for writ of administrative mandate at the Los Angeles County Superior Court which found no Board manifest abuse of discretion and denied the writ petition. Sternberg then filed an appeal to the Second District Court of Appeal in California which affirmed the decisions of the lower court and the Board.

In its analysis, the Court of Appeal noted that Business and Professions Code and California Code of Regulations are applied. Specifically, § 4036.5 defined the "pharmacist-in-charge" as "the supervisor or manager responsible for ensuring the pharmacy's compliance with all state and federal laws and regulations pertaining to the practice of pharmacy." The Court looked to the California statute to determine if there was a requirement of "knowledge" by the pharmacist-in-charge as a prerequisite to liability and found none; "[t]he Legislature's failure to include 'knowingly' or 'intentionally' or other qualifying words signals that it did not intend either guilty knowledge or intent to be elements of the licensing statute at issue." Furthermore, the Court determined that the Board's interpretation supported a "purpose of protecting the public by encouraging pharmacists-in-charge to take necessary precautions to adequately supervise and maintain the inventory of dangerous drugs." Moreover, the Court looked to the California Code which states that "[e]ach pharmacist while on duty shall be responsible for the security of the prescription department, including provisions for effective control against theft or diversion of dangerous drugs and devices, and records for such drugs and devices. Possession of a key to the pharmacy where dangerous drugs and controlled substances are stored shall be restricted to a pharmacist." The Court upheld the funding by the Board that Sternberg had "no controls to prevent theft; there was instead a lax oversight of the phone ordering system, failures in accepting deliveries and handling invoices, the lack of supervision when the pharmacist was on break, and the failure to conduct random checks of deliveries and invoices." In conclusion, the Court of Appeal held that "Sternberg failed to properly oversee the operations of the pharmacy and the

Board could have concluded that theft would have been averted if he supervised and randomly audited drug deliveries, conducted checks of his staff's work, and actively participated in the inventory and delivery process."

Pharmacists and pharmacies are under heightened scrutiny as the government seeks to control the opiate epidemic, and, therefore, opiate prescriptions will remain a risk in the foreseeable future.

In *USA v. Farmville Discount Drug, Inc.*, et al. [28], the US District Court for the Eastern District of North Carolina entered a consent judgment and permanent injunction, civil penalties, and a permanent surrender of a pharmacist's license to practice. The DOJ alleged that Farmville Discount Drug and Crocker repeatedly filled prescriptions in violation of the Controlled Substances Act. The DOJ alleged that defendants ignored "red flags" of drug diversion and drug-seeking behavior when filling prescriptions for controlled substances including, for example, oxycodone, hydrocodone, hydromorphone, and methadone, diazepam alprazolam, and zolpidem. The red flags allegedly ignored included (1) prescriptions filled for prescription-drug cocktails for long-distance patients who saw a doctor an hour away and lived an hour away; (2) filling hundreds of opioid prescriptions for multiple members of the same family; (3) filling prescriptions for a prescriber that had been cut off from other pharmacies; and (4) filling controlled-substance prescriptions for patients who shopped for physicians and pharmacies. Robert J. Murphy, Special Agent in Charge of the DEA Atlanta Field Division, stated that "DEA Diversion Investigators will continue to aggressively pursue the unlawful dispensing practices of healthcare providers."

The case of *Burton v. Walgreens* [29] illustrates a case of "spoliation of evidence" applied to a pharmacy. In *Burton*, plaintiff was prescribed Diovan, for his high blood pressure. On March 3, 2012, a Walgreen pharmacist erroneously filled plaintiff's prescription with a mix of Diovan and lithium pills which were different in shape but the same color. Burton continued to take the pills as instructed and began to experience numbness and weakness in his left hand requiring "hospitalization where he was diagnosed with an adverse reaction to lithium. Burton's wife noticed that the pills in the bottle did not match one another and returned the misfilled medications to Walgreens. Burton's symptoms worsened, and he was diagnosed with carpal tunnel syndrome and polyneuropathy, as a result of lithium, which ultimately required surgery. Burton then filed suit against Walgreens and during discovery asked Walgreens to produce the bottle with its contents intact so that he may test the pills inside to determine if some pills were in fact lithium to which Walgreens replied that it had destroyed the bottle and its contents in accordance with store policy. Burton filed motion for spoliation sanctions and a bench trial.

In its analysis, the court stated the legal standard for spoliation as "the destruction or significant alteration of evidence, or the failure to preserve property for another's use as evidence in pending or reasonably foreseeable litigation" noting that "[a] party must preserve evidence it knows or should know is relevant to a claim or defense of any party, or that may lead to the discovery of relevant evidence" and recognizing that "[b]efore imposing sanctions, the court should consider whether the alleged spoliation prejudiced plaintiff." Plaintiff Burton argued that Walgreens had purposefully and willfully destroyed the medication in violation of its policy to quarantine returned medication; but the court determined that Walgreens acted in accordance with its store policy which was to quarantine the misfilled medications in a depository safe and then returned medication to its prescription return center, where it was destroyed in compliance with store policy. Plaintiff Burton then argued that Walgreens had a duty to preserve the medications as evidence since it was on notice of "significant potential of litigation" when the incident report was filed, to which Walgreens responded stating that customers returned medications frequently and that it would be impractical to preserve medications just in case.

The court in *Burton* held that Walgreens indeed did have a duty to preserve the evidence but that plaintiff was not prejudiced by the spoliation and therefore declined to impose spoliation sanctions. The court also considered that "lithium is a common medication that has been used for decades and its effects are widely studied." Here, Walgreens (1) acted in accordance with its policies and procedures, and (2) the symptoms exhibited by plaintiff were not of the sort that would have resulted from the dose of lithium he ingested; this case could have turned differently if the facts were slightly different.

Pharmacists are also potentially liable under the False Claims Act. In 2018, the DOJ sentenced a pharmacist and his employee for their involvement in a $30 million healthcare fraud scheme against Tricare (the healthcare program for military service members, veterans, and their families); this case is the largest healthcare fraud case to go to trial involving the Tricare program. The District Court for the Southern District of Florida found the defendant pharmacist Francois guilty of conspiracy to commit healthcare fraud; 12 counts of healthcare fraud; conspiracy to pay kickbacks in connection with a federal healthcare program; 5 counts of paying kickbacks; 12 counts of money laundering; 8 counts of introducing misbranded drugs into interstate commerce; 4 counts of making false statements related to healthcare matters; and 1 count of making a false statement on a DEA form. The jury found the codefendant Tonge guilty of the same conspiracy charges, 11 counts of healthcare fraud, 3 counts of paying kickbacks, and 2 counts of money laundering. On March 9, 2018, Francois was sentenced to 204 months in prison to be followed by 3 years supervised release and was ordered to pay $31,259,252 in restitution. Tonge, 42, was sentenced to 188 months in prison, to be followed by 3 years of supervised release, and was also ordered to pay $31,259,252 in restitution [30].

Conclusions and Summary

The practice of pharmacy is regulated as a profession and is subject to both federal and state oversight. Understanding of the laws and regulations which govern pharmacy practice is mandatory and a basis of state licensure of pharmacists, through the MPJE. Nonetheless, legislation and regulations continue to evolve in response to external forces such as the opioid epidemic, scope of practice redefinition, reclassification of medications, the balancing of access to safe medications against the cost of pharmaceuticals, and occurrences which highlight gaps in the safety of the nation's drug supply.

References

1. FDCA. 21 USC.§ 351. Adulterated drugs and devices.
2. FDCA. 21 USC.§ 352. Misbranded drugs and devices.
3. United States Drug Enforcement Agency (DEA). Drug Scheduling. Available online at: https://www.dea.gov/drug-scheduling.
4. Poison Prevention Packaging Act of 1970 (PPPA).Pub. L. 91-601, 84 Stat. 1670-74. 15 U.S.C. 39A § 1471 et seq.
5. Prescription Drug Marketing Act (PDMA). P.L. 100-293, 102 Stat. 95.21 CFR §.
6. 21 CFR 1306.06.
7. Adams AJ. Transitioning pharmacy to "standard of care" regulation: analyzing how pharmacy regulates relative to medicine and nursing. Res Social Adm Pharm. 2019;15(10):1230–5.
8. Song Y, Barthold D. The effects of state-level pharmacist regulations on generic substitution of prescription drugs. Health Econ. 2018;27(11):1717–37.
9. Schmit CD, Penn MS. Expanding state laws and a growing role for pharmacists in vaccination services. J Am Pharm Assoc (2003). 2017;57(6):661–9.
10. Stimmel GL. Political and legal aspects of pharmacist prescribing. Am J Hosp Pharm. 1983;40(8):1343–4.
11. Pharmacy Technician Certification Board. State Regulations and Map. 31 Dec 2019. Available online at: https://www.ptcb.org/resources/state-regulations-and-map.
12. Doron S, Davidson LE. Antimicrobial stewardship. Mayo Clin Proc. 2011;86(11):1113–23.
13. Maliha G, Nepps ME, Tamma PD, Dodds Ashley E, Szymczak JE, Kolesar E, Hamilton KW. Legal implications of antibiotic stewardship programs. Infect Control Hosp Epidemiol. 2020;41(7):757–64.
14. Kauffman CA, Pappas PG, Patterson TF. Fungal infections associated with contaminated methylprednisolone injections. N Engl J Med. 2013;368:2495–500.
15. Smith RM, Derado G, Wise M, et al. Estimated deaths and illnesses averted during fungal meningitis outbreak associated with contaminated steroid injections, United States, 2012-2013. Emerg Infect Dis. 2015;21(6):933–40.
16. 18 U.S. Code § 371. Conspiracy to commit offense or to defraud United States.
17. FDA. U.S. Department of Justice Press Release. January 31, 2018: New England Compounding Center Pharmacist Sentenced for Role in Nationwide Fungal Meningitis Outbreak. 31 Jan 2019. Available online at: https://www.fda.gov/inspections-compliance-enforcement-and-criminal-investigations/press-releases/january-31-2018-new-england-compounding-center-pharmacist-sentenced-role-nationwide-fungal.
18. Drug Quality and Security Act. Hr. 3204. Public Law No: 113-54 (11/27/2013).
19. The consensus of the Pharmacy Practice Model Summit. Am J Health Syst Pharm. 2011;68(12):1148–52.
20. Healthcare Providers Service Organization (HPSO) and CNA Insurance. Pharmacist Liability Claim Report: 2nd Edition. 2019. Available online at: http://www.hpso.com/Documents/Risk%20Education/individuals/Claim-Reports/Pharmacist/HPSO-CNA-Pharmacist-Claim-Report-2019.pdf.
21. Peeples L. Another Fatal Vecuronium Error! Versed mix-up in radiology leads to lethal dose. Pharmacy Practice News. 8 Jan 2019. Available online at: https://www.pharmacypractice-news.com/Clinical/Article/01-19/Another-Fatal-Vecuronium-Error-/53755?enl=true&sub=F

09D4E1AEB1935236B7DD88EBF3511796624DD9967A417E04A63FAD9FB86. See also Patient Safety Solutions, Patient Safety Tip of the Week. December 11, 2018. Available online at: https://www.patientsafetysolutions.com/docs/December_11_2018_Another_NMBA_Accident.htm.

22. O'Donnell JT, O'Donnell JJ, Vogenberg FR. Forensic analysis in drug litigation finds most errors occur with commonly used therapies and practices. P T. 2019;44(3):118–21.
23. Cohen MR, Smetzer JL. ISMP medication error report analysis: Aggrastat-Argatroban mix-ups don't expect radiofrequency identification stock systems to be perfect paralyzed by mistakes: reassess the safety of neuromuscular blockers in your facility. Hosp Pharm. 2016;51(11):877–83. https://doi.org/10.1310/hpj5111-877.
24. Grissinger M. Paralyzed by mistakes - reassess the safety of neuromuscular blockers in your facility. P T. 2019;44(3):91–107.
25. O'Donnell JT, Vogenberg FR. Use of regulations, laws, standards, and best practices when prosecuting and defending hospitals in drug injury lawsuits. P T. 2018;43(12):747–71.
26. Oyler v Hy-Vee, Inc., 2017 Mo.App. LEXIS 1070 (October 24, 2017).
27. Sternberg v. California State Board of Pharmacy (2015) 239 Cal.App.4th 1159. California Court of Appeal, Second District, Division Eight, Case No. B255862. (Opinion filed August 6, 2015; Certified for publication August 26, 2015).
28. Consent Judgment and Permanent Injunction at https://www.justice.gov/usao-ednc/press-release/file/1242486/download. *See also* Department of Justice. Federal Court Orders North Carolina Pharmacy and Pharmacist to Pay $600,000 and to Permanently Cease Dispensing Opioids or Other Controlled Substances. 3 Feb 2020. Available online at: https://www.justice.gov/opa/pr/federal-court-orders-north-carolina-pharmacy-and-pharmacist-pay-600000-and-permanently-cease.
29. Burton v. Walgreen Co., Case No. 2:14-CV-84. United States District Court, D. Nevada. 10 July 2015.
30. Food and Drug Administration. Office of Criminal Investigations. U.S. Department of Justice Press Release. Southern District of Florida. 12 Mar 2018: Pharmacist and Pharmacy Employee Sentenced for Involvement in Over $30 Million Health Care Fraud. Available online at; https://www.fda.gov/inspections-compliance-enforcement-and-criminal-investigations/press-releases/march-12-2018-pharmacist-and-pharmacy-employee-sentenced-involvement-over-30-million-health-care.

Chapter 21
Legal Issues in Mental Health Relevant to Acute Care Practice

James E. Szalados

Ethical Issues in the Care of Patients with Mental Illness

The core ethical principles of autonomy, non-maleficence, beneficence, and justice apply to the care of all patients equally. However, questions regarding the mental capacity of a patient can lead to questions regarding their capacity for autonomous decision-making including both consent and refusal of care; shared decision-making; and needs to seek surrogate consent or refusal. Patients with mental illness may seek medications or procedures that may not be indicated, refuse necessary care, refuse admission to a facility, or sign out "against medical advice" when hospitalization and acute medical care are needed. Although the acute care team will generally always act in the best interests of the patient, the line between implied consent for emergent necessary care and battery can be very indistinct. In order to act within the boundaries of the law, providers must use their best judgment, document the circumstances, and seek consultation. Moreover, if the mentally ill patient has a disability, then he or she may fall into a protected class. The question of legal capacity often becomes one for a psychiatrist to determine.

The terms capacity and competence are frequently used interchangeably but have different legal meanings. Clinical competence is assessed by a physician, not a judge, and is referred to as capacity. Competence is more a legal term and refers to a judicial determination of legal status. Competence is generally presumed unless a court has otherwise determined that an individual is incompetent. Competence refers to a legal capacity. A legal definition of competence may read as "having

J. E. Szalados (✉)
Director, Surgical and Neurocritical Care Units, Rochester Regional Health System at Rochester General Hospital, Rochester, NY, USA

The Szalados Law Firm, Hilton, NY, USA
e-mail: james.szalados@rochesterregional.org; jszalados@aol.com

J. E. Szalados (ed.), *The Medical-Legal Aspects of Acute Care Medicine*,
https://doi.org/10.1007/978-3-030-68570-6_21

suitable or sufficient skill, knowledge, experience…for some purpose." Questions of legal competence arise in cases of an elderly person's ability to make a will, execute a contract, or an accused's competence to stand trial.[1] In general, once declared incompetent by a court, only a reassessment based on new evidence by a court can reverse that status. If a patient is considered incompetent under the law, then he or she lacks legal capacity and will have an appointed guardian.

Capacity, on the other hand, is a medical term that is determined by the treating physician and may be situational, in flux, or task-specific. A patient may lack capacity if he or she is acutely ill, has a head injury, or has been medicated; these situations are expected to resolve of "clear" and are not generally expected to be permanent. Capacity may be determined by the treating provider and based on levels of orientation, such as a mini-mental state examination. Capacity is fundamental to decision-making as either informed consent or informed refusal. The basic process of informed consent based on the legal requirements of disclosing the attendant risks, benefits, and alternatives of a planned procedure is meaningless unless the person consenting of refusing has the ability to comprehend the implications and consequences of his or her decision [1]. Thus, a prerequisite to informed consent or refusal is the ability to "(a) recognize there is a decision to be made, (b) understand the needed information, (c) understand the treatment options, (d) understand the likely consequences of each option (i.e. risks, burdens, and benefits), and (e) rationally manipulate the information to come up with a decision consistent with his or her values" [2]. Thus autonomy and choice are meaningless without the capacity for understanding the ramification of the choice. The legal definition of capacity is similar. Black's Law Dictionary defines "capacity" as a "legal qualification….which determines one's ability to sue or be sued, to enter into binding contract…" [3]. To the extent that informed consent has similarities to a contract, the legal definition, with a requisite soundness of mind, voluntariness, and insight as to one's actions, medical informed consent is similar to the medical definition of capacity to contract.

Involuntary Confinement

Involuntary confinement is a term that usually relates to confinement in a mental health facility; that is generally based on an assessment by a psychiatrist. In New York State, Section 9.60 of the NYS Mental Health Law, Kendra's Law, can compel an individual to undergo psychiatric treatment through a process of involuntary commitment.

More common in the acute care setting, however, is the mental hygiene attest or the emergency hold for medical stabilization (EHMS). The EHMS can be used in two general types of situations: (1) a brief (usually 72 hours) involuntary detention

[1] *See* 18 US Code § 4241. Determination of mental competency to stand trial to undergo postrelease proceedings.

of a person presumed to be mentally ill in order to determine whether an individual meets criteria for further involuntary civil commitment [4] and (2) involuntary hospitalization for a medical emergency under the presumption that a patient lacks the capacity to refuse care. For example, New York State Mental Hygiene law §9.39 states:

> The director of any hospital maintaining adequate staff and facilities for the observation, examination, care, and treatment of persons alleged to be mentally ill and approved by the commissioner to receive and retain patients pursuant to this section may receive and retain therein as a patient for a period of fifteen days any person alleged to have a mental illness for which immediate observation, care, and treatment in a hospital is appropriate and which is likely to result in serious harm to himself or others. "Likelihood to result in serious harm" as used in this article shall mean:
>
> 1. substantial risk of physical harm to himself as manifested by threats of or attempts at suicide or serious bodily harm or other conduct demonstrating that he is dangerous to himself, or
> 2. a substantial risk of physical harm to other persons as manifested by homicidal or other violent behavior by which others are placed in reasonable fear of serious physical harm.
>
> The director shall cause to be entered upon the hospital records the name of the person or persons, if any, who have brought such person to the hospital and the details of the circumstances leading to the hospitalization of such person [5].

In order for NY State Mental Hygiene Law to apply, the certifications of two examining physicians, accompanied by an application for the admission of such person, must accompany the admissions process.

Suicidal Ideation

A patient presenting with suicidal ideation must be assessed and treated, a psychiatric consultation, if possible, is essential. Patients with suicidal ideation often have a preexisting Diagnostic and Statistical Manual (DSM) of the American Psychiatric Association (APA) psychiatric diagnosis, including substance abuse disorder, depression, psychotic disease, and posttraumatic stress disorder. It is important to realize that suicidal ideation is unlikely to be the presenting compliant in acute medical and surgical care; rather, the patient may present with constitutional symptoms reflecting stress, and on further assessment, additional risk factors for suicide may be present. Inquiry can be important; evidence shows that inquiring about suicide does not increase suicidal ideation or attempts [6]. State laws may define reporting and hold mandates regarding suicidal patients.

Inpatient suicide is rare and should never occur. In 2018, the Joint Commission issued a National Patient Safety Goal for suicide prevention which states:

> The organization conducts an environmental risk assessment that identifies features in the physical environment that could be used to attempt suicide; the organization takes necessary action to minimize the risk(s) (for example, removal of anchor points, door hinges, and hooks that can be used for hanging).

For psychiatric hospitals and psychiatric units in general hospitals: The hospital conducts an environmental risk assessment that identifies features in the physical environment that could be used to attempt suicide; the hospital takes necessary action to minimize the risk(s) (for example, removal of anchor points, door hinges, and hooks that can be used for hanging).

For nonpsychiatric units in general hospitals: The organization implements procedures to mitigate the risk of suicide for patients at high risk for suicide, such as one-to-one monitoring, removing objects that pose a risk for self-harm if they can be removed without adversely affecting the patient's medical care, assessing objects brought into a room by visitors, and using safe transportation procedures when moving patients to other parts of the hospital.

Nonpsychiatric units in general hospitals are not expected to be ligature-resistant environments. Nevertheless, these facilities should assess clinical areas to identify objects that could be used for self-harm and should be routinely removed when possible from the area around a patient who has been identified as high risk for suicide. This information can be used for training staff who monitor high risk patients (for example, developing checklists to help staff remember which equipment should be removed when possible).

TJC. NPSG 15.01.01, EP 1 [7]

Tarasov and the Duty to Warn

In 1976, the Supreme Court of California, in *Tarasoff v. Regents of the University of California*, held that mental health professionals have a duty to protect individuals who are being threatened by a patient [8]. In the *Tarasoff* case, a university student named Tatiana Tarasoff was murdered by Indian graduate student, Prosenjit Poddar, at the University of California. Tarasoff and Poddar had an apparently superficial relationship, and when Tatiana rebuffed Poddar, he then sustained an emotional crisis for which he sought treatment at the University Medical Center by a counselor. During a counseling session, Poddar confessed his intention to kill Tatiana. Poddar was tried for first-degree murder but was found guilty of second-degree murder; he spent 5 years in prison until his conviction was successfully appealed and he was released. Tatiana's parents appealed the decision to the Supreme Court of California which held, inter alia:

> when a therapist determines, or pursuant to the standards of his profession should determine, that his patient presents a serious danger of violence to another, he incurs an obligation to use reasonable care to protect the intended victim against such danger. The court further held that the decision whether to warn was not a discretionary act within the immunity provisions … [9].

In the case of *Jablonski by Pahls v. United States* [10], Meghan Jablonski brought suit for the wrongful death of her mother, who has been murdered by the man she was living with, Phillip Jablonski. Following threats, the police intervened and Jablonski volunteered to undergo a psychiatric examination at the hospital. Jablonski was diagnosed with "antisocial personality" and deemed "potentially dangerous"; however, he refused voluntarily hospitalization and was released. The court looked to the elements of a Tarasoff cause of action: the plaintiff must prove (1) a psychotherapist-patient relationship existed, (2) that the psychotherapist knew, or should have known, that Jablonski was dangerous, (3) that Kimball was a foreseeable victim of Jablonski's violent tendencies, and (4) that the psychotherapist did not take the necessary steps to discharge his duty. Here, the Ninth Circuit Court of Appeals found that the Duty to Warn arises not only when a patient has expressed specific threats against an identifiable victim but also if that patient's prior history indicates that he or she is likely to direct violence against an identified person.

In 1985 the California Legislature enacted Section 43.92 of the California Civil Code to provide immunity for psychotherapists for failure to warn. However, the immunity does not apply if the patient communicated a serious threat of physical violence:

> (a) There shall be no monetary liability on the part of, and no cause of action shall arise against, any person who is a psychotherapist as defined in Section 1010 of the Evidence Code in failing to warn of and protect from a patient's threatened behavior or failing to predict and warn of and protect from a patient's violent behavior except where a patient communicated to the psychotherapist a serious threat of physical violence against a reasonable identifiable victim or victims."
>
> "(b) If there is a duty to warn and protect under the limited circumstances specified above, the duty shall be discharged by the psychotherapist making reasonable efforts to communicate the threat to the victim or victims and to a law enforcement agency."
>
> "Psychotherapist" is defined in Evidence Code Section 1010 to mean:
>
> "(a) A person authorized, or reasonably believed by the patient to be authorized, to practice medicine in any state or nation who devotes, or is reasonably believed by the patient to devote, a substantial portion of his or her time to the practice of psychiatry."
>
> California Civil Code § 43.92

Federal Laws Impacting Mental Health Care

The Mental Health Parity and Addiction Equity Act of 2008 (MHPAEA)[2] amended the Public Health Service Act, the Employee Retirement Income Security Act (ERISA), the Mental Health Parity Act of 1996 (MHPA), and the Internal Revenue Code. In general, the MHPAEA requires that health plans and health issuers take measures to ensure that financial benefits and requirements (e.g., co-pays and deductibles) and treatment limitations for patients with mental health or substance use disorder are no more restrictive benefits and requirements for medical or surgical benefits.

Treatment records of mental health facilities or programs are protected under both HIPAA and state law. Where state privacy and confidentiality laws are inconsistent, HIPAA will preempt (or supersede) any inconsistent provision of state law, unless the state requirements are "more stringent"; in such cases, state law may control. Standard HIPAA authorization forms make exceptions for mental health and substance abuse history disclosure, which must be authorized explicitly and

[2] Pub.L. 104–204

separately. The disclosure of mental health information though a request for medical records, without explicit authorization, is a HIPAA violation.

Medical Issues in the Care of the Psychiatric Patient

On October 4, 1984, an 18-year-old woman with history of depression named Libby Zion was admitted to the New York Hospital. Ms. Zion, a freshman at Bennington College in Vermont, was in New York City visiting her parents. Ms. Zion was under the care of a psychiatrist and had been prescribed phenelzine (Nardil®), a monoamine oxidase inhibitor (MAO-I), although she reportedly was also taking imipramine, flurazepam, diazepam, tetracycline, doxycycline, and aspirin/oxycodone following a dental extraction. Ms. Zion started to have "flu-like" symptoms and ran a fever of 102 °F and was later referred to the ED by her family physician. Where she presented with a fever of 103.5° an elevated white count. Ms. Zion was separately examined by the intern and a resident, and a provisional diagnosis of "viral syndrome with hysterical symptoms" was made. Ms. Zion was then administered to receive acetaminophen, antibiotics, and an intramuscular injection of 25 mg of meperidine. When Ms. Zion became more agitated, she received haloperidol and required physical restraint; her temperature continued to climb and was refractory to cooling measures until she sustained a cardiac arrest. It later became apparent that Ms. Zion had died of a lethal drug interaction, serotonin syndrome in the setting of the combined effects of phenelzine and meperidine [11]. Although the case subsequently became the basis for another reason, its impact on resident work hours, this case also illustrates the complex interactions between psychoactive medications and other medications commonly administered in the acute care setting. Moreover, in a patient with mental illness, it may not be possible to fully elicit a medication or substance abuse history; and the reactions to "standard" treatments, for example, haloperidol, may be atypical, sometimes refractory and sometimes exaggerated.

Serotonin syndrome is usually a result of a medication or a combination of medications which causes a buildup of serotonin, a neurotransmitter, in the body; with subsequent overactivity at central and peripheral serotonin receptors which then causes mental status changes, neuromuscular hyperactivity, and autonomic hyperactivity. Serotonin is normally metabolized by monoamine oxidase-A (MAO-A), an enzyme inhibited by the class of drugs known as MAO inhibitors. A large number of drugs can precipitate serotonin syndrome; however, for relevance, those most potentially likely implicated in the mentally ill patient are listed (Table 21.1).

Neuroleptic malignant syndrome (NMS) is a life-threatening reaction which, similar to serotonin syndrome, occurs in patients treated with antipsychotic (neuroleptic) agents. NMS is also characterized by mental status change, rigidity, fever, and dysautonomia. The differential diagnosis of NMS includes serotonin syndrome, malignant catatonia, acute intoxication with certain recreational drug, and central anticholinergic syndrome. Once again, a partial listing of medications associated

Table 21.1 Some drugs associated with serotonin syndrome

Mechanism of serotonin toxicity	Examples of drugs
Serotonin uptake inhibition	Amphetamines, phentermine Bupropion, trazodone Meperidine, methadone, tramadol Cocaine, MDMA (ecstasy) Desvenlafaxine, venlafaxine, duloxetine MAO-I's Citalopram, escitalopram, fluoxetine, paroxetine, sertraline Amitriptyline, desipramine, doxepin, imipramine, nortriptyline
Serotonin metabolism inhibitors	Buspirone MAO-I's Triptans
Increased serotonin synthesis	Amphetamine, phentermine, cocaine
Increased serotonin release	Mirtazapine
Serotonin receptor activation	LSD, lithium
CYP450 inhibitors	Oxycodone, risperidone, tramadol, oxycodone, methadone, citalopram

Table 21.2 Some drugs associated with neuroleptic malignant syndrome

Neuroleptics: Typical	Haloperidol Fluphenazine Chlorpromazine Prochlorperazine Thioridazine Thiothixene Perphenazine Promazine
Neuroleptics: Atypical	Clozapine Risperidone Olanzapine Quetiapine Ziprasidone Aripiprazole
Nonneuroleptics with antidopaminergic activity	Promethazine Amoxapine
Other	Lithium Phenelzine Desipramine Trimipramine

with NMS [12], especially those most relevant to patient with mental illness, is shown in Table 21.2.

The incidence and prevalence rates of both diagnosed and undiagnosed and untreated medical illnesses are higher in individuals with mental illness. The reason for such a health disparity remains unclear; however, possibilities include (1) potentially modifiable lifestyle factors and (2) access to medical care. Acute care providers must approach the patient with mental illness with a heightened scrutiny since: (1) history may be unreliable or unavailable; (2) past medical may be difficult to access, or unavailable; (3) providers may lack familiarity with psychoactive medication; and (4) there may be significant and unrecognized chronic comorbidity. Patients hospitalized with an acute medical or surgical diagnosis who have concomitant mental illness will benefit from referrals to social workers and care managers to ensure proper transitions of care planning and follow-up.

Disability of Patients with Mental Illness

Disability in mental illness occurs where there is symptomatic recovery with the available treatment modalities; however, long-term deficits continue which significantly interfere with self-care; interpersonal, social, and occupational functioning; and impaired quality of life. The International Classification of Impairments, Disabilities, and Handicaps defines disability as the interference with activities of the whole person in relation to the immediate environment [13]. Disability associated with mental illness is a major associated disease burden. It is important to realize that "mental illness" and "psychiatric disability" are not synonymous; not all persons with a diagnosis of mental illness are disabled, and in fact dome are highly functional. The APA lists more than 200 mental illness conditions in its Diagnostic DSM-V; these may include disorders, depression, bipolar disorder, schizophrenia, obsessive-compulsive disorder, gender dysphoria, and posttraumatic stress disorder (PTSD).

The Equal Employment Opportunity Commission (EEOC) notes that the ADA defines "mental impairment" as any "mental or psychological disorder, such as emotional or mental illness." Nonetheless, mental illness such as depression, bipolar disorder, anxiety disorders, and other mental health impairments may become disabilities, and therefore under the Americans with Disabilities Act (ADA), employers must make accommodations for workers with such conditions. Title I of the ADA prohibits employers with 15 or more employees from discriminating against qualified individuals with disabilities in job application procedures, hiring, firing, advancement, compensation, job training, and other employment matters. Not all conditions listed in the DSM translate to a disability as defined by the ADA or the Americans with Disabilities Act Amendments Act (ADAAA); for example, drug abuse diagnoses are not considered a disability under the ADA.

Patients with disabilities also fall into the designation of a protected class under the Civil Rights Act of 1964 which protects persons, or as patients, from being discriminated against based on certain characteristics: (1) age; (2) race; (3) national origin; (4) religious beliefs; (5) gender; (6) disability; (7) pregnancy; and (8) veteran status. In addition, some states already protect persons against discrimination on the basis of (1) gender identity; (2) sexual orientation; (3) political ideology; and, (4) service in a State Militia. Since gender dysphoria, for example, is a DSM diagnosis, it may, in some states, have protected class status. Under preemption, state laws may confer a greater amount of protections than federal laws; however, they may not be less strict or accord fewer protections than federal laws in the field regulated.

SARS-CoV-2 and COVID-19: Mental Health Implications

Following the SARS-CoV-2 coronavirus outbreak in 2019 and the subsequent COVID-19 pandemic of 2020, it is expected that the number of patients with mental illness presenting to acute care hospitals for general medical and surgical care will rise sharply, partly as the public experiences high levels of emotional distress and partly with exacerbation of preexisting previously latent borderline mental health conditions [14]. COVID-19 appears to be precipitating high levels of substance abuse, depression, suicide, and posttraumatic stress disorder (PTSD). Predictive analysis of the incidence of acute mental illness suggests an emerging global mental health crisis [15] and, probably, one that our health care system is ill-prepared to manage [16]. Furthermore, that suggests that many, if not most, of the acutely ill hospitalized population had serious chronic comorbidities prior to their hospitalization with COVID-19. Through the latter part of 2020, as the chronic mental health burden grows, and there is a threat of either a potential second wave of COVID-19, influenza, a COVID-19 mutation, or a novel virus, the superimposed preexisting mental health and superimposed acute medical illness will require novel and multidisciplinary approaches to care and long-term post-discharge planning.

Summary and Conclusions

Mental health laws serve dual purposes: (1) the protection of the individual from self-harm and (2) the protection of the public from the mentally ill. Mental hygiene laws must balance individual autonomy against the public interest, and therefore the laws are generally structured with deference to individuals, liberty interests.

References

1. Szalados JE. Morality, ethics, and the law: an overview of the foundations of contemporary clinical ethical analysis in Szalados JE. Ethics and law for neurosciences clinicians: foundations and evolving challenges. NJ: Rutgers University Press; 2019. p. 7.
2. Orr RD. Competence, capacity, and surrogate decision-making. The Center for Bioethics & Human Dignity. 3 Mar 2004. Available online at: https://cbhd.org/content/competence-capacity-and-surrogate-decision-making.
3. Garner BA, editor. Black's law dictionary. 7th ed. St. Paul: West; 1979. p. 199.
4. Hedman LC, Petrila J, Fisher WH, et al. State laws on emergency holds for mental health stabilization. Psychiatr Serv. 2016;67(5):529–35.

5. 2015 New York Laws MHY - Mental Hygiene Title B - Mental Health Act Article 9 - (9.01–9.63) Hospitalization of the Mentally Ill 9.41
6. Norris D, Clark MS. Evaluation and treatment of the suicidal patient. Am Fam Physician. 2012;85(6):602–5.
7. TJC. National Patient Safety Goal for suicide prevention. NPSG 15.01.01, EP 1. Issue 18, 27 Nov 2018. Available online at: https://www.jointcommission.org/-/media/tjc/documents/resources/patient-safety-topics/suicide-prevention/r3_18_suicide_prevention_hap_bhc_5_6_19_rev5.pdf?db=web&hash=887186D9530F7BB8E30C28FE352B5B8C.
8. Tarasoff v. Regents of the University of California, 17 Cal. 3d 425, 551 P.2d 334, 131 Cal. Rptr. 14 (Cal. 1976)
9. Tarasoff v. The University of California (1976). California official reports summary. Available online at: http://forensicmenta http://forensicmentalhealthservices.org/?p=6 lhealthservices.org/?p=6.
10. Jablonski Pahls v. United States. 712 F. 2d 391 (1983).
11. Volpi-Abadie J, Kaye AM, Kaye AD. Serotonin syndrome. Ochsner J. 2013;13(4):533–40.
12. Berman BD. Neuroleptic malignant syndrome: a review for neurohospitalists. Neurohospitalist. 2011;1(1):41–7.
13. Assessment, Classification and Epidemiology Group. International classification of impairment, disability and handicap (ICIDH). Geneva, Switzerland: World Health Organization; 1980.
14. Vindegaard N, Benros ME. COVID-19 pandemic and mental health consequences: systematic review of the current evidence. Brain Behav Immun. 2020:S0889-1591(20)30954-5.
15. Talevi D, Socci V, Carai M, Carnaghi G, Faleri S, Trebbi E, di Bernardo A, Capelli F, Pacitti F. Mental health outcomes of the CoViD-19 pandemic. Riv Psichiatr. 2020;55(3):137–44.
16. Xiang YT, Yang Y, Li W, Zhang L, Zhang Q, Cheung T, Ng CH. Timely mental health care for the 2019 novel coronavirus outbreak is urgently needed. Lancet Psychiatry. 2020;7:228–9.

Chapter 22
Clinical Labs: CLIA and Other Evolving Challenges

James E. Szalados

A History and Overview of the Clinical Laboratory Improvement Amendments (CLIA)

In 1967, Wilbur Cohen, Secretary of the US Department of Health, Education, and Welfare (HEW), and Dr. D.J. Sencer, Director of the US Public Health Service's Communicable Disease Center, testified before Congress at the House Committee on Interstate and Foreign Commerce, stating that clinical laboratory testing was then associated with an error rate of up to 25% [1]. Largely in response to that testimony, Congress passed the "Clinical Laboratory Improvement Act (CLIA) of 1967" (CLIA-1967), the first legislation to regulate clinical laboratory medicine in the USA [2]. CLIA-1967 was limited in its scope, addressing only laboratories transporting samples across state lines and therefore engaging in interstate commerce, providing services to Medicare and Medicaid patients; however, it defined personnel and staffing requirements. Since CLIA-1967 excluded testing in private physician laboratories, CLIA-1967 was applicable to very few clinical laboratories at the time.

In 1980, Dr. Joseph Boutwell, then Deputy Director of the Centers for Disease Control and Prevention's Bureau of Laboratories, publically opined that some of the most commonly performed medical laboratory tests were associated with a 14% error rate. The Office of the Assistant Secretary for Planning and Evaluation (ASPE) of HHS commissioned a study to assess the effectiveness of federal regulations

J. E. Szalados (✉)
Director, Surgical and Neurocritical Care Units, Rochester Regional Health System at Rochester General Hospital, Rochester, NY, USA

The Szalados Law Firm, Hilton, NY, USA
e-mail: james.szalados@rochesterregional.org; jszalados@aol.com

J. E. Szalados (ed.), *The Medical-Legal Aspects of Acute Care Medicine*,
https://doi.org/10.1007/978-3-030-68570-6_22

affecting clinical laboratories and their goal of protecting the public health and in 1986 released its reports entitled "Final Report on Assessment of Clinical Laboratory Regulations" [3]. Subsequently, in 1988, HCFA published proposed regulations entitled "Medicare, Medicaid and CLIA Programs; Revision of the Clinical Laboratory Regulations for the Medicare, Medicaid, and Clinical Laboratories Improvement Act of 1967 Programs." which ultimately led to Clinical Laboratory Improvement Amendments of 1988 and the legislative enactment of the "Clinical Laboratory Improvement Amendments of 1988 (CLIA-1988)" [4].

Through provisions in the Omnibus Budget Reconciliation Act of 1987 (OBRA-87), CLIA regulations were extended to include physician office laboratory (POL) testing. CLIA-1988 became a law on October 31, 1988 [5]. CLIA-1988 was passed with the intent of establishing quality standards for all laboratory-based testing, regardless of where the tests were performed, in order to ensure the accuracy, reliability, and timeliness of the test results. Prior to CLIA, federal regulation of laboratory testing applied only to testing performed in independent laboratories and hospitals; CLIA statutorily extended its regulatory reach to include all types of testing sites and based regulation on the complexity of tests, not the type of lab where the testing occurs, including POLs. Thus, the CLIA-1988 implemented regulations to address test complexity, required certification, proficiency testing, patient test management, personnel requirements, and quality assurance. Nonetheless, the phase in for CLIA-1988 continued in stages [6]. The "final" regulations implementing the CLIA were published on February 28, 1992, and have been in effect since September 1, 1992. On January 24, 2003, CMS published a further clarifying quality control requirements for laboratories and also qualification requirements for lab directors [7]. In 2020 CLIA was again updated to reflect changes to personnel requirements (training and experience in areas of responsibility), nontraditional test workflow (addressing big data and machine learning), and changes related to next-generation biomarker sequencing testing, workflows, and other best practices [8].

CLIA is established as a self-funded program financed by user fees collected from certifications and oversight functions. Three separate agencies within the Department of Health and Human Services (DHHS) are charged with the administration of the CLIA program: (a) CMS; (2) the Centers for Disease Control and Prevention (CDC); and (3) the Food and Drug Administration (FDA). Thus, CLIA is governed by a complex network of enabling statutes, legislation, and agency rules and regulations. The primary responsibility for management of the CLIA program rests with CMS which is charged with the registration of laboratories and accreditation of organizations, collections of user and other fees, laboratory, and other duties related to the enforcement of CLIA. In addition, CMS provides for inspectors and surveyors and approves proficiency testing of providers. CMS is authorized to impose a civil monetary penalty (CMP) ranging from $50 to $10,000 per day of noncompliance per violation and may also bring a civil suit to obtain a court order (restraining order) that prohibits a laboratory from continuing activities which may represent a "significant hazard to the public health" [9].

Within CMS, the Division of Clinical Laboratory Improvement and Quality, within the Quality, Safety, and Oversight Group, under the Center for Clinical

Standards and Quality (CCSQ), has responsibility for implementing the CLIA Program. Although CMS is responsible for monitoring regulatory compliance, it has delegated the conduct of compliance inspections, referred to as surveys, and the management of information required for applications, to state health departments. Clinical laboratories that were licensed in states that have enacted laws which impose requirements equal to or more stringent than those required under CLIA and where CMS has approved the licensure program qualify for exemption from CLIA. Currently, two states are exempt from CLIA certification, New York and Washington, which instead require state certificate or license [10].

The CDC manages and provides oversight for a Public Advisory Committee, the "CLIA Committee," which advises DHHS with respect to proposed regulatory changes. Prior to 2000, the CDC was also charged with responsibility for categorizing laboratory tests according to the test complexity (see below). This responsibility for the approval and complexity categorization of in vitro diagnostic (IVD) devices or tests which analyze human bodily fluids now falls to the Division of Clinical Laboratory Devices, located within the Office of Device Evaluation at the FDA's Center for Devices and Radiological Health, within the FDA.

Relevance of CLIA to Clinical Laboratory Medicine

All clinical laboratory testing in the USA is regulated by the Clinical Laboratory Improvement Amendments of 1988 (CLIA '88 or CLIA) and overseen by the Centers for Medicare and Medicaid Services (CMS). CMS has been delegated primary responsibility for CLIA oversight and enforcement; however, this CLIA oversight responsibility extends to all patients, even those patients outside the Medicare and Medicaid programs. At present, approximately 195,000 labs are certified under CLIA; these range from laboratories in physician offices performing less than 2000 tests per year to large hospital-based and independent labs performing millions of tests each year. CLIA-certified labs are identified by a ten-character alphanumeric code on the CLIA certificate, used to identify and track that lab throughout its entire history.

Laboratories that are considered "CLIA-exempt" are those labs (this designation is not applicable to a test system) which are licensed or approved by a state where CMS has determined that the state has enacted laws relating to laboratory requirements that are equal to or more stringent than CLIA requirements and the state licensure program has been approved by CMS [11].

Effective November 13, 2003, the Food and Drug Administration (FDA) has been authorized to oversee the CLIA test complexity categorization provisions. CLIA requires that clinical laboratories be certified prior to accepting specimens obtained from humans for the purposes of diagnosis, prevention, or treatment of any disease or the impairment of or to aid in the assessment of the health of humans. CLIA categorization follows a determination by the FDA once the agency has cleared or approved a marketing submission or the steps described in the FDA guidance entitled "Administrative Procedures for CLIA Categorization." Commercially available FDA-cleared or FDA-approved tests are scored by the FDA using criteria during the premarket approval process.

Tests developed by a laboratory or tests which have been modified from the approved manufacturer's instructions are considered to default to "high complexity" according to the CLIA regulations. The FDA defines a laboratory-developed test (LDT) as an in vitro diagnostic test manufactured by and used within one specific laboratory. LDTs are considered "devices" under the Federal Food, Drug, and Cosmetic Act (FFDCA) and subject to FDA regulatory oversight.

The FDA clears implantable medical devices using two main pathways: (a) premarket approval ("PMA") review and (b) 510(k). The PMA pathway is more time-consuming and more expensive and mandates clinical trials to demonstrate safety and efficacy [12]. The designation "FDA-cleared" refers to a test system which has been reviewed by the FDA and has been determined to be substantially equivalent to another test system already legally marketed for the same use; this designation may apply to waived, moderate-complexity, or high-complexity test systems. In such instances, prior to marketing a medical device, a developer must have received notification from the FDA reflecting a determination by the FDA that the device is considered substantially equivalent (SE) and thus "cleared" for commercial distribution. The 510(k) premarket notification [13] pathway is a premarket application or submission by a manufacturer to the FDA for consideration that the device be deemed as safe and effective, substantially equivalent, to a previously marketed device [14]. A device is considered substantially equivalent if, in comparison, it:

- … has the same intended use as the predicate; and
- has the same technological characteristics as the predicate; or
- has the same intended use as the predicate; and
- has different technological characteristics and does not raise different questions of safety and effectiveness; and
- the information submitted to FDA demonstrates that the device is as safe and effective as the legally marketed device.

The type of CLIA certificate a laboratory obtains depends upon the complexity of the tests it performs. CLIA regulations describe the following three levels of test complexity: waived tests, moderate-complexity tests, and high-complexity tests [15].

Waived tests are those relatively straightforward tests that are associated with a relatively small risk of error and are generally exempt from CLIA; however, waived tests must be performed in strict compliance with manufacturers' instructions. Waived tests are waived by regulation [16] or cleared or approved for home use. Such tests may be granted a certificate of waiver (COW) if they are deemed to use methodologies that are sufficiently simple and accurate as to render the likelihood of erroneous results negligible or if there is a determination that an incorrect use of the test poses no real risk of harm to the patient [17]. Training and experience required for the use of waived tests are considered to be reasonably obtained through on-the-job instruction. For example, waived tests include, but are not limited to, (1) non-automated dipstick or tablet reagent urinalysis for bilirubin, glucose, hemoglobin, ketone, leukocytes, nitrite, pH, protein, specific gravity, and urobilinogen (CPT 81002); (2) urine pregnancy tests by visual color (CPT 81025); (3) fecal occult blood (CPT 82270, 82272); and (4) blood glucose by glucose monitoring devices cleared by the FDA for home use (CPT 82962).

In addition, a number of portable point-of-care (POC) testing systems are considered waived under CLIA. "Point-of-care testing" describes the location where testing is performed, such as at the bedside or site of patient care; such POC is performed outside the laboratory setting. POC systems which have been granted at least some degree of CLIA waiver include those manufactured by, e.g., i-STAT Corporation; Abaxis, Inc.; ACON Laboratories, Inc.; Infopia Co., Ltd.; and HemoCue, Inc. [18]. Such testing is not necessarily limited to urinalysis and basic chemistry panels. For example, Axis-Shield Afinion AS100 Analyzer and Bayer A1CNow+ are used to detect the concentration of hemoglobin A1c in the blood to screen for and manage diabetes. Other tests include Rapid Pathogen Screening, Inc.'s InflammaDry which detects levels of the MMP-9 protein in human tear to aid in the diagnosis of dry eye; Aventir Biotech LLC's ForSure which provides rapid qualitative TSH assay for hypothyroidism screening; Alere's NMP22 BladderChek Test which is an immunoassay for the qualitative detection of urinary nuclear matrix protein NMP22 for the monitoring of bladder cancer patients; and BioFire Diagnostics' FilmArray 2.0 EZ Configuration Instrument which provides a multiplexed nucleic acid test for detection and identification of multiple respiratory pathogen nucleic acids in nasopharyngeal swabs. Thus, waived POC tests encompass a variety of tests which may actually allow detection of complex molecules and proteins [18].

CLIA regulations provide that the categorization of non-waived clinical laboratory test systems be based upon seven specific criteria:

1 – Knowledge

- Score 1. (A) Minimal scientific and technical knowledge is required to perform the test; and (B) Knowledge required to perform the test may be obtained through on-the-job instruction.
- Score 3. Specialized scientific and technical knowledge is essential to perform preanalytic, analytic or postanalytic phases of the testing.

2 - Training and experience

- Score 1. (A) Minimal training is required for preanalytic, analytic and postanalytic phases of the testing process; and (B) Limited experience is required to perform the test.
- Score 3. (A) Specialized training is essential to perform the preanalytic, analytic or postanalytic testing process; or Substantial experience may be necessary for analytic test performance.

3 - Reagents and materials preparation

- Score 1. (A) Reagents and materials are generally stable and reliable; and (B) Reagents and materials are prepackaged, or premeasured, or require no special handling, precautions or storage conditions.
- Score 3. (A) Reagents and materials may be labile and may require special handling to assure reliability; or (B) Reagents and materials preparation may include manual steps such as gravimetric or volumetric measurements.

4 - Characteristics of operational steps

- Score 1. Operational steps are either automatically executed (such as pipetting, temperature monitoring, or timing of steps), or are easily controlled.
- Score 3. Operational steps in the testing process require close monitoring or control, and may require special specimen preparation, precise temperature control or timing of procedural steps, accurate pipetting, or extensive calculations.

5 - Calibration, quality control, and proficiency testing materials

- Score 1. (A) Calibration materials are stable and readily available; (B) Quality control materials are stable and readily available; and (C) External proficiency testing materials, when available, are stable.
- Score 3. (A) Calibration materials, if available, may be labile; (B) Quality control materials may be labile, or not available; or (C) External proficiency testing materials, if available, may be labile.

6 - Test system troubleshooting and equipment maintenance

- Score 1. (A) Test system troubleshooting is automatic or self-correcting, or clearly described or requires minimal judgment; and (B) Equipment maintenance is provided by the manufacturer, is seldom needed, or can easily be performed.
- Score 3. (A) Troubleshooting is not automatic and requires decision-making and direct intervention to resolve most problems; or (B) Maintenance requires special knowledge, skills, and abilities.

7 - Interpretation and judgment

- Score 1. (A) Minimal interpretation and judgment are required to perform preanalytic, analytic and postanalytic processes; and (B) Resolution of problems requires limited independent interpretation and judgment.
- Score 3. (A) Extensive independent interpretation and judgment are required to perform the preanalytic, analytic or postanalytic processes; and (B) Resolution of problems requires extensive interpretation and judgment.

Source: US Food and drug administration (FDA). CLIA Categorizations. Categorization Criteria. Available online at: https://www.fda.gov/medical-devices/ivd-regulatory-assistance/clia-categorizations

Scores within each category are weighted from 1 through 3. A score of 1 indicates the lowest level of complexity, and a score of 3 indicates the highest level of complexity. The numerical sum of scores for the seven categories determines the classification of the test. A score of 12 or less is categorized as "moderate complexity," and a score greater than 12 is categorized as "high complexity." Moderate complexity test includes the subcategory of provider-performed microscopy (PPM). PPM tests must be personally performed by specified types of healthcare providers such as physicians, advanced-practice providers under the supervision of a physician, or dentists.

Laboratory testing that is classified as either "moderate" or "high" complexity is subject to regulations that set minimum qualifications for persons performing or supervising such testing and also corresponding responsibilities for each position in the lab. Such laboratories fall under the highly stringent requirements of CLIA for approved proficiency testing programs, external comparative evaluations of the accuracy of the laboratory's test results against known standards, systems and processes for monitoring testing equipment, procedures to ensure proper test performance and accurate results, and an ongoing quality monitoring program.

Laboratory complexity thus mandates personnel requirements. A moderately complex laboratory requires staffing which includes (a) a laboratory director, as licensed physician, who is responsible for the overall administration of the laboratory [19]; (b) a technical supervisor responsible for the technical and scientific oversight of the laboratory [20]; (c) a clinical consultant to serve as liaison between the laboratory and its clients in matters related to reporting and interpreting results [21]; and (d) a testing personnel who process specimens and report results. Moreover, highly complex laboratories require, in addition, fifth level of personnel structure, one or more general supervisor(s) [22] who under the direction of the laboratory director and supervision of the technical supervisor provide day-to-day supervision of testing personnel and reporting of test results. The general supervisor must be licensed by the state in which the laboratory is located, if such licensing is required, and must be qualified as either a laboratory director under § 493.1443 or a technical supervisor under § 493.1449.

A clinical laboratory that submits an application for a certificate of compliance (COC) or a certificate of accreditation (COA) for the purpose of performing moderate- or high-complexity testing is initially issued a certificate of registration (COR) and is valid for no more than 2 years or until a full compliance inspection can be performed. Once a laboratory meets all CLIA requirements, a COC or a COA is issued by an appropriate certifying entity. A laboratory may be accredited by one of six CMS-approved accrediting organizations, including:

1. American Association of Blood Banks (AABB)
2. American Osteopathic Association (AOA)
3. American Society for Histocompatibility and Immunogenetics (ASHI)
4. College of American Pathologists (CAP)
5. Commission on Office Laboratory Accreditation (COLA)
6. The Joint Commission (JC)

Clinical laboratories may select the accrediting organization of their choice. Although the accrediting organizations may differ with respect to the format of their respective inspection, the accreditation standards must comply with CLIA regulations.

CLIA, HIPAA, and HITECH

The HIPAA Privacy Rule (see Chap. 13) grants access by patients, patient's designees, and patient's personal representatives to the patient's protected health information (PHI), including an electronic copy. Limited exception under the Privacy Rule included a restriction to an individual's right to access his or her PHI when it was held by a CLIA-certified or a CLIA-exempt laboratory.

In 2014, a HIPAA/CLIA "Final Rule" effective April 7, 2014, was issued jointly by three agencies within HHS: (1) the Centers for Medicare and Medicaid Services

(CMS), which is generally responsible for laboratory regulation under CLIA; (2) the Centers for Disease Control and Prevention (CDC), which provides scientific and technical advice to CMS related to CLIA; and (3) the Office for Civil Rights (OCR), which is responsible for enforcing the HIPAA Privacy Rule [23]. The HIPAA/CLIA "Final Rule" amended "the Clinical Laboratory Improvement Amendments of 1988 (CLIA) regulations to specify that, upon the request of a patient (or the patient's personal representative), laboratories subject to CLIA may provide the patient, the patient's personal representative, or a person designated by the patient, as applicable, with copies of completed test reports that, using the laboratory's authentication process, can be identified as belonging to that patient. Subject to conforming amendments, the final rule retains the existing provisions that require release of test reports only to authorized persons and, if applicable, to the persons responsible for using the test reports and to the laboratory that initially requested the test" [24]. Under the Final Rule, HIPAA-covered laboratories, including HIPAA-covered reference laboratories, must have been in compliance with the rule effective October 6, 2014. The intent of the Final Rule was to facilitate the access by individuals to health information, potentially empowering them to better manage their health and healthcare.

Under the Final Rule, patients or their authorized personal representatives must be granted access to their requested laboratory results, mostly within 30 days, of the formal request. The right of individuals to access final test reports and other clinical laboratory data within a designated record was extended to cover data sets created prior to the effective date of the Final Rule, wherever that information was archived or stored. In addition, under the Final Rule, individuals (or their personal representatives) are accorded the right to access test reports directly from laboratories which are subject to HIPAA and, if applicable, to direct that copies of such test reports be transmitted to persons or entities as designated by the individual; the format of the information access may include direct access, paper copies, email, or mail. Importantly, where a HIPAA-covered entity reasonably believes that a non-CLIA laboratory test result may have clinical significance, the result is considered to be a part of a designated record set and therefore must be released upon the individual's request. The Final Rule also specifically preempted any conflicting state laws.

Although, under the Final Rule, HIPAA-covered laboratories may not delay providing test reports to an individual in order to first provide the results to a physician, the American College of Physicians issued a recommendation suggesting that directly accessed laboratory reports include a standard statement that provides general guidance on understanding lab results to limit misinterpretation—"both unwarranted concerns and inappropriate reassurances"—and encourages patients to review the results with the ordering physician or healthcare professional [25].

Potential Legal Liability Under CLIA and CLIA/HIPAA

Legal and Ethical Issues in the Disclosure of Individual Research Results

The Secretary of HHS is responsible for regulatory oversight of the system for the protection of human subjects in biomedical and behavioral research supported or conducted by the (HHS). The HHS Secretary's Advisory Committee on Human Research Protections (SACHRP) is tasked with providing expert advice and recommendations on issues and topics pertaining to or associated with the protection of human research subjects [26]. The Common Rule represents federal policy, from numerous agencies, which addresses the protection of human participants in any research conducted, funded, supported, or otherwise subject to regulation by the federal government [27]. The Common Rule neither explicitly encourages nor explicitly prohibits the return of results to study participants.

The legal and regulatory landscape regarding the disclosure of individual research results generated from human biological specimens is governed by numerous federal and state statutes and regulations [28]. At the present time, under US federal law, there is recognized right to access research results generated from the analysis of one's blood, fluid, or tissue specimens collected during the course of research. Although Colorado [29] and Alaska [30] have enacted statutes which confer some property rights to individuals as to specimens collected from them during the conduct of research, the majority of states have no such laws. Arguably, although silent on this issue, the Final Rule does present an arguable position through which research participants might access their individual research results.

In the recent past, there has been a significant regulatory shift to allow individuals greater access to their medical information, including laboratory results. Recall that the CLIA/HIPAA Final Rule eliminated the exception under HIPAA which had prohibited an individual's right to access his or her protected health information when held by a *CLIA-certified or CLIA-exempt laboratory*. Thus, on one side, the Final Rule imposed, on CLIA-certified or CLIA-exempt laboratories that process research results, in HIPAA-covered entities, a legal responsibility to provide the results to research subjects upon request. However, on the other hand, CLIA prohibits the release of research-related laboratory results generated in non-CLIA certified laboratories for a treatment purpose. That prohibition is based in the CLIA statute and is grounded in the long-standing concerns regarding the validity, reliability, and accuracy of results generated in non-CLIA-certified laboratories, in an effort to protect the public. Research testing usually does not always equate with more stringent clinical laboratory testing. Therefore, non-CLIA-certified laboratories which participate in the testing of human samples for research purposes may encounter ethical dilemmas where the testing reveals clinically relevant information which may be either urgent and/or not otherwise likely to be discovered. Under a strict interpretation of CLIA, such as under current CMS regulations, investigators would be prohibited from disclosing the results stemming from research unless they first became CLIA certified [31]. Another issue surrounds the "completeness" of test result; CLIA provides that, patients and their personal representatives can now access their "completed test reports" and although the term "completed test report" was not defined, in the preamble to the access rule, it is stated that "completeness" implies that "all results associated with an ordered test are finalized and ready for release" [32]. Whether completed test results from non-CLIA-certified labs fall under the rubric of test results that can be otherwise be accessed remains unclear.

Thus, at present, in the absence of federal guidance regarding either a duty to disclose, or a protection for non-disclosure, of the results of personal health information generated through biomedical research, there is no legal guidance on which investigators can reasonably rely. On the one hand, research participants may benefit from clinically actionable information they might not otherwise obtain [33]. Others argue that a right to one's laboratory data obtained through research is a bodily right and that a basic respect for persons is a basic ethical principle obligation from which obligations arise [34].

On the other hand, in addition to the legal and regulatory restraints under CLIA, the risks inherent in the disclosure of research data are many [35]. The greatest risk may potentially lie in the disclosure of erroneous or incorrect information leading to unnecessary anguish and costs; however, the ethical ramifications of not making critical, and potentially actionable, health information available to a research participant are a competing and plausible counterargument. Medical ethics is based in the patient-provider relationship which also gives rise to legal duties. Arguably, since biomedical research does not in itself imply a therapeutic relationship, one can post that there is no legal duty regarding diagnosis or treatment [36]. From a public policy point of view, research is not clinical medicine, and therefore research is intended to provide generalizable knowledge rather than an individual therapeutic benefit. In addition, if a researcher releases clinically relevant results to a research participant, that action may be construed as either the practice of medicine and/or as the basis for a therapeutic relationship, both in themselves giving rise to new legal duties not previously inherent in the research relationship. Biomedical research data is usually provisional by nature and could therefore be potentially harmful [37]. Similarly, and arguably, there is unlikely to be a fiduciary duty of the researcher to the research subject, unless the researcher is also in the role of the patient's treating provider. The further question of whether a "duty to warn" is implied within the biomedical research setting remains unclear, especially where the timely release of laboratory results may be actionable to the patient's health benefit.

Ethical and CLIA Issues Involved in Genetic Testing

The public health potential in genetic testing has led to increases in genetic research and innovation in laboratory-based genetic testing. Research participants are potentially at risk if the results generated through research suggest that the individual may have, or be at risk for, a yet undiagnosed genetically based condition. The Genetic Information Nondiscrimination Act of 2008 (GINA) prohibits discrimination in the context of health insurance and employment based on genetic information, which is defined as information about an individual's genetic tests, about the genetic tests of family members, or about the presence of a disease or disorder in family members [38]. However, GINA provides protection against misuse of genetic information only through the point in time when an individual manifests disease [39]. A disease may become manifest when either: (1) the patient experiences symptoms, (2) patient takes action based on the symptoms, or (3) when a physician makes a diagnosis and initiates a plan of action [40]. GINA was largely premised on the genetic science of the last century; therefore, it is dated both in scope and medical science.

Medical science has now elucidated substantial genetic links between genotype and disease states. At present, genetic tests are available for many thousands of diseases. Although the FDA has administrative oversight over laboratory tests and test kits, the FDA has not regulated test development but rather regulates only under CLIA. Thus, at least four issues become evident: (1) protection of research participants, especially during test development; (2) the validity of data generated by such tests, at all phases of development and marketing; (3) the confidentiality of the genetic information; and (4) the ultimate validity and confidentiality of genetic tests and services marketed directly to consumers. For example, if insurers and employers learn that an individual who has enrolled in a research study that uses positive test results from amyloid PET imaging or CSF measures of β-amyloid 42 as inclusion criteria has biomarkers indicative of AD pathology, that research participant may be at risk for discrimination. A certificate of confidentiality provides only nominal protection since such certificates only prohibit researchers from forced disclosure of identifiable sensitive information (such as mental health of substance abuse) gathered during research [41].

Federal regulations mandate laboratory standards related to personnel qualifications, quality control procedures, and proficiency testing programs to receive and maintain CLIA certification. CLIA does itself not require evaluation of the clinical validity or clinical utility of any particular test, and, in addition, there are no specific additional standards for laboratories performing genetic tests. Home tests generally fall under a CLIA waiver. The FDA regulates diagnostic test kits; specifically, during premarket review, the FDA will review the accuracy, clinical sensitivity, and specificity of a specific diagnostic kit. However, not all genetic tests are packaged as test kits, some tests are performed through laboratory-developed tests (LDT), which unlike the test kits, are generally not regulated by the FDA. LDTs are especially important during research regarding test development and validation. The FDA defines a laboratory-developed test (LDT) as an in vitro diagnostic test that is manufactured by and used within a single laboratory and considers these LDTs to be "medical devices"; therefore, LDTs will fall under FDA regulatory oversight, and such tests will be held to higher standards with respect to validity. The results of an LDT that has not been approved or cleared by the FDA are also prohibited from release to the public under CLIA.

Tort Law and Legal Liability in Clinical Laboratory Medicine

Clinical laboratories may become subject to medical liability actions either directly or indirectly. Errors in laboratory testing process may occur during either the preanalytic, analytic, and postanalytic phases or combinations thereof. Data suggests that errors occur more frequently due to preanalytical factors (46–68.2% of total errors), although a high error rate (18.5–47% of total errors) has also been found in the postanalytical phase. For example, with respect to the preanalytic phase, the failure to order the correct laboratory and other diagnostic tests account for the majority of missed and delayed diagnosis in the ambulatory setting and 58% of such errors in the emergency department [42] setting. On the other hand, others have found that systems process dysfunctions are significant causes of non-analytic errors including errors in ordering tests (12.9%), test implementation (17.9%), results reporting to clinicians (24.6%), clinicians responses (6.6%), patient notification of results (6.8%), and communication (5.7%); charting or filing errors accounted for 14.5% of errors [43].

Although errors due specifically to analytical factors have significantly decreased in incidence, with time, some processes such as immunoassays are still subject to errors and risk [44]. Nonetheless, it is primarily the analytical phase of clinical laboratory testing which falls under the direct control of the laboratory; whereas the pre- and postanalytical phases are more likely to be the responsibility of others such as clinicians, nurses, and others involved in specimen acquisition, patient identification, labeling, data entry, specimen collection, and transport.

Since it is estimated that over 70% of medical decisions are made on the basis of laboratory data, erroneous laboratory compromise diagnosis and treatment decisions and impact safe and effective patient care. Where laboratory results are delayed or erroneous providers, labs, and institutions may become jointly liable in actions alleging delay in diagnosis, failure to diagnose or erroneous diagnosis are common reasons for a medicolegal action [45]. The 2008 publication of Technical Specification (ISO/TS 22367) by the International Organization for Standardization recognized that laboratory errors cause a "failure of planned action to be completed as intended, or use of a wrong plan to achieve an aim, occurring at any part of the laboratory cycle, from ordering examinations to reporting results and appropriately interpreting and reacting to them" [46].

A significant area of clinical laboratory liability is that regarding the timely communication of critical laboratory results. Critical lab values (or "panic lab" values) may be defined as laboratory test results which are significantly outside the normal reference range and which therefore potentially indicate an immediate life-threatening state [47]. In general, since abnormal lab values fall on a range or continuum of deviation from accepted normal, the term "critical laboratory value limits" refers to the analysis-specific value limits which define a test result as a critically abnormal [48]. Another distinct form of critical lab is the STAT lab analysis that is sent with predetermined level of critical urgency; the STAT lab must be processed and reported immediately whether or not the values in themselves fall into the "critical lab value" range. The difference between a critical value and a STAT lab lies in the distinction that STAT labs are sent with a known urgency and the results are communicated urgently whether or not they are abnormal; whereas a critical lab value may arise from an unrecognized, or even routine, scenario. Finally, a "significant risk result" is defined by the JC as "a test result that is not life-threatening but requires timely medical attention and follow-up action within a medically justified timescale" [49].

CLIA 1988 first noted that "laboratories must develop and follow written procedures for reporting life-threatening laboratory results or panic values" [50]. The Joint Commission (JC), one of the entities responsible for laboratory accreditation in the USA, identified effective reporting of laboratory critical values as a National Patient Safety Goal (NSPG.02.03.01) [51]. Given its importance to patient safety, the recognition and reporting of critical labs is universally standardized and protocol-driven, although this responsibility usually falls on the laboratory technician who reports the values to a nurse, who then reports the values to a provider [52]. Given the complexity of the process, it is error-prone and, therefore, may implicate all elements of hospital- or office-based care.

References

1. Mahkorn S. Cutting red tape on clinical labs: why congress should deregulate doctors. The Heritage Foundation (Backgrounder #1056, 1995).
2. Clinical Laboratory Improvement Act of 1967 (81 Stat. 536, Public Law 90-174, Sec. 5).
3. Kenney ML. Quality assurance in changing times: proposals for reform and research in the clinical laboratory field. Clin Chem. 1987;33(2):328–36.
4. Clinical Laboratory Improvement Amendments of 1988. Public Law 100-578. United States Statutes at Large, Volume 102. 1988.
5. Clinical Laboratory Improvement Amendments of 1988 (CLIA) (42 U.S.C. 263a); (PL 100-578).
6. December 6, 1994 published in the Federal Register (59 FR 62606), May 12, 1997 published in the Federal Register (62 FR 25855), October 14, 1998 published in the Federal Register (63 FR 55031), and December 29, 2000 published in the Federal Register (65 FR 82941).
7. Centers for Disease Control and Prevention (CDC) (2) Centers for Medicare & Medicaid Services (CMS), HHS. Medicare, Medicaid, and CLIA programs; laboratory requirements relating to quality systems and certain personnel qualifications; final rule. Fed Regist. 2003;68(16):3639–714.

8. Clinical Laboratory Improvement Advisory Committee (01 October 2019). “Clinical Laboratory Improvement Advisory Committee (CLIAC) Recommendations Table” (PDF). Centers for Disease Control and Prevention. Retrieved 15 April 2020.
9. 42 U.S.C. § 263a(h)–(j); 42 C.F.R. § 493.1806(c)(3)–(d), 493.1834(a)–(d), 493.1846.
10. CMS. List of exempt states under the Clinical Laboratory Improvement Amendments (CLIA). 2017. Available online at: www.cms.gov/Regulations-and-Guidance/Legislation/CLIA/Downloads/ExemptStatesList.pdf.
11. 42 CFR 493.2.
12. 21 U.S.C. § 360e (2012).
13. 21 U.S.C. § 360c(2)(C)(ii)(II); § 360c(c)(2)(C).
14. FD&C Act 513(i)(1)(A).
15. 42 CFR 493.5(a).
16. 42 CFR 493.15(c).
17. CMS. CLIA. How to obtain a CLIA certificate of waiver. Available online at: https://www.cms.gov/Regulations-and-Guidance/legislation/CLIA/downloads/howobtaincertificateofwaiver.pdf.
18. Readers should carefully review the manufacturer as well as the specific assays (and CPT codes) granted waiver status. *See* CMS. TESTS GRANTED WAIVED STATUS UNDER CLIA. Available online at: https://www.cms.gov/Regulations-and-Guidance/Legislation/CLIA/Downloads/waivetbl.pdf.
19. 42 CFR § 493.1443 - Standard; Laboratory director qualifications.
20. 42 CFR § 493.1449 - Standard; Technical supervisor qualifications.
21. 42 CFR § 493.1419 - Standard; Clinical consultant responsibilities.
22. 42 CFR § 493.1461. Standard: General supervisor qualifications.
23. The final rule to the CLIA Program and HIPAA Privacy Rule amended 42 C.F.R. § 493; 45 C.F.R. § 164. See also, CLIA program and HIPAA Privacy Rule: Patients’ access to test reports. Fed Regist. 2014;79(25):7290–316. Federal Register.
24. CMS. CLIA program and HIPAA privacy rule; Patients’ access to test reports. 79 FR 7289. 6 Feb 2014. *Available online at*: https://www.federalregister.gov/documents/2014/02/06/2014-02280/clia-program-and-hipaa-privacy-rule-patients-access-to-test-reports.
25. American College of Physicians. Regulatory compliance. Summary of “CLIA Programs and HIPAA Privacy Rule; Patients’ access to test reports (CMS-2319-F)” Final Rule. *Available online at*: https://www.acponline.org/practice-resources/regulatory-resources/regulatory-compliance/summary-of-clia-programs-and-hipaa-privacy-rule-patients-access-to-test-reports-cms-2319-f-final.
26. The Secretary’s Advisory Committee on Human Research Protections (SACHRP) is authorized under 42 U.S.C. 217a, Section 222 of the Public Health Service (PHS) Act, as amended. The Committee is governed by the provisions of the Federal Advisory Committee Act (FACA), Public Law 92-463, as amended (5 U.S.C. App.), which sets forth standards for the formation and use of advisory committees.
27. 45 C.F.R. 46.
28. Barnes M, Stayin S, Forster D, Russell-Einhorn M, Peloquin D, Medina-Jordan A. The CLIA/HIPAA conundrum of returning test results to research participants. Med Res Law Policy Rep. 2015;14:491.
29. Colo. Rev. Stat. Ann. § 10-3-1104.7(1)(a).
30. Alaska Stat. § 18.13.010(a)(2).
31. National Academies of Sciences, Engineering, and Medicine; Health and Medicine Division; Board on Health Sciences Policy; Committee on the Return of Individual-Specific Research Results Generated in Research Laboratories; Downey AS, Busta ER, Mancher M, et al., editors. Returning individual research results to participants: guidance for a new research paradigm. Washington, DC: National Academies Press (US); 2018 Jul 10. 6, Reshaping the Legal and Regulatory Landscape to Support Return of Individual Research Results. Available from: https://www.ncbi.nlm.nih.gov/books/NBK525078/.

32. Federal Register, 2014, p. 7295.
33. Ravitsky V, Wilfond BS. Disclosing individual genetic results to research participants. Am J Bioeth. 2006;6(6):8–17. https://doi.org/10.1080/15265160600934772.
34. Shalowitz DI, Miller FG. Disclosing individual results of clinical research: implications of respect for participants. JAMA. 2005;294(6):737–40. https://doi.org/10.1001/jama.294.6.737.
35. Burke W, Evans BJ, Jarvik GP. Return of results: ethical and legal distinctions between research and clinical care. Am J Med Genet C Semin Med Genet. 2014;166C(1):105–11. https://doi.org/10.1002/ajmg.c.31393.
36. Clayton EW, McGuire AL. The legal risks of returning results of genomics research. Genet Med. 2012;14(4):473–7. https://doi.org/10.1038/gim.2012.10.
37. Miller FA, Christensen R, Giacomini M, Robert JS. Duty to disclose what? Querying the putative obligation to return research results to participants. J Med Ethics. 2008;34(3):210–3. https://doi.org/10.1136/jme.2006.020289.
38. Genetic Information Nondiscrimination Act of 2008, Public Law 110-233, 110th Cong. (May 21, 2008).
39. 29 U.S.C.A. § 1182(a)(3)(B) (2008); 42 U.S.C.A. § 2000ff-9 (2008).
40. Prince AE, Berkman BE. When does an illness begin: genetic discrimination and disease manifestation. J Law Med Ethics. 2012;40(3):655–64. https://doi.org/10.1111/j.1748-720X.2012.00696.x.
41. NIH. Notice of changes to NIH policy for issuing certificates of confidentiality. Notice Number: NOT-OD-17-109. September 7, 2017. Available online at: https://grants.nih.gov/grants/guide/notice-files/NOT-OD-17-109.html.
42. Kachalia A, Gandhi TK, Puopolo AL, et al. Missed and delayed diagnoses in the emergency department: a study of closed malpractice claims from 4 liability insurers. Ann Emerg Med. 2007;49(2):196–205. https://doi.org/10.1016/j.annemergmed.2006.06.035.
43. Hickner J, Graham DG, Elder NC, et al. Testing process errors and their harms and consequences reported from family medicine practices: a study of the American Academy of Family Physicians National Research Network. Qual Saf Health Care. 2008;17(3):194–200.
44. Plebani M. Errors in clinical laboratories or errors in laboratory medicine? Clin Chem Lab Med. 2006;44(6):750–9. https://doi.org/10.1515/CCLM.2006.123.
45. Dighe AS, Makar RS, Lewandrowski KB. Medicolegal liability in laboratory medicine. Semin Diagn Pathol. 2007;24(2):98–107. https://doi.org/10.1053/j.semdp.2007.03.008.
46. ISO/TS 22367:2008. Medical laboratories - reduction of error through risk management and continual improvement. Geneva: International Organization for Standardization; 2008.
47. Lundberg G. Critical (panic) value notification: an established laboratory practice policy (parameter). JAMA. 1990;263:709.
48. Lippi G, Mattiuzzi C. Critical laboratory values communication: summary recommendations from available guidelines. Ann Transl Med. 2016;4(20):400. https://doi.org/10.21037/atm.2016.09.36.
49. Joint Commission. 2016 National Patient Safety Goals 2016. Available online: https://www.jointcommission.org/hap_2016_npsgs/.
50. Centers for Medicare and Medicaid Services. Medicare, Medicaid and CLIA programs: regulations implementing the Clinical Laboratory Improvement Amendments of 1988 (CLIA) - HFCA final rule with comment period. Fed Regist. 1992;57:7002–186.
51. Joint Commission on Accreditation of Healthcare Organizations. 2010 National Patient Safety Goals. Available at: www.jointcommission.org/NR/rdonlyres/6447E5C3-E9EF-4431-885A-7FCF624DD73A/0/July2010NPSGs_Scoring_LAB.pdf.
52. Goldenstein R, Prosser D, Travis L. Analysis of critical laboratory value nurse-to-physician follow-up calls at a community hospital. J Nurs Care Qual. 2013;28(4):335–9. https://doi.org/10.1097/NCQ.0b013e31829229ff.

Chapter 23
Social Work, Care Managers, and Physician Advisors: Liability Related to Discharge Planning and Continuity of Care

James E. Szalados

Ethical Issues in Social Work

Social workers are licensed professionals who provide advice and guidance to vulnerable persons who are frequently at difficult points in their lives and who require counseling for complex decision-making. Hospitals are the most common setting for the employment of healthcare social workers. In the area of healthcare, social work has a focus on patient autonomy with respect to choices intended to further personal as well as societal well-being. Social work is concerned with the complexity of the human experience. Social workers are our interval members of the healthcare team and focus on preservation of personal autonomy, family relationships, community support, and support structures for patients who may have difficulty making appropriate choices for themselves.

Healthcare social workers work with patients and their families in the context of a particular illness and provide emotional support and counseling regarding choices and decisions. Social workers practicing within the hospital setting are also referred to as a "clinical social workers" or "medical social workers." Thus, within hospitals and healthcare systems, social workers are frequently closely on with members of the acute care team. Social workers typically make early contact with patients and families, seek to align goals of care with available resources, and explore post-discharge family and support structures. Typically, social workers help coordinate post-discharge planning and help identify optimal post-discharge rehabilitation or, in addition, social workers are actively involved in end-of-life care and palliative

J. E. Szalados (✉)
Director, Surgical and Neurocritical Care Units, Rochester Regional Health System at Rochester General Hospital, Rochester, NY, USA

The Szalados Law Firm, Hilton, NY, USA
e-mail: james.szalados@rochesterregional.org; jszalados@aol.com

J. E. Szalados (ed.), *The Medical-Legal Aspects of Acute Care Medicine*,
https://doi.org/10.1007/978-3-030-68570-6_23

care and are therefore closely involved with clinical healthcare decision-making. Patient advocacy relates to the ethical principle of beneficence.

The National Association of Social Workers (NASW) established a Code of Ethics in 1996, subsequently revised in 2017 to articulate their shared ethical principles and ethical standards. The mission of the profession of social work is rooted in a set of six core values: (1) service; (2) social justice; (3) dignity and worth of the person; (4) importance of human relationships; (5) integrity; and (6) competence. The NASW Code articulate set of values, principles, and standards to guide decision-making and conduct to help address complex situations. Furthermore, the NASW Code of Ethics serves six purposes:

1. The Code identifies core values on which social work's mission is based.
2. The Code summarizes broad ethical principles that reflect the profession's core values and establishes a set of specific ethical standards that should be used to guide social work practice.
3. The Code is designed to help social workers identify relevant considerations when professional obligations conflict or ethical uncertainties arise.
4. The Code provides ethical standards to which the general public can hold the social work profession accountable.
5. The Code socializes practitioners new to the field to social work's mission, values, ethical principles, and ethical standards.
6. The Code articulates standards that the social work profession itself can use to assess whether social workers have engaged in unethical conduct. NASW has formal procedures to adjudicate ethics complaints filed against its members.* In subscribing to this Code, social workers are required to cooperate in its implementation, participate in NASW adjudication proceedings, and abide by any NASW disciplinary rulings or sanctions based on it.
   NASW Code of Ethics. 2017 [1]

Since social workers have expertise in understanding and optimizing the social situations from which patients are admitted, and will subsequently be discharged to, social workers have an important role on the integrated healthcare team. Where social workers focus on strategies to help assist with complex care coordination, post-discharge planning, and the management of post-discharge care challenges, nurses and providers can better focus on the acute process of disease management. Thus, in order to provide optimal care to patients, the team model of care should integrate the perspectives and opinions of clinical social workers.

Legal Issues in Social Work

Social workers are healthcare professionals who must practice in accordance with professional standards applicable to the professional social work; in addition, social workers are also interval members of a healthcare team. Thus, social workers are held to a standard of care and, deviation from the applicable standard of care may be actionable as professional malpractice or negligence. In general, liability exposure for social workers is highly dependent on the specific population served; for example, psychiatric patients, pediatric patients, elderly patients, and indigent patients will all have varying needs and associated risks for liability.

Social workers are subject to the same federal and state statutes which govern healthcare providers, such as HIPAA and EMTALA; however, in some cases social workers are held to even higher standards, especially in the cases of statutes governing the obligations of social workers to investigate and report cases of suspected abuse and neglect of children, elders, and other vulnerable patients and minors' right to consent to mental health counseling and to drug and alcohol abuse treatment. Thus, similar to other members of the healthcare team, social workers are at risk for errors of commission (such as the breach of confidentiality) and also omission (failure to report); in many cases, such liability arises out of conflicting ethical and legal duties.

Ethical obligations and legal obligations are frequently at odds. On the one hand, the "rule of law" demands that, if justice is to prevail, laws must be applied to every similarly situated person equally. Accordingly, Wasserstrom writes that "given what we know of the possibilities of human error and the actualities of human frailty, and given the tendency of democratic societies to make illegal only those actions which would, even in the absence of law, be unjustified, we can confidently conclude that the consequences will on the whole and in the long run be best if no one ever takes it upon himself to 'second guess' the laws and to conclude that in his case his disobedience is justified." Nonetheless, the countervailing view is that blind obedience, especially where the circumstances so dictate, for the good of another person, under the ethical principle of justice, should be approached with discretion. Under such logic, thoughtful social workers, as professionals, should exercise careful discretion and judgment and perhaps violate such laws which may constrain the ability of a professional to best care for those who entrust them with their care. Accordingly, Rawls argued that "we are not required to acquiesce in the crushing of fundamental liberties by democratic majorities which have shown themselves blind to the principles of justice upon which justification of the Constitution depends" [2]. Reamer argues that reasonable, thoughtful, and principled practitioners might reasonably disagree about the appropriate course of action and that where difficult and controversial situations pose ethical conflicts, social workers may be obligated to make decisions that, in their best judgment, is both defensible and consistent with their professional ethical standards.

In the N.Y. case of *Community Service Society v. Welfare Inspector General of New York* [3], the N.Y. Appellate Division decision unanimously upheld the right of a social service agency and its workers to maintain privileged confidential relationship with a client on the grounds of social worker-client privilege, thereby finding grounds for privileged communications between a social worker and his or her client.

In the case of *Jaffee v. Redmond*, the US Supreme Court recognized the federal psychotherapist-patient privilege as it applied to licensed clinical social workers [4]. Here, a police officer, Mary Lu Redmond, was the first responding officer to a "fight in progress" call at an apartment complex where there had been a stabbing, and as Redmond called for an ambulance, several men ran out, one brandishing a pipe and another brandishing a butcher knife, and Redman shot the man with the butcher knife. During pretrial discovery, the court learned that after the shooting Redmond had participated in approximately 50 counseling sessions with a clinical social worker licensed by the State of Illinois. Where the plaintiff sought discovery of these sessions, defendants asserted that the contents of the conversations between were protected against disclosure under the psychotherapist-patient privilege; an argument that was rejected by the district judge. The district judge, during his instructions to the jury, advised that the refusal to turn over the clinical notes had no "legal justification" and that the jury could therefore presume that the contents of the notes would have been unfavorable; the jury then found against Redman. On appeal, the Court of Appeals for the Seventh Circuit reversed and remanded for a new trial reasoning that reason and experience, " the touchstones for acceptance of a privilege under Rule 501 of the Federal Rules of Evidence, compelled recognition of a psychotherapist patient privilege." The Supreme Court held that "confidential communications between a licensed psychotherapist and her patients in the course of diagnosis or treatment are protected from compelled disclosure under Rule 501 of the Federal Rules of Evidence" in part because the court also recognized that "social workers provide a significant amount of mental health treatment" [5].

In Maine, case of *Harrison v. Granite Bay Care, Inc.*, a social worker was terminated on the grounds of allegedly "creating disharmony in the workplace" when she reported what she considered to be violations of state employment law to her supervisor and, thereafter, to Maine's Department of Health and Human Services. Although the district court granted a motion for summary judgment against the social worker, on appeal, the First Circuit vacated the judgment finding a misapplication of whistleblower statute. Here the issue is whether the filing of a mandatory report with DHHS constitutes protected activity under the Maine Whistleblower Protection Act. The final outcome of this case remains pending at present.

The Maryland case of *In re Adoption/Guardianship No. CCJ14746* addressed the issue of whether licensed clinical social workers may provide expert witness testimony concerning the diagnosis and treatment of emotional and mental disorders [6]. Here, upon hearing the facts of the case, the Court of Special Appeals affirmed the judgment of the Circuit Court for Washington County finding that the clinical social worker in that case was specifically authorized to diagnose mental disorders and, therefore, was qualified to testify as an expert. In this case, petitioner Munson invoked the language of the state social work act which itself made a critical distinction between a licensed social worker and a licensed clinical social worker, where a licensed clinical social worker was specifically authorized by the Maryland Legislature to render diagnoses based on a recognized manual of mental and emotional disorders [7].

Ethical and Legal Issues in Case and Care Management

Care management is fundamental to population health; case management is fundamental to the management of the health of a defined population. Care management is a team-based, patient-centered approach which aims to assist patients and their support systems in the management of medical conditions more effectively so as to coordinate complex care, decrease the cost of care, and improve outcomes. Hospital-based care managers are patient advocates who help drive appropriate plans of care especially when multiple disciplines are involved in the care of complex patients.

Although distinctions between "case managers" and "care managers and care coordinators" have been drawn, the positions are sufficiently similar [8] as to be discussed as an aggregate in general terms. The Case Management Society of America (CMSA) defines case management as "provided by healthcare professionals working with people to identify issues and barriers that may prevent them from getting better and uncovering mutually agreed upon solutions to achieve their healthcare goals" [9].

The Agency for Healthcare Research and Quality (AHRQ) describes care coordination as "deliberately organizing patient care activities and sharing information among all of the participants concerned with a patient's care to achieve safer and more effective care" [10].

The Commission for Case Manager Certification (CCMC) describes advocacy in case management as a process that promotes beneficence, justice, autonomy, self-determination, and independence for patients and their families or caregivers. The Commission articulates in its statement that the profession adheres to the ideals of service and advocacy for patients regardless of race, ethnicity, religion, age, gender, sexual orientation, national origin, marital status, or disability. Furthermore, the service and advocacy ideal of case managers is the education of patients about their rights, benefits, and healthcare and human services, facilitating informed decision-making, and considerations for the client's values, beliefs, interests, and culture. In its Social Justice Statement and its Code of Professional Conduct for Case Managers, the Commission commits to responsibilities to (1) place the public interest above our own at all times; (2) respect the rights and inherent dignity of others; (3) always maintain objectivity in our relationships with clients; and (4) act with integrity, dignity, and fidelity with clients and others.

Case managers work with members of the interdisciplinary healthcare team to promote the best interests of the patient and his or her family; therefore, from an ethical standpoint, case managers must weigh and balance the potential risks and benefits of possible actions, interventions, treatments, and decisions when considering care options. In addition, since case managers are also employees who are tasked with directing access and utilization in the context of insurers, patient finances, and inpatient throughput management, there are potential ethical conflicts which arise because of competing imperatives.

Case managers function at the intersection of numerous federal and state statutes and regulations which include, for example, HIPAA, CMS mandates, insurance law, and workers compensation. Important areas of potential liability for care managers include denial of service, premature or improper discharge, or premature or improper transfer. Furthermore, it is important to realize that the case managers (like social workers) have important and legislatively mandated functions as part of the health-care patient management team.

The Federal Register is the legal repository for laws that are finalized by Congressional action. Title 42 (Public Health) Chapter IV (Hospitals) addresses most of the federal statutes that govern healthcare, specifically hospitals. 42 CFR § 440.169 statutorily defines case management services:

(a) Case management services means services furnished to assist individuals, eligible under the State plan who reside in a community setting or are transitioning to a community setting, in gaining access to needed medical, social, educational, and other service

....

(d) The assistance that case managers provide in assisting eligible individuals obtain services includes -

(1) Comprehensive assessment and periodic reassessment of individual needs, to determine the need for any medical, educational, social, or other services. These assessment activities include the following:

(i) Taking client history.
(ii) Identifying the needs of the individual, and completing related documentation.
(iii) Gathering information from other sources, such as family members, medical providers, social workers, and educators (if necessary) to form a complete assessment of the eligible individual.

(2) Development (and periodic revision) of a specific care plan based on the information collected through the assessment, that includes the following:

(i) Specifies the goals and actions to address the medical, social, educational, and other services needed by the eligible individual.

(ii) Includes activities such as ensuring the active participation of the eligible individual and working with the individual (or the individual's authorized health care decision maker) and others to develop those goals.

(iii) Identifies a course of action to respond to the assessed needs of the eligible Individual.

(3) Referral and related activities (such as scheduling appointments for the individual) to help the eligible individual obtain needed services, including activities that help link the individual with medical, social, and educational providers or other programs and services that are capable of providing needed services to address identified needs and achieve goals specified in the care plan.

(4) Monitoring and follow-up activities, including activities and contacts that are necessary to ensure that the care plan is effectively implemented and adequately addresses the needs of the eligible individual and which may be with the individual, family members, service providers, or other entities or individuals and conducted as frequently as necessary, and including at least one annual monitoring, to help determine whether the following conditions are met:

(i) Services are being furnished in accordance with the individual's care plan.
(ii) Services in the care plan are adequate.
(iii) There are changes in the needs or status of the eligible individual. Monitoring and follow-up activities include making necessary adjustments in the care plan and service arrangements with providers.

(e) Case management may include contacts with non-eligible individuals that are directly related to the identification of the eligible individual's needs and care, for the purposes

of helping the eligible individual access services, identifying needs and supports to assist the eligible individual in obtaining services, providing case managers with useful feedback, and alerting case managers to changes in the eligible individual's needs.
72 FR 68091, Dec. 4, 2007, as amended at 74 FR 31196, June 30, 2009

Similarly, CMS defines the process of "discharge planning." Discharge planning is a federally mandated process to transition through the levels of care and is a vital component of a successful transition from hospitals and PAC settings. The most appropriate location to which a patient should be discharged should be based on the patient's clinical care requirements, available support network, and patient and caregiver treatment preferences and goals of care. Therefore, the role of case management in the continuity of care following an acute care hospitalization is obvious. CMS defined "discharge planning" in a final rule [11], published September 26, 2019, which also empowered patients to make informed decisions about their care as they are discharged from acute care into post-acute care (PAC). The final rule revised hospital discharge planning requirements affect long-term care hospitals (LTCHs), inpatient rehabilitation facilities, inpatient psychiatric facilities, children's hospitals, cancer hospitals, IRFs, critical access hospitals (CAHs), and home health agencies (HHAs). The intent of the rule was to promote the seamless exchange of patient information between healthcare settings and to ensure that each patient's healthcare information accompanies them after discharge from a hospital or PAC provider [12]. Compliance with the rule is a Condition of Participation (CoP) for the Medicare and Medicaid programs.

CFR Title 42, Subsection 482.43 addresses Condition of Participation as they relate to discharge planning:

The hospital must have an effective discharge planning process that focuses on the patient's goals and treatment preferences and includes the patient and his or her caregivers/support person(s) as active partners in the discharge planning for post-discharge care. The discharge planning process and the discharge plan must be consistent with the patient's goals for care and his or her treatment preferences, ensure an effective transition of the patient from hospital to post-discharge care, and reduce the factors leading to preventable hospital readmissions.

(a) Standard: Discharge planning process. The hospital's discharge planning process must identify, at an early stage of hospitalization, those patients who are likely to suffer adverse health consequences upon discharge in the absence of adequate discharge planning and must provide a discharge planning evaluation for those patients so identified as well as for other patients upon the request of the patient, patient's representative, or patient's physician. [CMS did not finalize the proposed design requirements.]
  (1) Any discharge planning evaluation must be made on a timely basis to ensure that appropriate arrangements for post-hospital care will be made before discharge and to avoid unnecessary delays in discharge.
  (2) A discharge planning evaluation must include an evaluation of a patient's likely need for appropriate post-hospital services, including, but not limited to, hospice care services, post-hospital extended care services, home health services, and non-health care services and community based care providers, and must also include a determination of the availability of the appropriate services as well as of the patient's access to those services.
  (3) The discharge planning evaluation must be included in the patient's medical record for use in establishing an appropriate discharge plan and the results of the evaluation must be discussed with the patient (or the patient's representative).

(4) Upon the request of a patient's physician, the hospital must arrange for the development and initial implementation of a discharge plan for the patient.
(5) Any discharge planning evaluation or discharge plan required under this paragraph must be developed by, or under the supervision of a registered nurse, social worker, or other appropriately qualified personnel.
(6) The hospital's discharge planning process must require regular re- evaluation of the patient's condition to identify changes that require modification of the discharge plan. The discharge plan must be updated, as needed, to reflect these changes.
(7) The hospital must assess its discharge planning process on a regular basis. The assessment must include ongoing, periodic review of a representative sample of discharge plans, including those patients who were readmitted within 30 days of a previous admission, to ensure that the plans are responsive to patient post-discharge needs.
(8) The hospital must assist patients, their families, or the patient's representative in selecting a post-acute care provider by using and sharing data that includes, but is not limited to, HHA, SNF, IRF, or LTCH data on quality measures and data on resource use measures. The hospital must ensure that the post-acute care data on quality measures and data on resource use measures is relevant and applicable to the patient's goals of care and treatment preferences.

(b) Standard: Discharge of the patient and provision and transmission of the patient's necessary medical information. The hospital must discharge the patient, and also transfer or refer the patient where applicable, along with all necessary medical information pertaining to the patient's current course of illness and treatment, post-discharge goals of care, and treatment preferences, at the time of discharge, to the appropriate post-acute care service providers and suppliers, facilities, agencies, and other outpatient service providers and practitioners responsible for the patient's follow-up or ancillary care.
(c) Standard: Requirements related to post-acute care services. For those patients discharged home and referred for HHA services, or for those patients transferred to a SNF for post-hospital extended care services, or transferred to an IRF or LTCH for specialized hospital services, the following requirements apply, in addition to those set out at paragraphs (a) and (b) of this section:

(1) The hospital must include in the discharge plan a list of HHAs, SNFs, IRFs, or LTCHs that are available to the patient, that are participating in the Medicare program, and that serve the geographic area (as defined by the HHA) in which the patient resides, or in the case of a SNF, IRF, or LTCH, in the geographic area requested by the patient. HHAs must request to be listed by the hospital as available.

(i) This list must only be presented to patients for whom home health care post-hospital extended care services, SNF, IRF, or LTCH services are indicated and appropriate as determined by the discharge planning evaluation.
(ii) For patients enrolled in managed care organizations, the hospital must make the patient aware of the need to verify with their managed care organization which practitioners, providers or certified suppliers are in the managed care organization's network. If the hospital has information on which practitioners, providers or certified supplies are in the network of the patient's managed care organization, it must share this with the patient or the patient's representative.
(iii) The hospital must document in the patient's medical record that the list was presented to the patient or to the patient's representative.

`(2) The hospital, as part of the discharge planning process, must inform the patient or the patient's representative of their freedom to choose among participating Medicare providers and suppliers of post-discharge services and must, when possible, respect the patient's or the patient's representative's goals of care and treatment preferences, as well as other preferences they express. The hospital must not specify or otherwise limit the qualified providers or suppliers that are available to the patient.

(3) The discharge plan must identify any HHA or SNF to which the patient is referred in which the hospital has a disclosable financial interest, as specified by the Secretary, and any HHA or SNF that has a disclosable financial interest in a hospital under Medicare.

CFR Title 42, Subsection 482.43

Furthermore, Sect. 484.58 was added to the CoP added to read:

(a) Standard: Discharge planning. An HHA must develop and implement an effective discharge planning process. For patients who are transferred to another HHA or who are discharged to a SNF, IRF or LTCH, the HHA must assist patients and their caregivers in selecting a post-acute care provider by using and sharing data that includes, but is not limited to HHA, SNF, IRF, or LTCH data on quality measures and data on resource use measures. The HHA must ensure that the post-acute care data on quality measures and data on resource use measures is relevant and applicable to the patient's goals of care and treatment preferences.

(b) Standard: Discharge or transfer summary content.

1. The HHA must send all necessary medical information pertaining to the patient's current course of illness and treatment, post- discharge goals of care, and treatment preferences, to the receiving facility or health care practitioner to ensure the safe and effective transition of care.
2. The HHA must comply with requests for additional clinical information as may be necessary for treatment of the patient made by the receiving facility or health care practitioner.

The Improving Medicare Post-Acute Care Transformation Act of 2014 (IMPACT Act) [13] further mandates hospitals, including short-term acute care hospitals, CAHs, and PAC providers (LTCHs, IRFs, HHAs, and SNFs), to develop and implement quality measures and resource use measures to assist patients and their families in their decision-making during the discharge planning process. IMPACT requires the standardization of PAC assessment data so as to facilitate comparison across PAC settings, to be used by hospitals as a means to facilitate coordinated care and improved Medicare beneficiary outcomes. These data sets include the Long-Term Care Hospital CARE Data Set (LCDS) for LTCHs, the Minimum Data Set (MDS) for SNFs, the Outcome and Assessment Information Set (OASIS) for HHAs, and the Inpatient Rehabilitation Facility Patient Assessment Instrument (IRF PAI) for IRFs. Meaningful measures prioritized by CMS include:

- Promote effective communication and coordination of care
- Promote effective prevention and treatment of chronic disease
- Work with communities to promote best practices of healthy living
- Make care affordable
- Make care safer by reducing harm, cost in the delivery of care
- Strengthen person and family engagement as partners in their care [14]

CMS also published a proposed rule on June 16, 2016, in the Federal Register, titled "Medicare and Medicaid Programs; Hospital and Critical Access Hospital (CAH) Changes to Promote Innovation, Flexibility, and Improvement in Patient Care" which proposed to update CoPs to mandate improved communication between providers and patients and patient access to their medical records.

Liability for case managers stems primarily from failures to communicate or document in accordance with the relevant laws, regulations, or rules. Although verbal communication is a foundation for decision-making in case management, contemporaneous documentation of the details and the outcomes of the discussions is necessary in the event that that is a post-action review. Such reviews often arise from patient or caregiver complaints and may escalate internally to quality assurance or to risk management or externally to state boards or CMS. Alternatively, if there is a demonstrable deviation from standards of care which results in a patient harm, litigation is possible. Thus, case managers must be familiar with and understand the national standards of care published by the Case Management Society of America, adhere the standards, and carefully document why services were provided or denied. In addition, since case managers are hospital employees, case managers should also be careful so as to respect the boundaries of such job description, which, at times, may result in ethical dilemmas. Nonetheless, the conduct and decisions of case managers, similar to other employees such as social workers, physician advisors, and nurses, can implicate the hospital in regulatory inquiries and/or litigation.

Ethical and Legal Issues Facing Physician Advisors

In contract to social workers and case managers, physician advisors are a new member to the multidisciplinary care management team. Although there is likely no one single definition for a physician advisor, one legal definition of a physician advisor might be, for example, "a physician licensed to practice medicine who provides medical advice or information to a private review agent or a utilization review entity in connection with its utilization review activities" [15]. The physician advisor is a clinical leader that facilitates the coordination of clinical care and cost-of-care initiatives. In general, the physician advisor functions as a liaison between the clinical medical staff and care management so as to provide advice and support regarding the medical necessity of inpatient services which may include (1) a secondary level of physician review regarding medical necessity and status determinations; (2) concurrent and retrospective payer denial appeals and management; (3) recovery audit contractor (RAC) denials and appeals; (4) clinical documentation improvement (CDI) to best reflect comorbidities and case mix index; (5) utilization management issues including length of stay, optimal resource utilization, and level of care transfers; and (6) discharge planning and readmissions management. Acute care hospitals and healthcare systems have rapidly embraced the physician advisor model because of demonstrated return on investment (ROIs) realized from such programs. Thus, an effective physician advisor program will improve hospital reimbursement and maintain the spirit of medical staff self-governance [16] required by the Joint Commission through a paradigm of clinical peer communication and coaching.

In general, the level of clinical documentation by clinicians has been suboptimal; understandably, charting has been seen as subordinate to actual hands-on patient care. Nonetheless, it is the medical record that supports not only the level but also quality of the care that was provided. Thus, the quality of medical record documentation is fundamental to supporting claims and reimbursement but also providing the foundation for a successful defense in the event of malpractice litigation. Nonetheless, for every hour a clinician spends with a patient, the clinician then spends 2 hours on EHR documentation; thus, providers already typically spend 27% of their total working time on direct face-to-face patient interactions and about 49.2% of their time on EHR documentation [17].

In order to understand the importance of clinical documentation, and therefore a key tenet of the physician advisor paradigm, it is important to understand the coding and claims submission process (see Chap. 11). The clinical documentation entered by providers into the medical record is subsequently extracted by clinical coders. The data extracted by clinical coders is then translated into claims, case mix, quality reporting data, and disease management. Importantly, a chart which does not accurately reflect all of a patient's chronic and acute comorbidities can underrepresent the severity of illness and overestimate the expected outcomes of care resulting in an adverse quality-of-care assessment. In essence, a patient who looks healthier on the record, because of poor documentation, is expected to have less complications, lower mortality risk, and less need for post-discharge support; the insufficiency of documentation in turn results in underpayment to the health system, poorer quality or outcome metrics, and potential liability exposure. Clinical documentation is also at the foundation for value-based care initiatives.

Liability for physician advisor activities has not been clearly established, although there are potential concerns. The physician advisor team typically manages the CDI process through a process termed the "physician query" which is an EMR chart-based communication questioning the provider's wording of a clinical issue. The query will typically suggest an alternate wording to better describe a clinical issue or problem; however, the query may also raise a previously undocumented problem. The intent of the query is to more accurately portray a patient's clinical situation. Moreover, clinicians' compliance with queries is monitored and enforced, typically by amendments to medical staff bylaws. The query raises at least three potential liability exposures: (1) a potential false claims issue where queries may be exploited to artificially exaggerate the severity of illness, and therefore reimbursement; (2) rephrasing a provider's clinical impressions in such a way as to change the provider's liability in the event of malpractice litigation; and (3) medical staff disciplinary proceedings which are based in query compliance and standardized documentation, rather than quality of care.

Conclusions

Traditionally, the oversight for inpatient care has been managed by the medical staff, through peer review and quality improvement processes, and by clinical support staff including social workers and case managers through the utilization review process. The increased complexity of the private payer review and the regulatory review environment now necessitates a coordinated multidisciplinary process by which utilization and financial metrics can be best aligned with the mission of acute care organizations. It is important that providers understand that the multidisciplinary structure is supportive, and not adverse, to their clinical work. In addition, it is important that clinicians respect and collaborate with their multidisciplinary partners, since, to a large extent, such partnership unloads a multitude of administrative tasks from busy clinicians while working in parallel to support important quality, satisfaction, and financial metrics. Nonetheless, social workers, case managers, and physician advisors usually all operate as hospital employees but mostly within national standards, policies, and job descriptions. Although there is, at present, no established line of case precedent in this area, regulations and potentially applicable national standards provide important guidance to minimize the risk of liability exposures.

References

1. NASW Code of Ethics. 2017. Available online at: https://www.socialworkers.org/About/Ethics/Code-of-Ethics/Code-of-Ethics-English.
2. Reamer F. Ethical and legal standards in social work: consistency and conflict. Fam Soc. 2005;86(2):163–9. https://doi.org/10.1606/1044-3894.2237.
3. Community Service Society v. Welfare Inspector General of New York (New York Supreme Court, Appellate Division, 411 N.Y.S.2d 188 (N.Y. 1978))411 N.Y.S.2d 188 (N.Y. 1978)).
4. Jaffee v. Redmond (United States Supreme Court, 518 U.S. 1 (1996))518 U.S. 1 (1996)).
5. *Citing* U. S. Dept. of Health and Human Services, Center for Mental Health Services, Mental Health, United States, 1994 pp. 85–87, 107–114.
6. In re Adoption/Guardianship No. CCJ14746 (Maryland Court of Appeals, 759 A.2d 755 (2000))759 A.2d 755 (2000)).
7. Maryland Code (1981, 1994 Repl. Vol., 1999 Supp.) § 19-302(d)(2) of the Health Occupations Article.
8. Care Excellence. Case managers play a critical role in healthcare. Available online at: https://careexcellence.org/blog/case-manager-roles/.
9. Case Management Society of America. Available online at: http://solutions.cmsa.org/acton/fs/blocks/showLandingPage/a/10442/p/p-0003/t/page/fm/0.
10. The Agency for Healthcare Research and Quality. Available online at: https://www.ahrq.gov/ncepcr/care/coordination.html.
11. 84 FR 51836. Pp. 51836-51884. 42 CFR 482. 2019.
12. CMS. CMS' Discharge planning rule supports interoperability and patient preferences. 26 Sept 2019. Available online at: https://www.cms.gov/newsroom/fact-sheets/cms-discharge-planning-rule-supports-interoperability-and-patient-preferences.
13. Improving Medicare Post-Acute Care Transformation Act of 2014. Pub. L. 113–185.
14. CMS. IMPACT Act of 2014 Data Standardization & Cross Setting Measures. Available online at: https://www.cms.gov/Medicare/Quality-Initiatives-Patient-Assessment-Instruments/Post-Acute-Care-Quality-Initiatives/IMPACT-Act-of-2014/IMPACT-Act-of-2014-Data-Standardization-and-Cross-Setting-Measures.
15. Law Insider. Definition of Physician advisor. Available online at: https://www.lawinsider.com/dictionary/physician-advisor#:~:text=Definition%20of%20Physician%20advisor.%20Physician%20advisor%20means%20a,entity%20in%20connection%20with%20its%20utilization%20review%20activities.

16. Hurst K. Professional self-regulation in the context of Clinical Governance. Int J Health Care Qual Assur. 2003;16:199–212.
17. Sinsky C, Colligan L, Li L, et al. Allocation of physician time in ambulatory practice: a time and motion study in 4 specialties. Ann Intern Med. 2016;165(11):753–60.

Chapter 24
Employment and Human Resources Law: An Overview

James E. Szalados

The Definitions of Employee and Independent Contractor

Two workers, performing the same work, for the same wage, may be legally classified as either "employee" or "independent contractor." According to the IRS, under common-law rules, anyone who performs services for [an employer] is [an] employee if [the employer] can control what will be done and how it will be done [1]. On the other hand, *Black's Law Dictionary* defines an employee to be "a person in the service of another under any contract of hire, express or implied, oral or written, where the employer has the power or right to control and direct the employee in the material details of how the work is to be performed" [2]. Although the question of whether one who works for another is actually an "employee" would seem simple, but it is not. In fact, the legal definition of "employee" is more concerned with than the compensation received by the worker.

An employee must be distinguished from an "independent contractor." The IRS defines "independent contractor" as "...an individual is an independent contractor if the payer has the right to control or direct only the result of the work and not what will be done and how it will be done" [3], whereas *Black's Law Dictionary* defines an "independent contractor" as one who "in the exercise of an independent employment, contracts to do a piece of work according to his own methods and is subject to his employer's control only as to the end product or final result of his work" [4].

There are other less common classifications of workers. For example, business owners who provide services to other businesses are generally considered self-employed and are thus neither employees nor contractors. Specific classes of

J. E. Szalados (✉)
Director, Surgical and Neurocritical Care Units, Rochester Regional Health System at Rochester General Hospital, Rochester, NY, USA

The Szalados Law Firm, Hilton, NY, USA
e-mail: james.szalados@rochesterregional.org; jszalados@aol.com

J. E. Szalados (ed.), *The Medical-Legal Aspects of Acute Care Medicine*,
https://doi.org/10.1007/978-3-030-68570-6_24

workers may also be reclassified by statute. Thus, workers who would be classified as independent contractors under common law rules may nevertheless be treated as employees by statute ("statutory employees") under specific circumstances. Similarly, a worker may be classified as a "statutory nonemployee." Finally, the classification of government workers is complex; in general an "officer, employee, or elected official" of government is an employee for income tax withholding purposes unless a law or Section 218 Agreement applies.

The Employer-Employee Relationship

There are significant ramifications associated with the classification of a worker; these impact both the employer and the worker. Workers may be classified as independent contractors either appropriately or inappropriately by misunderstanding or intent. An employer can eliminate the employer's share and withhold the worker's share of taxes and withholdings and, thereby, eliminate significant costs associated with salaries, benefits, and employment taxes by classifying a worker as an independent contractor including:

- Social Security (FICA) [5] and Medicare taxes (employer's share)
- Fair Labor Standards Act (FLSA) [6] mandated overtime and minimum wage payments
- Federal (FUTA [7]) and state (SUTA) unemployment compensation taxes
- Workers' compensation insurance premiums
- Employee health insurance premiums
- Employee retirement benefits, vacation, holiday, and sick pay
- Employee fringe benefits (stock options)

In addition, numerous legislative protections which apply to employees and do not, or may not fully, apply to independent contractors including:

- Title VII of the Civil Rights Act of 1964 [8] which prohibits employer discrimination against employees on the basis of race, color, religion, sex, or national origin
- Age Discrimination in Employment Act (ADEA) [9] which prohibits employer discrimination against employees on the basis of their age
- Employment Retirement Security Act (ERISA) [10] which defines parameters of qualified employee benefit plans, including the level of benefits and amount of service required for vesting of those benefits, typically in the context of retirement
- Americans with Disabilities Act (ADA) [11] prohibits employer discrimination against otherwise qualified individuals with disabilities.
- Family and Medical Leave Act (FMLA) [12] requires employers to provide eligible employees with up to 12 weeks of unpaid leave per year when those employees are faced with certain critical life situations.
- The National Labor Relations Act (NLRA) [13] which grants employees the right to organize and governs labor-management relations

Furthermore, it is how the worker is treated, not how the agreement or contract is worded or structured that is relevant. An "employment contract" or "employment agreement" does not, in itself, despite wording to the contrary, define the classification status of a worker. Similarly, labels or similar categorical assignments or workers by employers have little meaning in the legal context. Rather, regulators and "investigators will use a totality of the circumstances" test [14] to assess each element of the conditions and manner in which the work is, or has been, performed. Federal and state regulators, especially the IRS, take the issue of worker and will investigate and will regularly challenge worker classifications and take actions to recover back taxes and contributions owed. In addition, private suit can be brought by employees to recover benefits of employment, benefits owed, and violations of anti-discrimination laws. In the case of *United States v. Polk* [15], US Court of Appeals for the Ninth Circuit found that an employer could be held criminally liable for its failure to pay FICA employment taxes, despite arguments by the employer that workers were all subcontractors.

There is one absolute no uniform test or set of criteria which will distinguish employees from independent contractors. US government agencies such as the IRS, the US Department of Labor (DOL), and the National Labor Relations Board (NLRB) may each use their own factor and criteria (Tables 24.1 and 24.2). Nonetheless, US courts have developed, and employ, three tests to determine worker's status: (1) the common-law test; (2) the economic realities test; and (3) a hybrid test (Table 24.3). The outcome of the tests may vary based on the test that is used, the statute or Federal Law(s) applied, or even the jurisdiction in which the case is adjudicated.

The common-law test [16] is basis of the traditional legal concept of agency and looks at ten individually non-dispositive factors to determine a worker's classification. Nonetheless, the common-law test emphasizes the "right of control." The IRS looks for three categories of evidence regarding the degree of control and independence: "(1) *Behavioral*: Does the company control or have the right to control what the worker does and how the worker does his or her job?; (2) Financial: Are the business aspects of the worker's job controlled by the payer? (these include things like how worker is paid, whether expenses are reimbursed, who provides tools/supplies, etc.); and, (3) Type of Relationship: Are there written contracts or employee type benefits (i.e. pension plan, insurance, vacation pay, etc.)? Will the relationship continue and is the work performed a key aspect of the business?" [17]. The IRS 20-factor test [18] (Table 24.4) is derived from the common-law test. The IRS 20 factor test remains valid today. In *Walker v. Altmeyer* [19], the US Court of Appeals for the Second Circuit weighed the elements of supervision and control in its determination of worker classification. Subsequently the US Supreme Court opined, in the cases of *Nationwide Mutual Insurance Co. v. Darden* [20], that Federal laws, at the time, did not clearly define an "employee" and ruled that the relationship between employer and worker should be evaluated on the basis of the common-law test, with a focus on the "right to control" the worker.

The economic realities test focuses on the economic dependence of the worker on the employer and is thus most relevant in the context of the Fair Labor Standards

Table 24.1 The basics of worker classification: employee versus independent contractor

Description	Employee	Contractor
Employment laws	Federal and state employment statutes	Not employee – therefore employment laws generally do not apply
Hiring process	A potential employee submits an application through the human resources department according to applicable laws and policies. If the application is approved, a job offer follows. Once the offer of employment is accepted, the employer is obligated to obtain additional personal data such as date of birth, marital status, and citizenship status	A potential contractor may be contacted by an entity to submit a proposal ("RFP"), if chosen as the contractor, then a contract regarding the details of the project is signed by the parties and the project commences
Tax documents include	Name, address, social security number, tax filing status, and exemptions on a W-4	Name, address, taxpayer identification number, and W-9 withholding information
Payer's tax reporting requirements	Reports salary and benefits paid to the employee on W-2	Reports payments of $600 or more per calendar year on a Form 1099
Other reporting	State and federal unemployment insurance	None
Payments for value of work or contract	Either hourly wage or annual salary	Contractual agreement
Payments accrue	Per pay period, the intervals for which must remain the same unless formally changed	Contractor reimbursed by accounts payable per contract terms on receipt of invoice

Act governing minimum wage and overtime obligations. The economic realities test intends to protect workers who are financially dependent on their employer(s). The implication, under the economic realities test, is that independent contractors have a larger degree of economic independence, and, thus, may simultaneously or in rapid sequence work for and be compensated by many different employers. Totality of circumstances is again important under the economic realities test because of intrinsic ambiguities; for example, a worker might be determined to be an employee for the purposes of the FLSA, but an independent contractor under FICA. The different conclusions based on the test applied can be, to some extent, illustrated in the case of *Donovan v. DialAmerica Marketing, Inc.* [21], where the Court of Appeals first ruled that under the economic realities test, workers were employees; however, on appeal, the Appellate Court ruled that the workers were independent contractors under the FLSA. Similarly, in the case of *Brock v. Superior Care, Inc.*, the US Court of Appeals for the Second Circuit ruled that the employer, Superior Care, Inc., had violated the overtime-pay protections within the FLSA when it failed to pay overtime compensation to nurses who were determined to be employees using a totality of the circumstances analysis of the economic realities test.

The hybrid test incorporates elements of both the common-law and the economic realities tests, with, as foundation, the view accepted by courts which have heard such matters, that the totality of the circumstances is fundamental to the legal

Table 24.2 General tests for worker classification (employee versus independent contractor)

Test	General rule	Applicable laws
Common-law test (IRS)	There is an employment relationship where employer has right of control over work processes (through an assessment of *the totality of the circumstances*)	Federal Insurance Contributions Act Federal Unemployment Tax Act Income tax withholding Employment Retirement and Income Security Act National Labor Relations Act Immigration Reform Control Act (IRS test)
Economic realities test	There is an employment relationship where employment relationship exists where the employee is dependent on the employer for continued employment	Fair Labor Standards Act Title VII Age Discrimination in Employment Act Americans with Disabilities Act Family and Medical Leave Act
Hybrid test	Employment relationship is evaluated under both common law and economic reality test factors, with a focus on who has the right to control the means and manner of a worker's performance	Title VII Age Discrimination in Employment Act Americans with Disabilities Act

analysis. The hybrid test considers, but does focus on the economic realities of the work relationship; and rather, but focuses on the employer's right to control the work process as the more determinative factor in its determinations. The "hybrid test" is the test most frequently applied by the courts to controversies surrounding employer discrimination that are brought under Title VII of the Civil Rights Act of 1964. In the case of *Diggs v. Harris Hospital—Methodist, Inc.* [22], the US Court of Appeals for the Fifth Circuit held that Jacqulyn Diggs, an African-American physician, could not sustain a claim under Title VII for discrimination, since the court determined that Diggs was an independent contractor, and not an employee, under the hybrid test, finding that (1) medical staff privileges at Harris Hospital were not necessary to Diggs' medical practice; (2) the hospital did not direct the manner or means by which medical care was provided; and (3) the hospital did not pay a salary, licensing fees, professional dues, insurance premiums, taxes, or retirement benefits to, or on behalf of, Diggs. The *Diggs* court thus concluded that Diggs was an independent contractor not under Title VII protection.

In the event that an employer misclassifies an employee, the IRS has established the Voluntary Classification Settlement Program (VCSP) which is an optional

Table 24.3 Worker status as defined by common-law tests

Factor	Employee if …	Independent contractor if …
Right of control	Employer controls the details of the work	Worker independently controls details of the work
Business relationship	Worker is fully engaged in employer's business	Worker operates as a separate business
Supervision level	Employer supervises worker ("respondeat superior")	Worker operates without direct supervision
Skill level	Skill level required is ordinary for employees in that business	Skill level is specialized, is unique, or based in training, education, experience
Tools and materials	Employer provides instrumentalities, tools, and a workplace structure	Worker provides his or her instrumentalities and tools and is based elsewhere
Continuing relationship	Worker is employed for extended continuous period	Worker is employed for specific project or "as needed"
Method of payment	Worker is paid a wage	Worker is paid by the project
Integration	Work is an integral element of employer's usual business	Work is not part of employer's usual ongoing business
Intent	Employer and worker intend to create an employer-employee relationship	Employer and worker do not intend to create an employer-employee relationship or intend to create an independent contractor relationship
Dedicated engagement	Worker dedicated to one employer for the time required by employer. Worker may be a 'part time' employee or have more than one job; these do not overlap	Worker may provide services simultaneously to more than one business or employer

program that provides an opportunity to reclassify workers as employees for future tax periods for employment tax purposes, with partial relief from federal employment taxes, provided that employers agree to prospectively classify those workers as employees [17].

Exempt and Non-exempt Employee Status

Employees are further classified into exempt or non-exempt categories under the Fair Labor Standards Act. The main implication of an employee's status as exempt is that exempt employees are not entitled to a specific minimum wage or to overtime pay. Nonetheless, although the FLSA provides no guarantees regarding minimum wage and overtime pay for exempt employees, individual employers have authority to determine what compensation, if any, will be provided to exempt employees in return for overtime work. Furthermore, there are three general requirements under the FLSA necessary to meet exempt status: (1) exempt employees are paid by a salary rather than an hourly rate; (2) exempt employees must meet the minimum salary

Table 24.4 The IRS 20-factor test [56]

Factor	Description
Level of instruction	A worker is required to comply with employer's rules and policies regarding hours of work, place of work, and the process of work to be performed as an employee [57]
Amount of training	Training a worker by requiring an experienced employee to work with the worker, by requiring the worker to attend meetings, or by using other methods indicates that the person(s) for whom the services are performed want the services performed in a particular manner or by use of a particular method and thereby indicates the requisite control to establish an employer-employee relationship [58]
Degree of business integration	Integration of the worker's services into the business operations generally shows that the worker is subject to direction and control [59]
Extent of personally rendered services	Employers that insist on a particular person performing the work assert a degree of control that suggests an employment relationship. In contrast, independent contractors typically are free to assign the work [60]
Control of assistants	If a company hires, supervises, and pays a worker's assistants, this control indicates a possible employment relationship. If the worker retains control over hiring, supervising, and paying helpers, this arrangement suggests an independent contractor relationship [61]
Continuity of relationship	A continuous relationship between a company and a worker indicates a possible employment relationship. However, an independent contractor may contract for an ongoing relationship or through for multiple, sequential projects
Flexibility of schedule	Those whose hours or days of work are dictated by a company are apt to qualify as its employees [62]
Demands for full-time work	If the worker must devote substantially his or her full time to the business of the employer, there is control over the amount of time the worker spends working. An independent contractor is free to work when and for whom he or she chooses [63]
Services performed on employer's premises	Requiring someone to work on company premises – particularly if the work can be performed elsewhere – indicates a possible employment relationship [64]
Sequence of work	If a company requires work to be performed in specific order or sequence, this control suggests an employment relationship [63]
Requirements for oral or written reports	If a worker regularly must provide written or oral reports on the status of a project, this arrangement indicates a possible employment relationship [65]
Method of payment	Hourly, weekly, or monthly pay schedules are characteristic of employment relationships, unless the payments simply are a convenient way of distributing a lump-sum fee. Payment on commission or project completion is more characteristic of independent contractor relationships [66]
Payment of business or travel expenses	Independent contractors typically bear the cost of travel or business expenses, and most contractors set their fees high enough to cover these costs. Direct reimbursement of travel and other business costs by a company suggests an employment relationship [67]

(continued)

Table 24.4 (continued)

Factor	Description
Provision of tools and materials	Workers who perform most of their work using company-provided equipment, tools, and materials are more likely to be considered employees. Work largely done using independently obtained supplies or tools supports an independent contractor finding [68]
Investment in facilities	If the worker invests in facilities that are used by the worker in performing services and are not typically maintained by other employees of the employer, that factor tends to indicate that the worker is an independent contractor [68]
Realization of profit or loss	A worker who can realize a profit or suffer a loss as a result of the worker's services is generally an independent contractor, but the worker who cannot is an employee [69].
Work for multiple companies	People who simultaneously provide services for several unrelated companies are likely to qualify as independent contractors [70]
Availability to public	If a worker regularly makes services available to the general public, this supports an independent contractor determination [64]
Control over discharge	This right is a factor indicating that the worker is an employee and the person possessing the right is an employer. An independent contractor, conversely, cannot be fired so long as he or she produces a result that meets the contract specifications [71]
Right of termination	Most employees unilaterally can terminate their work for a company without liability. Independent contractors cannot terminate services without liability, except as allowed under their contracts [69]

threshold set by the FLSA; for example, in the year 2020, employees must earn a minimum or $684 per week or $35,568 per year to be considered exempt; and (3) exempt employees have high-level responsibilities. Under the FLSA, job titles and job descriptions are not considered when classifying an employee as exempt or non-exempt since a job title may not reflect the actual job duties; duties rather than title or job description serve to classify an employee as either exempt or nonexempt. Nonetheless, exempt employees will usually fall into one of three categories: (a) professional; (2) administrative; or (3) executive.

In order for an employee to meet the professional exemption status, he or she will typically perform job duties that require educational qualifications such as specialized education and exercise professional discretion and judgment. The creative professional exemption applies to employees in a creative or artistic endeavors where they are required to use their talent, imagination, and inventiveness within the scope of their employment.

The administrative exemption applies to employees who direct business operations and exercise independent judgment and discretion over important business decisions.

Executive exemption status requires that the employee be responsible for managing at least part of a business wherein he or she supervises two or more full-time employees or four part-time employees regularly and makes key decisions regarding the job status of other employees such as hiring, terminating, or delegating.

The Employment Contract

The contract clause, found in Article I, Section 10 of the Constitution, prohibits the states from impairing the obligations of contracts, although in the case of *Ogden v. Saunders*, the Supreme Court clarified that the clause applied only to retroactive impairments of existing contracts, not to general police power regulation that affects future contracts [23]. Nonetheless, the Supreme Court later found that a liberty of contract was an enforceable constitutional right under the due process clause in the case of *Frisbie v. United States* [24]. The Court in Frisbee opined that "among the inalienable rights of the citizen is that of the liberty of contract." Today, "freedom of contract" is well recognized as "the ability of parties to bargain and create the terms of their agreement as they desire without outside interference from government" [25]. With any contract, there are recognized defenses to contract formation which include (1) mutual or unilateral mistake, (2) duress or undue influence, (3) unconscionability, (4) misrepresentation or fraud, (5) impossibility or impracticability, (6) capacity, (7) illegality, and (7) frustration of purpose.

An employment contract is an agreement that covers the working relationship of a company and an employee. The employment contract may be entitled either a "contract" or "agreement." The written contract memorializes the intent of the parties at the time that contract was made and will be interpreted by what is actually within the contract without regard to prior oral or written promises (see Chap. 28). Once a contract is signed, it becomes legally binding on both parties, typically the employer and the employee after which a violation of the terms becomes legally actionable in breach.

Agency and Vicarious Liability

The power of agency is a special designation conferred upon an employee. Most typical employment contracts will contain specific written provisions expressly prohibiting a power of agency to the employee. Agency refers to a relationship between one people who is designated as the "agent," who then is legally authorized to act on behalf of another person, company, or government – the "master" or "principal." A key element of the principal-agent relationship is the concept of control wherein the agent agrees to act under the direction of the principal. A legally binding agency relationship must be created through the explicit consent of both the agent and the principal. Agency mostly refers to an authorization of an employee by an employer to enter into contracts on the employer's behalf but can extend to management, operational, and financial functions. The scope and extent of agency authority is usually clearly defined through writings in a contract. Thus, the power of agency is almost always, or should be, documented in writing and through the mutual written agreement and consent of both parties.

The agent's authority may be actual or apparent. An agency relationship is formed either by (a) express agreement through a contract according to a power of agency; (b) by ratification of unauthorized actions by the principal, essentially retroactively creating a de facto express agency; (c) implication, as implied or inferred from the conduct of the parties; or (d) apparent agency by holding oneself as an agent in a relationship which does not in fact exist. If the principal grants express powers to the agent to act on his or her behalf, then the agent is empowered with real or "actual" authority. Through the exercise of an agent's actual authority, it is as if the principal himself or herself were acting, and the principal is then legally bound by the agent's acts. For example, an agent empowered through express agreement with actual authority can legally bind the principal, a person or entity, in debt, contract, or other liability. One important example or actual agency is that of a healthcare agent (e.g., healthcare proxy, durable power of attorney for healthcare).

Where the principal either knowingly or mistakenly allows a purported agent to assume that he or she is actually empowered with authority to act when such authority in reality does not exist, this is known as apparent authority. Principals must look out for such situations and intervene and disavow apparent or implied authority before liability is incurred. If others reasonably and in good faith rely on such implied or apparent authority, the principal will be held liable.

Agency can give rise to vicarious liability or imputed liability. The issue of apparent agency has a long and important history in American tort law; specifically, at issue is that which could constitute "apparent agency" in the context of alleged medical malpractice. The issue of agency rarely arises in the malpractice setting where the providers are employed. An employer of an employee who injures someone through negligence while in the scope of employment is generally vicariously liable for damages. *Respondeat superior*, which means "let the master answer," is the legal principle by which a plaintiff may impute liability to an employer for the negligence by one or more of its employees where the negligent act occurred within the scope of employment. Whether or not an employer-employee relationship exists depends primarily on whether the employer has the "right of control" over the employee [26]. Through such imputed liability, physicians may be held liable for negligent acts by their staff, interns, or medical students while under that physician's supervision and guidance; and medical groups or medical practices may be held liable for the negligence of partners and associates.

On the other hand, where the providers against whom medical malpractice is alleged are not employees, but rather independent contractors, a showing of apparent agency is one way for the plaintiff to impute liability upon the hospital or healthcare institution. Historically, hospitals were considered charitable institutions and were therefore considered to be exempt from the general rule that a corporation was to be held responsible for the negligent acts of its employees. The doctrine which declared charitable institutions immune from liability was first articulated in the case of *McDonald v. Massachusetts* [27]. The doctrine of charitable immunity was unchallenged until 1957, in the New York case of *Bing v. Thunig* [28], where the plaintiff, Isabel Bing, was severely burned during surgery in the operating room of St. John's Episcopal Hospital, where the ignition of gases formed by the evaporation of antiseptic which had been applied to plaintiff's body at and about the immediate site of the operation was then ignited when the surgeon applied heated cautery to the site. The court in *Bing* articulated a reversal from the doctrine of charitable immunity:

> The doctrine of *respondeat superior* is grounded on firm principles of law and justice. Liability is the rule, immunity the exception. It is not too much to expect that those who serve and minister to members of the public should do so, as do all others, subject to that principle and within the obligation not to injure through carelessness. It is not alone good morals but sound law that individuals and organizations should be just before they are generous, and there is no reason why that should not apply to charitable hospitals.
>
> The conception that the hospital does not undertake to treat the patient, does not undertake to act through its doctors and nurses, but undertakes instead simply to procure them to act upon their own responsibility, no longer reflects the fact. Present-day hospitals, as their manner of operation plainly demonstrates, do far more than furnish facilities for treatment. They regularly employ on a salary basis a large staff of physicians, nurses and internes, as well as administrative and manual workers, and they charge patients for medical care and treatment, collecting for such services, if necessary, by legal action. Certainly, the person who avails himself of "hospital facilities" expects that the hospital will attempt to cure him, not that its nurses or other employees will act on their own responsibility.
>
> *Bing v. Thunig* at 666.

The Illinois Supreme Court in the case of *Gilbert v. Sycamore Municipal Hospital* [29] defined a multifactor test to help determine whether a hospital could be held vicariously liable for the alleged acts of its independent contractor physicians. Specifically, the court in *Gilbert* opined that in order for a plaintiff to hold a hospital liable under the theory of "apparent agency," a plaintiff must show that:

> (1) The hospital, or its agent, acted in a manner that would lead a reasonable person to conclude that the individual who was alleged to be negligent was an employee or agent of the hospital; (2) where the acts of the agent create the appearance of authority, the plaintiff must also prove that the hospital had knowledge of and acquiesced in them; and (3) the plaintiff acted in reliance upon the conduct of the hospital or its agent, consistent with ordinary care and prudence.
>
> *Gilbert v. Sycamore Municipal Hospital* at 525.

The Idaho Supreme Court reaffirmed the apparent authority theory in *Navo v. Bingham Memorial Hospital* [30]. In this case, Navo broke his ankle and had an initial surgical procedure at Bingham Memorial Hospital, and the ankle subsequently became infected; when Navo underwent a second surgery, he suffered an adverse reaction to the anesthesia and later died. The patient's family brought suit against the hospital, alleging that the hospital was liable for both its own actions and the acts of the certified registered nurse anesthetist who provided the anesthesia. On the basis of several factors, including a hospital admission consent form that stated that anesthesia providers were independent contractors, and an anesthesia consent form explaining separate bills for hospital and anesthesia services, the trial court granted summary judgment to the hospital, finding that Navo had failed to adequately plead a case of apparent authority. On appeal the court reversed finding that there were genuine issues of fact as to whether the conduct of Bingham Memorial

Hospital could have reasonably led Navo to believe that the CRNA was acting on the hospital's behalf [31].

To prove a case of vicarious liability against a hospital, a plaintiff must prove that the employee or agent was either the hospital's actual agent or apparent agent [32]. A hospital is not likely to liable for the acts of providers who provides medical care as an independent agent beyond the control of the hospital. However, the question of control, and this agency liability, is generally a question of fact; a court may decide the issue as a matter of law if only one conclusion may be drawn from the undisputed fact [33]. Courts will look at a variety of factors in making a determination as to whether or not there is apparent agency, giving rise to vicarious liability, in the case of negligence by independent contractor medical staff. The factors include:

- The hospital contract with the contractor to provide relevant services to hospital patients.
- The hospital controls or assigns the contractor.
- The hospital relies on the contractor to provide a key service as part of usual hospital's services (anesthesiology, laboratory, radiology, and emergency medicine).
- The hospital represents to the public that the contractor was a manager of the clinical service line.
- The hospital advertisements "hold out" the services provided by the contractor as a "hospital service."
- The hospital fails to disclose that a service is performed by independent contractors.
- The hospital's consent forms did not identify the contractor as an independent contractor or expressly disclaim liability for the contractor's services.
- The hospital's logo or letterhead is displayed on consent forms and other documents used by the contractor.
- The hospital allows contractors to use hospital scrubs and name tags bearing the hospital's name or logo.

Thus, apparent agency and apparent authority are legal theories by which courts may impose liability on a group, practice, or healthcare institution, as the employer of an independent contractor where the employer has acted in such a way as to "hold out" the independent contractor as its employee such that there is the reasonable belief that the independent contractor is actually the employee of the employer [34].

Employee at Will

Employment relationships are presumed to be mutually "at-will" in all US states except Montana. At the present time, in contrast to all other US states, Montana only allows at-will termination of an employee while that employee is within an introductory, or probationary, period of employment. "At-will" termination otherwise allows that in an employer-employee relationship, even where there may be a contract or employment for a fixed term, either party can terminate the employment relationship at any time, for no reason, except an illegal reason, without incurring legal liability. In contracts, this is referred to as "termination without cause" and is generally subject only to the notice period outlined in the contract. It is important to note that "termination without cause" is an exercise of one's statutory rights, either employer or employee, and is materially different from "termination for cause" which occurs within a disciplinary or contract breach situation and may lead to legal liabilities. The at-will presumption is a default rule which potentially may be modified by contract; for example, an employment contract may specify a specific term of employment absent a "without cause" or, it may be limited in its construction and specify only a "for cause" termination; although such contracts are exceedingly rare. Finally, "at-will" employment can be used by either employer or employee to terminate a poor relationship without escalation to legal controversy which may stem from a "for cause" termination of an employment contract.

The extension of the "at-will" doctrine of employment also allows an employer to change the terms of the employment relationship with little or no required reason or notice: including, for example, job duties, wages, certain benefits, or paid time off; however, such radical changes also are exceedingly rare because they are subject to federal and state employment laws.

Brief Summary of Key Statutes and Laws Relating to Human Resources

Title VII of the Civil Rights Act of 1964

Title VII of the Civil Rights Act of 1964 [35] and subsequent amendments, including the Civil Rights Act of 1991, prohibits employers from discriminating against individuals on the basis of color, race, sex, religion, or national origin. The 1964 Act established the Equal Employment Opportunity Commission to enforce the act and provides for civil penalties in the event of discrimination [36]. Title VII applies only to businesses with 15 or more employees. Compliance with Title VII requires that businesses establish, implement, and document fair and nondiscriminatory practices with respect to interviews, hiring, training, pay, benefits, and termination in the course of human resources management. The Civil Rights Act of 1991 [37] and the Lily Ledbetter Fair Pay Act of 2009 [38] amended Title VII. In addition, Section 102 of the Civil Rights Act [39] further amended Title VII to provide for the recovery of compensatory and punitive damages in cases of intentional violations of Title VII, the Americans with Disabilities Act of 1990, and Section 501 of the Rehabilitation Act of 1973.

The Fair Labor Standard Act (FLSA) of 1938

The FLSA [40] is administered by the Department of Labor Wage and Hour Division. FLSA establishes the federal minimum wage, work hour and rest time, standards for overtime pay, and child labor and classifies employees as either exempt or non-exempt.

The Family and Medical Leave Act (FMLA) of 1993

The FMLA [41] is administered by the Department of Labor. The FMLA only applied to companies which employ at least 50 employees within 75 miles but grants such employees who have worked a minimum of 1250 hours in the past year to take an unpaid, job-protected leave for family and medical reasons. During an FMLA leave, the employee remains entitled to group health insurance coverage. Eligible employees are entitled to (1) 12 workweeks of leave in a 12-month period for (a) the birth of a child and to care for the newborn child within 1 year of birth; (b) the placement with the employee of a child for adoption or foster care and to care for the newly placed child within 1 year of placement; (c) care for the employee's spouse, child, or parent who has a serious health condition; (d) a serious health condition that makes the employee unable to perform the essential functions of his or her job; or (e) a qualifying exigency arising out of the fact that the employee's spouse, son, daughter, or parent is a covered military member on "covered active duty." Alternatively ("or") eligible employees are entitled to 26 workweeks of military caregiver leave during a single 12-month period to care for a covered service member with a serious injury or illness if the eligible employee is the service member's spouse, son, daughter, parent, or next of kin.

The Americans with Disabilities Act of 1990

Four federal agencies share the responsibility for the administration and enforcement of the ADA [42]. The EEOC enforces regulations when it comes to private employment. The ADA only applies to businesses which employ 15 or more employees. Title I of the ADA prohibits local governments, state governments, labor unions, employment agencies, and private employers from discriminating against individuals with disabilities who are qualified during hiring, job application procedures, advancement, firing, job training, compensation, and other privileges, terms, and conditions of employment. Title II of the ADA focuses on eliminating discrimination in the realm of local and state governments. This includes any services, programs, and activities provided through these entities. Title III adds these standards to privately owned businesses and commercial facilities. This means the standards for equal opportunities extend through education, public accommodation, and public transportation. The Title IV amendment of 2008 extended employee protections to digital communications, including closed captioning and guidelines for internet accessibility and other digital services. Title V is a blanket section that spans certain conditions and provisions on how ADA can be implemented.

The Age Discrimination in Employment Act (ADEA)

The ADEA [43] prohibits employers from discriminating against individuals aged 40 or older in wages, hiring, promotions, layoffs, benefits, terminations, and other terms or conditions when it comes to employment. The EEOC administers the ADEA.

The Occupational Safety and Health Act (OSHA) of 1970

OSHA [44] established the Occupational Safety and Health Administration and mandates that employers provide a healthy and safe work environment for their workers. The primary goal of this law is to reduce workplace hazards and implement safety and health programs for both employers and their employees. OSHA conferred rights on employees including the right to (a) receive training and information regarding workplace hazards and applicable OSHA standards and laws; (b) receive and review documentation on work-related illnesses and injuries at the job site; (c) submit complaints to OSHA in a confidential manner confidentially; (d) receive copies of any tests done to measure workplace hazards; and (e) nondiscrimination and protecting against retaliation for OSHA-related complaints or inquiries.

The Patient Protection and Affordable Care Act (PPACA)

PPACA [45] establishes an employer and individual mandate that requires all employees to buy healthcare coverage and all employers who have at least 50 employees to offer health insurance to their employees.

The Employee Retirement Income Security Act (ERISA) of 1974

ERISA [46] built upon the foundations of the Labor Management Relations Act of 1947 [47] (LMRA) which allowed, but did not require, labor and management to establish jointly administered health and welfare trusts, sometimes called

Taft-Hartley trusts [48]. ERISA provides for federal preemption of most state regulations and regulatory powers as they relate to employee benefits [49]. ERISA not only preempts state laws that conflict with ERISA but also all state laws which "relate to" employee benefit plans. ERISA was enacted both to ensure the fiscal integrity of pension plans and to define the federal role in the regulation of private employment-based health benefit plans. ERISA is primarily concerned with reporting, disclosure, and fiduciary duties related to the establishment and administration of employee health benefit plans. There is also a large body of case law relating to ERISA.

In 1985, Congress amended ERISA and the Internal Revenue Code to allow qualified health plan participants and beneficiaries who would otherwise lose their benefits due to certain defined events to elect continued coverage, widely referred to as COBRA continuation coverage, or simply COBRA coverage, an abbreviation of the Consolidated Omnibus Reconciliation Act of 1985 [50]. COBRA coverage continuation requirements apply to employers with 20 or more employees

The Equal Pay Act (EPA)

The EPA [51] prohibits wage discrimination between men and women based on sex when men and women perform equivalent jobs which require equal skill, at the same establishment, and under comparable working conditions. The EEOC administers the EPA.

The Pregnancy Discrimination Act (PDA)

The PDA [52] is an amendment to Title VII of the Civil Rights Act of 1964 and prohibits employers from discriminating against employees who are pregnant or suffering from pregnancy-related conditions. Women affected by pregnancy or related conditions must be treated in the same manner as other applicants or employees who are similar in their ability or inability to work. The PDA applies to businesses with at least 15 employees. The EEOC administers the PDA.

The Norris-Laguardia Act of 1932

The Norris-Laguardia Act [53] protects the rights of unions to organize and prohibits employers from forcing job applicants to promise not to join a union in exchange for employment. The Act also restricted the use of court injunctions in labor disputes against strikes, picketing, and boycotts. The Act laid the foundation for an even more important labor bill, the National Labor Relations Act of 1935.

The National Labor Relations Act (NLRA) of 1935

The NLRA [54], previously known as the Wagner Act of 1935, expanded on the protections granted in the Norris-Laguardia Act and defines relations between management and unions. The NLRA defines and protects the rights of employers, employees, and labor unions; encourages collective bargaining; and eliminates unfair labor practices. The NLRA was subsequently modified through the Taft-Hartley Amendments of 1947 and the Landrum-Griffin Act of 1959 (Labor-Management Reporting and Disclosure Act (LMRDA)).

Genetic Information Nondiscrimination Act (GINA) of 2000

GINA [55] protects Americans from discrimination based on their genetic information in both health insurance (Title I) and employment (Title II). Title I amends the Employee Retirement Income Security Act of 1974 (ERISA), the Public Health Service Act (PHSA), and the Internal Revenue Code (IRC), through the Health Insurance Portability and Accountability Act of 1996 (HIPAA), as well as the Social Security Act, to prohibit health insurers from engaging in genetic discrimination. Title II of GINA is implemented by the Equal Employment Opportunity Commission (EEOC) and prevents employers from using genetic information in employment decisions and prevents employers from requesting and requiring genetic information from employees or those applying for jobs.

Summary and Conclusions

Employment, human resources, and labor laws are highly specialized areas of law which are likely to impact both healthcare practices and also providers and staff. The multitude of federal and state regulations and laws which impact employment can potentially incur significant liability for the underprepared. As with all other areas of law, expert legal advice is advised before, during, and after any potential actions involving worker relations.

References

1. IRS. Employee (Common-Law Employee). Available online at: https://www.irs.gov/businesses/small-businesses-self-employed/employee-common-law-employee.
2. Black HC. Black's law dictionary. St. Paul: West Publishing Co; 1991. p. 363.
3. IRS. Independent contractor defined. Available online at: https://www.irs.gov/businesses/small-businesses-self-employed/independent-contractor-defined.

4. IRS. Independent contractor defined. Available online at: https://www.irs.gov/businesses/small-businesses-self-employed/independent-contractor-defined, p. 530.
5. 26 U.S.C. 3101 et seq.
6. 29 U.S.C. 201 et seq.
7. Federal Unemployment Tax Act (FUTA). 26 U.S.C. 3301 et seq.
8. 42 U.S.C. 2000(e) et seq.
9. 29 U.S.C. 621 et seq.
10. 29 U.S.C. 1001 et seq.
11. 42 U.S.C. 12101 et seq.
12. 29 U.S.C. 2601 et seq.
13. 29 U.S.C. 151 et seq.
14. The Department of Labor (DOL) notes that proper classification depends on the totality of the circumstances of the activity or situation, not a specific rule or test. See, DOL Fact Sheet 13, Employment Relationship Under the Fair Labor Standards Act (July 2008), https://www.dol.gov/agencies/whd/fact-sheets/13-flsa-employment-relationship.
15. *United States v. Polk* 550 F.2d 566 (9th Cir. 1977).
16. Pub. 15-A p. 7 "Common-Law Rules" section. See generally, Pub. 15-A pp. 7-10.
17. IRS. Independent Contractor (Self-Employed) or Employee? Available online at: https://www.irs.gov/businesses/small-businesses-self-employed/independent-contractor-self-employed-or-employee.
18. Rev. Rul. 87-41, 1987-1 C.B. 296, 298.
19. *Walker v. Altmeyer*. 137 F.2d 531 (2nd Circuit 1943).
20. *Nationwide Mutual Insurance Co. v. Darden*. 112 S.Ct. 1344, 1348–49 (1992).
21. *Donovan v. DialAmerica Marketing, Inc.*, 757 F.2d 1376 (3rd Cir. 1985).
22. *Diggs v. Harris Hospital—Methodist, Inc.*, 847 F.2d 270 (9th Cir. 1988).
23. Ogden v. Saunders, 25 U.S. 213 (1827).
24. Frisbie v. United States, 157 U.S. 160 (1895).
25. Cornell Law School. Legal Information Institute. Freedom of Contract. Online at: https://www.law.cornell.edu/wex/freedom_of_contract.
26. St Joseph Hosp v Wolff, 94 SW3d 513, 541–42 (Tex 2002); Baptist Mem'l Hosp Sys v Sampson, 969 SW2d 945, 947 (Tex 1998).
27. McDonald v. Massachusetts General Hospital, 120 Mass. 432 (1876).
28. Bing v. Thunig, 2 N.Y.2d 656, 666 (N.Y. 1957).
29. Gilbert v. Sycamore Municipal Hospital. 156 Ill.2d 511 (1993).
30. Navo v. Bingham Memorial Hospital, 160 Idaho 363, 373 P.3d 681 (2016).
31. Navo v. Bingham Mem'l Hosp. No. 42540 (Idaho Apr. 26, 2016).
32. Wallace v. Alexian Brothers Medical Center, 389 Ill. App. 3d 1081, 1085-86 (1st Dist. 2009).
33. James v. Ingalls Memorial Hospital, 299 Ill. App. 3d 627, 632 (1st Dist. 1998).
34. Baptist Memorial Hospital System v. Sampson. 969 SW2d 945, 41 Tex Sup Ct J 833.
35. Title VII of the Civil Rights Act of 1964, 42 U.S.C. §2000e. *Online at*: http://www.eeoc.gov/laws/statutes/titlevii.cfm.
36. EEOC Management Directive-110. *Online at*: https://www.eeoc.gov/federal/directives/md110.cfm.
37. Pub. L. 102-166.
38. Pub. L. 111-2.
39. 42 U.S.C. 1981. Section 1977.
40. Fair Labor Standards Act of 1938 (FLSA) (29 U.S.C., Chapter 8).
41. FMLA. Public Law 103-3 (February 5, 1993). Codified at 29 U.S.C. sec. 2601.
42. ADA. 42 U.S.C. § 12101.
43. Age Discrimination in Employment Act, 29 U.S.C. §621. *Online at*: https://www.eeoc.gov/laws/statutes/adea.cfm.
44. Occupational Safety and Health Act of 1970. Public Law 91-596. 84 STAT. 1590. 91st Congress, S.2193. December 29, 1970 and as amended through January 1, 2004.

45. PPACA. Public Law 111–148. 2010.
46. ERISA. 29 U.S.C.A. §1001 et seq., P.L. 93-406, 88 Stat. 829.
47. The Labor Management Relations Act (LMRA) was enacted on June 23, 1947, 61 Stat. 157.
48. Taft-Hartley. 29 U.S.C.A. §186(c)(5).
49. ERISA. 29 USCS ch 144[a].
50. COBRA. P.L. 99-272, 100 Stat. 82 (1986).
51. Equal Pay Act, 29 U.S.C. § 206(d). *Online at*: https://www.eeoc.gov/laws/statutes/epa.cfm.
52. Pregnancy Discrimination Act (PDA). Title VII. 29 CFR Part 16.
53. Norris-LaGuardia Act. 29 U.S.C.A. § 101 et seq.
54. National Labor Relations Act of 1935. 29 U.S.C. § 151–169.
55. Genetic Information Nondiscrimination Act, 42 U.S.C. §2000ff. *Online at*: https://www.eeoc.gov/laws/statutes/gina.cfm
56. Rev. Rul. 87-41, 1987-1 C.B. 296, 298. See also, Simmons SL (1988) "Determining Status as an Employee Rev. Ruling 87-41," Akron Tax Journal: Vol. 5, Article 14. Available online at: https://ideaexchange.uakron.edu/akrontaxjournal/vol5/iss1/14. See also: State of Oregon. IRS 20 Factor Test – Independent Contractor or Employee? *Available online at:* https://www.oregon.gov/ODA/shared/Documents/Publications/NaturalResources/20FactorTestforIndependentContractors.pdf.
57. Rev. Rul. 68-598, 1968-2 C.B. 464, and Rev. Rul. 66-381, 1966-2 C.B. 449.
58. Rev. Rul. 70-630, 1970-2 C.B. 229.
59. *United States v. Silk,* 331 U.S. 704 (1947), 1947-2 C.B. 167.
60. Rev. Rul. 55-695, 1955-2 C.B. 410.
61. Rev. Rul. 63-115, 1963-1 C.B. 178, with Rev. Rul. 55-593, 1955-2 C.B. 610.
62. Rev. Rul. 73-591, 1973-2 C.B. 337.
63. Rev. Rul. 56-694, 1956-2 C.B. 694.
64. Rev. Rul. 56-660, 1956-2 C.B. 693.
65. Rev. Rul. 70-309, 1970-1 C.B. 199, and Rev. Rul. 68-248, 1968-1 C.B. 431.
66. Rev. Rul. 74-3 89, 1974-2 C.B. 330.
67. Rev. Rul. 55-144, 1955-I C.B. 483.
68. Rev. Rul. 71-524, 1971-2 C.B. 346.
69. Rev. Rul. 70-309, 1970-1 C.B. 199.
70. Rev. Rul. 70-572, 1970-2 C.B. 221.
71. Rev. Rul. 75-41, 1975-1 C.B. 323.

Chapter 25
Anatomy of Healthcare Contracts: Pitfalls and Avoidance of Liability

James E. Szalados

Introduction

Generally defined, a contract is an enforceable agreement. The lives of professionals and the day-to-day affairs of professional entities are closely governed by contracts. Some contracts are obvious, such as a contract of employment. However, many contracts are more subtle and can become a source of liability even if we do not perceive them as contracts, for example, medical staff bylaws, the rules and regulations of a medical staff, shareholder or partnership agreements, software user agreements, insurance policies, leases, operating agreements, managed care provider agreements, licensing agreements, mortgages, informed consent documents, codes of conduct, and other "agreements" (Table 25.1). Thus, not all contracts are obvious or are labelled as contracts; on the other hand, not every document labelled as a "contract" truly represents a legally binding contract. Sometimes, one encounters a document for which its title or nomenclature either does not identify it as contract or may only implicitly imply that it is a contract. A very general introductory rule is that where a document specifies (1) parties who (2) each agree to perform some service or provide some compensation and where (3) failure to perform as agreed has legal consequences will likely represent a contract.

Contracts are legal documents. The fundamental purpose of a contract is to formally define obligations in a legally binding way; but a more implicit and equally important function of a contract is to shift risk between parties. Similar to insurance (see Chap. 10), contracts are used to manage risk and are frequently used to shift risks, between parties in a transaction. Parties to a contract will shift as much risk as

J. E. Szalados (✉)
Director, Surgical and Neurocritical Care Units, Rochester Regional Health System at Rochester General Hospital, Rochester, NY, USA

The Szalados Law Firm, Hilton, NY, USA
e-mail: james.szalados@rochesterregional.org; jszalados@aol.com

J. E. Szalados (ed.), *The Medical-Legal Aspects of Acute Care Medicine*,
https://doi.org/10.1007/978-3-030-68570-6_25

Table 25.1 A general sampling of types of contracts

Acquisition agreements
Ambulatory surgery center agreements
Ancillary service agreements
Billing and collection services agreements
Business associate agreements
Call coverage agreements
Clinical trial agreements
Code of conduct
Corporate, LLC, and shareholder agreements
Compliance agreements
Employee handbook
Employment agreements (contracts)
Equipment leases
Group purchasing organization agreements
Group-provider contracts
Harassment (and sexual harassment) policy
Healthcare technology agreements
Hospital service management agreements
Hospital-based provider contracts
IDTF (independent diagnostic testing facility)/ supervision agreements
IPA (independent physician association) agreements
Joint venture agreements
Locums tenens agreements
Medical directorship agreements
Medical office and facility leases
Medical staff bylaws
Merger agreements
Military service agreements
Office sharing agreements
Pharmacy services agreements
Physician recruitment and retention agreements
Practice management agreements
Relocation agreements
Residency or postgraduate training program agreements
Rules and regulations (department or institution)
Service line management agreements
Visa sponsorship agreements

possible onto the other party, to minimize their own potential liabilities and to maximize their own benefits, with the least attendant risk. Thus, in any contract, there are both mutual obligations, and duties, and there should be mutual benefits. Attorneys are retained to (1) identify risks and benefits that should be managed through contract; (2) develop or write a new contract; (2) review a proposed contract document for the purpose of mapping and counselling a party about real and potential risks and benefits; (3) negotiate changes in a proposed contract to shift or more reasonably allocate risk between parties; (4) renegotiate existing contracts to more favorably allocate the risks, obligations, or benefits; (5) litigate breaches, or perceived breaches of contract; and (6) negotiate potential impeding beaches of contract. More often than not, if there is a sense that a private or business deal should, or even could, be memorialized in the form of a contract, then consultation with an attorney is advised. The world has changed much since the days when contracts were binding on a nod and a handshake. The importance of a written memorialization of the exact terms of an agreement cannot be overemphasized.

Attorneys involved in contract law may have either a transactional or litigator focus, although some attorneys may work in dual roles. Transactional attorneys will focus primarily on the focus on the business issues and the legal issues arising through the course of business dealings ("the deal"); the focus of a transactional attorney is the drafting, structuring, reviewing, and negotiating contract provisions, with a focus on avoiding future litigation. Many transactional attorneys are overly optimistic about completing the deal. On the other hand, the mindset of a good transactional attorney is that of a litigator who sees the "glass as half empty" and is focused on the "what if's" such as hidden risks and liabilities within a deal and the associated contract. Transactional attorneys tend to focus on contract construction, whereas litigating attorneys tend to focus on issues of interpretation and how the contract may or may not withstand challenges relating to the interpretation, or perceptions, of the parties, in the event of dispute.

It is an often overlooked tenet that the terms of contract matter most when the relationship between the parties turns contentious and the potential for dispute or litigation arises. Contracts should be analyzed at the onset for those terms and conditions which could become unfavorable in the event of contract breach or termination. Providers frequently sign contracts with a focus on the compensation and the perks but neglect to consider the implications of clauses which contain at will termination, indemnification, or non-compete clauses; and they often fail to recognize that important benefits and partnership clauses are lacking.

The terms and clauses that are included in a contract are extremely important; however, equally important to a successful relationship are the potential terms and clauses which are not, but could or should be, included so as to protect a party from future liability. In some instances, missing terms may and can be supplied by a court if they are either consistent with parties' intentions or if they are statutorily or legally required; however, important missing terms can have serious ramifications. The importance of reviewing any and all potential agreements with an attorney who has experience in contract and/or healthcare law cannot be underscored. In the event of untimely termination or breach, contract litigation can be very costly.

The laws of contracts are governed by the laws of each state, and therefore there is some variation in the way that contract law is defined, interpreted, enforced between the various states. However, to a large extent, contract law is generally uniform among the states. Within the USA, 49 states are common law jurisdictions; the exception is Louisiana which is a civil law jurisdiction which is based in civil law derived from Napoleonic Code. The fundamental difference is that in common law jurisdictions, the emphasis is upon case law in the form of precedent and published judicial opinions, whereas in civil law jurisdictions systems, the emphasis is upon legislatively defined, or codified, statutes. Nonetheless, because of subtle differences in the laws of contracts between the states, contracts contain a "choice of law" or "governing law" clause, or provision, through which the parties agree at the outset, regarding the particular state in which disagreements will be litigated.

The law governing commercial transactions such as the sale of goods is largely governed by the Uniform Commercial Code (UCC) which is a federal construct intended primarily to harmonize the contract laws of the various states and thereby facilitate interstate commerce; with few exceptions, it will not be in detail covered in this chapter.

In general, there are two main types of contracts relevant to healthcare providers:

1. Contracts between the provider and his/her employer
2. Contracts between the provider, the group, and third parties

Although the language and the clauses of healthcare contracts may be similar, the party writing the contract will generally have both tactical and strategic advantage. The focus here will necessarily be on contract between providers and groups; however, many of the clauses are applicable to other forms of healthcare contracting.

The Language of Contracts

Attorneys will draft contracts using words and language that best describes the intentions of the party drafting the contract. The language should be as specific as possible, but not so specific as to make the completion of the contract impossible. The language should also be concise and clear, since overly verbose contracts can be difficult to follow; and they may contain difficult to identify contradictions. The language should be used to effectively communicate the needs and intentions of the parties between themselves.

Legal documents, such as contracts, have traditionally been written in "legalese" – using words and phrases that are at best poorly understood and ambiguous to a layperson. Terms that appear as plain English may have a more specific or different meaning when they appear within a contract clause. Such plain English terms that have important legal ramifications are referred to as "legal terms of art." "Legal terms of art" are sometimes referred to as "magic words" by lawyers. Since contracts reflect the innate complexities of the specific transactions they address, specialized legal terminology is often used by attorneys to most efficiently express the intentions of the parties. However, for laypersons, "terms of art" are sometimes viewed as adding unavoidable complexity to the interpretation of the contract. Increasingly, "terms of art" are being replaced by plain language in contracts and other legal documents.

The party ("offeror") who writes the contract has an inherent strategic advantage because they have "set the stage" for further negotiating; they have done so to put themselves in their most favored position at the outset. The party ("offeree") who receives the contract is then out in a position to decide whether to accept clauses as they are written, to challenge clauses, or even to rewrite elements of the contract in a more favorable fashion.

Therefore, contract language exists at two levels: (1) rules of contract construction and (2) rules of interpretation [1]. The rules of contract construction necessarily incorporate various types of meaning, including plain meaning, ordinary use meaning, subjective meaning, objective meaning, purpose, belief, and intent. Rules of contract construction can effect both the intended and unintended legal consequences of a contract. For example, preamble clauses and/or associated recitals may be used to define the intent of the parties and also define meanings of other clauses within the contract. Also, under a presumption of negative implication, where one thing is clearly expressed, the expression of one thing generally implies the exclusion of others *(expressio unius est exclusio alterius)*. Punctuation within a clause may also not be arbitrary, and the type and placing of punctuation may also be used as an indicator of intended meaning. Within the body of a contract, where a conflict arises between general and specific provision, the specific provision is generally given greater weight and therefore usually controls (*generalia specialibus non derogant*). Terms should be clearly defined, within the contract, if possible; where terms generate ambiguity, if litigated, evidence of customary usage and practices specific to a business or industry can be introduced during litigation to define the unexplained or ambiguous term [2].

With respect to contract interpretation, the overarching issue is to ascertain and "give effect to the expressed intentions of the parties" [3] at the time that the contract was drafted and signed. Ambiguity arises when a term, provision, or clause in a contract can reasonably be interpreted in more than one way. Thus, "contract language is not ambiguous merely because the parties dispute what it means. To be ambiguous, a disputed contract term must be fairly or reasonably susceptible to more than one meaning" [4]. The determination of whether a contract or provision is ambiguous is a determination of law for the court to make on a case-by-case basis; therefore, ambiguity can be a source of unpredictability and should be avoided if possible; "No ambiguity exists where the contract language has 'a definite and precise meaning, unattended by danger of misconception in the purport of the [contract] itself, and concerning which there is no reasonable basis for a difference of opinion" [5]. Finally, contracts are expected to be construed in a commercially reasonable manner; courts should not interpret a contract in a way that would be "commercially unreasonable, or contrary to the reasonable expectations of the parties" [6].

Thus the choice of words, the terms and clauses, and the structure of language within a contract is extremely important; however, equally important to a successful relationship are the potential terms and clauses which are not, but could or should be, included so as to protect a party from future liability. In some jurisdictions, terms and conditions, which are not written into a contract, but are legislatively or statutorily required, may be operative and binding; generally these statutory conditions may be known to the attorneys but not a layperson reading a contract. Thus, where a statute regulates the content of a specific type of contract, the statutory requirements may be legally considered to be integral to the contract, such as a gap-filling function, even if they are not written into the body of the contract. Where provisions of a contract run contrary to statute, such provisions may be considered void or nonbinding. Contracts also contain words such as "must," "shall," or "should." Mandatory words impose a duty, whereas permissive words allow for discretion.

"Boilerplate provisions" are often trivialized and overlooked since they frequently seem to recite the obvious. These clauses may appear generic and superficially identical to similar clauses in other contracts one has looked at; sometimes the clauses are in fact identical to those in other contracts, and sometimes they are only similar. Thus, a superficial reading, even by those experienced in contract law, can result in an erroneous interpretation. Boilerplate provisions are actually substantive portions of a contract which deserve close attention to their details since they may incur hidden liability. Experienced attorneys will read, and then reread, contracts both word-by-word and sentence-by-sentence to find the inherent meaning and the inherent risks within each covenant.

During contract negotiations, words or clauses may be altered to incorporate the needs of a party, usually the offeree. Versions of a contract sometimes include additional details or omit some details previously present. During negotiations, each contract should be compared side-by-side to all prior versions to assure that important details have not been altered, added, or omitted. Tracking functions in word-processing programs are helpful, but there is no substitute for a careful legal review.

Not only must the language within the contract but also the legal and regulatory contexts be considered in contract drafting, interpretation, and enforcement. Where certain statutes exists and are legally in force at the time a contract is formed, the contract is deemed to incorporate such statutes, even if the law is later changed. Legally imposed rules in contracts include mandatory rules and default rules. A mandatory rule involves legally binding rules which apply regardless of the wording of the contract; such rules include legally defined defenses to contract formation or statutorily mandated provisions such as minimum wage, good faith, public policy, civil rights provisions, or medical leave provisions. A default rule becomes operative unless the contract explicitly states otherwise, such as implied warranties or rules governing the calculation of damages for breach of contract.

The Elements of a Contract

To be valid, a contract must generally contain all of the following elements: (a) offer; (b) consideration; and (c) acceptance; in addition, there must be no valid defenses to contract formation. One of the threshold issues in contract litigation is often the question of whether a valid and enforceable (prima facie) contract actually was formed. In order to litigate or challenge the existence of the contract, one party must provide evidence that one or more elements required for contract formation was not met. Litigation regarding contracts must commence within the applicable statute of limitations, as defined by state law.

An offer is an expression, by an offeror, of a willingness to enter into a contract on specified terms. In a contract, at least one of the parties must promise either to perform, or refrain from performing, some specified action in the future. Offers must be specific and communicate its terms with sufficient definiteness and certainty to form the basis for a contract. Offers must be firm, not ambiguous, or vague.

Consideration does not pertain to a process of deliberation or reflection per se, although a careful weighing of the implications of the contract is important and better discussed as a "meeting of minds" under "acceptance" or as potential defenses to contract formation. Rather, the legal definition of "consideration" as it pertains to contracts refers to something of value promised in exchange for the specified action or non-action. Consideration is the thing of value which induces parties to enter into a contract. Consideration can take the form of money or effort, a promise to perform some service, an agreement not to do something, or reliance on another's promise. The existence of consideration distinguishes a contract from a gift. There is also no consideration where one performs a voluntary act or completes a pre-existing obligation.

Acceptance by the offeree refers to an absolute unconditional agreement to each and every term contained within the offer. Acceptance of an offer presupposes a "meeting of the minds" between the parties so that each party understands what is being offered and what is being accepted. The "meeting of minds" is sometimes referred to as a "mutuality" of agreement, wherein the parties affirm, through acceptance, that they understood and agreed to the basic substance and terms of the contract. The acceptance must be unambiguous, affirmative, and communicated to the offeror within the parameters outlined by the offeror; such parameters include the form of the response and the time limits required for the response. Acceptance may be expressed through words, deeds, or performance. The acceptance of various forms and levels of risk is one of the most important analyses which will determine the progress of negotiations and whether a final contract will ever be agreed upon.

The "mailbox rule" is a default rule of law that establishes precisely when an acceptance affects a legal change in status. A mailed acceptance is deemed to be effective at the time that it is relinquished from the offeree's possession, even without regard to whether it ever reaches the offeror. The rule, however, is only operational as long as the offer does not stipulate or provide otherwise; the offeror can stipulate, for example, that an acceptance shall be effective only upon receipt; and the offeror can also stipulate that alternate modes of delivery, such as email or fax, are valid methods of acceptance.

Defenses to Contract Formation

A well-written and duly executed contract that otherwise meets all the requisite elements for a contract may still be deemed unenforceable by the courts if a party raises and can prove one or more of the six defenses to contract formation. The defenses to contract formation are (1) incapacity (a promisor lacks mental capacity); (2) operation of the statute of frauds; (3) illegality; (4) mutual mistake; (5)

duress; and (6) unconscionability. Where a valid defense is raised, a court deems the contract unenforceable or may declare the contract canceled, revoked, or voided. If a defense is raised, the contract is potentially voidable, but not automatically void. A voided contract effectively declares a contract to have never been formed.

Capacity to contract can be affected by age, mental illness, intoxication, and intellectual challenge. In order for a person to enter into a contract, it must be shown that the contractor has the ability to understand not only the nature and quality of the transaction [7] but also its significance and consequences. The importance of the capacity requirement rests in the obligation of legal system to protect those who would potentially be unfairly taken advantage of. Minors who enter into contracts form voidable contracts [8]; contracts are voidable if the minor disaffirms, or requests, the contract voided. However, minors who contract for necessities, such as general goods or services necessary for subsistence, healthcare, basic comfort, or education, may be legally deemed to have a limited circumstantial capacity to contract.

The "statute of frauds" is a general rule of law, which may vary by state or jurisdiction, which requires that some types of contracts be written (and not based in oral or verbal agreement alone) and that the contract be signed by all parties to an agreement. The statute of frauds requires that the agreement must (a) be in written form; (b) reasonably identify the subject matter of the contact; (c) provide the essential terms of the agreement (such as term, quantity, or price); and (d) bear the signature of both parties. The statute of frauds is operable primarily in contracts (i) of marriage and prenuptial agreements, (ii) which cannot be performed within 1 year, (iii) for the transfer of an interest in land, (iv) by the executor of a will to pay a debt of the estate with his own money, (v) for the sale of goods totaling $500.00 or more, and (vi) where one becomes a guarantor for another's debt or other obligation.

Contracts are only enforceable when they are legal; contracts for matters that are illegal are not enforceable. For example, a contract for the sale of illegal goods is not a valid contract; a contract for the performance of an act that is illegal (a crime) will not be enforced by the courts. In some instances, the subject matter of a contract may not be illegal per se; however, its performance as specified may be detrimental to public interest, welfare, or safety [9]. In the case of matters contrary to public interests, courts may dtermine that a contract is contrary to public policy and deem such contracts to be either void or voidable [10].

Duress occurs when an individual is threatened or coerced into signing the contract and therefore his bargain is not made willingly. Freedom to contract includes the freedom to not contract. The unconscionability defense may be upheld where a court finds that the substantive terms of a contract are unfair, one sided, or oppressive through a gross inequality of bargaining power.

Preliminary Negotiations

Preliminary negotiations can pose significant risk to parties in the law of contracts. Potential offerors must be careful to avoid terminology presented in such clear and definite terms so as to create the power of acceptance in the potential offeree. On the other hand, potential offerees must be careful so as to not misinterpret a preliminary negotiation as an offer (or conversely, to overlook an actual offer within a perceived letter of intent).

One common example of preliminary negotiation is the "letter of intent" (also referred to as an "intent to negotiate" or a "memorandum of understanding" or "memorandum of agreement"); other important examples include invitations to deal, estimates, oral agreement on terms to be reduced to writing, and agreements with one or more terms left open.

Letters of intent are generally used to signal parties' agreement to the basic elements of ongoing discussions and negotiations with the intention of later coming to an agreement to contract. Letters of intent are even sometimes accompanied by a confidentiality agreement. In furtherance of commercial transactions, letters of intent serve important business purposes: (1) a commitment to commence more serious negotiations to complete a business transaction; (2) a commitment to a timeline of negotiations which may include an opportunity or deadline within which a deal must be closed; (3) an understanding that parties will incur effort and costs associated with due diligence such as consultation with an accountant, consultant, and/or attorney; (4) to estimate the opportunities, expenses, and risks associated with the future potential contract; and (5) to design, negotiate, or determine the optimal formal terms and conditions which would facilitate mutual acceptance [11].

Confidentiality agreements do not preclude legal counsel, unless for some reason it is specifically prohibited. Legal representation during all phases of contract negotiation is not only prudent but is generally expected. Disclosure that an attorney has been retained to review a contract should not be seen as adversarial; rather, it should be perceived by both sides as prudent practice. Attorney-client privilege is generally deemed to attach to the contract review, the contents of the contract, and negotiations or correspondence involved in the contracting process. The holder of the privilege is the client.

Some letters of intent emphatically state that that they are not formal agreements, some do not. Legal issues arise when letters of intent are misconstrued to represent offers to contract or are not recognized to be actual offers. Enforceability is only an issue when one party insists it didn't intend to be bound. Depending on the situation, the presentation, the terms, and the stipulations, some letters of intent may actually represent enforceable contracts whereas some may not. Parties may rely on letters of intent and incur financial liabilities or hardship in situations where there was not contract; the issue will then center on whether or not such reliance was in fact justified. For example, a provider responds to an advertisement and is interested in the job, and after an interview, he or she receives a letter of intent and perceives it to be a contract; soon thereafter he or she arranges to relocate believing that he or she has been hired, enters into a lease or buys a home, and then learns that the letter of intent represented not a final contract but only an invitation to negotiate which later fails to materialize.

In the event that a letter of intent is deemed to be a binding contract by a court, then the parties are faced with the difficult situation of a contract which contains general terms but lacks specific terms; the parties are then left to work out the details in an already contentious relationship. The timely involvement of legal counsel can potentially help avoid problems with letters of intent.

A General Overview of Contract Clauses

General Contract Clauses

A contract may be entitled either a "contract" or an "agreement," but if it meets the legal form and content requirements, as outlined above, it is likely a contract. The parties to a contract are referred to by name and often by address; the names and addresses as they were at the time of signing should be verified correct. Where there are multiple named parties, one should verify the nature of the promises, and therefore the obligations, owed to each named party.

There is usually a "contract date" which is contained within the opening sentences of a contract, although this date is not legally required to be within a contract. In general, the contract date should reflect the date that the last party signed the contract; however, the contract date in the first paragraph may not be reliable since it may predate further negotiations and subsequent alterations.

Employee or Independent Contractor

The contract should clearly identify the status of the parties; in general, the distinction will be whether the relationship is that of "employee" or "independent contractor" either status confers potential risks and benefits, but the relationship should be clear at the time of contracting. Furthermore, it is important that the nature of the relationship adheres to the nomenclature used; a party identified as an employee but treated as an independent contractor will likely be treated as an independent contractor under the law. Thus, written language within the contract stating the worker is an "independent contractor" is not in itself determinative. The cost of employing an independent contract contractor is lower since expenses such as overtime and minimum wage payments; benefits such as health insurance premiums, retirement benefits, vacation, holiday, and sick pay; workers' compensation insurance; and employer's shares for social security (FICA) and Medicare taxes and for Federal and state unemployment compensation taxes (FUTA and SUTA) can potentially be eliminated. The penalties for misclassification of workers can be severe [12] and attach primarily to the employer, although the employee can be liable for unpaid taxes [13]. Independent contractors generally assume expenses and liabilities which would ordinarily be the responsibility of the employer.

In a very general sense, an independent contractor is self-employed and contracts to provide services. The IRS uses a number of general and specific criteria to distinguish between employees and independent contractors and uses a variety of tests such as the common law 20-factor test or the IRS 3-factor test. In general, the nature of the employment relationship will hinge upon issues such as (a) behavioral control, relating to the degree of control that the employer has on the way the work is done; (b) financial control, relating to pay and reimbursement for expenses; and (c) relationship control, as based within the entire relationship context.

The issue of employee versus independent contractor frequently arises in locums, medical director relationships, or part-time employment.

The Contract Term and Termination Clauses

The term in the contract is usually defined; there are associated dates. The contract is binding as of the date that it is executed ("date of execution"). The date of contract execution appears next to, underneath, or otherwise in proximity to a signature and should always reflect the date on which that party signed the document. The signors to a contract may not all sign on the same date; the date of execution reflects the date on which the last signor signed the contract.

The "effective date" of the contract is the future date at which the relationship will start. In general, the effective date is the day on which obligations and liabilities related to the employment will begin. The effective date is a date upon which the parties have promised each other to begin a legal relationship, even if that date is in the future. However, once a contract is signed, the parties can be expected to reasonably rely on expectation that obligations and liabilities will actually begin as of the effective date. If a party fails to begin its performance as of the effective date, that party will be in breach.

In some circumstances, a contract may be written to enforce backdated rights relating back to a relationship that pre-existed the writing or execution of a contract. The backdated contract can require the parties to behave as if the contract had been in force since the earlier effective date. The practice of backdating should be reserved for rare circumstances, for example, situations in which the parties had already behaved as though the contract had been in existence; there is mutual agreement regarding ongoing fulfillment of all the existing contractual terms. In effect, a backdated contract should generally be reserved for situations where an oral contract was made, the lawful performance under the contract had begun for both parties, and the written document was being prepared to memorialize the contract terms. A contract should never be backdated in order to avoid taxes or other obligations.

The term of a contract defines how long the contract, as written, is intended to remain in force. Since courts mostly do not honor perpetual contracts, all contracts indicate the duration, or term, of the contract. The term of a contract of employment is usually for 1, 2, or 3 years at the onset, with one various possible provisions for renewal or renegotiation.

Contracts often renew through an "evergreen clause" which, in general, will state that the contract or agreement "shall renew automatically for successive terms of one (1) year, unless either party provides written notice to the other of its intent to not renew or terminate the agreement not less than thirty (30) days before the end of the existing term." Evergreen terms must be careful to stipulate another fixed term of renewal in order to avoid being construed as a perpetual contract. Evergreen clauses provide a sense of security to the employee or contractor; and since contract renegotiation can be time-consuming and costly, especially where the number of employees is large, automatic renewal can be cost-effective. On the other hand, new hires, especially providers, are relatively unknown with respect to potential ability and performance. Providers may be in a better negotiating position after they have built a track record and reputation; therefore, in some instances, contract renegotiation can be highly beneficial to the provider.

Termination clauses allow parties to terminate a contract. There are two types of termination clauses in contracts: (1) "for cause" and (2) "without cause" or "not-for-cause." "For cause" termination occurs in the event that one party cannot fulfill its obligations under the contract. Examples of "for cause" termination in provider contracts may include loss of license or other mandatory credentials but may also include more vaguely worded transgressions such as "attitude," "unprofessional behavior," or "activities in adverse interest to the employer." Where possible, vague transgressions should be clearly defined or removed from a contract. Violations for which a contract may be terminated "for cause" are often accompanied by "cure" provisions where a transgression can be corrected or "cured" within a period of time to avoid termination. A "cure provision" requires one party to provide the other with written notice of any deficiency or potential breach and delineates a period of time (usually 10–30 days) to remedy the breach and ensure continuity of the relationship.

Termination "without cause" clauses generally allow either the employer or the employee to terminate the contract for no reason at all, without penalty, if timely noticed. Contracts will generally provide for a "without cause" termination of the contract by either party as long as that party provides the other with a 30-day, 60-day, or 90-day notice, delivered in accordance with the rules specified within the contract. The "without cause" provision allows either party to exit an undesirable relationship. On the other hand, a "without cause" termination provision will effectively transform a contract into a 30-day, 60-day, or 90-day contract, *regardless* of the stated "term" of the contract as discussed above. Termination without cause is especially dangerous because it means that the contract can be terminated by either party on a whim, without recourse.

Noncompete Agreements

Few provisions within provider contracts are as commonly overlooked, or as often enforced, as are postemployment "restrictive covenants" or "covenants not-to-compete." In general, these clauses should be viewed as enforceable and binding in almost every jurisdiction. Noncompete covenant serves an important purpose for hospitals and group practices by disincentivizing or prohibiting newly hired providers from locally establishing themselves at the practice's expense and then leaving the practice and establishing a competing practice.

An example of a restrictive covenant would read: "should the Agreement be terminated between employer and employee, the employee will not work within a twenty-five (25) air miles of any of the employer's offices for a period of two (2) years following the termination date of the employment." The area represented by the noncompete clause is sometimes referred to as a "restricted area." In such a case, especially if the employer has multiple offices in various locations within the community, the geographic area involved in the restrictive covenant may encompass the entire city or even county. The scope of some restrictive covenant applies not only to the practice of the employees specialty or profession but may also include teaching, administrative activity, or consulting activities, for example.

Some restrictive covenants or noncompetition clauses may also apply during the period of employment. Such clauses prohibit moonlighting at other institutions in furtherance of organizational loyalty. An example of such a clause might read as "employee shall devote his or her entire and exclusive professional time and efforts to the organization and shall not engage in any outside activities ...." For professionals, external activities may be important for both personal and group reputation and may be compensated through bonuses and/or honoraria. The employment agreement should specify whether or not such activities are permitted, if so what types of activities are permitted, and specify how such income is to be treated (as compensation paid directly to the individual or more treated as group income). Similarly, how discoveries, publications, or patents are treated should be also be addressed in contracts since if a professional does develop an idea of value while employed, the issues of future ownership claims for patents or royalties are likely to be contentious if not addressed in advance.

Although, depending on specific circumstances, some exceptions and defenses have been successfully used to defeat or prevent the enforcement of a restrictive covenant, such litigation is costly and often occurs while the provider is restricted from practicing through temporary injunction. In some situations, the contract will define "liquidated damages" which actually represents the price demanded by the practice for a practitioner's violation of the covenant. Although it is the practice's best interest to make the covenant as broad and restrictive as possible, practitioners would be better off if the covenant is removed or reduced to the extent possible. In addition, providers should negotiate so that restrictive covenants are only unilateral; thus, the covenant would apply only if the provider terminates the contract and, more importantly, does not apply if the employer terminates the contract.

Indemnification Clauses

Indemnification is a contractual term of art which prospectively allocates liability or financial compensation in the event of an act or omission. Indemnification is also referred to as a "hold harmless" clause. Indemnification is a clear example of how contracts can be used to shift risk and liability. To be held "harmless" means to be freed from potential blame or liability. When coupled with an agreement to defend, the indemnifier is agreeing to pay the other party's legal expenses as it defends a claim made by a third party.

Indemnification provisions are generally heavily negotiated and also frequently litigated contract clauses. Indemnification can be unilateral, in which case one party indemnified the other, or bilateral where both parties mutually indemnify each other. Unilateral indemnification provisions oblige one party to indemnify the other without reciprocation. Equally mutual or bilateral indemnification provisions oblige each party indemnifies the other to an equal extent. Unequally mutual or bilateral indemnification provisions oblige each party to indemnify the other; however, in this case the scope or substance of the indemnification obligations will be different. The concept of contractual indemnification can be intuitively difficult, and therefore indemnification clauses are often poorly constructed and do not reflect the actual intentions of the parties at the time of contract formation.

An example of a bilateral indemnification clause could read: "Each party agrees to indemnify, defend, and hold harmless the other party from and against any loss, cost, or damage of any kind (including reasonable attorneys' fees) as arising out of its breach of this Agreement and/or its negligence or willful misconduct."

An example of a unilateral indemnification clause might read: "Party A agrees to defend, indemnify, and hold harmless Party B from and against any loss, cost, or damage of any kind (including reasonable attorneys' fees) as arising out of its breach of this Agreement and/or its negligence or willful misconduct."

In a healthcare contract, the contractual risk stems from the fact that in the ordinary course of clinical activities, such indemnification clauses can result in one-way indemnification whereby providers agree to protect their employers, groups, or their hospitals from joint liability claims. For example, if a patient files a medical malpractice case against the physician, wherein the plaintiff alleges vicarious liability against the hospital, and the physician has agreed to indemnify the hospital, he or she can be liable for the hospital's attorney fees, court costs, and even and settlement or verdict entered against the hospital. Clauses may sometimes set limits on the costs of defense for indemnification claims.

Form providers, an additional area of risk, stems from a lack of coverage for indemnification agreements within professional liability or malpractice insurance policies; thus, fully allocating risk for joint liability onto a provider.

Optimally, when agreeing to indemnify, the extent of indemnification should be narrowly limited to one's own mistakes or misconduct. Wording is extremely important here such that the term "to the extent arising out of" better limits liability than the slightly differently worded term "in any way arising out of or related to." Similarly, the wording of an agreement to defend is important since agreeing to defend "all reasonable claims" is narrower and may limit liability to a greater extent than an agreement to defend against "all claims." Another issue is the limitation of the duration of effect of the indemnification clause; the duration may be limited to the term of the contract, the applicable statute of limitations, or other reasonable term depending on circumstances.

Non-solicitation or Noninterference Covenants

Non-solicitation covenants prohibit employees from soliciting clients or employees of the employer during a specified period of time. Non-solicitation clauses are often cross-referenced with clauses addressing intellectual property.

A sample non-solicitation clause may read: "During the Term of this Agreement and for a period of two (2) years thereafter, the employee will not, directly or indirectly, in any capacity, or permit any other person to do so on the employee's behalf, (i) solicit or attempt to solicit any person who has been or is a client of Employer or its Affiliates; (ii) solicit, hire, or attempt to solicit or hire, any employee of Employer or its Affiliates; (iii) copy or take patient files or address lists; or (iv) interfere with or attempt to disrupt the relationship, contractual or otherwise of Employer or its Affiliates with any client employee, independent contractor, or third party."

Non-solicitation provisions usually apply for the same duration of time as do restrictive covenants and may also be accompanied by liquidated damages clauses. Furthermore, in addition to triggering a breach of contract, violation of non-solicitation clauses may also trigger causes of action under "tortious interference with contract."

Entire Agreement Clauses and the Parol Evidence Rule

"Entire agreement" (or "merger") clauses are used to put both parties on notice that the content of contemporaneous or prior, oral or written, inducements, discussions, negotiations, or correspondence in any form are formally deemed not part of the final agreement unless specifically included within the final draft. "Entire agreement" clauses have the effect of excluding or limiting liabilities, subject of course to liabilities which are not specifically referred to but nonetheless imposed under law [see above].

An example of an "entire agreement" clause might read as: "This Agreement contains the entire agreement and understanding among the parties hereto with respect to the subject matter hereof and supersedes all prior and contemporaneous agreements, understandings, inducements, and conditions, express or implied, oral or written, of any nature whatsoever with respect to the subject matter hereof."

The entire agreement clause is related to the "parol evidence rule." The "parol evidence rule" prevents the introduction of evidence of prior or contemporaneous negotiations and agreements that contradict, modify, or vary the contractual terms of a written contract when the written contract is intended to be a complete and final expression of the parties' agreement. In principle, only the provisions "within the four corners of the contract" apply. Courts look at the "four corners of the contract" to determine what is within and what is not within the contract when examining a potential claim for breach. The "entire agreement" clause in the contract explicitly applies the "parol evidence rule" to the agreement. Any prior tentative agreements resulting from preliminary negotiations are considered to be subsumed within the provisions of the final duly executed contract through the "integration doctrine" which reinforces that the signed contract is the true final and complete expression of the parties' understanding of their risks, benefits, and liabilities. The intent of an "entire agreement" clause is to explicitly prevent prior negotiations or preliminary agreements from construed as contract terms. However, poorly drafted clauses can also potentially negate all other simultaneous active agreements between the parties.

Alternative Dispute Resolution Provisions

Alternative dispute resolution (ADR) allows parties to predetermine the format through which parties resolve disputes arising from a contract. ADR generally takes one of two forms: (a) arbitration or (b) mediation. ADR clauses generally contractually address disputes "arising under or related to" the contract. Contract clauses which prescribe mandatory ADR also thereby preclude litigation of a contract dispute through the court system or waive a party's right to bring suit in court. The importance of recognizing the ADR clause in a contract is to ensure that one does not unknowingly waive a right.

Contract litigation through the court system is costly and will involve all the elements of a traditional civil lawsuit including discovery such as the taking of depositions and document requests, witness subpoenas, motion practice, and trial, with possible appeals. However, the costs of ADR are not inconsequential. Where an employee must litigate a contract dispute with a larger group or institution, the individual is usually disadvantaged because of the time and costs associated with the litigation process.

Mediation is a form of nonbinding dispute resolution involving a neutral third party who tries to help the disputing parties reach a mutually agreeable solution. During mediation, a mediator, usually a judge or attorney, facilitates discussion and dialogue between the parties in hopes of achieving an outcome that both parties will agree upon. Then, if the parties still cannot resolve their differences after mediation, the option to proceed with either arbitration or litigation remains an option.

Arbitration, on the other hand, is a form of dispute resolution involving one or more neutral third parties, known as arbitrators, who are usually agreed to by the disputing parties, hear evidence presented by both sides, and then makes a decision. Arbitration may be either nonbinding (so that in a manner similar to mediation, the option for litigation remains open) or binding (where the arbitrator's decision is considered final and courts will enforce the judgment). The form of arbitration should be specified beforehand within the contract clause. In general, where an arbitration clause is agreed upon, binding arbitration may be more common.

Potentially Missing Clauses

A key clause commonly omitted from provider contracts are the expectations or conditions for a path to promotion, partnership, or shareholder status. Such discussions sometimes occur orally during the contract negotiation period; however, in order to minimize the risk of liability, employers may be reluctant to elaborate such opportunities within the written contract. A promise of "partner" or "shareholder" status after the passage of a period of time will not be enforceable unless all of the requisite terms and requirements are specified, and demonstrated to be met, in order to have the promise enforced. Contracts implying or promising equity status should define the circumstances under which one may be considered for or automatically offered partnership; the timing and methods for calculating a proposed stock purchase, and the period over which the stock purchase price is expected in payment.

Although the actual terms of ownership or buy-in will be stipulated separately in "buy-sell" and/or "partnership" agreements, which are unlikely to be disclosed or not signed until the opportunity for partnership or ownership arises, the options and potential assurances, at least as contingencies for later consideration, should be both discussed during the employment negotiations which are detailed within the written employment contract. Ownership may also entail risks, such as enhanced liability exposure. There are additional elements of due diligence that should be explored, even if these elements are not included within the written contract. An attorney should be able to help advise how best to evaluate potential risks and opportunities for personal and corporate growth inherent within a company.

Arguably, however, if a promise of promotion or shareholder status is made, and later such a promise requires judicial intervention to enforce it, the future relationship that needs to be predicated on litigation may not be a satisfying one.

Sign on bonuses should be negotiated. In addition, relocation assistance, reimbursement to travel in order to find a new home, should be explored. The type of professional liability insurance which may be obtained and paid for should be clear at the onset to minimize the risk of future liability in the event that the contract expires or is terminated (see Chap. 10).

Contract Assignability

In recent years, healthcare entities have seen an unprecedented increase in merger and acquisition (M&A) activity. Healthcare entities are consolidating market share primarily to maintain a competitive advantage in regional markets. However, M&A activity is also occurring within hospital systems where private groups are being acquired by, or are merging with, other groups within, or outside of, a system, or being acquired by hospitals or systems. Smaller subspecialty groups such as cardiologists, pulmonologists, or anesthesiologists are most likely to be affected by such

M&A activity. By default, and unless prescribed or limited by agreement, contractual rights are, in general, freely assignable or delegable.

An assignment clause may read: "No party may assign either this Agreement or any of its rights, interests, or obligations hereunder without the prior written approval of the other parties." In such a case, neither party may assign the contract without the consent of the other. Of course, in personal service contracts typical of employment agreements, the employed person is hired for his or her special skills, and therefore employees are intuitively not in a position to assign the contract.

Assignability is more likely to apply to the contractor in the event of a future, yet unforeseen, acquisition, consolidation, or merger. If the ownership structure of the employer were to change significantly in the case of M&A, and the contract is assignable by the contractor, the contractual obligations of the contractee may continue unchanged, assuming that newly formed entity continues to have a need for the contracted for services and is willing to continue the relationship without renegotiating the terms of the contract. On the other hand, if the contract is "non-assignable," the contractee's relationship is terminated by operation of contract.

Anti-kickback Statute and "Stark" Law Compliance

Healthcare industry requires careful review with attention to regulatory risk areas such as anti-kickback laws, physician self-referral (Stark) law, and antitrust laws. A detailed discussion of these laws is beyond the scope of this chapter (see Chap. 4); however, providers entering into arrangements such as medical director positions or consulting relationships with industry should review the proposed contract carefully for potential risks under applicable federal and state statutes.

Breach of Contract

Breach of contract represents failure, without justification, to perform any promise that forms all or part of the contract. Breaches of contract may take several forms: (1) an "actual breach" where one party explicitly refuses to comply with the terms of the contract and (2) an "anticipatory breach" where one party voices an intention, or acts in such a way as to suggest a plan to not comply with the terms of the contract. In addition, breaches may be "minor" and reasonably amenable to a "cure" or they may be "material" and so egregious as to render the foundations of "good faith in dealing" to be suspect.

Courts will look at the elements of the contract, the promises made, and the promises putatively broken. Courts will then look to see if potential defenses to a claim breach of contract apply. If a contract is deemed to be in breach, and there are no valid defenses, then the issue becomes one of allocation and assessment of damages.

- The elements necessary for a prima facie case of breach of contract are:
- Valid contract formation
- Performance or lack of duty to perform by one party
- The other party's failure to perform
- Harm that resulted in quantifiable loss

Remedies for breach of contract include (a) award of damages, (b) specific performance, (c) rescission, and (d) restitution. The usual remedy in civil courts is an award of damages. Specific performance, rescission, and restitution are equitable remedies that are less commonly employed in the circumstances of corporate or business practice.

Interpretation of Contracts by the Courts

The meaning of a contract is, in general, determined by examining the intentions of the parties at the time of the contract's creation. The process by which an analysis of a claim for breach of contract proceeds includes the following line of reasoning:

1. Is there a valid contract?
2. If so, what did the contract require of each of the parties?
3. Was the contract modified at any point?
4. Did the claimed breach of contract occur?
5. If so, was the breach material to the contract?
6. Does the breaching party have a legal defense to enforcement of the contract?
7. What damages were caused by the breach?

Potential Valid Defenses Against a Breach of Contract Claim

There are many potential affirmative defenses by which to argue a breach of contract claim. For example:

Enforcement of the contract would violate public policy.

Performance of the contract has become impossible or the purpose of the contract has become frustrated.

The contract limits the amount of damages that can be recovered.

There are valid defenses to contract formation, such as lack or capacity (contract is voidable or void), or faulty formation, such as lack of consideration (no contract exists).

However, an important clause is increasingly appearing within contracts, especially following the Coronavirus Pandemic of 2020. "Force majeure" is a contract clause which functions as an affirmative defense, to excuse one or both parties' performance obligations in situations or circumstances which arise unexpectedly and which are beyond the parties' control and make performance of the contract impractical or impossible [14]. In some states, such as New York, the clause must list the specific event claimed to be preventing performance [15]. "Force majeure" events that may be enumerated within a contract will include:

1. Acts of God, such as natural catastrophes including floods, fires, earthquakes, hurricanes, epidemics, or explosions
2. Social or societal events such as acts of war or terrorism
3. Governmental or regulatory changes such as expropriation, condemnation, and changes in laws and regulations, strikes, and labor disputes

Damages

Liquidated damages are specified within the contract. For example, liquidated damages are commonly specified in the event of breach of a restrictive covenant. In such cases, a party desiring to breach the covenant can reasonably estimate, in advance, the cost of doing so. Here, the clauses in the contract could specify the compensation owed. Liquidated damages are helpful to avoid litigation on a specific contract breach, since, if liquidated damages not specified, resolution through a process of ADR or litigation in court will provide an award amount in the event of breach. Nonetheless, if the amount specified in a liquidated damages clause is unreasonable or excessive, it may be later contested. Liquidated damages clauses are usually accompanied by a clause which stipulates in clear language that the amount is deemed reasonable to both parties at the time of contract formation.

An "injunctive relief" clause may also accompany the liquidated damages or any other clause within a contract. For example, even if a party would agree to pay liquidated damages to violate a restrictive covenant, he or she may still be barred from doing so if there is an injunctive relief agreement. Injunctive relief clause specifically prohibits one or both parties from acting in a certain way.

Furthermore, there are two general categories of damages that may be awarded to compensate an aggrieved party in a breach of contract claim: (a) compensatory damages and (b) special damages.

Compensatory damages (also called "actual damages") are intended to compensate the non-breaching party for their losses arising from the other party's breach. Within the realm of "compensatory damages" are two types of potential awards: (1) general damages which compensate for losses directly related to the subject matter of the contract such as loss of revenue and (2) specific damages which compensate for indirect losses such as reputation. For example, if a healthcare provider fails to report for work, there may be damages related to the hiring of a locums replacement, closure of an office or service line, furloughs of support employees, and inability to make good on promises of services advertised to the community.

Punitive damages (also called "exemplary damages") may be awarded to in the event that a breach of contract involves an actor whose conduct is willful, malicious, or fraudulent. Punitive damages, if awarded, would be in addition to compensatory damages. Punitive damages are rarely awarded for breach of contract.

Summary

In summary, a healthcare contract is one of the most important financial commitments that providers, groups, or institutions will make. Legal counsel is vital to minimize misunderstandings and liability. The right to contract is an important freedom. However, the time to scrutinize the terms of a contract is before the contract is signed (Table 25.2).

Table 25.2 Contract pearls for providers

Avoid the temptations of "reading up" on contracts, comparing new contracts to those from a prior transaction, or getting "legal advice" from lay friends or peers. Each contract and its attendant fact patterns are different
Legal representation during contract negotiations is a right and is expected
Retain legal counsel early, in the negotiations phase, before a contract is offered if possible
There is no "standard" contract or agreement; all contracts are modifiable
Every element in a contract is negotiable; the ability to negotiate depends on the bargaining position and the skill of the negotiator
Ascertain that the final contract you are presented with includes all prior promises (i.e., verbal, email), concessions from preliminary negotiations
Verify that all attachments such as exhibits, addenda, or schedules are specifically referred to in the contract ("incorporation by reference")
Be sure that any absolute contingencies required of you at the time of signing have been met
Check that each blank in the contract has been completed, cross out blank pages
Obtain and review copies of each and document referred to in the Agreement; these are "incorporated by reference" and deemed legally to be a part of the final agreement. Examples of such documents may include benefit plans, staff bylaws, policies and procedures, employee handbook, code of conduct, policies regarding discrimination and harassment, loan repayment schedules, visa sponsorship promises, and compliance agreements. Retain copies of all contract-related documents
Be prepared to comply with each and every provision of the contract. Assume that breaches will be litigated and that the cost of litigation will be expensive; therefore, individuals will be at a disadvantage if contract litigation becomes necessary

References

1. Rowley KA. Contract Construction and Interpretation: From the “Four Corners” to Parol Evidence (and everything in Between), 69 Miss. L.J. 73 (1999).
2. Hoag v. Chancellor, Inc., 246 A.D.2d 224, 677 N.Y.S.2d 531; See also Boody v. Giambra, 192 Misc.2d 128, 744 N.Y.S.2d 803).
3. In re Motors Liquidation Co.460 B.R. 603 Bkrtcy.S.D.N.Y., November 28, 2011. See also Cordis Corp. v. Boston Scientific Corp. 868 F.Supp.2d 342, 2012 WL 2320799 D.Del.,2012, June 19, 2012 (The primary consideration in interpreting a contract is to “attempt to fulfill, to the extent possible, the reasonable shared expectations of the parties at the time they contracted.”).
4. Alta Berkeley VI C.V. v. Omneon, Inc. 41 A.3d 381 Del.Supr., 2012,
5. Chesapeake Energy Corp. v. Bank of New York Mellon Trust Co., N.A. 957 F.Supp.2d 316 S.D.N.Y., 2013.
6. Samba Enters., LLC v. iMesh, Inc., No. 06 Civ. 7660 (DLC), 2009 U.S. Dist. LEXIS 23393, 2009 WL 705537, at *5 (S.D.N.Y.Mar. 19, 2009).
7. J.I.Case Threshing Machine Co. v. Myers, 111 N.W. 602, (Neb. 1907).(“the nature and quality of the act to be performed, or its consequences.”).
8. Restatement (Second) of Contracts § 14 (1981).
9. McGrath v. SNH Dev., Inc., 158 N.H. 540, 543 (N.H. 2009).
10. 17A Am. Jur. 2d Contracts §§ 217, 231.
11. Szalados JE. Employment Contracts 101. Law and Ethics in Neurocritical Care. 102–103.
12. Misclassification of Employees as Independent Contractors. Wage and Hour Division. U.S. Department of Labor. Available online at: https://www.dol.gov/agencies/whd/flsa/misclassification.
13. What’s the difference between an independent contractor and an employee? Office of Child Support Enforcement. U.S. Department of Health and Human Services. 23 Oct 2018. Available online at: https://www.acf.hhs.gov/css/resource/the-difference-between-an-independent-contractor-and-an-employee.
14. Ner Tamid Congregation of N. Town v. Krivoruchko, 638 F. Supp. 2d 913, 931 (N.D. Ill. 2009), as amended (July 9, 2009).
15. Phibro Energy, Inc. v. Empresa De Polimeros De Sines Sarl, 720 F. Supp. 312, 318 (S.D.N.Y. 1989) (citing Kel Kim Corp. v. Central Markets, Inc., 70 N.Y.2d at 902-03).

Chapter 26
Corporate and Partnership Structures Used in Healthcare Entity Formation

James E. Szalados

Considerations Regarding Choice of the Business Structure

Historically, the business structure environment of physician practices was organized either as a sole proprietorship or as a small group of physicians organized as a form of partnership. Physicians, providers, and allied healthcare professionals are frequently organized into a form of legal business entity: (1) individual providers or professionals, frequently independent contractors, (2) practices, (3) affiliates practices, (4) hospitals, and (5) healthcare systems. The key considerations which must be balanced in a decision to form a legal business entity include (1) protection against liability, (2) employer status and administrative responsibility, (3) tax structure and potential corporate benefits, (4) shared ownership, shareholder, and partnership opportunities, and (5) access to capital.

The legal definition of a "company" is a formal business entity that is organized in furtherance of a business undertaking; a company may be organized in one of many different forms. Companies are business entities. The main legal forms of organization for a professional practices are (1) sole proprietorship, (2) general partnership, (3) limited partnership, (4) C corporation (standard corporation), (5) S corporation, (6) limited liability company (LLC), and (7) limited liability partnership (LLP). In general, given the potential advantages and disadvantages of each, consultation with an attorney, tax advisor, and financial advisor is important prior to choosing or establishing a legal form. Specifically, the designation as a professional corporation or service corporation does not usually affect either the level of liability risk or taxation for providers or professionals. Nonetheless, professional service

J. E. Szalados (✉)
Director, Surgical and Neurocritical Care Units, Rochester Regional Health System at Rochester General Hospital, Rochester, NY, USA

The Szalados Law Firm, Hilton, NY, USA
e-mail: james.szalados@rochesterregional.org; jszalados@aol.com

J. E. Szalados (ed.), *The Medical-Legal Aspects of Acute Care Medicine*,
https://doi.org/10.1007/978-3-030-68570-6_26

corporations are regulated by the state with unique requirements. For example, states will usually require that all the owners of a professional service corporation be members of the same profession; for example, combinations of professionals such as physicians, lawyers, nurse practitioners, or therapists would not be eligible to jointly own a professional service corporation. Finally, the law of corporations, similar to many of the laws that govern medical providers and allied healthcare professionals, may vary by state; however, especially with respect to taxation and compliance, it may also be governed by federal statutes and regulations.

Corporations, as legal persons, have been legally accorded some of the rights of natural persons; this is a notion that is variably termed the "corporate persona" or "corporate personhood." Thus, corporations may own property, enter into contracts, assume debt, and both sue and be sued for incurred liabilities. Corporate personhood was not always the case; in the Supreme Court case of *Bank of the United States v. Deveaux*, Chief Justice Marshall stated: "[t]hat invisible, intangible, and artificial being, that mere legal entity, a corporation aggregate, is certainly not a citizen; and consequently cannot sue or be sued in the courts of the United States, unless the rights of the members, in this respect, can be exercised in their corporate name" [2]. Deveaux was overruled in the 1844, Supreme Court ruling in *Louisville, C. & C.R.R. v Letson* when, after elaborate argument, a divided Court held that "a corporation created by and doing business in a particular state, is to be deemed to all intents and purposes as a person, although an artificial person, an inhabitant of the same state, for the purposes of its incorporation, capable of being treated as a citizen of that state, as much as a natural person" [3]. The Supreme Court opinion in the case of *Santa Clara County v Southern Pacific Railroad Co.* extended the Equal Protection Clause of the 14th Amendment to corporations through the dicta of Chief Justice Morrison Waite wherein he noted that "[t]he Court does not wish to hear argument on the question whether the provision in the Fourteenth Amendment to the Constitution which forbids a state to deny to any person within its jurisdiction the equal protection of the laws applies to these corporations. We are all of opinion that it does" [4].

Courts allow incorporation in any state; the state of incorporation does not need to be the state in which the business has its principal headquarters. Nonetheless, the business entity must be registered in the state where the business is located. Foreign companies are those that are incorporated in one state and then are registered and do their primary business in another state. In the case of a foreign corporation, the corporation may be taxed separately in two states and be subject to reporting and registration fees in two states. A foreign corporation is one that is incorporated in another jurisdiction, For example, Delaware is a common choice for the state of incorporation. Where there is a conflict between the choices of law that may govern in the event of a legal disagreement, the principles of Conflict of Laws will apply. Conflict of Laws is a procedural application of defined principles which determine which of the relevant states' substantive law will govern in the resolution of a conflict.

Business Structures

The ownership of any business requires the requisite permits and licenses. A healthcare professional may be providing services under a healthcare license within another entity, either as independent contractor or as employee, where the services are offered directly to the public. In general, a license represents a legal permit to engage in business within a regulated field; thus, a license may be required of drivers, liquor store owners, allied health professionals, and providers. In general, a license implies that a licensing agency has performed some level of due diligence and determined that a licensee is competent to engage in that licensed activity. Permits represent more of a registration with a county of state that allows a level of oversight and regulation, such as building permits, construction permits, and health permits (Table 26.1).

Table 26.1 General comparison table for business entities

Entity	Individual risk	Main advantages	Main disadvantages
DBA or sole proprietorship	Owner is personally liable for the debts and obligations of the entity Requires malpractice insurance	Simple and inexpensive to create and manage Marketing Tax deductions: health insurance, business expenses Single owner	Unlimited business risk Employment taxes on all income Self-employment tax Owner must pay estimated taxes
General partnership	Joint and several unlimited (see text) Requires malpractice insurance	Two or more owners Relatively simple to operate Pass through taxation Profits and losses are attributed to individual partners Income is allocated based on partnership agreement	Unlimited business risk Employment taxes on all medical service income Dissolves if a partner leaves or dies Owners must pay estimated taxes
Limited partnership	Limited to individuals (see text) Requires malpractice insurance for all partners	Income can be allocated different from ownership Pass through taxation Limited liability for business risk for limited partners Centralized management of businesses Protects against personal liability for business claims but does not protect against malpractice claims	Registration with Secretary of State General partner of the LP has unlimited liability. Employment taxes on all medical service income Owners must pay estimated taxes

(continued)

Table 26.1 (continued)

Entity	Individual risk	Main advantages	Main disadvantages
C corporation (standard corporation)	Protects against business risks except for malpractice claims Protects personal assets from liability Requires malpractice insurance	Protects against personal liability for business claims, except for malpractice claims Exists separate from owners, with no specified end Owner gets a W-2	Registration with Secretary of State Double taxation Costs of operation and management Mandatory meetings
S corporation	Limited to individuals Requires malpractice insurance	Protects against personal liability for business claims Does not protect against malpractice claims Exists separate from owners, with no specified end Owner gets a W-2 Provides for taxation of profits and losses as partners, while providing a corporate shield against business claims	Registration with Secretary of State Income must be allocated the same as ownership More expensive to operate Must have malpractice insurance
LLC	Requires malpractice insurance Depending on the state, can consist of individuals, corporations, or other LLCs	Not taxed as a separate entity Pass through taxation LLC members protected from personal liability for business debts and claims	Registration with Secretary of State Professional service income is all subject to employment taxes Owner does not get a W-2 and must pay estimated taxes
LLP	Requires malpractice insurance	Protects against liability for acts of other partners Can provide protection against personal liability for business partner's liabilities and can be limited to the amount of the investment Pass through taxation	Owner does not get a W-2 and must pay estimated taxes

"Doing Business As" (DBA)

In general, when a natural person starts an unincorporated business, the name of the business will usually default to the name of the owner; this means that the business and the owner are treated as a single entity under the law. A DBA is the recognized acronym for "doing business as" and is a legal means that is required for businesses operating under a name other than the name of the owner or another legal business name. In essence, a DBA is a fictitious name used for the purpose of conducting business. In most jurisdictions and in most circumstances, the DBA should not contain words such as "company," "incorporated," or other implication that it is an actual company. Thus, although laws will vary by jurisdiction, in general, a sole proprietorship may neither need nor benefit from a DBA, unless there is a specific reason to do so. Nonetheless, if the sole proprietorship operates under a name different from that of its owner, a DBA is necessary. Where a DBA opens a bank account under the DBA name, the bank will likely require a copy of the fictitious name certificate. In many cases, the DBA will be filed with the Office of the County Clerk after a filing fee is paid. The discontinuation or amendment of a DBA likely requires that the County Clerk's Office is appropriately notified. Under most circumstances, the taxation of the DBA is usually taxed as a sole proprietorship (see the below section).

The Sole Proprietorship

The sole proprietorship is the most basic and the most common business form in the USA; it is an unincorporated business that is owned and operated by one individual. Formation of a sole proprietorship requires no formal state filings and, once again, the business and the owner are treated as a single entity under the law. Where a person does work under his or her own name, that person may functionally be sole proprietorship for the purposes of business entity definition, but may, for example, receive earnings as an independent contractor for wage and taxation purposes. In a sole proprietorship, the legal and financial entities of the owner and the business are the same. The owner of a sole proprietorship is not shielded from legal or financial liability and the sole proprietorship may be liable for both income taxes (Schedule C) and also a self-employment tax (Social Security and Medicare taxes); however, the sole proprietorship is also able to deduct business expenses.

Partnerships

In general, a partnership is a legal form of business operation between two or more individuals who share management and profits. Partnerships require two or more partners. Partnerships are classified as either (1) general, (2) limited partnerships, or (3) limited liability partnerships. A fourth type of partnership, the limited liability limited partnership (LLLP), is not uniformly recognized in all states. The partnership agreement is a key element of a partnership formation since partnerships are groups of individuals subject to disagreements. In any partnership, the partnership agreement should contain at least (1) the ownership percentages, capital contributions, profit and loss allocations, and distributions; (2) the authority of the partners to bind the business; (3) management function assignments; and (4) procedures in the event of death or disability, disputes, part withdrawal, and procedures whereby new partners may be added. Disputes can undermine the effective function of a partnership and be costly. The Uniform Partnership Act (UPA) provides governance for business partnerships in approximately 37/50 US states. The UPA applies only to general liabilities and limited liability partnerships (LLPs); the UPA does not apply to limited partnerships (LPs). A partner relationship is generally created by contract; such a contract may be either express or implied. If the existence of a partnership is challenged, in order to determine the existence of a *de facto* partnership, the courts will look to the (1) intention of the parties, (2) sharing of profits and losses, (3) joint administration and control of business operation, (4) capital investment by each partner, and (5) common ownership of property. Partnership agreements are similar to corporate operating agreements. The partnership agreement should detail, for example, the process for decision-making, the grounds for removing a partner, the process for dissolution, and responsibilities of the partners. Partnerships do not pay income taxes as an entity but rather the profits "pass through" the business entity to the individual partners, generally similar to sole proprietorships, limited liability companies, and C-corps. General partnerships, limited partnerships, and limited liability partnerships file a Form 1065 with the IRS, in addition to a Schedule K for each partner which details lists that partner's share of income and expenses.

General partnerships are usually created by beginning business activities as partners, and no state filing is required. A partnership agreement and licenses and permits are required, as in any other business. In a general partnership, all members share equally in both profits and liabilities. Partners may be defined by percentages based on investment or contribution. In a general partnership, the withdrawal of one partner subjects the partnership to dissolution. The partner-owners of a general partnership are considered to be the same as the business, similar to the sole proprietorship above, and thus personal assets can therefore be considered to be business assets without a liability shield. In a general partnership, any one partner may be sued for any or all business debts (joint and several liabilities). In addition, in a general partnership, each partner has full agency powers (unless specifically restricted in the Partnership Agreement) and therefore any partner may legally bind the partnership to debts and obligations. A partnership doing business under a trade name must file a certificate of "doing business under a fictitious name" or DBA notice.

In a limited partnership (LP), there is at least one general partner and that partner has unlimited liability, whereas the other (limited) partners have limited liability. The number of limited partners may be limited by state statutory law. The general partner manages the business. Limited liability refers to the protection of personal assets from the liabilities and obligations of the partnership. The liability of limited partners is limited to the extent of their investment in the LP. An LP requires a formal written agreement between the managing general partner or partners, and all of the limited partners. Limited partners will usually join the partnership through an investment of funds into the partnership which then entitles the partner to a predetermined share of profits. Unlike the general partnership, the withdrawal of as limited partner from an LP does not incur automatic dissolution of the LP, although a "buy out" of the limited partner's assets may be necessary. Limited partnerships must file with the Secretary of State in the state where the partnership is created.

Limited liability partnerships (LLPs) can only be created by certain types of professional service businesses, and professionals will generally elect to form a limited liability partnership. In a limited liability partnership (LLP), there are no general partners. In an LLP, all partners have limited liability for business debts; the personal assets of the partners are shielded from business debts and liabilities. In the LLP, each partner's liabilities are limited to the amount of their investment. In the event that the partnership fails, creditors cannot attach to a partner's personal assets or income. However, like the PC, the LLP does not shield partners for liability for professional malpractice. LLPs are usually governed by complex partnership, or operating, agreements that provide structure for the operations and decision-making of the LLP. For example, an LLP may employ junior partners who may have the opportunity to become full partners. Partners in an LLP may withdraw or retire without dissolving the LLP; similarly the LLP may add new partners. LLPs also must file with the Secretary of State in the state where the partnership is created.

Professional Corporation

The professional corporation (PC) or professional service corporation (PSC) is a corporate entity created by state statutes, as a variation of the general corporate form, for use by specific and specified licensed professionals such as attorneys, accountants, and physicians. In most jurisdictions, licensed professionals must incorporate as a PC as a matter of law. Thus, where most businesses have the discretion to incorporate as an S-corp, C-corp, or LLC; professionals with the notable exception of businesses owned and operated by professionals to provide services within the scope of the profession, must usually incorporate as a professional corporation (PC), professional LLC (PLLC), or, professional S-corp or professional C-corp. In a PC, all the shareholders must be members of the same profession, although employees may be of different backgrounds such as nurses, managers, lawyers, or accountants. The Internal Revenue Service (IRS) rules (Sec. 269A(b)(1)) require that a PC be incorporated under state law and meet the requirements of both the function test and the ownership test. The function test requires that substantially all of the business activities of the professional corporation involve services within specific profession or occupation that defines the business. The ownership test requires that substantially all the stock of the PC be held directly or indirectly by qualified people: (1) employees who are currently performing professional services for the corporation; (2) retired employees; (3) or their heirs or estates. If a professional corporation organized under state law does not qualify as a PSC, then it is treated as a general partnership for federal tax purposes.

Moreover, in a professional corporation, the owners perform services for the business as employees. The owners of traditional corporations are generally shielded from liability, whereas the owners of professional corporations are shielded from liability with the notable exception of liability due to professional negligence. Claims are brought against themselves, despite the fact that their business is properly incorporated. Otherwise, the differences between a professional C-corp and professional S-corp are the same as the differences between traditional C-corps and S-corps, the key difference being the taxation of earnings (see below).

Limited Liability Company

The limited liability company (LLC) is neither a partnership nor a corporation; rather it is a hybrid of partnership and corporation. The ownership of an LLC is by its members, rather than by partners; however, the members are analogous to partners or shareholders. The LLC may be composed of an unlimited number of members and an LLC may have non-US residents as members. LLCs may acquire and own subsidiaries without restriction and LLCs can be owned as a subsidiary of another LLC or corporation. The LLC, as a business entity, is separate from its owners, who are generally protected from personal liability for business debts and claims. The owners of an LLC are liable only to the extent of their investment in the LLC. The LLC is also a "pass-through" entity for the purposes of income tax. Although the LLC provides a shield against liability, that liability protection may not extend to negligence, personally or individually guaranteed obligations or loans, or illegal activities. Finally, where the LLC is functionally an extension of the persona of its owner, especially in the case of a single member LLC, courts may pierce the liability shield of the LLC. LLCs are formed by registration of the LLC with the Secretary of State in the state where the LLC is established.

C-Corporation

A C-corporation (C-corp) is a corporation. C-corps are formed by registration of the LLC with the Secretary of State in the state where the corporation is established. In order to form a corporation, Articles of Incorporation must be filed which define the name of the corporation and a general description of the purpose of the organization (which may be as simple as, for example, "to engage in any lawful activity") and detail about stock or shares. Furthermore, a corporation must have bylaws which describe the procedures and operating policies of the corporation. Similar to other business entities discussed, the owners are separate from the corporation and are therefore insulated from the debts of the corporation through limited liability. C-corps offer stock to shareholders, who then become owners of the corporation. However, unlike the entities discussed above, the C-corp is taxed as an entity, subject to corporate taxation; the shareholders or owners are then also taxed separately on their earnings. Corporations are thus subject to double taxation. When a corporation achieves $10 million in assets and 500 shareholders, it is required to register with the SEC under the Securities Exchange Act of 1934. In addition, corporations are subject to additional organization and management mandates such as requirements to organize and hold meetings with a Board of Directors and to hold annual shareholder meetings. A C-corp has perpetual existence, and the corporation will continue to exist even if the founder, majority owner, director, or chief executive officer dies, leaves, or retires.

S-Corporation

An S-corporation (S-corp) is a corporation, in a sense it is a business entity structure which is a slightly smaller and simpler version of the classic C-corp. The S-corp structure offers investment and growth opportunity, liability protections, and perpetual existence. However, unlike the C-corp, the S-corp allows for pass through taxation and reduced management and tax filing requirements. During the formation of the S-corp, the founders elected to be taxed under Subchapter S of the Internal Revenue Code. The owners of an S-corp may opt to receive both a salary and stock-based dividend payments from the corporation. Unlike C-corps, an S-corp may have only one class of stock and there are strict regulations with respect to qualifications for shareholder status and the number of potential shareholders. If growth or complexity justify, an S-corp can easily be converted to a C-corp, since it already organized as a corporation.

Important Issues in Corporate Law

"Pass-Through" Taxation

Pass-through taxation is an option for all business entities except C-Corps. LLCs have the option of being taxed as "pass through" or to be taxed as a C-corp. "Pass-through" taxation allows the income generated by the business to "pass through" the income of the business to the owner or owners and to the business owners' personal tax returns, avoiding double taxation in corporate income tax. Thus, with "pass-through" income, there is one single layer of income tax and has generally been taxed as ordinary income up to a maximum rate of 37%. The vast majority of businesses in the USA are "pass-through" entities.

The 2017 Tax Cuts and Jobs Act (TCJA) [5] created a new 20% deduction for certain pass-through income through 2025. With modifications in IRC Code section 199A, the "qualified business income" deduction effectively reduced the top marginal tax rate on qualifying pass-through income from the top ordinary rate of 37% to 29.6, subject to qualifying rules [6]. For example, in order to qualify, total taxable income must be $163,300 or less for single filers or $326,600 for joint filers. In addition, professionals are generally excluded from TCJA since they are deemed to be a "specified service trade or business."

The Corporate Veil

Fundamental premises of US corporate law are that (1) shareholders in a corporation are not liable for the obligations of the enterprise beyond the capital that they contributed in exchange for their shares and (2) the corporation is an entity separate from its shareholders, directors, or officers [7]. Limited liability permits parties to allocate the risk of an enterprise and the encouragement of investment in business enterprise to promote growth. The corporate veil is a legal doctrine that establishes a layer of protection between the assets of a corporation and the assets of the shareholders of the corporation with respect to potential liability for a company's debts and obligations. In certain cases, a court may choose to remove that layer of protection and impute personal liability to the owners or shareholders to satisfy an obligation; when a court does so, it is "piercing the corporate veil." On the one hand, the corporate form is a legal entity with legal "personhood," whereas instances may arise where statutory or legal goals or remedies require such judicial action. In keeping with the recognition that business entities are commonly founded specifically to limit the personal liability of its owners, there are few, if any, cases where a court pierces the corporate veil solely based on undercapitalization. Veil piercing is most common in closely held corporations where the corporation may be reasonably be construed to simply be the alter ego of a single, or limited number of owners, so as to functinally be a DBA or sole proprietorship.

States and jurisdictions will vary in the criteria used to pierce a corporate veil. For example, in Florida, courts must typically show that (1) either a corporation is simply the alter ego or mere instrumentality of the parent corporation or the shareholders or (2) realized parent company or shareholders are engaged in improper conduct. In New York, courts will hold a principal of a corporation vicariously liable under the doctor and of *respondeat superior* where the court finds that the corporation is in fact an agent of the shareholders [8]. In *Walkovsky v. Carlton*, the NY Appellate Court stated the doctrine: " That the corporate 'veil' may be swept aside and another defendant held liable only if, at the very inception of the controversy or of the act which gave rise to the liability, the corporate 'veil' had been utilized by such defendant in order to defraud the plaintiff and to insulate himself from judgment by reason of the fraud" [9].

Legal and Ethical Duties of Directors or Board Members

Directors and board members are considered to be fiduciaries of a business organization, as fiduciaries, directors, and board members must (1) act at all times in good faith so as to promote the success of the company, (2) exercise independent judgment, reasonable care, skill, and diligence, (3) act within the scope of one's duties to ensure that the organization's resources are used in a reasonably appropriate and legally accountable manner, and (4) avoid conflicts of interest. Thus, the duties of a fiduciary are generally (1) the Duty of Care, (2) the Duty of Loyalty, and (3) the Duty of Obedience. "In essence, the duty of care consists of an obligation to act on an informed basis; the duty of loyalty requires the board and its directors to maintain, in good faith, the corporation's and its shareholders' best interests over anyone else's interests" [10].

The business judgment rule is most often a consideration in lawsuits where a director or the board of directors of a corporation takes a course of action that adversely affects the corporation, and a plaintiff sues, alleging that the director violated his or her duty of care. Courts will uphold the decisions of directors as long as the decisions are made (1) in good faith, (2) with the care that a reasonably prudent person would use, and (3) with the reasonable belief that one is acting in the best interests of the corporation. The burden of proof in such a case rests with the plaintiff that the business judgment rule does not apply because of gross negligence, bad faith, or a conflict of interest. Such lawsuits may be brought against a board, director, or corporate officer, by a shareholder on behalf of a corporation as a "shareholder derivative suit."

Therefore, the business judgment rule is in fact a standard of judicial review for corporate director conduct. The business-judgment rule presumes that "in making a business decision the directors of a corporation acted on an informed basis, in good faith, and in the honest belief that the action was in the best interest of the company" [11]. The business-judgment rule is "a rule of law that insulates an officer or director of a corporation from liability for a business decision made in good faith if he is not interested in the subject of the business judgment, is informed with respect to the subject of the business judgment to the extent he reasonably believes to be appropriate under the circumstances, and rationally believes that the business judgment is in the best interests of the corporation" [12].

Conclusions

Healthcare, as a business, is largely predicated corporate and business law which prescribes a variety of legal business entities through which practitioners may organize the delivery of care. Business law intersects with all aspects of healthcare as well as tax laws; thus, business law is highly complex. Providers and practitioners seeking to organize a business entity should consult proactively with legal counsel to determine which, if any, business structure is best suited to their business goals.

References

1. Michelson D. Financial Management OR Efficiencies Margin + mission: A prescription for curing healthcare's cost crisis. Becker's Hospital CFO Report. January 6, 2016. Available online at: https://www.beckershospitalreview.com/finance/margin-mission-a-prescription-for-curing-healthcare-s-cost-crisis.html. See also: The Legacy of Sister Irene Kraus: No Margin, No Mission. Teletracking Technologies, Inc. October 18, 2018. Available online at: https://www.teletracking.com/resources/no-margin-no-mission-sister-irene-kraus.
2. Bank of the United States v. Deveaux, 9 U.S. (5Cr.) 61, 86 (1809).
3. Louisville, C. & C.R.R. v Letson, 43 U.S. (2 How.) 497, 588 (1844).
4. Santa Clara County v. Southern Pacific Railroad Company, 118 U.S. 394 (1886).

5. Tax Cuts and Jobs Act. Public Law No: 115-97. December 22, 2017.
6. Gale W, Krupkin A. Navigating the new pass-through provisions: a technical explanation. Washington, DC: Urban-Brookings Tax Policy Center; 2018.
7. MODEL BUSINESS CORP. § 6.22(b) American Bar Foundation (2003). Available online at: http://www.lexisnexis.com/documents/pdf/20080618091347_large.pdf.
8. Legal Business Institute. Piercing the Corporate Veil. Cornell Law School Available online at: https://www.law.cornell.edu/wex/piercing_the_corporate_veil#:~:text=New%20York,business%20in%20an%20individual%20capacity.
9. Walkovsky v. Carlton. 24 A.D.2d 582 (1965).
10. Shoen v. SAC Holding Corp., 137 P.3d 1171, 1178 (Nev. 2006) (citing Cede & Co. v. Technicolor, Inc., 634. A.2d 345, 360-61 (Del. 1993)).
11. In re Walt Disney Co. Derivative Litig., 906 A.2d 27, 52 (Del. 2006) (quoting Aronson v. Lewis, 473 A.2d 805, 812 (Del. 1984).
12. Am. Soc'y for Testing & Materials v. Corrpro Cos., 478 F. 3d 557, 572 (3d Cir. 2007).

Chapter 27
Statutory Controls and Regulation of Pharmaceuticals and Medical Devices

James E. Szalados

The Administrative Procedures Act and the Regulatory Authority of the FDA

The FDA as an agency was not specifically created by Congress; rather, it was merged into the US Department of Health, Education, and Welfare (HEW) which was cabinet-level department of the US government that existed from 1953 through 1979. The FDA represents one of the policymaking and enforcement units within HHS and remains a part of the US Public Health Service (PHS). The FDA Commissioner, not a statutorily created position, is charged with enforcing the Federal Food, Drug, and Cosmetic Act (FDCA), subsequent amending statutes, and other relevant statutes.[1] The FDA Commissioner is appointed by the President with the advice and consent of the Senate. In its regulatory oversight powers, the FDA must act in accordance with the Administrative Procedure Act (APA). Regulatory

[1] For example, other statutes that FDA enforces are the Filled Milk Act, 21 U.S.C. §61; the Federal Import Milk Act, 21 U.S.C. §141; the Tea Importation Act, 21 U.S.C. §41; the Federal Caustic Poison Act, ch. 489, 44 Stat. 1406, 15 U.S.C §§401–11; the Fair Packaging and Labeling Act, 15 U.S.C. §1451; and some portions of the Public Health Service Act, 42 U.S.C. §§241–361. The FDA also administers, among others, the Best Pharmaceuticals for Children Act (Pub. L. No. 107-109 (Jan. 4, 2002)); the Pediatric Research Equity Act (Pub. L. No. 108-15 (Dec. 3, 2003)); and, the Minor Use and Minor Species Animal Health Act (Food Allergen Labeling and Consumer Protection Act) (Pub. L. No. 108-282 (Aug. 2, 2004)).

J. E. Szalados (✉)
Director, Surgical and Neurocritical Care Units, Rochester Regional Health System at Rochester General Hospital, Rochester, NY, USA

The Szalados Law Firm, Hilton, NY, USA
e-mail: james.szalados@rochesterregional.org; jszalados@aol.com

J. E. Szalados (ed.), *The Medical-Legal Aspects of Acute Care Medicine*,
https://doi.org/10.1007/978-3-030-68570-6_27

power is not granted by the Constitution but rather through an authorizing statute which delegates a specific field of regulation. In order for the FDA, as a federal agency, to develop rules with the force of law, it must have the authority to engage in rulemaking, adjudication, summary judgment, and publication of statutory guidelines. A rule is defined to mean "the whole or a part of an agency statement of general or particular applicability and future effect designed to implement, interpret, or prescribe law or policy or describing the organization, procedure, or practice requirements of an agency" [4]. However, rules made by an agency must be within the field over which it was granted Congressional authority, within the bounds of its enabling statute, and in accordance with the APA. The rulemaking process must conform to standards of due process, transparency, and public participation. The term "rulemaking" refers to the "agency process for formulating, amending, or repealing a rule" [5]. The FDA has used both notice and comment rulemaking and also adjudicative rulemaking, which is a formal, case-by-case, evidentiary, on-the-record, quasi-judicial, or judicial rulemaking in developing its policies.

The notice and comment rulemaking process requires publication of proposed rules in the *Federal Register*, followed by a period of public notice with opportunities for public comment, before publication of the final rule. These rules may be either legislative (or substantial) and provide the agency with authority to promulgate rules that extend existing laws or they may be nonlegislative (or interpretational) such as guidance documents, policy statements, or agency manuals that are nonbinding and lack the force of law. Agency rule, once enacted, will apply uniformly; however, they will only apply prospectively.

The FDA may also issue "guidance documents" which will usually relate to administrative procedures or to the design, production, manufacturing, and testing of regulated products; the intent of such documents is to achieve consistency in regulatory approach. The purposes of guidance documents are to provide (1) assistance to the regulated industry by clarifying the requirements imposed by Congress or issued in FDA regulations and explaining how industrial users may comply with such requirements and (2) specific review and enforcement approaches to help ensure that the FDA carries out its legislative mandate in an "effective, fair, and consistent manner." To that end, the FDA has determined that all guidance documents must include the following:

(1) The umbrella term "guidance"
(2) Information that identifies the center or office producing the document
(3) The regulatory activity to which the document applies and/or the intended users of the document [6]

Such guidance documents are not binding on the FDA *or the public*; rather, they represent the FDA's current position on a specific subject matter. Guidance documents are specific documents which conform to a specific format; they do not include agency reports, general information provided to consumers, documents relating to solely internal FDA procedures, speeches, journal articles and editorials, media interviews, warning letters, or other communications or actions taken by individuals at FDA or directed to individual persons or firms. Thus, since guidance documents are neither regulations nor laws, they are not enforceable, either through administrative action or the courts.

The FDA also employs its summary judgment authority when necessary to enforce agency positions based upon the merits, when there are “no genuine and substantial issues of fact,” or when “data and information submitted are insufficient to justify the factual determination” [7].

Rules enacted by the FDA, as an agency, are subject to legal challenge and therefore judicial review. The federal judiciary has final authority on issues of statutory construction and may reject those agency administrative interpretations or constructions that it rules to be contrary to congressional intent. When a court is faced with a “pure question of statutory interpretation,” it relies on traditional methods of statutory construction to determine the intent of Congress. Courts:

> have long recognized that considerable weight should be accorded to an executive department’s construction of the statutory scheme which it is entrusted to administer, and the principle of deference to administrative interpretations “has been consistently followed . . . whenever decision as to the meaning or reach of a statute has involved reconciling conflicting policies, and a full understanding of the force of the statutory policy in the given situation has depended upon more than ordinary knowledge respecting the matters subjected to agency regulations.” [8]

A court which is reviewing an agency action will employ a two-step analysis of agency mandate and congressional intent; this process is the “*Chevron* analysis.” The judicial review of an agency’s statutory interpretation will first focus on congressional intent; here the first question is whether Congress has previously directly addressed the precise question at issue. If a prior intent of Congressional intent is clearly established, then the court, and the agency, must defer to Congress. If, however, the court does not find congressional intent to legislate in that area, or if the statute as written is “silent or ambiguous,” then the reviewing court must determine if the agency’s ruling is permissible on the basis of its enabling statute [9].

The FDA will at times also assemble advisory committees, through which independent advisory opinions may be heard at public hearings on matters of potentially controversial public policy or technical issues. An advisory committee typically “has a fixed membership, a defined purpose of providing advice to the agency on a particular subject, regular or periodic meetings, and an organizational structure” [10]. FDA advisory committees may be either policy advisory committees or technical advisory committees. A policy advisory committee advises the FDA on broad and general matters of policy, whereas a technical advisory committee advises the FDA on specific technical or scientific issues.

A Brief History of the FDA and the FDCA

The FDA has its origin in the Federal Food and Drugs Act of 1906 (also known as the Wiley Act or the Pure Food and Drugs Act), administered under the authority of the US Bureau of Chemistry and the first federal legislation to address standards for the preparation and the marketing of medicines [11]. Prior to 1906, medicinal products (then consisting largely of proprietary alcoholic tonics, patent medicines, and sometimes even toxic compounds sold as "remedies") were basically unregulated in terms of their content, purity, and safety. The 1906 Act was first time that marketing of compounds known to be poisonous or potentially harmful to human health, as either medicines or food additives, was prohibited by law in the USA. The Sherley Amendment of 1912 expanded the statutory prohibitions to include any "false and fraudulent" statements relating to unsubstantiated "therapeutic effects" [12]. The Bureau of Chemistry was renamed as the US Food, Drug, and Insecticide Administration in 1927; and in 1930 the name was shortened to Food and Drug Administration (FDA).

The Federal Food, Drug, and Cosmetic Act (FDCA) became law on June 25, 1938, when it superseded and repealed the Wiley Act. Although the 1938 FDCA was actually drafted in 1933 by the US Department of Agriculture, it was later formally enacted into law in response to a national public health crisis caused by a medicinal antibiotic compound, the "elixir of sulfanilamide."

In 1951, the Durham-Humphrey Amendment to the FDCA defined the types of drugs that could not be safely used without medical supervision, thereby effectively creating a defined class of drugs which became known as "prescription drugs," and by exclusion simultaneously defined those drugs that could be used without medical supervision and thus could be sold over the counter (OTC) without a prescription [13]. Statutorily defined criteria for prescription drugs included (1) habit-forming drugs; (2) drugs that could be used only under the supervision of a licensed healthcare practitioner; and (3) drugs that can be used only under professional supervision because they were approved as the result of a new drug application (NDA). On the other hand, OTC status was accorded to medications if (1) a patient could self-diagnose safely or could understand drug usage requirements and restrictions and (2) the drug was not known to cause any significant side effects [14].

In 1962, the FDCA was further amended by the Kefauver-Harris Amendments which explicitly required the FDA to review all NDAs to assess them for *safety* in humans *and* to ascertain that a drug manufacturer had provided "substantial evidence" through "adequate and well-controlled investigations" to demonstrate that a potential new drug is also *effective* for its intended use [15]. Additionally, the 1962 Amendments required that the FDA retroactively review and assess the safety and effectiveness for drugs that were previously approved by the agency from 1938 to 1962. In order to accomplish the requisite safety and effectiveness retroactive review of a large number of compounds, the FDA contracted with the National Research Council (NRC) of the National Academy of Sciences through a project known as the Drug Efficacy Study Implementation (DESI). The FDA was empowered to withdraw drugs which had been granted prior approval to be unsafe or ineffective. The 1962 FDCA Amendments added the requirements that (1) a new drug or medical device could not be marketed until it was approved by the FDA and (2) the FDA approval must be issued prior to initiation of human clinical testing of a new drug. These amendments mandated an affirmative FDA premarket approval for new drugs as a prerequisite to any commercial development and marketing.

The Food and Drug Administration Modernization Act of 1997 (FDAMA) further reiterated demonstration by manufacturers of a new drug's effectiveness prior to FDA approval for marketing; specifically, the FDAMA emphasized the term "substantial evidence" to represent the statutorily required standard of proof for drug "effectiveness" [16]. The FDAMA iterated a four-part FDA mission statement that stressed not only its duty to protect the public health but also the *promotion* of the public health.

In 1998, the FDA published the "Pediatric Rule," which asserted FDA's authority to compel drug manufacturers to complete pediatric testing for pharmaceuticals. However, the Association of American Physicians and Surgeons, the Competitive Enterprise Institute, and Consumer Alert subsequently litigated and successfully challenged the validity of the Pediatric Rule in the US District Court for the District of Columbia, and as a result the Pediatric Rule was invalidated in 2002 upon the holding by the court that the FDA lacked statutory authority to pass such a regulation.

Nonetheless, the Best Pharmaceuticals for Children Act of 2002 [17] was subsequently enacted to address persistent concerns that the vast majority of prescription medications were never tested in and therefore not specifically approved for use in children. The BPCA was passed after the FDAMA and provided for pediatric exclusivity of 6 months' duration with respect to marketing exclusivity for pharmaceutical companies who conducted pediatric studies and subsequently brought products to market. In 2003, the Medicare Prescription Drug Improvement and Modernization Act (MMA, also known as the Medicare Modernization Act) was enacted [18].

The Kennedy-Enzi Bill, "Enhancing Drug Safety and Innovation Act of 2006," was developed as legislative groundwork for the Food and Drug Administration Amendments Act of 2007 (FDAAA) and was intended "to amend the Public Health Service Act and the Federal Food, Drug, and Cosmetic Act to improve drug safety and oversight …" [19].

On September 27, 2007, President George W. Bush signed into law the Food and Drug Administration Amendments Act of 2007 ("FDAAA") which amended both the FFDCA and the Public Health Service Act [20]. Title I amended the FDCA to require new drug and biologics sponsors to develop and comply with "Risk Evaluation and Mitigation Strategies" (REMS), as a requisite to obtaining and maintaining FDA approval status [21]. Under REMS, manufacturers were required to submit a pharmacovigilance statement, and associated justification, indicating (1) whether routine adverse event reporting will be adequate to assess "serious risk" and to identify "unexpected serious risk" presented by the drug after approval or (2) whether post-marketing studies or clinical trials are needed. Title IV amended the FDCA with a process for the screening of potential advisory committee members for conflicts of interest. Title III of the FDAAA statutorily created the Pediatric Medical Device Safety and Improvement Act which incentivized device manufacturers to create products that specifically meet the needs of pediatric patients. In Title IV, The FDAAA reauthorized the Pediatric Research Equity Act and empowered the FDA with broader authority to mandate pediatric testing. Title VI of the FDAAA created the Reagan-Udall Foundation as a nonprofit corporation and explicitly "not be an agency or instrumentality of the US Government" "to advance the mission of the [FDA] to modernize medical, veterinary, food, food ingredient, and cosmetic product development, accelerate innovation, and enhance product safety." The goals of the Foundation broadly included policy and program development and funding within the areas of safety, research, and education by:

(1) taking into consideration the Critical Path reports and priorities published by the Food and Drug Administration, identify unmet needs in the development, manufacture, and evaluation of the safety and effectiveness, including postapproval, of devices, including diagnostics, biologics, and drugs, and the safety of food, food ingredients, and cosmetics, and including the incorporation of more sensitive and predictive tools and devices to measure safety;
(2) establish goals and priorities in order to meet the unmet needs …
(3) in consultation with the Secretary, identify existing and proposed Federal intramural and extramural research and development programs relating to the goals and priorities established under paragraph (2), coordinate Foundation activities with such programs, and minimize Foundation duplication of existing efforts;
(4) … award grants to, or enter into contracts, memoranda of understanding, or cooperative agreements with, scientists and entities, which may include the Food and Drug Administration, university consortia, public-private partnerships, institutions of higher education, entities described in section 501(c) (3) of the Internal Revenue Code …
(5) recruit meeting participants and hold or sponsor (in whole or in part) meetings as appropriate to further the goals and priorities established under paragraph (2);
(6) … release and publish information and data and, to the extent practicable, license, distribute, and release material, reagents, and techniques to maximize, promote, and coordinate the availability of such material, reagents, and techniques for use by the Food and Drug Administration, nonprofit organizations, and academic and industrial researchers to further the goals and priorities established under paragraph (2); …

Title VI of the FDAAA established the Office of the Chief Scientist, a person appointed by the Secretary with the responsibilities to:

(1) oversee, coordinate, and ensure quality and regulatory focus of the intramural research programs of the Food and Drug Administration;
(2) track and, to the extent necessary, coordinate intramural research awards made by each center of the Administration or science-based office within the Office of the Commissioner, and ensure that there is no duplication of research efforts supported by the Reagan-Udall Foundation for the Food and Drug Administration;
(3) develop and advocate for a budget to support intramural research;
(4) develop a peer review process by which intramural research can be evaluated;
(5) identify and solicit intramural research proposals from across the Food and Drug Administration through an advisory board composed of employees of the Administration that shall include--
    (A) representatives of each of the centers and the science-based offices within the Office of the Commissioner; and
    (B) experts on trial design, epidemiology, demographics, pharmacovigilance, basic science, and public health; and
(6) develop postmarket safety performance measures that are as measurable and rigorous as the ones already developed for premarket review… [22]

In addition, Title VI empowered the FDA to enter into collaborative agreements, known as "Critical Path Public-Private Partnerships, with one or more eligible entities to implement the Critical Path Initiative of the Food and Drug Administration by developing innovative, collaborative projects in research, education, and outreach for the purpose of fostering medical product innovation, enabling the acceleration of medical product development, manufacturing, and translational therapeutics, and enhancing medical product safety" [23].

Title VII of the FDAAA addressed bias and conflicts of interest building upon the Draft Guidance on Disclosure of Conflicts of Interest for Special Government Employees Participating in FDA Product Specific Advisory Committees first published in 2002. Title VII contained a legislative mandate requiring "disclosure of any financial interest prior to any meeting of an advisory committee regarding a particular matter (as that term is used in section 208 of title 18, United States Code), each member of the committee who is a full-time Government employee or special Government employee shall disclose to the Secretary financial interests" [24].

Title IX of the FDAAA required that information regarding the safety of pharmaceuticals be reported to FDA so that the Agency can take appropriate action to protect the public health when necessary. The FDA recognized that its decisions regarding drug approvals represented a complex balancing of interests: on the one hand, warnings which overstate or exaggerate risks may deter appropriate use and are in effect of no more utility than labeling which understate risks or side effects, since both will adversely affect public health and safety. The withdrawal of the biological product rofecoxib raised questions about the integrity of the US drug safety system. In response, and at the request of the Center for Drug Evaluation and Research (CDER) of the Food and Drug Administration (FDA), the Institute of Medicine (IOM) issued a comprehensive review and set of recommendations for reforms. Title IX granted the FDA the express discretionary authority to impose Risk Evaluation and Mitigation Strategies ("REMS"), mandatory reporting requirements intended to ensure that the benefits of a prescription drug or biologic outweigh the product's risks which were applicable both prior to approval and also within the course of the post-approval period.

The FDAAA defines an "adverse drug experience" to include "any adverse event associated with the use of a drug in humans, whether or not considered drug related" and included:

(A) An adverse event occurring in the course of the use of the drug in professional practice;
(B) An adverse event occurring from an overdose of the drug, whether accidental or intentional;
(C) An adverse event occurring from abuse of the drug;
(D) An adverse event occurring from withdrawal of the drug; and
(E) Any failure of expected pharmacological action of the drug [25]

The Biologics Price Competition and Innovation Act of 2009 (BPCI) [26] are comprised of statutory provisions within the Patient Protection and Affordable Care Act (PPACA) which became law on March 23, 2010. A biological product (biologic) is a pharmaceutical product that is derived from, or contains components of, biologic organisms which include a wide range of products such as vaccines, blood and blood components, allergenics, somatic cells, gene therapy, tissues, and recombinant therapeutic proteins [27]. As defined by the FDA, the term "protein" refers to any alpha amino acid polymer with a specific, defined sequence greater than 40 amino acids in size [28]. The BPCI amended the Public Health Service Act to create an expedited approval pathway for biological products which are "highly similar" (biosimilar) to, or "interchangeable" with, an already FDA-approved biological product. A biological product may be considered to be "biosimilar" if data demonstrates that the biosimilar product is "highly similar" to the reference product, notwithstanding minor differences in clinically inactive components, and there are no clinically meaningful differences between the biological product and the reference product in terms of safety, purity, and potency. The BPCI is conceptually similar to the Drug Price Competition and Patent Term Restoration Act of 1984 ("Hatch-Waxman Act") which, at that time, provided for expedited pathways for the approval of drugs under Federal Food, Drug, and Cosmetic Act (FFDCA) [29].

In response to the terrorist attacks on America on September 11, 2001, the Congress enacted the Public Health Security and Bioterrorism Preparedness and Response Act (PHSBPRA or BPRA) in 2002. The US Department of Agriculture (USDA) subsequently identified food defense as an area of domestic vulnerability. Food defense refers to the protection of food products from contamination or adulteration intended to cause public health harm or economic disruption. BPRA required the FDA to implement regulations and oversight actions regarding food defense: (1) administrative detention of imported food; (2) establishment and maintenance of records; (3) food facility registration; and (4) prior notice of imported food. The FDA Food Safety Modernization Act (FSMA) of 2011 [30] was enacted in the face of public concerns regarding the safety of the US Food Supply. However, the regulatory burdens associated with compliance with the FSMA ushered in the Tester-Hagan Amendment to the Food Safety Modernization Act, which then created certain exemptions for small farms. The intent of the FSMA was to be proactive rather than reactive with respect to risk identification and mitigation as they relate to food safety.

The FDA Safety and Innovation Act (FDASIA) and the Medical Device User Fee and Modernization Act [31] was passed into law in 2012. FDASIA granted the FDA with a tool for expedited drug development, known as the "breakthrough therapy" designation, designed to expedite the development and review of new drugs with only preliminary clinical evidence that indicates the drug may offer a substantial improvement over available therapies for patients with serious or life-threatening diseases [32].

The integrity and security of the US drug supply which was addressed in part by the Drug Quality and Security Act (DQSA) of 2013 [33] further amended the FDCA to address drug compounding and to create a drug track-and-trace program. The Drug Quality and Security Act represented a legislative response to an outbreak of fungal meningitis in 2012 attributed to medication compounding at the New England Compounding Center [34]. The DQSA is substantively comprised of two titles. Title I of the DQSA represents the Compounding Quality Act (CQA). The CQA implemented a voluntary compliance program for compounding pharmacies, enabling such facilities to register with the FDA as outsourcing facilities, and thereby have access to FDA oversight for Good Manufacturing Practices (GMPs) and thereby exemptions from some approval and labeling requirements. The Drug Supply Chain Security Act (DSCSA) was enacted as Title II of DQSA, providing for steps to build an electronic, interoperable system to identify and trace prescription drugs distributed in the USA. The DSCSA Pilot Project Program began on February 8, 2019. The goal of DSCSA is to implement medication tracking and tracing; serialization, verification, and detection of suspicious products; and strict guidelines for wholesaler licensing and reporting.

The 21st Century Cures Act of 2016 (Cures Act) [35] was passed with the intent of helping to accelerate the development, approval, and marketing of medical products. In order to accomplish the goal of more rapid and efficient translation of basic science into a pharmaceutical product, the Cures Act deemphasized reliance on the gold standard double-blind randomized clinical trial and included a provision which allowed for consideration of "real-world evidence," which includes "sources other than randomized clinical trials" such as "patient experience data" for administrative determinations of safety and efficacy. In addition, §3011 addressed novel trial designs, modeling and simulations, the nature quantitative and qualitative data, and potential methodologies to best satisfy the NDA substantial evidence standard. For example, §3022 discusses the use of real-world evidence to help support regulatory decision-making. The Cures Act defines "real-world evidence" as that data regarding the use, benefits, or risks of a drug that are "derived from sources other than randomized clinical trials," which could include, for example, post-marketing safety surveillance, observational studies, and drug or patient registries. The deadline for implementation of the provisions of the Cures Act regulations is November 2, 2020.

The Cures Act also mandated that patients be provided access to of their health information contained within their electronic medical records without charge by their healthcare provider. Information blocking, as defined in the regulations for healthcare providers, prohibits practices that a healthcare provider knows are unreasonable and are likely to interfere with, prevent, or materially discourage access, exchange, or use of electronic health information. The eight types of clinical documents that patients must be allowed to access are (1) consultation notes; (2) discharge summary notes; (3) history and physical; (4) imaging narratives; (4) laboratory report narratives; (6) pathology report narratives; (7) procedure notes, and (8) progress notes, as outlined by the US Core Data for Interoperability (USCDI) standards.

The Cures Act specifically excluded personal health records, EHRs, and other health IT from its definition of a medical "device" so long as three criteria were met: they (1) are entered or reviewed by healthcare professionals (or those working under their supervision); (2) are certified under the Office of the National Coordinator (ONC) for Health Information Technology; and (3) are not intended for the analysis of patient records, including medical images, for the purpose of the diagnosis, cure, mitigation, prevention, or treatment of a disease or condition [36]. Nonetheless, the FDA has determined that Medical Device Data Systems (MDDS) and Medical Image Storage Devices are, in themselves, exclusive of the software, medical devices [37].

The FDA Reauthorization Act of 2017 (FDARA) [38] was passed with the intent of lowering prescription drug costs and, when passed, represented the sum of a number of bipartisan health-related bills. The FDARA required that the FDA accelerate the process whereby it approves generic drugs; enacted the "Right to Try Act" whereby terminally ill patients could legally access experimental drugs and medications prior to FDA approval; and amended the FFDCA to revise and extend the user-fee programs for drugs, medical devices, generic drugs, and biosimilar biological products. User fees are fees paid for by medical drug and device developers and manufacturers with every new product application.

Classification of Pharmaceuticals

Consumers in the USA may legally access pharmaceuticals either (1) by presenting a valid prescription issued by a licensed healthcare provider to a pharmacist or (2) by purchasing either with or without a prescription called an over-the-counter (OTC) purchase. Whether or not a prescription is required to obtain any given drug is a determination made by the US Food and Drug Administration (FDA). In addition, prescription and nonprescription drugs may be available as either generic or brand name products; and, in some cases, they may also be available as both. State laws regulate prescriptive authority through scope of practice laws and licensure. Although there is no federal legislation regarding prescriptive authority, licensed individuals may obtain a federal license specifically to prescribe controlled substances under the federal Controlled Substances Act (CSA) administered in part by the US Drug Enforcement Agency (DEA).

The word "drug" is a legal term of art under the FDCA, and as such it legislatively encompasses a great deal more than its strict medical connotation or definition. A drug is defined as (a) a substance recognized by an official pharmacopoeia or formulary; (b) a substance intended for use in the diagnosis, cure, mitigation, treatment, or prevention of disease; (c) a substance (other than food) intended to affect the structure or any function of the body; and (d) a substance intended for use as a component of a medicine but not a device or a component, part or accessory of a device. Biological products are included within this definition and are generally covered by the same laws and regulations, but differences exist regarding their manufacturing processes [39]. The current FDA classification of drugs is based upon (1) mechanism of action; (2) physiologic effect; and (3) chemical structure.

Overview of FDA Regulation of Medical Devices

FDA rules and regulations regarding the development, approval, marketing, and post-marketing follow-up for medical devices largely parallel the applicable rules for pharmaceuticals. The Medical Device Amendments Act of 1976 (MDA) [40] expanded the authority of the FFDCA, and thus the FDA, to include medical devices. The MDA intended to provide patients, the end-users, of medical devices with a reasonable assurance that the devices meet both safety and efficacy standards. In the case of devices, FDA approval is believed to more heavily favor safety over efficacy. In a manner similar to pharmaceuticals, medical devices must be manufactured under a quality assurance program (GMPs), be suitable for the intended use, be adequately packaged, be properly labeled, and have establishment registration and device listing forms on file with the FDA. The statutory authority for the FDA to regulate both medical devices and electronic radiation-emitting products is also within the FFDCA [41].

The FDA defines a medical device as:

> an instrument, apparatus, implement, machine, contrivance, implant, in vitro reagent, or other similar or related article, including a component part or accessory which is: recognized in the official National Formulary, or the United States Pharmacopoeia, or any supplement to them,
>
> intended for use in the diagnosis of disease or other conditions, or in the cure, mitigation, treatment, or prevention of disease, in man or other animals, or
>
> intended to affect the structure or any function of the body of man or other animals, and which does not achieve its primary intended purposes through chemical action within or on the body of man or other animals and which is not dependent upon being metabolized for the achievement of any of its primary intended purposes. [42]

The Classification Regulation Panels [43] are the basis for the Center for Devices and Radiological Health's (CDRH's) Classification Product Code structure and organization. The FDA Center for Devices and Radiological Health (CDRH) is responsible for regulating the manufacture, repackage, relabel, and/or import of medical devices. Medical devices are classified into Class I, II, and III based upon their potential risk to the patient or user. The FDA has established classifications for approximately 1700 different generic types of devices; these are then grouped into 16 medical specialties referred to as panels. Device classification depends on the intended use of the device and also upon indications for use. Both risk and therefore regulatory oversight and control increase from Class I to Class III. Class I devices are associated with general controls, either with or without exemptions; Class II devices are associated with both general controls and special controls, either with or without exemptions; and Class III devices have both general controls and requirements for premarket approval. The term "exemption" in this context refers to exemption from premarket notification [510(k)] requirements and Medical Device Good Manufacturing Practices (GMPs) that may also be termed Quality System (QS) Regulations.

Class I devices normally represent minimal potential risk of harm and are not life-supporting or life-sustaining. Examples of Class I devices include tongue depressors, exam gloves, handheld surgical instruments, and bandages, for example. Class II devices are subject to special controls, in addition to the general controls required of Class I devices. Class II devices include, for example, infusion pumps, sutures, X-ray machines, and home pregnancy tests. Class III devices are generally considered to be the most complex and, in general, are used to sustain or support life, are implanted, or present potential unreasonable risk of illness or injury; examples of Class III devices might include, for example, pacemakers, hear valves, and stents.

The FDA maintains a post-marketing safety-surveillance process for medical devices which relies heavily on physicians and providers, healthcare institutions, manufacturers, and patients to report medical device failures and complications through the Medical Device Reporting System. Medical Device Reporting Regulations represent a set of mandatory requirements for manufacturers, importers, and device user facilities to report certain device-related adverse events and product problems to the FDA, and the failure to report malfunctions can result in punitive damages, rendering a device misbranded and the rescission of FDA approval.

Manufacturers must submit reports to the FDA whenever there are data to suggest that a device (1) may have caused or contributed to a death or serious injury or (2) has malfunctioned and that the device or a similar device marketed by the manufacturer or importer would be likely to cause or contribute to a death or serious injury if the malfunction were to recur. Adverse event data are logged by both manufacturers and the FDA. The Standards Management Staff of the FDA is charged with the responsibility to ensure that evolving medical device standards are published to provide formal notice to designers and manufacturers and thereby facilitate the incorporation of new regulatory standards into product design and manufacture [44].

In 2009, the FDA began the "Sentinel Initiative," a program designed to integrate the electronic health records (EHRs) of healthcare institutions with FDA databases in order to perform continuous and online post-marketing safety analyses. Since medical devices, in contrast to pharmaceuticals, had previously lacked unique device identifiers (UDIs), the FDA was authorized, through the FFDCA Amendments Act of 2007, to develop a comprehensive UDI system for medical devices that is expected to soon be integrated with EHRs as well as administrative and claims databases to identify patients who have been exposed to specific devices and thereby track rare post-exposure risks.

The MDA expressly pre-empts states from imposing any requirement that is different from, or in addition to, any requirement applicable under the MDA (see below).

Technological advances in tissue engineering, cell biology, pharmacology, gene therapy, and materials science have resulted in the development of products which do not fit neatly into statutory distinctions as either drugs, medical devices, or biologics; such products are referred to as "combinations" or "combination products" since they combine the attributes of drugs, biologics, and/or medical devices [45]. Examples of combination products may include, for example, antibiotic- or heparin-bonded catheters or implants. A combination product is defined to be:

(1) A product comprised of two or more regulated components, i.e., drug/device, biologic/device, drug/biologic, or drug/device/biologic, that are physically, chemically, or otherwise combined or mixed and produced as single entity;
(2) Two or more separate products packaged together in a single package or as a unit and comprised of drug and device products, device and biological products, or biological and drug products;
(3) A drug, device, or biological product packaged separately that according to its investigational plan or proposed labeling is intended for use only with an approved individually specified drug, device, or biological product where both are required to achieve the

intended use, indication, or effect and where upon approval of the proposed product the labeling of the approved product would need to be changed, e.g., to reflect a change in intended use, dosage form, strength, route of administration, or significant change in dose; or

(4) Any investigational drug, device, or biological product packaged separately that according to its proposed labeling is for use only with another individually specified investigation drug, device, or biological product where both are required to achieve the intended use, indication, or effect [46].

The FDA Safety and Effectiveness Standards

Regulation of new drug and device development by the FDA addresses two principal goals in the agency's mission statement: (1) FDA standards require empirical demonstration of both the safety and efficacy of new drugs prior to their approval for marketing; and (2) enforcement of the regulatory scheme is necessary to keep unapproved products from the market. Traditionally, the responsibility for the approval of new drugs or devices by the FDA is reflective of a high degree of administrative tension between two important but competing public health risks: (1) the risk that a drug will be approved prematurely without an adequate demonstration of safety and efficacy and (2) the risk of unnecessary delay in the availability of necessary medications required for disease treatment [47]. It is well recognized that, in general, all pharmacologic agents are inherently toxic. Thus, the FDA recognizes that all drugs have varying levels of efficacy, safety, and toxicity, largely depending on the context and the dosages in which they are administered. The requirement of a demonstration of efficacy addresses the question of whether a drug does what it purports to do, the penultimate test of clinical utility. Given such a delicate balancing test, the FDA may be more likely to approve a drug or device associated with higher risks if its potential benefits are substantial, for example, a unique but potentially toxic drug that effectively treats a severe life-threatening disease. Approval of a drug or device by the FDA is thus contingent on the demonstration of both safety and efficacy; "any person who wishes to introduce or deliver for introduction into interstate commerce any new drug, biological product, or new animal drug must demonstrate that the product is safe and effective for its intended uses" [48]. The traditional standard by which a new drug or device was evaluated by the FDA was on the basis of data from adequate and well-controlled studies, so as to posit substantial evidence or adequate scientific evidence to support approval. In addition, traditionally, the FDA has interpreted the substantial evidence requirement to mean that at least two adequate and well-controlled studies have been completed and recognizes that uncontrolled clinical studies represent merely corroborating evidence. The gold standard for clinical trials has been the double-blinded randomized clinical trial. The adequate and well-controlled studies must include data from both animal (preclinical) studies and human (clinical) studies.

The FDA enforces its quality standards through its oversight of "good manufacturing procedures" (GMPs). The FDA issues and regularly updates GMP regulations for drugs, and GMP regulations represent accepted practices and procedures for manufacturing, processing, and packing the products to assure their quality and purity. The FDA polices GMP violations through inspections; and the FDA inspectors have the authority to sanction violators and/or suspend productions through their injunctive police powers.

Adverse drug events (ADEs) are integral to the labeling of a medication; often the products are relabeled in the post-marketing surveillance process to add new warnings or restrictions. The "black box" warning represents the highest level of five possible warning categories that may appear in a package insert. Such a black box warning can impact drug sales, marketing, and even the prescription process; and the black box warnings can be a source of litigation, representing a litigation risk primarily to the "learned intermediaries" who assume the risks associated with the warnings. Recently, patient safety advocates argue that the patient should be specifically informed and that the patient's written informed consent should be obtained, prior to initiating treatment with a drug that has an associated black box warning. Informed consent regarding the prescribing of drugs with black box warnings remains controversial.

Overview of the FDA Approval Process

The development and marketing of a new drug or device is complex and uncertain; a developer or manufacturer will engage in a process of research and development (R&D); through the R&D process, the developer must cover its operating costs, produce shareholder value, and allocate sufficient funds from profits to pay for the sunk costs of unapproved drugs and also fund future R&D. Importantly, R&D is characterized by false starts, resulting in uncompensated returns due to products which do not meet the requisite safety and efficacy requirements.

Drugs are generally developed from new chemical entities (NCEs) which are hypothesized to possess biological activity and therefore potential medicinal utility. A specific line of research conducted today is known as "translational" which is a term that reflects a deliberate effort to apply laboratory research findings to clinical applications. Preliminary research regarding the properties of an NCE begins with process of chemical studies and laboratory animal experimentation focusing on acute and short-term toxicity studies to determine a basic safety profile. The FDA regulates "good laboratory practices" (GLPs) during drug testing in the laboratory stage. Usually, there are simultaneous preclinical studies designed to determine if the NCE has a potential therapeutic value. Once the basic properties of a NCE become sufficiently understood at a preclinical laboratory level, the FDA will use its risk-benefit calculus to decide whether the potential benefits outweigh the risks so as to justify further studies in humans. Clinical trials represent the process by which a drug is tested to ensure that the NCE can be deemed "safe and effective" in humans.

In order to begin clinical trials, a manufacturer (referred to as a sponsor) must file (1) an (investigational new drug (IND) or device (IDE) application and (2) a new drug application (NDA) supported by the results of a series of the laboratory studies. The IND is synonymous with "Notice of Claimed Investigational Exemption for a New Drug" [49]. Sponsors include companies, research institutions, and other drug developers. The IND includes all preclinical research data and a scientific design of the human studies to be conducted. An IDE, or investigational device exemption, allows for an investigational device to be used in a clinical study in order to collect safety and effectiveness data required to support a premarket approval (PMA) application or a premarket application to the FDA. There are three general types of IND applications: (1) the investigator IND; (2) the emergency use IND; and (3) the compassionate use IND. The investigator IND is submitted by a medical sponsor who both initiates and conducts the clinical investigation and under whose immediate direction the investigational drug is administered or dispensed. A clinical trial is based on a research protocol, or set of rules, which define the population from which participants will be recruited and delineates the procedures, medications, dosages, and monitoring and subsequent statistical methods that will be used. Clinical research protocols presuppose that the IND has been favorably reviewed by the FDA and approved by institutional review boards (IRBs) for the participating research institutions. IRBs are entities which approve and supervise the conduct of human subjects research, locally approve the protocols, ensure that research subject participants are accorded the opportunity informed consent, ensure that the researchers are free from bias or conflict of interest, and continuously monitor the study for adverse outcomes.

Phase I clinical trials are designed to establish the safety of a new drug, including safe dosage range, and Phase I trials represent the first administration of a potential drug to a small test population of healthy human adult volunteers. Phase I trials are conducted following the IND approval by the FDA. Phase I trials focus on safety rather than efficacy. The primary objective of Phase II trials is to confirm the safety profile in humans. Phase I trials typically involve approximately 20–100 normal, healthy volunteers and will usually occur over a period of several months. Phase I testing will determine basic metabolic, basic pharmacologic, and toxicological properties of the IND with an emphasis on dose ranges and tolerance and metabolism (absorption, distribution, elimination, and excretion) of the compound and potentially generate preliminary data about safety.

If Phase I testing does not reveal significant safety concerns, the IND will proceed to Phase II clinical trials, which are conducted on a much larger adult population of adults, usually patients who have been diagnosed with a specific medical condition of interest for which the IND is presumptively effective. The focus of Phase II trials shifts from safety to efficacy; however, the monitoring for safety issues never ceases. Phase II trials are usually double-blinded randomized and controlled studies which evaluate the safety and effectiveness of the IND compared to placebos, existing alternative drugs, or other accepted standard agents for comparison.

Phase III clinical trials are large-scale studies often conducted with multi-institutional involvement and typically provide the power necessary for proper scientific conclusions to be reached regarding safety and efficacy in large diverse populations of patients.

The FDA also requires that a sponsor verify its proposed production methods, and the facilities and controls for the manufacturing, processing, and packaging of a new drug are adequate to preserve its identity, strength, quality, and purity. The requirements are part of the demonstration of good manufacturing practices (GMPs). The subsequent decision to pursue an NDA and proceed with marketing is based on reasonably full reports of preclinical and clinical trials substantiating the drug's safety and effectiveness, a description of the drug's components, chemical formulation, manufacturing controls, and the conditions under which the drug will be used, and samples of the drug and a description of the proposed labeling containing dosage instructions, appropriate warnings of adverse drug reactions, and indications of harmful drug interactions [50]. The Prescription Drug User Fee Act (PDUFA III), passed in 1992 and subsequently reaffirmed and as amended, requires manufacturers to pay fees to the FDA for the evaluation of NDAs and supplements.

Once the testing phase for a NCE under the IND approval is successfully completed, the sponsor can file for FDA approval, that application is known as an NDA, a new drug approval application. The NDA is strict and must be adhered to in all subsequent marketing, and the FDA will not tolerate deviations from the NDA, following its submission and approval. Such deviations, unless they fall into specific exceptions, will be considered to represent "misbranding." The exceptions under which NDA may be modified include an additional abbreviated new drug application (ANDA) which must be further approved by the FDA by the filing of a supplemental NDA (sNDA) or supplemental ANDA (sANDA) [51]. The sANDA "must be submitted for any change in the drug substance, drug product, production process, quality controls, equipment, or facilities that has a substantial potential to have an adverse effect on the identity, strength, quality, purity, or potency of the drug product as these factors may relate to the safety or effectiveness of the drug product" [51]. Following submission of an NDA, the FDA must determine if it will review that application, as it is submitted, within 60 days. The final decisions for approval or denial of NDAs is typically rendered by the FDA within 6–12 months; 10 months on average.

The Approval Process for Biologics

The Vaccine Act of 1813 provided for a public supply of smallpox vaccine. The US post office was an integral component of the Vaccine Act as citizens could only apply to receive a vaccine at a post office, which was obligated to assist the vaccine agent in the distribution of vaccine. The Vaccine Act was repealed in 1822. The Biologics Act of 1902 exerted jurisdiction over "viruses, therapeutic serums, toxins, anti-toxins, or analogous products" as "biologics" that were intended for the "prevention and cure of diseases of man" [52] – authority which was expanded subsequently with the passage of the Public Health Service Act of 1912 (PHSA) [53]. The

Center for Biologics Evaluation and Research (CBER) regulates products under a variety of regulatory authorities including the PHSA and the FDCA.

Sponsors of biologic products, such as vaccines, must file an IND to initiate the premarket testing phases. For a vaccine, the IND must also describe the vaccine, its method of manufacture, quality control tests for release, and data about the vaccine's safety and ability to elicit a protective immune response (immunogenicity) derived from preclinical animal testing studies. The development of potential vaccines generally follows the same pathway as for drugs, devices, and other biologics [54]. Vaccines, like NCEs and devices, must progress through Phases I–III of clinical trials to determine a reasonable safety and efficacy profile. For vaccines, Phase I trials focus on safety and immunogenicity in studies performed on a small group of healthy volunteers. If all the phases of clinical trials are successful, the sponsor may submit a biologics license application (BLA) [55]; the BLA is the biologics analog of the NDA. After the FDA has reviewed the BLA, the findings presented to the Vaccines and Related Biological Products Advisory Committee (VRBPAC) of the FDA. VRBPAC is comprised of external non-FDA experts who will further advise the FDA regarding concerns about the biological product prior to its approval for marketing [56].

Labeling, Marketing, and Misbranding

The NDA for a pharmaceutical, the BLA for a biological product, or the 510(k) for a device will define the intended use, based on the safety and efficacy data submitted to the FDA. The "labeling" of a product is thus an FDA term of art which means that the FDA has approved a product for a certain indication or indications. The "FDA has the authority to control certain aspects of the label, to enforce the requirement of truthful and non-misleading label representations, and to ensure that the label contains adequate directions for use and appropriate safety warnings" [14]. The package insert that physically accompanies the FDA-approved product describes and determines the uses for which the product has been demonstrated to be safe and effective. The label will be approved only if it conforms precisely to the uses for which the product has been proven safe and effective and contains specific information including directions for safe and effective use, warnings, precautions, clinical pharmacology information, indications, contraindications, and associated adverse reactions. In addition to the package insert, all other labeling, defined as "any supplementary or explicative information from the vendor, whether or not it physically accompanies the drug," must comply with these restrictions. As a result, the manufacturer functionally is barred from disseminating any promotional or informational materials describing any uses of the drug (including different indications, doses, or routes of administration) that have not been approved by FDA and included in the package insert. The "alteration, mutilation, destruction, obliteration, or removal of the whole or any part of the labeling of, or the doing of any other act with respect to, a food, drug, device, or cosmetic, if such act is done while such article is held for sale (whether or not the first sale) after shipment in interstate commerce and results in such article being adulterated or misbranded," is prohibited by law [57]. A drug is thus considered to be misbranded if (1) it has a false or misleading label; (2) it lacks "a label containing (a) the name and place of business of the manufacturer, packer, or distributor and (b) an accurate statement of the quantity of the contents in terms of weight, measure, or numerical count"; or (3) "any word, statement, or other information required by or under authority of [the FDCA] to appear on the label or labeling is not prominently placed thereon," or otherwise violates the specified labeling standards iterated in 21 U.S.C. §352. A drug is also considered misbranded if appropriate and adequate directions for use, sufficient warnings regarding interactions and contraindications, or information regarding unsafe dosages, methods of administration, or duration of use are lacking on the label.

The Lanham Act [58] prohibits commercial advertising or promotion that misrepresents the nature, characteristics, qualities, or geographic origin of the advertiser's or another person's goods, services, or commercial activities. The intent of the Lanham Act is:

> to regulate commerce within the control of Congress by making actionable the deceptive and misleading use of marks in such commerce; to protect registered marks used in such commerce from interference by State, or territorial legislation; to protect persons engaged in such commerce against unfair competition; to prevent fraud and deception in such commerce by the use of reproductions, copies, counterfeits, or colorable imitations of registered marks; and to provide rights and remedies stipulated by treaties and conventions respecting trademarks, trade names, and unfair competition entered into between the United States and foreign nations. [59]

The "Practice of Medicine" Exception: "Off-Label" Uses of Drugs and Medical Devices

The "off-label use" of a drug, biological, or device refers to its discretionary use by a licensed medical provider with prescriptive authority, in a reasonable manner, but in a manner that is either inconsistent with or not described in the product's FDA-approved labeling. Off-label use, by definition, has not been subject to preclinical or clinical testing or to review by the FDA, and therefore safety and efficacy data has not been established. Nonetheless, there may be a reasonable presumption of safety and efficacy or a favorable risk versus benefit calculus in the opinion of the provider. The unapproved or off-label use of drugs has not been recognized by the FDA as an acceptable alternative to documentation of the safety and effectiveness of drugs through the IND and NDA; however, with subsequent revisions of the FDCA, such data is increasingly accepted. The FDA does not consider itself nor is it authorized to regulate the practice of medicine, and therefore the FDA does not regulate the prescribing of drugs for off-label uses [60]. When a drug has been approved by the FDA for market for any (approved) indication, the actual prescription choices regarding those drugs are left to the discretion of the medical provider who may prescribe an approved drug for any medical condition, irrespective of whether FDA has determined that the drug is safe and effective with respect to that specific indication. Off-label use by prescribers has traditionally been very common in some patient populations and, in some instances, has permeated clinical practice to become a new standard of patient care. Nonetheless, the provider will accept the risks and liabilities, should they arise, stemming from such unapproved use. However, the FDA has established strict policies prohibiting medical companies from promoting non-FDA-approved uses of their drugs or devices under the NDA and marketing and branding provisions of the FDCA. The FDA has stated that "once a [drug] product has been approved for marketing, a physician may prescribe it for uses or in treatment regimens of patient populations that are not included in approved labeling." The FDA also noted that off-label ("unapproved" or "unlabeled") uses may in fact be appropriate in some circumstances and may represent a kind of therapeutic innovation [61].

The "learned intermediary" doctrine in essence states that the provider prescribing any drug is legally considered to be fully aware of (1) the characteristics of the drug he or she is prescribing, (2) the dosage of the drug that may be safely administered, and (3) other relevant medications the patient is taking for the purposes of drug interactions. The doctrine states that pharmaceutical manufacturers are limited in their "duty to warn" regarding the intended and approved use of a drug; that duty, under the *doctrine*, is owed only to the prescribing providers. When the manufacturer has discharged their duty through advising the provider, that provider steps into the shoes of the manufacturer as a "learned intermediary" and thereby assumes the risks related to prescribing that drug. Therefore, the prescriber assumes the "duty to warn" from the manufacturer as a "learned intermediary" [62]. However, the manufacturer has a strict duty to warn the provider, and the manufacturer remains liable if the warnings pit provided to the learned intermediary are determined inadequate [63]. Thus, "unless the individual prescribing physician receives specific, relevant warnings, she cannot make a careful, balanced assessment of the risks and benefits to her patient, nor can the patient herself be adequately informed" [64].

Biologicals and the Immunization of Vaccines from Liability

Following the approval and marketing of vaccines, post-marketing monitoring begins with the Vaccine Adverse Event Reporting System (VAERS), a national system used by scientists at FDA and the Centers for Disease Control and Prevention (CDC) to collect reports of adverse events (possible side effects) that happen after vaccination. Reports of possible adverse events attributable to vaccines led to waning interests in vaccinations and also industry research in the field of vaccine development. In response to a vaccine liability crisis in the 1980s, and as an effort to both support vaccine research and to provide relief to vaccine manufacturers in the face of litigation, the Congress enacted the National Childhood Vaccine Injury Act of 1986 which established the National Vaccine Injury Compensation Program (VICP) in 1988 as a federal "no-fault" compensation system for those harmed by vaccines covered under the Act. In 2015, the Act was further amended based on the recommendations of the 2012 Institute of Medicine (IOM) report, "Adverse Effects of Vaccines: Evidence and Causality" [65]. The VICP served as a streamlined and less adversarial alternative to the traditional civil law system for resolving claims that arise from vaccine injury [66] The VICP covers all vaccines recommended by the Centers for Disease Control and Prevention for routine administration to children. The Program is jointly administered by the US Department of Health and Human Services (HHS), the US Department of Justice, and the US Court of Federal Claims (CFC). Within the HHS, the program is administered by the Health Resources and Services Administration.

In particular, the VICP states:

(1) No vaccine manufacturer shall be liable in a civil action for damages arising from a vaccine-related injury or death associated with the administration of a vaccine after October 1, 1988, if the injury or death resulted from side effects that were unavoidable even though the vaccine was properly prepared and was accompanied by proper directions and warnings

....

(c) Direct warnings: No vaccine manufacturer shall be liable in a civil action for damages arising from a vaccine-related injury or death associated with the administration of a vaccine after October 1, 1988, solely due to the manufacturer's failure to provide direct warnings to the injured party (or the injured party's legal representative) of the potential dangers resulting from the administration of the vaccine manufactured by the manufacture.

...

(e) Preemption

- No State may establish or enforce a law which prohibits an individual from bringing a civil action against a vaccine manufacturer for damages for a vaccine-related injury or death if such civil action is not barred by this part.
- 42 U.S. Code § 300aa–22

Litigation

In general, private litigation regarding prescription drugs are disfavored because they might subvert the regulatory jurisdiction of the FDA and negatively impact the availability of drugs and devices to health consumers. Product liability litigation against manufacturers or pharmaceuticals intends to compensate those injured by a faulty or defective product. Under a product liability theory, the manufacturer or seller of a drug or device is liable to the consumer if the product contains an inherent defect that is unreasonably dangerous and if that defect causes injury to a foreseeable user of the product. Product liability is generally considered to be a strict liability offense, meaning that liability is not predicated on the degree of carefulness used in the design, manufacturing, or marketing of a product. Under strict liability, a manufacturer is liable when it is shown that the product is defective. Strict liability does not apply to medical providers. Therefore, "strict liability shall attach to one who sells a product 'in a defective condition, unreasonably dangerous' to the consumer"; "to prevent a product from being unreasonably dangerous, direction or warnings as to its use must be given in appropriate cases"; and "the lack of adequate warning is what renders the product 'defective'" [67]. Product defects are categorized as either (1) design defects; (2) manufacturing defects; or (3) marketing defects. A design defect exists when the defect is determined to be inherent within the design of a product. In a product liability case, the plaintiff must establish that an alternative design, even a hypothetical one, would be (1) safer, (2) as economically feasible, and (3) as practical as the original design, while retaining the primary purpose. On the other hand, manufacturing defects represent unintended manufacturing errors which occur during manufacture or assembly of a device. Marketing defects also involve inadequate warnings and/or instructions and are typically exemplified by inadequate or faulty user instructions and by failures to warn learned intermediaries.

Nonetheless, prescription drugs may be an exception to the general rule of strict liability because they have been classified as "unavoidably unsafe" products. The FDA, and the courts, have repeatedly stated their recognition of the fact that prescription drugs, even when administered exactly as indicated, may inflict harm. The prescription drug exception "intends to shield from strict liability products which cannot be designed more safely; however, if such products are mis-manufactured or unaccompanied by adequate warnings, then the seller may be liable even if the plaintiff cannot establish the seller's negligence" [68]. Courts will generally apply the test for pharmaceutical or device product liability on a case-by-case basis.

Liability claims may also be predicated in a tort law theory of negligence. Negligence is defined as a failure to exercise proper or ordinary care; and a manufacturer may be held liable if a plaintiff can establish that a lack of reasonable care during the production, design, or assembly of the manufacturer's product caused a foreseeable harm and resulting damages.

The Restatement (Second) of Torts recognizes that:

> there are some products which, in the present state of human knowledge, are quite incapable of being made safe for their intended and ordinary use. These are especially common in the field of drugs. . . . Such a product, properly prepared, and accompanied by proper directions and warning, is not defective, nor is it unreasonably dangerous . . . which for this very reason cannot legally be sold except to physicians, or under the prescription of a physician [69].

Paracelsus, the renaissance physician, stated that "[a]ll things are poisons, for there is nothing without poisonous qualities. It is only the dose which makes a thing poison" [70]. Thus, drugs will always, by their nature, carry some element of inherent risk, "for a drug, by its very nature, cannot be totally safe for everyone. The basic tenet of pharmacology is that any drug action is a toxicity…We cannot provide a certificate of safety" [71].

The Restatement further notes that:

> the seller is not liable when he delivers the product in a safe condition, and subsequent mishandling or other causes make it harmful by the time it is consumed. The burden of proof that the product was in a defective condition at the time that it left the hands of the particular seller is upon the injured plaintiff; and unless evidence can be produced which will support the conclusion that it was then defective, the burden is not sustained. Safe condition at the time of delivery by the seller will, however, include proper packaging, necessary sterilization, and other precautions required to permit the product to remain safe for a normal length of time when handled in a normal manner. [72]

Issues which can cause a pharmaceutical product to be considered "defective" include improper packaging (i.e., lack of childproof capping), improper labeling, impurities or contamination, or the lack of appropriate warnings. Under the "duty-to-warn" theory, a product sold without adequate warnings is considered to be sold in a defective condition [73]. Under the "learned intermediary doctrine" however, the duty to warn runs from the manufacturer to the prescribing provider, not the patient [74]. A classic case which illustrates the "learned intermediary doctrine" is that of *Heindel v. Pfizer Inc.* [75], where Pfizer, the manufacturer of the nonsteroidal anti-inflammatory drugs or NSAIDs under the brand names of Celebrex® and Vioxx®, was sued for complications, including cardiac and renal toxicity, associated with their use. The court held that the "manufacturer of prescription drugs need only direct information and warnings to prescribing physicians" and granted the manufacturers' motion for summary judgment.

The FDA requires that medical device litigation be brought in federal court. In fact, the FDAAA articulates an express preemption clause related to medical devices which provides that "no state...may establish or continue in effect with respect to a device...any requirement (1) which is different from, or in addition to, any requirement applicable under [the Food & Drug Act], and (2) which relates to the safety or effectiveness of the device or to any other matter included in a requirement applicable to the device.." In *Riegel v. Medtronic*, the Supreme Court held that state-law tort claims against a manufacturer of an allegedly defective medical device, which had received premarket approval from the FDA, were preempted under 21 U.S.C.S. § 360k(a) of the Medical Device Amendments of 1976 [76].

Conclusions

The FDA is the federal agency to which the responsibility for the US cosmetic, food, drug, and device supply has been delegated by the Congress. Arguably, the depth and breadth of such single agency oversight may border on unmanageable. On the one hand, the demand for more rapid and expeditious release of drugs and devices which may positively impact human health and well-being is at odds with the risks of less than optimal testing and the legal liabilities associated with potential harms. The previous gold standard of multiphase trials and the reliance on the double-blinded randomized clinical trials as the basis for a demonstration of reasonable safety and efficacy are devolving. The importance of devices and biologics is increasingly relevant as advances in genomics and proteomics allow us to target the innate variations in biologic makeup between individuals and thereby provide peronalized medicine. Finally, the laws regarding vaccines and vaccinations will continue to challenge not only our ethical and moral decisions but also the legal system and regulatory oversight environment. The laws and regulations relating to drugs, devices, and biologics is ever-evolving, and the regulations continue to be "forced" into effect by evolving technologies.

References

1. 5 U.S.C. §§551, 553, 701–06, generally; see also 21 U.S.C. §§701(a), 701(e), specifically.
2. Szalados JE. Statutory and regulatory controls. In: Clark ME. ed. Pharmaceutical law: regulation of research, development, and marketing. BNA Books; Arlington, VA, 2007. p. 1–120.
3. Szalados JE. Statutory and regulatory controls for drug development. In: Clark ME, editor. Pharmaceutical law: regulation of research, development, and marketing – 2008 Supplement. BNA Books; Arlington, VA, 2008. p. 1–22.
4. 5 U.S.C. §551(4) (2005).
5. 5 U.S.C. §551(5) (2005).
6. The Food and Drug Administration's development, issuance, and use of guidance documents, notice, 62 Fed. Reg. 8961, 8967 (Feb. 27, 1997).
7. 21 C.F.R. §12.24(b) (2006);
8. Chevron, 467 U.S. at 844–45, citing, inter alia, National Broad. Co. v. United States, 319 U.S. 190 (1943); Labor Bd. v. Hearst Publ'ns, Inc., 322 U.S. 111 (1944); Republic Aviation Corp. v. Labor Bd., 324 U.S. 793 (1945); Securities & Exch. Comm'n v. Chenery Corp., 332 U.S. 194 (1947); Labor Bd. v. Seven-Up Bottling Co., 344 U.S. 344 (1953).
9. Chevron v. Natural Resources Defense Council, Inc., 467 U.S. 837 (1984).
10. The Federal Advisory Committee Act forms the basis for convening an advisory committee. See 21 C.F.R. §14 and 5 U.S.C. §561 ("Agencies have the authority to establish negotiated rulemaking committees under the laws establishing such agencies and their activities and under the Federal Advisory Committee Act (5 U.S.C. App.).").
11. Pure Food and Drugs Act, Pub. L. No. 59-384, ch. 3915, 34 Stat. 768 (1906); 21 U.S.C. §§1–15 (1934). See S. 88, 59th Cong., 2d Sess. (1906), passed into law June 30, 1906. This Act was repealed in 1938 by U.S.C §329(a).
12. Pure Food and Drugs Act of Aug. 23, 1912, ch. 352, 37 Stat. 416.
13. Pub. L. No. 82-215, 65 Stat. 648 (1951).
14. 21 U.S.C. §352(f) (2005).
15. Drug Amendments of 1962, Pub. L. No. 87-781, 76 Stat. 780 (1962) (codified at 21 U.S.C. §§321, 331–32, 348, 351–53, 355, 357–60, 372, 374, and 381) (2005).
16. Pub. L. No. 105-115, 111 Stat. 2296 (1997).
17. Pub.L. 107-109 (2002).
18. Pub.L. 108–173, 117 Stat. 2066.
19. H.R. 3580: Food and Drug Administration Amendments Act of 2007 Enacted — Signed on Sep 27, 2007.
20. H.R.3580 - Food and Drug Administration Amendments Act of 2007. Public Law No: 110-85. Available online at: https://www.congress.gov/bill/110th-congress/house-bill/3580.
21. FDA. Food and Drug Administration Amendments Act (FDAAA) of 2007. Available online at: https://www.fda.gov/regulatory-information/selected-amendments-fdc-act/food-and-drug-administration-amendments-act-fdaaa-2007.

22. FDAA, Title VI Sec 602 (b)(1) – (6), 121 Stat. 823, (2008).
23. FDAA, Title VI Sec 603 (a), 121 Stat. 823, (2008).
24. FDAA, Title VII Sec 701 (c)(1), 121 Stat. 823, (2008).
25. FDAA, Title VII Sec 701 (c)(1), 121 Stat. 823, (2008). Public Law No: 110-85.
26. Biologics Price Competition and Innovation Act of 2009 (BPCI), PL 111-148, Title VII, Subtitle A.
27. DHHS. FDA. Definition of the term "Biological Product" docket no. FDA-2018-N-2732. Available online at: https://www.fda.gov/media/135421/download.
28. 85 FR 10057, February 21, 2020.
29. FDA. Implementation of the Biologics Price Competition and Innovation Act of 2009. Available online at: https://www.fda.gov/drugs/guidance-compliance-regulatory-information/implementation-biologics-price-competition-and-innovation-act-2009.
30. FDA Food Safety Modernization Act PL 111-353 (Jan. 4, 2011).
31. 21 U.S.C. §§ 301 et seq.
32. Szalados JE. Regulatory law and the clinical practice of the neurosciences. In: Szalados JE, editor. Ethics and law for neurosciences clinicians: foundations and evolving challenges. New Brunswick: Rutgers University Press; 2019.
33. Drug Quality and Security Act PL 113–54 (2013).
34. Brechtelsbauer ED, Pennell B, Durham M, Hertig JB, Weber RJ. Review of the 2015 Drug Supply Chain Security Act. Hosp Pharm. 2016;51(6):493–500.
35. 21st Century Cures Act PL 115-52 (2016).
36. FDA. Changes to existing medical software policies resulting from section 3060 of the 21st Century Cures Act: guidance for industry and food and drug administration staff. 2019. Available online at: https://www.fda.gov/media/109622/download.
37. FDA. Medical device data systems, medical image storage devices, and medical image communications devices: guidance for industry and food and drug administration staff. 2019. Available online at: https://www.fda.gov/media/88572/download.
38. FDA Reauthorization Act of 2017 (FDARA) PL 115-52 (2017).
39. FDA. Drugs@FDA Glossary of terms. Available online at: https://www.fda.gov/drugs/drug-approvals-and-databases/drugsfda-glossary-terms.
40. Medical Device Amendments, H.R.11124, 94th U.S. Congress (December 11, 1975).
41. FDA Regulations addressing medical devices can be found in Title 21 Code of Federal Regulations (CFR) Part 800 to Part 1299. This reference is abbreviated to 21 CFR 800 to 1299.
42. FFDCA. 21 USC § 321(h).
43. Classification regulation panels. 21 CFR Parts 862-892.
44. Federal Food, Drug, and Cosmetics Act. Subchapter H. Quality system regulation. 21 Code of Federal Regulations 820.1(a)(1)(2018).
45. Definition of primary mode of action of a combination product, 69 Fed. Reg. 25,527, 25,528–30 (May 7, 2004) (to be codified at 21 C.F.R. pt. 3).
46. 21 C.F.R. §3.2(e) (2006).
47. Szalados, 2008, supra.
48. 59 Fed. Reg. 59,820. See also 21 U.S.C. §§355(a) and 360b(a); and the Public Health Service Act, 42 U.S.C. §262.
49. 21 C.F.R. §312.3 (1998).
50. Lloyd G. Millstein, specific requirements, content, and format of an NDA, in new drug approval process: clinical and regulatory management 261 (Richard A. Guarino ed., 1987).
51. 21 C.F.R. §§314.70(b)(1), (2) (1994).
52. Pub. L. No. 57-244, 32 Stat. 728 (1902).
53. Ch. 288, 37 Stat. 309 (1912) (codified at 42 U.S.C. §201 et seq. (2005)).
54. Parkman PD, Hardegree MC. Regulation and testing of vaccines. In: Plotkin SA, Orenstein WA, editors. Vaccines. 3rd ed. Philadelphia: Saunders; 1999. p. 1131–43.
55. 42 U.S.C. §262 and 21 C.F.R. §600 et seq.

56. National Vaccine Advisory Committee. United States vaccine research: a delicate fabric of public and private collaboration. Pediatrics. 1997;100(6):1015–20.
57. 21 U.S.C. §355 (d)(7)(e) (2005).
58. 60 Stat. 427, popularly known as the "Lanham Act" or the "Trademark Act of 1946" and appears generally as 15 U.S.C. §1051 et seq.
59. 60 Stat. 427, popularly known as the "Lanham Act" or the "Trademark Act of 1946" and appears generally as 15 U.S.C. §1051 et seq., §1127.
60. Shane M. Ward, the first amendment inequity of the Food and Drug Administration's Regulation of off-label drug use information on the internet, 56 Food & Drug L.J. 41 (2001).
61. 12 FDA DRUG BULL. 4–5, (1982).
62. Ehlis v. Shire Richwood, Inc., 367 F.3d 1013, 1016 (8th Cir. 2004); *see also* Mazur v. Merck & Co., 964 F.2d 1348, 1356 (3d Cir. 1992).
63. Wyeth-Ayerst Lab. Co. v. Medrano, 28 S.W.3d 87, 91 (Tex. App.–Texarkana 2000, no writ).
64. Desmarais v. Dow Corning Corp., 712 F. Supp. 13, 18 (D. Conn. 1989).
65. Stratton K, Ford A, Rusch E, Clayton EW, Committee to review adverse effects of vaccines, Institute of Medicine, editors. Adverse effects of vaccines: evidence and causality. Washington, DC: National Academies Press (US); 2011.
66. Pub L No. 100-203 §§4301 *et seq* 101 Stat. 1330-221, codified at 42 USCA §§300aa-1 et seq (1989).
67. The Restatement 2d, Torts Section 402A provides: "Special liability of seller of product for physical harm to user or consumer (1) One who sells any product in a defective condition unreasonably dangerous to the user or consumer or to his property is subject to liability for physical harm thereby caused to the ultimate user or consumer, or to his property, if (a) the seller is engaged in the business of selling such a product, and (b) it is expected to and does reach the user or consumer without substantial change in the condition in which it is sold. (2) The rule stated in Subsection (1) applies although (a) the seller has exercised all possible care in the preparation and sale of his product, and (b) the user or consumer has not bought the product from or entered into any contractual relation with the seller".
68. Toner v. Lederle Lab., 112 Idaho 328, 336 (1987).
69. Restatement (Second) of Torts §402A. See also Prosser & Keeton, Law of Torts §99, at p. 695 (5th ed. 1984).
70. Paracelsus, the byname of Philippus Aureolus Theophrastus Bombastus von Hohenheim, (1493–1591) was a German-Swiss physician and alchemist who established the role of chemistry in medicine.
71. National Academy of Sciences, How safe is safe? The design of policy on drugs and food additives 28 (1974).
72. Restatement (Second) of Torts §402A.
73. Brochu v. Ortho Pharm. Corp., 642 F.2d 652, 661 (1st Cir. 1981).
74. Sterling Drug, Inc. v. Cornish, 370 F.2d 82 (8th Cir. 1966).
75. Heindel v. Pfizer Inc., 381 F. Supp. 2d 364 (D.N.J. 2004).
76. Riegel v. Medtronic, Inc., 128 S. Ct. 999 (U.S. 2008).

Chapter 28
Ethical Principles and Laws Governing Clinical Research

Marcin Karcz

Introduction

Clinical research is distinct from clinical practice in that each has different, yet not mutually exclusive, purposes, goals, and methods [1]. Clinical practice involves diagnosis, prevention, treatment, and care for a particular individual or group of individuals with the goal of meeting the health needs of and benefiting that individual. Clinical practice is based on evidence or experience, is designed to enhance the patient's well-being, and has a reasonable expectation of success. Usual methods in clinical practice are evidence-based and guided by standard practice and experience. The risks of interventions or procedures employed in clinical practice are justified by the prospect of therapeutic benefit to the individual. In contrast, clinical research aims to generate useful knowledge and is not designed to meet the health needs of, nor necessarily to benefit, individual patient participants. Although an individual may receive quality patient care and treatment when participating in research, this is not the goal of research, and much research does not directly benefit individual participants. Further, frequently used research methodologies, such as randomization, blinding, dose escalation, placebo controls, and others are rarely found and might be considered unacceptable, in clinical practice. In clinical research, some risk is justified by the importance of the knowledge to be gained rather than benefit to the individual participant.

M. Karcz (✉)
Columbia University Vagelos College of Physicians and Surgeons, New York, NY, USA
e-mail: mak9177@nyp.org

J. E. Szalados (ed.), *The Medical-Legal Aspects of Acute Care Medicine*,
https://doi.org/10.1007/978-3-030-68570-6_28

Ethics and Clinical Research

There are several fundamental considerations that need to be considered when conducting clinical research ethically. Clinical research is vital in generating practical knowledge useful for advancing or improving medical care and health, yet respect for the rights, welfare, dignity, and freedom of choice of individual humans is crucial. Research with human beings is essential to improving and advancing medical care and providing health professionals with the knowledge and evidence necessary to appropriately and safely care for patients. The pursuit of knowledge through research should however be rigorous to inform effective and safe clinical practice. Progress would not be possible without rigorous clinical research. Conducting clinical research designed to enhance the understanding of human health and illness may be more than a social good; arguably it is a social imperative [2]. Although progress in medical care and health is a societal good, some contend it is an optional good [3], and that other considerations, such as the primacy of the individual, should take precedence. Whether improvement in medical care or health through clinical research is an option or an imperative, limits are necessary. Human research participants are the means to securing practical knowledge, but because people should not be treated merely as a means to an end, but always as ends in themselves [4], the need to respect and protect human research participants is paramount. The primary ethical tension in clinical research, therefore, is that a few individuals are asked to accept some research burden, risk, or inconvenience to benefit others, including future persons and society. Ethical requirements aim to minimize the possibility of exploiting research participants by ensuring that they are treated with respect while contributing to the generation of knowledge, and their rights and welfare are protected throughout the process of research.

Historical Overview of Ethical Perspectives in Clinical Research

There was little basis for a distinction between experimentation and therapy historically because most therapy was experimental, and systematic evidence of the effectiveness of medical interventions was rare [5]. Experimental therapies were used in the hopes of benefiting ill patients, but such therapy frequently contributed to or caused morbidity or mortality. Systematic research was sporadic. Most researchers were medical practitioners, motivated to do what they thought best for their patients, and trusted to do the right thing. Fraud and abuse were minimized to some extent through peer censorship because no specific codes of ethics, laws, or regulations governed the conduct of research. Early regulations, such as the Pure Food and Drug Act of 1906 in the United States, prohibited unsubstantiated claims on medicine labels. Yet, research began to grow as an enterprise only after the development of early antibiotics such as penicillin and the passage of the Food, Drug, and

Cosmetic Act in 1938, which required evidence of safety before a product was marketed [6].

Societal Benefits

There was a dramatic shift in clinical research around the time of the Second World War, with tremendous growth in the research enterprise. Pharmaceutical companies were established; large amounts of both public and private money were devoted to research; and research became increasingly centralized, coordinated, standardized in method, and valued. Human subject research entered what has since been described as an unashamedly utilitarian phase [7]. Individuals often were included in research because they were available and marginalized, and seen as making a contribution to society. The federal government and the pharmaceutical industry supported intensive research efforts to develop vaccines and antibiotics for infectious diseases to help soldiers, as infectious diseases were a significant problem for the armed services. During this era, research was commonly conducted in prisons, orphanages, and homes for the emotionally or developmentally disturbed, as well as with other institutionalized groups. The distinction between research and therapy was fairly clear: subjects not necessarily in need of therapy were accepting a personal burden to make a contribution to society. A utilitarian justification served as the basis of claims that some individuals could be used for the greater common good. Revelations of Nazi medical experiments and war crimes, and the Nuremberg trial of Nazi doctors, raised public and professional concerns about the justification and scope of research with human subjects [8].

Human Subject Protection in Research

Stories of abuse of human subjects in the late 1960s and early 1970s in the United States led to intense scientific and public scrutiny and reflection, and debate about the scope and limitations of research involving human subjects. A renowned Harvard anesthesiologist, Henry Beecher, published a landmark article in the *New England Journal of Medicine* in 1966 [9] highlighting ethical problems in 22 research studies conducted in reputable US institutions. Exposition of studies such as the hepatitis B studies at Willowbrook, the U.S. Public Health Service Tuskegee syphilis studies, and others generated intense public attention and concern. Congressional hearings and action led to passage of the 1974 National Research Act and establishment of the US National Commission for the Protection of Human Subjects of Biomedical and Behavioral Research [10]. This extremely influential body authored multiple reports and recommendations about clinical research, including reports on research with children and on institutional review boards. Included in its legacy is the Belmont Report, in which ethical principles underlying the conduct of human subject research and their application are explained [11]. The Commission's work emphasized the need to protect individuals participating in research from potential exploitation and harm, and provided the basis for subsequent federal regulations codified in 1981 in Title 45, US Code of Federal Regulations, Part 46, titled "Protection of Human Subjects," and similar FDA regulations. In 1991, the Department of Health and Human Services regulations became the currently operative Common Rule [12], which governs the conduct of human subject research funded by 17 US federal agencies. The major thrust of these federal regulations and of many existing codes of research ethics continues to be protection of subjects from the burdens and harms of research.

Benefits of Research in General

Public perspectives on clinical research were altered by events in the late 1980s and the 1990s. It was asserted by some vocal activists that research participation, rather than simply harm to be protected from, can actually offer advantages that individuals want access to [13]. According to this perspective, as adopted by human immunodeficiency virus (HIV) and breast cancer activists and others, participation in research is a benefit, protectionism is discrimination, and exclusion from research can be unjust. Empirical studies have demonstrated that oncology patients, for example, who participate in clinical trials benefit through improved survival [14, 15]. Activism and changes in public attitudes about research led to substantive changes in the way research is done and drugs are approved. In addition to the possible benefits of participation for individuals, it was claimed that certain traditionally underrepresented groups were being denied the benefits of the application of knowledge gained through research [16]. Since 1994, the US National Institutes of Health (NIH) has required that those who receive research funding must include previously underrepresented women and ethnic minorities [17]. Since 1998, NIH guidelines have required the inclusion of children in research or justification for their exclusion [18].

Research Benefits for the Community

The growth of genetics research in subsequent years, as well as research with stored biospecimens and data, and international collaborative research have highlighted the value of greater public and community involvement in research. Clinical research is a collaborative social activity that requires the support and investment of involved communities, and it also comes with inherent risks and potential benefits for communities and groups. As such, involvement of the community in helping to set research priorities, in planning and approving research, in evaluating risks and benefits during and after a trial, and in influencing particular aspects of recruitment, informed consent, and the realization of community benefits demonstrates respect for the community and can facilitate successful research.

Research Ethics and Regulations Codes

Several influential documents have helped to shape our sense of the contours of ethical research throughout history. Most were written in response to specific crises or historical events, yet all have accepted an underlying assumption that research, as a means to progress in medical care or health is a social good. The Nuremberg Code, a ten-point code on the ethics of human experimentation, was written as the concluding part of the judgment at the Nuremberg Trials (1949) [19]. Established in response to Nazi experimentation, the Nuremberg Code recognized the potential value of research knowledge to society but emphasized the absolute necessity of voluntary consent of the subject. The Nuremberg Code established that ethical research must prioritize the rights and welfare of the subject. Most subsequent codes and guidelines for the ethical conduct of research have maintained this emphasis and all have incorporated requirements for informed consent. The World Medical Assembly (WMA) introduced the Declaration of Helsinki in 1964 as a guide to the world's physicians involved in human subject research [20]. The Declaration of Helsinki recognizes that some, but not all, medical research is combined with clinical care and emphasizes that patients' participation in research should not put them at a disadvantage with respect to medical care. The Declaration of Helsinki also recognizes legitimate research with people who cannot give their own informed consent, such as children and the cognitively impaired, but for whom informed permission could be obtained from a legal guardian. The Declaration of Helsinki has had considerable influence on the formulation of international, regional, and national legislation and regulations governing clinical research. The Declaration of Helsinki has been revised multiple times by the WMA and is considered a living document. Certain provisions of the Helsinki Declaration, such as post trial obligations and the use of placebo controls, have been topics of continued debate among international researchers. The Belmont Report, published by the US National Commission for the Protection of Human Subjects of Biomedical and Behavioral Research, describes three broad ethical principles that guide the conduct of research and form the "basis on which specific rules could be formulated, criticized, and interpreted" [11]. These three principles are respect for persons, beneficence, and justice. Respect for persons requires respect for the autonomous decision-making of capable individuals as applied in the process of informed consent and also calls for protection of those with diminished autonomy. Beneficence requires protecting individuals from deliberate and unnecessary harm, as well as maximizing benefits and minimizing harms, and is applied to clinical research through careful risk/benefit evaluation. Justice demands a fair distribution of the benefits and burdens of research and is applied in the Belmont Report to fairness in the processes and outcomes of selecting research subjects.

In 1982, the Council of International Organizations of Medical Sciences (CIOMS), in conjunction with the World Health Organization (WHO), issued International Ethical Guidelines for Biomedical Research Involving Human Subjects, which were subsequently revised [21]. The CIOMS guidelines acknowledge that background circumstances sometimes differ between low-income, middle-income, and high-income countries, and there may be differences in the primacy of focus on the individual and individual rights. CIOMS set out to apply the Helsinki principles to the "special circumstances of many technologically developing countries." CIOMS adopted the three ethical principles spelled out in the US National Commission's Belmont Report and maintains most of the tenets of Nuremberg and Helsinki but has provided additional and valuable guidance and commentary on externally sponsored research and research with vulnerable populations. The 2015 revision restructures and expands many previously existing guidelines and adds new guidelines on compensation for research-related injury, research with stored biospecimens and data, and implementation science, among others [21].

Federal regulations found in Title 45, US Code of Federal Regulations (USCFR), Part 46 (45CFR46) [12], were propagated in 1981 for research funded by Department of Health and Human Services (DHHS) and at Title 21 USCFR, Part 50 and 56 for the US Food and Drug Administration (FDA) [22]. FDA regulations are similar, but not identical, to those found in the Common Rule [23]. Compliance with these and other FDA regulations is required for research investigating FDA-regulated products, such as drugs, biologics, and medical devices. DHHS regulations were extended in 1991 as the Federal Common Rule, applicable to research funded by 17 US federal agencies (not including the FDA). Based on recommendations of the National Commission, the Common Rule stipulates both the membership and the function of IRBs, and the criteria that an IRB should apply when reviewing a research protocol to determine whether to approve it. The Common Rule also delineates the information that should be included in an informed consent document, how consent should be documented, and criteria for waiver or alteration of informed consent. Subparts B, C, and D of 45CFR46 describe additional protections for DHHS-funded research with fetuses and pregnant women, prisoners, and children, respectively. In 2017, a final revision to the Common Rule was published in the Federal Register, with the most extensive changes to the Common Rule since 1991 [24]. The International Conference on Harmonization (ICH) sought to harmonize regulatory guidelines for product registration trials for the United States, the European Union, and Japan. The ICH Good Clinical Practice (GCP) Guidelines provide widely accepted guidance promoting the ethical conduct of research and reporting of accurate and reliable data [25]. The World Health Organization produced good clinical research guidelines that incorporated ICH Good Clinical Practice (GCP) Guidelines and also included types of clinical research beyond drug registration trials [26]. Countries around the world to guide the conduct of research are adopting good clinical practice guidelines.

Bioethical Perspectives in Research

The historical evolution of clinical research ethics and the development of guidelines and regulations were largely in response to particular events or scandals. The Nuremberg Code, for example, was a response to atrocities performed by Nazi research doctors during the Second World War. The formation of the National Commission for the Protection of Human Subjects of Biomedical and Behavioral Research was in response to revelations of the U.S. Public Health Service syphilis studies in Tuskegee. The systems for protection of human subjects, the focus of the ethics of clinical research, and the existing regulations grew out of these efforts. Another essential way to inform our thinking about the ethics of clinical research, and one that has gained traction in recent decades, is research on bioethical questions. Bioethics research is usually conducted using one or more of the following methodologies: historical inquiry, conceptual analysis, empirical studies, or policy analysis [27]. Bioethics research on voluntariness, an essential part of informed consent, could better our understanding of what voluntariness means and how to maximize it in the process of informed consent. Such research might include an analysis of the concept. Recognizing that all decisions and actions can be influenced by one's understanding, previous experiences, religion and culture, and the influences of respected others, distinguishing what makes a choice sufficiently voluntary from a choice that is controlled is important. Conceptual bioethics research also might examine the concepts of coercion, undue influence, and manipulation, which are different possible controlling influences [28]. Empirical research might seek to elucidate how people actually choose research participation, what sources of influence and pressure they identify, whether they perceive they could say no to participation and under what circumstances, experiences of manipulation or undue influence, and other phenomena. Requirements for rigorous and ethical research on topics in bioethics are similar to those for ethical clinical research.

Outline of Ethical Principles in Clinical Research

A systematic outline of principles for ethical clinical research was derived from guidance provided in various ethical codes, guidelines, literature, and bioethics research. This proposed summary of principles is meant to apply sequentially and universally to clinical research [29]. According to this outline, ethical clinical research should satisfy the following requirements: social or scientific value, scientific validity, fair subject selection, favorable risk/benefit ratio, independent review, informed consent, and respect for enrolled subjects [30]. Application of these principles to specific cases will always involve judgment and specification on the part of investigators, sponsors, review boards, and others involved in clinical research.

The Principal of Scientific Value and Validity

The first requirement of ethical research is that the research question must be worth asking, that is, the question must have potential social, scientific, or clinical value. The anticipated usefulness of knowledge to be gained in understanding or improving health or health care is the core of determining value and not whether study results are positive or negative. A study should have sufficient social value to justify asking individuals to assume risk or inconvenience in research and to justify the expenditure of resources [31]. A valuable research question then ethically requires validity and rigor in research design and implementation to produce valid, reliable, interpretable, and generalizable results. Poorly designed research, for example, with an inappropriate design, inadequate power, insufficient or sloppy data, or inappropriate or unfeasible methods is harmful because human and material resources are wasted and individuals are exposed to risk for no benefit [30].

The Principle of Subject Selection

Fair subject selection requires that subjects be chosen for participation in clinical research based first on the scientific question, balanced by considerations of risk, benefit, and vulnerability. As described in the Belmont Report, fairness in both the processes and the outcomes of subject selection prevents exploitation of vulnerable individuals and populations and promotes equitable distribution of research burdens and benefits. Fair procedures means that investigators should identify groups or individuals who would be appropriate for scientific reasons, that is, for reasons related to the problem being studied and justified by the design and the particular questions being asked not because of their easy availability or manipulability, or because subjects are favored or disfavored [11]. Extra care should be taken to justify the inclusion of vulnerable subjects, as well as to justify excluding those who stand to benefit from participation. Exclusion without adequate justification can be unfair; therefore, eligibility criteria should be as broad as possible, consistent with the scientific objectives and the anticipated risks of the research. Distributive justice is concerned with a fair distribution of benefits and burdens; thus, expected benefit and burden in a particular study is an important consideration for subject selection. Scientifically appropriate individuals or groups may be fairly selected consistent with attention to equitably distributing benefits and burdens, as well as minimizing risks and maximizing benefits.

Persons are considered vulnerable when their ability to protect or promote their own interests is compromised, often because of an impaired capacity to provide informed consent. Although disagreement remains about the meaning of vulnerability in research and who is actually vulnerable [32], there is support for the idea that among scientifically appropriate subjects, the less vulnerable should be selected first. For example, an early drug safety study should be conducted with adults before children, and with consenting adults before including those who cannot consent. Certain groups, such as pregnant women, fetuses, prisoners, and children, are further protected by specific regulations requiring additional safeguards in research. According to US regulations, determination of the permissibility of research with children depends on the level of research risk and the anticipated benefits. Accordingly, research that poses minimal risk to children is acceptable; however, research with more than minimal risk must be counterbalanced by a prospect of direct therapeutic benefit for the children in the study. Research with small amounts of additional risk (minor increment over minimal), but without the prospect of direct therapeutic benefit for the children, can sometimes be justified by the importance of the question for children with the disorder under study.

Finally, research without a prospect of benefit that poses greater than minimal risk to participating children can only be conducted if approved by a special panel convened by the US Secretary of the DHHS [33]. Enrolling children in research also requires permission from their parents or legal guardians, along with the child's assent whenever possible. Fair subject selection also requires considering the outcomes of subject selection. As an example, if women, minorities, or children are not included in studies of a particular intervention, then study results may be difficult to apply to these groups in practice, and interventions could actually be harmful. Therefore, study populations recruited for research should be representative of the populations likely to use the strategies tested in the research [34]. Similarly, it has been argued that justice requires subjects to be among the beneficiaries of research. This means that subjects should be selected as participants in research from which they or others like them can benefit and should not be asked to bear the burdens of research from which they can reap no benefits. This understanding of justice has raised important and challenging questions in the conduct of collaborative international research. Some have argued that if an experimental drug or vaccine is found effective in a certain tested population, there should be prior assurance that population will have access to the drug or vaccine [35]. Alternatively, subjects or communities should be assured of and involved in negotiation about fair benefits derived from research that are not necessarily limited to the benefits of available products of research [36].

Risk/Benefit Assessment in Research

The ratio of risks to benefits in research is favorable when risks are justified by benefits to participants or to society, and when research is designed in a way that minimizes risk and enhances benefit for participating subjects. The ethical principle of beneficence obliges that people are protected from deliberate or unnecessary harm and obtain maximal benefits. A widely accepted principle states that one should not deliberately harm another individual regardless of the benefits that might be made available to others as a result. However, as the Belmont Report reminds us, offering benefit to people and avoiding harm requires learning what is of benefit and what is harmful, even if in the process some people may be exposed to the risk of harm. To a great extent, clinical research is an activity designed to learn about the benefits and harms of unproven methods of diagnosing, preventing, treating, and caring for human beings. The challenge for clinical investigators and review groups is to decide in advance when it is justifiable to seek certain benefits despite the research risks, what level of risk is acceptable, whether risks have been minimized to the extent possible, and when it is better to forego the possible benefits because of the risks. This is called a risk/benefit assessment. The calculation and weighing of risks and benefits in research can be complicated. When designing a study, investigators consider whether the inherent risks are justified by the expected value of the information and any possible benefit to the participants. Studies should be designed so that risks to participants are minimized and benefits are enhanced. When reviewing a study, an IRB identifies possible risks and benefits and determines whether the relationship of risks to benefits is favorable enough that the proposed study should go forward or instead be modified or rejected. When reviewing studies with little or no expected benefit for individual subjects, the IRB determines whether the anticipated risks or burdens to study subjects are justified only by the potential value of the knowledge to be gained, a particularly challenging risk/benefit assessment. Prospective subjects make their own risk/benefit assessment of whether the risks of participating in a given study are acceptable to them and are worth their participation. A risk/benefit assessment can include consideration of many types of risks and benefits, including physical, psychological, social, economic, and legal. For example, in a genetics study, physical risks may be limited to a blood draw for example, so assessment of potential psychological and social risks is more important. Investigators, reviewers, and potential subjects may not only have dissimilar perspectives about research but also are likely to assign different weights to risks and benefits. For example, IRBs consider only health-related benefits of the research in justifying risks, whereas subjects are likely to consider access to care and financial compensation as important benefits that may tip the balance in favor of participation. Acknowledging that risk/benefit assessment is not a straightforward or easy process does not in any way diminish its importance. An important step in evaluating the ethics of clinical research involves not only careful attention to potential benefits to individuals or society of a particular study in relation to its risks, but also consideration of the risks of not conducting the research.

Independent Review of the Risks of Research

Independent review is a process that allows evaluation of the research for adherence to established ethical guidelines by individuals with varied expertise and no personal or business interests in the research. Such a review is carried out by an IRB or research ethics committee (REC). Using criteria detailed in US federal regulations [12, 22], IRBs evaluate the value of doing the study, the risks involved, the fairness of subject selection, whether the risks have been sufficiently minimized and are justified, and the plans for obtaining informed consent. They then decide whether to approve a study, with or without modifications, to table a proposal for major revisions or more information, or to disapprove a study as unacceptable. Independent review of the risks of proposed research by someone other than the investigator has been described as a central protection for research participants [37]. Nonetheless, there is concern that the current IRB system in the United States is outdated given the current profile of clinical research, and also is bureaucratic, beset with conflicts, and in need of reform [38]. Both the 2017 revisions to the Common Rule and recent NIH policy require single IRB review for domestic multisite studies [24, 39].

The Principle of Informed Consent

Once a proposal is deemed valuable, valid, with acceptable risks in relation to benefits and fair subject selection, individuals are recruited and are asked to give their informed consent. The process of informed consent shows respect for persons and their autonomy, giving prospective subjects the opportunity to make autonomous decisions about participating and remaining in research, and respecting their choices about participation. We show lack of respect when we do not provide the necessary information to make a considered judgment, pressure an individual to make a particular judgment or deny him or her the freedom to act on judgments. The process of informed consent involves the following: disclosure of study information, comprehension of the information, voluntariness with respect to the decision, and authorization [40]. Information provided to subjects about a research study should be adequate, balanced, and presented in an understandable manner. Information should be provided in the language of the subject, at an appropriate level of complexity given the subject's age, educational level, and culture. US federal regulations detail the types of information that should be included in informed consent [12, 22]. This is essentially information that a reasonable person needs to know to make an informed decision about initial or ongoing research participation. Ideally, individuals receive the necessary information, understand it, process it in the context of their own situation and life experiences, and make a voluntary choice free from coercion or undue influence. The process of initial research informed consent usually culminates with the signing of a consent form. However, respect for persons requires that subjects continue to be informed throughout a study and are free to modify or withdraw their consent at any time.

Although widely accepted as central to the ethical conduct of research, achieving informed consent is challenging. Determining the appropriate amount and complexity of information for disclosure is not straightforward. Written consent documents have become long and complex, and large amounts of information may actually hinder understanding by subjects. Scientific information is often complex, research methods are unfamiliar to many people, and subjects have varying levels of education, understanding of science, and knowledge about their diseases and treatments, and are dissimilar in their willingness to enter into dialogue. Besides the amount and detail of information, understanding may be influenced by who presents the information and the setting. In some cases, information may be more accessible to potential subjects if presented in group sessions or through print, video, or other media presentations. Determining whether a subject has the capacity to consent and understands the particular study information is challenging. Capacity to provide consent is study specific. Individuals who are challenged in some areas of decision-making may still be capable of consenting to a particular research study. Similarly, individuals may not have the capacity to consent to a particular study, even if generally able to function in other areas of their lives. Assessing capacity might take into account an individual's educational level and familiarity with science and research, as well as evidence of cognitive or decisional impairment. In some but not all cases, mental illness, depression, sickness, desperation, or pain may interfere with a person's capacity to understand or process information.

Empirical research on informed consent shows that participants do not always have a good understanding of the purpose or potential risks of the research studies for which they gave their consent [41]. Informed consent to participation in research should be voluntary, and free of controlling influences, coercion, and undue influence [40]. Terminal or chronic illness, exhaustion of other treatment options, and lack of health insurance may limit a participant's options but do not necessarily render decisions involuntary. Payment and other incentives, trust in health care providers, dependence on the care of clinicians, family pressures, and other factors commonly influence decisions about research participation. Most of the time, these are acceptable influences, but some worry that under certain circumstances, they can become controlling. Given these multiple factors, it is important to ensure that prospective subjects have and perceive that they have the option to say no to research participation and to do so with impunity. Research has demonstrated that active and ongoing dialogue and discussion between the research team and subjects, opportunities to have questions answered, waiting periods between the presentation of information and the actual decision to participate, the opportunity to consult with family members and trusted others, a clear understanding of alternatives, and other strategies can serve to enhance the process of informed consent [42, 43].

Participant Respect in Research

Research participants deserve continued respect after enrollment, throughout the duration of the study, and when the study ends. Respect for subjects is demonstrated through appropriate clinical monitoring and attention to participants' well-being throughout the study. Adverse effects of research interventions and any research-related injuries should be treated. Private information collected about subjects should be handled confidentially, and participants informed about the limits of confidentiality. Research subjects should be reminded of their right to withdraw from the research at any time without penalty. A change in clinical status or life circumstances, as well as new information from the study or other studies, may be relevant to a person's willingness to continue participation. Investigators should make plans regarding the end of the trial, including participants' continued access to successful interventions when indicated and to study results after the study is finished.

Ethical Principles Governing Randomized Controlled Trials

Randomized controlled trials (RCTs) remain the principal method and gold standard for demonstrating safety and efficacy in the development of new drugs and biologics, and other interventions. An RCT has several characteristic features. RCTs are controlled, randomized, and usually blinded, and the significance of the results is determined statistically according to a predetermined algorithm. An RCT typically involves comparison of two or more interventions to demonstrate that they are similar or that one is superior in the treatment, diagnosis, or prevention of a specific disorder. RCTs present a spectrum of unique ethical problems [44]. The ethical justification to begin an RCT is usually described as that of a null hypothesis, also often referred to as clinical equipoise [45]. In an RCT comparing two interventions, clinical equipoise is satisfied if there is no convincing evidence about the relative merits of each of the interventions. The goal of an RCT is therefore to provide credible evidence about the relative value of each intervention. Equipoise rests on a therapeutic commitment that patients should not receive a treatment known in advance to be inferior, nor should they be denied effective treatment that is otherwise available. Doubt based on lack of evidence about which intervention is superior justifies giving subjects an equal chance to get either one and makes it ethically acceptable to assign half or some portion of subjects to different treatments provided in an RCT. There remains some disagreement about the meaning, justification, and application of equipoise in clinical research. Some argue that equipoise is based on a mistaken confluence of research with therapy and therefore should be abandoned [46]. Another controversy in RCTs involves what should count as convincing evidence. Some worry that the common acceptance of statistical significance at the $P = 0.05$ level potentially discounts clinically significant observations. Statisticians recently criticized overreliance and misuse of the p-value, reiterating that it cannot tell you the probability that results are true or due to random chance, but only the probability of seeing results given a particular hypothetical explanation [47]. People also disagree about the extent to which preliminary data, data from previous studies, data from uncontrolled studies and pilot studies, and historical data do or should influence the balance of evidence. In some cases, the existence of these other types of data may make equipoise impossible. However, data from small, uncontrolled, or observational studies can lead to false or inconclusive impressions about safety or efficacy. RCTs are usually monitored by data and safety monitoring committees who see data at specified time points during the trial and can recommend altering or stopping a trial based on prespecified boundaries for safety, efficacy, or futility [48].

Another important scientific and ethical consideration in RCTs is the selection of outcome variables by which the relative merits of an intervention will be determined. Different conclusions may be reached depending on whether the efficacy of an intervention is a measure of survival or of tumor shrinkage, symptoms, surrogate end points, quality of life, or some composite measure. The choice of end points in a clinical trial is never simply a scientific decision. In an RCT, subjects are assigned to treatment through a process of randomization, rather than on the basis of individual needs and characteristics. The goal of random assignment is to control for confounding variables by keeping two or more treatment arms similar in relevant and otherwise uncontrollable aspects. Also, RCTs are often single blind (subject does not know which intervention he or she is receiving) or double blind (both subject and investigator are blinded to the intervention). Random assignment and blinding are methods used in clinical trials to reduce bias and enhance study validity. Although compatible with the goals of an RCT, random assignment to treatment and blinding to treatment assignment may seem incompatible with the best interests or autonomy interests of the patient-subject. In some placebo-controlled blinded studies, both subjects and investigators can guess (often because of side effects) whether they are receiving active drug or placebo, potentially thwarting the goal of reducing bias [49].

The necessity and adequacy of blinding and randomization should be assessed in the design and review of each proposed research protocol. When randomization and blinding are deemed useful and appropriate for a particular protocol, there are two ethical considerations, which need to be considered. The first being the preferences for an intervention and information about which intervention a subject is receiving may be relevant to autonomous decisions. The second consideration is that the information which intervention the subject is receiving may be important in managing an adverse event or a medical emergency. With respect to the first concern, subjects should be informed about the purpose of the research and should be asked to consent to random assignment and a temporary suspension of knowledge about which intervention they are receiving. To balance the need for scientific objectivity with respect for a research subject's need for information to make autonomous decisions, investigators should provide subjects with adequate information about the purpose and methods of randomization and blinding. Subjects are asked to consent to a suspension of knowledge about their treatment assignment until completion of the protocol or some other predetermined point, at which time they should be informed about which intervention they received in the clinical trial. In some cases, knowledge of which medications a subject is receiving may be important in the treatment of adverse events or other medical emergencies. To balance the need for scientific objectivity with concern for subject safety, investigators should consider in advance the conditions under which a blind may be broken to treat an adverse event. Specifically, the protocol should specify where the code will be located, the circumstances, if any, under which the code will be broken, who will break it, how the information will be handled, and how breaking of a blind will influence the analysis of data.

Research subjects should always have information about whom they should contact in the event of an emergency. The IRB should be satisfied that these plans provide adequate protection for patient safety. Plans also should be made for what will happen at the end of a trial. Some argue that those who volunteer for RCTs, especially in externally sponsored international research, deserve assurance in advance about access to interventions proven to be beneficial in the RCT. Investigators should plan for whether and how subjects randomized to an intervention that is benefiting them will continue to receive that intervention, and how those randomized to the inferior intervention might be given an opportunity to receive the better one. Considerable disagreement remains regarding the extent of the obligation of researchers or sponsors to ensure post trial access. A participant may be concerned about participating in an RCT if one of the potential treatment assignments is placebo. Some people perceive randomization to placebo in clinical trials as problematic because it potentially deprives the individual of treatment that he or she may need. On the other hand, without proof of the safety and efficacy of an experimental treatment, it is possible that those randomized to placebo are simply deprived of potentially toxic side effects or of a useless substance [50]. Scientifically, comparison of an experimental drug to placebo can allow efficient and rigorous establishment of efficacy. The alternative is an RCT that compares the investigational drug to an already established therapy, if one exists, which can be designed to test superiority or non-inferiority of the two agents – that is if the experimental drug is similar to the standard therapy control within a non-inferiority margin. Some authors suggest that both scientific design and possible risk to subjects should be determinants of the acceptability of placebo [51]. Most accept that the use of a placebo control in research is justified under the following circumstances: (1) there is no proven effective treatment for the condition under study; (2) withholding treatment poses negligible risks to participants; (3) there are compelling methodological reasons for using placebo, and withholding treatment does not pose a risk of serious harm to participants; and, more controversially, (4) there are compelling methodological reasons for using placebo, the research is intended to develop interventions that can be implemented in the population from which trial participants are drawn, and the trial does not require participants to forgo treatment they would otherwise receive [52]. Most agree, however, that if the outcome for the patient of no treatment or placebo treatment is death, disability, or serious morbidity, a placebo control should not be used [53].

Conclusion

Ethical principles and guidance related to the conduct of clinical research with human participants help to minimize the possibility of exploitation and promote respect for and protection of the rights and welfare of individuals who serve as human subjects of research. This chapter has reviewed the historical evolution of research ethics, a systematic ethical framework for the conduct of clinical research, and ethical considerations of some of the unique features of RCTs. In addition to adherence to principles, codes of ethics, and regulations, the ethical conduct of human clinical research depends on the thoughtfulness, integrity, and sagacity of all involved. Scientific validity is important to evaluating the ethics of clinical research. Without rigorous scientific validity, the research outcomes are not reliable so persons are unnecessarily asked to accept risk and burden. Unethical research however can actually cause death. Individuals thus harmed through participation in research where there are breaches in ethical practice, should be compensated and efforts must be made by the research sponsors to assist them with any resulting health problems. In addition, affected patients should be made aware of the nature of the unethical practice and any ongoing effects fully explained to them. It should always be remembered that at center of the research method is the importance of good ethical practice, honesty, and professional integrity. The scientific community should always adhere to exemplary ethical standards of intellectual honesty in the conduct, formulation, and reporting of medical research.

References

1. Brody H, Miller FG. The clinician-investigator: unavoidable but manageable tension. Kennedy Inst Ethics J. 2003;13(4):329–45.
2. Eisenberg L. The social imperatives of medical research. Science. 1977;198:1105–10.
3. Jonas H. Philosophical reflections on experimenting with human subjects. In: Freund P, editor. Experimentation with human subjects. New York: Braziller; 1970. p. 219–47.
4. Beauchamp TL. Methods and principles in biomedical ethics. J Med Ethics. 2003;29:269–74.
5. Emanuel E, Grady C. Four paradigms of clinical research and research oversight. In: Emanuel G, Crouch L, Miller W, editors. Oxford textbook of clinical research ethics. NY: Oxford University Press; 2008. p. 222–30.
6. US FDA. Milestones in U.S. Food and Drug Law History. 2018. https://www.fda.gov/about-fda/fdas-evolving-regulatory-powers/milestones-us-food-and-drug-law-history. Accessed 14 June 2019.
7. Rothman D. Ethics and human experimentation - Henry Beecher revisited. N Engl J Med. 1987;317:1195–9.
8. Wiendling P. The Nazi medical experiments. In: Grady, Crouch, Lie, Miller, Wendler, editors. Oxford textbook of clinical research ethics. New York: Oxford University Press; 2008. p. 18–30.
9. Beecher HK. Ethics and clinical research. N Engl J Med. 1966;274:1354–60.
10. Porter J, Koski G. Regulations for the protection of humans in research in the United States. In: Emanuel, Grady, Crouch, Lie, Miller, Wendler, editors. Oxford textbook of clinical research ethics. New York: Oxford University Press; 2008. p. 156–67.
11. Department of Health, Education, and Welfare; National Commission for the Protection of Human Subjects of Biomedical and Behavioral Research. The Belmont report. Ethical principles and guidelines for the protection of human subjects of research. J Am Coll Dent. 2014;81(3):4–13.
12. U.S. Department of Health and Human Services. Protection of human subjects. 2009. https://www.hhs.gov/ohrp/sites/default/files/ohrp/humansubjects/regbook2013.pdf.pdf. Accessed 16 May 2019.

13. National Research Council (US) Panel on Monitoring the Social Impact of the AIDS Epidemic. In: Jonsen AR, Stryker J, editors. The social impact of AIDS in the United States. Washington, DC: National Academies Press; 1993.
14. Herbert-Croteau N, Brisson J, Lemaire J, Latreille J. The benefit of participating to clinical research. Breast Cancer Treat Res. 2005;91(3):279–81.
15. Bleyer A, Montello M, Budd T, Saxman S. National survival trends of young adults with sarcoma: lack of progress is associated with lack of clinical trial participation. Cancer. 2005;103(9):1891–7.
16. Dresser R. Wanted: single, white male for medical research. Hast Cent Rep. 1992;22(1):21–9.
17. National Institutes of Health. Guidelines for the inclusion of women and minorities as subjects in clinical research. 2001. https://grants.nih.gov/grants/guide/notice-files/NOT-OD-02-001.html. Accessed 6 May 2019.
18. National Institutes of Health. NIH policy and guidelines on the inclusion of children as participants in research involving human subjects. 2015. https://grants.nih.gov/grants/guide/notice-files/not98-024.html . Accessed 17 May 2019.
19. National Institutes of Health. The nuremberg code. https://history.nih.gov/research/downloads/nuremberg.pdf. Accessed 23 May 2019.
20. World Medical Association. Declaration of Helsinki. https://www.wma.net/policies-post/wma-declaration-of-helsinki-ethical-principles-for-medical-research-involving-human-subjects/ Accessed 23 May 2019.
21. Council for International Organizations of Medical Sciences (CIOMS). International ethical guidelines for health-related research involving human subjects. 2016. https://cioms.ch/wp-content/uploads/2017/01/WEB-CIOMS-EthicalGuidelines.pdf. Accessed 27 Apr 2019.
22. U.S. Food and Drug Administration. Code of federal regulations title 21. 2018. https://www.accessdata.fda.gov/scripts/cdrh/cfdocs/cfcfr/CFRsearch.cfm?CFRPart=50. Accessed 6 May 2019.
23. US FDA. Comparison of FDA and DHHS humans subject protection regulations. 2000. https://www.fda.gov/science-research/good-clinical-practice-educational-materials/comparison-fda-and-hhs-human-subject-protection-regulations. Accessed 23 May 2019.
24. Department of Homeland Security, et al. Final rule. Federal policy for the protection of human subjects. 2017. https://www.federalregister.gov/documents/2017/01/19/2017-01058/federal-policy-for-the-protection-of-human-subjects. Accessed 26 May 2019.
25. ICH Harmonised Tripartite Guideline. Guideline for good clinical practice E6(R1) 1996. https://www.ich.org/fileadmin/Public_Web_Site/ICH_Products/Guidelines/Efficacy/E6/E6_R1_Guideline.pdf . Accessed 28 May 2019.
26. World Health Organization (WHO) Handbook for good clinical research practice (GCP): guidance for implementation. 2005. https://apps.who.int/iris/handle/10665/43392. Accessed 17 Apr 2019.
27. Emanuel E. Researching a bioethical question. In: Gallin JI, Ognibene FP, editors. Principles and practice of clinical research. 3rd ed. London: Elsevier Inc.; 2012. p. 31–42.
28. Largent E, Grady C, Miller F, Wertheimer A. Misconceptions about coercion and undue influence: reflections on the views of IRB members. Bioethics. 2013;27(9):500–7.
29. Emanuel E, Wendler D, Grady C. What makes clinical research ethical? J Am Med Assoc. 2000;283(20):2701–11.
30. Emanuel E, Wendler D, Grady C. An ethical framework for biomedical research. In: Emanuel, Grady, Crouch, Lie, Miller, Wendler, editors. Oxford textbook of clinical research ethics. New York: Oxford University Press; 2008. p. 123–35.
31. Freedman B. Scientific value and validity as ethical requirements for research: a proposed explanation. IRB Rev Hum Subjects Res. 1987;9(5):7–10.
32. Levine C, Faden R, Grady C, Hammerschmidt D, Eckenwiler L, Sugarman J, Consortium to Examine Clinical Research Ethics. The limitations of "vulnerability" as a protection for human research participants. Am J Bioeth. 2004;4(3):44e9.

33. Office for Human Research Protections (OHRP). 45 CFR 46. 2016. https://www.hhs.gov/ohrp/regulations-and-policy/regulations/45-cfr-46/index.html. Accessed 10 June 2019.
34. Meltzer L, Childress J. Fair participant selection. In: Emanuel G, Crouch L, Miller W, editors. Oxford textbook of clinical research ethics. New York: Oxford University Press; 2008. p. 377–85.
35. Emanuel E. Benefits to host countries. In: Emanuel, Grady, Crouch, Lie, Miller, Wendler, editors. Oxford textbook of clinical research ethics. New York: Oxford University Press; 2008. p. 719–28.
36. Participants in the 2001 Conference on Ethical Aspects of Research in Developing Countries. Fair benefits for research in developing countries. Science. 2002;298:2133–4.
37. National Bioethics Advisory Commission. Ethical and policy issues in research involving human participants: Volume 1. Report and recommendations. https://bioethicsarchive.georgetown.edu/nbac/human/overvol1.pdf . Accessed 16 May 2019.
38. Emanuel E, Wood A, Fleischman A, et al. Oversight of human participants research: identifying problems to evaluate reform proposals. Ann Intern Med. 2004;141(4):282–91.
39. National Institutes of Health. Final NIH policy on the use of a single institutional review board for multi-site research; 2016. https://grants.nih.gov/grants/guide/notice-files/not-od-16-094.html. Accessed 2 June, 2019.
40. Faden R, Beauchamp T. A history and theory of informed consent. New York: Oxford University Press; 1986: Chapter 5–9.
41. Mandava A, Pace C, Campbell B, Emanuel E, Grady C. The quality of informed consent: mapping the landscape. A review of empirical data from developing and developed countries. J Med Ethics. 2012;38:356–65.
42. Flory J, Emanuel E. Interventions to improve research participants' understanding in informed consent for research: a systematic review. J Am Med Assoc. 2004;292:1593–601.
43. Nishimura A, Carey J, Erwin PJ, Tilburt JC, Murad MH, McCormick JB. Improving understanding in the research informed consent process: a systematic review of 54 interventions tested in randomized control trials. BMC Med Ethics. 2013;14:28.
44. Levine RJ. Ethics and regulation of clinical research. 2nd ed. New Haven: Yale University Press; 1988.
45. Freedman B. Equipoise and the ethics of clinical research. N Engl J Med. 1987;317(3):141e5.
46. Miller F, Brody H. A critique of clinical equipoise: therapeutic misconception in the context of clinical trials. Hast Cent Rep. 2003;33(3):20–8.
47. Wasserstein RL, Lazar NA. The ASA statement on p-values: context, process, and purpose. Am Statist. 2016;70(2):129–33.
48. FDA. The Establishment and operation of clinical trial data monitoring committees for clinical trial sponsors. 2006. http://www.fda.gov/regulatoryinformation/guidances/ucm127069.htm. Accessed 17 June 2019.
49. Fisher S, Greenberg R. How sound is the double-blind design for evaluating psychotropic drugs? Nerv Ment Dis. 1993;181(6):345–50.
50. Levine R. The use of placebos in randomized clinical trials. IRB Rev Hum Subjects Res. 1985;7(2):1–4.
51. Emanuel EJ, Miller FG. The ethics of placebo-controlled trialsda middle ground. N Engl J Med. 2001;345(12):915–9.
52. Millum J, Grady C. The ethics of placebo-controlled trials: methodological justifications. Contemp Clin Trials. 2013;36(2):510–4.
53. Miller F, Brody H. What makes placebo-controlled trials unethical? Am J Bioeth. 2002;2(2):3–9.

Chapter 29
State of Emergency: The Laws Governing Natural Disasters and Other Mass Casualty Incidents

James E. Szalados

Disasters and Mass Casualty Events

A "mass casualty incident" (MCI), also referred to as a multiple-casualty incident or multiple-casualty situation, may occur as a result of natural disasters, epidemics, large-scale industrial disasters, or acts of violence.

The term "disaster" refers to a low-probability but high-impact event which causes a large number of individuals to become acutely ill or injured. Recent examples of natural disasters include, the impact of Hurricane Katrina on the east coast of the United States in 2005, the 2010 earthquake in Haiti, or the Australian fires of 2019. Recent outbreaks of infectious diseases include Ebola, cholera, measles, Middle East respiratory syndrome (MERS), and the 2020 COVID-19 (SARS-CoV-2 or 2019-nCoV) coronavirus. Notable recent industrial disasters include the nuclear meltdown at the Chernobyl nuclear power plant in Prypiat, Ukraine, in 1986, and the 1984 leak of methyl isocyanate at Union Carbide in Bhopal, Madhya Pradesh, India. In some cases, a natural disaster occurs which then directly causes an industrial disaster, such as the 2011 Tōhoku, Japan, earthquake and tsunami which precipitated the Fukushima Daiichi nuclear accident. Finally, overwhelming acts of civilian terrorism and violence may perhaps be best highlighted by the Tokyo subway sarin attack of 1995 and the 9/11 World Trade Center bombing in Manhattan, New York.

J. E. Szalados (✉)
Director, Surgical and Neurocritical Care Units, Rochester Regional Health System at Rochester General Hospital, Rochester, NY, USA

The Szalados Law Firm, Hilton, NY, USA
e-mail: james.szalados@rochesterregional.org; jszalados@aol.com

J. E. Szalados (ed.), *The Medical-Legal Aspects of Acute Care Medicine*,
https://doi.org/10.1007/978-3-030-68570-6_29

Terrorist threats are generally classified into five categories: chemical, biological, radiological, nuclear, and explosive (CBRNE). Some events are sudden, some evolve slowly, some are silent and insidious, and some sudden events produce lingering effects, such as toxins or radiation. The common features of MCIs are that they (a) cause widespread fear and sometimes panic, (b) disrupt the public infrastructure, and (c) overwhelm healthcare resources. Indicators and triggers represent the information and actions taken at specific thresholds that guide incident recognition, response, and recovery.

There is no absolute definition or specific criteria for an MCI. US Federal statute defines a mass killing as three or more persons killed in a single incident [1]. The Department of Justice, Community Oriented Policing Services Division, defines MCI to be an event in which four or more individuals are shot, whether wounded or killed, excluding the perpetrator [2].

In the healthcare context, the number of casualties in an MCI is less critical than is the ratio of immediately presenting acute casualties to available resources; for example, resource limitation may be a result of providers, operating rooms, mechanical ventilators, isolating rooms, blood or blood products, medications, or beds. Thus, a smaller medical center, or a smaller community, may be more easily overwhelmed than a university medical center in a larger metropolitan city. A healthcare-centric definition of an MCI may best be therefore an event that overwhelms the local healthcare system. In an MCI, the number of acutely injured or sick *rapidly and acutely overwhelms all* available local healthcare resources and capabilities in a *very short period of time* [3]. Thus, the definition of an MCI is partially contextual, depending on the availability and flexibility of resources; however, the outcomes will largely depend on the extent of preparedness.

The definition of a "mass effect incident" (MEI) is one which acutely affects the ability of an organization to continue its normal operations, such as the delivery of routine healthcare services in such a way as to hinder their ability to accommodate surge capacity. MEIs can be more insidious than MCIs since they may not receive widespread media attention and may not precipitate the imminent sense of urgency of MCIs; nonetheless, MEIs can seriously impact the health and welfare of medically fragile persons, especially the very young, the aged, and those with chronic health conditions requiring continuous support and resources. The 2020 COVID-19 (SARS-CoV-2 also referred to as 2019-nCoV) coronavirus pandemic was an example of an MEI since the disease was relatively unrecognized as an emerging lethal pandemic for a long period of time, thereby facilitating its global spread and contagion. Thus, COVID-19 was not declared a pandemic until it was well established internationally rapidly escalating in an unprepared world.

In order to retain system functionality in a time of chaos, advance preparation is essential. Situational awareness facilitates accurate perception and comprehension of the circumstances, not only within the active arena but also with respect to available local, state, regional, and federal resources and support. Whereas provider focus may be on casualty management, adjunct administrative and legal perspectives are essential to maintain operational integrity and coordination both within the hot zone and with external resources. It is imperative that all healthcare professionals be aware of state and federal emergency management resources and support, as well as the regulatory and legal authorities under which response operations are conducted [4]. Providers must also know and understand their roles within the hospital and the community. The Hospital Emergency Incident Command System (HEICS) is an example of a hospital-scaled NIMS which can facilitate internal preparedness and coordination within a standardized structure approach disaster management. In turn, hospitals must be prepared to interface with their relevant incident command at all levels; to deal with transitions, including local, state, and federal levels; and to interface with referring community clinics and hospitals, public health, and EMS.

Coordination of actions during a crisis requires teamwork and leadership. Teamwork during a crisis [Chapter 8] requires the effective participation of support staff, professionals and specialists, administrators, attorneys, and local, regional, and or national incident command leadership. Teamwork can make the difference between chaos and an effective mission. There are two main types of leadership styles: directive, such as a military chain of command, and empowering that is more common in groups of professionals. More recent leadership theories postulate that empowering (shared) leadership is more effective when tasks are complex; since it is more important it is that team members be empowered and engaged, and share responsibility for the management of information, communication, and adaptability to achieve success [5]. However, the response is coordinated and must be effective, since in MCIs the stakes are high as measured in human life and suffering and also in community integrity and health.

The Development of an Integrated Response System

The principal philosophy of MCI management espouses that every such event is managed initially at the most local geographic, organizational, and jurisdictional levels [6]. Thereafter, as necessary, the response for an MCI is escalated through the responsible hierarchy in proportion to the impact and requirements of the event. When local response capabilities are exhausted or overwhelmed, state government and agencies become involved, enabling the allocation of statewide resources to the affected area; when the state declares a state of emergency the federal government is involved and then formally assumes leadership and responsibility.

States have the primary responsibility for the health and welfare of their citizens. Article I § 8 of the US Constitution enumerates the powers granted to US Congress and the Tenth Amendment of the US Constitution provides that "The powers not delegated to the United States by the Constitution, nor prohibited by it to the States, are reserved to the States respectively, or to the people." Although the Constitution twice mentions "General Welfare," once in the Preamble and subsequently in the Taxing and Spending Clause, the Supreme Court has ruled that such references were "never been regarded as the source of any substantive power conferred on the Government of the United States or on any of its Departments" [7]. Under the narrowest interpretation of police power, as limited by substantive due process, it is understood that states can exercise the power to protect the public health and safety. Thus, from a constitutional perspective, states have "plenary" authority to protect the public's health under their reserved powers in the Tenth Amendment. The Supreme Court has made it clear that states have a deep reservoir of public health powers, conceiving of state police powers as "an immense mass of legislation... Inspection laws, quarantine laws, and health laws of every description...are components of this mass" [8]. State governments have ultimate responsibility for the health and well-being of their citizens and can therefore allocate funding and statewide emergency resources, utilize National Guard troops, and draw on state supplies of drugs and vaccines. The Supreme Court regards federal police powers as constitutionally limited and curtailed expansion of a national public health authority [9].

System and surge resiliency is optimized by (a) prior preparedness through a hazard-vulnerability analysis (HVA) and (b) an integrated, trained, and ready incident command system (ICS). The "Medical Surge and Mass Prophylaxis" capabilities are the first lines of response to bioterrorism, pandemic influenza, and other public health emergencies. In the circumstance that an MCI cannot be managed effectively at local and state levels, it may be declared an "incident of national significance." An "incident of national significance" is defined as one with high impact requiring an extensive and well-coordinated response by federal, state, local, tribal, and nongovernmental authorities to save lives, minimize damage, and provide the basis for long-term community and economic recovery; it is declared by the Secretary of the Department of Homeland Security, activates the "National Response Plan," and shifts command structure to the federal government through the "National Incident Management System" (NIMS). Activation of the NRP and NIMS mobilizes federal resources, including federal funding, stockpiles, and the deployment of disaster management assistance teams (DMATs).

Much of the rules, regulations, and planning for MCIs have been developed through Presidential Orders. Presidential Directives represent a specific type of Executive Order. Directives have been issued since the Presidential term of Ronald Regan in 1981 (then termed "National Security Decision Directives") and continue through to the present. During the term of President G.W. Bush, Presidential Directives were denoted as "Homeland Security Presidential Directives" (HSPDs). Presidential Directives speak to the Executive Branch's national security policy and have the effect of law. These Directives are issued by the office of the President with the advice and consent of the National Security Council and outline responsibilities for the Executive Branch. Important Presidential Directives applicable to disaster management include the following:

- PPD-1: Organization of the National Security Council System
- PPD-2: Implementation of the National Strategy for Countering Biological Threats
- NSPM-4: Organization of the National Security Council and the Homeland Security Council
- HSPD-4/NSPD-17: National Strategy to Combat Weapons of Mass Destruction
- HSPD-5: Management of Domestic Incidents

- HSPD-6: Directive on Integration and Use of Screening Information to Protect against Terrorism
- HSPD-7: Critical Infrastructure Identification, Prioritization, and Protection
- PPD-8: National Preparedness
- HSPD-9: Defense of United States Agriculture and Food
- HSPD-10/NSPD-33: Biodefense for the 21st Century
- HSPD-18: Medical Countermeasures Against Weapons of Mass Destruction
- HSPD-21: Public Health and Medical Preparedness

Effective management of an emergency presupposes an effective plan. The Medical Surge Capacity and Capability (MSCC) Management System was developed in February 2003 as a systematic approach for managing the medical and public health response to an emergency or disaster; the details were subsequently updated in 2007 [10]. Homeland Security Presidential Directive, (HSPD)-5 mandated under § 15 to develop and administer a National Incident Management System (NIMS) and under § 16 to develop a National Response Plan (NRP).

Inter-agency collaboration is essential at all times, especially in times of crisis. The stated objective of HSPD-5 was to "ensure that all levels of government across the Nation have the capability to work efficiently and effectively together, using a national approach to domestic incident management" [11]. The intent of the program was to unify the treatment of crisis management and consequence management into a single integrated function under the authority of the Secretary of Homeland Security, pursuant to the Homeland Security Act of 2002, to coordinate all federal operations within the United States to prepare for, respond to, and recover from terrorist attacks, major disasters, and other emergencies. HSPD-5 recognized that the initial responsibility for incidents rests with the state and local authorities and also recognized that private and nongovernmental sectors also have important roles and responsibilities during such incidents. The authority of the secretary to assume responsibility is predicated upon four conditions:

1. Federal department or agency acting under its own authority has requested the assistance of the secretary.
2. The resources of state and local authorities are overwhelmed and federal assistance has been requested by the appropriate state and local authorities.
3. More than one federal department or agency has become substantially involved in responding to the incident.
4. The secretary has been directed to assume responsibility for managing the domestic incident by the president [11].

The NIMS is intended to provide a consistent nationwide model for federal, state, and local governments to achieve a functional interagency collaboration during the preparation, response, and recovery from incidents regardless of cause, size, or complexity. NIMS mandated the development and implementation of core concepts, principles, terminology, and technologies. Moreover, NIMS outlines the structure and operations of the Incident Command System (ICS), the unified command mandate; training, qualification, and certification requirements; resource identification and management; and the management of information and data flow.

The NRP integrates domestic prevention, preparedness, response, and recovery efforts into a single all-discipline, all-hazards plan.

1. The NRP, using the NIMS, shall, with regard to response to domestic incidents, provide the structure and mechanisms for national-level policy and operational direction for federal support to state and local incident managers and for exercising direct federal authorities and responsibilities, as appropriate.
2. The NRP will include protocols for operating under different threats or threat levels; incorporation of existing federal emergency and incident management plans (with appropriate modifications and revisions) as either integrated components of the NRP or as supporting operational plans; and additional operational plans or annexes, as appropriate, including public affairs and intergovernmental communications.
3. The NRP will include a consistent approach to reporting incidents, providing assessments, and making recommendations to the president, the secretary, and the Homeland Security Council.
4. The NRP will include rigorous requirements for continuous improvements from testing, exercising, experience with incidents, and new information and technologies.

Multiple Presidential Directives reinforced the need for a coordinated response system. Presidential Policy Directive (PPD-8) was promulgated in March 2011 with the intent of strengthening the security and resilience through the delineation of a National Preparedness Goal and the further development of the National Preparedness System as a scalable, flexible, and adaptable coordinating structures to align key roles and responsibilities [12]. PPD-8 was intended to leverage all available national resources and authorities from state and local governments, private and nonprofit sectors, and the public for the delivery of essential core capabilities [13]. In order to achieve these goals, national preparedness, necessitated planning and execution at strategic, operational, and tactical viewpoints. The strategic objective was outlined within the Implementation Plan and the National Preparedness Goal in PPD-8. The operational objective was outlined within the National Planning Frameworks and elements of the National Preparedness System. The tactical viewpoint was the basis for translation of the National Response Framework (NRF), the National Disaster Recovery Framework (NDRF), and the National Infrastructure Protection Plan (NIPP).

The National Preparedness Goal also categorized 31 core capabilities to assess and respond to the greatest risks [14]. The mission area of PPD-8 addressed the five elements of preparedness: prevention, protection, mitigation, response, and recovery. Each elements in the framework identifies risk, summarizes relevant roles and responsibilities, and leverages concepts from the NIMS to define and manage the structural and operational complexity.

Practical Considerations

Healthcare Facility Surge Accommodation

Healthcare facilities can potentially increase available capacity on short notice by stopping elective admissions and discharging noncritical patients either directly home or via transfer to lower acuity facilities. Key capacity limitations generally include resources such as intensive care unit (ICU) beds, operating rooms, and negative pressure rooms.

A comprehensive discussion of creative options for managing surge in a disaster situation is well beyond the scope of this chapter. There is much room for creative solutions for managing surge, in the ED, the floors, and the ICU. In order to devise creative solutions, those "boots on the ground" providers who are actually "in the arena" need to be engaged in devising and implementing such solutions; this is a fundamental task of leadership preparation for MCIs. For example, New York State (NYS) provides for the temporary suspension of state statutes and regulations in the event of an emergency declaration or proclamation by the local, state, or federal government. For example, NYS would provide for rapid endorsement of out-of-state RNs [15], allow out-of-state licensed nurses to provide general nursing care; [16] allow hospital facilities affected by the disaster/emergency to rapidly discharge, transfer, or receive patients, provided all reasonable measures to protect patient health and safety are taken; [17] and expedite medical staff appointment and privileging [18].

By further example, staffing assignment reassignment and support must consider the possibility that staff may be affected, cannot find transportation to and from work, or cannot leave their children or families. Transportation via police or EMS, child care, and possibly arrangements with local hotels may be necessary to provide sleeping arrangements. Critical Incident Debriefings may be necessary to minimize PTSD and burnout (see below). Local gymnasia or storage facilities can become makeshift wards. A shortage of ventilators may mandate volunteers who can hand-ventilate intubated patients.

Healthcare Facility Security

The vulnerability of hospital communication capabilities was made obvious during Hurricane Katrina and also 9/11. The loss of power, cell towers, or the overwhelming through communications crowding can incapacitate internal and external communications.

In the event of chemical, biological, or nuclear-based MCIs, there is a risk of secondary contamination though exposure of responders to the patient, his or her clothing, or other objects or fomites. The Tokyo sarin MCI demonstrated that the failure of hospital providers to properly use personal protective equipment together with a decision to contain contaminated patients in a poorly ventilated hospital chapel caused secondary sarin exposure to numerous healthcare workers .Protocols for decontamination in the field or outside the physical hospital are important to conserve the most fragile healthcare resources – the provider and support personnel.

The integrity of the communications infrastructure, both internally within the organization and externally with others is fundamental to an effective disaster response. The vulnerability of cell communications was clearly demonstrated during 9/11. Options for closed internal communications, generator power, water, and food must be considered and planned for in advance. The security, and conversely the vulnerability of a facility, will be defined by its self-sustainability with respect to operations involving its power grid, water supply, and equipment availability and functionality.

The International Association for Healthcare Security and Safety (IAHSS) is an organization endorsed by the Joint Commission (TJC) and serves to assist healthcare administrators in the management and direction of security, safety, and emergency management programs in healthcare facilities [19]. TJC requires each accredited institution to implement plans consistent with standards such as the Environment of Care, Emergency Management, and Emergency Operations Plan.

Hospitals as Targets

Hospitals can be targeted by terrorism directly or indirectly. Family members and friends searching for loved ones can pose security challenges, as can the press. In some situations, a hospital may need to be placed on lock down. Facility planning for direct attacks should be a part of each facility's MCI disaster scenario with attendant protocols to limit public access; identity verification, perimeter security; and to safeguard critical resources such as air, medical gasses, food, water, communications, and power. Hacking has recently exposed the healthcare systems' vulnerability to cyberattacks which can disable the EMR, communications, telemetry, and all connected devices through the internet of things (IoT).

The Model State Emergency Health Powers Act (MSEHPA) and the Ethics of Public Health Responses to MCIs

Despite the network of Presidential Directives and other regulations, and the diverse plans and agencies developed with the intent of effectively responding to an MCI, the coordination of public health response among the states remains limited. State public health laws have been and remain inconsistent both within states and among them; moreover, they mostly date to the early twentieth century and are therefore infective and counterproductive and often obsolescent and ineffective [20]. The Robert Wood Johnson (RWJ) Foundation initiated Turning Point in collaboration with the W.K. Kellogg Foundation (Kellogg) in 1997 [21]. The Turning Point Public Health Statute Modernization National Collaborative developed the Model State Public Health Act with the intent of strengthening the US public health infrastructure in order for states, local communities, and their public health agencies to better respond to public health challenges.

In response to the anthrax outbreak of 2001, the Centers for Disease Control and Prevention (CDC) called upon the Center for Law and the Public's Health (CLPH) at Georgetown and Johns Hopkins Universities to draft a Model State Emergency Health Powers Act (MSEHPA) [22]. Because it was commissioned by the CDC, the Model Act provided states with an outline of necessary powers which would be needed in order to detect and contain a bioterrorism or naturally occurring MCI such as a pandemic. The Model Act is structured to reflect five basic public health functions to be facilitated by law: (1) preparedness, comprehensive planning for a public health emergency; (2) surveillance, measures to detect and track public health emergencies; (3) management of property, ensuring adequate availability of vaccines, pharmaceuticals, and hospitals, as well as providing power to abate hazards to the public's health; (4) protection of persons, powers to compel vaccination, testing, treatment, isolation, and quarantine when clearly necessary; and (5) communication, providing clear and authoritative information to the public [23]. Under MSEHPA, state powers over property and persons would necessarily take effect only after a state's governor declares a "public health emergency." MSEHPA would then provide comprehensive powers to manage property, protect persons, and safeguard the public's health and security such as the examination or testing of persons, isolate or quarantine, and vaccinations. MSEHPA incorporates protections against abuse of power by the states: (1) the governor must adhere to strict criteria, including consultation with public health experts and the community before he or she can declare an emergency; (2) the state legislature, by majority vote, can override the governor's declaration of an emergency at any time; and (3) the judiciary can terminate the governor's exercise of power if it deems a violation of standards, procedures, or the state constitution.

Following its publication in October 2001 and revision in December 2001, possibly because of the public rights controversy, MSEHPA was formally released to state legislatures for consideration and many subsequently initiated legislative and/or administrative efforts to adopt it in whole or in part, although not all states do so. In fact, in general, states did not respond to the recommendations articulated by MSEHPA with either the breadth or consistency envisioned by the Center for Law and the Public's Health. Some argue that although the controversy regarding the Model Act is unlikely to lead to repeal of statutes enacted in response to MSEHPA, the controversy did signal that many citizens remain deeply suspicious about how a government could use or abuse its powers during health emergencies.

The ethical argument which underlies MSEHPA is identical to the ethical arguments which are fundamental not only to public health but also to healthcare in general: the issues of autonomy, paternalism, and justice [See Chapter 1]. On one hand, the principle of autonomy was articulated by Justice Benjamin Cardozo in *Schloendorff* where he stated that "every human being of adult years and sound mind shall have the right to determine what shall be done with his own body ...." [24]. Cardozo's words subsequently became the foundation for the Doctrine of Informed Consent [25].

On the other hand, with respect to the common good, the Supreme Court ruled in 1905 that "the liberty secured by the Constitution of the United States to every person within its jurisdiction does not impart an absolute right in each person to be, at all times and in all circumstances, wholly freed from restraint. There are manifold restraints to which every person is necessarily subject for the common good" [26]. Dworkin defined paternalism as "interference with a person's liberty of action justified by reason referring exclusively to the welfare … of the person being coerced" [27].

Thus, the relevant analysis here may not be paternalism *versus* autonomy but rather justice *versus* autonomy. The principle of justice speaks to a moral obligation to act on the basis of fair adjudication between competing claims; it involves fairness, entitlement, and equality. In healthcare ethics, the principle of justice can be subdivided into three categories: fair distribution of scarce resources (distributive justice), respect for people's rights (rights-based justice), and respect for morally acceptable laws (legal justice) [28]. In an MCI, some individual rights will need to be, at least temporarily, subjugated in order to best care for the community, for example as in instances of quarantine and triage. Population-based, public health, ethical models may, at times, be in conflict with traditional framework of medical ethics.

MSEHPA was criticized on the basis of the broad state police powers it proposed – controversy on issues of individual freedoms, personal privacy, and a lack of oversight provisions. Although Annas has posited that the "argument that, in a public health emergency, there must be a trade-off between effective public health measures and civil rights is simply wrong." It is nonetheless imperative to reconcile the competing viewpoints and yet to maintain a sense of moral integrity. Although there is no uniformly acceptable answer whereby individual rights can be curtailed in a free society, the need to limit societal impact cannot be disregarded. Ethics can provide a framework for publicly discussing and managing such a controversy. Childress annotated five "justificatory conditions" to be considered when weighing public health interventions as against individual autonomy: (1) effectiveness, (2) proportionality, (3) necessity, (4) least infringement, and (5) public justification [29].

Ethical and Legal Issues in Mass Casualty Events

Ethical decision-making requires an understanding of and a sensitivity to the ethical implications of problems and situations. Ethical analysis can help provide a common framework for difficult real-time decision-making and to manage transparency retroactively where decisions may be questioned. The after-action review (AAR) is an example of a structured review for review, analysis, and identification of future opportunities. In spite of the chaos which characterizes MCIs, ethical, moral, and legal duties cannot be disregarded. High-level, abstract ethical frameworks are more often than not impractical during times of crisis when emotions are high, and the circumstances can be overwhelming. In order for ethical guidance to be useful, it must be part of the preparation and planning of all expected responders, be clearly articulated, morally justified, and be practical and implementable in the arena. When governments, governmental agencies, healthcare systems, and providers begin to plan for mass casualty events, such theoretically sound and practically useful ethical guidance should be at the foundation of prospective laws, regulations, and action plans [30].

The Emergency Medical Treatment and Labor Act (EMTALA)

The Emergency Medical Treatment and Active Labor Act (EMTALA) was enacted as law in 1986 by Congress as part of the Consolidated Omnibus Budget Reconciliation Act [31] (COBRA) of 1985. EMTALA requires all hospitals which have an Emergency Department (ED) and who participate in Medicare to provide any individual who presents to an ED regardless of ability to pay, with a medical screening examination (MSE), medical stabilization, and an appropriate transfer if necessary.

Specifically, EMTALA Mandates

1. An appropriate medical screening exam (MSE) to determine if the individual has an emergency medical condition (EMC). If there is no EMC, a hospital has no further EMTALA obligation.
2. If there is an EMC, a hospital must either (i) treat and stabilize the EMC within the capability of the hospital, including the admission of the individual or (ii) appropriately transfer the individual to a hospital that has the capability and capacity to stabilize the MCE if the presenting hospital is unable to do so.[1]

EMTALA defines "stabilized" with respect to an EMC to mean "that no material deterioration of the condition is likely, within reasonable medical probability, to result from or occur during the transfer of the individual from a facility" [32]. EMTALA further defines an EMC to be either:

1. A medical condition manifesting itself by acute symptoms of sufficient severity (including severe pain, psychiatric disturbances and/or symptoms of substance abuse) such that the absence of immediate medical attention could reasonably be expected to place the individual's health (or, with respect to a pregnant woman,

[1] Note: Section 945 of the Medicare Prescription Drug, Improvement, and Modernization Act of 2003 enacted an advisory group regarding EMTALA law is governed primarily by section 1867 of the Social Security Act and regulations found at 42 CFR 489.24.

the health of the woman or her unborn child) in serious jeopardy; or serious impairment to bodily functions; or serious dysfunction of any bodily organ or part; or
2. With respect to a pregnant woman who is having contractions, that there is inadequate time to effect a safe transfer to another hospital before delivery, or that the transfer may pose a threat to the health or safety of the woman or the unborn child [33].

The Inspector General (OIG) of the Department of Health and Human Services and Centers for Medicaid and Medicare Services (CMS) enforces EMTALA. The civil statute of limitations for EMTALA enforcement is 2 years. Penalties for EMTALA violations include:

- Termination of the hospital or physician's Medicare provider agreement.
- Hospital fines up to $50,000 per violation ($25,000 for a hospital with fewer than 100 beds).
- Physician fines $50,000 per violation, including on-call physicians.
- The hospital may be sued for personal injury in civil court under a "private cause of action."
- A receiving facility, having suffered financial loss as a result of another hospital's violation of EMTALA, can bring suit to recover damages.

Physicians and hospitals are liable under EMTALA regardless of intent or motive. On January 21, 1999, the US Supreme Court issued its decision in the case of *Roberts v Galen* of Virginia, Inc. [34], a case which had been granted certiorari from a decision by the US Circuit Court for the Sixth Circuit in April 1997. The Court of Appeals had ruled that in alleging a violation of EMTALA's stabilization requirement, a plaintiff must show that the hospital's actions resulted from an improper motive such as indigence, race, or sex. The US Supreme court disagreed, reversed, and held that proof of improper motive was not within the meaning of the EMTALA statute.

In disaster, mass casualty, or emergency situations, EMTALA remains in effect and its provisions must be followed; under such circumstances, EDs and hospitals remain responsible for MSE evaluations and thereafter patients can be transferred or referred to other hospitals in accordance with the hospital emergency plan or the community response plan. During extraordinary ED surges and MCIs, the MSE does not have to take place in the ED and a hospital may set up alternative sites on its campus to perform MSEs which must be conducted by qualified personnel as defined in the Practice Act of the relevant state. In addition, hospitals may set up screening at off-campus, appropriately staffed hospital-controlled sites. In an MCI event, individuals requiring additional emergent medical attention must be transferred within the campus or to the campus as medically necessary and in conformity with Medicare Conditions of Participation and/or in coordination with local emergency medical services (EMS). On the other hand, communities, not hospitals, may set up screening clinics at sites not under the control of a hospital and where there is no applicable EMTALA obligation.

An EMTALA waiver allows hospitals to legally direct or relocate individuals from an ED to an alternative off-campus site, in accordance with a State emergency or pandemic preparedness plan, for the MSE and to effect the transfer of individuals with unstable EMC that would be otherwise prohibited under EMTALA, as long as the transfer is necessitated by the emergency circumstances. In an MCI and under certain similar circumstances enumerated below, EMTALA obligations regarding MSE and stabilization sanctions can be waived:

1. The President declares an emergency or disaster under the Stafford Act or the National Emergencies Act; and
2. The Secretary of Health and Human Services declares that a Public Health Emergency (PHE) exists and also authorizes EMTALA waivers under section 1135 of the Social Security Act. Notice of EMTALA waivers will be provided through CMS to covered entities; and
3. Unless EMTALA waivers are granted for an entire geographic area, the hospital applies for a waiver; and
4. The hospital must have activated its emergency operations plan; and
5. The State must have activated its emergency operations plan or pandemic plan for an area that covers the affected hospital [35].

The waiver of EMTALA requirements is generally considered effective for 72 hours after an emergency is declared and the facility's emergency plan is activated. However, despite waiver, the hospital remains responsible for ensuring the safety of patients under its care. In addition, an EMTALA waiver may be made retroactive to the effective date of the emergency period and the date of the activation of the hospital emergency operations plan, but in no circumstances before the effective date of the emergency declaration [36].

The Health Insurance Portability and Accountability Act (HIPAA)

The Health Insurance Portability and Accountability Act of 1996 [37] (HIPAA; sometimes referred to as the Kennedy–Kassebaum Act) was enacted in response to advances in electronic and information technology as a legislative safeguard to patients' protected health information (PHI), while also simultaneously ensuring, and requiring, that such PHI can be disclosed and utilized by facilities, practitioners, and individuals, as necessary, to provide treatment to the patient. The HIPAA Privacy Rule applies to organizations known as HIPAA-covered entities and these include healthcare providers, healthcare facilities, health plans, healthcare clearinghouses, and business partners or associates. The HIPAA Security Rule specifically focuses on safeguarding electronic protected health information (ePHI) [38].

HHS expanded HIPAA under an omnibus rule in 2013 to modify HIPAA according to Health Information Technology for Economic and Clinical Health (HITECH)

Act of 2009 [39]. HIPAA is enforced through the HHS Office for Civil Rights (OCR) which prosecutes HIPAA compliance violations to a maximum of $1.5 million per incident. The OCR further clarified the HIPAA security rule in 2016 through the development of a crosswalk between HIPAA, HiTECH, and the National Institute of Standards and Technology's Cybersecurity Framework to identify cybersecurity gaps and comply with cybersecurity standards.

The use, sharing, and safeguarding of ePHI during an MCI can be a challenge. In any situation where providers and hospitals must share ePHI, reasonable safeguards must be in place to limit the information provided so as to disclose only the minimum necessary information accomplish the intended purpose [40]. For example, in 2005, during Hurricane Katrina, the US DHHS published specific guidance for providers stating that (a) healthcare providers could share patient information as necessary to provide treatment; (b) healthcare providers could share patient information as necessary to identify, locate, and notify family members, guardians, or anyone else responsible for the individual's care of the individual's location, general condition, or death; and (c) "when a health care provider is sharing information with disaster relief organizations that, like the American Red Cross, are authorized by law or by their charters to assist in disaster relief efforts, it is unnecessary to obtain a patient's permission to share the information if doing so would interfere with the organization's ability to respond to the emergency" [41]. In addition, HIPAA allows that hospitals may release information to law enforcement as required by law and law enforcement [42].

Triage

The word "triage" derives from the French word "trier" meaning "to sort" [43]. Although the first known context in which the term "triage was used was in reference to goods sorted as to quality and price, the term is now widely understood to apply to the sorting and prioritization of patients in need of emergency medical attention. Triage is commonly used in military and civilian situations and is even utilized every daily in emergency departments to prioritize the ordering of patients based on their acuity. The goal of triage is to optimize the relationship between the perceived degree of injury and statistical likelihood of functional survival as offset by the estimation of scarce resources which will need to be consumed [44]. Triage is also addressed in Chapter 5.

The key modern ethical principle used to justify triage is that of distributive justice. The underlying philosophical debate in triage is that of utilitarianism under which the goal is the survival (or the "greatest good") of the greatest number and the notion of egalitarianism which advocates that all individuals be treated fairly and equally. However, ethics, as moral philosophy, is both a branch of philosophy, which addresses questions about morality, and is also the foundation of the codes of behavior and rules of conduct encompassing providers' obligations to patients, colleagues, and society. Aristotelian ethical theory distinguishes two types of knowledge:

"sophia" and "phronesis." "Sophia" represents absolute knowledge or universal truths which can be physically, mathematically, or logically derived such as equations or plainly evident diagnoses. On the other hand, "phronesis" refers to a more complex form of knowledge, more a type of wisdom, which requires not only the fund of knowledge but also experience and careful consideration and reflection [45]. "Phronesis" is therefore a practical wisdom [46] that cannot be learned or taught from textbooks and is rather a virtue based on both learning and extensive real-world experience. In the end, a purely ethical analysis of triage leads to dilemmas: (1) Is it compassion or logic that guides medical rationing? (2) Can rationing reasonably be relegated to a computer using physiologic parameters as the input guiding triage or does ethical triage require practical wisdom and a moral compass that cannot be distilled into an algorithm? [47]

Triage as it is used to objectively prioritize and allocate resources during a civilian mass-casualty scenario has fostered the development of multiple static (single assessment) and dynamic (serial assessment) triage measures, tools, and techniques [48]. Operationally, triage is a simple notion based on the first impression and initial examination of the patient. Primary triage occurs at the scene of an MCI and secondary triage at the casualty clearing station or staffing area. Usually, triage occurs rapidly and in the absence of extensive physiologic, laboratory, or radiologic data. Patients who are obviously at the extremes of the risk of death spectrum, either those with non-life-threatening injuries and thus relatively low risk of death, or those with massive injury who are at imminent risk of death even with interventions, are given low priorities in triage. Triage is also a dynamic process subject to unanticipated or anticipated changes in any patient's clinical status and therefore requires ongoing assessment and re-prioritization.

Algorithm-based approaches utilize decision-support guidance intended to provide objectivity; minimize confusion, debate, and delay; optimize timely care; and provide transparency [49]. Nonetheless, algorithms and scores are not universally accepted. For example, the Move, Assess, Sort, Send (MASS), Simple Triage and Rapid Treatment (START), and the Sort, Assess, Life-saving interventions, Treatment and/or Transport (SALT) are both used but also criticized [50]. The CDC published "Guidelines for Field Triage of Injured Patients" in which it steps and details, and the use of basic scoring systems, as a type of standard operating procedure (SOP) to guide triage decision-making [51]. Public health triage refers to triage protocols that distribute vaccinations or countermeasures in the event of an infectious disease outbreak, natural disaster, or other MCI [52]. In 2009, during the H1N1 pandemic, the Institute of Medicine (IOM) and the National Academy of Medicine, at the request of the Office of the Assistant Secretary for Preparedness and Response (ASPR) at DHHS convened an *ad hoc* committee to address how resource allocation and triage decisions could be fairly made under crisis conditions [53], subsequently culminating in the creation of a toolkit for planners [54]. Despite use of an algorithm or SOP, triage decisions can be subjective and discretionary. Nonetheless, both algorithms and SOPs increase the likelihood that decision-making in triage situations is transparent, fair, and efficient. Arguably, the more objective the process of difficult clinical decision-making is, the less it is vulnerable to bias and, therefore, the more defensible it is in the event of retrospective review such as an AAR [55].

Legally, cases against providers predicated on triage decisions alone are rare and even more rarely are they successful without evidence of carelessness or gross negligence. However, certainly in civilian emergencies, there can be provider and hospital liability under the EMTALA which imposes specific triage obligations on healthcare providers to (a) perform a medical screening examination to determine whether an emergency medical condition exists; (b) to provide necessary stabilizing treatment when an emergency medical condition exists; and (c) to stabilize the patient or, if the physician certifies that the benefits of transfer outweigh the risks, arrange for proper transfer to another hospital.

Quarantine

The practice of isolating people inflicted with a disease is described in the Old Testament Book of Leviticus where lepers were isolated from society in an effort to contain leprosy. Isolation separates those people diagnosed with a communicable disease from the healthy. Isolation poses no risk to the isolated, since they already have the disease, although arguably they are technically isolated and may not have appropriate access to treatment and other resources.

On the other hand, the practice of quarantine separates and restricts the movement of people who were exposed to a contagious disease during a period of observation to see if they manifest the disease. Thus, the key difference between isolation and quarantine is that isolation affects only those known to be sick, whereas quarantine restricts the movement of a group of people, of whom some are known to be ill, in confinement with others who are potentially healthy (or potentially ill). Isolation isolates the sick to prevent transmission to the healthy. Quarantine confines the sick with the healthy, knowing that the healthy may also subsequently become sick, in order to avoid transmission outside the group which has been quarantined. Thus quarantine poses a risk to those who are not yet infected housed with the ill but who are likely to contact the illness because of the closed quarters or proximity.

The term "quarantine" is derived from the Latin word for "forty." The practice of quarantine dates back to the fourteenth century when ships arriving in Venice from infected ports were required to sit in precautionary isolation for a period of 40 days before landing in an effort to protect coastal cities from plague. In the United States, in 1793, in response to a yellow fever outbreak in Philadelphia, a quarantine station named Lazaretto was constructed along the Delaware River in order to contain the potentially infected. Shortly thereafter, Congress enacted the National Quarantine Act of 1878 [56]. The following year, in 1879, the National Board of Health (NBH) was created by an Act of the 45th US Congress titled "An Act to Prevent the Introduction of Infectious or Contagious Disease into the United States and to establish a National Board of Health" [57].

Today, under their Police Powers, states have the primary responsibility for maintaining public health and therefore the responsibility for controlling the spread of diseases within state borders; accordingly every state, the District of Columbia, and most territories have enacted laws authorizing both isolation and quarantine and isolation. The federal government is also authorized to mandate quarantine through the Public Health Service Act [58] and Executive Orders addressing Quarantinable Communicable Diseases [59]. A comprehensive list of specific laws and regulations governing the control of communicable diseases within the United States has been catalogued by the CDC [60]. The US DHHS also has statutory responsibility for preventing the introduction, transmission, and spread of communicable diseases in the United States; these functions are delegated to the Division of Global Migration and Quarantine which has the authority to:

1. Operate quarantine stations at ports of entry
2. Establish standards for medical examination of persons destined for the United States
3. Administer interstate and foreign quarantine regulations, which govern the international and interstate movement of persons, animals, and cargo

On January 31, 2020, President Donald Trump released a proclamation in response to the COVID-19 outbreaks suspending entry into the United States from certain countries, specifically outlining medical screening and quarantine where appropriate [61]. Not long thereafter, Governor Cuomo instituted a quarantine of the city of New Rochelle, NY [62].

The ethical justification of quarantine and quarantine laws stems from a general moral obligation to prevent harm to others. Similar to triage, quarantine may be ethically justified if the primary focus is on population-based, public health, rather than the rights of the individual.

Upshur outlines the principles which must be met for a quarantine to be ethically justified:

1. The harm principle must be met; there should be clear and measurable harm to others.
2. The proportionality, or least restrictive means, principle should be observed; meaning that public health authorities should use the least restrictive measures in proportion to achieving the desired goal.
3. Reciprocity must exist; if society requires that individuals curtail their liberties for the good of others, society has a reciprocal obligation to assist them in return.
4. The transparency principle holds that public health authorities have an obligation to communicate clearly the justification for their actions and establish for a process of appeal of governmental action [63].

Inherent in the justification of quarantine (and also triage) is the notion of due process. Due process is especially important in the context of quarantine, since it arguably results in particularly extreme deprivations of liberty such as the arbitrary and indefinite confinement of individuals presumably against their will. Moreover, federal law requires that HHS and the CDC appoint a medical expert to examine persons under quarantine to establish whether ongoing quarantine is justified; however, the timeline for such an evaluation is not specified [64]. In the case of Foucha [65], the US Supreme Court ruled that involuntary commitment of those with mental illness does not violate the Due Process Clause of the Fourteenth Amendment if there is sufficient evidence to conclude that they present a danger to themselves or others.

Standards of Care for MCI Casualties

In general, the legal definition of negligence is defined as a deviation from "the standard of conduct to which one must conform… [and] is that of a reasonable man under like circumstances" [66]. Medical standards of care describe the types and levels of medical care dictated by professional norms, professional requirements, and institutional objectives [67]. On the other hand, the legal definition for the medical standard of care can be generally defined as the level and nature of care that a reasonably competent and skilled healthcare professional would be expected to provide under the circumstances.

In the event of an MCI and a subsequent surge which mandates triage, quarantine, resource redistribution, and mass casualty care, hospitals and providers may find it necessary to shift to a sufficiency-of-care mode, in which the focus is on saving as many lives as possible rather than ensuring that each patient receives the usual standard of care. Constrained resources during MCIs may require that patients be managed as a population to maximize overall, rather than individual, outcomes. The utilitarian philosopher Jeremy Bentham stated that "it is the greatest good to the greatest number of people which is the measure of right and wrong" [68]. Although the applicability of Bentham's philosophy to everyday life can be debated, it has applicability in situations where scarce resources are overwhelmed.

The immediate public health goals in the event of an MCI can be delineated as the needs to:

1. Minimize death and serious illness by distributing finite resources to those who have the greatest opportunity to benefit
2. Maximize appropriate care for the largest number of patients
3. Maximize self-care by the public by using media to deliver public health messages
4. Delineate which health care facilities should provide what level of care based on the capacities and capabilities of the facility
5. Provide a legal framework for developing triage decisions
6. Engage the public and build trust in the community by being inclusive, transparent, open, and honest about the limited resources and the resulting crisis standard [69]

The principles of Crisis Standards of Care (CSC) articulated by the IOM in 2009 are based on ethical principles and the law. In order to be meaningful and effective, CSC "must be applied across all levels of the health care system horizontally (virtual, outpatient, inpatient) and vertically (hospital, health care coalition, state/region, federal) with plans to maximize services and capacity while sharing information, leveraging resources, and distributing patients to ensure the greatest equity and consistency of care" [70]. CSC are based on the following seven key principles:

1. Fairness
2. Duty to Care
3. Duty to Steward Resources
4. Transparency
5. Consistency
6. Proportionality
7. Accountability [71]

CSC represents a dynamic process which can involve complex and difficult decisions, trade-offs, and potentially unconventional acts (such as the denial or withdrawal of health care services because of limited resources). Nonetheless, Tenet Health Systems as the operator of Memorial Medical Center in New Orleans settled claims brought by Hurricane Katrina victims for $25 million where they alleged not only for Tenet's failure to respond but also for its failure to plan and properly prepare [72].

There are no comprehensive national liability protections for health care practitioners or entities in all settings. Volunteers who act in good faith and without willful misconduct, gross negligence, or recklessness may be protected under Good Samaritan Statutes or the Uniform Emergency Volunteer Health Practitioners Act (UEVHPA). Notably, although protection from liability for actions during an MCI is afforded to volunteers, governmental actors, firefighters, and EMS, healthcare providers are not similarly indemnified, with the exceptions of a few states including Virginia [73][2] and Louisiana [74].[3]

Provider Post-Traumatic Stress Disorder and Burnout

The American Psychiatric Association (APA) generally defines post-traumatic stress disorder (PTSD) as a psychiatric disorder that can occur in people who have experienced or witnessed a traumatic event such as a natural disaster, a serious accident, a terrorist act, war/combat, rape, or other violent personal assault. The United

[2] "In the absence of gross negligence or willful misconduct, any health care provider who responds to a disaster shall not be liable for any injury or wrongful death of any person arising from the delivery or withholding of health care when (i) a state or local emergency has been or is subsequently declared in response to such disaster, and (ii) the emergency and subsequent conditions caused a lack of resources, attributable to the disaster, rendering the health care provider unable to provide the level or manner of care that otherwise would have been required in the absence of the emergency and which resulted in the injury or wrongful death at issue."

[3] "During a state of public health emergency, any health care providers shall not be civilly liable for causing the death of, or, injury to, any person or damage to any property except in the event of gross negligence or willful misconduct."

Nations International Strategy for Disaster Reduction (UNISDR) defines disaster as "a serious disruption of the functioning of a community or a society at any scale due to hazardous events interacting with conditions of exposure, vulnerability and capacity, leading to one or more of the following: human, material, economic and environmental losses and impacts" [75].

The APA diagnostic criteria for PTSD were updated in the fifth edition of the Diagnostic and Statistical Manual of Mental Disorders (DSM-5) in 2013. PTSD in DSM-5 included a newly revised clinical entity category, "Trauma- and Stressor-Related Disorders," comprised of multiple criteria, all of which must be met for a diagnosis. The relevant diagnostic criteria and additional required specifications are as follows:

- Criterion A stressor: exposure to death, threatened death, actual or threatened serious injury, or actual or threatened sexual violence
- Criterion B intrusion symptoms: the traumatic event is persistently re-experienced
- Criterion C avoidance: avoidance of trauma-related stimuli
- Criterion D negative alterations in cognitions and mood: negative thoughts or feelings that began or worsened after the trauma
- Criterion E alterations in arousal and reactivity: trauma-related arousal and reactivity that began or worsened after the trauma
- Criterion F duration: symptoms last for more than 1 month
- Criterion G functional significance: symptoms create distress or functional impairment
- Criterion H exclusion: symptoms are not due to medication, substance use, or other illness

Specifications:

- Dissociative Specification: as either depersonalization or derealization
- Delayed Specification: full diagnostic criteria are not met until at least six months after the trauma(s), although onset of symptoms may occur immediately [76]

Epidemiological evidence indicates that PTSD is under-recognized and therefore potentially undertreated. Diagnosis and treatment of PTSD are confounded by the fact that PTSD as a diagnosis commonly coexists with or is confused with other diagnoses such as major depressive disorders, anxiety disorders, and substance abuse.

Rates of post-disaster PTSD often studies "incidence" rather than "prevalence;" however, this may underestimate the impact of PTSD especially in those geographical areas where populations are repeatedly exposed to large-scale traumatic events such as natural disasters, wars, or violence. PTSD can cause occupational, psychiatric, medical, and psychosocial disabilities, and its consequences are significant not only to survivors and their families but also to healthcare providers, the healthcare system, and society [77]. PTSD is especially common among first responders involved in rescue and recovery. Following the 1989 Hillsborough football stadium disaster in Sheffield, UK, reportedly 44.3% of police officers were diagnosed with severe PTSD and 44.1% manifested moderate symptom severity [78].

Resilience is the ability to cope with stress. Resilience occurs at the personal level and also at the community level; communities can enhance reliance [79]. Although supportive communities enhance reliance, they require psychological, economic, and physical resources to do so. Thus, Kendra observes that (1) most disaster-related resilience work focuses on communities and (2) at a foundation level, resilience is part of "[society's] ongoing search for survival" [80]. In the end, MCIs profoundly impact the psyche of each of the individual and cut deeply into the social fabric of the community. Long after the MCI, these scars will remain and cannot be ignored.

Conclusions

Coordinated and effective response to MCIs requires planning, preparation, training, and a mindset of resilience. MCIs strike to the heart of individuals and society and they continue to increase in both size and scope. The state of system-wide emergency preparedness in most countries is, at best, poor. The state of legislative and regulatory preparedness is likewise disjointed, ineffective, and inadequate. Despite widespread concerns by providers and facilities regarding potential liability during MCI events, there remain minimal state-specific, and no comprehensive national level liability protections for health care practitioners or facilities in the event of a disaster response. On the other hand, formal liability protections do exist for civilian volunteers, all levels of government agencies and actors, emergency managers, police, firefighters, and EMS. Never before have the legal and regulatory bases for the provider component of the emergency response system been so much in need of comprehensive reform to ensure the effective and timely response of the healthcare system.

References

1. 28 U.S.C. § 530C(b)(1)(M)(i)(I).
2. Mass shootings: preparing for violent events (July 2019). Online at: https://cops.usdoj.gov/html/dispatch/07-2019/mass_shootings.html. Verified 11 Oct 2020.
3. Ben-Ishay O, Mitaritonno M, Catena F, Sartelli M, Ansaloni L, Kluger Y. Mass casualty incidents - time to engage. World J Emerg Surg. 2016;11:8. Published 2016 Feb 3. https://doi.org/10.1186/s13017-016-0064-7.
4. U.S Department of Health and Human Services. Topic collection: healthcare-related disaster legal/ regulatory/ federal policy. Online at: https://asprtracie.hhs.gov/technical-resources/83/healthcare-related-disaster-legal-regulatory-federal-policy/1. Verified 11 Oct 2020.
5. Pearce CL, Sims HP Jr. Vertical versus shared leadership as predictors of the effectiveness of change management teams: An examination of aversive, directive, transactional, transformational, and empowering leader behaviors. Group Dyn. 2002;6(2):172–97.
6. DHS (U.S. Department of Homeland Security). National response plan. Washington, DC: DHS; 2004.

7. Jacobson v. Massachusetts, 197 U.S. 11, 22 (1905).
8. Gibbons v. Ogden, 22 U.S. (9 Wheat.) 1 (1824)
9. United States v. Lopez, 514 U.S. 549 (1995).
10. U.S. Department of Health and Human Services. Medical surge capacity and capability: a management system for integrating medical and health resources during large-scale emergencies. 2nd ed. September 2007. Available online at https://www.phe.gov/Preparedness/planning/mscc/handbook/Documents/mscc080626.pdf. Verified 11 Oct 2020.
11. U.S. Department of Homeland Security. Homeland Security Presidential Directive-5. February 28, 2003. Available online at: https://www.dhs.gov/sites/default/files/publications/Homeland%20Security%20Presidential%20Directive%205.pdf. Verified 11 Oct 2020.
12. Department of Homeland security. Presidential Policy Directive / PPD-8: National Preparedness. Available online at: https://www.dhs.gov/presidential-policy-directive-8-national-preparedness. Verified 11 Oct 2020.
13. Jared T. Brown, Presidential Policy Directive 8 and the National Preparedness System: Background and Issues for Congress. Congressional Research Service. October 21, 2011. Available online at: https://fas.org/sgp/crs/homesec/R42073.pdf. Verified 11 Oct 2020.
14. Federal Emergency Response Administration. PPD-8 Overview Presentation: Presidential Policy Directive 8 / PPD-8: National Preparedness. January 16, 2013. Available online at: https://www.fema.gov/media-library-data/20130726-1904-25045-2748/draft_ppd_8_eric_runnels_cfscc_20120928_fd_.pdf. See also: National Preparedness Goal. Homeland Security. 2011. Online at: https://www.doi.gov/sites/doi.gov/files/uploads/National_Preparedness_Goal_pdf.pdf. Verified 11 Oct 2020.
15. Thus suspending NY PHL Articles 28-E & 36; Ed. Law Article 13. See also, Healthcare Association of New York State (HANYS). Temporary Suspension or Modification of Statutes and Regulations in New York State During Emergencies. August 2014. Available online at: https://www.urmc.rochester.edu/MediaLibraries/URMCMedia/flrtc/preparedness-response-tools/documents/HANYS-healthcare_emergency_guidebook_regs.pdf. Verified October 11, 2020.
16. Thus suspending NY Ed. Law Article 139.
17. Thus suspending 10 NYCRR §400.9; 10 NYCRR §405.9 (f)(7).
18. Thus suspending 10 NYCRR §405.2(e).
19. The Joint Commission. International Association for Healthcare Security and Safet https://www.jointcommission.org/en/resources/patient-safety-topics/workplace-violence-prevention/international-association-for-healthcare-security-and-safety/. Verified 11 Oct 2020.
20. Gostin LO, Sapsin JW, Teret SP. at al. The Model State Emergency Health Powers Act: planning for and response to bioterrorism and naturally occurring infectious diseases. JAMA. 2002;288(5):622–8.
21. Hassmiller S. Turning point: the Robert Wood Johnson Foundation's effort to revitalize public health at the state level. J Public Health Manag Pract. 2002;8(1):1–5.
22. The Center for Law and Public Health at Georgetown and Johns Hopkins Universities in collaboration with the National Governors Association, the National Conference of State Legislatures, Association of State and Territorial Health Officials, the National Association of City and County Health Officers, and the National Association of Attorneys General. The Model State Emergency Health Powers Act. October 23, 2001. Available online at: https://www.aapsonline.org/legis/msehpa.pdf.
23. Gostin LO. Public Health Law In An Age Of Terrorism: Rethinking Individual Rights And Common Goods. HEALTH AFFAIRSVOL. 21, NO. 6: Nov/Dec 2002.
24. Schloendorff v Society of New York Hospital. 105 N.E. 92 (N.Y. 1914).
25. Salgo V (1957) Leland Stanford Jr. Univ. Bd. Trustees. 154 Cal. App. 2d 560, 317 P.2d 170.
26. Jacobson v. Massachusetts. 197 U.S. 11, 25 S.Ct. 358, 49 L.Ed. 643.
27. Dworkin G. The theory and practice of autonomy: Cambridge, Cambridge University Press; 1988.
28. Gillon R, Lloyd A, editors. Principles of health care ethics. Chichester: Wiley; 1994.

29. Childress JF, Faden RR, Gaare RD, et al. J Law Med Ethics. 2002. Summer;30(2):170–8.
30. Leider JP, DeBruin D, Reynolds N, et al. Ethical guidance for disaster response, specifically around crisis standards of care: a systematic review. Am J Public Health. 2017;107(9):e1–9.
31. Consolidated Omnibus Budget Reconciliation Act of 1985. 29 U.S.C. § § 1161-1168.
32. 42 U.S.C. § 1395dd(a).
33. 42 U.S.C. §1395dd(E). (See 42 CFR 489.24(b)) Reference: PT31 EMT 5D Worksheet, CMS/ OIG investigative report form.
34. Roberts v. Galen of Virginia, Inc., 525 U.S. 249, 119 S.Ct. 685, 142 L.Ed.2d 648 (1999).
35. U.S. Department of Health & Human Services. Technical Resources, Assistance Center, and Information Exchange (TRACIE). Healthcare Emergency Preparedness Information Gateway. Updated may 7, 2018. Available online at: https://files.asprtracie.hhs.gov/documents/aspr-tracie-fact-sheet-emtala-and-disasters.pdf. Verified 11 Oct 2020.
36. Department of Health and Human Services. Centers for Medicare & Medicaid Service. Center for Medicaid and State Operations/Survey and Certification Group. Emergency Medical Treatment and Labor Act (EMTALA) Requirements and Options for Hospitals in a Disaster. S&C-09-52. August 14, 2009. Online at https://www.cms.gov/Medicare/Provider-Enrollment-and-Certification/SurveyCertificationGenInfo/downloads/SCLetter09_52.pdf. Verified 11 Oct 2020.
37. Health Insurance Portability and Accountability Act of 1996 (HIPAA; Pub.L. 104–191, 110 Stat. 1936, enacted August 21, 1996).
38. Department of Health and Human Services, Health Insurance Reform: Security Standards; Final Rule (HIPAA Security Rule), 45 C.F.R. Parts 160, 162 and 164 (2003).
39. Health Information Technology for Economic and Clinical Health (HITECH) Act, Title XIII of Division A and Title IV of Division B of the American Recovery and Reinvestment Act of 2009 (ARRA), Pub. L. No. 111-5, 123 Stat. 226 (Feb. 17, 2009), codified at 42 U.S.C. §§300jj et seq.; §§17901 et seq.
40. 45 C.F.R. § 164.514(d)(3).
41. U.S. Department of Health and Human Services Office for Civil Rights. Hurricane Katrina Bulletin: HIPAA Privacy and Disclosures in Emergency Situations. September 2, 2005. Available online at: https://www.hhs.gov/sites/default/files/katrinanhipaa.pdf. Verified October 11, 2020.
42. 45 C.F.R. § 164.512(f)(1).
43. Swan KG, Swan KG Jr. Triage: the past revisited. Mil Med. 1996;161:448–52.
44. Szalados JE. Triage. In: Szalados JE, Smith W, Wright W, editors. Law and ethics in neurocritical care: Neurocritical Care Society; 2019.
45. Aristotle, Nicomachean Ethics. trans. Terence Irwin. 2nd ed. Hackett, 1999. ISBN 0-87220-464-2.
46. Schwartz B, Sharpe K. Practical wisdom: Riverhead Publishers; 2010. ISBN-13: 978-1594487835.
47. Ytzhak A, Sagi R, Bader T, et al. Pediatric ventilation in a disaster: clinical and ethical decision making. Critical Care Medicine. 2012;40(2)
48. Jenkins JL, McCarthy ML, Sauer LM, et al. Mass-casualty triage: time for an evidence-based approach. Prehosp Disaster Med. 2008;23:3–8.
49. Kennedy K, Aghababian RV, Gans L, et al. Triage: techniques and applications in decision making. Ann Emerg Med. 1996;28:136–44.
50. Benson M, Koenig KL, Schultz CH. Disaster triage: START, then SAVE—a new method of dynamic triage for victims of a catastrophic earthquake. Prehosp Disaster Med. 1996;11:117–24.
51. CDC. Guidelines for field triage of injured patients: recommendations of the National Expert Panel on Field Triage. MMWR. 2009;58. [No. RR-1. 2011.
52. Howard MJ, Brillman JC, Burkle FM. Infectious disease emergencies in disasters. Emerg Med Clin North Am. 1996;14:413–28.

53. Institute of Medicine. Guidance for establishing crisis standards of care for use in disaster situations: A letter report. Washington, DC: The National Academies Press; 2009. https://doi.org/10.17226/12749. Verified 11 Oct 2020.
54. Institute of Medicine. Crisis standards of care: a systems framework for catastrophic disaster response: Volume 1: Introduction and CSC framework. Washington, DC: The National Academies Press; 2012. https://doi.org/10.17226/13351. *See also*: Institute of Medicine. 2013. Crisis standards of care: A toolkit for indicators and triggers. Washington, DC: The National Academies Press. https://doi.org/10.17226/18338. Verified 11 Oct 2020.
55. Szalados JE. Triaging the fittest: practical wisdom versus logical calculus? Crit Care Med. 2012;40(2):697–8. https://doi.org/10.1097/CCM.0b013e318238789b.
56. National Quarantine Act. Sess. 2, Ch. 66, 20 Stat. 37. 1878
57. Reports of the actions of the 45th Congress, Sess. 3, Ch. 202, March 3, 1879. An Act to Prevent the Introduction of Infectious or Contagious Diseases into the United States and to Establish a National Board of Health.
58. 42 U.S.C. 264. Part G - Quarantine and Inspection. Regulations to Control Communicable Diseases. 2011.
59. *See ie*. Executive Order 13295 of April 4, 2003 "Revised List of Quarantinable Communicable Diseases" 68 FR 17255; Executive Order 13375 of April 1, 2005 "Amendment to Executive Order 13295 Relating to Certain Influenza Viruses and Quarantinable Communicable Diseases" 70 FR 17299; and Executive Order 13674 of July 31, 2014 "Revised List of Quarantinable Communicable Diseases" 79 FR 45671.
60. Centers for Disease Control and Prevention. Specific Laws and Regulations Governing the Control of Communicable Diseases. Available online at: https://www.cdc.gov/quarantine/specificlawsregulations.html. Verified October 11, 2020.
61. Donald J. Trump. Proclamation on Suspension of Entry as Immigrants and Nonimmigrants of Persons who Pose a Risk of Transmitting 2019 Novel Coronavirus. January 31, 2020. Available online at: https://www.whitehouse.gov/presidential-actions/proclamation-suspension-entry-immigrants-nonimmigrants-persons-pose-risk-transmitting-2019-novel-coronavirus/. Verified 11 Oct 2020.
62. Jon Campbell. MSN News. Coronavirus in New York: Another New Rochelle family tests positive as 1,000 local people quarantined. Online at: https://www.msn.com/en-us/news/us/coronavirus-in-new-york-another-new-rochelle-family-tests-positive-as-1-000-local-people-quarantined/ar-BB10JF4r. Verified 11 Oct 2020.
63. Upshur R. The ethics of quarantine. AMA J Ethics. Virtual Mentor. 2003;5(11):393–5. https://doi.org/10.1001/virtualmentor.2003.5.11.msoc1-0311.
64. Control of Communicable Diseases. 42 CFR Parts 70 and 71. Fed Reg 82, No. 12. Thursday, January 19, 2017.
65. *Foucha v. Louisiana*, 504 U.S. 71 (1992).
66. Restatement of Torts, Second. Section 283.
67. AHRQ Agency for Health Research and Quality. Altered standards of care in mass casualty events: Bioterrorism and other public health emergencies. Rockville: AHRQ; 2005. Publication no. 05-0043.
68. A comment on the commentaries and a fragment on government, ed. JH Burns, HLA Hart, in The collected works of Jeremy Bentham [hereafter CW] (London, 1977), p. 393.
69. Kaji, A. ACEP Disaster Preparedness and Response Committee. American College of Emergency Physicians. Guidelines for crisis standards of care during disasters. June 2013. Available online at: https://www.acep.org/globalassets/uploads/uploaded-files/acep/clinical-and-practice-management/ems-and-disaster-preparedness/disaster-preparedness-grant-projects/crisis-standards-of-care-0613.pdf.
70. Hick, J. L., D. Hanfling, M. K. Wynia, and A. T. Pavia. 2020. Duty to Plan: Health Care, Crisis Standards of Care, and Novel Coronavirus SARS-CoV-2. NAM Perspectives. Discussion paper. National Academy of Medicine. Washington, DC. https://doi.org/10.31478/202003b. Verified 11 Oct 2020.

71. *See supra*, Institute of Medicine. 2009. Guidance for establishing crisis standards of care for use in disaster situations: A letter report.
72. Hodge JG, Brown EF. Assessing liability for health care entities that insufficiently prepare for catastrophic emergencies. J Am Med Assoc. 2011;306:308–9.
73. Va. Code Ann. § 8.01-225.02 (2008).
74. La. Rev. Stat. Ann. § 29:771 (2003).
75. UNISDR (United Nations International Strategy for Disaster Reduction) UNISDR Terminology on Disaster Risk Reduction. Geneva (2017). Available online at: http://www.unisdr.org/we/inform/terminology. Verified 11 Oct 2020.
76. American Psychiatric Association. Diagnostic and statistical manual of mental disorders. 5th ed. Washington, DC; 2013.
77. Brunello N, Davidson JR, Deahl M, Kessler RC, Mendlewicz J, Racagni G, Shalev AY, Zohar J. Posttraumatic stress disorder: diagnosis and epidemiology, comorbidity and social consequences, biology and treatment. Neuropsychobiology. 2001;43:150–62.
78. Smith EM, North CS, Spitznagel EL. Post-traumatic stress in survivors of three disasters. J Soc Behav Person. 1993;8:353–68.
79. FEMA (Federal Emergency Management Agency) A Whole Community Approach to Emergency Management: Principles, Themes, and Pathways for Action. FDOC 104-008-1. Washington, DC. (2011). p. 24.
80. Kendra JM, Clay LA, Gill KB. Resilience and disasters. In: Rodriguez H, Donner W, Trainor JE, editors. Handbook of disaster research. 2nd ed. Cham: Springer International Publishing AG; 2018. p. 87–107.

Chapter 30
New and Evolving Frontiers in Resuscitation: Ethical and Legal Concerns

Samuel A. Tisherman

Introduction

Ethical and legal issues regarding research on critically ill patients, particularly those in extremis, are complex. The patients' underlying conditions, comorbidities, and age often make the risk of successful recovery with standard therapies low. Frailty has been recognized more and more as an underlying risk factor for poor outcomes from critical illness, surgery, or trauma [1].

Consequently, clinicians and researchers are eager to develop new treatment strategies to improve these outcomes, often leading to high-risk interventions in an already high-risk situation with a vulnerable patient. Frailty would decrease the capacity of a research subject to tolerate adverse effects resulting from research. Nonetheless, without trying new approaches, the field of resuscitation will never move forward.

The potential critically ill research subject who may best receive benefit from a novel therapy is also the subject most likely to suffer consequences of an adverse effect or a negative trial. Research should be relevant, not possible to carry out in non-critically ill patients, and should offer potential benefits that outweigh the known and assumable risks [2].

S. A. Tisherman (✉)
Department of Surgery, Program in Trauma, University of Maryland School of Medicine, RA Cowley Shock Trauma Center, Baltimore, MD, USA
e-mail: stisherman@som.umaryland.edu

J. E. Szalados (ed.), *The Medical-Legal Aspects of Acute Care Medicine*,
https://doi.org/10.1007/978-3-030-68570-6_30

Definition of Research

In managing any particular patient, physicians typically begin with strategies based upon their training and experience. In some circumstances, there are national guidelines or recommendations that are typically generated by national organizations based upon a thorough evaluation of the literature. For resuscitation, clinical trials are particularly challenging and costly. Consequently, guideline developers must rely upon weak data and consensus in order to develop guidelines. These are ideally reassessed on a regular basis. A good example of a well-accepted set of guidelines are those developed by the American Heart Association for the management of patients who suffered a cardiac arrest [3]. From a legal perspective, an important question is whether or not guidelines like this should represent the "standard of care" [4].

Outcomes from acute events such as a cardiac arrest are often poor because of delays in recognition, delays in the call for assistance, the underlying disease itself, and the patient's comorbidities. Typical guidelines can only take the clinicians to a certain point at which continuing the standard management is futile. At this point, is it appropriate for a clinician to attempt a different resuscitation strategy that may not be in accordance with the published guidelines? There is certainly the potential for legal risk if the patient has a poor outcome and the standard of care was not met. At what point does trying something slightly different in certain patients shift from a provider trying something new in individual patients to actual research?

The National Institutes of Health defines research as a "systematic investigation, including research development, testing and evaluation, designed to develop or contribute to generalizable knowledge" [5]. At times, interventions thread a fine line between quality improvement projects and true research. One question to ask is, "Is the intent of the project to improve the outcomes of specific patients at a specific institution or to produce widely applicable data for publication?" Typically, any prospective assignments of patients to receive different treatments would constitute research.

In rare, specific circumstances, an investigational drug or device may be offered to individuals for compassionate use via expanded access programs. For example, hemoglobin-based oxygen carriers that have not been approved by the FDA for general use in the USA have been offered for individuals with life-threatening anemia who cannot receive blood transfusions [6]. Such use of non-approved therapies typically requires emergency approval by the local Institutional Review Boards (IRB).

Consent for Resuscitation Research

Investigators who conduct clinical research must protect the rights and welfare of human subjects [7]. The principal investigator must assure that every reasonable precaution is taken to reduce risks of harm to research subjects. There are numerous layers of organizations, including, but not limited to, Institutional Review Boards (IRBs), Human Research Protection Offices, and the Food and Drug Administration (FDA) that have oversight for research studies. Individual clinical trials may have dedicated medical monitors or data safety and monitoring boards (DSMBs). Safety of research subjects is paramount.

In addition, research subjects have specific rights regarding consent for research. The investigator or his/her designee must explain the rationale for the research, the potential risks and benefits, and the voluntary aspect of consent to the potential research subject. In some circumstances, a legally authorized representative (LAR) is able to provide consent. The potential subject or the LAR should have an opportunity to ask questions and take time to decide whether or not to participate. In the acute care setting, with time-sensitive interventions, the process becomes challenging.

Acute care medicine, including the management of shock states, trauma, and cardiac arrest, requires rapid interventions to optimize the patient's chance for survival. These patients are unable to provide informed consent even for standard procedures because of their critical condition. Time-sensitive research-related interventions must be initiated rapidly with no opportunity to obtain consent from the patient or the patient's LAR. In most cases, the LAR is not available. Even if the LAR is present, the acuity of the situation and the emotional state of the LAR preclude any meaningful informed consent conversation.

For standard emergency interventions, the providers can readily document that the procedure is necessary to saving the patient's life, that the patient is unable to provide consent because of the condition, and that there is no time for obtaining consent from the LAR. The providers should nonetheless make an effort to contact the LAR to inform them of the situation and the planned interventions. In the end, though, life-saving interventions can proceed without consent.

The situation is more complicated for conducting resuscitation research. The experimental interventions need to be initiated rapidly. There may be a relatively brief window of opportunity for the intervention to be potentially beneficial. The potential subject cannot provide consent because of the acute medical issue. LARs are often not available or capable of giving consent [8]. Can truly informed consent be obtained? Who would give consent? Will the process jeopardize the potential benefit of the intervention?

Resuscitation researchers, ethicists, and federal agencies have struggled with developing an ethical approach for conducting emergency research under an exception from informed consent [9]. Prior to 1991, there was no specific guidance from federal agencies. Researchers studying novel therapies in emergency situations, such as cardiac arrest or major trauma, developed the concept of "deferred consent" [10]. They enrolled subjects into trials, proceeded with the designated interventions, and subsequently approached the LAR for consent.

In 1991, the US Department of Health and Human Services developed the Common Rule, designed to protect human subjects from harm and to promote uniformity in compliance across federal agencies [11]. This regulation prevented research without prospective, informed consent, which essentially shut down resuscitation research. Fortunately for resuscitation researchers, in 1996, the Final Rule, which allowed for an exception from informed consent, was approved [12]. Research could now be performed without informed consent in emergency circumstances under certain conditions. Investigators needed to demonstrate that (1) the subject has an acutely life-threatening condition, (2) currently available treatments are untested or unsatisfactory, (3) the potential subject cannot consent because of the acute condition, (4) there must not be time within the proposed therapeutic window of the intervention to contact the LAR to obtain prospective consent, and (5) the subject might directly benefit from participation in the research.

These new regulations mandated community consultation and public disclosure as protective measures for members of the community who may be enrolled without their consent in a resuscitation trial. The hope was that this process would help mitigate the risks and enhance the benefits of research. Shared responsibility between the investigators and community members can help legitimize the research endeavors. Community consultation is a two-way process aimed at gathering feedback from the community regarding the appropriateness and acceptability of the design of the proposed research, including its risks and benefits. Investigators typically reach out to civic groups or invite community members to a "town hall." They may also conduct surveys of community members. Public disclosure, on the other hand, is a one-way process by which investigators attempt to inform the community about the study. This process is overseen by the local IRB, as well as by an independent DSMB, the FDA, and funding agencies. The goal of this process is to provide sufficient information to the community such that they are aware of the plans for the research, the expected benefits and risks, as well as information regarding conducting the study without informed consent.

Even non-interventional clinical studies may benefit from an exception from informed consent [13]. Such studies represent minimal risk to the subject. Losing potential subjects because of a lack of consent could lead to consent bias in that subjects with a lower severity of illness would be more likely to consent. The number of subjects could be significantly decreased.

Experiences with Community Consultation and Public Disclosure

The Resuscitation Outcomes Consortium (ROC) was developed by the National Heart, Lung, and Blood Institute to conduct clinical trials related to cardiac arrest and trauma. The experience of this group exemplifies some of the challenges with the process of community consultation and public disclosure [14]. Within this consortium, there was significant variability among centers regarding their approach to community consultation and public disclosure, though there were common points of information that were utilized during discussions with community groups. The public disclosure portion of the process typically included press releases, newspaper, radio, and television interviews. Centers created websites that provide information and often provided a mechanism for community members to comment on this study. Paid advertisements were also utilized. The utility of this public disclosure process could be questioned. Several surveys have demonstrated that only about 5–10% of potentially eligible subjects in a community were actually aware of the study [15, 16].

For the community consultation portion, many sites sponsored town hall events with community members and IRB representatives, but these were generally poorly attended and yielded little feedback. Investigators found that they could engage with community members and leaders better when they presented the study to a group that was already scheduled to meet for a given purpose. Focus groups of cardiac arrest or trauma survivors were very engaged and provided excellent feedback. Several sites utilize a random digit dialing, structured telephone survey of the community, chosen to match the demographics for potential subjects, which was performed by an independent professional group [17]. This process yielded hundreds of survey responses in a relatively short period of time, but this could be rather costly for the investigators. Other researchers have utilized social media to reach out to the community [18, 19].

Community members' opinions regarding the exception from informed consent vary considerably. They may be more willing to receive a new drug outside of a research study and particularly outside of a randomized, controlled trial [20]. They may also be less willing to participate in a study of a very invasive procedure compared to a less invasive procedure. The methodology for conducting community consultation can impact the responses. In one study, the method of consultation (phone survey, interview, or community meeting), framing of questions (positive or negative), and community demographics (ethnicity, age) affected the outcome [21]. In addition, victims of trauma may have a different opinion than their families or the general community [22]. For critical care research, there may be a tendency for LARs to overestimate the willingness of a subject to participate in a study, particularly as the risk of the intervention increases [23].

Do investigators need to reach out to the broader community or could they use community leaders as surrogates for the rest of the community? A survey of patients in an urban emergency department suggested that most respondents could identify with specific communities and could identify leaders who could represent their views [24]. The communities were most often identified as geographic, religious, or medical, whereas the ideal leaders for consultation most often had geographic, religious, or political affiliations.

One other part of the community consultation and public disclosure process includes providing a process for individuals to opt out of the research before potential enrollment. Typically, the investigators offered the individual a bracelet. One center issued a pocket card that could be recognized by EMS personnel. The general experience has been that very few individuals request to opt out, though media coverage of a study may influence community reactions and requests for opt-out bracelets [25]. A survey of community members who requested to opt out demonstrated that these individuals generally supported resuscitation research, but opposed conducting the research without consent [26].

Once a subject is enrolled in a study under the exception from informed consent, researchers are required to obtain and document consent from the subject or LAR for continued participation in the study. Optimal timing of this notification and consent process depends upon the status of the subject and the availability of the LAR. Even if the subject dies in the meantime, researchers need to notify the LAR at an appropriate time. Contacting the LAR is often difficult because of poor or inaccurate contact information [27]. If the consent is obtained from an LAR and the subject is subsequently able to engage in the consent process, the subject then has the option of continuing participation or not.

If the subject or the LAR refuses continued participation, researchers may be allowed to utilize that subject's data up to the point of this refusal, but this depends upon following regulations stipulated in the Health Insurance Portability and Accountability Act and other federal or state regulations. In addition, researchers may utilize public information, such as vital statistics, to find out if a subject has died. For the welfare of subjects, a process for assuring proper identification of any adverse effects of the intervention, even after the patient has been removed from the study, should be arranged if possible. Appropriately collecting as much outcome data as possible for a subject that is enrolled in a clinical trial is critical for the statistical evaluation of the intervention. Perhaps just as important, however, is collecting data that would support the safety or the adverse effects of an intervention. As a general rule with these studies, the actual risk to the subject from the intervention has already occurred by the time consent for continued participation is discussed. Ongoing participation generally has minimal risks involved.

One of the major challenges with community consultation is how to define the community and how to appropriately reach that community for consultation. For example, community consultation for a study of patients who suffer a nontraumatic cardiac arrest, which typically occurs in older adults, could be conducted at community events typically attended by this age group or organizations to which they frequently belong. In general, trauma could affect essentially any age group, particularly people under the age of 45. Here, too, there may be organizations or events that would lend themselves to the conduct of community consultation. Blunt trauma, e.g., motor vehicle crashes or falls, can impact all age groups regardless of gender, race, or socioeconomic status. In contrast, penetrating trauma, e.g., gunshot wounds or stab wounds, frequently affect young, minorities, males. Reaching this demographic group can be significantly more difficult. Since the vast majority of trauma studies include patients who have suffered blunt trauma, this is not usually a problem, even if a small percentage of the expected subjects would have suffered penetrating trauma. The Emergency Preservation and Resuscitation for Cardiac Arrest from Trauma study, on the other hand, is an example of a study that is only enrolling patients who have suffered penetrating trauma. These researchers therefore had to tailor the committee consultation process to engage this part of the community [28]. Surveys were placed in trauma clinic, which should include patients who represent the population at risk. Researchers went to events that were specifically targeted to the communities at risk. Organizations that represent this community were directly approached for discussions. Random digit dialing telephone surveys were utilized based upon the phone numbers within the trauma registry.

Oversight of Community Consultation and Public Disclosure

Federal regulations mandate that a federal agency must approve clinical trials that involve the exception from informed consent. For the most part, this oversight has been conducted by the FDA. For projects that are funded by the Department of Defense, approval is also required at the level of the secretary of the designated service, even though military personnel are typically excluded from enrollment because they are considered a vulnerable population that is not free to choose whether or not to participate. There has been some work on developing processes for conducting research within the Department of Defense [29].

At the local level, the IRB must approve the community consultation and public disclosure plan and then review the findings before allowing the research to proceed. There has been a strong push for developing a national IRB that could set standards for studies conducted under the exception from informed consent for research in the emergency setting. This would be extremely helpful for multicenter studies in which individual IRBs may have variable experience and expertise with resuscitation research. A realistic alternative might be development of regional or centralized IRBs for approval and execution of community consultation and public disclosure plans, as well as study oversight and monitoring. Creation of specialized, community IRBs could include community leaders and scientists. This group could obtain advice from more experienced IRBs as they gain their own experience with this process.

At this point, the current process is relatively well accepted by researchers, IRBs, and communities, though it may not be optimal. Further research on this process, along with ongoing discussions between regulatory agencies and researchers, will be necessary for this process to further evolve.

Challenges with High-Risk Interventions for Resuscitation and Critical Care

Advances in technologies for the support of failing organs have saved countless lives. Ventilators for supporting patients with respiratory failure and hemodialysis machines for supporting patients with acute kidney injury are ubiquitous in ICUs in the developed world. Though these resources may be limited in developing countries or during disasters and pandemics, ethical issues with their initiation or discontinuation do occur but are relatively uncommon.

In contrast, there are more advanced organ support technologies that are extremely expensive, require enormous amounts of resources, and are limited to very advanced medical systems. For example, extracorporeal membrane oxygenation (ECMO), which is essentially a scaled-down version of the heart lung machine like that used for cardiac surgery, can support the lungs in venovenous (VV) mode or both the heart and lungs in veno-arterial (VA) mode. Demonstrating clear benefit of ECMO has been very difficult [30, 31]. More recently, the use of this technology as extracorporeal CPR (ECPR) for resuscitation of patients with refractory cardiac arrest has gained significant interest in many centers [32]. Ever since ECMO became available, however, its use has led to ongoing scientific, ethical, and financial debate. The use of ECMO in neonates and children has become relatively standard, whereas the use in adults has not.

The decision to initiate ECMO often must be made quickly, with little time to discuss the pros and cons with the patient's family. Invariably, the patient is in extremis and unable to participate in the discussion. ECMO centers develop guidelines for making the decision to offer ECMO or ECPR in certain cases, but the decision is usually not straightforward. The challenge with ECMO is that the device itself does not directly improve the patient's underlying disease process. It supports patients long enough for them to either improve on their own or transition to a long-term solution such as a transplant (heart or lung) or ventricular assist device. Once the patient is supported on ECMO, the most common outcomes include clinical improvement with weaning from ECMO, bridge to a long-term support device or transplant, or deterioration to death from multiple organ failure or a catastrophic event (such as intracerebral hemorrhage). The most challenging outcome, however, is that the patient remains relatively stable on ECMO, perhaps even awake, but clinical improvement to allow weaning from ECMO is extremely unlikely and no other destination therapy is available [33]. Because of these potential scenarios, early ethics committee consultation is extremely important when employing expensive, labor-intensive interventions without clear benefit and sometimes without a clear destination for the individual patient.

Challenges During Disasters and Pandemics

Planning for disasters and pandemics is critical, but the topic is outside the purview of this review. There are, however, significant challenges that arise with resuscitation strategies and research once the event has already occurred. In general, if the event has overwhelmed the healthcare system, triage decisions must be made regarding how to save the most patients or the most patient-years. These decisions focus on standard therapies, such as the use of ventilators, the use of medications that could be in limited supply, or providing cardiopulmonary resuscitation. Whether or not to provide more advanced therapies presents a unique challenge. The use of ECMO provides an example of just such an intervention that is worth discussing. If an institution or healthcare system does not have the ability to provide ECMO and transporting a patient to an ECMO center is not possible, there is really no decision to make. ECMO is just not offered. On the other hand, if an institution does have ECMO capability, including the necessary personnel, equipment, facilities, and systems [34], how should this resource best be utilized during a challenging event such as a pandemic? Experience with previous influenza outbreaks, such as H1N1, and COVID-19 can provide useful context [35].

For patients with severe respiratory failure from influenza or COVID-19, standard ventilatory support, even with the addition of rescue therapies such as prone positioning, may not prevent death from hypoxemia. ECMO could provide the necessary support to allow recovery. The decision to offer ECMO to patients who are infected with the viral agent is difficult. It could be life-saving, or it could just put more healthcare workers at risk of infection and waste valuable resources. In addition, during such events, should the use of ECMO in other circumstances be limited? If only one more circuit is available, should it be used for a COVID-19 patient or a trauma patient with severe pulmonary contusions? These are difficult questions without easy answers. Having predetermined criteria for ECMO and utilizing experts in ethics and legal matters when necessary are critical [34].

During disasters or pandemics, healthcare personnel and systems are almost totally focused on saving lives. In order to improve outcomes during the event or during future events, there needs to be some effort to conduct research. Data collection as in a registry could be accomplished readily if electronic health records are still available and the necessary information is entered by healthcare workers anyway. Asking these frontline staff to enter additional information is not feasible. If an institution develops a standard treatment protocol for these patients, based upon the typical standard of care and current knowledge about the disease, collecting data on outcomes as in a quality improvement fashion could be invaluable and would not represent research that would require regulatory approvals.

The greater challenge in terms of logistics and ethics is actually trying to conduct prospective research. When patients and providers are desperate to save more people, they may be willing to try unproven (or even potentially dangerous) treatments. This approach is troubling both ethically and scientifically. Another approach could be asking pharmaceutical companies for compassionate use of certain therapies that may have benefit. Depending upon the approval status of such therapies, this may or may not present an ethical concern.

It is possible, however, to conduct research even in the middle of a pandemic. Researchers need to quickly design appropriate trials with the most promising agents based upon previous basic science or clinical literature. These studies still require funding and appropriate approvals from the FDA and IRB. Institutions have the ability to expedite the usual processes in order to start trials in a timely fashion while maintaining the standard safeguards for research subjects. The classic approach to randomized clinical trials has been questioned as typically large numbers of patients are needed, significantly prolonging the duration of the trial. The use of adaptive trial designs has been successfully employed to facilitate clinical trials [36]. During a pandemic, such an approach could make even more sense. Creative researchers, with support from drug companies, the FDA, and local IRBs, can rapidly initiate ethically and scientifically rigorous trials and, hopefully, discover effective therapies, even in the midst of a pandemic.

References

1. Shah R, Attwood K, Arya S, Hall DE, Johanning JM, Gabriel E, et al. Association of frailty with failure to rescue after low-risk and high-risk inpatient surgery. JAMA Surg. 2018;153(5):1–10.
2. Estella A. Ethics research in critically ill patients. Med Intensiva [Internet]. 2018;42(4):247–54. Available from: www.elsevier.es/medintensiva.
3. Link MS, Berkow LC, Kudenchuk PJ, Halperin HR, Hess EP, Moitra VK, et al. Part 7: adult advanced cardiovascular life support: 2015 American Heart Association guidelines update for cardiopulmonary resuscitation and emergency cardiovascular care. Circulation. 2015;132(18):S444–64.
4. Ely JW, Hartz AJ, James PA, Johnson CA. Determining the standard of care in medical malpractice: the physician's perspective. SSRN Electron J 2005. https://doi.org/10.2139/ssrn.347600.
5. Department of Health and Human Services. Protection of Human Subjects [Internet]. 2009. Available from: https://www.hhs.gov/ohrp/sites/default/files/ohrp/policy/ohrpregulations.pdf.
6. MacKenzie CF, Dubé GP, Pitman A, Zafirelis M. Users guide to pitfalls and lessons learned about HBOC-201 during clinical trials, expanded access, and clinical use in 1,701 patients. Shock. 2019;52(1S):92–9.
7. Protection of Human Subjects. 21CFR50 Food and Drug Administration, Department of Health and Human Services.
8. Dutton RP, Stansbury LG, Hemlock B, Hess JR, Scalea TM. Impediments to obtaining informed consent for clinical research in trauma patients. J Trauma Inj Infect Crit Care. 2008;64(4):1106–12.
9. Abramson NS, Safar P, Meisel A. Informed consent in resuscitation research. J Am Med Assoc. 1981;246(24):2828–30.
10. Abramson NS, Safar P. Deferred consent: use in clinical resuscitation research. Ann Emerg Med. 1990;19(7):781–4.
11. Federal Policy for the Protection of Human Subjects. Fed Regist. 2017;82(12):7149–274.
12. Protection of human subjects; informed consent–FDA. Final rule. Fed Regist. 1996;61(192):51528–9.
13. Fox EE, Bulger EM, Dickerson AS, Del Junco DJ, Klotz P, Podbielski J, et al. Waiver of consent in noninterventional, observational emergency research: the PROMMTT experience. J Trauma Acute Care Surg. 2013;75(1 SUPPL1):3–8.
14. Tisherman SA, Powell JL, Schmidt TA, Aufderheide TP, Kudenchuk PJ, Spence J, et al. Regulatory challenges for the resuscitation outcomes consortium. Circulation. 2008;118(15):1585–92.
15. Triner W, Jacoby L, Shelton W, Burk M, Imarenakhue S, Watt J, et al. Exception from informed consent enrollment in emergency medical research: attitudes and awareness. Acad Emerg Med. 2007;14(2):187–91.
16. Jacoby LH, Young B, Watt J. Public disclosure in research with exception from informed consent: the use of survey methods to assess its effectiveness. J Empir Res Hum Res Ethics. 2008;3(1):79–87.
17. Bulger EM, Schmidt TA, Cook AJ, Brasel KJ, Griffiths DE, Kudenchuk PJ, et al. The random dialing survey as a tool for community consultation for research involving the emergency medicine exception from informed consent. Ann Emerg Med. 2009;53(3):341–50, 350.e1-2.
18. Harvin JA, Podbielski JM, Vincent LE, Liang MK, Kao LS, Wade CE, et al. Impact of social media on community consultation in exception from informed consent clinical trials. J Surg Res [Internet]. 2019;234:65–71. Available from: https://doi.org/10.1016/j.jss.2018.09.007.

19. Stephens SW, Williams C, Gray R, Kerby JD, Wang HE, Bosarge PL. Using social media for community consultation and public disclosure in exception from informed consent trials. J Trauma Acute Care Surg. 2016;80(6):1005–9.
20. Abboud PA, Heard K, Al-Marshad AA, Lowenstein SR. What determines whether patients are willing to participate in resuscitation studies requiring exception from informed consent? J Med Ethics. 2006;32(8):468–72.
21. Contant C, McCullough LB, Mangus L, Robertson C, Valadka A, Brody B. Community consultation in emergency research. Crit Care Med. 2006;34(8):2049–52.
22. Sims CA, Isserman JA, Holena D, Sundaram LM, Tolstoy N, Greer S, et al. Exception from informed consent for emergency research: consulting the trauma community. J Trauma Acute Care Surg. 2013;74(1):157–66.
23. Newman JT, Smart A, Reese TR, Williams A, Moss M. Surrogate and patient discrepancy regarding consent for critical care research. Crit Care Med. 2012;40(9):2590–4.
24. Merchant RM, Rubright JD, Pryor JP, Karlawish JHT. Who can speak for the emergently ill? Testing a method to identify communities and their leaders. Acad Emerg Med. 2008;15(6):581–3.
25. Nelson MJ, DeIorio NM, Schmidt T, Griffiths D, Daya M, Haywood L, et al. Local media influence on opting out from an exception from informed consent trial. Ann Emerg Med. 2010;55(1):1–8.
26. Nelson MJ, DeIorio NM, Schmidt TA, Zive DM, Griffiths D, Newgard CD. Why persons choose to opt out of an exception from informed consent cardiac arrest trial. Theatr Res Int. 2013;84(6):825–30. https://doi.org/10.1016/j.resuscitation.2013.01.030.
27. Spence JM, Notarangelo V, Frank J, Long J, Morrison LJ. Responses to written notification during out-of-hospital care trials using waiver of informed consent. Acad Emerg Med. 2005;12(11):1099–103.
28. Tisherman SA. Defining "community" and "consultation" for emergency research that requires an exception from informed consent. AMA J Ethics. 2018;20(5):467–74.
29. Hatzfeld JJ, Childs JD, Dempsey MP, Chapman GD, Dalle Lucca JJ, Brininger T, et al. Evolution of biomedical research during combat operations. J Trauma Acute Care Surg. 2013;75(2 SUPPL. 2):115–9.
30. Peek GJ, Mugford M, Tiruvoipati R, Wilson A, Allen E, Thalanany MM, et al. Efficacy and economic assessment of conventional ventilatory support versus extracorporeal membrane oxygenation for severe adult respiratory failure (CESAR): a multicentre randomised controlled trial. Lancet. 2009;374(9698):1351–63.
31. Combes A, Hajage D, Capellier G, Demoule A, Lavoué S, Guervilly C, et al. Extracorporeal membrane oxygenation for severe acute respiratory distress syndrome. N Engl J Med. 2018;378(21):1965–75.
32. Fagnoul D, Combes A, De Backer D. Extracorporeal cardiopulmonary resuscitation. Curr Opin Crit Care. 2014;20(3):259–65.
33. Makdisi T, Makdisi G. Extra corporeal membrane oxygenation support: ethical dilemmas. Ann Transl Med. 2017;5(5):1–5.
34. Ramanathan K, Antognini D, Combes A, Paden M, Zakhary B, Ogino M, et al. Planning and provision of ECMO services for severe ARDS during the COVID-19 pandemic and other outbreaks of emerging infectious diseases. Lancet Respir Med [Internet]. 2020;2600(20). Available from: https://doi.org/10.1016/S2213-2600(20)30121-1.
35. Zangrillo A, Biondi-Zoccai G, Landoni G, Frati G, Patroniti N, Pesenti A, et al. Extracorporeal membrane oxygenation (ECMO) in patients with H1N1 influenza infection: a systematic review and meta-analysis including 8 studies and 266 patients receiving ECMO. Crit Care. 2013;17(1):1–8.
36. Bhatt DL, Mehta C. Adaptive designs for clinical trials. N Engl J Med. 2016;375(1):65–74.

Chapter 31
Defining Standards of Care and the Role of Expert Testimony in Jurisprudence

Wendy L. Wright

Introduction

Most clinicians fear being named in a medical malpractice lawsuit, but the particulars are often misunderstood, especially by those who have never participated in a malpractice trial. In the United States, the basis of medical malpractice is professional negligence. The legal elements required to prove that a clinician was indeed negligent depend on the ability of a plaintiff's (patient's) attorney to prove that the health care provider breached their professional duty, causing damages. Breach of duty, in the case of medical malpractice, is another way to say that the clinician did not provide the standard of care [17]. Determining the applicable standard of care is a complicated legal issue that usually requires testimony of a medical expert witness. Therefore, understanding how the standard of care is determined and the role of expert witness testimony should be of interest to everyone practicing medicine.

Tort Law, Professional Negligence, and Medical Malpractice

An important goal of the American legal system is to establish an expectation of societal norms in order to provide stability [17, 30]. The legal system, therefore, should provide clarity and certainty [17]. Ostensibly, if one is aware of defined standards of law, one will be able to predict which actions (or inactions) will lead to government-imposed sanctions and penalties. On the other hand, if laws are not well defined, or if the sanctions and penalties are applied inconsistently, justice cannot be applied equally and impartially.

W. L. Wright (✉)
Emory University Hospital Midtown, Emory University School of Medicine, Atlanta, GA, USA
e-mail: wwrigh2@emory.edu

J. E. Szalados (ed.), *The Medical-Legal Aspects of Acute Care Medicine*,
https://doi.org/10.1007/978-3-030-68570-6_31

The basis of medical malpractice is rooted in tort law. A tort is a type of civil wrong that has a legal remedy, usually consisting of compensation or repayment to the wronged person. A civil wrong is contrasted from a criminal wrong, in which the crime is considered to be an offense to the public, and involves condemnation and punishment from the State. One major category of torts is negligent torts [30]. Negligence in a legal context is defined as the failure to exercise the degree of care appropriate to specific circumstances, which then leads to some form of damage or harm [28]. Professional negligence is a specific form of negligent tort, in which a professional, defined as one who has a particular degree of skill based on education and training, breaches a duty of care that is owed to the client. Medical malpractice is a specific form of professional negligence based on the duty a health care provider has in relation to a patient [31].

Medical malpractice laws share the common goals of other torts, including to compensate someone who has suffered a loss, to act as a deterrent for negligent actions, and to encourage judicial handling of disputes rather than self-help (which can include vigilante or renegade justice). When a patient (or their family) feels that they have unjustly suffered some type of harm or damage at the hands of a medical professional, they hire a plaintiff's attorney, whose role is then to prove all of the necessary elements of medical malpractice based on the preponderance of the evidence [31]. The elements of medical malpractice are, again, based on the standard elements of negligence but are applied specifically based on the expectations of the duty the medical professional owes to a patient. Those elements are often listed as duty, breach, causation, and damages [31].

Elements of Medical Malpractice

All medical malpractice actions begin with an event, such as an adverse patient outcome, an injury, or a medical error. The event in question may lead to a dispute among the patient/family (plaintiff) and the health care provider/practice group/hospital (defendant). The plaintiff may contend that they were injured as a result of the negligence of the health care provider; the defendant may argue that the damage was unavoidable (for example, as part of the natural progression of disease, or an adverse event that occurred despite appropriate care). If the plaintiff chooses to seek damages, they will hire an attorney and allow the dispute to play out in court. In order for defendants to be found guilty of malpractice, the plaintiff must prove all four of the following elements based on the preponderance of the evidence (Table 31.1).

The US legal system is an adversarial system, meaning that if a dispute is going to be settled in a lawful forum such as the court system, the two disputing parties will have legal representation who will advocate for them, with a judge presiding to ensure correct procedures, and often a jury to hear the case in order to decide on a verdict. Before the actual trial, a great deal of work is done to gather information regarding the dispute, including the depositions of the parties and of expert

Table 31.1 Elements of medical malpractice

Element	Requirement to prove malpractice	Examples
Duty	It must be established that the clinician had the legal responsibility to care for the patient	The existence of a doctor-patient relationship The nurse assigned to the patient
Breach	The standard of care was violated	Failure to administer antibiotics in a timely fashion Delay in needed procedure or diagnostic test
Causation	The error, omission, or action in question caused the damages	Localized infection causes sepsis, leading to irreversible organ damage Failure to diagnose a surgical emergency leads to patient death
Damages	The patient/family suffered a loss in some way	Usually physical (such as death, loss of limb, loss of vision, etc.) or economic loss (such as loss of future earnings and accumulation of additional medical expenses) In some cases, pain and suffering, or some other type of emotional damage may also be considered to be present in addition to physical or economic losses

witnesses. Attorneys may file motions, such as to dismiss a case or to exclude certain evidence. Most malpractice disputes do not actually make it to trial; rather, they are dismissed or are settled before trial [20]. If the case does go to trial, expert witnesses will be called to help the jury understand the medical information in the case, so that they may decide which party will prevail.

Although each element of negligence must be proven, the standard of care deserves focused discussion. Establishing standard of care is necessary to demonstrate a breach of duty. A lay jury, however, is not likely in a position to know what standard would apply to a particular situation; therefore, this element usually requires expert witness testimony. Understanding how standard of care evolved, how it is determined, and what factors must be considered when establishing the relevant standard will help to better inform the legal system as to when malpractice occurred (and may help the health care provider avoid breaching the standard of care).

Evolution of the Standard of Care

Defining the standard of care is essential if a health care provider wishes to reliably and consistently avoid breaching their professional duty. Like many legal concepts, the standard of care has evolved over time. Early in the history of the United States, malpractice suits were rare [23]. Initially they were based on English jurisprudence and comprised chiefly of common law writ proceedings [4]. As more medical schools and training programs opened up, medical doctors found themselves competing with each other in an unregulated, unlicensed market place. Unfortunately, medical professionals were also competing with untrained non-professionals peddling services to unwitting customers [18]. By the mid-nineteenth century, some courts were equating malpractice actions with contract law, with the failure to deliver services as promised essentially constituting a breach of contract. Later in the nineteenth century, as the writ system collapsed, tort law emerged, and medical negligence evolved as part of tort doctrine. Therefore, a medical professional became liable for a breach in the standard of care, rather than for a breach of contract [29]. Part of the reason for this evolution was based on the medical profession's effort to achieve professional status and distinguish medical practice from ordinary commercial transactions. Medical professionals argued that the establishment of a contract assumed equal footing between parties and was therefore unsuitable for the doctor-patient relationship, in which the doctor has the education and training to understand the risks and benefits of proposed treatment that the patient is not expected to understand as fully [18]. By assuming the role of the professional, the health care provider, therefore, has a duty toward a patient that is higher than would be expected of an untrained member of the public. Health care professionals are expected to achieve and maintain a level of skill and knowledge that allows them to understand the level of care that should be reasonably expected from a patient seeking medical treatment; failing to meet this level, or standard, of care, leaves the health care professional liable for harm that may befall the patient as a result.

At the close of the nineteenth century, the standard of care was felt largely to be based on custom [17]. If a practice was considered customary, or felt to be something that was "usually done," failing to provide such level of care could be considered a breach. Early in the twentieth century, the Supreme Court added an additional a requirement, essentially stating that failure to do anything that seemed "reasonable" could be considered negligence, when, in 1903, Associate Justice Oliver Wendell Holmes, Jr., included the following statement in a Supreme Court opinion: "what usually is done may be evidence of what ought to be done, but what ought to be done is fixed by a standard of reasonable prudence, whether it is usually complied with or not [26]." In *The TJ Hooper* case, Judge Learned Hand ruled that the standard for negligence was based on if something (in this case, a new technology) was "reasonable" and didn't matter if it was customary [27]. In the medical profession, this would be a hard standard with which to comply, considering on the rapid evolution of technology and the differences in opinion in what would could be "reasonable."

The case of *Helling v. Carey* added to these worrisome precedents. The case involved a 32-year-old woman who suffered severe, permanent eye damage due to glaucoma. At the time, routine screening for glaucoma for patients under 40 was not customary among ophthalmologists. However, the court held the defendant ophthalmologists liable for damages, concluding that reasonable prudence required the timely administration of an eye pressure test, regardless of the standards the ophthalmologic community set. The ruling stated that custom is not the definitive factor in determining negligence; to the contrary, custom was not enough, and there are some things that are not customary, but may be reasonable, merely based on prudence. This case in particular was worrisome to the medical community because it suggested that it is up to the legal profession and the jury, not the medical profession, to decide what is "reasonable" and "unreasonable" [11]. The ruling in *Helling* prompted state legislatures to pass statutes that defined the standard of care in their jurisdiction. Washington was first and said the standard of care is not met when "the defendant or defendants [fail] to exercise that degree of skill, care and learning possessed by other persons in the same profession…" [19].

The modern definition continued to emerge with a series of landmark rulings, in many ways defining what the standard of care is *not*. In *Hall v. Hilburn*, the court ruled that a physician treating a patient takes on an "obligation enforceable by law to use minimally sound medical judgement and render minimally competent care in the course of service [the physician] provides. A physician does not guarantee recovery…A competent physician is not liable *per se* for a mere error of judgement, mistaken diagnosis or the occurrence of an undesirable result [10]." This ruling makes two important points that are commonly misunderstood by the medical community. First, the standard of care is only meant to apply a minimal standard of competency. This may seem antithetical to medical professionals, who are highly educated and motivated to be excellent. However, a line must be set somewhere, so that that medical professionals have a clear and consistent line that they know not to cross, lest they will be held legally liable. When considered from this vantage point, one can see that setting the line at the level of "minimal competence" makes sense, so that the standards do not allow for "incompetent" clinicians, and yet do not exclude those who meet the required education and training elements. The second important point to take away from the *Hall* ruling is that the standard of care is not ideal care, or perfect care, although the phrase is commonly misused by medical professionals who mistakenly conflate "standard of care" with "gold standard." This second point is further emphasized in the case of *McCourt v. Abernathy*, in which the court ruled that "negligence may not be informed from a bad result – a physician is not an insurer of health and is not required to guarantee results, rather must meet the standard skill possessed generally by others practicing in [their] field under similar circumstances" [16].

Johnston v. St Francis Medical Center was a critical ruling that helped further define the modern concept of standard of care. In this case, the court ruled that physician conduct and judgment cannot be judged in hindsight, but rather must be judged based on what a competent physician would have done under same or similar circumstances [13]. The stipulation that the judgment is based on the "same or similar circumstances" added the important elements of timing, practice setting, and patient-specific factors. For example, a case that is coming to court several years after the dispute arose needs to be judged based on the relevant standard of care at the time of the incident. Furthermore, health care professionals at a small, rural hospital with less access to specialty services, diagnostic equipment, and surgical equipment should not be held to the same standard as those at a large, urban, tertiary referral hospital. The medical decisions made at the time and in the circumstances also have to take into account the history, condition, and risk factors of an individual patient. For example, if a certain situation would normally dictate a diagnostic study, but the patient is too hemodynamically unstable to undergo the test, a clinician should not be held liable for a breach of standard of care for failing to obtain the diagnostic test. Therefore, the relevant standard of care is highly fact-specific.

Hence, the evolution of standard of care has passed through phases from that which is customary, to that which is customary plus anything that seems reasonable, to a more modern definition, generally speaking, of that which a minimally competent physician in the same field would do under similar circumstances. Standard of care does not mean perfection in practice; bad outcomes are to be expected, and it is not reasonable to expect that all disease entities are diagnosed within a specified time frame. Since tort law is regulated by individual states, each state has a legal definition of malpractice and of standard of care.

Defining Standard of Care

Standard of care is a legal term of art. Its specific definition applied to a malpractice case depends on the jurisdiction in which the dispute occurs. However, a generic definition of standard of care can be conceptualized as the care that would be provided by a reasonable and prudent clinician in the same or similar circumstances [32]. Care that does not meet this standard is considered a breach. The definition usually includes qualifiers such as "reasonable" and "prudent" to indicate that a provider is both trained and qualified, as well as meeting professional obligations to maintain competency and skill, such as participating in continung medial education. Some states will include (or substitute) "careful," "cautious," or "skilled" into their definitions. It is important to note that the definition does not refer to what the "average" clinician would do, otherwise half of the medical care provided would breach the standard of care.

Within the definition of standard of care, one will often find phrases such as "in the same or similar circumstances." This element of the definition implies a timing aspect and acknowledges that not all resources are available to all clinicians. With respect to the timing, the standard of care applied to the case must reflect the standard of care at the time of the incident in question, rather than what may have been accepted in the remote past, or how thinking might have evolved since then. Additionally, the clinician's actions (or omissions) need to be assessed based on what the clinician knew (or should have known) at the time, and not influenced by hindsight, or based on how the case subsequently unfolded. "Same or similar circumstances" should also imply that the care be judged based on the resources available to the clinician. For example, if a clinician is practicing at a hospital where a certain subspecialist or equipment was not available, the clinician should be held to a standard of care based on their own resources and geography (though transferring the patient to a facility providing a higher level of care may be within the range of acceptable options that would qualify as meeting standard of care).

Despite the fact that standard of care is supposed to be a fixed standard, based on "reasonableness" as assessed by educated, trained professional in good standing, the conflict of opinion among expert witnesses is often at the core of a medical malpractice dispute. Considering clinical equipoise, and that the definition of standard of care is dependent on patient factors, timing, circumstances, setting, and the training and experience of the provider, it is not too surprising that disagreement ensues. Importantly, there is not often a single right answer or action that would constitute the accepted standard of care, but more likely there is a range of acceptable, reasonable, prudent options that would meet the standard of care, rather than fall below it and constitute a breach [32]. Smith [21] describes it not as a "duty determined by a given set of circumstances that present in a particular patient, with a specific condition, at a definite time and place," rather than a guideline or a list of options.

Establishing Standard of Care

As stated previously, one must first establish an accepted standard of care in order to prove that it was breached [5]. However, establishing a particular standard of care for each individual situation is a complicated issue, largely because each malpractice case is heavily fact-specific. Health care providers (and attorneys) have many sources to turn to that might give some insight into what the relevant standard of care might be, but these can be difficult to apply at the level of the individual incident in question.

A common starting point when looking for the standard of care has traditionally been local practice patterns, but this is becoming less relevant as medical professionals have access to a robust amount of medical education materials to help inform decisions [32]. The original idea behind the locality rule was that a local community would have similar access to medical educational materials, would learn from each other, and would model behavior to one another; therefore, expectations were based on the resources and practice patterns that evolved in that area. Restated, the "locality rule" is generally described as the expectation that a defendant physician provide the same degree of care and skill that is required of other physicians practicing in the same or similar community [4]. The locality rule was originally widely adopted in the United States, mostly as a way to protect rural physicians from having to uphold the same standard of care that was provided in academic health science centers and modern, urban clinics [9]. In the mid-1960s, case law emerged that held specialists to the standard of other specialists, regardless of locality [3]. Modern critics call the locality rule "archaic" and "anachronistic" in light of the standardization of medical education, wealth of information readily available for access globally, and in the context for national standards for board certification [6]. Indeed, the locality rule seems increasingly difficult to justify, but some states do maintain some reliance on the locality rule [4, 14]. In contrast to the locality rule is the national standard. National standards assume the same level of training and diligence among practitioners, but neither assumes nor requires the same availability of medical facilities [4]. The application of local vs. national standards is just one of the complexities in establishing standard of care.

It seems desirable to seek a written source of proof of standard of care, such as a textbook, journal article, guideline, practice parameter, hospital policy, or professional society statement [32]. The problems with many of these written sources can be reflected when one considers the use of clinical practice guidelines, or CPGs, as a source to establish standard of care [4, 17]. Several legal cases have addressed the use of CPGs, but currently there is no set standard for how these documents are used in court [8]. Normally, such documents would be considered "hearsay" since the authors are not available to testify or be cross-examined. However, CPGs may be used as "learned treatises," therefore bypassing the hearsay rule, if they are considered to be of scientific validity. The validity of CPGs (and other written materials) is boosted if the informational material includes multiple sources of scientific merit and is not dependent on the opinion of a relatively small group of people. If clear evidence is sparse, this should be acknowledged [17].

The hope of many was that CPGs would shield clinicians form frivolous lawsuits, eventually decreasing the practice of defensive medicine [15]. However, there are several pitfalls to consider. First, CPGs become quickly outdated because of new research and emerging practices [4]. This is also considered a problem with other written materials, especially textbooks. Another problem is that CPGs may conflict with one another, even if they were created contemporaneously. Some may lack enough scientific evidence to support their recommendations, and some are published by groups without fiduciary responsibilities to patients, such as insurance companies or the pharmaceutical industry. Additionally, some guidelines may be authored by individual clinicians or groups of clinicians with potentially conflicting industry relations [4].

With these things in mind, CPGs should probably not be used to set standard of care for any individual malpractice case [4]. Ideally, the CPGs would allow for some flexibility and consideration of the complexities of care that clinicians inevitably face in real-life scenarios [17]. Some CPG writing groups are now being careful to add in disclaimer statements, specifically stating that the CPG does *not* indicate a standard of care, but this act alone is likely not protective. Though CPGs might not set the standard of care, they can be persuasive, especially if they are from strong, evidence-based sources, like professional medical societies [12]. The CPGs and other written material may, for example, lend credibility to (or detract credibility from) expert medical witness testimony [17], but generally, they are just a part of the larger body of evidence [12].

Role of the Expert Witness

A responsible clinician may use sources such as local practice patterns, professional society statements, medical literature, and clinical practice guidelines to maintain education and competence. While these sources may be persuasive to a jury, when establishing a heavily fact-specific issue like applicable standard of care, expert witnesses are necessary. A medical expert witness assists a court (or other lawful forum convened for the purpose of dispute resolution) by explaining relevant medical processes and scientific information so that the court may determine the facts of the case. Neither the judge nor the jury is likely to have medical training, so expert witnesses must be able to explain information in a way that makes sense to a lay audience. Fortunately, this skill is quite inherent to medical practice, since most clinicians need to be able to explain relevant medical information to patients and families on a regular basis. State laws generally require that an expert witness be qualified by knowledge, skill, experience, training, or education in order to help the finders of fact (usually the jury) understand the evidence. The testimony of the expert witness must be based on sufficient facts or data and should be the product of reliable principles and methods that are relevant to the facts of the specific case in which the opinion is rendered [32].

As discussed previously, medical malpractice has four required elements: duty, breach, causation, and damages. All four elements must be proven by the plaintiff to a reasonable degree of medical certainty, sometimes described as "more likely than not," or "greater than 50% certainty." An expert witness may serve to elucidate any of the elements or combination of elements [32]. Therefore, for each element, such as standard of care, an expert will generally be asked to describe the level of certainty for the opinion; if the expert does not feel that the opinions expressed are beyond a reasonable degree of medical certainty/more likely than not/greater than 50% certainty, this should be made clear.

Duty has traditionally been an element that was not heavily disputed; rather, clinicians would be professionally obligated to render care based on the existence of a clinician-patient relationship. This was originally based on the notion that the patient and doctor entered into what was essentially a contract, though usually an implied contract. This relationship may not be as clearly established with hospitalized patients, who may have little to no option for their nurse, advanced practice provider, or hospital-based physician. Aspects of duty have become less clear with the rise of telemedicine and with evolving practice patterns, including the use of hospitalist-based physicians and advanced practice providers. For example, if a hospitalist is caring for a patient while assigned clinical duties, does the doctor-patient relationship end when the clinical duties are handed off to another hospitalist? As with many disputes surrounding malpractice, this may be one of the points argued within a particular lawsuit.

A malpractice case usually requires a plaintiff's expert witness opinion that the standard of care was breached in order to proceed to trial, and the defense attorney will generally put forward an expert witness whose opinion is that the standard of care was not breached. In fact, in many cases, the plaintiff's expert witness claiming a breach of standard of care may be the only barrier to a malpractice case being filed [32]. Most jurisdictions require that, in order to testify about standard of care, the expert witness be in the same profession, specialty or field of practice as the defendant clinician [4]. In the strictest form of the locality rule, some jurisdictions require an expert witness to practice in the same community or in a community similar to the community in which they are offering opinions [9]. Similarly, some jurisdictions will call for the application of a local standard of care, which means that local practice patterns will influence what range of clinical decisions meet the duty of standard of care, but some require that a national standard be used [32]. The needed facts upon which the standard of care will be based should be largely found in the medical record, where patient's history, condition, risk factors, diagnostic studies, and responses to treatments should be carefully and contemporaneously documented, as should discussions of risks and benefits, goals of care, and informed consent documents. In the face of inadequate documentation, health care provider depositions may fill in the gaps, but health care providers should remember to provide thorough documentation. Besides offering higher quality patient care, there can be some legal protections if the documentation supports that the defendant met the standard of care [7].

Another element of malpractice that usually requires medical expert opinion is that of causation. In order to prove medical malpractice, the plaintiff's attorney must prove that negligence caused harm to the patient. Causation is a very complex legal issue, often beyond the knowledge of a lay jury, so an expert witness is called in to explain the relevant issues. Sometimes, the act of negligence directly causes the harm or injury, but sometimes it is part of the chain of causation [32]. The issues can be more complicated, such as when the negligence may have "substantially increased" the likelihood of an injury, or lead to a "loss of chance" for treatment [24].

Sometimes medical expert witnesses will be asked to give an expert opinion on damages. In a civil court proceeding like a medical malpractice trial, the only option for compensation for "damages" is financial remuneration. This may include medical bills, future medical treatments, loss of income, pain and suffering, and others [25].

Practical Aspects of Expert Witness Testimony

Providing much-needed assistance to the courts by serving as an expert witness may not be the right choice for all health care professionals, but some professional societies, such as the American College of Physicians, encourage broad participation [22]. In fact, some hold it up as a professional duty. The legal system (and, by extension, the citizens it applies to) would likely benefit from the balance brought by a wider variety of educated voices, rather than relying on a relatively few physicians or other health care professionals who spend a disproportionate amount of time testifying (and, therefore, less time practicing, potentially leaving them less attuned to relevant standards of care). Many professional societies have recommended qualifications and expectations, and codes of ethics that address the implications of unethical testimony [1, 22]. Additionally, state laws may specify qualifications. The retaining attorney will usually pose questions about time in practice, professional training, licensure, practice setting, etc., before deciding to retain an expert. Hospitals and health care systems may have policies that apply to employees wishing to engage in legal consulting, which may include requiring the employee to have the employer's permission to participate [32].

As far as qualifications, the American College of Physicians (ACP) has recommendations that generally reflect those of many other professional societies. Interested parties should check specifically with their professional societies; in the absence of any further guidance, what follows should be considered advisory, but may be neither necessary nor sufficient. Per the ACP, the expert witness should have a valid, unrestricted license to practice in their state. The expert witness should be certified by an appropriate Board or should be fully trained in a specialty or subspecialty that is appropriate to the subject matter of the case; the expert should be qualified by experience or should have demonstrated competence; they should have evidence of continuing medical education; they should be familiar with the clinical practice of the specialty or the subject matter of the case at the time of the alleged incident in dispute; and they should have been actively involved in the clinical practice of the specialty or the subject matter of the case for three of the five years prior to the date of the testimony [22].

The ACP also offers general guidelines that are helpful to anyone considering acting as an expert witness. They say that an expert witness should testify honestly, fully, and impartially about their qualifications and regarding the medical information involved in the case. They suggest that one should review the standards of practice prevailing at the time of the alleged occurrence [22]. The author finds this to be controversial, since, in theory, a qualified expert should be very familiar with the relevant standards. One might posit that if the expert has to review the standards, they might not be qualified enough to offer an opinion; however, the suggestion to fully prepare and ensure accuracy is respectable. When testifying, the expert should be prepared to state whether testimony is based on personal experience, specific scientific references, or generally accepted within the specialty [22]. The American Academy of Neurology (AAN) guidelines state that if an expert is engaged expert witness testimony for more than 20% of their professional time, the expert should be prepared to demonstrate clinical competency and that their opinion is objective, rather than being influenced by financial considerations [1].

Some elements of the expert opinions, such as causation or damages, may be based on a medical evaluation. This is usually done by performing a detailed review of the medical records, but a face-to-face evaluation of the patient may be required. Due to variations among jurisdictions, it is very important to listen to the instructions of the retaining attorney. If the attorney who has retained the expert witness feels that the expert opinions are helpful to their client's case, the attorney may ask the expert witness to report them formally to the court. This may require a written report or a deposition. Though many malpractices cases settle before going to trial, an expert witness should always enter into a case with the mindset that they may need to provide formal trial testimony before the court and that they will see the case through to the end [32].

Serving as a medical expert witness can be time-consuming. Experts should be prepared to commit the necessary time to familiarize themselves with the case and provide the needed testimony. Compensation for expert witness work should be reasonable and reflective of the time that it takes to gather the information needed to render the expert opinion, as well as for preparing for deposition and, if applicable, for a court appearance. Under no circumstances should compensation be dependent on the outcome of the case [22, 32].

In order to be effective as an expert witness, one must be able to communicate well and must be able to explain medical and scientific principles to a lay audience. One must be prepared for the fact that the legal system in the United States is designed to be adversarial (that is, one party is pitted against the other in a struggle to show that their version of the "facts" of the actual case constitute the "truth"). Unfortunately for the expert witness, this usually means entering a hostile situation. Therefore, the expert witness would do well to testify on opinions with which they are comfortable and should expect the opposing attorney to try to undermine their credibility [32].

Probably the most important piece of information when formulating an expert opinion is to remember that the clinician is there to act as an educator for the court. The expert witness may be retained by the plaintiff's (patient's) attorney or by the defense (clinician, hospital) attorney, but the expert is not an advocate "for" the plaintiff or "for" the defense. Rather, the expert is there to present the truth, in so far as the medical and scientific facts are understood. The attorneys will use the information to advocate for their clients, and the jury will use this information to come to a verdict [32].

Implications of Providing Improper or Unethical Expert Witness Testimony

A medical malpractice dispute, by definition, has two opposing sides. This means that expert witnesses will provide testimony that is in conflict with other expert witnesses. Keep in mind that there is necessarily a dispute between parties, or else there would be no basis for a malpractice case; similarly, there is necessarily a disagreement between the expert witnesses retained by the plaintiff's attorney and the defense attorney, otherwise the case would settle or would be dismissed. Some fear that an expert witness is essentially acting as a mercenary, testifying a certain way because they are being paid by the retaining attorney's client. The author proposes an alternative point of view: the retaining attorney would not hire the expert witness if the witness's opinion was not helpful to the client's case. Therefore, the adversarial legal system almost creates a selection bias, of sorts, when it pits expert witnesses against one another. The reasons that educated, trained, licensed, credentialed professionals have conflicting expert opinions about a point that is supposed to be "objective" are many. Sometimes expert witnesses will offer the opinion based on what they do in practice, or what the ideal treatment would have been in a particular case, simply as a result of not understanding the legal definition of "standard of care." Sometimes the expert witness will present an opinion based on what should have been done in hindsight, or what care is recommended in a generic set of circumstances. These opinions may not reflect what a reasonable, prudent clinician would have done if presented with the same or similar circumstances.

Sometimes, however, clinicians do present expert witness testimony in an unethical way. For example, they may serve as an expert witness, even though the area is not within their usual area of practice or expertise. They may provide testimony that reflects scientific information or practice that evolved after the actual case. They may present an area of clinical equipoise as an issue that has been settled or misrepresent medical literature in a way that advances their own opinions or causes. This may cause one of the parties to suffer an injustice. For example, if a defense attorney presents an expert witness that is improperly shielding a defendant, an injured patient may not be compensated. If a plaintiff's attorney presents an expert witness that is improperly prosecutorial, an innocent defendant may pay an unfair price in monetary damages, reputational loss, and emotional distress. In addition to the implications for the individual case, there is a possibility for the improper testimony to contribute to the body of case law, impacting future cases.

Since tort law is a common law system, unethical expert witness testimony can have lasting implications. Unethical testimony may set unsound precedents, causing future clinicians to be held to standards inconsistent with the way medicine is practiced. Expert witnesses should remember that depositions and court testimony are a matter of public record and, therefore, subject to peer review [22, 32]. If caught providing unethical testimony, other courts may not allow an expert's testimony in the future, and the experts may face sanctions from their professional societies based on formal grievance processes [1]. Expert witnesses who lie under oath could even face perjury charges [32]. If one is offering expert witness testimony, this guiding principle may be helpful: an expert witness should live up to the standard of care that they are testifying to if they are faced with the same or similar circumstances; or, similarly, they be comfortable with the reality that this standard may be applied to them someday, either as defendant or as a patient. Testifying to an unrealistic or unsound standard may have lasting implications if that standard becomes part of case law.

The idea that expert witness testimony drives case law, thereby setting legal precedent and evolving the standard of care, is exemplified in the case of *Austin v. American Ass'n of Neurological Surgeons* [2]. A neurosurgeon suspended from the American Association of Neurological Surgeons (AANS) sued for damages, citing the economic impact of his damaged reputation. He claimed the suspension was out of revenge for expert witness testimony he gave, specifically that the majority of neurosurgeons would agree that recurrent laryngeal nerve injury as the result of anterior cervical fusion surgery could only be due to negligence on the part of the surgeon. To the contrary, recurrent laryngeal injury is a known complication of cervical spine surgery. Whether negligence is the cause of the injury is a fact-driven dispute, and one that should be decided by a jury, if a patient chooses to seek damages. The 7th Circuit Court ruled that the physician did not have an important economic interest in AANS membership, and he could not obtain damages. Additionally, they ruled that the AANS did not act in bad faith; rather, the irresponsible expert witness testimony could have set an unreasonable precedent that other surgeons would then be held to and, as such, the testimony itself constituted the "practice of medicine." The Supreme Court refused to hear the case on appeal. Therefore, the

AANS and other professional societies maintain a vested interest in making sure that expert witness testimony is truthful, impartial, accurate, and relevant.

Conclusion

The standard of care is a duty to provide the care that a skilled, qualified clinician would provide in the same or similar circumstances. Proving medical malpractice hinges on establishing that a health care provider breached their duty to meet the standard of care, causing damages to a patient. Because determination of the standard of care is heavily fact-specific, expert witness testimony is needed to establish what standard of care should be applied to the specific case. In educating the court about the relevant medical issues, the expert witness must take into account the timing, geography, practice setting, patient factors, and clinical expertise when testifying to the relevant standards. Improper or unethical expert witness may cause impractical or unrealistic standards of care to evolve, confounding justice, so expert witnesses may face penalties such as sanctions from professional societies if they are found to have provided inaccurate testimony.

References

1. American Academy of Neurology qualifications and guidelines for the physician expert witness. Neurology 2006;66:13–4.
2. A*ustin v. American Ass'n of Neurological Surgeons* 253 F.3d 967 (7th Cir 2001).
3. *Brune v. Belinkoff*, 235 N.E.2d 793 (Mass. 1968).
4. Cooke BK, Worsham E, Reisfield GM. The elusive standard of care. J Am Acad Psychiatry Law. 2017;45(3):358–64.
5. Field RI. The malpractice crisis turns 175: what lessons does history hold for reform? Drexel L Rev. 2011;4:7–39.
6. Ginsberg M. The locality rule lives! Why? Using modern medicine to eradicate an "unhealthy" law. Drake L Rev. 2013;61:321–73.
7. Grady A. The importance of standard of care and documentation. Virtual Mentor. 2005 Nov;7(11):756–8.
8. Hall C. Policies, guidelines and protocols. In: Szalados J, Wright W, Smith W, editors. Law and ethics in neurocritical care. Chicago: Neurocritical Care Society; 2019. p. 146–7.
9. Hall GE. The "locality" rule. JAMA. 1969;207:627–8.
10. *Hall v. Hilburn*, 466 So. 2d 856 (Miss. 1985).
11. *Helling v. Carey*, 83 Wash. 2d 514, 519 P.2d 981 (1974).
12. Hyams AL, Shapiro DW, Brennan TA. Medical practice guidelines in malpractice litigation: an early retrospective. J Health Pol'y & L. 1996;21:289–313.
13. *Johnston v. St. Francis Medical Center, Inc.*, No. 3 5, 236-CA, Oct. 31, 2001.
14. Lewis MH, Gohagen JK, Merenstein DJ. The locality rule and the physician's dilemma; local medical practices vs the national standard of care. JAMA. 2007;297:2633–7.
15. Mehlman MJ. Professional power and the standard of care in medicine. Ariz St L J. 2012;44:1166–233.
16. *McCourt v Abernathy*, 457 S.E.2d 603 (S.C. 1995).

17. Moffett P, Moore G. The standard of care: legal history and definitions: the bad and good news. WestJEM. 2011 Feb;12(1):109–12.
18. Mohr JC. American medical malpractice litigation in historical perspective. JAMA. 2000;283:1731–7.
19. Revised Code of Washington. Section 4.24.290.
20. Rubin JB, Bishop TF. Characteristics of paid malpractice claims settled in and out of court in the USA: a retrospective analysis. BMJ Open. 2013;3:e002985.
21. Smith H. A model for validating an expert's opinion in medical negligence cases. J Leg Med. 2005;26(2):207–31.
22. Snyder L (author; developed for the Health and Public Policy Committee by the Clinical Practice Subcommittee: Farmer RG, Cleaveland CR, Fryhofer SA, Gordon DL, Myers WA, Rosenow EC, et al.). Guidelines for the physician expert witness. Ann. Intern. 1990;113(10):789.
23. Spiegel AD, Kavaler F. America's first medical malpractice crisis, 1835–1865. J Community Health. 1997;22:283–308.
24. Szalados J. Lost chance doctrine. In: Szalados J, Wright W, Smith W, editors. Law and ethics in neurocritical care. Chicago: Neurocritical Care Society; 2019a. p. 28–9.
25. Szalados J. Economic loss and damages. In: Szalados J, Wright W, Smith W, editors. Law and ethics in neurocritical care. Chicago: Neurocritical Care Society; 2019b. p. 26–7.
26. *Texas & P. Ry. v. Behymer*, 189 U.S. 468, 470, 47 L. Ed. 905, 23 S. Ct. 622 (1903).
27. *The T.J. Hooper*, 60 F:2d 737 (2d Cir.), cert. denied, 287 U.S. 662 (1932).
28. Thomas T. Professional negligence. In: Szalados J, Wright W, Smith W, editors. Law and ethics in neurocritical care. Chicago: Neurocritical Care Society; 2019. p. 16–7.
29. White EG. The intellectual origins of torts in America. Yale L J. 1977;86:671–93.
30. Wright W. Overview of tort law. In: Szalados J, Wright W, Smith W, editors. Law and ethics in neurocritical care. Chicago: Neurocritical Care Society; 2019a. p. 14–5.
31. Wright W. Medical malpractice. In: Szalados J, Wright W, Smith W, editors. Law and ethics in neurocritical care. Chicago: Neurocritical Care Society; 2019b. p. 18–9.
32. Wright W. Expert witness testimony. In: Szalados J, Wright W, Smith W, editors. Law and ethics in neurocritical care. Chicago: Neurocritical Care Society; 2019c. p. 34–7.

Chapter 32
The Second Victim in Medical Malpractice Litigation: The Stress of Litigation

Wendy L. Wright

Introduction

When a medical error or adverse event leads to patient harm, the patient and family are considered the first victims. Increasingly recognized, however, is the impact on the health care providers involved in the care of the patient at the time of the event. A health care provider can suffer a complex psychological harm driven by guilt, shame, fear, anxiety, and isolation [54], which can ripple through their professional and personal lives, increasing the risk that they will not be able to function to the best of their abilities and further compromising patient safety. Wu described this phenomenon as the "second victim" of medical errors [55]. As there is a growing emphasis on disclosure and apology after medical errors as a way to increase quality and safety, a parallel movement is looking at care that should be rendered to wounded healers [54].

The attention to the second victim is important when establishing a "fair and just culture." A fair and just culture is one that openly examines its own weaknesses in order to improve [21]. It is critical that caregivers feel supported when voicing concerns about patient safety issues, including when their own errors are revealed [21, 28]. A fair and just culture moves away from a traditional model of "blame and shame" in the setting of medical errors in order to foster a culture of continuous improvement [23]. Otherwise, health care providers might be tempted to not reveal errors or raise patient safety concerns, for fear of negative consequences, which would undermine potential opportunities for improvement.

W. L. Wright (✉)
Emory University Hospital Midtown, Emory University School of Medicine, Atlanta, GA, USA
e-mail: wwrigh2@emory.edu

J. E. Szalados (ed.), *The Medical-Legal Aspects of Acute Care Medicine*,
https://doi.org/10.1007/978-3-030-68570-6_32

The Second Victim of Medical Errors

First described by Wu in 2000, the second victim phenomenon was defined in further detail by Scott et al. in 2009. The second victim is a health care provider traumatized by an error or adverse event, feeling personally responsible for an unexpected or undesired outcome [40]. Physicians, advanced practice providers, nurses, pharmacists, and other members of the health care team are all at risk for causing errors and may therefore become second victims [14]. The second victim can be any member of the medical team, the entire medical team, or groups of teams involved in the care of the patient. [54]. They may second guess their clinical skills and knowledge base and may feel as if they have failed their patient [40]. Clinicians involved in a medical error may feel singled out and exposed. They may agonize over what to say and do in the aftermath of an error and may fear that the error or their role in the adverse event will be discovered. However, analysis of an error is essential to promote quality improvement. Modern ethical practice favors disclosure of errors, but health care providers may dread the prospect of potential negative consequences, including the patient's anger [49].

Medical Errors and Adverse Events

At the heart of the second victim phenomenon is a medical professional's sense of responsibility for patients and the culpability when there is an error or adverse event. The definitions of error and adverse event are not standardized. Adverse medical events may happen unrelated to error; a medical error may (or may not) cause an adverse event. Adverse events may include events that the health care provider has no control over, such as the death of young person, and may not reflect any error or aspect of care for which a health care provider would be culpable. That is not to say that a health care provider does not feel grief or suffering after an adverse event, but, unfortunately, death, debility, and loss are inherent parts of the occupation with which a clinician must learn to cope in order to continue in the field.

The possible spectrum of medical errors and adverse events may hinder the study and recognition of the second victim, as one should try to narrow down the types of incidents that are likely to be triggers for symptoms. Some studies add medication errors. Others include only "serious" adverse events [45], which revisits the debate over error (implying on some level that a mistake was made) versus adverse event (for example, the failure of a planned treatment course to reverse an illness, through no fault of the treating team). Even "near miss" events, which, by definition, should cause no harm to a patient, may be a source of embarrassment and may cause a crisis of confidence in a health care provider. In order to narrow the discussion, this chapter will focus more on medical errors, since they are more likely to trigger second victim phenomena and medical malpractice litigation.

Lander proposed a broad definition of medical error, which is anything that the health care provider reflects upon and concludes, "I don't want this to happen again" [26]. The advantages of this definition include that it encourages clinician introspection. This can drive personal improvement from the clinician and may inspire quality improvement efforts within the institution. However, one can imagine how this definition would include adverse events (for which the health care provider may not be culpable) or even near misses (which, by definition, would not result in patient harm). Therefore, it might be a little too broad to serve as a basis of the discussion at hand. The Institute of Medicine (IOM) defines a medical error as "the failure of a planned action to be completed as intended or the use of a wrong plan to achieve an aim" [17, 22]. This is also useful definition, in that it may not only help the clinician and the hospital learn how to avoid a similar error in the future, but it could also refer to situations where no harm befalls the patient. Committing an error with no harm befalling the patient may still result in negative feelings on the part of the responsible clinician. However, an incident without harm is unlikely to lead to a medical malpractice lawsuit. An older definition of medical error proposed by [30] is "a mistake resulting in an unanticipated negative consequence of a medical intervention." For the sake of focusing the discussion on the second victim and malpractice litigation, this chapter uses the Mizhari definition of medical error.

Symptoms of the Second Victim

The second victim of medical errors is often troubled by the impact of the error on the first victims (the patient and family). Symptoms are reflective of psychological distress and most often include guilt, anger, irritation, fear, depressed mood, embarrassment, humiliation, shame, regret, grief, sadness, self-doubt, disappointment, frustration, loss of self-confidence, remorse, and anxiety [45]. Second victims may exhibit behavioral symptoms such as insomnia and nightmares. They may relive the incident intrusively and repeatedly. They may have cognitive symptoms such as disturbance in concentration. Some report that they lose confidence in their practices and fear making another error. They may also perceive a loss of trust by their colleagues [36]. At times, the guilt and fear can disrupt a clinician's therapeutic relationship with first victim, leaving the patient and family to feel abandoned by the clinician [6]. Worse patient outcomes and greater sense of personal responsibility are associated with more intense reactions and greater personal anguish in resident physicians [17].

Long-term effects may include burnout, depression [18, 45, 52], decreased quality of life, concentration difficulties, and persistent anxiety [45]. Over time, second victims can have continuing emotional distress and even go on to develop posttraumatic stress disorder (PTSD) [33, 36, 39]. Second victims may seek solace in drugs or alcohol or, tragically, can be driven to suicidal ideation [54].

The psychological distress can impact both the professional lives and the personal lives of clinicians [1, 3, 13, 36, 42]. Second victims who are burned out or have reduced job satisfaction can degrade working relationships, causing communication issues and degrading the culture of safety. Loss of clinical confidence can be a safety issue, increasing mistakes and further driving the spiral. Their job performance can be impaired and they may pose additional safety hazards if they find maladaptive ways of coping [45], such as alcohol or drug use [23, 55, 25].

Prevalence and At-Risk Populations

Since the second victim phenomenon is relatively recently described, the prevalence has not been widely studied. Current estimates range from 10.4% [26] to 46% [16]. It seems likely that the prevalence is underestimated. Negative emotions felt and symptoms experienced by health care providers involved in adverse medical events are a pervasive problem [54]. A majority of perioperative nurses reported being angry at themselves for committing an error and exhibited some measure of emotional distress [9]. In an older study, some reported shattered confidence and a level of distress so extreme that they felt they were unfit to be a nurse any longer [2].

Female second victims report more distress than male second victims. They report they are more afraid of receiving blame and more prone to losing confidence. Female second victims report that they experience more loss of reputation. They are, however, more likely to discuss the error to learn whether colleagues would make the same decision and more likely to attend training programs designed to assist recovery [24, 31, 56].

Medical students and residents can be deeply impacted as second victims [27, 57]. A study by Wu in 1993 concluded that medical residents should be encouraged to accept responsibility for medical mistakes. They should be given the opportunity to discuss a mistake and should be discouraged from forgetting about it or avoiding thinking about it [57]. On the upside, a study by Engel found that residents who are confronted with a mistake and feel personal responsibility are inherently more motivated to change their future practices. However, the downside is that confrontation and discussion may challenge their emotional well-being [17]. Faculty who oversee residents should have a fair and just approach to engaging residents in the discussion of medical errors. A "blame and shame approach" may do more long-term harm than good. Supervisors of trainees do need a reliable way to assess skills acquisition and clinical improvement, so trainees should not feel compelled to hide mistakes to minimize the feared negative consequences. A resident may not be emotionally or psychologically mature enough to disclose an error, so this skill is something that should be taught and modeled during training.

Risk Factors and Triggers for Second Victim Phenomena

Some circumstances pose higher risk for generating second victim symptoms. These include unexpected death of a patient, death of a young patient, ethically challenging cases, and proximity to or long professional relationship with the patient [54]. These circumstances may apply with variable frequency to hospital-based clinicians, depending on job description, but inpatient clinicians certainly have exposure to deaths and ethically challenging cases. Since nurses are often the ones that spend the most time on the frontlines, and usually spend more time with patients, it stands to reason that they will be at higher risk of developing second victim symptoms if they commit an error.

When a medical error causes an adverse event, it is important that this error be disclosed to the patient or family. Disclosure of the error to the patient is stressful and may initiate or exacerbate second victim symptoms. In addition to the psychological distress when facing the first victim, clinicians may feel conflicted when disclosing an error due to the potential for legal implications or uncertainty about the cause of the error. It may be tempting to the distressed clinician to avoid involvement in the disclosure, but Lander et al. [26] suggest that failure to address the emotional need to accept responsibility actually hampers completion of the necessary steps to deal with the aftermath of an error. Respectful disclosure should include support for the patient and clinician, resolution of the event, and steps for learning and improvement [11]. Some states have laws that require disclosure, but not all confer legal protection that excludes the disclosure from being entered into evidence in a malpractice trial. Since the laws vary from one state to the next, the legal landscape regarding this issue is uneven and unclear [15].

The clinician may experience further moral and psychological injury while bracing for the investigation into the adverse event. At this point, they may become reluctant to disclose information out of fear of privacy violations and due to ambiguity about what can be discussed with whom [54]. The impact of second victim symptoms increases when a health care provider receives a patient complaint. A complaint following an error or adverse medical event can further strain the doctor-patient relationship and can cause a loss of confidence on the part of the clinician [3, 13].

Medical Malpractice Defendant as Second Victim

Second victim symptoms can worsen, re-emerge, or present for the first time when a health care provider is sued for medical malpractice. Not only does a lawsuit reinforce the idea that the clinician did something wrong or shameful, but it also adds the fear of a formal assignment of guilt of professional negligence by a jury of one's peers. There is significant fear of financial loss, reputational injury, and professional insecurity, especially by those who have never tangled with the legal system before being named in a malpractice suit. The sued clinician is suddenly faced with a significant investment of time in what is generally a painful, humiliating process marked with uncertainty. The author reflects on personal experience when stating that facing a malpractice lawsuit (which was fortunately later dismissed) is emotionally devastating and one of the most traumatic episodes in one's professional life.

A new entity called "medical malpractice stress syndrome (MMSS)" has emerged in the literature over the last few years [35]. MMSS can affect the health and practice of health care professionals [34]. MMSS symptoms are remarkably similar to PTSD [35], including shame, guilt, anger, frustration, irritability, and isolation [47]. Physical symptoms might include fatigue, GI upset, and chest pain [4]. Symptoms can result in the setting of a formal complaint or investigation, even if a lawsuit does not result [4]. The primary cause of the stress is the perception of a complaint or malpractice suit as an attack on one's personal integrity [4]. Although most malpractice cases do not actually make it all the way to trail, lawsuits are time consuming, costly, and take an emotional toll even if the defendant is later dismissed or found not liable for negligence [5]. Defendants may end up developing a sense of outrage if they feel they are unfairly accused [35] or if they are the victims of unscrupulous expert witness testimony [5]. As Avitzur [5] wisely notes "even when you win, you lose," illustrating that a defendant found not liable for professional negligence still suffers a loss.

Healing the Second Victim

Clinicians impacted as a second victim may respond in a variety of ways. Some coping strategies are constructive, such as taking responsibility for an error, disclosing the error, and reflecting on the error [19]. Some are destructive, such as denying involvement in the error [30]. Professionals by nature have a strong sense of personal responsibility, and this sense is linked to the ability to take responsibility for the medical error [17, 23, 32]. Clinicians can feel a deep sense of regret, fear, and anxiety when they have a role in a medical error that led to an adverse outcome. Health care professionals have and ethical and professional responsibilty to care for themselves in a way that allows them to care for their patients. Adhering to general principles of wellness is always advisable [54]. Recovery may be hindered if discussion of the event is discouraged, either passively by lack of appropriate forums or actively by risk managers or hospital attorneys [55].

Scott et al. [40] describe the stages of recovery for second victims. Immediately after an adverse medical event, the medical team may be occupied by trying to decipher what happened and by managing the medical care of the patient. This stage is often marked by the chaos of accident response. When the situation stabilizes, the clinicians involved may experience intrusive reflections, including feelings of inadequacy and self-doubt. They may ask themselves "what-if" questions. At some point, the clinicians will look to restore personal integrity. They may want to turn to trusted advisors to relate their experiences and try to understand the impact of the medical error on their professional and personal lives. However, they might not know where to seek support [38]. For example, a clinician may feel they are unable to discuss the case with colleagues or friends for fear of consequences (such as those discussions being used in an investigation or litigation) [55]. If colleagues are unsupportive, this may impair the recovery of the second victim [38]. Commonly, second victims will need to endure questioning from others regarding medical errors, whether that be from colleagues to elicit areas of improvement or risk managers who are trying to gauge risk of malpractice litigation. Further questioning, in the form of deposition or trial testimony, will follow if a lawsuit is filed.

At some point, the clinician is expected to "move on" from the experience. Scott [38] describes three general patterns of existence for the second victim at the end of the recovery process. The first is dropping out, which is when the clinician leaves the profession, changes roles, or changes practice settings to minimize the chances of undergoing second victim trauma. The second is surviving, which is when the clinician is able to carry on with normal duties, but is having a hard time moving past the medical error. The last is thriving, which is when the health care professional is able to learn from the event or turn it into a positive experience. The success or failure of the recovery process is likely related to the coping strategies employed, including the ability of the clinician to successfully seek support.

Destructive Coping Strategies

Considering the pain and trauma that a second victim endures, it is not a surprise that some of the coping mechanisms employed may end up being defensive and potentially even destructive. One defensive technique is keeping the error to one's self in order to avoid the negative repercussions of the error [45]. However, this will hamper the culture of safety by not allowing for quality improvement initiatives based on that error and is likely to still result in negative emotions such as guilt in the second victim. A second victim may try to distance themselves from the incident, perhaps by distancing themselves from the patient and family, avoiding participation in the investigation of the event, or avoiding similar patients. These escape behaviors are associated with the second victim's perception that job overload contributed to the mistake and with the perception that the institution responded judgmentally to the error [29, 56, 57]. Another escape behavior is to discount their role in the error or the severity of the error [30]. Though these behaviors may avoid short-term suffering, there is a strong relationship between escape or avoidance and emotional distress [9].

Some clinicians make changes in their practice. This can be either by destructive or by constructive mechanisms. Destructive coping occurs when the clinician is less confident or more worried. They order more tests than usual or become less decisive. As mentioned earlier, the change to their practice may be to leave their practice setting or leave medicine all together.

Constructive Coping Strategies

Constructive coping strategies start with accepting responsibility for the medical error [9, 23]. Clinicians may look to incorporate changes in practice that avoid future errors, such as seeking more advice, paying more attention to detail, increasing educational efforts, confirming data personally, slowing down, and following hospital policies more closely [45]. It is generally agreed that discussion of the error is beneficial [32]. Some clinicians may ask a colleague what they would have done and solicit insight about alternative approaches [45].

One coping strategy is referred to as planful problem-solving. This is a problem-focused strategy in which the individual tries to learn from the mistake by seeking information to try to determine what happened and participating in problem-solving that will help reduce the chance of error recurrence [9, 57]. When an error comes to light, the case is reviewed which may lead to changes in system processes and practices; when second victims contribute to the solution design, it not only helps address vulnerabilities in the system but also helps the second victim heal [44]. However, the discussion of the problem and the subsequent investigation may heighten emotional distress [9, 43, 56], so colleagues should watch for worsening or re-emergence of second victim symptoms.

In contrast to a problem-focused strategy, some coping strategies are emotion-focused [1, 2, 9]. Emotion-focused strategies try to reduce the emotional turmoil caused by the medical error. Meeting with the patient or family harmed by a medical error to disclose the error has been identified as an important way for reducing the negative impact of the event on physicians. However, disclosure is not a guaranteed method for obtaining relief or absolution [1, 7]. Some studies indicate that disclosure can lead to better outcomes, improved relationships with patients, and improved health care delivery systems [48]. Some show that there is a positive impact on the emotional distress of the second victim and a reduced likelihood of future mistakes [43, 50, 55, 56]. However, disclosure can lead to additional stress on the second victim [50]. Clinicians may be hesitant to disclose an error for fear of reputational loss, loss of patients, or incurring a negative emotional reaction from the patient [20]. Clinicians also fear that error disclosure opens them up to malpractice litigation. Some state laws now require disclosure of medical errors, but not all confer legal protections surrounding disclosure [15]. In order to make disclosure as beneficial as possible to all parties, the discussion should be organized and facilitated by those trained to do so [43, 55, 56] and by those trained to assess a worsening or re-emergence of second victim symptoms.

Another valuable emotion-focused strategy is seeking emotional support and error disclosure [45]. Engel et al. [17] report that talking with family and friends seems less therapeutic than talking with colleagues. Despite the importance of self-care, clinicians face significant barriers to seeking help, as shown in Table 32.1.

Even if second victims know where to turn for support, they may not receive adequate support [22, 39, 50]. In light of these barriers, and recognizing the

Table 32.1 Barriers to second victims seeking help

Fear of embarrassment
Fear of reputational injury
Which can lead to negative financial consequences
Fear of punishment or other negative consequences based on the triggering event
Including loss of job, additional scrutiny at place of work
Feelings of inadequacy or guilt over the triggering event
Lack of clarity regarding sources of help
Including not understanding which conversations are peer-review protected and which would be discoverable in a legal proceeding
Lack of accessible mental health resources
Can be based on location or due to limited hours of availability
Shame associated with receiving help for mental health reasons

long-term impact of the second victim phenomenon, health care organizations have a responsibility to support clinicians after a medical error.

Organizational Support After Medical Error

Health care organizations have three priorities after a medical error leads to an adverse event. The first is to care for the patient and family who are the direct victims (first victims) of the error [10, 14]. Health care organizations have a responsibility to try to understand how and why medical errors and adverse events happen. Ideally, this information should be used to improve quality of care [10]. The second is to care for the frontline clinicians (second victims) who are exposed to the event [10, 14]. Hospitals should also establish resources to respectfully and compassionately help clinicians deal with the emotional impact of medical errors and adverse events [11]. The third is to formulate a response plan to address the needs of the organization which might suffer a loss [10, 14].

Since ongoing emotional distress is related to an increased likelihood of adverse events [51] and lack of emotional support makes the emotional distress worse [2], health care organizations need to provide emotional support to second victims. Ideally, the support would be available immediately [39], which would require around-the-clock availability [10, 41, 48], and support would come from someone with whom the second victim has a trusting relationship [36, 40]. It should be immediately obvious that this is a very difficult prescription to fill. In some cases, the second victim's only option is to seek support externally, such as at national or international peer conferences [17, 22, 48] because health care institutions fail to provide the necessary elements of support [10, 22, 37].

A fair and just culture that supports mutual criticism and constructive feedback at the workplace reduces the impact of the adverse event [1]. However, discussion of errors is still not common. In one study, 30% of faculty members and nearly 50%

of trainees reported that they were not comfortable discussing errors [6]. Clinicians report that they are afraid of damage to professional reputation, and some felt colleagues minimize the mistakes or avoid their emotional concerns [12]. Open discussion should be organized and facilitated [43, 55, 56]. The second victim should be reassured that their professional abilities are still important to the organization and their professional teams [17, 37]. Support can be provided by asking about the emotional impact of the error and by asking how the colleague is coping [29, 55]. A supportive colleague should seek to be present in the conversation, practice active listening, allow the second victim to share the personal impact of the story, and avoid condemnation without knowing the whole story [39]. The facilitators of the discussion should guarantee confidentiality and facilitate a higher level of support when needed [41, 48, 50].

Resources for Support

Even if second victims are hesitant to reach out for support, or do not know where to turn for support, there are often resources for support available. Individual support can come from managers, supervisors, therapists, counselors, clergy, and colleagues. Staff should be guided on how they can support each other and whether any supplemental support programs are available [54]. The highest level of peer support is conferred when the clinician can discuss the error with a trusted mentor to discuss what went wrong [1]. Risk managers and department supervisors should be trained to identify the need for support and refer providers to the second victim programs as needed [50]. Group settings can be a source of emotional support [19, 57]. Debriefing after an adverse event caused by medical error may help identify second victims and give them a forum in which to discuss their feelings [54]. Classically, morbidity and mortality conferences were a setting where errors were discussed [17, 22], but these conferences notoriously exemplified the "blame and shame" culture that should be left behind. Wu [55] has recommended the use of "error conferences" as a way to help heal second victims.

Scott et al. [41] described the need for a three-tiered support system. The first stage is emotional "first aid." This is described as basic care to ensure that the second victim is okay. This could be organized at the department or local level. Scott et al. found that this was sufficient for 60% of the participants studied. The second tier is support by trained peer. This includes intensive mentoring of clinicians by frontline managers, with referrals to patient safety specialists or risk managers as needed. This level of support was needed by 30% of the participants studied. The third tier consisted of referral to professional counselors, which was needed by about 10% of participants.

The Joint Commission [46] suggests that second victim support programs incorporate several elements. One is peer support, specifically the ability of a trained peer colleague to respond to the adverse event and begin supporting health care workers. Some examples include Medically Induced Trauma Support Services [8] and

Critical Incident Stress Management [53]. Other Joint Commission recommendations for elements to include are leadership support; the promotion of discussion of feelings in an appropriate format; confidential, non-judgmental follow-up for clinicians continuing to struggle for a prolonged time period after an incident; and provision of external resources such as outside counselors as needed. Developing such a system takes a significant dedication of time, training, and resources, but it must be a priority for a hospital that wants to maintain a fair and just culture and support second victims [54].

One widely available resource for support is an employee assistance program (EAP). EAPs can offer counseling services and make outside referrals if needed. However, there are barriers and limitations that hinder the second victim. One is not wanting (or not being able) to take time away from work to seek assistance. EAP programs carry with them the stigma of accessing mental health services, and clinicians fear negative judgments by colleagues. Clinicians may have doubts about the confidentiality of the process [46].

Coping with the Stress of Litigation

The Joint Commission [46] specifically recommends support for clinicians involved in litigation. Efforts to discuss the second victims' feelings with colleagues and friends may be actively discouraged by defense attorneys, which contributes to worsening stress and feelings of isolation [54, 55]. Laws are often unclear or even silent regarding legal protection of information discussed in second victim support groups, which can hamper efforts to provide second victim support [15]. Some have called for safeguards around second victim programs, since the impact of the second victim's depression and anxiety extends beyond the first victim to other patients in the second victim's care [15]. In the absence of such safeguards, defendants in medical malpractice suits often suffer in silence [5].

Since malpractice lawsuits typically last for a few years, the resulting stress must be managed effectively, lest it will take its toll on one's health, relationships, and profession. Ansari-Winn [4] offers recommendation for managing medical malpractice stress syndrome. She suggests seeking support from a mental health professional if the stress is interfering with relationships, contributing to drug or alcohol abuse, and causing physical symptoms, or if there is a history of emotional conditions that required treatment. Consulting with a personal physician may be helpful if the stress is causing a worsening of chronic medical conditions. Support groups are available to provide support, education, and coaching on the legal process. Even though most defendants would choose to avoid the legal process, engaging in one's defense will help the second victim gain a stronger sense of control. Importantly, the second victim who is facing a malpractice lawsuit should make time for self-care. They should engage in hobbies, exercise, eat a healthy diet, and spend time with family and friends.

Conclusion

As awareness regarding the second victim phenomenon increases, health care institutions need to make a more concerted effort to heal the wounded healers. The stigma that remains regarding the access and use of mental health care services [55] needs to be broken as part of the evolution from the "blame and shame" culture to a culture of continuous improvement [23]. The emotional stress of the second victim is likely to be significantly more impactful when a medical malpractice lawsuit results. Since second victim support is an integral part of patient safety, more research and training regarding second victims of medical errors are needed [44].

References

1. Aasland OG, Førde R. Impact of feeling responsible for adverse events on doctors' personal and professional lives: the importance of being open to criticism from colleagues. Qual Saf Health Care. 2005;14:13–7.
2. Arndt M. Medication errors. Research in practice: how drug mistakes affect self-esteem. Nurs Times. 1994;90:27–30.
3. Ashok J, Ogden J. General practitioners' experience of patients' complaints: qualitative study. Br Med J. 1999;318:1596–9.
4. Ansari-Winn D. 4 keys to manage medical malpractice stress syndrome. KevinMD.com. 2014. Available at https://www.kevinmd.com/blog/2014/03/4-keys-manage-medical-malpractice-stress-syndrome.html. Accessed 12 Dec 2019.
5. Avitzur O. The ordeal of medical malpractice: even when you win, you lose. Neurol Today. 2010;10(4):20–1.
6. Bell SK, Moorman DW, Delbanco T. Improving the patient, family, and clinician experience after harmful events: the "when things go wrong" curriculum. Acad Med. 2010;85:1010–7.
7. Berlinger N, Wu AW. Subtracting insult from injury: addressing cultural expectations in the disclosure of medical error. J Med Ethics. 2005;31:106–8.
8. Carr S. Disclosure and apology. What's missing? Advancing programs that support clinicians. Boston: Medically Induced Trauma Support Services, Inc.; 2009.
9. Chard R. How perioperative nurses define, attribute causes of, and react to intraoperative nursing errors. AORN J. 2010;91:132–45.
10. Conway J, Federico F, Stewart K, Campbell M. Respectful management of serious clinical adverse events. IHI innovation series white paper. Cambridge, MA: Institute for Healthcare Improvement; 2010.
11. Conway JB, Weingart SN. Leadership: assuring respect and compassion to clinicians involved in medical error. Swiss Med Wkly. 2009;139:3.
12. Christensen JF, Levinson W, Dunn PM. The heart of darkness: the impact of perceived mistakes on physicians. J Gen Intern Med. 1992;7:424–31.
13. Cunningham W. The immediate and long-term impact on New Zealand doctors who receive patient complaints. N Z Med J. 2004;117:U972.
14. Denham C. TRUST: the 5 rights of the second victim. J Patient Saf. 2007;3:107–19.
15. de Wit ME, Marks CM, Natterman JP, Wu AW. Supporting second victims of patient safety events: shouldn't these communications be covered by legal privilege? J Law Med Ethics. 2013:4;852–8.
16. Edrees HH, Paine LA, Feroli ER, Wu AW. Health care workers as second victims of medical errors. Polskie Archiwum Medycyny Wewn˛etrznej. 2011;121:101–8.

17. Engel KG, Rosenthal M, Sutcliffe KM. Residents' responses to medical error: coping, learning, and change. Acad Med. 2006;81:86–93.
18. Fahrenkopf AM, Sectish TC, Barger LK, Sharek PJ, Lewin D, Chiang VW, Edwards S, Wiedermann BL, Landrigan CP. Rates of medication errors among depressed and burnt out residents: prospective cohort study. BMJ. 2008;336(7642):488–91.
19. Fischer MA, Mazor KM, Baril J, Alper E, DeMarco D, Pugnaire M. Learning from mistakes. Factors that influence how students and residents learn from medical errors. J Gen Intern Med. 2006;21:419–23.
20. Fisseni G, Pentzek M, Abholz HH. Responding to serious medical error in general practice—consequences for the GPs involved: analysis of 75 cases from Germany. Fam Pract. 2008;25:9–13.
21. Frankel AS, Leonard MW, Denham CR. Fair and just culture, team behavior, and leadership engagement: the tools to achieve high reliability. Health Serv Res. 2006 Aug;41(4 Pt 2):1690–709.
22. Gallagher TH, Waterman AD, Ebers AG, Fraser VJ, Levinson W. Patients' and physicians' attitudes regarding the disclosure of medical errors. J Am Med Assoc. 2003;289(8):1001–7.
23. Goldberg RM, Kuhn G, Andrew LB, Thomas HA. Coping with medical mistakes and errors in judgment. Ann Emerg Med. 2002;39:287–92.
24. Kaldjian LC, Forman-Hoffman VL, Jones EW, Wu BJ, Levi BH, Rosenthal GE. Do faculty and resident physicians discuss their medical errors? J Med Ethics. 2008;34:717–22.
25. King MB, Cockcroft A, Gooch C. Emotional distress in doctors: sources, efects and help sought. JRSM. 1992;85:605–08.
26. Lander LI, Connor JA, Shah RK, Kentala E, Healy GB, Roberson DW. Otolaryngologists' responses to errors and adverse events. Laryngoscope. 2006;116:1114–20.
27. Martinez W, Lo B. Medical students' experiences with medical errors: an analysis of medical student essays. Med Educ. 2008;42:733–41.
28. Marx D. Patient safety and the "just culture": a primer for health care executives. New York: Columbia University; 2001. http://www.chpso.org/sites/main/files/file-attachments/marx_primer.pdf. Accessed 13 Aug 2019.
29. Meurier CE, Vincent CA, Parmar DG. Learning from errors in nursing practice. J Adv Nurs. 1997;26:111–9.
30. Mizrahi T. Managing medical mistakes: ideology, insularity and accountability among internists-in-training. Soc Sci Med. 1984;19:135–46.
31. Muller D, Ornstein K. Perceptions of and attitudes towards medical errors among medical trainees. Med Educ. 2007;41:645–52.
32. Penson RT, Svendsen SS, Chabner BA, Lynch TJ, Levinson W. Medical mistakes: a workshop on personal perspectives. Oncologist. 2001;6:92–9.
33. Rassin M, Kanti T, Silner D. Chronology of medication errors by nurses: accumulation of stresses and PTSD symptoms. Issues Ment Health Nurs. 2005;26:873–86.
34. Reyes R, Reyes C. At your defense: medical malpractice stress syndrome takes its toll. Emerg Med News. 2017;39(2):19.
35. Ryll N. Living through litigation: malpractice stress syndrome. J Radiol Nurs. 2015;34(1):35–8.
36. Schelbred AB, Nord R. Nurses' experiences of drug administration errors. J Adv Nurs. 2007;60:317–24.
37. Schwappach DL, Boluarte TA. The emotional impact of medical error involvement on physicians: a call for leadership and organizational accountability. Swiss Med Wkly. 2008;39(1–2):9–15.
38. Scott SD. Patient safety primer: second victims: support for clinicians involved in errors and adverse events. 2011. Available at: https://psnet.ahrq.gov/primers/primer/30/second-victims-support-for-clinicians-involved-in-errors-and-adverse-events. Accessed Aug 20, 2018.
39. Scott SD, Hirschinger LE, Cox KR. Sharing the load. Rescuing the healer after trauma. Register Nurse J. 2008;71:38–43.
40. Scott SD, Hirschinger LE, Cox KR, McCoig M, Brandt J, Hall LW. The natural history of recovery for the healthcare provider "second victim" after adverse patient events. Qual Saf Health Care. 2009;18:325–30.

41. Scott SD, Hirschinger LE, Cox KR, McCoig M, Hahn-Cover K, Epperly KM, Hall LW. Caring for our own: deploying a systemwide second victim rapid response team. Jt Comm J Qual Patient Saf. 2010;36:233–40.
42. Sirriyeh R, Lawton R, Gardner P, Armitage G. Coping with medical error: a systematic review of papers to assess the effects of involvement in medical errors on healthcare professionals' psychological well-being. Qual Saf Health Care. 2010;19:e43.
43. Smith ML, Forster HP. Morally managing medical mistakes. Camb Q Healthc Ethics. 2000;9:38–53.
44. Seys D, Scott S, Wu A, Van Gerven E, Vleugels A, Euwema M, et al. Supporting involved health care professionals (second victims) following an adverse health event: a literature review. Int J Nurs Stud. 2013;50:678–87.
45. Seys D, Wu AW, Van Gerven E, Vleugels A, Euwema M, Panella M, et al. Health care professionals as second victims after adverse events: a systemic review. Eval Health Prof. 2012;36(2):135–62.
46. The Joint Commission. Supporting second victims. Available at https://www.jointcommission.org/assets/1/23/Quick_Safety_Issue_39_2017_Second_victim_FINAL2.pdf. Accessed 20 Aug 2018.
47. Tunajek S. Dealing with litigation stress syndrome. Am Assoc Nurse Anesth AANA News Bull. 2007:22–3.
48. van Pelt F. Peer support: healthcare professionals supporting each other after adverse medical events. Qual Saf Health Care. 2008;17:249–52.
49. Vincent C. Understanding and responding to adverse events. N Engl J Med. 2003;348:1051–6.
50. Waterman AD, Garbutt J, Hazel E, Dunagan WC, Levinson W, Fraser VJ, Gallagher TH. The emotional impact of medical errors on practicing physicians in the United States and Canada. Jt Comm J Qual Patient Saf. 2007;33:467–76.
51. West CP, Huschka MM, Novotny PJ, Sloan JA, Kolars JC, Habermann TM, Shanafelt TD. Association of perceived medical errors with resident distress and empathy: a prospective longitudinal study. J Am Med Assoc. 2006;296(9):1071–8.
52. West CP, Tan AD, Habermann TM, Sloan JA, Shanafelt TD. Association of resident fatigue and distress with perceived medical errors. J Am Med Assoc. 2009;302:1294–300.
53. Wolf ZR. Stress management in response to practice errors: critical events in professional practice. PA-PSRS Patient Saf Adv. 2005;2(4):1–2.
54. Wright W, Pendleton K. "Second victim" of medical errors and clinician after care. In: Szalados J, Wright W, Smith W, editors. Law and ethics in neurocritical care. Chicago: Neurocritical Care Society; 2019. p. 234–7.
55. Wu AW. Medical error: the second victim. The doctor who makes the mistake needs help too. BMJ. 2000;320:726–7.
56. Wu AW, Folkman S, McPhee SJ, Lo B. Do house officers learn from their mistakes? J Am Med Assoc. 1991;265:2089–94.
57. Wu AW, Folkman S, McPhee SJ, Lo B. How house officers cope with their mistakes. West J Med. 1993;159:565–9.

Chapter 33
Liability for Advanced Care Practitioners

Brenton LaRiccia, Cheryl Lustik, and Nicole Keenan

Background

Physician assistants (PAs), nurse practitioners (NPs), and certified registered nurse anesthetists (CRNAs), sometimes collectively referred to as advanced care practitioners (ACPs), advanced practice providers (APPs), or nonphysician providers (NPPs), are among a number of growing professions that manage patients at a high level collaboratively with their respective physician teams. As ACPs are integrated into hospitals, nursing homes, and clinics, they are exposed to similar liability issues as physicians and other healthcare professionals.

Liability for ACPs is complicated by regulations specific to each profession, scope of practice laws that vary from state to state, supervision or collaboration with physicians in patient care, and practice variations across institutions. Physician assistants and nurse practitioners are typically hired for the same positions and are usually considered interchangeable from a clinical perspective. Clinical services train both PA and NP graduates through a variety of onboarding models which incorporate both professions, including hospital- or practice-based orientation programs, transition to practice programs [1], and postgraduate fellowship or residency programs [2]. The differences between NPs and PAs lie in education and state regulatory requirements.

In this chapter, we will provide an overview of PA, NP, and CRNA scope of practice, related regulatory requirements, as well as liability issues and malpractice trends related to ACPs, and the potential liability that physicians face for the acts or omissions of ACPs [3].

B. LaRiccia (✉) · C. Lustik · N. Keenan
University of Rochester Medical Center, Rochester, NY, USA
e-mail: Brenton_lariccia@urmc.rochester.edu; Cheryl_Lustik@URMC.Rochester.edu; Nicole_Tripoli-Keenan@URMC.Rochester.edu

J. E. Szalados (ed.), *The Medical-Legal Aspects of Acute Care Medicine*,
https://doi.org/10.1007/978-3-030-68570-6_33

Physician Assistants

Physician assistants (PAs) are medical practitioners who are educated in a medical model similar to physicians. The first PA program was developed in 1965 by Eugene A. Stead Jr. MD at Duke University Medical Center [4]. PAs typically have 2000 or more hours of clinical rotations prior to graduating from an accredited PA program [5]. There are approximately 123,000 PAs practicing in the United States, and they are employed in every type of medical setting, including outpatient clinics, nursing homes, urgent care, operating rooms, hospital wards, and intensive care units to name a few [5]. PAs are governed by individual state medical boards and are subject to regulations which vary from state to state. PAs provide high-quality, cost-effective care relative to their salaries and benefits [6].

PA Scope of Practice

Physician assistants practice medicine and provide services that a physician might otherwise provide, including taking medical history, performing physical exams, ordering and interpreting diagnostic laboratory and imaging tests, assisting in surgery, and performing procedures in both the office setting and the hospital [2, 4, 6]. After completion of their medical education through an accredited PA program and after passing the PA boards administered by the National Commission on Certification of PAs, a PA is eligible to apply for positions in any area of medicine across the age spectrum and also in any specialty of medicine or surgery, including areas such as pediatrics, psychiatry, critical care, emergency medicine, and cardiology, to name a few. This professional flexibility allows PAs to develop a career in one specialty and sometimes move into another specialty.

PA scope of practice varies by state. PAs are typically regulated by the state medical board with the exception of Arizona, California, Iowa, Massachusetts, Rhode Island, Tennessee, and Utah, which have separate PA regulatory boards [7]. A minority of states [8] require that a certain number or percentage of PA charts are cosigned by physicians. A majority of states [9] have a physician-to-PA ratio limit for supervision or collaboration [7]. For example, in New York, physicians may not supervise more than four PAs in private practice or more than six PAs in a hospital setting. The other states with PA to physician ratios typically have regulations that limit the ratio to between three and seven PAs depending on the practice setting, similar to New York [7].

PA Supervision

Physician assistant supervision requirements are determined state by state. Supervision regulations for PAs often require written supervisory agreements with an identified physician, and depending on the state, the supervisory relationship is determined at the practice level. Currently 47 states require supervision by physicians, and 2 states require collaborative agreements (Arkansas and Illinois) [7]. New Mexico requires PA supervision for providers with less than 3 years of experience or specialty care PAs, and Michigan requires a "participating" physician [7]. PA scope of practice is determined at the practice level in 47 states. Most state supervision requirements include language similar to New York, "Supervision shall be continuous but shall not necessarily require the physical presence of the supervising physician at the time and place where the services are performed" [7, 10]. Wisconsin, New Jersey, and New Mexico are the three exceptions in which the scope of practice is not determined at a practice site [7].

Missouri has certain supervision specifications for PAs. Although state regulations do provide some latitude at the practice level, the supervising physician must be on-site 66% of the time a PA is practicing in a calendar quarter, and PAs are limited geographically to a 30-mile radius from their supervising physician [7]. Mississippi also has geographic limitations on PA distance from supervising physicians, and Arkansas requires that the supervising physician be able to reach the PA practice location within 1 hour [7].

Some states have specific criteria for new graduate PAs. Mississippi requires on-site physician presence for the first 120 days (or 960 hours) of the new PAs practice [7]. Nebraska requires that the supervising physician is present 20% of the time a newly licensed PA is practicing for the first 3 months and 10% of the time thereafter [7].

PA Prescriptive Authority

PAs are able to prescribe Schedule II–V medications in 44 states but cannot prescribe Schedule II medications in Alabama, Arkansas, Georgia, Hawaii, Iowa, or West Virginia [7].

PA Practice Environment

PAs and other ACP continue to address barriers to practice. Optimal team practice is a policy passed by the American Academy of PAs to address state regulations that are considered limiting to PA practice. The primary goals of this initiative are to (1) ensure PAs have a voice on state medical boards that regulate PAs or to develop state PA boards (some already exist); (2) remove the requirement for a specific physician supervisor, replaced by collaboration; and (3) allow PAs to participate in the same payment arrangements that are currently available to physicians and NPs [11]. The federal government has expressed support for these initiatives through a joint report from the departments of Health and Human Services, Treasury, and Labor entitled

"Reforming America's Healthcare System Through Choice and Competition" [12]. Regulatory changes that may occur as a result of this initiative could reduce physician liability for the actions of PAs in cases where the physician is not directly involved in the care of the patient in question [11].

Nurse Practitioners

A nurse practitioner (NP) is an advanced practice registered nurse (APRN) who has earned at least a master's degree and completed additional training in a specialty area of medicine [13]. Dr. Loretta Ford, co-founder of the NP role in 1965, partnered with Dr. Henry Silver to create the first pediatric NP program in the United States at the University of Colorado [14]. Since the start of NP programs, the profession has blossomed into certified and state-recognized graduate degree programs throughout the country [15]. According to the American Association of Nurse Practitioners [16], there are currently 350 academic institutions in the United States offering graduate NP degree programs and over 248,000 licensed NPs, a workforce that is growing at a fast rate.

The strengths of NPs are communication and adherence to evidence-based practice guidelines [17]. Additionally, patients and families acknowledge the importance of having an ongoing relationship with their NP. For example, patients enjoy working with NPs for health education, routine health care, and supportive interventions, including advice on how to cope with diseases [18]. Furthermore, patients describe NPs' contributions to team effectiveness, including easing access to care, consulting, communicating concerns of the patient to the physician, and making clinical decisions [19].

NPs have demonstrated high-quality care outcomes as members of healthcare teams. Specifically, NPs manage manifestations of patients' acute and chronic diseases to reduce rates of unnecessary hospitalizations, readmissions, and emergency room visits [20]. Furthermore, NPs bring a unique perspective to health services by emphasizing health promotion, disease prevention, and health education [16].

Nurse Practitioner Scope of Practice

The purpose of nursing regulation is to ensure nurses are competent to practice safely and ensure a consistent quality of nursing practice [21]. All 50 states, plus the District of Columbia, have independent regulatory rules that govern the education and practice of NPs [21]. Although NPs are certified nationally, state scope of practice laws determines the extent to which NPs can practice independently, specifically the required level of education, physician involvement, and prescriptive authority.

The lack of uniformity exists despite national organizations' support of NPs practicing to the full extent of their training and education [14, 21]. Since 2008, several national organizations have published recommendations to accelerate NPs' scope of practice. For example, the National Council of State Boards of Nursing published a report in 2008, the *Consensus Model for APRN Regulation: Licensure, Accreditation, Certification, & Education* which defined national standards to provide guidance for states to adopt uniform regulation on licensure, accreditation, certification, and education of APRN's [8]. Additionally, the Institute of Medicine (2011), *The Future of Nursing: Leading Change and Advancing Health* [22], recommended APRNs practice to the full extent of their education and certification. The IOM (2011) recommended removing barriers to APRN's scope of practice and changing public policy on all levels of government [14]. The recommendation reflected the recognition that variability of the scope of practice regulations across states is large, with legislation in some states specific and detailed and in others, vague and open to interpretation [23]. Furthermore, in 2012, the report by the National Governors Association proposed states consider revising the restrictions on the NP scope of practice to assure adequate reimbursement for the services provided [14]. Despite support from key national organizations, there remains the lack of successful establishment of standardization of NPs' scope of practice at the state level.

Nurse Practitioner Practice Environment

The variation between states in NP scope of practice often involves the requirement of NPs to have a collaborating relationship with physicians or restrictions on NPs prescribing authority [5, 14]. Though substantial variation exits, the scope of practice is broadly categorized into three groups: [1] full practice authority – under the licensure authority of the state board of nursing, NPs are permitted to practice and prescribe with no involvement with an outside health provider; [2] reduced practice – state law limits at least one element of NP practice, such as requiring a collaborative practice agreement with another healthcare provider in order for the NP to provide patient care, or limiting the setting of NP practice; [3] restricted practice – state practice and licensure laws restrict NP provision of care to require supervision, delegation, or team management by another healthcare provider [5, 13]. According to the AANP [5], as of December 2018, 22 states and the District of Columbia permit NPs full practice authority, 16 states permit reduced practice, and 12 states permit restricted practice.

Full Practice

Full practice authority (FPA) means that NPs can practice in accordance with their educational preparation and physician involvement is not required [14]. FPA is not without controversy. Proponents claim FPA removes barriers that fully improve efficiency by enabling NPs to provide essential care to the fullest extent of their education [13, 24]. Particularly, states granting NPs greater scope of practice authority are more likely to establish NP-based rural health clinics, providing care to underserved and rural communities. With less restrictive state regulations, NPs and their collaborating physician do not need to be geographically close, thereby potentially expanding practice locations [8]. Additionally, FPA benefits physicians and patients. NPs can manage patient's medical conditions and authorize prescriptions, thereby decreasing physician's time spent on these tasks. Patients benefit by improving access to care, decreasing wait time, and improving patient satisfaction [24]. On the contrary, national medical organizations such as the American Academy of Family Physicians and the American Medical Association, denounce the movement to grant NPs FPA [14, 25]. The medical organizations oppose state legislation allowing for the independent practice by anyone who is not a licensed physician; however, they support team-based care that includes NPs [14, 26].

Reduced Practice

The second category of scope of practice for NPs is reduced practice. Under this regulation, NP practice is restricted with NPs maintaining a collaborative agreement with a physician that includes plans for consultation, coverage, and quality assurance [5, 8]. Prescribing privileges vary; some states permit NPs to prescribe medicines only if they are collaborating with or supervised by a physician. Other states allow NPs to prescribe, administer, dispense, and procure medications, including controlled substances with no physician oversight [5, 27].

As a transition strategy to less restrictive practices, several states are adopting systematic processes that allow NPs greater independence as they gain more experience. In 2015 New York State implemented the Nurse Practitioners Modernization Act which removed the required collaborative practice agreement between NPs and physicians for NPs with more than 3600 hours of practice [28]. A transition to practice requirement is not new as both Maine and Colorado adopted periods of formal collaboration before granting FPA [14]. The length of the transition periods varies (18 months to 2 years) as do the practice hours (2000–3600). According to Poghosyan et al. [28], there is a slow translation from the policy change into practice secondary to several factors: lack of knowledge about the law, unawareness of NP competencies, and organizational bylaws, specifically within hospitals and medical centers that are not reformed to accommodate the change.

Restrictive Practice

In 12 states, NPs' practice is restrictive, meaning both engagement in practice and prescriptive authority are limited [5]. NPs must work under a collaborative practice agreement with a physician, and this can include outlining the geographic practice area [29]. For instance, in Missouri, NPs need to practice within a certain radius of their collaborating physician, and the physician must be available to periodically review the NP services through a chart review, and be available, or designate a substitute, for consultation [29]. Under restrictive practice, controlled substance authority is limited, although varies among states depending on the abuse potential of the medication. For example, according to the DEA [27] NPs in Arkansas have limited prescriptive authority of schedule II substances (medications that have a high abuse potential with severe psychic or physical dependence liability). Specifically, prescribing are limited to hydrocodone products only. States such as Missouri, Nebraska, and South Carolina limit NPs to prescribe a 5-day supply of opiates for schedules II or III; other states (Illinois, North Carolina, and Pennsylvania) limit NP prescriptive authority to a 30-day supply. Lastly, the licensing authority of Georgia and Oklahoma does not grant prescriptive authority for class II opiates to NPs [27].

Nurse Practitioner Scope of Practice Trends

Over the last 20 years, state regulations on NPs' scope of practice have loosened, granting more authority to NPs, while at the same time, many states have increased entry-to-practice requirements [23]. For example, from 2000 to 2010, the scope of practice expanded for NPs evidenced by a decrease in physician involvement in treatment and diagnosis as well as prescription oversite [23]. As state regulations granted more authority, many states such as Tennessee, New Hampshire, Colorado, and Arkansas began requiring a Master of Science in Nursing as entry into practice for NP [23].

The trend in state regulation of NP is less restrictive over time, though variation persists. As a key positive factor for reported day-to-day practice autonomy is the NP ability to prescribe medications independently. NPs who work in states with FPA report the highest level of day-to-day practice autonomy in four measures: utilization of skills, billing independence, physician relationship, and independent patient management [13]. There were significant differences reported in autonomy of daily practice between NPs in restrictive practice states and NPs practicing in reduced practice states that have restricted practice authority [13]. In other words, little day-to-day practice autonomy is gained with NP scope of practice is limited by prescriptive authority.

Certified Registered Nurse Anesthetists

Certified registered nurse anesthetists are registered nurses who continue on to specialized training in anesthesia. The minimum requirements to become a nurse anesthetist include a baccalaureate or graduate degree in nursing; an unencumbered license as a registered nurse or advanced practice registered nurse in the United States; a minimum of 1-year full-time work in a critical care setting; graduation with a minimum of a master's degree from an accredited nurse anesthesia program; and completion of an average of 9369 clinical hours [30]. Upon meeting the requirements for graduation from an accredited program, the student is then eligible to obtain certification as a nurse anesthetist by passing an initial certification exam administered by the National Board for Certification and Recertification for Nurse Anesthetists.

The type of recognition nurse anesthetists obtain is dependent on what state they are practicing in. In all but six states, nurse anesthetists are recognized as advanced practice registered nurses. States which do not have an umbrella title for nurse anesthetists include Arizona, Michigan, Nevada, New Mexico, New York, and Pennsylvania [31]. There are also differences among states regarding who the primary source or authority for recognition is. Nurse anesthetists in California, Indiana, Puerto Rico, and Tennessee are recognized by the Nurse Practice Act. This is in contrast to Massachusetts, North Carolina, and Pennsylvania in which nurse anesthetists are recognized by the State Board of Nursing Rules and Regulations. All other states except for New York recognize nurse anesthetists under both the Nursing Practice Act and the State Board of Nursing Rules and Regulations. Currently in New York, nurse anesthetists are not recognized by the state under nursing acts but by the Department of Health [31].

CRNA Practice Environment

Nurse anesthetists practice in many different settings such as hospitals, ambulatory centers, and office-based centers. There is a federal requirement that a physician is to oversee the practice of anesthesia administered by nurse anesthetists. This is accomplished by either working independently (not in conjunction with an anesthesiologist but under the supervision of a surgeon) or as part of an anesthesia care team (generally two to six nurse anesthetists working with one attending physician anesthesiologist). If the nurse anesthetist is working independently, they normally have a contract with a surgeon stating that the surgeon will oversee them. Surgeons have no obligation however to control the anesthetic process and most times rely on the nurse anesthetist to be the anesthesia expert. This arrangement does not automatically leave the surgeon liable for the actions of the nurse anesthetist, nor does it mean they escape liability when working with a physician anesthesiologist. If the surgeon "affords the anesthesia provider the discretion and judgement in the performance of his or her professional duties...[and] claims no control over the administration of anesthesia, he or she should face no increased risk of liability" [32]. There are many cases in which surgeons have not been held liable for working with nurse anesthetists, and many cases involving anesthesia mishaps with surgeons were sued when working with physician anesthesiologists [33]. Although it is required that nurse anesthetists may only administer anesthesia under the supervision of a physician, this does not establish control nor create liability. If the nurse anesthetist is found to be negligent that does not necessarily hold the surgeon liable [33].

There are two different ways in which nurse anesthetists can work with physician anesthesiologists in a care team model. There is a billing differentiation under Centers for Medicare and Medicaid Services rules which determine whether nurse anesthetists work under medical direction or medical supervision. In order to bill under medical direction, a physician anesthesiologist can oversee two, three, or four concurrent cases and must perform the seven steps of medical direction. These steps include performing a pre-anesthetic examination and evaluation; prescribing the anesthesia plan; personally participating in the most demanding procedures in the anesthesia plan including induction and emergence; ensuring that any procedures in the anesthesia plan that he or she does not perform are performed by a qualified anesthetist; monitoring the course of anesthesia administration at frequent intervals; remaining physically present and available for immediate diagnosis and treatment of emergencies; and providing indication post-anesthesia care.

If the physician anesthesiologist is not able to meet one of these seven steps of medical direction, performs a task that is not permitted while medically directing, or is involved in more than four concurrent cases, then the model is classified as medical supervision [34]. In the anesthesia care team model therefore, since the physician anesthesiologist is essentially controlling the anesthetic plan, they would be held more liable than the nurse anesthetist for any anesthesia mishap.

In a 2001 ruling by the Centers for Medicare and Medicaid Services, there was a decision to let individual states opt-out of the federal supervision requirement which mandated a nurse anesthetist be under the supervision of a physician while providing anesthesia services [35]. This ruling was based on the agency's finding that there is a "lack of evidence to support the requirement for [surgeon or anesthesiologist] supervision of Certified Registered Nurse Anesthetists" [35]. As of 2016 there have been 17 states and Guam which have decided to opt-out of this requirement [36]. For a state to be eligible to "opt-out," the state's governor must send a letter of attestation to Centers for Medicare and Medicaid Services stating the governor has consulted with both the state's boards of medicine and nursing and that it is in the state's best interest to opt-out of the federal requirement of physician supervision and that the opt-out is consistent with state law [36].

Although there are differences in training required to become a registered nurse versus a physician, the classroom and clinical training in anesthesia care for both certified registered nurse anesthetists and anesthesiologists is similar [37]. There have been several studies conducted showing that adverse events related to anesthesia are rare regardless of the provider [9, 35, 38, 39].

Malpractice and Liability

Malpractice refers to "acts of negligence or incompetence on the part of a professional" [40]. Liability refers to being legally responsible or accountable [40]. Physicians and institutions can be held responsible for the actions of ACPs. Under the principle of *respondent superior*, there are circumstances in which the employer can be held liable for the negligence of its employees. This principle does not necessarily apply when an employee is an independent contractor [41].

Legal Theories

Although the risk of malpractice may not increase with the employment of ACPs, a physician or employer can be exposed to liability [42]. In general, ACPs may be held directly liable for their actions or omissions, and this is represented by ACPs as being listed as the sole healthcare provider in paid malpractice claims 76.81% of the time [43]; however, the collaborating physician may also be held liable even if the physician did not commit an error [44]. There are several legal theories commonly used to attach liability to a physician or employer for an ACP errors: negligent hiring, negligent supervision, and vicarious liability [42, 45].

Negligent Hiring

Physicians or employers can be found negligent if an ACP is hired and verification of the ACPs background is not completed [46]. To determine whether the ACP is competent and capable of performing the necessary skills, a review of the ACP educational background is required, as well as appropriate licensure and certification, prior work history, and reviewing references or recommendations from prior employees or professors [42, 45].

Negligent Supervision

State laws and regulations determine the required level of supervision, including whether the physician must be in the same physical location as the ACP [42, 45]. Negligent supervision arises when the ACP has limited or absent supervision by the physician or there is limited or absent documentation of supervision [46]. Many states restrict the number of ACPs with whom a physician may collaborate, as supervising multiple ACPs increases the potential for liability [7, 14, 42].

Vicarious Liability

A physician may be held vicariously liable for wrongful actions of the ACP, even though the physician did not perform the actions, because the ACP is working on behalf of the physician [42, 45]. Vicarious liability to the physician is state dependent; in some states, liability depends on whether the physician has the right to control the work done by the ACP, as opposed to a more strict interpretation of the statue that a physician will most always be found liable because the ACP acted on behalf of the physician [42, 45].

Mitigating the Risk of Liability

Physicians and employers can safely incorporate ACPs into clinical practice and lessen the exposure to liability. Listed below are suggested actions to minimize exposure to liability.

Negligent Hiring

First, when interviewing and hiring an ACP, check credentials and references to ensure truth and accuracy. Check NPDB for malpractice payments or reported adverse actions. Always talk with the ACPs prior employer. Next, hire only qualified ACPs with the necessary educational requirement and training needed for the position they are hired. Last, be aware of guidelines or policies adopted by the employer relevant to ACP practices within the organization.

Negligent Supervision

First, follow the collaborative or supervisory practice agreement between physician and ACPs, subject to state regulations. Second, develop a system to regularly review patient charts and the quality of ACPs work for quality assurance purposes, again following state regulatory requirements. Third, adhere strictly to the list of duties and responsibilities delegated to the ACP. Last, physicians should ensure the ratio of ACPs permitted by the state to physicians is appropriate.

Vicarious Liability

First, properly train and teach the ACP in the specialty area they will be practicing. Second, set high standards for the ACP, perform periodic performance evaluations, provide meaningful ongoing assessment of competency, and ensure procedures and policies are being followed. Third, physicians should act as a positive role model, stressing documentation that is appropriate, accurate, and timely. Last, and undoubtedly the most important, the physician and ACP should engage in effective communication. The ACP must feel comfortable initiating conversation, asking for clarification, and understanding expectations.

Malpractice Trends for Advanced Care Providers

The National Practitioner Data Bank (NPDB), created in 1990, contains details of health care providers' medical malpractice payments and reported adverse actions [42]. The NPDB was created in response to the Healthcare Quality and Information

Act of 1986, stipulating mandatory reporting of all payment events to compile a complete record of events [43].

Physician Assistants

From January 1, 2005, to December 31, 2014, NPDB recorded 178,035 malpractice claims or adverse actions [40]. PAs accounted for 3064 (2.9%) of these claims. These claims against PAs were primarily adverse action claims compared to malpractice reports (71.9% vs. 28.1%, $p < 0.001$). The malpractice claim rate for PAs ranged from 1.4 to 2.4 per 1000 PAs in this time period. The adverse action rate for PAs ranged from 2.8 to 6.9 per 1000 [40]. The risk ratio of physicians to PAs, a metric of probability that one group will experience an event compared to another group, declined over this time period, as did the risk ratio of physicians to NPs. PAs and NPs were less likely per capita than physicians to have either malpractice payments or adverse actions [40].

Nurse Practitioners

The most common types of medical errors committed by NPs have been evaluated. When NPs were liable, the medical malpractice claims were diagnosis- or treatment-related events [40, 43]. Within the diagnosis-related claims group, the most common errors were failure to diagnosis (26.59%), delay to diagnosis (11.31%), and misdiagnosis (3.15%). The most common error of treatment-related events was a delay in treatment, accounting for 2.97% of paid claims [43].

The patient care setting (i.e., outpatient, inpatient, or both) was collected in the NPDB beginning in 2004. The most common medical errors committed by NPs that were reported to the NPDB occurred in the outpatient setting. Over 80% of diagnosis-related claims and over 60% of treatment-related claims occurred in the outpatient setting between 2004 and 2014 [43].

The most common patient outcomes in NP paid malpractice claims identified by NPDB through years 1990–2014 were serious. Errors leading to death (37.77%), significant permeant injury (10.95%), or minor temporary injury (10.67%) accounted for 59.39% of patient outcomes for NP paid malpractice claims [43]. Across a 10-year period from 2005 through 2014, physicians and NPs had an increase in the rate of adverse actions [40]. Adverse actions involve healthcare-related criminal convictions, civil infarctions, revocation of provider license, or exclusions from Medicare or Medicaid participation.

From 2005 to 2014, there was a decrease in the rate of malpractice reports for physicians and an unchanged rate for NPs [40]. However, physicians continue to have a higher rate of malpractice rates compared NPs. For example, in 2014, the malpractice rate for physicians was 11.2 per 1000 providers compared to 1.2 per 1000 for NPs [40].

Despite risk control recommendations for NPs to enhance patient safety and employ risk management strategies (education and training, communication, protocols, and response), the number of paid NP malpractice claims has increased over the last several years [40, 42, 45]. For example, in the 1990s, NP malpractice claims averaged fewer than 20 per year compared to approximately 180 in 2011 [43]. The increased frequency is reflective of the increase in the NP workforce along with more states allowing FPA for NPs. Due to scope of practice regulations, NPs who commit malpractice can be held liable and, in addition, may pass a substantial portion of their liability to their supervising physician [44]. However, NPs are less likely than physicians to have malpractice payments or adverse reactions compared to physicians.

Certified Registered Nurse Anesthetists

CRNA adverse events and malpractice payments are also captured in the NPDB databank. A retrospective analysis of the NPDB data between January 31, 2004, and December 31, 2010, revealed a total of 2664 anesthesia-related malpractice payments, 369 (13.8%) of which were related to CRNAs [47]. The most frequently coded severity of injury categories were death (34%), minor permanent injury (14%), grave permanent injury (11%), and major permanent injury (11%), respectively [30]. The three most common malpractice allegation categories were improper performance (15%), failure to monitor (14%), and problem with intubation (12%) [30].

There are several limitations of the NPDB: (a) potential coding errors, (b) delays in reporting claim payments, (c) payments that do result in payment are not captured, and (d) claims against corporations are not included [40, 43]. The lower rates of PA, NP, and CRNA occurrences in the NPDB database could be related to ACPs being dropped from cases that involve multiple team members including physicians. The lower rates may also be partially due to the "corporate shield" where individual providers are not reported if malpractice payments are paid on behalf of the hospital or corporation [47].

Regardless of the trending ACP malpractice data and valuable insight into common themes of ACP medical malpractice, the malpractice data from the NPDB cannot conclusively indicate that incorporation of ACPs into healthcare practices increases or decreases liability.

Summary

ACPs have a major role in making high-quality, patient-centered healthcare available to the broadest range of consumers. ACP scope of practice is state specific, ranging from full practice authority, reduced, or restricted practice for NPs [5], and PA and CRNA scope of practice varies between states, as described above. The trend in state regulation of ACPs is less restrictive over time, though variation persists. Influence from federal agencies to reduce barriers to practice and lobbying efforts by the ACP professional organizations will continue to shape the landscape.

Physician liability extending from ACP errors or clinical misjudgments is a concern; however, malpractice claims are lower for ACPs compared to physician colleagues [44]. There are several steps that physicians, ACPs, and healthcare organizations can enact to mitigate the risk of malpractice and liability.

Future Trends

A recent combined report from the US Departments of Health and Human Services, Treasury, and Labor, titled "Reforming America's Healthcare System Through Choice and Competition" highlights the myriad challenges facing the healthcare system and offers insight into a number of proposed regulatory changes previously mentioned [12]. This report includes recommendations to broaden the scope of practice for PAs, NPs, and other professions to "increase access and drive down costs for consumers, while still ensuring safe care" [12]. In addition, the report recommends reducing or eliminating collaborative/supervisory agreements when possible. Depending on how these changes may be enacted, ACPs may be exposed to more liability [48].

As employers of ACPs navigate the regulatory changes related to the scope of practice at the state and national level, they can minimize their liability exposure through ensuring a robust hiring, credentialing, and orientation process, as well as ensuring that supervision or collaboration complies with current state regulations with regard to ACP practice [45]. In addition, routine quality review of procedural activity and documentation, as well as other patient safety efforts and adherence to practice guidelines and protocols, can both ensure quality patient care delivery and potentially reduce liability for employed ACPs [45].

References

1. Nicely KLW, Fairman J. Postgraduate nurse practitioner residency programs: supporting transition to practice. Acad Med. 2015;90(6):707–9.
2. Grabenkort WR, Meissen HH, Gregg SR, Coopersmith CM. Acute care nurse practitioners and physician assistants in critical care: transforming education and practice. Crit Care Med. 2017;45(7):1111–4.
3. Markovic M, Amsler EF, Keller L. Physician assistant: a risk-benefit analysis. Education. 2017;6542:1.
4. Assistants AAoP. History of the PA profession 2019. Available from: https://www.aapa.org/about/history/.
5. Practitioners AAoN. State practice environment 2018. Available from: https://www.aanp.org/advocacy/state/state-practice-environment.
6. AAPA. What is a PA? 2019. Available from: https://www.aapa.org/what-is-a-pa/.
7. Center AMAAR. Physician assistant scope of practice 2018. Available from: https://www.ama-assn.org/sites/ama-assn.org/files/corp/media-browser/public/arc-public/state-law-physician-assistant-scope-practice.pdf.
8. Xue Y, Ye Z, Brewer C, Spetz J. Impact of state nurse practitioner scope-of-practice regulation on health care delivery: systematic review. Nurs Outlook. 2016;64(1):71–85.
9. Forrest W. Outcome: the effect of the provider. In: Health care delivery in anesthesia. Philadelphia: George F Stickley Co; 1980. p. 137–42.

10. Regulations NYSHD. 10 NYCRR 94.2 Physician assistants and specialist assistants. In: Department H, editor. 2015. p. 1–18.
11. Sobel J. Seven things you should know about optimal team practice. J Am Acad PAs. 2019;32(5):12–3.
12. Azar A, Mnuchin S, Acosta A. Reforming America's healthcare system through choice and competition. 2018.
13. Park J, Athey E, Pericak A, Pulcini J, Greene J. To what extent are state scope of practice laws related to nurse practitioners' day-to-day practice autonomy? Med Care Res Rev. 2018;75(1):66–87.
14. Brom HM, Salsberry PJ, Graham MC. Leveraging health care reform to accelerate nurse practitioner full practice authority. J Am Assoc Nurse Pract. 2018;30(3):120–30.
15. Twine N. The first year as a nurse practitioner: an integrative literature review of the transition experience. J Nurs Educ Pract. 2018;8(5):54–62.
16. Practitioners AAoN. Number of nurse practitioners hits new record high 2018. Available from: https://www.aanp.org/news-feed/number-of-nurse-practitioners-hits-new-record-high.
17. Nevidjon B, Rieger P, Miller Murphy C, Rosenzweig MQ, McCorkle MR, Baileys K. Filling the gap: development of the oncology nurse practitioner workforce. J Oncol Pract. 2010;6(1):2–6.
18. Laurant MG, Hermens RP, Braspenning JC, Akkermans RP, Sibbald B, Grol RP. An overview of patients' preference for, and satisfaction with, care provided by general practitioners and nurse practitioners. J Clin Nurs. 2008;17(20):2690–8.
19. Kilpatrick K, Jabbour M, Fortin C. Processes in healthcare teams that include nurse practitioners: what do patients and families perceive to be effective? J Clin Nurs. 2016;25(5–6):619–30.
20. Mason H, DeRubeis MB, Foster JC, Taylor JM, Worden FP, editors. Outcomes evaluation of a weekly nurse practitioner-managed symptom management clinic for patients with head and neck cancer treated with chemoradiotherapy. Oncology nursing forum; 2013: NIH Public Access.
21. Rounds LR, Zych JJ, Mallary LL. The consensus model for regulation of APRNs: implications for nurse practitioners. J Am Acad Nurse Pract. 2013;25(4):180–5.
22. Nursing IoMCotRWJFIotFo. The future of nursing: leading change, advancing health. Washington, DC: National Academic Press; 2011.
23. Gadbois EA, Miller EA, Tyler D, Intrator O. Trends in state regulation of nurse practitioners and physician assistants, 2001 to 2010. Med Care Res Rev. 2015;72(2):200–19.
24. Dillon D, Gary F. Full practice authority for nurse practitioners. Nurs Adm Q. 2017;41(1):86–93.
25. Pittman D. Independent NPs must go, AAFP says. September 19, 2012 Available from: https://www.medpagetoday.com/nursing/Nursing/34843.
26. SPLINTER NPC, CARE UP-C. Family medicine updates. Ann Fam Med. 2012;10:572–3.
27. Control DOoD. Mid-level practitioners authorization by state. 2019. Available from: https://www.deadiversion.usdoj.gov/drugreg/practioners/index.html.
28. Poghosyan L, Norful AA, Laugesen MJ. Removing restrictions on nurse practitioners' scope of practice in New York State: Physicians' and nurse practitioners' perspectives. J Am Assoc Nurse Pract. 2018;30(6):354–60.
29. Policy SoP. Nurse practitioners overview 2019. Available from: http://scopeofpracticepolicy.org/practitioners/nurse-practitioners/.
30. Anesthetists AAoN. Education of nurse anesthetists in the US 2018. Available from: https://www.aana.com/membership/become-a-crna/education-of-nurse-anesthetists-in-the-u.s.
31. Anesthetists AAoN. Statutory/regulatory nurse anesthetist recognition 2019. Available from: https://www.aana.com/docs/default-source/sga-aana-com-web-documents-(all)/recognition.pdf?sfvrsn=fbe448b1_10.
32. Silberman MJ. Navigating the "captain of the ship" argument. AANA J. 2016;84(6):392.
33. Blumenreich GA. Another article on the surgeon's liability for anesthesia negligence. AANA J. 2007;75(2):89.
34. Byrd JR, Merrick SK, Stead SW. Billing for anesthesia services and the QZ modifier: a lurking problem. ASA Newsl. 2011;75(6):36–8.

35. Centers for Medicare & Medicaid Services (CMS). Medicare and Medicaid programs; hospital Conditions of Participation: anesthesia services. Final rule. Fed Regist. 2001;66(219):56762.
36. Anesthetists AAoN. Fact sheet concerning state opt-outs and November 13, 2001 CMS Rule September 2018. Available from: https://www.aana.com/docs/default-source/sga-aana-com-web-documents-(all)/801-fact-sheet-concerning-state-opt-outs-pdf.pdf?sfvrsn=450743b1_8.
37. Dulisse B, Cromwell J. No harm found when nurse anesthetists work without supervision by physicians. Health Aff. 2010;29(8):1469–75.
38. Abenstein J, Warner MA. Anesthesia providers, patient outcomes, and costs. Anesth Analg. 1996;82(6):1273–83.
39. Bechtoldt JA. Committee on anesthesia study. Anesthetic-related deaths: 1969-1976. N C Med J. 1981;42(4):253–9.
40. Brock DM, Nicholson JG, Hooker RS. Physician assistant and nurse practitioner malpractice trends. Med Care Res Rev. 2017;74(5):613–24.
41. Russell G, Thornton J. Responsibility for the acts of others. Baylor University Medical Center Proceedings. 2010;23(3):313–5.
42. Bernard CD. Physician liability for the actions of midlevel providers. Med Econ. 2015;92(4):43–5.
43. Sweeney CF, LeMahieu A, Fryer GE. Nurse practitioner malpractice data: informing nursing education. J Prof Nurs. 2017;33(4):271–5.
44. McMichael BJ, Safriet BJ, Buerhaus PI. The extraregulatory effect of nurse practitioner scope-of-practice laws on physician malpractice rates. Med Care Res Rev. 2018;75(3):312–26.
45. Moses RE, Feld AD. Physician liability for medical errors of nonphysician clinicians: nurse practitioners and physician assistants. Am J Gastroenterol. 2007;102(1):6.
46. Waterhouse BE, Paterick TE, Sanbar SS. Liability of physicians supervising nonphysician clinicians. J Med Pract Manag MPM. 2014;29(5):309.
47. Jordan LM, Quraishi JA, Liao J. The national practitioner data bank and CRNA anesthesia-related malpractice payments. AANA J. 2013;81(3):178–82
48. Hooker RS. FPAR and labor complexities. J Am Acad PAs. 2017;30(6):1–2.

A Glossary of Terms[1]

Adjudicate To arrive at or to pronounce a formal judgment, settlement, or decision about a disputed matter.

Affidavit A voluntary written or transcribed statement or declaration of facts confirmed under oath, for use in court or other formal proceeding.

Affirmation Affirmation of truth of statement by attorney, physician, osteopath, or dentist. "The statement of an attorney admitted to practice in the courts of the state, or of a physician, osteopath or dentist, authorized by law to practice in the state, who is not a party to an action, when subscribed and affirmed by him to be true under the penalties of perjury, may be served or filed in the action in lieu of and with the same force and effect as an affidavit" (CPLR Rule 2106).

Allegation An unproven accusation. A claim or assertion which must be proven. In a pleading it may be a statement by one party to an action as an accusation or as a defense describing what that party intends to prove.

Allied Healthcare Professionals Healthcare professionals with specialized training, education, and knowledge who provide direct patient care or complementary patient care under the direct or indirect supervision of a physician, surgeon, or dentist. Examples may include registered nurses, radiology technicians, dietitians, medical technologists, occupational therapists, physical therapists, respiratory therapists, and speech-language pathologists.

Alternative Dispute Resolution Methods other than litigation to resolve a legal dispute, such as negotiation, mediation, and arbitration.

Annual Aggregate Limit For claims-made carriers, the annual aggregate limit is the maximum amount the carrier will pay for all claims arising from incidents that occurred and were reported during a given policy year.

[1] The material contained herein is provided for reference and *educational purposes only and does in no way constitute legal advice*. This material is generic and has been compiled from a variety of sources. Definitions may vary by state. Consult an attorney with questions regarding the law.

J. E. Szalados (ed.), *The Medical-Legal Aspects of Acute Care Medicine*,
https://doi.org/10.1007/978-3-030-68570-6

Answer Written response in which the defendant admits or denies the allegations contained in the complaint. A pleading that responds to each allegation in the complaint by denying or admitting it or admitting in part and denying in part.

Appeal A request to a higher court to review the decision of a lower or trial court.

Appellant A person who brings an appeal.

Appellee The person against whom the appeal is brought.

Arbitration The use of an arbitrator to settle a dispute. The hearing and settlement of a legal dispute between the plaintiff and defendant by a neutral third-party arbitrator whose decision will be final. It is potentially a more efficient, faster, and cheaper route than litigation.

Assumption of Risk A defendant's allegation that the injured plaintiff recognized the danger of the plaintiff's course of action but, nonetheless, freely, willingly, or willingly chose to assume the risks arising from that danger; an affirmative defense in a personal injury or negligence claim. Assumption of risk may be express or may be implied from the plaintiff's words and actions.

Attorney-Client Privilege A legal doctrine that prevents communications between an attorney and his or her client from being disclosed or forced to de disclosed. The privilege is usually asserted in the face of a legal demand for the communications, such as a discovery request or a demand that the lawyer testify under oath. This privilege presumes the existence of an attorney-client relationship.

Breach of Duty Failure to conduct oneself in accordance with one's legal relationship to another.

Burden of Proof The obligation to prove one's claim is supported by the facts. The burden of proof is initially upon the plaintiff or the prosecution. The burden of proof may also refer to the level of proof required.

Case Law Case law is a law that is derived from prior judicial decisions; it is common law and is a collection of precedents derived from prior judicial decisions on a particular issue or topic. Case law varies by jurisdiction and thus may have a persuasive or binding effect.

Causation In a negligence case, the plaintiff must show that their injury was directly caused by something the defendant did (or failed to do). Causation involves two different issues: cause in fact and proximate cause. Cause in fact is the "actual cause." Cause in fact is determined by the "but for" test. Proximate cause is the "legal cause."

Civil Generally pertains to disputes, not involving crimes, including family matters, contracts, medical malpractice, collection of debts, and compensation for personal injury or property loss.

Civil Complaint The first pleading in a civil case filed by the plaintiff. It alleges the material facts and legal theories to support the plaintiff's claim against the defendant. The complaint is the official document that starts a lawsuit.

Civil Lawsuit A lawsuit in which one does not need to prove criminal liability.

Claim A demand for money, for property, or for enforcement of a right provided by law. A set of operative facts creating an enforceable right.

Claims-Made Insurance Claims-made is a form of insurance in which coverage is limited to liability for those claims that arise from incidents or events that occur and are reported to the insurance company while the policy is in force.

Common Law Law that derives its authority solely from usages and customs of the past; this also includes case law precedent.

Comparative Negligence The doctrine of comparing degrees of fault among the responsible parties. Comparative negligence does not relieve the defendant from liability, but it reduces the number of damages that may be owed to the plaintiff, in proportion to the plaintiff's negligence.

Complainant Also known as the *plaintiff*.

Contractual Liability Liability arising from the assumption of risk through a contract or agreement.

Contingency Fee A fee arrangement in which the plaintiff and his or her attorney agree that the fees due to the attorney are due only if the case is resolved in the plaintiff's favor. The contingency fee is usually a fixed percentage of the judgment granted if in the favor of the plaintiff. The attorney's fee is usually paid directly from the award.

Continuance A postponement or an adjournment of a scheduled session of a court.

Cross-Examination The interrogation of an opponent's witness during a trial, hearing, or deposition. Cross-examination is limited to matters that were raised during direct examination.

Damages Monetary compensation claimed by a person who has suffered a loss or injury to his person, property, or rights as a result of the negligence or unlawful conduct of another.

Compensatory Damages that cover actual losses and are intended to make the plaintiff "whole" again.

Exemplary See Punitive Damages, under Damages

General Damages Monetary damages that are subjective in value, including pain and suffering, future problems and crippling effect of an injury, loss of ability to perform various acts, shortening of life span, mental anguish, loss of companionship, humiliation from scars, loss of anticipated business, and other harm that is not easily assessed a value. Still considered compensatory.

Punitive Damages Damages that are intended to punish a defendant in order to assist them in learning their lesson. Rare in civil litigation but does happen in extreme cases of negligence or intentional wrongdoing.

Special Damages Monetary damages actually caused by the injury, including medical and hospital bills, ambulance charges, loss of wages, property repairs, and replacement costs. Often considered compensatory.

Date of Incident The date on which a situation of alleged malpractice took place. It can also be called the date of occurrence.

Date of Reporting The date on which an incident was reported to the insurance company.

Declarations Page The portion of an insurance policy states information such as the name and address of the insured, the policy period, the amount of insurance coverage, premiums due for the policy period, and any coverage restrictions.

Decree An order of the court. A final decree is one that is dispositive of the litigation.

Deductible The amount of money the insured person is responsible for paying toward a claim. Once the deductible has been reached, the insurance company will cover the remainder of the costs.

Default Failure of either party to file required documents or appear in a civil case within a certain period of time.

Manufacturing Defects The pharmaceutical drug is manufactured improperly, or the drug has become contaminated during the process and causes harm to the patient.

Design Defects When a defect is inherent in the design of the product itself.

Failure to Warn A failure to provide sufficient or appropriate instructions, warnings, or recommendations for the use of a biological, drug, or device to the consumer or the learned intermediary.

Defendant The person or party sued in a civil case or accused in a criminal case.

Demand Letter A formal letter sent to the opposing party formally requesting some action or a request to cease an action, under threat of legal action.

Deposition Is a sworn out-of-court testimony under oath. A deposition is part of the discovery process.

Direct Examination Questioning of a witness by the party who calls the witness, in order to support the allegations or the defense.

Directed Verdict A directed verdict is a ruling entered by a trial judge after determining that there is no legally sufficient evidentiary basis for a reasonable jury to reach a different conclusion. Directed verdicts have been largely replaced by judgment as a matter of law (JMOL).

Disciplinary Hearing A hearing or professional review conducted by an organizational, local, or state or federal administrative agency such as a licensing or regulatory authority.

Disclosure The release of documents about a person or legal entity; information requested or otherwise sought by the opposing party; to divulge information that is relevant to the case.

Discovery The pretrial process in which one party discovers the evidence that will be relied upon at trial by the opposing party; this typically involves interviews, depositions, interrogatories, requests for documents and records, request for a plaintiff to receive a medical exam, electronic discovery, and request for admissions.

Dismissal with Prejudice An order to dismiss a case in which the plaintiff is legally barred from suing or appealing the same cause of action.

Dismissal Without Prejudice An order to dismiss a case in which the court preserves the plaintiff's right to sue the same cause of action again in the future.

Duty of Care A requirement that a person acts toward others and the public with the watchfulness, attention, caution, and prudence that a reasonable person in the same circumstances would use. Failure to meet the standard or reasonable duty of care is negligence.

Economic Damages Out-of-pocket expenses. These may include medical bills past or future, lost wages or earnings, rehabilitation, vocational retraining, or property damages.

Electronic Discovery (e-discovery) the location and process of obtaining data or information that is stored in an electronic or digital format.

Established Customary Standard of Care This refers to evidence, usually by expert testimony, of that level of skill and care that the average professional would provide in a similar situation under similar circumstances.

Evidence A fact presented in court through the testimony of a witness, an object, or written documents.

Excess Judgement The amount of additional damages that an insurer is required to pay above an insurance policy limit.

Exhibit A document or object that is offered into evidence during a deposition, trial, or hearing.

Expert Witness Testimony given by someone who is qualified to speak with authority about scientific, technical, or professional matters.

Fault An intentional or negligent failure to act in a reasonable fashion, either according to law or according to duty. Fault is a wrong act or error that causes injury to another person. The fault may arise out of ignorance, carelessness, negligence, or even unskillfulness.

Fraud Intentional deception resulting in damage to another, whether to his or her person, rights, property. or reputation. Fraud usually consists of a misrepresentation, as an affirmative statement or a concealment or nondisclosure of a material fact.

Gross Negligence Intentional failure to perform a standard of duty by recklessly disregarding another person's health or property; also known as willful negligence.

Hold Harmless and Indemnification Agreement A method of risk transfer in which one party assumes, by contract, the liability for the negligence of another party.

Indemnity An agreement wherein one party financially protects another against an anticipated loss, such as an insurer who indemnifies an insured.

Independent Medical Examination A second independent medical opinion by an impartial party usually at the request of defendant/insurance company.

Informed Consent A process whereby a healthcare provider informs a patient of the potential benefits, major risks, and alternatives involved in any surgical procedure, medical procedure, or other course of treatment and obtains the patient's consent to proceed.

Insurance A contractual relationship through which one agrees to reimburse an insured for damage or injury caused by certain stated hazards, dangers, or events.

Insured The individual protected (indemnified) under an insurance policy.

Interrogatories A form of discovery in which one party submits a series of written questions to the other party and to which the latter provides written answers under oath

Joint and Several Liability If parties are "jointly and severally liable" for a certain obligation, it means that each party is liable to pay the full obligation, regardless of their proportion of responsibility. The party who pays the full obligation, however, can seek from other parties their contribution or share of the liability.

Judgment The official final decision issued by a court regarding a legal controversy or matter.

Judgment Notwithstanding the Verdict A judgment by the court, overruling a decision of a jury. One type of judgment as a matter of law (JMOL).

Jury Instructions Directions, or legal rules, issued by the judge to the jury before deliberation, including their instructions for reaching a verdict, the laws pertaining to the case, and what must be proven and by whom.

Legal Malpractice When an attorney breaches their legal duty; generally, all cases of legal malpractice involve four elements: duty, breach, causation, and damages.

Liability A legal responsibility or obligation.

Liability Risk Liability loss or exposure where negligent acts may occur for which an organization may be held responsible. The act must be injury to or property damage of others. Insurance coverage for this type of risk is called "third-party insurance."

Lien An encumbrance, upon real or personal property, which secures the payment of a debt or the performance of a duty.

Limitation of Risk The maximum amount an insurer can be obligated to pay in any event.

Litigant One of the parties involved in a legal action.

Litigation The process of settling a dispute through the court system.

Litigation Risk The likelihood of winning a personal injury lawsuit in court (rather than settling out of court) usually assessed by one's attorney in the face of unpredictability of trial.

Loss of consortium Damages awarded to the family member of a deceased person for loss of companionship.

Mandate Command from a court directing the enforcement of a judgment, sentence, or decree.

Maximum Medical Improvement (MMI) The point at which an injured person's condition or injury stabilizes and no further improvement or recovery is expected.

Medical Negligence Failure of a physician or other medical professional to meet the standards of conduct for duties relating to that profession.

Mediation A settlement of a dispute or controversy through a neutral independent party with experience in dispute resolution to aid them in the resolution of a controversy without litigation.

Medical Malpractice Negligence by a professional healthcare provider, such as a medical professional or hospital, who departs from the applicable standard of care, and that act or omission directly causes injury.

Medical Professional Liability Insurance (MPLI) An insurance product that offers financial protection to healthcare providers for liability arising from errors and omissions in the practice of their profession.

Motion A formal request that a judge make a ruling or take some action.

Named Insured Any individual whose name actually appears on the insurance policy, as opposed to those who may be covered, but are not specifically named on the documents.

Negligence Failure to exercise that degree of care that a reasonable person would exercise under the same circumstances.

Noneconomic Damages Pain, suffering, inconvenience, loss of consortium, physical impairment, disfigurement, and other nonpecuniary damages.

Nose Coverage Retroactive or prior acts coverage which extends the effective date of claims-made policies to a date prior to the effective date of a policy

Notary A person with legal training who is licensed by the state to perform acts in legal affairs, in particular, certifying or attesting to witnessing signatures on documents.

Notice of Claim A letter from the patient or his attorney notifying a healthcare provider of the intent to sue.

Notice to Insurer Written notice to the insurance company about an incident.

Nursing Malpractice An intentional act or negligence committed by a member of the nursing profession that causes physical, financial, cognitive, emotional, or psychosocial damage to a patient under their care.

Occurrence Insurance A type of policy in which the insured is covered for any incident that occurs (or that did occur) while the policy is (or was) in force, regardless of when the incident is reported or when it becomes a case in controversy.

Opening Statement The initial statement made by each attorney at the beginning of a trial outlining the facts each intends to establish during the trial.

Out-of-Court Settlement An agreement reached between the plaintiff and defendant which does not require the approval of a court or judge before a trial takes place.

Paralegal A non-attorney, who is educated as a paralegal and trained and certified to assist a lawyer.

Parties Persons, corporations, or associations who have started a lawsuit or who are defendants in a lawsuit.

Pecuniary Damages Referring to the loss of past and future income.

Peer and Quality Review The credentialing and privileging processes used to evaluate and measure the competence of professional peers.

Plaintiff The party who initiates a legal action; in a personal injury lawsuit, the person who alleges that he or she has suffered monetary damages due to the negligence of another party.

Pleadings Written documents stating the allegations and claims of the opposing parties.

Prayer for Relief A request addressed to the court by the plaintiff requesting specific remedies or damages.

Precedent When a previously decided case(s) is recognized as the basis and authority for determining future cases; the basis for case law.

Preponderance of Evidence A preponderance of evidence means that the proof one has presented will simply tip the scales in the plaintiff's favor.

Prior Acts Coverage A claims-made policy feature that protects the Insured for claims arising from medical incidents which took place before the inception of the current policy for which a claim is not made until after the policy is in force.

Probable Claim Event A policy provision that allows an Insured to trigger coverage under its medical professional liability policy by reporting a medical incident that is reasonably expected to later result in a claim; this is also known as awareness or incident reporting provision or a discovery clause.

Proceeding Any hearing or court appearance related to a legal case.

Professional Services Services for which a person is licensed, trained, and qualified to perform in the capacity of a healthcare provider.

Proximate Cause The primary or moving reason why an injury or damage occurred, and without which the accident would not have happened, if the injury in question can be foreseen as a natural occurrence of the action.

Punitive Damages Refers to damages awarded to penalize a defendant for grossly negligent, malicious, reckless, or intentional conduct.

Rebuttal Evidence that attempts to explain, counteract, or disprove facts given in evidence by the other party.

Redirect Examination Opportunity to present rebuttal evidence after cross-examination.

Reasonable Care The level of treatment by a healthcare professional/establishment that would be considered adequate by a fair and sensible person.

Res Ipsa Loquitur Latin for "the thing speaks for itself." *Res ipsa* permits the jury to infer negligence based on evidence that the injury is of a kind that does not ordinarily occur in the absence of negligence.

Respondent Superior A type of vicarious liability that holds an employer liable for an employee's negligent actions. Latin for "let the master answer."

Retainer Advance payment of fees, or fees and costs, made by a client to an attorney when the client retains the attorney to act on his or her behalf.

Request for Admission A request made by a party in a lawsuit to another in that lawsuit to admit to the truthfulness of a fact or the genuineness of a piece of evidence.

Request for Documents A request made by a party in a lawsuit to another in that lawsuit to provide specific documents or other physical evidence.

Risk Identification and Analysis This step of the risk management process includes the identification and analysis of situations or problems that may give rise to events or incidents of potential liability.

Risk Retention Group (RRG) RRGs are insurance companies owned and controlled by a group engaged in similar or related businesses for the purpose of ensuring the liability exposures of its members.

Settlement Conclusion of a legal matter; negotiated agreement by opposing parties in a civil suit before or after litigation has begun but before the court.

Sovereign Immunity Doctrine This doctrine provided that no governmental body could be sued unless it gave its permission to be sued.

Statute of Limitations A law that determines the period of time that one has to file legal action.

Stipulation An agreement, admission, or concession made in a judicial proceeding by the parties or their attorneys, thus relieving a party of its obligation to produce evidence in support of an argument or allegation.

Strict Liability The responsibility of wrongdoing to another party regardless of their direct involvement in the incident.

Subpoena A legal document issued by the court ordering a person to appear as specified and give testimony and/or produce evidence.

Subrogation A process by which a third party is put in the place of a creditor so that the rights and securities of the creditor pass to that third person.

Tail Coverage (Extended Reporting Coverage) Coverage that protects the physician against all claims that arise from professional services performed while the claims-made policy was in effect but which were reported after the termination of the policy.

Tort A civil wrong, giving rise to a cause of action, independent of contract.

Transcript The official verbatim record of a proceeding.

Trier of Facts The jury; or in a nonjury trial, the judge. The person or group that analyzes the evidence in order to make a decision about the case or issue in dispute.

Verdict A formal decision about the outcome of a case made by a judge or jury.

Vicarious Liability A doctrine that provides that a party is held responsible for the negligence of another based solely on the relationship between the parties, such as employer and employee or principal and agent.

Voir Dire Commonly known as jury selection.

Wrongful Death A death that occurs because of someone else's malice, negligence, or recklessness. A lawsuit filed against an individual or company for the death of a person due to negligent or wrongful behavior. Wrongful death cases are generally filed by a surviving family member (typically spouse), who can recover damages for, for example, mental and physical suffering, lost wages, funeral and medical expenses for the deceased, loss of income and earning capacity, and loss of consortium.

Index

J. E. Szalados (ed.), *The Medical-Legal Aspects of Acute Care Medicine*,
https://doi.org/10.1007/978-3-030-68570-6

I

MIX
Papier aus verantwortungsvollen Quellen
Paper from responsible sources
FSC® C105338
FSC
www.fsc.org

If you have any concerns about our products,
you can contact us on
ProductSafety@springernature.com

In case Publisher is established outside the EU,
the EU authorized representative is:
Springer Nature Customer Service Center GmbH
Europaplatz 3, 69115 Heidelberg, Germany

Printed by Libri Plureos GmbH
in Hamburg, Germany